CANADIAN
MORTGAGE
PAYMENT
TABLES

Stoddart

Revised edition published in 1994 by
Stoddart Publishing Co. Limited
34 Lesmill Road
Toronto, Ontario
M3B 2T6
(416)445-3333

Reprinted October 1994

Original edition published in 1990 by
Stoddart Publishing Co. Limited

CANADIAN CATALOGUING IN PUBLICATION DATA
Main entry under title:
Canadian mortgage payment tables
Rev. ed.
ISBN 0-7737-5650-7
1. Interest – Canada – Tables.   2. Mortgage loans –
Canada – Tables.

HG1634.C35 1994   332.8′2′0212   C94-930038-1

Monthly payments are computed on the basis of nominal
annual interest rates computed semiannually in advance.
Although great care was taken in the preparation of these
tables, there is no warranty of complete accuracy.

Cover Design: David Montle
Computation: PSL Consulting Services

Printed and bound in the United States of America

CONTENTS

Weekly, Biweekly, Semimonthly, Monthly
Payment Tables with amounts necessary to
amortize a mortgage loan of $1000

HOW TO USE THIS BOOK

The monthly mortgage payment tables in this book reflect the lower interest rates of the 1990s, showing blended monthly payments for loans up to $1,000,000 amortized over 1 to 30 years at interest rates from 4% to 18.50% in 1/8% increments.

In order to determine the monthly payment on a mortgage of $25,000 amortized over 25 years at 8.25%, for example, find the table for 8.25%, then locate the amortization period for 25 years along the top of the table and follow that column down to the line for the amortization amount for $25,000, shown in bold type in the left hand column. The monthly payment is $194.81.

The tables at the back of the book show regular weekly, biweekly, semimonthly, and monthly payments for a loan of $1000. To calculate the payments for larger loans, multiply the payment by the mortgage amount and divide by 1000. Regular payments result in smaller payments but do not substantially decrease the time to pay off a loan. Accelerated payments are not shown in this book; however, they can easily be derived by taking the regular monthly payments and dividing by 4 for weekly accelerated payments, and by 2 for biweekly payments.

4%

MONTHLY PAYMENT
NECESSARY TO AMORTIZE A LOAN

Amortization Amount	1 Year	2 Years	3 Years	4 Years	5 Years	6 Years	7 Years
25	2.13	1.09	0.74	0.56	0.46	0.39	0.34
50	4.26	2.17	1.48	1.13	0.92	0.78	0.68
100	8.51	4.34	2.95	2.26	1.84	1.56	1.37
200	17.03	8.68	5.90	4.51	3.68	3.13	2.73
300	25.54	13.02	8.85	6.77	5.52	4.69	4.10
400	34.05	17.36	11.80	9.03	7.36	6.25	5.46
500	42.57	21.71	14.75	11.28	9.20	7.82	6.83
600	51.08	26.05	17.71	13.54	11.04	9.38	8.19
700	59.59	30.39	20.66	15.80	12.88	10.94	9.56
800	68.11	34.73	23.61	18.05	14.72	12.50	10.92
900	76.62	39.07	26.56	20.31	16.56	14.07	12.29
1000	85.13	43.41	29.51	22.56	18.40	15.63	13.65
2000	170.27	86.82	59.02	45.13	36.80	31.26	27.31
3000	255.40	130.23	88.53	67.69	55.20	46.89	40.96
4000	340.54	173.64	118.04	90.26	73.61	62.52	54.61
5000	425.67	217.05	147.55	112.82	92.01	78.15	68.27
6000	510.81	260.46	177.06	135.39	110.41	93.78	81.92
7000	595.94	303.87	206.57	157.95	128.81	109.41	95.58
8000	681.08	347.28	236.07	180.51	147.21	125.04	109.23
9000	766.21	390.69	265.58	203.08	165.61	140.67	122.88
10000	851.35	434.10	295.09	225.64	184.02	156.30	136.54
11000	936.48	477.51	324.60	248.21	202.42	171.93	150.19
12000	1021.62	520.92	354.11	270.77	220.82	187.56	163.84
13000	1106.75	564.33	383.62	293.34	239.22	203.19	177.50
14000	1191.89	607.74	413.13	315.90	257.62	218.82	191.15
15000	1277.02	651.15	442.64	338.46	276.02	234.45	204.80
16000	1362.16	694.56	472.15	361.03	294.43	250.08	218.46
17000	1447.29	737.97	501.66	383.59	312.83	265.71	232.11
18000	1532.43	781.38	531.17	406.16	331.23	281.34	245.77
19000	1617.56	824.80	560.68	428.72	349.63	296.97	259.42
20000	1702.70	868.21	590.19	451.29	368.03	312.60	273.07
21000	1787.83	911.62	619.70	473.85	386.43	328.23	286.73
22000	1872.97	955.03	649.21	496.42	404.84	343.86	300.38
23000	1958.10	998.44	678.71	518.98	423.24	359.49	314.03
24000	2043.24	1041.85	708.22	541.54	441.64	375.12	327.69
25000	2128.37	1085.26	737.73	564.11	460.04	390.75	341.34
26000	2213.51	1128.67	767.24	586.67	478.44	406.38	354.99
27000	2298.64	1172.08	796.75	609.24	496.84	422.01	368.65
28000	2383.78	1215.49	826.26	631.80	515.25	437.65	382.30
29000	2468.91	1258.90	855.77	654.37	533.65	453.28	395.96
30000	2554.05	1302.31	885.28	676.93	552.05	468.91	409.61
35000	2979.72	1519.36	1032.83	789.75	644.06	547.06	477.88
40000	3405.39	1736.41	1180.37	902.57	736.07	625.21	546.15
45000	3831.07	1953.46	1327.92	1015.39	828.07	703.36	614.41
50000	4256.74	2170.51	1475.47	1128.22	920.08	781.51	682.68
55000	4682.42	2387.56	1623.01	1241.04	1012.09	859.66	750.95
60000	5108.09	2604.62	1770.56	1353.86	1104.10	937.81	819.22
65000	5533.77	2821.67	1918.11	1466.68	1196.11	1015.96	887.49
70000	5959.44	3038.72	2065.65	1579.50	1288.12	1094.11	955.76
75000	6385.11	3255.77	2213.20	1692.32	1380.12	1172.26	1024.02
80000	6810.79	3472.82	2360.75	1805.15	1472.13	1250.41	1092.29
85000	7236.46	3689.87	2508.29	1917.97	1564.14	1328.57	1160.56
90000	7662.14	3906.92	2655.84	2030.79	1656.15	1406.72	1228.83
95000	8087.81	4123.98	2803.39	2143.61	1748.16	1484.87	1297.10
100000	8513.49	4341.03	2950.93	2256.43	1840.17	1563.02	1365.37
200000	17026.97	8682.05	5901.87	4512.86	3680.33	3126.04	2730.73
300000	25540.46	13023.08	8852.80	6769.30	5520.50	4689.05	4096.10
400000	34053.94	17364.11	11803.74	9025.73	7360.67	6252.07	5461.46
500000	42567.43	21705.13	14754.67	11282.16	9200.83	7815.09	6826.83
1000000	85134.86	43410.27	29509.34	22564.32	18401.66	15630.18	13653.65

MONTHLY PAYMENT
NECESSARY TO AMORTIZE A LOAN

4%

Amortization Amount	8 Years	9 Years	10 Years	15 Years	20 Years	25 Years	30 Years
25	0.30	0.28	0.25	0.18	0.15	0.13	0.12
50	0.61	0.55	0.51	0.37	0.30	0.26	0.24
100	1.22	1.10	1.01	0.74	0.60	0.53	0.48
200	2.43	2.21	2.02	1.48	1.21	1.05	0.95
300	3.65	3.31	3.03	2.21	1.81	1.58	1.43
400	4.87	4.41	4.04	2.95	2.42	2.10	1.90
500	6.09	5.51	5.05	3.69	3.02	2.63	2.38
600	7.30	6.62	6.07	4.43	3.63	3.16	2.85
700	8.52	7.72	7.08	5.17	4.23	3.68	3.33
800	9.74	8.82	8.09	5.90	4.83	4.21	3.80
900	10.96	9.92	9.10	6.64	5.44	4.73	4.28
1000	12.17	11.03	10.11	7.38	6.04	5.26	4.76
2000	24.35	22.05	20.22	14.76	12.08	10.52	9.51
3000	36.52	33.08	30.33	22.14	18.13	15.78	14.27
4000	48.70	44.10	40.44	29.52	24.17	21.04	19.02
5000	60.87	55.13	50.54	36.90	30.21	26.30	23.78
6000	73.04	66.15	60.65	44.28	36.25	31.56	28.53
7000	85.22	77.18	70.76	51.66	42.30	36.82	33.29
8000	97.39	88.20	80.87	59.04	48.34	42.08	38.04
9000	109.57	99.23	90.98	66.42	54.38	47.34	42.80
10000	121.74	110.25	101.09	73.80	60.42	52.60	47.55
11000	133.91	121.28	111.20	81.18	66.47	57.86	52.31
12000	146.09	132.31	121.31	88.56	72.51	63.12	57.06
13000	158.26	143.33	131.42	95.95	78.55	68.38	61.82
14000	170.44	154.36	141.52	103.33	84.59	73.64	66.57
15000	182.61	165.38	151.63	110.71	90.64	78.90	71.33
16000	194.78	176.41	161.74	118.09	96.68	84.16	76.08
17000	206.96	187.43	171.85	125.47	102.72	89.42	80.84
18000	219.13	198.46	181.96	132.85	108.76	94.68	85.59
19000	231.31	209.48	192.07	140.23	114.81	99.94	90.35
20000	243.48	220.51	202.18	147.61	120.85	105.20	95.10
21000	255.65	231.54	212.29	154.99	126.89	110.46	99.86
22000	267.83	242.56	222.40	162.37	132.93	115.72	104.61
23000	280.00	253.59	232.50	169.75	138.98	120.98	109.37
24000	292.18	264.61	242.61	177.13	145.02	126.24	114.12
25000	304.35	275.64	252.72	184.51	151.06	131.51	118.88
26000	316.52	286.66	262.83	191.89	157.10	136.77	123.63
27000	328.70	297.69	272.94	199.27	163.15	142.03	128.39
28000	340.87	308.71	283.05	206.65	169.19	147.29	133.15
29000	353.04	319.74	293.16	214.03	175.23	152.55	137.90
30000	365.22	330.76	303.27	221.41	181.27	157.81	142.66
35000	426.09	385.89	353.81	258.31	211.49	184.11	166.43
40000	486.96	441.02	404.35	295.22	241.70	210.41	190.21
45000	547.83	496.15	454.90	332.12	271.91	236.71	213.98
50000	608.70	551.27	505.44	369.02	302.12	263.01	237.76
55000	669.57	606.40	555.99	405.92	332.34	289.31	261.54
60000	730.44	661.53	606.53	442.82	362.55	315.61	285.31
65000	791.31	716.66	657.08	479.73	392.76	341.91	309.09
70000	852.18	771.78	707.62	516.63	422.97	368.21	332.86
75000	913.05	826.91	758.17	553.53	453.18	394.52	356.64
80000	973.92	882.04	808.71	590.43	483.40	420.82	380.41
85000	1034.79	937.17	859.25	627.33	513.61	447.12	404.19
90000	1095.66	992.29	909.80	664.23	543.82	473.42	427.97
95000	1156.53	1047.42	960.34	701.14	574.03	499.72	451.74
100000	1217.40	1102.55	1010.89	738.04	604.25	526.02	475.52
200000	2434.79	2205.10	2021.77	1476.08	1208.49	1052.04	951.04
300000	3652.19	3307.65	3032.66	2214.12	1812.74	1578.06	1426.56
400000	4869.58	4410.20	4043.55	2952.15	2416.99	2104.08	1902.07
500000	6086.98	5512.75	5054.44	3690.19	3021.23	2630.10	2377.59
1000000	12173.96	11025.49	10108.87	7380.39	6042.46	5260.20	4755.19

3

4.125%

Amortization Amount	1 Year	2 Years	3 Years	4 Years	5 Years	6 Years	7 Years
25	2.13	1.09	0.74	0.57	0.46	0.39	0.34
50	4.26	2.17	1.48	1.13	0.92	0.78	0.69
100	8.52	4.35	2.96	2.26	1.85	1.57	1.37
200	17.04	8.69	5.91	4.52	3.69	3.14	2.74
300	25.56	13.04	8.87	6.79	5.54	4.71	4.11
400	34.08	17.39	11.83	9.05	7.38	6.27	5.48
500	42.60	21.73	14.78	11.31	9.23	7.84	6.86
600	51.11	26.08	17.74	13.57	11.07	9.41	8.23
700	59.63	30.43	20.69	15.83	12.92	10.98	9.60
800	68.15	34.77	23.65	18.10	14.77	12.55	10.97
900	76.67	39.12	26.61	20.36	16.61	14.12	12.34
1000	85.19	43.46	29.56	22.62	18.46	15.69	13.71
2000	170.38	86.93	59.13	45.24	36.91	31.37	27.42
3000	255.57	130.39	88.69	67.86	55.37	47.06	41.13
4000	340.76	173.86	118.26	90.48	73.83	62.74	54.84
5000	425.96	217.32	147.82	113.10	92.29	78.43	68.55
6000	511.15	260.79	177.38	135.72	110.74	94.12	82.26
7000	596.34	304.25	206.95	158.34	129.20	109.80	95.97
8000	681.53	347.72	236.51	180.95	147.66	125.49	109.68
9000	766.72	391.18	266.08	203.57	166.11	141.18	123.39
10000	851.91	434.65	295.64	226.19	184.57	156.86	137.10
11000	937.10	478.11	325.20	248.81	203.03	172.55	150.81
12000	1022.29	521.58	354.77	271.43	221.49	188.23	164.52
13000	1107.48	565.04	384.33	294.05	239.94	203.92	178.23
14000	1192.67	608.51	413.90	316.67	258.40	219.61	191.94
15000	1277.86	651.97	443.46	339.29	276.86	235.29	205.65
16000	1363.06	695.44	473.02	361.91	295.31	250.98	219.36
17000	1448.25	738.90	502.59	384.53	313.77	266.67	233.07
18000	1533.44	782.37	532.15	407.15	332.23	282.35	246.78
19000	1618.63	825.83	561.72	429.77	350.69	298.04	260.50
20000	1703.82	869.30	591.28	452.39	369.14	313.72	274.21
21000	1789.01	912.76	620.84	475.01	387.60	329.41	287.92
22000	1874.20	956.23	650.41	497.63	406.06	345.10	301.63
23000	1959.39	999.69	679.97	520.24	424.51	360.78	315.34
24000	2044.58	1043.16	709.54	542.86	442.97	376.47	329.05
25000	2129.78	1086.62	739.10	565.48	461.43	392.16	342.76
26000	2214.97	1130.09	768.66	588.10	479.89	407.84	356.47
27000	2300.16	1173.55	798.23	610.72	498.34	423.53	370.18
28000	2385.35	1217.02	827.79	633.34	516.80	439.21	383.89
29000	2470.54	1260.48	857.36	655.96	535.26	454.90	397.60
30000	2555.73	1303.95	886.92	678.58	553.71	470.59	411.31
35000	2981.69	1521.27	1034.74	791.68	646.00	549.02	479.86
40000	3407.64	1738.60	1182.56	904.77	738.29	627.45	548.41
45000	3833.60	1955.92	1330.38	1017.87	830.57	705.88	616.96
50000	4259.55	2173.25	1478.20	1130.97	922.86	784.31	685.51
55000	4685.51	2390.57	1626.02	1244.06	1015.14	862.74	754.06
60000	5111.46	2607.90	1773.84	1357.16	1107.43	941.17	822.62
65000	5537.42	2825.22	1921.66	1470.26	1199.72	1019.60	891.17
70000	5963.37	3042.55	2069.48	1583.35	1292.00	1098.04	959.72
75000	6389.33	3259.87	2217.30	1696.45	1384.29	1176.47	1028.27
80000	6815.28	3477.20	2365.12	1809.55	1476.57	1254.90	1096.82
85000	7241.24	3694.52	2512.94	1922.64	1568.86	1333.33	1165.37
90000	7667.19	3911.85	2660.76	2035.74	1661.14	1411.76	1233.92
95000	8093.15	4129.17	2808.58	2148.84	1753.43	1490.19	1302.48
100000	8519.10	4346.50	2956.40	2261.93	1845.72	1568.62	1371.03
200000	17038.21	8693.00	5912.81	4523.87	3691.43	3137.24	2742.05
300000	25557.31	13039.50	8869.21	6785.80	5537.15	4705.87	4113.08
400000	34076.41	17385.99	11825.61	9047.74	7382.86	6274.49	5484.11
500000	42595.51	21732.49	14782.02	11309.67	9228.58	7843.11	6855.13
1000000	85191.03	43464.99	29564.03	22619.35	18457.16	15686.22	13710.27

MONTHLY PAYMENT
NECESSARY TO AMORTIZE A LOAN **4.125%**

Amortization Amount	8 Years	9 Years	10 Years	15 Years	20 Years	25 Years	30 Years
25	0.31	0.28	0.25	0.19	0.15	0.13	0.12
50	0.61	0.55	0.51	0.37	0.31	0.27	0.24
100	1.22	1.11	1.02	0.74	0.61	0.53	0.48
200	2.45	2.22	2.03	1.49	1.22	1.07	0.97
300	3.67	3.32	3.05	2.23	1.83	1.60	1.45
400	4.89	4.43	4.07	2.98	2.44	2.13	1.93
500	6.12	5.54	5.08	3.72	3.05	2.66	2.41
600	7.34	6.65	6.10	4.47	3.66	3.20	2.90
700	8.56	7.76	7.12	5.21	4.28	3.73	3.38
800	9.78	8.87	8.13	5.95	4.89	4.26	3.86
900	11.01	9.97	9.15	6.70	5.50	4.80	4.34
1000	12.23	11.08	10.17	7.44	6.11	5.33	4.83
2000	24.46	22.17	20.33	14.88	12.21	10.66	9.65
3000	36.69	33.25	30.50	22.33	18.32	15.98	14.48
4000	48.92	44.33	40.67	29.77	24.43	21.31	19.30
5000	61.16	55.42	50.84	37.21	30.54	26.64	24.13
6000	73.39	66.50	61.00	44.65	36.64	31.97	28.96
7000	85.62	77.58	71.17	52.09	42.75	37.30	33.78
8000	97.85	88.67	81.34	59.54	48.86	42.63	38.61
9000	110.08	99.75	91.51	66.98	54.97	47.95	43.44
10000	122.31	110.83	101.67	74.42	61.07	53.28	48.26
11000	134.54	121.92	111.84	81.86	67.18	58.61	53.09
12000	146.77	133.00	122.01	89.30	73.29	63.94	57.91
13000	159.01	144.08	132.18	96.75	79.40	69.27	62.74
14000	171.24	155.17	142.34	104.19	85.50	74.59	67.57
15000	183.47	166.25	152.51	111.63	91.61	79.92	72.39
16000	195.70	177.33	162.68	119.07	97.72	85.25	77.22
17000	207.93	188.42	172.84	126.51	103.82	90.58	82.05
18000	220.16	199.50	183.01	133.96	109.93	95.91	86.87
19000	232.39	210.58	193.18	141.40	116.04	101.24	91.70
20000	244.62	221.67	203.35	148.84	122.15	106.56	96.52
21000	256.85	232.75	213.51	156.28	128.25	111.89	101.35
22000	269.09	243.83	223.68	163.73	134.36	117.22	106.18
23000	281.32	254.92	233.85	171.17	140.47	122.55	111.00
24000	293.55	266.00	244.02	178.61	146.58	127.88	115.83
25000	305.78	277.08	254.18	186.05	152.68	133.20	120.65
26000	318.01	288.17	264.35	193.49	158.79	138.53	125.48
27000	330.24	299.25	274.52	200.94	164.90	143.86	130.31
28000	342.47	310.33	284.69	208.38	171.01	149.19	135.13
29000	354.70	321.42	294.85	215.82	177.11	154.52	139.96
30000	366.94	332.50	305.02	223.26	183.22	159.85	144.79
35000	428.09	387.92	355.86	260.47	213.76	186.49	168.92
40000	489.25	443.33	406.69	297.68	244.29	213.13	193.05
45000	550.40	498.75	457.53	334.89	274.83	239.77	217.18
50000	611.56	554.17	508.37	372.10	305.37	266.41	241.31
55000	672.72	609.58	559.20	409.31	335.90	293.05	265.44
60000	733.87	665.00	610.04	446.52	366.44	319.69	289.57
65000	795.03	720.42	660.88	483.73	396.98	346.33	313.70
70000	856.18	775.83	711.71	520.94	427.51	372.97	337.83
75000	917.34	831.25	762.55	558.15	458.05	399.61	361.96
80000	978.49	886.67	813.39	595.36	488.59	426.25	386.09
85000	1039.65	942.08	864.22	632.57	519.12	452.90	410.23
90000	1100.81	997.50	915.06	669.79	549.66	479.54	434.36
95000	1161.96	1052.92	965.90	707.00	580.20	506.18	458.49
100000	1223.12	1108.33	1016.73	744.21	610.73	532.82	482.62
200000	2446.24	2216.67	2033.47	1488.41	1221.47	1065.64	965.24
300000	3669.35	3325.00	3050.20	2232.62	1832.20	1598.46	1447.85
400000	4892.47	4433.33	4066.94	2976.82	2442.93	2131.27	1930.47
500000	6115.59	5541.67	5083.67	3721.03	3053.66	2664.09	2413.09
1000000	12231.18	11083.33	10167.34	7442.06	6107.33	5328.18	4826.18

4.25%

MONTHLY PAYMENT
NECESSARY TO AMORTIZE A LOAN

Amortization Amount	1 Year	2 Years	3 Years	4 Years	5 Years	6 Years	7 Years
25	2.13	1.09	0.74	0.57	0.46	0.39	0.34
50	4.26	2.18	1.48	1.13	0.93	0.79	0.69
100	8.52	4.35	2.96	2.27	1.85	1.57	1.38
200	17.05	8.70	5.92	4.53	3.70	3.15	2.75
300	25.57	13.06	8.89	6.80	5.55	4.72	4.13
400	34.10	17.41	11.85	9.07	7.41	6.30	5.51
500	42.62	21.76	14.81	11.34	9.26	7.87	6.88
600	51.15	26.11	17.77	13.60	11.11	9.45	8.26
700	59.67	30.46	20.73	15.87	12.96	11.02	9.64
800	68.20	34.82	23.70	18.14	14.81	12.59	11.01
900	76.72	39.17	26.66	20.41	16.66	14.17	12.39
1000	85.25	43.52	29.62	22.67	18.51	15.74	13.77
2000	170.49	87.04	59.24	45.35	37.03	31.48	27.53
3000	255.74	130.56	88.86	68.02	55.54	47.23	41.30
4000	340.99	174.08	118.48	90.70	74.05	62.97	55.07
5000	426.24	217.60	148.09	113.37	92.56	78.71	68.84
6000	511.48	261.12	177.71	136.05	111.08	94.45	82.60
7000	596.73	304.64	207.33	158.72	129.59	110.20	96.37
8000	681.98	348.16	236.95	181.40	148.10	125.94	110.14
9000	767.22	391.68	266.57	204.07	166.61	141.68	123.90
10000	852.47	435.20	296.19	226.74	185.13	157.42	137.67
11000	937.72	478.72	325.81	249.42	203.64	173.17	151.44
12000	1022.97	522.24	355.43	272.09	222.15	188.91	165.20
13000	1108.21	565.76	385.04	294.77	240.67	204.65	178.97
14000	1193.46	609.28	414.66	317.44	259.18	220.39	192.74
15000	1278.71	652.80	444.28	340.12	277.69	236.14	206.51
16000	1363.95	696.32	473.90	362.79	296.20	251.88	220.27
17000	1449.20	739.84	503.52	385.47	314.72	267.62	234.04
18000	1534.45	783.36	533.14	408.14	333.23	283.36	247.81
19000	1619.70	826.87	562.76	430.81	351.74	299.10	261.57
20000	1704.94	870.39	592.38	453.49	370.25	314.85	275.34
21000	1790.19	913.91	621.99	476.16	388.77	330.59	289.11
22000	1875.44	957.43	651.61	498.84	407.28	346.33	302.87
23000	1960.69	1000.95	681.23	521.51	425.79	362.07	316.64
24000	2045.93	1044.47	710.85	544.19	444.31	377.82	330.41
25000	2131.18	1087.99	740.47	566.86	462.82	393.56	344.18
26000	2216.43	1131.51	770.09	589.54	481.33	409.30	357.94
27000	2301.67	1175.03	799.71	612.21	499.84	425.04	371.71
28000	2386.92	1218.55	829.33	634.88	518.36	440.79	385.48
29000	2472.17	1262.07	858.94	657.56	536.87	456.53	399.24
30000	2557.42	1305.59	888.56	680.23	555.38	472.27	413.01
35000	2983.65	1523.19	1036.66	793.60	647.95	550.98	481.85
40000	3409.89	1740.79	1184.75	906.98	740.51	629.69	550.68
45000	3836.12	1958.39	1332.84	1020.35	833.07	708.41	619.52
50000	4262.36	2175.99	1480.94	1133.72	925.64	787.12	688.35
55000	4688.60	2393.58	1629.03	1247.09	1018.20	865.83	757.19
60000	5114.83	2611.18	1777.13	1360.47	1110.76	944.54	826.02
65000	5541.07	2828.78	1925.22	1473.84	1203.33	1023.25	894.86
70000	5967.30	3046.38	2073.31	1587.21	1295.89	1101.96	963.69
75000	6393.54	3263.98	2221.41	1700.58	1388.45	1180.68	1032.53
80000	6819.77	3481.58	2369.50	1813.95	1481.02	1259.39	1101.36
85000	7246.01	3699.18	2517.59	1927.33	1573.58	1338.10	1170.20
90000	7672.25	3916.78	2665.69	2040.70	1666.15	1416.81	1239.03
95000	8098.48	4134.37	2813.78	2154.07	1758.71	1495.52	1307.87
100000	8524.72	4351.97	2961.88	2267.44	1851.27	1574.24	1376.70
200000	17049.44	8703.94	5923.75	4534.89	3702.55	3148.47	2753.40
300000	25574.16	13055.92	8885.63	6802.33	5553.82	4722.71	4130.10
400000	34098.87	17407.89	11847.50	9069.77	7405.09	6296.94	5506.80
500000	42623.59	21759.86	14809.38	11337.21	9256.37	7871.18	6883.50
1000000	85247.19	43519.72	29618.76	22674.43	18512.73	15742.35	13767.00

Amortization Amount	8 Years	9 Years	10 Years	15 Years	20 Years	25 Years	30 Years
25	0.31	0.28	0.26	0.19	0.15	0.13	0.12
50	0.61	0.56	0.51	0.38	0.31	0.27	0.24
100	1.23	1.11	1.02	0.75	0.62	0.54	0.49
200	2.46	2.23	2.05	1.50	1.23	1.08	0.98
300	3.69	3.34	3.07	2.25	1.85	1.62	1.47
400	4.92	4.46	4.09	3.00	2.47	2.16	1.96
500	6.14	5.57	5.11	3.75	3.09	2.70	2.45
600	7.37	6.68	6.14	4.50	3.70	3.24	2.94
700	8.60	7.80	7.16	5.25	4.32	3.78	3.43
800	9.83	8.91	8.18	6.00	4.94	4.32	3.92
900	11.06	10.03	9.20	6.75	5.56	4.86	4.41
1000	12.29	11.14	10.23	7.50	6.17	5.40	4.90
2000	24.58	22.28	20.45	15.01	12.35	10.79	9.80
3000	36.87	33.42	30.68	22.51	18.52	16.19	14.69
4000	49.15	44.57	40.90	30.02	24.69	21.59	19.59
5000	61.44	55.71	51.13	37.52	30.86	26.98	24.49
6000	73.73	66.85	61.36	45.02	37.04	32.38	29.39
7000	86.02	77.99	71.58	52.53	43.21	37.78	34.28
8000	98.31	89.13	81.81	60.03	49.38	43.17	39.18
9000	110.60	100.27	92.03	67.54	55.55	48.57	44.08
10000	122.89	111.41	102.26	75.04	61.73	53.97	48.98
11000	135.17	122.55	112.49	82.54	67.90	59.36	53.87
12000	147.46	133.70	122.71	90.05	74.07	64.76	58.77
13000	159.75	144.84	132.94	97.55	80.24	70.16	63.67
14000	172.04	155.98	143.16	105.06	86.42	75.55	68.57
15000	184.33	167.12	153.39	112.56	92.59	80.95	73.47
16000	196.62	178.26	163.62	120.06	98.76	86.35	78.36
17000	208.91	189.40	173.84	127.57	104.93	91.74	83.26
18000	221.19	200.54	184.07	135.07	111.11	97.14	88.16
19000	233.48	211.69	194.29	142.58	117.28	102.54	93.06
20000	245.77	222.83	204.52	150.08	123.45	107.93	97.95
21000	258.06	233.97	214.75	157.58	129.62	113.33	102.85
22000	270.35	245.11	224.97	165.09	135.80	118.73	107.75
23000	282.64	256.25	235.20	172.59	141.97	124.12	112.65
24000	294.92	267.39	245.42	180.10	148.14	129.52	117.54
25000	307.21	278.53	255.65	187.60	154.31	134.92	122.44
26000	319.50	289.67	265.88	195.10	160.49	140.31	127.34
27000	331.79	300.82	276.10	202.61	166.66	145.71	132.24
28000	344.08	311.96	286.33	210.11	172.83	151.10	137.13
29000	356.37	323.10	296.55	217.62	179.00	156.50	142.03
30000	368.66	334.24	306.78	225.12	185.18	161.90	146.93
35000	430.10	389.95	357.91	262.64	216.04	188.88	171.42
40000	491.54	445.65	409.04	300.16	246.90	215.86	195.91
45000	552.98	501.36	460.17	337.68	277.76	242.85	220.40
50000	614.43	557.07	511.30	375.20	308.63	269.83	244.88
55000	675.87	612.77	562.43	412.72	339.49	296.81	269.37
60000	737.31	668.48	613.56	450.24	370.35	323.80	293.86
65000	798.75	724.19	664.69	487.76	401.22	350.78	318.35
70000	860.20	779.89	715.82	525.28	432.08	377.76	342.84
75000	921.64	835.60	766.95	562.80	462.94	404.75	367.33
80000	983.08	891.31	818.08	600.32	493.80	431.73	391.81
85000	1044.53	947.01	869.21	637.84	524.67	458.71	416.30
90000	1105.97	1002.72	920.34	675.36	555.53	485.69	440.79
95000	1167.41	1058.43	971.47	712.88	586.39	512.68	465.28
100000	1228.85	1114.13	1022.60	750.40	617.25	539.66	489.77
200000	2457.71	2228.27	2045.20	1500.80	1234.51	1079.32	979.54
300000	3686.56	3342.40	3067.79	2251.20	1851.76	1618.98	1469.30
400000	4915.42	4456.53	4090.39	3001.60	2469.02	2158.64	1959.07
500000	6144.27	5570.66	5112.99	3752.00	3086.27	2698.30	2448.84
1000000	12288.54	11141.33	10225.98	7504.00	6172.55	5396.60	4897.68

4.375%

MONTHLY PAYMENT
NECESSARY TO AMORTIZE A LOAN

Amortization Amount	1 Year	2 Years	3 Years	4 Years	5 Years	6 Years	7 Years
25	2.13	1.09	0.74	0.57	0.46	0.39	0.35
50	4.27	2.18	1.48	1.14	0.93	0.79	0.69
100	8.53	4.36	2.97	2.27	1.86	1.58	1.38
200	17.06	8.71	5.93	4.55	3.71	3.16	2.76
300	25.59	13.07	8.90	6.82	5.57	4.74	4.15
400	34.12	17.43	11.87	9.09	7.43	6.32	5.53
500	42.65	21.79	14.84	11.36	9.28	7.90	6.91
600	51.18	26.14	17.80	13.64	11.14	9.48	8.29
700	59.71	30.50	20.77	15.91	13.00	11.06	9.68
800	68.24	34.86	23.74	18.18	14.85	12.64	11.06
900	76.77	39.22	26.71	20.46	16.71	14.22	12.44
1000	85.30	43.57	29.67	22.73	18.57	15.80	13.82
2000	170.61	87.15	59.35	45.46	37.14	31.60	27.65
3000	255.91	130.72	89.02	68.19	55.71	47.40	41.47
4000	341.21	174.30	118.69	90.92	74.27	63.19	55.30
5000	426.52	217.87	148.37	113.65	92.84	78.99	69.12
6000	511.82	261.45	178.04	136.38	111.41	94.79	82.94
7000	597.12	305.02	207.71	159.11	129.98	110.59	96.77
8000	682.43	348.60	237.39	181.84	148.55	126.39	110.59
9000	767.73	392.17	267.06	204.57	167.12	142.19	124.41
10000	853.03	435.74	296.74	227.30	185.68	157.99	138.24
11000	938.34	479.32	326.41	250.03	204.25	173.78	152.06
12000	1023.64	522.89	356.08	272.75	222.82	189.58	165.89
13000	1108.94	566.47	385.76	295.48	241.39	205.38	179.71
14000	1194.25	610.04	415.43	318.21	259.96	221.18	193.53
15000	1279.55	653.62	445.10	340.94	278.53	236.98	207.36
16000	1364.85	697.19	474.78	363.67	297.09	252.78	221.18
17000	1450.16	740.77	504.45	386.40	315.66	268.58	235.01
18000	1535.46	784.34	534.12	409.13	334.23	284.37	248.83
19000	1620.76	827.91	563.80	431.86	352.80	300.17	262.65
20000	1706.07	871.49	593.47	454.59	371.37	315.97	276.48
21000	1791.37	915.06	623.14	477.32	389.94	331.77	290.30
22000	1876.67	958.64	652.82	500.05	408.50	347.57	304.12
23000	1961.98	1002.21	682.49	522.78	427.07	363.37	317.95
24000	2047.28	1045.79	712.16	545.51	445.64	379.17	331.77
25000	2132.58	1089.36	741.84	568.24	464.21	394.96	345.60
26000	2217.89	1132.94	771.51	590.97	482.78	410.76	359.42
27000	2303.19	1176.51	801.19	613.70	501.35	426.56	373.24
28000	2388.49	1220.09	830.86	636.43	519.91	442.36	387.07
29000	2473.80	1263.66	860.53	659.16	538.48	458.16	400.89
30000	2559.10	1307.23	890.21	681.89	557.05	473.96	414.72
35000	2985.62	1525.11	1038.57	795.53	649.89	552.95	483.83
40000	3412.13	1742.98	1186.94	909.18	742.74	631.94	552.95
45000	3838.65	1960.85	1335.31	1022.83	835.58	710.94	622.07
50000	4265.17	2178.72	1483.68	1136.48	928.42	789.93	691.19
55000	4691.68	2396.60	1632.04	1250.13	1021.26	868.92	760.31
60000	5118.20	2614.47	1780.41	1363.77	1114.10	947.91	829.43
65000	5544.72	2832.34	1928.78	1477.42	1206.94	1026.91	898.55
70000	5971.23	3050.21	2077.15	1591.07	1299.79	1105.90	967.67
75000	6397.75	3268.09	2225.51	1704.72	1392.63	1184.89	1036.79
80000	6824.27	3485.96	2373.88	1818.37	1485.47	1263.89	1105.91
85000	7250.78	3703.83	2522.25	1932.01	1578.31	1342.88	1175.03
90000	7677.30	3921.70	2670.62	2045.66	1671.15	1421.87	1244.15
95000	8103.82	4139.57	2818.99	2159.31	1764.00	1500.87	1313.27
100000	8530.33	4357.45	2967.35	2272.96	1856.84	1579.86	1382.38
200000	17060.67	8714.89	5934.71	4545.91	3713.68	3159.72	2764.77
300000	25591.00	13072.34	8902.06	6818.87	5570.51	4739.57	4147.15
400000	34121.33	17429.79	11869.41	9091.83	7427.35	6319.43	5529.54
500000	42651.67	21787.24	14836.76	11364.78	9284.19	7899.29	6911.92
1000000	85303.34	43574.47	29673.53	22729.56	18568.38	15798.58	13823.85

Amortization Amount	8 Years	9 Years	10 Years	15 Years	20 Years	25 Years	30 Years
25	0.31	0.28	0.26	0.19	0.16	0.14	0.12
50	0.62	0.56	0.51	0.38	0.31	0.27	0.25
100	1.23	1.12	1.03	0.76	0.62	0.55	0.50
200	2.47	2.24	2.06	1.51	1.25	1.09	0.99
300	3.70	3.36	3.09	2.27	1.87	1.64	1.49
400	4.94	4.48	4.11	3.03	2.50	2.19	1.99
500	6.17	5.60	5.14	3.78	3.12	2.73	2.48
600	7.41	6.72	6.17	4.54	3.74	3.28	2.98
700	8.64	7.84	7.20	5.30	4.37	3.83	3.48
800	9.88	8.96	8.23	6.05	4.99	4.37	3.98
900	11.11	10.08	9.26	6.81	5.61	4.92	4.47
1000	12.35	11.20	10.28	7.57	6.24	5.47	4.97
2000	24.69	22.40	20.57	15.13	12.48	10.93	9.94
3000	37.04	33.60	30.85	22.70	18.71	16.40	14.91
4000	49.38	44.80	41.14	30.26	24.95	21.86	19.88
5000	61.73	56.00	51.42	37.83	31.19	27.33	24.85
6000	74.08	67.20	61.71	45.40	37.43	32.79	29.82
7000	86.42	78.40	71.99	52.96	43.67	38.26	34.79
8000	98.77	89.60	82.28	60.53	49.90	43.72	39.76
9000	111.11	100.80	92.56	68.10	56.14	49.19	44.73
10000	123.46	111.99	102.85	75.66	62.38	54.65	49.70
11000	135.81	123.19	113.13	83.23	68.62	60.12	54.67
12000	148.15	134.39	123.42	90.79	74.86	65.59	59.64
13000	160.50	145.59	133.70	98.36	81.10	71.05	64.61
14000	172.84	156.79	143.99	105.93	87.33	76.52	69.58
15000	185.19	167.99	154.27	113.49	93.57	81.98	74.55
16000	197.54	179.19	164.56	121.06	99.81	87.45	79.51
17000	209.88	190.39	174.84	128.63	106.05	92.91	84.48
18000	222.23	201.59	185.13	136.19	112.29	98.38	89.45
19000	234.57	212.79	195.41	143.76	118.52	103.84	94.42
20000	246.92	223.99	205.70	151.32	124.76	109.31	99.39
21000	259.27	235.19	215.98	158.89	131.00	114.77	104.36
22000	271.61	246.39	226.27	166.46	137.24	120.24	109.33
23000	283.96	257.59	236.55	174.02	143.48	125.71	114.30
24000	296.30	268.79	246.84	181.59	149.71	131.17	119.27
25000	308.65	279.99	257.12	189.16	155.95	136.64	124.24
26000	321.00	291.19	267.40	196.72	162.19	142.10	129.21
27000	333.34	302.39	277.69	204.29	168.43	147.57	134.18
28000	345.69	313.59	287.97	211.85	174.67	153.03	139.15
29000	358.03	324.78	298.26	219.42	180.91	158.50	144.12
30000	370.38	335.98	308.54	226.99	187.14	163.96	149.09
35000	432.11	391.98	359.97	264.82	218.33	191.29	173.94
40000	493.84	447.98	411.39	302.65	249.52	218.62	198.79
45000	555.57	503.98	462.82	340.48	280.72	245.95	223.64
50000	617.30	559.97	514.24	378.31	311.91	273.27	248.48
55000	679.03	615.97	565.66	416.14	343.10	300.60	273.33
60000	740.76	671.97	617.09	453.97	374.29	327.93	298.18
65000	802.49	727.97	668.51	491.80	405.48	355.25	323.03
70000	864.22	783.96	719.94	529.63	436.67	382.58	347.88
75000	925.95	839.96	771.36	567.47	467.86	409.91	372.73
80000	987.68	895.96	822.78	605.30	499.05	437.24	397.57
85000	1049.41	951.96	874.21	643.13	530.24	464.56	422.42
90000	1111.14	1007.95	925.63	680.96	561.43	491.89	447.27
95000	1172.87	1063.95	977.06	718.79	592.62	519.22	472.12
100000	1234.60	1119.95	1028.48	756.62	623.81	546.55	496.97
200000	2469.21	2239.90	2056.96	1513.24	1247.62	1093.09	993.93
300000	3703.81	3359.84	3085.44	2269.86	1871.44	1639.64	1490.90
400000	4938.41	4479.79	4113.92	3026.48	2495.25	2186.18	1987.87
500000	6173.02	5599.74	5142.40	3783.10	3119.06	2732.73	2484.83
1000000	12346.03	11199.48	10284.80	7566.20	6238.12	5465.45	4969.67

4.5%

MONTHLY PAYMENT
NECESSARY TO AMORTIZE A LOAN

Amortization Amount	1 Year	2 Years	3 Years	4 Years	5 Years	6 Years	7 Years
25	2.13	1.09	0.74	0.57	0.47	0.40	0.35
50	4.27	2.18	1.49	1.14	0.93	0.79	0.69
100	8.54	4.36	2.97	2.28	1.86	1.59	1.39
200	17.07	8.73	5.95	4.56	3.72	3.17	2.78
300	25.61	13.09	8.92	6.84	5.59	4.76	4.16
400	34.14	17.45	11.89	9.11	7.45	6.34	5.55
500	42.68	21.81	14.86	11.39	9.31	7.93	6.94
600	51.22	26.18	17.84	13.67	11.17	9.51	8.33
700	59.75	30.54	20.81	15.95	13.04	11.10	9.72
800	68.29	34.90	23.78	18.23	14.90	12.68	11.10
900	76.82	39.27	26.76	20.51	16.76	14.27	12.49
1000	85.36	43.63	29.73	22.78	18.62	15.85	13.88
2000	170.72	87.26	59.46	45.57	37.25	31.71	27.76
3000	256.08	130.89	89.18	68.35	55.87	47.56	41.64
4000	341.44	174.52	118.91	91.14	74.50	63.42	55.52
5000	426.80	218.15	148.64	113.92	93.12	79.27	69.40
6000	512.16	261.78	178.37	136.71	111.74	95.13	83.28
7000	597.52	305.40	208.10	159.49	130.37	110.98	97.17
8000	682.88	349.03	237.83	182.28	148.99	126.84	111.05
9000	768.24	392.66	267.55	205.06	167.62	142.69	124.93
10000	853.59	436.29	297.28	227.85	186.24	158.55	138.81
11000	938.95	479.92	327.01	250.63	204.87	174.40	152.69
12000	1024.31	523.55	356.74	273.42	223.49	190.26	166.57
13000	1109.67	567.18	386.47	296.20	242.11	206.11	180.45
14000	1195.03	610.81	416.20	318.99	260.74	221.97	194.33
15000	1280.39	654.44	445.92	341.77	279.36	237.82	208.21
16000	1365.75	698.07	475.65	364.56	297.99	253.68	222.09
17000	1451.11	741.70	505.38	387.34	316.61	269.53	235.97
18000	1536.47	785.33	535.11	410.13	335.23	285.39	249.85
19000	1621.83	828.96	564.84	432.91	353.86	301.24	263.74
20000	1707.19	872.58	594.57	455.70	372.48	317.10	277.62
21000	1792.55	916.21	624.29	478.48	391.11	332.95	291.50
22000	1877.91	959.84	654.02	501.26	409.73	348.81	305.38
23000	1963.27	1003.47	683.75	524.05	428.35	364.66	319.26
24000	2048.63	1047.10	713.48	546.83	446.98	380.52	333.14
25000	2133.99	1090.73	743.21	569.62	465.60	396.37	347.02
26000	2219.35	1134.36	772.94	592.40	484.23	412.23	360.90
27000	2304.71	1177.99	802.66	615.19	502.85	428.08	374.78
28000	2390.07	1221.62	832.39	637.97	521.47	443.94	388.66
29000	2475.42	1265.25	862.12	660.76	540.10	459.79	402.54
30000	2560.78	1308.88	891.85	683.54	558.72	475.65	416.42
35000	2987.58	1527.02	1040.49	797.47	651.84	554.92	485.83
40000	3414.38	1745.17	1189.13	911.39	744.96	634.20	555.23
45000	3841.18	1963.32	1337.77	1025.31	838.08	713.47	624.64
50000	4267.97	2181.46	1486.42	1139.24	931.21	792.75	694.04
55000	4694.77	2399.61	1635.06	1253.16	1024.33	872.02	763.44
60000	5121.57	2617.75	1783.70	1367.09	1117.45	951.29	832.85
65000	5548.37	2835.90	1932.34	1481.01	1210.57	1030.57	902.25
70000	5975.16	3054.05	2080.98	1594.93	1303.69	1109.84	971.66
75000	6401.96	3272.19	2229.62	1708.86	1396.81	1189.12	1041.06
80000	6828.76	3490.34	2378.27	1822.78	1489.93	1268.39	1110.47
85000	7255.56	3708.48	2526.91	1936.70	1583.05	1347.67	1179.87
90000	7682.35	3926.63	2675.55	2050.63	1676.17	1426.94	1249.27
95000	8109.15	4144.78	2824.19	2164.55	1769.29	1506.22	1318.68
100000	8535.95	4362.92	2972.83	2278.48	1862.41	1585.49	1388.08
200000	17071.90	8725.85	5945.67	4556.95	3724.82	3170.98	2776.16
300000	25607.84	13088.77	8918.50	6835.43	5587.23	4756.47	4164.24
400000	34143.79	17451.69	11891.33	9113.90	7449.64	6341.96	5552.33
500000	42679.74	21814.62	14864.16	11392.38	9312.05	7927.45	6940.41
1000000	85359.48	43629.23	29728.33	22784.75	18624.10	15854.90	13880.81

10

Amortization Amount	8 Years	9 Years	10 Years	15 Years	20 Years	25 Years	30 Years
25	0.31	0.28	0.26	0.19	0.16	0.14	0.13
50	0.62	0.56	0.52	0.38	0.32	0.28	0.25
100	1.24	1.13	1.03	0.76	0.63	0.55	0.50
200	2.48	2.25	2.07	1.53	1.26	1.11	1.01
300	3.72	3.38	3.10	2.29	1.89	1.66	1.51
400	4.96	4.50	4.14	3.05	2.52	2.21	2.02
500	6.20	5.63	5.17	3.81	3.15	2.77	2.52
600	7.44	6.75	6.21	4.58	3.78	3.32	3.03
700	8.68	7.88	7.24	5.34	4.41	3.87	3.53
800	9.92	9.01	8.28	6.10	5.04	4.43	4.03
900	11.16	10.13	9.31	6.87	5.67	4.98	4.54
1000	12.40	11.26	10.34	7.63	6.30	5.53	5.04
2000	24.81	22.52	20.69	15.26	12.61	11.07	10.08
3000	37.21	33.77	31.03	22.89	18.91	16.60	15.13
4000	49.61	45.03	41.38	30.51	25.22	22.14	20.17
5000	62.02	56.29	51.72	38.14	31.52	27.67	25.21
6000	74.42	67.55	62.06	45.77	37.82	33.21	30.25
7000	86.83	78.80	72.41	53.40	44.13	38.74	35.30
8000	99.23	90.06	82.75	61.03	50.43	44.28	40.34
9000	111.63	101.32	93.09	68.66	56.74	49.81	45.38
10000	124.04	112.58	103.44	76.29	63.04	55.35	50.42
11000	136.44	123.84	113.78	83.92	69.34	60.88	55.46
12000	148.84	135.09	124.13	91.54	75.65	66.42	60.51
13000	161.25	146.35	134.47	99.17	81.95	71.95	65.55
14000	173.65	157.61	144.81	106.80	88.26	77.49	70.59
15000	186.05	168.87	155.16	114.43	94.56	83.02	75.63
16000	198.46	180.12	165.50	122.06	100.86	88.56	80.67
17000	210.86	191.38	175.84	129.69	107.17	94.09	85.72
18000	223.27	202.64	186.19	137.32	113.47	99.63	90.76
19000	235.67	213.90	196.53	144.94	119.78	105.16	95.80
20000	248.07	225.16	206.88	152.57	126.08	110.69	100.84
21000	260.48	236.41	217.22	160.20	132.39	116.23	105.89
22000	272.88	247.67	227.56	167.83	138.69	121.76	110.93
23000	285.28	258.93	237.91	175.46	144.99	127.30	115.97
24000	297.69	270.19	248.25	183.09	151.30	132.83	121.01
25000	310.09	281.44	258.59	190.72	157.60	138.37	126.05
26000	322.50	292.70	268.94	198.35	163.91	143.90	131.10
27000	334.90	303.96	279.28	205.97	170.21	149.44	136.14
28000	347.30	315.22	289.63	213.60	176.51	154.97	141.18
29000	359.71	326.48	299.97	221.23	182.82	160.51	146.22
30000	372.11	337.73	310.31	228.86	189.12	166.04	151.26
35000	434.13	394.02	362.03	267.00	220.64	193.72	176.48
40000	496.15	450.31	413.75	305.15	252.16	221.39	201.69
45000	558.16	506.60	465.47	343.29	283.68	249.06	226.90
50000	620.18	562.89	517.19	381.43	315.20	276.74	252.11
55000	682.20	619.18	568.91	419.58	346.72	304.41	277.32
60000	744.22	675.47	620.63	457.72	378.24	332.08	302.53
65000	806.24	731.76	672.35	495.86	409.76	359.76	327.74
70000	868.26	788.04	724.07	534.01	441.28	387.43	352.95
75000	930.27	844.33	775.78	572.15	472.80	415.10	378.16
80000	992.29	900.62	827.50	610.29	504.32	442.78	403.37
85000	1054.31	956.91	879.22	648.44	535.84	470.45	428.58
90000	1116.33	1013.20	930.94	686.58	567.36	498.13	453.79
95000	1178.35	1069.49	982.66	724.72	598.88	525.80	479.00
100000	1240.37	1125.78	1034.38	762.87	630.41	553.47	504.22
200000	2480.73	2251.56	2068.76	1525.74	1260.81	1106.95	1008.43
300000	3721.10	3377.33	3103.14	2288.60	1891.22	1660.42	1512.65
400000	4961.46	4503.11	4137.52	3051.47	2521.62	2213.89	2016.86
500000	6201.83	5628.89	5171.90	3814.34	3152.03	2767.36	2521.08
1000000	12403.66	11257.78	10343.79	7628.68	6304.05	5534.73	5042.16

4.625%

Amortization Amount	1 Year	2 Years	3 Years	4 Years	5 Years	6 Years	7 Years
25	2.14	1.09	0.74	0.57	0.47	0.40	0.35
50	4.27	2.18	1.49	1.14	0.93	0.80	0.70
100	8.54	4.37	2.98	2.28	1.87	1.59	1.39
200	17.08	8.74	5.96	4.57	3.74	3.18	2.79
300	25.62	13.11	8.93	6.85	5.60	4.77	4.18
400	34.17	17.47	11.91	9.14	7.47	6.36	5.58
500	42.71	21.84	14.89	11.42	9.34	7.96	6.97
600	51.25	26.21	17.87	13.70	11.21	9.55	8.36
700	59.79	30.58	20.85	15.99	13.08	11.14	9.76
800	68.33	34.95	23.83	18.27	14.94	12.73	11.15
900	76.87	39.32	26.80	20.56	16.81	14.32	12.54
1000	85.42	43.68	29.78	22.84	18.68	15.91	13.94
2000	170.83	87.37	59.57	45.68	37.36	31.82	27.88
3000	256.25	131.05	89.35	68.52	56.04	47.73	41.81
4000	341.66	174.74	119.13	91.36	74.72	63.65	55.75
5000	427.08	218.42	148.92	114.20	93.40	79.56	69.69
6000	512.49	262.10	178.70	137.04	112.08	95.47	83.63
7000	597.91	305.79	208.48	159.88	130.76	111.38	97.57
8000	683.32	349.47	238.27	182.72	149.44	127.29	111.50
9000	768.74	393.16	268.05	205.56	168.12	143.20	125.44
10000	854.16	436.84	297.83	228.40	186.80	159.11	139.38
11000	939.57	480.52	327.61	251.24	205.48	175.02	153.32
12000	1024.99	524.21	357.40	274.08	224.16	190.94	167.25
13000	1110.40	567.89	387.18	296.92	242.84	206.85	181.19
14000	1195.82	611.58	416.96	319.76	261.52	222.76	195.13
15000	1281.23	655.26	446.75	342.60	280.20	238.67	209.07
16000	1366.65	698.94	476.53	365.44	298.88	254.58	223.01
17000	1452.07	742.63	506.31	388.28	317.56	270.49	236.94
18000	1537.48	786.31	536.10	411.12	336.24	286.40	250.88
19000	1622.90	830.00	565.88	433.96	354.92	302.32	264.82
20000	1708.31	873.68	595.66	456.80	373.60	318.23	278.76
21000	1793.73	917.36	625.45	479.64	392.28	334.14	292.70
22000	1879.14	961.05	655.23	502.48	410.96	350.05	306.63
23000	1964.56	1004.73	685.01	525.32	429.64	365.96	320.57
24000	2049.97	1048.42	714.80	548.16	448.32	381.87	334.51
25000	2135.39	1092.10	744.58	571.00	467.00	397.78	348.45
26000	2220.81	1135.78	774.36	593.84	485.68	413.69	362.39
27000	2306.22	1179.47	804.15	616.68	504.36	429.61	376.32
28000	2391.64	1223.15	833.93	639.52	523.04	445.52	390.26
29000	2477.05	1266.84	863.71	662.36	541.72	461.43	404.20
30000	2562.47	1310.52	893.49	685.20	560.40	477.34	418.14
35000	2989.55	1528.94	1042.41	799.40	653.80	556.90	487.83
40000	3416.62	1747.36	1191.33	913.60	747.20	636.45	557.52
45000	3843.70	1965.78	1340.24	1027.80	840.60	716.01	627.21
50000	4270.78	2184.20	1489.16	1142.00	933.99	795.57	696.89
55000	4697.86	2402.62	1638.07	1256.20	1027.39	875.12	766.58
60000	5124.94	2621.04	1786.99	1370.40	1120.79	954.68	836.27
65000	5552.02	2839.46	1935.91	1484.60	1214.19	1034.24	905.96
70000	5979.09	3057.88	2084.82	1598.80	1307.59	1113.79	975.65
75000	6406.17	3276.30	2233.74	1713.00	1400.99	1193.35	1045.34
80000	6833.25	3494.72	2382.65	1827.20	1494.39	1272.91	1115.03
85000	7260.33	3713.14	2531.57	1941.40	1587.79	1352.46	1184.72
90000	7687.41	3931.56	2680.48	2055.60	1681.19	1432.02	1254.41
95000	8114.48	4149.98	2829.40	2169.80	1774.59	1511.58	1324.10
100000	8541.56	4368.40	2978.32	2284.00	1887.99	1591.13	1393.79
200000	17083.12	8736.80	5956.63	4568.00	3735.98	3182.26	2787.58
300000	25624.68	13105.20	8934.95	6852.00	5603.97	4773.40	4181.37
400000	34166.25	17473.60	11913.27	9136.00	7471.96	6364.53	5575.16
500000	42707.81	21842.00	14891.58	11420.00	9339.95	7955.66	6968.95
1000000	85415.62	43684.01	29783.16	22840.00	18679.90	15911.32	13937.89

Amortization Amount	8 Years	9 Years	10 Years	15 Years	20 Years	25 Years	30 Years
25	0.31	0.28	0.26	0.19	0.16	0.14	0.13
50	0.62	0.57	0.52	0.38	0.32	0.28	0.26
100	1.25	1.13	1.04	0.77	0.64	0.56	0.51
200	2.49	2.26	2.08	1.54	1.27	1.12	1.02
300	3.74	3.39	3.12	2.31	1.91	1.68	1.53
400	4.98	4.53	4.16	3.08	2.55	2.24	2.05
500	6.23	5.66	5.20	3.85	3.19	2.80	2.56
600	7.48	6.79	6.24	4.61	3.82	3.36	3.07
700	8.72	7.92	7.28	5.38	4.46	3.92	3.58
800	9.97	9.05	8.32	6.15	5.10	4.48	4.09
900	11.22	10.18	9.36	6.92	5.73	5.04	4.60
1000	12.46	11.32	10.40	7.69	6.37	5.60	5.12
2000	24.92	22.63	20.81	15.38	12.74	11.21	10.23
3000	37.38	33.95	31.21	23.07	19.11	16.81	15.35
4000	49.85	45.26	41.61	30.77	25.48	22.42	20.46
5000	62.31	56.58	52.01	38.46	31.85	28.02	25.58
6000	74.77	67.90	62.42	46.15	38.22	33.63	30.69
7000	87.23	79.21	72.82	53.84	44.59	39.23	35.81
8000	99.69	90.53	83.22	61.53	50.96	44.84	40.92
9000	112.15	101.85	93.63	69.22	57.33	50.44	46.04
10000	124.61	113.16	104.03	76.91	63.70	56.04	51.15
11000	137.08	124.48	114.43	84.61	70.07	61.65	56.27
12000	149.54	135.79	124.84	92.30	76.44	67.25	61.38
13000	162.00	147.11	135.24	99.99	82.81	72.86	66.50
14000	174.46	158.43	145.64	107.68	89.18	78.46	71.61
15000	186.92	169.74	156.04	115.37	95.55	84.07	76.73
16000	199.38	181.06	166.45	123.06	101.93	89.67	81.84
17000	211.84	192.38	176.85	130.75	108.30	95.28	86.96
18000	224.31	203.69	187.25	138.45	114.67	100.88	92.07
19000	236.77	215.01	197.66	146.14	121.04	106.48	97.19
20000	249.23	226.32	208.06	153.83	127.41	112.09	102.30
21000	261.69	237.64	218.46	161.52	133.78	117.69	107.42
22000	274.15	248.96	228.87	169.21	140.15	123.30	112.53
23000	286.61	260.27	239.27	176.90	146.52	128.90	117.65
24000	299.07	271.59	249.67	184.59	152.89	134.51	122.76
25000	311.54	282.91	260.07	192.29	159.26	140.11	127.88
26000	324.00	294.22	270.48	199.98	165.63	145.72	132.99
27000	336.46	305.54	280.88	207.67	172.00	151.32	138.11
28000	348.92	316.85	291.28	215.36	178.37	156.92	143.22
29000	361.38	328.17	301.69	223.05	184.74	162.53	148.34
30000	373.84	339.49	312.09	230.74	191.11	168.13	153.45
35000	436.15	396.07	364.10	269.20	222.96	196.16	179.03
40000	498.46	452.65	416.12	307.66	254.81	224.18	204.61
45000	560.76	509.23	468.13	346.11	286.66	252.20	230.18
50000	623.07	565.81	520.15	384.57	318.52	280.22	255.76
55000	685.38	622.39	572.16	423.03	350.37	308.24	281.33
60000	747.69	678.97	624.18	461.49	382.22	336.27	306.91
65000	809.99	735.56	676.19	499.94	414.07	364.29	332.48
70000	872.30	792.14	728.21	538.40	445.92	392.31	358.06
75000	934.61	848.72	780.22	576.86	477.77	420.33	383.63
80000	996.91	905.30	832.24	615.31	509.63	448.35	409.21
85000	1059.22	961.88	884.25	653.77	541.48	476.38	434.79
90000	1121.53	1018.46	936.27	692.23	573.33	504.40	460.36
95000	1183.83	1075.04	988.28	730.69	605.18	532.42	485.94
100000	1246.14	1131.62	1040.30	769.14	637.03	560.44	511.51
200000	2492.28	2263.25	2080.59	1538.28	1274.07	1120.89	1023.03
300000	3738.43	3394.87	3120.89	2307.43	1911.10	1681.33	1534.54
400000	4984.57	4526.50	4161.18	3076.57	2548.13	2241.77	2046.05
500000	6230.71	5658.12	5201.48	3845.71	3185.17	2802.22	2557.56
1000000	12461.42	11316.24	10402.96	7691.42	6370.33	5604.43	5115.13

4.75%

Amortization Amount	1 Year	2 Years	3 Years	4 Years	5 Years	6 Years	7 Years
25	2.14	1.09	0.75	0.57	0.47	0.40	0.35
50	4.27	2.19	1.49	1.14	0.94	0.80	0.70
100	8.55	4.37	2.98	2.29	1.87	1.60	1.40
200	17.09	8.75	5.97	4.58	3.75	3.19	2.80
300	25.64	13.12	8.95	6.87	5.62	4.79	4.20
400	34.19	17.50	11.94	9.16	7.49	6.39	5.60
500	42.74	21.87	14.92	11.45	9.37	7.98	7.00
600	51.28	26.24	17.90	13.74	11.24	9.58	8.40
700	59.83	30.62	20.89	16.03	13.12	11.18	9.80
800	68.38	34.99	23.87	18.32	14.99	12.77	11.20
900	76.92	39.36	26.85	20.61	16.86	14.37	12.60
1000	85.47	43.74	29.84	22.90	18.74	15.97	14.00
2000	170.94	87.48	59.68	45.79	37.47	31.94	27.99
3000	256.42	131.22	89.51	68.69	56.21	47.90	41.99
4000	341.89	174.96	119.35	91.58	74.94	63.87	55.98
5000	427.36	218.69	149.19	114.48	93.68	79.84	69.98
6000	512.83	262.43	179.03	137.37	112.41	95.81	83.97
7000	598.30	306.17	208.87	160.27	131.15	111.77	97.97
8000	683.77	349.91	238.70	183.16	149.89	127.74	111.96
9000	769.25	393.65	268.54	206.06	168.62	143.71	125.96
10000	854.72	437.39	298.38	228.95	187.36	159.68	139.95
11000	940.19	481.13	328.22	251.85	206.09	175.65	153.95
12000	1025.66	524.87	358.06	274.74	224.83	191.61	167.94
13000	1111.13	568.60	387.89	297.64	243.57	207.58	181.94
14000	1196.60	612.34	417.73	320.53	262.30	223.55	195.93
15000	1282.08	656.08	447.57	343.43	281.04	239.52	209.93
16000	1367.55	699.82	477.41	366.32	299.77	255.49	223.92
17000	1453.02	743.56	507.25	389.22	318.51	271.45	237.92
18000	1538.49	787.30	537.08	412.12	337.24	287.42	251.91
19000	1623.96	831.04	566.92	435.01	355.98	303.39	265.91
20000	1709.43	874.78	596.76	457.91	374.72	319.36	279.90
21000	1794.91	918.51	626.60	480.80	393.45	335.32	293.90
22000	1880.38	962.25	656.44	503.70	412.19	351.29	307.89
23000	1965.85	1005.99	686.27	526.59	430.92	367.26	321.89
24000	2051.32	1049.73	716.11	549.49	449.66	383.23	335.88
25000	2136.79	1093.47	745.95	572.38	468.39	399.20	349.88
26000	2222.27	1137.21	775.79	595.28	487.13	415.16	363.87
27000	2307.74	1180.95	805.63	618.17	505.87	431.13	377.87
28000	2393.21	1224.69	835.46	641.07	524.60	447.10	391.86
29000	2478.68	1268.43	865.30	663.96	543.34	463.07	405.86
30000	2564.15	1312.16	895.14	686.86	562.07	479.04	419.85
35000	2991.51	1530.86	1044.33	801.34	655.75	558.87	489.83
40000	3418.87	1749.55	1193.52	915.81	749.43	638.71	559.80
45000	3846.23	1968.25	1342.71	1030.29	843.11	718.55	629.78
50000	4273.59	2186.94	1491.90	1144.76	936.79	798.39	699.75
55000	4700.95	2405.63	1641.09	1259.24	1030.47	878.23	769.73
60000	5128.30	2624.33	1790.28	1373.72	1124.15	958.07	839.71
65000	5555.66	2843.02	1939.47	1488.19	1217.83	1037.91	909.68
70000	5983.02	3061.72	2088.66	1602.67	1311.50	1117.75	979.66
75000	6410.38	3280.41	2237.85	1717.15	1405.18	1197.59	1049.63
80000	6837.74	3499.10	2387.04	1831.62	1498.86	1277.43	1119.61
85000	7265.10	3717.80	2536.23	1946.10	1592.54	1357.27	1189.58
90000	7692.46	3936.49	2685.42	2060.58	1686.22	1437.11	1259.56
95000	8119.82	4155.19	2834.61	2175.05	1779.90	1516.94	1329.53
100000	8547.17	4373.88	2983.80	2289.53	1873.58	1596.78	1399.51
200000	17094.35	8747.76	5967.61	4579.06	3747.15	3193.57	2799.02
300000	25641.52	13121.64	8951.41	6868.59	5620.73	4790.35	4198.53
400000	34188.70	17495.52	11935.21	9158.12	7494.31	6387.13	5598.03
500000	42735.87	21869.40	14919.02	11447.65	9367.89	7983.92	6997.54
1000000	85471.74	43738.80	29838.03	22895.30	18735.77	15967.84	13995.09

Amortization Amount	8 Years	9 Years	10 Years	15 Years	20 Years	25 Years	30 Years
25	0.31	0.28	0.26	0.19	0.16	0.14	0.13
50	0.63	0.57	0.52	0.39	0.32	0.28	0.26
100	1.25	1.14	1.05	0.78	0.64	0.57	0.52
200	2.50	2.27	2.09	1.55	1.29	1.13	1.04
300	3.76	3.41	3.14	2.33	1.93	1.70	1.56
400	5.01	4.55	4.18	3.10	2.57	2.27	2.08
500	6.26	5.69	5.23	3.88	3.22	2.84	2.59
600	7.51	6.82	6.28	4.65	3.86	3.40	3.11
700	8.76	7.96	7.32	5.43	4.51	3.97	3.63
800	10.02	9.10	8.37	6.20	5.15	4.54	4.15
900	11.27	10.24	9.42	6.98	5.79	5.11	4.67
1000	12.52	11.37	10.46	7.75	6.44	5.67	5.19
2000	25.04	22.75	20.92	15.51	12.87	11.35	10.38
3000	37.56	34.12	31.39	23.26	19.31	17.02	15.57
4000	50.08	45.50	41.85	31.02	25.75	22.70	20.75
5000	62.60	56.87	52.31	38.77	32.18	28.37	25.94
6000	75.12	68.25	62.77	46.53	38.62	34.05	31.13
7000	87.64	79.62	73.24	54.28	45.06	39.72	36.32
8000	100.15	91.00	83.70	62.04	51.50	45.40	41.51
9000	112.67	102.37	94.16	69.79	57.93	51.07	46.70
10000	125.19	113.75	104.62	77.54	64.37	56.75	51.89
11000	137.71	125.12	115.09	85.30	70.81	62.42	57.07
12000	150.23	136.50	125.55	93.05	77.24	68.09	62.26
13000	162.75	147.87	136.01	100.81	83.68	73.77	67.45
14000	175.27	159.25	146.47	108.56	90.12	79.44	72.64
15000	187.79	170.62	156.93	116.32	96.55	85.12	77.83
16000	200.31	182.00	167.40	124.07	102.99	90.79	83.02
17000	212.83	193.37	177.86	131.83	109.43	96.47	88.21
18000	225.35	204.75	188.32	139.58	115.87	102.14	93.39
19000	237.87	216.12	198.78	147.33	122.30	107.82	98.58
20000	250.39	227.50	209.25	155.09	128.74	113.49	103.77
21000	262.91	238.87	219.71	162.84	135.18	119.17	108.96
22000	275.42	250.25	230.17	170.60	141.61	124.84	114.15
23000	287.94	261.62	240.63	178.35	148.05	130.51	119.34
24000	300.46	273.00	251.10	186.11	154.49	136.19	124.53
25000	312.98	284.37	261.56	193.86	160.92	141.86	129.71
26000	325.50	295.75	272.02	201.62	167.36	147.54	134.90
27000	338.02	307.12	282.48	209.37	173.80	153.21	140.09
28000	350.54	318.50	292.94	217.12	180.23	158.89	145.28
29000	363.06	329.87	303.41	224.88	186.67	164.56	150.47
30000	375.58	341.25	313.87	232.63	193.11	170.24	155.66
35000	438.18	398.12	366.18	271.41	225.29	198.61	181.60
40000	500.77	454.99	418.49	310.18	257.48	226.98	207.54
45000	563.37	511.87	470.80	348.95	289.66	255.36	233.49
50000	625.97	568.74	523.11	387.72	321.85	283.73	259.43
55000	688.56	625.62	575.43	426.49	354.03	312.10	285.37
60000	751.16	682.49	627.74	465.27	386.22	340.47	311.31
65000	813.76	739.37	680.05	504.04	418.40	368.85	337.26
70000	876.35	796.24	732.36	542.81	450.59	397.22	363.20
75000	938.95	853.11	784.67	581.58	482.77	425.59	389.14
80000	1001.55	909.99	836.98	620.35	514.96	453.96	415.09
85000	1064.14	966.86	889.30	659.13	547.14	482.34	441.03
90000	1126.74	1023.74	941.61	697.90	579.33	510.71	466.97
95000	1189.33	1080.61	993.92	736.67	611.51	539.08	492.92
100000	1251.93	1137.49	1046.23	775.44	643.70	567.46	518.86
200000	2503.86	2274.97	2092.46	1550.89	1287.39	1134.91	1037.72
300000	3755.79	3412.46	3138.69	2326.33	1931.09	1702.37	1556.57
400000	5007.73	4549.94	4184.92	3101.77	2574.78	2269.82	2075.43
500000	6259.66	5687.43	5231.15	3877.22	3218.48	2837.28	2594.29
1000000	12519.32	11374.85	10462.30	7754.43	6436.96	5674.56	5188.58

4.875%

Amortization Amount	1 Year	2 Years	3 Years	4 Years	5 Years	6 Years	7 Years
25	2.14	1.09	0.75	0.57	0.47	0.40	0.35
50	4.28	2.19	1.49	1.15	0.94	0.80	0.70
100	8.55	4.38	2.99	2.30	1.88	1.60	1.41
200	17.11	8.76	5.98	4.59	3.76	3.20	2.81
300	25.66	13.14	8.97	6.89	5.64	4.81	4.22
400	34.21	17.52	11.96	9.18	7.52	6.41	5.62
500	42.76	21.90	14.95	11.48	9.40	8.01	7.03
600	51.32	26.28	17.94	13.77	11.28	9.61	8.43
700	59.87	30.66	20.93	16.07	13.15	11.22	9.84
800	68.42	35.03	23.91	18.36	15.03	12.82	11.24
900	76.98	39.41	26.90	20.66	16.91	14.42	12.65
1000	85.53	43.79	29.89	22.95	18.79	16.02	14.05
2000	171.06	87.59	59.79	45.90	37.58	32.05	28.10
3000	256.58	131.38	89.68	68.85	56.38	48.07	42.16
4000	342.11	175.17	119.57	91.80	75.17	64.10	56.21
5000	427.64	218.97	149.46	114.75	93.96	80.12	70.26
6000	513.17	262.76	179.36	137.70	112.75	96.15	84.31
7000	598.70	306.56	209.25	160.65	131.54	112.17	98.37
8000	684.22	350.35	239.14	183.61	150.33	128.20	112.42
9000	769.75	394.14	269.04	206.56	169.13	144.22	126.47
10000	855.28	437.94	298.93	229.51	187.92	160.24	140.52
11000	940.81	481.73	328.82	252.46	206.71	176.27	154.58
12000	1026.33	525.52	358.72	275.41	225.50	192.29	168.63
13000	1111.86	569.32	388.61	298.36	244.29	208.32	182.68
14000	1197.39	613.11	418.50	321.31	263.08	224.34	196.73
15000	1282.92	656.90	448.39	344.26	281.88	240.37	210.79
16000	1368.45	700.70	478.29	367.21	300.67	256.39	224.84
17000	1453.97	744.49	508.18	390.16	319.46	272.42	238.89
18000	1539.50	788.28	538.07	413.11	338.25	288.44	252.94
19000	1625.03	832.08	567.97	436.06	357.04	304.46	267.00
20000	1710.56	875.87	597.86	459.01	375.83	320.49	281.05
21000	1796.09	919.67	627.75	481.96	394.63	336.51	295.10
22000	1881.61	963.46	657.64	504.91	413.42	352.54	309.15
23000	1967.14	1007.25	687.54	527.87	432.21	368.56	323.21
24000	2052.67	1051.05	717.43	550.82	451.00	384.59	337.26
25000	2138.20	1094.84	747.32	573.77	469.79	400.61	351.31
26000	2223.72	1138.63	777.22	596.72	488.58	416.64	365.36
27000	2309.25	1182.43	807.11	619.67	507.38	432.66	379.41
28000	2394.78	1226.22	837.00	642.62	526.17	448.68	393.47
29000	2480.31	1270.01	866.90	665.57	544.96	464.71	407.52
30000	2565.84	1313.81	896.79	688.52	563.75	480.73	421.57
35000	2993.48	1532.78	1046.25	803.27	657.71	560.86	491.83
40000	3421.11	1751.74	1195.72	918.03	751.67	640.98	562.10
45000	3848.75	1970.71	1345.18	1032.78	845.63	721.10	632.36
50000	4276.39	2189.68	1494.65	1147.53	939.59	801.22	702.62
55000	4704.03	2408.65	1644.11	1262.29	1033.54	881.34	772.88
60000	5131.67	2627.62	1793.58	1377.04	1127.50	961.47	843.14
65000	5559.31	2846.58	1943.04	1491.79	1221.46	1041.59	913.41
70000	5986.95	3065.55	2092.51	1606.55	1315.42	1121.71	983.67
75000	6414.59	3284.52	2241.97	1721.30	1409.38	1201.83	1053.93
80000	6842.23	3503.49	2391.43	1836.05	1503.34	1281.96	1124.19
85000	7269.87	3722.46	2540.90	1950.81	1597.30	1362.08	1194.45
90000	7697.51	3941.42	2690.36	2065.56	1691.25	1442.20	1264.72
95000	8125.15	4160.39	2839.83	2180.31	1785.21	1522.32	1334.98
100000	8552.79	4379.36	2989.29	2295.07	1879.17	1602.44	1405.24
200000	17105.57	8758.72	5978.59	4590.13	3758.34	3204.89	2810.48
300000	25658.36	13138.08	8967.88	6885.20	5637.52	4807.33	4215.72
400000	34211.14	17517.44	11957.17	9180.26	7516.69	6409.78	5620.96
500000	42763.93	21896.80	14946.47	11475.33	9395.86	8012.22	7026.20
1000000	85527.86	43793.60	29892.93	22950.65	18791.72	16024.44	14052.39

Amortization Amount	8 Years	9 Years	10 Years	15 Years	20 Years	25 Years	30 Years
25	0.31	0.29	0.26	0.20	0.16	0.14	0.13
50	0.63	0.57	0.53	0.39	0.33	0.29	0.26
100	1.26	1.14	1.05	0.78	0.65	0.57	0.53
200	2.52	2.29	2.10	1.56	1.30	1.15	1.05
300	3.77	3.43	3.16	2.35	1.95	1.72	1.58
400	5.03	4.57	4.21	3.13	2.60	2.30	2.11
500	6.29	5.72	5.26	3.91	3.25	2.87	2.63
600	7.55	6.86	6.31	4.69	3.90	3.45	3.16
700	8.80	8.00	7.37	5.47	4.55	4.02	3.68
800	10.06	9.15	8.42	6.25	5.20	4.60	4.21
900	11.32	10.29	9.47	7.04	5.85	5.17	4.74
1000	12.58	11.43	10.52	7.82	6.50	5.75	5.26
2000	25.15	22.87	21.04	15.64	13.01	11.49	10.53
3000	37.73	34.30	31.57	23.45	19.51	17.24	15.79
4000	50.31	45.73	42.09	31.27	26.02	22.98	21.05
5000	62.89	57.17	52.61	39.09	32.52	28.73	26.31
6000	75.46	68.60	63.13	46.91	39.02	34.47	31.58
7000	88.04	80.04	73.65	54.72	45.53	40.22	36.84
8000	100.62	91.47	84.17	62.54	52.03	45.96	42.10
9000	113.20	102.90	94.70	70.36	58.54	51.71	47.36
10000	125.77	114.34	105.22	78.18	65.04	57.45	52.63
11000	138.35	125.77	115.74	85.99	71.54	63.20	57.89
12000	150.93	137.20	126.26	93.81	78.05	68.94	63.15
13000	163.51	148.64	136.78	101.63	84.55	74.69	68.41
14000	176.08	160.07	147.31	109.45	91.06	80.43	73.68
15000	188.66	171.50	157.83	117.27	97.56	86.18	78.94
16000	201.24	182.94	168.35	125.08	104.06	91.92	84.20
17000	213.81	194.37	178.87	132.90	110.57	97.67	89.46
18000	226.39	205.81	189.39	140.72	117.07	103.41	94.73
19000	238.97	217.24	199.91	148.54	123.57	109.16	99.99
20000	251.55	228.67	210.44	156.35	130.08	114.90	105.25
21000	264.12	240.11	220.96	164.17	136.58	120.65	110.51
22000	276.70	251.54	231.48	171.99	143.09	126.39	115.78
23000	289.28	262.97	242.00	179.81	149.59	132.14	121.04
24000	301.86	274.41	252.52	187.62	156.09	137.88	126.30
25000	314.43	285.84	263.05	195.44	162.60	143.63	131.56
26000	327.01	297.27	273.57	203.26	169.10	149.37	136.83
27000	339.59	308.71	284.09	211.08	175.61	155.12	142.09
28000	352.17	320.14	294.61	218.90	182.11	160.86	147.35
29000	364.74	331.58	305.13	226.71	188.61	166.61	152.61
30000	377.32	343.01	315.65	234.53	195.12	172.35	157.88
35000	440.21	400.18	368.26	273.62	227.64	201.08	184.19
40000	503.09	457.34	420.87	312.71	260.16	229.80	210.50
45000	565.98	514.51	473.48	351.80	292.68	258.53	236.81
50000	628.87	571.68	526.09	390.89	325.20	287.25	263.13
55000	691.75	628.85	578.70	429.97	357.72	315.98	289.44
60000	754.64	686.02	631.31	469.06	390.24	344.71	315.75
65000	817.53	743.19	683.92	508.15	422.76	373.43	342.06
70000	880.41	800.35	736.53	547.24	455.28	402.16	368.38
75000	943.30	857.52	789.14	586.33	487.79	430.88	394.69
80000	1006.19	914.69	841.74	625.42	520.31	459.61	421.00
85000	1069.07	971.86	894.35	664.50	552.83	488.33	447.31
90000	1131.96	1029.03	946.96	703.59	585.35	517.06	473.63
95000	1194.85	1086.19	999.57	742.68	617.87	545.78	499.94
100000	1257.73	1143.36	1052.18	781.77	650.39	574.51	526.25
200000	2515.47	2286.72	2104.36	1563.54	1300.79	1149.02	1052.50
300000	3773.20	3430.09	3156.54	2345.31	1951.18	1723.53	1578.75
400000	5030.94	4573.45	4208.72	3127.08	2601.57	2298.04	2105.00
500000	6288.67	5716.81	5260.90	3908.85	3251.97	2872.55	2631.25
1000000	12577.35	11433.62	10521.81	7817.70	6503.93	5745.10	5262.51

5%

Amortization Amount	1 Year	2 Years	3 Years	4 Years	5 Years	6 Years	7 Years
25	2.14	1.10	0.75	0.58	0.47	0.40	0.35
50	4.28	2.19	1.50	1.15	0.94	0.80	0.71
100	8.56	4.38	2.99	2.30	1.88	1.61	1.41
200	17.12	8.77	5.99	4.60	3.77	3.22	2.82
300	25.68	13.15	8.98	6.90	5.65	4.82	4.23
400	34.23	17.54	11.98	9.20	7.54	6.43	5.64
500	42.79	21.92	14.97	11.50	9.42	8.04	7.05
600	51.35	26.31	17.97	13.80	11.31	9.65	8.47
700	59.91	30.69	20.96	16.10	13.19	11.26	9.88
800	68.47	35.08	23.96	18.40	15.08	12.86	11.29
900	77.03	39.46	26.95	20.71	16.96	14.47	12.70
1000	85.58	43.85	29.95	23.01	18.85	16.08	14.11
2000	171.17	87.70	59.90	46.01	37.70	32.16	28.22
3000	256.75	131.55	89.84	69.02	56.54	48.24	42.33
4000	342.34	175.39	119.79	92.02	75.39	64.32	56.44
5000	427.92	219.24	149.74	115.03	94.24	80.41	70.55
6000	513.50	263.09	179.69	138.04	113.09	96.49	84.66
7000	599.09	306.94	209.64	161.04	131.93	112.57	98.77
8000	684.67	350.79	239.58	184.05	150.78	128.65	112.88
9000	770.26	394.64	269.53	207.05	169.63	144.73	126.99
10000	855.84	438.48	299.48	230.06	188.48	160.81	141.10
11000	941.42	482.33	329.43	253.07	207.33	176.89	155.21
12000	1027.01	526.18	359.37	276.07	226.17	192.97	169.32
13000	1112.59	570.03	389.32	299.08	245.02	209.05	183.43
14000	1198.18	613.88	419.27	322.08	263.87	225.14	197.54
15000	1283.76	657.73	449.22	345.09	282.72	241.22	211.65
16000	1369.34	701.57	479.17	368.10	301.56	257.30	225.76
17000	1454.93	745.42	509.11	391.10	320.41	273.38	239.87
18000	1540.51	789.27	539.06	414.11	339.26	289.46	253.98
19000	1626.10	833.12	569.01	437.12	358.11	305.54	268.09
20000	1711.68	876.97	598.96	460.12	376.95	321.62	282.20
21000	1797.26	920.82	628.91	483.13	395.80	337.70	296.31
22000	1882.85	964.67	658.85	506.13	414.65	353.79	310.42
23000	1968.43	1008.51	688.80	529.14	433.50	369.87	324.53
24000	2054.02	1052.36	718.75	552.15	452.35	385.95	338.64
25000	2139.60	1096.21	748.70	575.15	471.19	402.03	352.75
26000	2225.18	1140.06	778.64	598.16	490.04	418.11	366.86
27000	2310.77	1183.91	808.59	621.16	508.89	434.19	380.97
28000	2396.35	1227.76	838.54	644.17	527.74	450.27	395.07
29000	2481.94	1271.60	868.49	667.18	546.58	466.35	409.18
30000	2587.52	1315.45	898.44	690.18	565.43	482.43	423.29
35000	2995.44	1534.69	1048.18	805.21	659.67	562.84	493.84
40000	3423.36	1753.94	1197.91	920.24	753.91	643.25	564.39
45000	3851.28	1973.18	1347.65	1035.27	848.15	723.65	634.94
50000	4279.20	2192.42	1497.39	1150.30	942.39	804.06	705.49
55000	4707.12	2411.66	1647.13	1265.33	1036.63	884.46	776.04
60000	5135.04	2630.91	1796.87	1380.36	1130.86	964.87	846.59
65000	5562.96	2850.15	1946.61	1495.39	1225.10	1045.27	917.14
70000	5990.88	3069.39	2096.35	1610.42	1319.34	1125.68	987.69
75000	6418.80	3288.63	2246.09	1725.45	1413.58	1206.09	1058.24
80000	6846.72	3507.87	2395.83	1840.48	1507.82	1286.49	1128.79
85000	7274.64	3727.12	2545.57	1955.52	1602.06	1366.90	1199.33
90000	7702.56	3946.36	2695.31	2070.55	1696.30	1447.30	1269.88
95000	8130.48	4165.60	2845.05	2185.58	1790.54	1527.71	1340.43
100000	8558.40	4384.84	2994.79	2300.61	1884.77	1608.11	1410.98
200000	17116.79	8769.68	5989.57	4601.21	3769.55	3216.23	2821.96
300000	25675.19	13154.53	8984.36	6901.82	5654.32	4824.34	4232.94
400000	34233.59	17539.37	11979.15	9202.42	7539.10	6432.46	5643.93
500000	42791.99	21924.21	14973.93	11503.03	9423.87	8040.57	7054.91
1000000	85583.97	43848.42	29947.87	23006.06	18847.74	16081.15	14109.82

MONTHLY PAYMENT
NECESSARY TO AMORTIZE A LOAN
5%

Amortization Amount	8 Years	9 Years	10 Years	15 Years	20 Years	25 Years	30 Years
25	0.32	0.29	0.26	0.20	0.16	0.15	0.13
50	0.63	0.57	0.53	0.39	0.33	0.29	0.27
100	1.26	1.15	1.06	0.79	0.66	0.58	0.53
200	2.53	2.30	2.12	1.58	1.31	1.16	1.07
300	3.79	3.45	3.17	2.36	1.97.	1.74	1.60
400	5.05	4.60	4.23	3.15	2.63	2.33	2.13
500	6.32	5.75	5.29	3.94	3.29	2.91	2.67
600	7.58	6.90	6.35	4.73	3.94	3.49	3.20
700	8.84	8.04	7.41	5.52	4.60	4.07	3.74
800	10.11	9.19	8.47	6.30	5.26	4.65	4.27
900	11.37	10.34	9.52	7.09	5.91	5.23	4.80
1000	12.64	11.49	10.58	7.88	6.57	5.82	5.34
2000	25.27	22.99	21.16	15.76	13.14	11.63	10.67
3000	37.91	34.48	31.74	23.64	19.71	17.45	16.01
4000	50.54	45.97	42.33	31.52	26.29	23.26	21.35
5000	63.18	57.46	52.91	39.41	32.86	29.08	26.68
6000	75.81	68.96	63.49	47.29	39.43	34.90	32.02
7000	88.45	80.45	74.07	55.17	46.00	40.71	37.36
8000	101.08	91.94	84.65	63.05	52.57	46.53	42.70
9000	113.72	103.43	95.23	70.93	59.14	52.34	48.03
10000	126.36	114.93	105.81	78.81	65.71	58.16	53.37
11000	138.99	126.42	116.40	86.69	72.28	63.98	58.71
12000	151.63	137.91	126.98	94.57	78.86	69.79	64.04
13000	164.26	149.40	137.56	102.46	85.43	75.61	69.38
14000	176.90	160.90	148.14	110.34	92.00	81.42	74.72
15000	189.53	172.39	158.72	118.22	98.57	87.24	80.05
16000	202.17	183.88	169.30	126.10	105.14	93.06	85.39
17000	214.80	195.37	179.89	133.98	111.71	98.87	90.73
18000	227.44	206.87	190.47	141.86	118.28	104.69	96.06
19000	240.07	218.36	201.05	149.74	124.85	110.50	101.40
20000	252.71	229.85	211.63	157.62	131.43	116.32	106.74
21000	265.35	241.34	222.21	165.51	138.00	122.14	112.08
22000	277.98	252.84	232.79	173.39	144.57	127.95	117.41
23000	290.62	264.33	243.37	181.27	151.14	133.77	122.75
24000	303.25	275.82	253.96	189.15	157.71	139.59	128.09
25000	315.89	287.31	264.54	197.03	164.28	145.40	133.42
26000	328.52	298.81	275.12	204.91	170.85	151.22	138.76
27000	341.16	310.30	285.70	212.79	177.42	157.03	144.10
28000	353.79	321.79	296.28	220.67	184.00	162.85	149.43
29000	366.43	333.28	306.86	228.56	190.57	168.67	154.77
30000	379.07	344.78	317.44	236.44	197.14	174.48	160.11
35000	442.24	402.24	370.35	275.84	229.99	203.56	186.79
40000	505.42	459.70	423.26	315.25	262.85	232.64	213.48
45000	568.60	517.16	476.17	354.66	295.71	261.72	240.16
50000	631.78	574.63	529.07	394.06	328.56	290.80	266.85
55000	694.95	632.09	581.98	433.47	361.42	319.88	293.53
60000	758.13	689.55	634.89	472.87	394.28	348.96	320.21
65000	821.31	747.02	687.80	512.28	427.13	378.04	346.90
70000	884.49	804.48	740.70	551.69	459.99	407.12	373.58
75000	947.66	861.94	793.61	591.09	492.84	436.20	400.27
80000	1010.84	919.40	846.52	630.50	525.70	465.28	426.95
85000	1074.02	976.87	899.43	669.91	558.56	494.36	453.64
90000	1137.20	1034.33	952.33	709.31	591.41	523.44	480.32
95000	1200.37	1091.79	1005.24	748.72	624.27	552.52	507.01
100000	1263.55	1149.25	1058.15	788.12	657.13	581.60	533.69
200000	2527.10	2298.51	2116.30	1576.25	1314.25	1163.21	1067.38
300000	3790.65	3447.76	3174.45	2364.37	1971.38	1744.81	1601.07
400000	5054.20	4597.02	4232.60	3152.50	2628.50	2326.42	2134.76
500000	6317.76	5746.27	5290.75	3940.62	3285.63	2908.02	2668.45
1000000	12635.51	11492.54	10581.49	7881.24	6571.25	5816.05	5336.91

19

Amortization Amount	1 Year	2 Years	3 Years	4 Years	5 Years	6 Years	7 Years
25	2.14	1.10	0.75	0.58	0.47	0.40	0.35
50	4.28	2.20	1.50	1.15	0.95	0.81	0.71
100	8.56	4.39	3.00	2.31	1.89	1.61	1.42
200	17.13	8.78	6.00	4.61	3.78	3.23	2.83
300	25.69	13.17	9.00	6.92	5.67	4.84	4.25
400	34.26	17.56	12.00	9.22	7.56	6.46	5.67
500	42.82	21.95	15.00	11.53	9.45	8.07	7.08
600	51.38	26.34	18.00	13.84	11.34	9.68	8.50
700	59.95	30.73	21.00	16.14	13.23	11.30	9.92
800	68.51	35.12	24.00	18.45	15.12	12.91	11.33
900	77.08	39.51	27.00	20.76	17.01	14.52	12.75
1000	85.64	43.90	30.00	23.06	18.90	16.14	14.17
2000	171.28	87.81	60.01	46.12	37.81	32.28	28.33
3000	256.92	131.71	90.01	69.18	56.71	48.41	42.50
4000	342.56	175.61	120.01	92.25	75.62	64.55	56.67
5000	428.20	219.52	150.01	115.31	94.52	80.69	70.84
6000	513.84	263.42	180.02	138.37	113.42	96.83	85.00
7000	599.48	307.32	210.02	161.43	132.33	112.97	99.17
8000	685.12	351.23	240.02	184.49	151.23	129.10	113.34
9000	770.76	395.13	270.03	207.55	170.13	145.24	127.51
10000	856.40	439.03	300.03	230.62	189.04	161.38	141.67
11000	942.04	482.94	330.03	253.68	207.94	177.52	155.84
12000	1027.68	526.84	360.03	276.74	226.85	193.66	170.01
13000	1113.32	570.74	390.04	299.80	245.75	209.79	184.18
14000	1198.96	614.65	420.04	322.86	264.65	225.93	198.34
15000	1284.60	658.55	450.04	345.92	283.56	242.07	212.51
16000	1370.24	702.45	480.05	368.98	302.46	258.21	226.68
17000	1455.88	746.36	510.05	392.05	321.37	274.35	240.84
18000	1541.52	790.26	540.05	415.11	340.27	290.48	255.01
19000	1627.16	834.16	570.05	438.17	359.17	306.62	269.18
20000	1712.80	878.06	600.06	461.23	378.08	322.76	283.35
21000	1798.44	921.97	630.06	484.29	396.98	338.90	297.51
22000	1884.08	965.87	660.06	507.35	415.88	355.03	311.68
23000	1969.72	1009.77	690.07	530.42	434.79	371.17	325.85
24000	2055.36	1053.68	720.07	553.48	453.69	387.31	340.02
25000	2141.00	1097.58	750.07	576.54	472.60	403.45	354.18
26000	2226.64	1141.48	780.07	599.60	491.50	419.59	368.35
27000	2312.28	1185.39	810.08	622.66	510.40	435.72	382.52
28000	2397.92	1229.29	840.08	645.72	529.31	451.86	396.69
29000	2483.56	1273.19	870.08	668.78	548.21	468.00	410.85
30000	2569.20	1317.10	900.09	691.85	567.12	484.14	425.02
35000	2997.41	1536.61	1050.10	807.15	661.63	564.83	495.86
40000	3425.60	1756.13	1200.11	922.46	756.15	645.52	566.69
45000	3853.80	1975.65	1350.13	1037.77	850.67	726.21	637.53
50000	4282.00	2195.16	1500.14	1153.08	945.19	806.90	708.37
55000	4710.20	2414.68	1650.16	1268.38	1039.71	887.59	779.20
60000	5138.40	2634.19	1800.17	1383.69	1134.23	968.28	850.04
65000	5566.61	2853.71	1950.18	1499.00	1228.75	1048.97	920.88
70000	5994.81	3073.23	2100.20	1614.31	1323.27	1129.66	991.71
75000	6423.01	3292.74	2250.21	1729.61	1417.79	1210.35	1062.55
80000	6851.21	3512.26	2400.23	1844.92	1512.31	1291.04	1133.39
85000	7279.41	3731.78	2550.24	1960.23	1606.83	1371.73	1204.22
90000	7707.61	3951.29	2700.26	2075.54	1701.35	1452.41	1275.06
95000	8135.81	4170.81	2850.27	2190.84	1795.86	1533.10	1345.90
100000	8564.01	4390.32	3000.28	2306.15	1890.38	1613.79	1416.74
200000	17128.02	8780.65	6000.57	4612.30	3780.77	3227.59	2833.47
300000	25692.02	13170.97	9000.85	6918.46	5671.15	4841.38	4250.21
400000	34256.03	17561.30	12001.14	9224.61	7561.53	6455.18	5666.94
500000	42820.04	21951.62	15001.42	11530.76	9451.92	8068.97	7083.68
1000000	85640.08	43903.25	30002.84	23061.52	18903.83	16137.94	14167.35

MONTHLY PAYMENT
NECESSARY TO AMORTIZE A LOAN
5.125%

Amortization Amount	8 Years	9 Years	10 Years	15 Years	20 Years	25 Years	30 Years
25	0.32	0.29	0.27	0.20	0.17	0.15	0.14
50	0.63	0.58	0.53	0.40	0.33	0.29	0.27
100	1.27	1.16	1.06	0.79	0.66	0.59	0.54
200	2.54	2.31	2.13	1.59	1.33	1.18	1.08
300	3.81	3.47	3.19	2.38	1.99	1.77	1.62
400	5.08	4.62	4.26	3.18	2.66	2.35	2.16
500	6.35	5.78	5.32	3.97	3.32	2.94	2.71
600	7.62	6.93	6.38	4.77	3.98	3.53	3.25
700	8.89	8.09	7.45	5.56	4.65	4.12	3.79
800	10.16	9.24	8.51	6.36	5.31	4.71	4.33
900	11.42	10.40	9.58	7.15	5.98	5.30	4.87
1000	12.69	11.55	10.64	7.95	6.64	5.89	5.41
2000	25.39	23.10	21.28	15.89	13.28	11.77	10.82
3000	38.08	34.65	31.92	23.84	19.92	17.66	16.24
4000	50.78	46.21	42.57	31.78	26.56	23.55	21.65
5000	63.47	57.76	53.21	39.73	33.19	29.44	27.06
6000	76.16	69.31	63.85	47.67	39.83	35.32	32.47
7000	88.86	80.86	74.49	55.62	46.47	41.21	37.88
8000	101.55	92.41	85.13	63.56	53.11	47.10	43.29
9000	114.24	103.96	95.77	71.51	59.75	52.99	48.71
10000	126.94	115.52	106.41	79.45	66.39	58.87	54.12
11000	139.63	127.07	117.05	87.40	73.03	64.76	59.53
12000	152.33	138.62	127.70	95.34	79.67	70.65	64.94
13000	165.02	150.17	138.34	103.29	86.31	76.54	70.35
14000	177.71	161.72	148.98	111.23	92.94	82.42	75.76
15000	190.41	173.27	159.62	119.18	99.58	88.31	81.18
16000	203.10	184.83	170.26	127.13	106.22	94.20	86.59
17000	215.79	196.38	180.90	135.07	112.86	100.09	92.00
18000	228.49	207.93	191.54	143.01	119.50	105.97	97.41
19000	241.18	219.48	202.19	150.96	126.14	111.86	102.82
20000	253.88	231.03	212.83	158.90	132.78	117.75	108.24
21000	266.57	242.58	223.47	166.85	139.42	123.64	113.65
22000	279.26	254.14	234.11	174.79	146.06	129.52	119.06
23000	291.96	265.69	244.75	182.74	152.69	135.41	124.47
24000	304.65	277.24	255.39	190.68	159.33	141.30	129.88
25000	317.35	288.79	266.03	198.63	165.97	147.19	135.29
26000	330.04	300.34	276.68	206.57	172.61	153.07	140.71
27000	342.73	311.89	287.32	214.52	179.25	158.96	146.12
28000	355.43	323.45	297.96	222.46	185.89	164.85	151.53
29000	368.12	335.00	308.60	230.41	192.53	170.73	156.94
30000	380.81	346.55	319.24	238.35	199.17	176.62	162.35
35000	444.28	404.31	372.45	278.08	232.36	206.06	189.41
40000	507.75	462.06	425.65	317.80	265.56	235.50	216.47
45000	571.22	519.82	478.86	357.53	298.75	264.93	243.53
50000	634.69	577.58	532.07	397.25	331.95	294.37	270.59
55000	698.16	635.34	585.27	436.98	365.14	323.81	297.65
60000	761.63	693.10	638.48	476.70	398.33	353.24	324.71
65000	825.10	750.85	691.69	516.43	431.53	382.68	351.76
70000	888.57	808.61	744.89	556.15	464.72	412.12	378.82
75000	952.04	866.37	798.10	595.88	497.92	441.56	405.88
80000	1015.50	924.13	851.31	635.60	531.11	470.99	432.94
85000	1078.97	981.89	904.51	675.33	564.31	500.43	460.00
90000	1142.44	1039.65	957.72	715.05	597.50	529.87	487.06
95000	1205.91	1097.40	1010.93	754.78	630.70	559.30	514.12
100000	1269.38	1155.16	1064.13	794.50	663.89	588.74	541.18
200000	2538.76	2310.32	2128.27	1589.01	1327.78	1177.48	1082.35
300000	3808.14	3465.48	3192.40	2383.51	1991.67	1766.22	1623.53
400000	5077.52	4620.65	4256.54	3178.01	2655.56	2354.96	2164.71
500000	6346.90	5775.81	5320.67	3972.52	3319.45	2943.71	2705.88
1000000	12693.81	11551.61	10641.35	7945.03	6638.91	5887.41	5411.77

21

5.25%

MONTHLY PAYMENT
NECESSARY TO AMORTIZE A LOAN

Amortization Amount	1 Year	2 Years	3 Years	4 Years	5 Years	6 Years	7 Years
25	2.14	1.10	0.75	0.58	0.47	0.40	0.36
50	4.28	2.20	1.50	1.16	0.95	0.81	0.71
100	8.57	4.40	3.01	2.31	1.90	1.62	1.42
200	17.14	8.79	6.01	4.62	3.79	3.24	2.85
300	25.71	13.19	9.02	6.94	5.69	4.86	4.27
400	34.28	17.58	12.02	9.25	7.58	6.48	5.69
500	42.85	21.98	15.03	11.56	9.48	8.10	7.11
600	51.42	26.37	18.03	13.87	11.38	9.72	8.54
700	59.99	30.77	21.04	16.18	13.27	11.34	9.96
800	68.56	35.17	24.05	18.49	15.17	12.96	11.38
900	77.13	39.56	27.05	20.81	17.06	14.58	12.80
1000	85.70	43.96	30.06	23.12	18.96	16.19	14.23
2000	171.39	87.92	60.12	46.23	37.92	32.39	28.45
3000	257.09	131.87	90.17	69.35	56.88	48.58	42.68
4000	342.78	175.83	120.23	92.47	75.84	64.78	56.90
5000	428.48	219.79	150.29	115.59	94.80	80.97	71.13
6000	514.18	263.75	180.35	138.70	113.76	97.17	85.35
7000	599.87	307.71	210.40	161.82	132.72	113.36	99.58
8000	685.57	351.66	240.46	184.94	151.68	129.56	113.80
9000	771.27	395.62	270.52	208.05	170.64	145.75	128.03
10000	856.96	439.58	300.58	231.17	189.60	161.95	142.25
11000	942.66	483.54	330.64	254.29	208.56	178.14	156.48
12000	1028.35	527.50	360.69	277.40	227.52	194.34	170.70
13000	1114.05	571.46	390.75	300.52	246.48	210.53	184.93
14000	1199.75	615.41	420.81	323.64	265.44	226.73	199.15
15000	1285.44	659.37	450.87	346.76	284.40	242.92	213.38
16000	1371.14	703.33	480.93	369.87	303.36	259.12	227.60
17000	1456.83	747.29	510.98	392.99	322.32	275.31	241.83
18000	1542.53	791.25	541.04	416.11	341.28	291.51	256.05
19000	1628.23	835.20	571.10	439.22	360.24	307.70	270.28
20000	1713.92	879.16	601.16	462.34	379.20	323.90	284.50
21000	1799.62	923.12	631.21	485.46	398.16	340.09	298.73
22000	1885.32	967.08	661.27	508.57	417.12	356.29	312.95
23000	1971.01	1011.04	691.33	531.69	436.08	372.48	327.18
24000	2056.71	1054.99	721.39	554.81	455.04	388.68	341.40
25000	2142.40	1098.95	751.45	577.93	474.00	404.87	355.63
26000	2228.10	1142.91	781.50	601.04	492.96	421.07	369.85
27000	2313.80	1186.87	811.56	624.16	511.92	437.26	384.08
28000	2399.49	1230.83	841.62	647.28	530.88	453.46	398.30
29000	2485.19	1274.78	871.68	670.39	549.84	469.65	412.53
30000	2570.89	1318.74	901.74	693.51	588.80	485.85	426.75
35000	2999.37	1538.53	1052.02	809.10	663.60	566.82	497.88
40000	3427.85	1758.32	1202.31	924.68	758.40	647.79	569.00
45000	3856.33	1978.11	1352.60	1040.27	853.20	728.77	640.13
50000	4284.81	2197.90	1502.89	1155.85	948.00	809.74	711.25
55000	4713.29	2417.70	1653.18	1271.44	1042.80	890.72	782.38
60000	5141.77	2637.49	1803.47	1387.02	1137.60	971.69	853.50
65000	5570.25	2857.28	1953.76	1502.61	1232.40	1052.66	924.63
70000	5998.73	3077.07	2104.05	1618.19	1327.20	1133.64	995.75
75000	6427.21	3296.86	2254.34	1733.78	1422.00	1214.61	1066.88
80000	6855.69	3516.65	2404.63	1849.36	1516.80	1295.59	1138.00
85000	7284.17	3736.44	2554.92	1964.95	1611.60	1376.56	1209.13
90000	7712.66	3956.23	2705.21	2080.53	1706.40	1457.54	1280.25
95000	8141.14	4176.02	2855.50	2196.12	1801.20	1538.51	1351.38
100000	8569.62	4395.81	3005.78	2311.70	1896.00	1619.48	1422.50
200000	17139.23	8791.62	6011.57	4623.41	3792.00	3238.97	2845.00
300000	25708.85	13187.43	9017.35	6935.11	5688.00	4858.45	4267.50
400000	34278.47	17583.24	12023.14	9246.82	7584.00	6477.93	5690.00
500000	42848.09	21979.05	15028.92	11558.52	9480.00	8097.42	7112.50
1000000	85696.17	43958.09	30057.84	23117.04	18960.00	16194.83	14225.00

Amortization Amount	8 Years	9 Years	10 Years	15 Years	20 Years	25 Years	30 Years
25	0.32	0.29	0.27	0.20	0.17	0.15	0.14
50	0.64	0.58	0.54	0.40	0.34	0.30	0.27
100	1.28	1.16	1.07	0.80	0.67	0.60	0.55
200	2.55	2.32	2.14	1.60	1.34	1.19	1.10
300	3.83	3.48	3.21	2.40	2.01	1.79	1.65
400	5.10	4.64	4.28	3.20	2.68	2.38	2.19
500	6.38	5.81	5.35	4.00	3.35	2.98	2.74
600	7.65	6.97	6.42	4.81	4.02	3.58	3.29
700	8.93	8.13	7.49	5.61	4.69	4.17	3.84
800	10.20	9.29	8.56	6.41	5.37	4.77	4.39
900	11.48	10.45	9.63	7.21	6.04	5.36	4.94
1000	12.75	11.61	10.70	8.01	6.71	5.96	5.49
2000	25.50	23.22	21.40	16.02	13.41	11.92	10.97
3000	38.26	34.83	32.10	24.03	20.12	17.88	16.46
4000	51.01	46.44	42.81	32.04	26.83	23.84	21.95
5000	63.76	58.05	53.51	40.05	33.53	29.80	27.44
6000	76.51	69.67	64.21	48.05	40.24	35.76	32.92
7000	89.27	81.28	74.91	56.06	46.95	41.71	38.41
8000	102.02	92.89	85.61	64.07	53.66	47.67	43.90
9000	114.77	104.50	96.31	72.08	60.36	53.63	49.38
10000	127.52	116.11	107.01	80.09	67.07	59.59	54.87
11000	140.27	127.72	117.72	88.10	73.78	65.55	60.36
12000	153.03	139.33	128.42	96.11	80.48	71.51	65.84
13000	165.78	150.94	139.12	104.12	87.19	77.47	71.33
14000	178.53	162.55	149.82	112.13	93.90	83.43	76.82
15000	191.28	174.16	160.52	120.14	100.60	89.39	82.31
16000	204.04	185.77	171.22	128.15	107.31	95.35	87.79
17000	216.79	197.38	181.92	136.15	114.02	101.31	93.28
18000	229.54	209.00	192.62	144.16	120.72	107.27	98.77
19000	242.29	220.61	203.33	152.17	127.43	113.22	104.25
20000	255.04	232.22	214.03	160.18	134.14	119.18	109.74
21000	267.80	243.83	224.73	168.19	140.85	125.14	115.23
22000	280.55	255.44	235.43	176.20	147.55	131.10	120.72
23000	293.30	267.05	246.13	184.21	154.26	137.06	126.20
24000	306.05	278.66	256.83	192.22	160.97	143.02	131.69
25000	318.81	290.27	267.53	200.23	167.67	148.98	137.18
26000	331.56	301.88	278.24	208.24	174.38	154.94	142.66
27000	344.31	313.49	288.94	216.25	181.09	160.90	148.15
28000	357.06	325.10	299.64	224.25	187.79	166.86	153.64
29000	369.81	336.71	310.34	232.26	194.50	172.82	159.13
30000	382.57	348.33	321.04	240.27	201.21	178.78	164.61
35000	446.33	406.38	374.55	280.32	234.74	208.57	192.05
40000	510.09	464.43	428.06	320.36	268.28	238.37	219.48
45000	573.85	522.49	481.56	360.41	301.81	268.16	246.92
50000	637.61	580.54	535.07	400.45	335.35	297.96	274.35
55000	701.37	638.60	588.58	440.50	368.88	327.75	301.79
60000	765.13	696.65	642.08	480.55	402.41	357.55	329.22
65000	828.90	754.70	695.59	520.59	435.95	387.35	356.66
70000	892.66	812.76	749.10	560.64	469.48	417.14	384.10
75000	956.42	870.81	802.60	600.68	503.02	446.94	411.53
80000	1020.18	928.87	856.11	640.73	536.55	476.73	438.97
85000	1083.94	986.92	909.62	680.77	570.09	506.53	466.40
90000	1147.70	1044.98	963.12	720.82	603.62	536.33	493.84
95000	1211.46	1103.03	1016.63	760.86	637.16	566.12	521.27
100000	1275.22	1161.08	1070.14	800.91	670.69	595.92	548.71
200000	2550.45	2322.17	2140.28	1601.82	1341.38	1191.84	1097.42
300000	3825.67	3483.25	3210.41	2402.73	2012.07	1787.75	1646.12
400000	5100.90	4644.34	4280.55	3203.64	2682.76	2383.67	2194.83
500000	6376.12	5805.42	5350.69	4004.55	3353.45	2979.59	2743.54
1000000	12752.24	11610.84	10701.38	8009.09	6706.91	5959.18	5487.08

5.375%

Amortization Amount	1 Year	2 Years	3 Years	4 Years	5 Years	6 Years	7 Years
25	2.14	1.10	0.75	0.58	0.48	0.41	0.36
50	4.29	2.20	1.51	1.16	0.95	0.81	0.71
100	8.58	4.40	3.01	2.32	1.90	1.63	1.43
200	17.15	8.80	6.02	4.63	3.80	3.25	2.86
300	25.73	13.20	9.03	6.95	5.70	4.88	4.28
400	34.30	17.61	12.05	9.27	7.61	6.50	5.71
500	42.88	22.01	15.06	11.59	9.51	8.13	7.14
600	51.45	26.41	18.07	13.90	11.41	9.75	8.57
700	60.03	30.81	21.08	16.22	13.31	11.38	10.00
800	68.60	35.21	24.09	18.54	15.21	13.00	11.43
900	77.18	39.61	27.10	20.86	17.11	14.63	12.85
1000	85.75	44.01	30.11	23.17	19.02	16.25	14.28
2000	171.50	88.03	60.23	46.35	38.03	32.50	28.57
3000	257.26	132.04	90.34	69.52	57.05	48.76	42.85
4000	343.01	176.05	120.45	92.69	76.06	65.01	57.13
5000	428.76	220.06	150.56	115.86	95.08	81.26	71.41
6000	514.51	264.08	180.68	139.04	114.10	97.51	85.70
7000	600.27	308.09	210.79	162.21	133.11	113.76	99.98
8000	686.02	352.10	240.90	185.38	152.13	130.01	114.26
9000	771.77	396.12	271.02	208.55	171.15	146.27	128.54
10000	857.52	440.13	301.13	231.73	190.16	162.52	142.83
11000	943.27	484.14	331.24	254.90	209.18	178.77	157.11
12000	1029.03	528.16	361.35	278.07	228.19	195.02	171.39
13000	1114.78	572.17	391.47	301.24	247.21	211.27	185.68
14000	1200.53	616.18	421.58	324.42	266.23	227.53	199.96
15000	1286.28	660.19	451.69	347.59	285.24	243.78	214.24
16000	1372.04	704.21	481.81	370.76	304.26	260.03	228.52
17000	1457.79	748.22	511.92	393.93	323.28	276.28	242.81
18000	1543.54	792.23	542.03	417.11	342.29	292.53	257.09
19000	1629.29	836.25	572.14	440.28	361.31	308.78	271.37
20000	1715.05	880.26	602.26	463.45	380.32	325.04	285.66
21000	1800.80	924.27	632.37	486.62	399.34	341.29	299.94
22000	1886.55	968.28	662.48	509.80	418.36	357.54	314.22
23000	1972.30	1012.30	692.60	532.97	437.37	373.79	328.50
24000	2058.05	1056.31	722.71	556.14	456.39	390.04	342.79
25000	2143.81	1100.32	752.82	579.32	475.41	406.30	357.07
26000	2229.56	1144.34	782.93	602.49	494.42	422.55	371.35
27000	2315.31	1188.35	813.05	625.66	513.44	438.80	385.63
28000	2401.06	1232.36	843.16	648.83	532.45	455.05	399.92
29000	2486.82	1276.38	873.27	672.01	551.47	471.30	414.20
30000	2572.57	1320.39	903.39	695.18	570.49	487.55	428.48
35000	3001.33	1540.45	1053.95	811.04	665.57	568.81	499.90
40000	3430.09	1760.52	1204.52	926.90	760.65	650.07	571.31
45000	3858.85	1980.58	1355.08	1042.77	855.73	731.33	642.72
50000	4287.61	2200.65	1505.64	1158.63	950.81	812.59	714.14
55000	4716.37	2420.71	1656.21	1274.49	1045.89	893.85	785.55
60000	5145.14	2640.78	1806.77	1390.36	1140.97	975.11	856.97
65000	5573.90	2860.84	1957.34	1506.22	1236.06	1056.37	928.38
70000	6002.66	3080.91	2107.90	1622.08	1331.14	1137.63	999.79
75000	6431.42	3300.97	2258.47	1737.95	1426.22	1218.89	1071.21
80000	6860.18	3521.04	2409.03	1853.81	1521.30	1300.15	1142.62
85000	7288.94	3741.10	2559.59	1969.67	1616.38	1381.40	1214.04
90000	7717.70	3961.17	2710.16	2085.54	1711.46	1462.66	1285.45
95000	8146.46	4181.23	2860.72	2201.40	1806.54	1543.92	1356.86
100000	8575.23	4401.29	3011.29	2317.26	1901.62	1625.18	1428.28
200000	17150.45	8802.59	6022.58	4634.52	3803.25	3250.36	2856.55
300000	25725.68	13203.88	9033.86	6951.78	5704.87	4875.55	4284.83
400000	34300.90	17605.18	12045.15	9269.05	7606.50	6500.73	5713.11
500000	42876.13	22006.47	15056.44	11586.31	9508.12	8125.91	7141.38
1000000	85752.26	44012.95	30112.88	23172.61	19016.25	16251.82	14282.77

24

Amortization Amount	8 Years	9 Years	10 Years	15 Years	20 Years	25 Years	30 Years
25	0.32	0.29	0.27	0.20	0.17	0.15	0.14
50	0.64	0.58	0.54	0.40	0.34	0.30	0.28
100	1.28	1.17	1.08	0.81	0.68	0.60	0.56
200	2.56	2.33	2.15	1.61	1.36	1.21	1.11
300	3.84	3.50	3.23	2.42	2.03	1.81	1.67
400	5.12	4.67	4.30	3.23	2.71	2.41	2.23
500	6.41	5.84	5.38	4.04	3.39	3.02	2.78
600	7.69	7.00	6.46	4.84	4.07	3.62	3.34
700	8.97	8.17	7.53	5.65	4.74	4.22	3.89
800	10.25	9.34	8.61	6.46	5.42	4.83	4.45
900	11.53	10.50	9.69	7.27	6.10	5.43	5.01
1000	12.81	11.67	10.76	8.07	6.78	6.03	5.56
2000	25.62	23.34	21.52	16.15	13.55	12.06	11.13
3000	38.43	35.01	32.28	24.22	20.33	18.09	16.69
4000	51.24	46.68	43.05	32.29	27.10	24.13	22.25
5000	64.05	58.35	53.81	40.37	33.88	30.16	27.81
6000	76.86	70.02	64.57	48.44	40.65	36.19	33.38
7000	89.68	81.69	75.33	56.51	47.43	42.22	38.94
8000	102.49	93.36	86.09	64.59	54.20	48.25	44.50
9000	115.30	105.03	96.85	72.66	60.98	54.28	50.07
10000	128.11	116.70	107.62	80.73	67.75	60.31	55.63
11000	140.92	128.37	118.38	88.81	74.53	66.34	61.19
12000	153.73	140.04	129.14	96.88	81.30	72.38	66.75
13000	166.54	151.71	139.90	104.95	88.08	78.41	72.32
14000	179.35	163.38	150.66	113.03	94.85	84.44	77.88
15000	192.16	175.05	161.42	121.10	101.63	90.47	83.44
16000	204.97	186.72	172.19	129.17	108.40	96.50	89.01
17000	217.78	198.39	182.95	137.25	115.18	102.53	94.57
18000	230.59	210.06	193.71	145.32	121.95	108.56	100.13
19000	243.41	221.73	204.47	153.39	128.73	114.60	105.69
20000	256.22	233.40	215.23	161.47	135.50	120.63	111.26
21000	269.03	245.07	225.99	169.54	142.28	126.66	116.82
22000	281.84	256.74	236.75	177.61	149.06	132.69	122.38
23000	294.65	268.41	247.52	185.69	155.83	138.72	127.95
24000	307.46	280.09	258.28	193.76	162.61	144.75	133.51
25000	320.27	291.76	269.04	201.84	169.38	150.78	139.07
26000	333.08	303.43	279.80	209.91	176.16	156.82	144.63
27000	345.89	315.10	290.56	217.98	182.93	162.85	150.20
28000	358.70	326.77	301.32	226.06	189.71	168.88	155.76
29000	371.51	338.44	312.09	234.13	196.48	174.91	161.32
30000	384.32	350.11	322.85	242.20	203.26	180.94	166.89
35000	448.38	408.46	376.66	282.57	237.13	211.10	194.70
40000	512.43	466.81	430.46	322.94	271.01	241.25	222.51
45000	576.49	525.16	484.27	363.30	304.89	271.41	250.33
50000	640.54	583.51	538.08	403.67	338.76	301.57	278.14
55000	704.59	641.86	591.89	444.04	372.64	331.72	305.96
60000	768.65	700.21	645.69	484.40	406.51	361.88	333.77
65000	832.70	758.56	699.50	524.77	440.39	392.04	361.59
70000	896.76	816.92	753.31	565.14	474.27	422.19	389.40
75000	960.81	875.27	807.12	605.51	508.14	452.35	417.21
80000	1024.86	933.62	860.93	645.87	542.02	482.51	445.03
85000	1088.92	991.97	914.73	686.24	575.90	512.66	472.84
90000	1152.97	1050.32	968.54	726.61	609.77	542.82	500.66
95000	1217.03	1108.67	1022.35	766.97	643.65	572.98	528.47
100000	1281.08	1167.02	1076.16	807.34	677.52	603.13	556.29
200000	2562.16	2334.04	2152.31	1614.68	1355.05	1206.27	1112.57
300000	3843.24	3501.06	3228.47	2422.02	2032.57	1809.40	1668.86
400000	5124.32	4668.09	4304.63	3229.36	2710.10	2412.54	2225.14
500000	6405.40	5835.11	5380.79	4036.70	3387.62	3015.67	2781.43
1000000	12810.80	11670.22	10761.57	8073.41	6775.24	6031.35	5562.85

25

5.5%

MONTHLY PAYMENT
NECESSARY TO AMORTIZE A LOAN

Amortization Amount	1 Year	2 Years	3 Years	4 Years	5 Years	6 Years	7 Years
25	2.15	1.10	0.75	0.58	0.48	0.41	0.36
50	4.29	2.20	1.51	1.16	0.95	0.82	0.72
100	8.58	4.41	3.02	2.32	1.91	1.63	1.43
200	17.16	8.81	6.03	4.65	3.81	3.26	2.87
300	25.74	13.22	9.05	6.97	5.72	4.89	4.30
400	34.32	17.63	12.07	9.29	7.63	6.52	5.74
500	42.90	22.03	15.08	11.61	9.54	8.15	7.17
600	51.49	26.44	18.10	13.94	11.44	9.79	8.60
700	60.07	30.85	21.12	16.26	13.35	11.42	10.04
800	68.65	35.25	24.13	18.58	15.26	13.05	11.47
900	77.23	39.66	27.15	20.91	17.17	14.68	12.91
1000	85.81	44.07	30.17	23.23	19.07	16.31	14.34
2000	171.62	88.14	60.34	46.46	38.15	32.62	28.68
3000	257.43	132.20	90.50	69.68	57.22	48.93	43.02
4000	343.23	176.27	120.67	92.91	76.29	65.24	57.36
5000	429.04	220.34	150.84	116.14	95.36	81.54	71.70
6000	514.85	264.41	181.01	139.37	114.44	97.85	86.04
7000	600.66	308.47	211.18	162.60	133.51	114.16	100.38
8000	686.47	352.54	241.34	185.83	152.58	130.47	114.73
9000	772.28	396.61	271.51	209.05	171.65	146.78	129.07
10000	858.08	440.68	301.68	232.28	190.73	163.09	143.41
11000	943.89	484.75	331.85	255.51	209.80	179.40	157.75
12000	1029.70	528.81	362.02	278.74	228.87	195.71	172.09
13000	1115.51	572.88	392.18	301.97	247.94	212.02	186.43
14000	1201.32	616.95	422.35	325.20	267.02	228.32	200.77
15000	1287.13	661.02	452.52	348.42	286.09	244.63	215.11
16000	1372.93	705.09	482.69	371.65	305.16	260.94	229.45
17000	1458.74	749.15	512.86	394.88	324.23	277.25	243.79
18000	1544.55	793.22	543.02	418.11	343.31	293.56	258.13
19000	1630.36	837.29	573.19	441.34	362.38	309.87	272.47
20000	1716.17	881.36	603.36	464.56	381.45	326.18	286.81
21000	1801.98	925.42	633.53	487.79	400.52	342.49	301.15
22000	1887.78	969.49	663.69	511.02	419.60	358.80	315.49
23000	1973.59	1013.56	693.86	534.25	438.67	375.10	329.83
24000	2059.40	1057.63	724.03	557.48	457.74	391.41	344.18
25000	2145.21	1101.70	754.20	580.71	476.81	407.72	358.52
26000	2231.02	1145.76	784.37	603.93	495.89	424.03	372.86
27000	2316.83	1189.83	814.53	627.16	514.96	440.34	387.20
28000	2402.63	1233.90	844.70	650.39	534.03	456.65	401.54
29000	2488.44	1277.97	874.87	673.62	553.10	472.96	415.88
30000	2574.25	1322.03	905.04	696.85	572.18	489.27	430.22
35000	3003.29	1542.37	1055.88	812.99	667.54	570.81	501.92
40000	3432.33	1762.71	1206.72	929.13	762.90	652.36	573.63
45000	3861.38	1983.05	1357.56	1045.27	858.27	733.90	645.33
50000	4290.42	2203.39	1508.40	1161.41	953.63	815.44	717.03
55000	4719.46	2423.73	1659.24	1277.55	1048.99	896.99	788.74
60000	5148.50	2644.07	1810.08	1393.69	1144.35	978.53	860.44
65000	5577.54	2864.41	1960.92	1509.84	1239.72	1060.08	932.14
70000	6006.58	3084.75	2111.76	1625.98	1335.08	1141.62	1003.84
75000	6435.63	3305.09	2262.60	1742.12	1430.44	1223.17	1075.55
80000	6864.67	3525.43	2413.44	1858.26	1525.81	1304.71	1147.25
85000	7293.71	3745.78	2564.28	1974.40	1621.17	1386.26	1218.95
90000	7722.75	3966.10	2715.12	2090.54	1716.53	1467.80	1290.66
95000	8151.79	4186.44	2865.96	2206.68	1811.89	1549.35	1362.36
100000	8580.83	4406.78	3016.80	2322.82	1907.26	1630.89	1434.06
200000	17161.67	8813.56	6033.59	4645.65	3814.51	3261.78	2868.13
300000	25742.50	13220.35	9050.39	6968.47	5721.77	4892.67	4302.19
400000	34323.34	17627.13	12067.18	9291.30	7629.03	6523.56	5736.26
500000	42904.17	22033.91	15083.98	11614.12	9536.28	8154.45	7170.32
1000000	85808.34	44067.82	30167.95	23228.24	19072.57	16308.90	14340.64

Amortization Amount	8 Years	9 Years	10 Years	15 Years	20 Years	25 Years	30 Years
25	0.32	0.29	0.27	0.20	0.17	0.15	0.14
50	0.64	0.59	0.54	0.41	0.34	0.31	0.28
100	1.29	1.17	1.08	0.81	0.68	0.61	0.56
200	2.57	2.35	2.16	1.83	1.37	1.22	1.13
300	3.86	3.52	3.25	2.44	2.05	1.83	1.69
400	5.15	4.69	4.33	3.26	2.74	2.44	2.26
500	6.43	5.86	5.41	4.07	3.42	3.05	2.82
600	7.72	7.04	6.49	4.88	4.11	3.66	3.38
700	9.01	8.21	7.58	5.70	4.79	4.27	3.95
800	10.30	9.38	8.66	6.51	5.48	4.88	4.51
900	11.58	10.56	9.74	7.32	6.16	5.49	5.08
1000	12.87	11.73	10.82	8.14	6.84	6.10	5.64
2000	25.74	23.46	21.64	16.28	13.69	12.21	11.28
3000	38.61	35.19	32.47	24.41	20.53	18.31	16.92
4000	51.48	46.92	43.29	32.55	27.38	24.42	22.56
5000	64.35	58.65	54.11	40.69	34.22	30.52	28.20
6000	77.22	70.38	64.93	48.83	41.06	36.62	33.83
7000	90.09	82.11	75.75	56.97	47.91	42.73	39.47
8000	102.96	93.84	86.58	65.10	54.75	48.83	45.11
9000	115.83	105.57	97.40	73.24	61.60	54.94	50.75
10000	128.69	117.30	108.22	81.38	68.44	61.04	56.39
11000	141.56	129.03	119.04	89.52	75.28	67.14	62.03
12000	154.43	140.76	129.86	97.66	82.13	73.25	67.67
13000	167.30	152.49	140.69	105.79	88.97	79.35	73.31
14000	180.17	164.22	151.51	113.93	95.81	85.45	78.95
15000	193.04	175.95	162.33	122.07	102.66	91.56	84.59
16000	205.91	187.68	173.15	130.21	109.50	97.66	90.23
17000	218.78	199.41	183.97	138.35	116.35	103.77	95.86
18000	231.65	211.14	194.79	146.48	123.19	109.87	101.50
19000	244.52	222.87	205.62	154.62	130.03	115.97	107.14
20000	257.39	234.59	216.44	162.76	136.88	122.08	112.78
21000	270.26	246.32	227.26	170.90	143.72	128.18	118.42
22000	283.13	258.05	238.08	179.04	150.57	134.29	124.06
23000	296.00	269.78	248.90	187.17	157.41	140.39	129.70
24000	308.87	281.51	259.73	195.31	164.25	146.49	135.34
25000	321.74	293.24	270.55	203.45	171.10	152.60	140.98 ←
26000	334.61	304.97	281.37	211.59	177.94	158.70	146.62
27000	347.48	316.70	292.19	219.73	184.79	164.81	152.25
28000	360.35	328.43	303.01	227.86	191.63	170.91	157.89
29000	373.22	340.16	313.84	236.00	198.47	177.01	163.53
30000	386.08	351.89	324.66	244.14	205.32	183.12	169.17
35000	450.43	410.54	378.77	284.83	239.54	213.64	197.37
40000	514.78	469.19	432.88	325.52	273.76	244.16	225.56
45000	579.13	527.84	486.99	366.21	307.98	274.68	253.76
50000	643.47	586.49	541.10	406.90	342.20	305.20	281.95
55000	707.82	645.14	595.21	447.59	376.42	335.72	310.15
60000	772.17	703.78	649.32	488.28	410.63	366.23	338.34
65000	836.52	762.43	703.43	528.97	444.85	396.75	366.54
70000	900.86	821.08	757.54	569.66	479.07	427.27	394.73
75000	965.21	879.73	811.65	610.35	513.29	457.79	422.93
80000	1029.56	938.38	865.76	651.04	547.51	488.31	451.13
85000	1093.91	997.03	919.86	691.73	581.73	518.83	479.32
90000	1158.25	1055.68	973.97	732.42	615.95	549.35	507.52
95000	1222.60	1114.33	1028.08	773.11	650.17	579.87	535.71
100000	1286.95	1172.97	1082.19	813.80	684.39	610.39	563.91
200000	2573.90	2345.95	2164.39	1627.60	→ 1368.78	1220.78	1127.81 ←
300000	3860.85	3518.92	3246.58	2441.39	2053.17	1831.17	1691.72
400000	5147.80	4691.90	4328.78	3255.19	2737.57	2441.57	2255.63
500000	6434.75	5864.87	5410.97	4068.99	3421.96	3051.96	2819.53
1000000	12869.50	11729.74	10821.94	8137.98	6843.91	6103.91	5639.06

27

22500.⁰⁰ (153988)

Amortization Amount	1 Year	2 Years	3 Years	4 Years	5 Years	6 Years	7 Years
25	2.15	1.10	0.76	0.58	0.48	0.41	0.38
50	4.29	2.21	1.51	1.16	0.96	0.82	0.72
100	8.59	4.41	3.02	2.33	1.91	1.64	1.44
200	17.17	8.82	6.04	4.66	3.83	3.27	2.88
300	25.76	13.24	9.07	6.99	5.74	4.91	4.32
400	34.35	17.65	12.09	9.31	7.65	6.55	5.76
500	42.93	22.06	15.11	11.64	9.56	8.18	7.20
600	51.52	26.47	18.13	13.97	11.48	9.82	8.64
700	60.11	30.89	21.16	16.30	13.39	11.46	10.08
800	68.69	35.30	24.18	18.63	15.30	13.09	11.52
900	77.28	39.71	27.20	20.96	17.22	14.73	12.96
1000	85.86	44.12	30.22	23.28	19.13	16.37	14.40
2000	171.73	88.25	60.45	46.57	38.26	32.73	28.80
3000	257.59	132.37	90.67	69.85	57.39	49.10	43.20
4000	343.46	176.49	120.89	93.14	76.52	65.46	57.59
5000	429.32	220.61	151.12	116.42	95.64	81.83	71.99
6000	515.19	264.74	181.34	139.70	114.77	98.20	86.39
7000	601.05	308.86	211.56	162.99	133.90	114.56	100.79
8000	686.92	352.98	241.78	186.27	153.03	130.93	115.19
9000	772.78	397.10	272.01	209.56	172.16	147.29	129.59
10000	858.64	441.23	302.23	232.84	191.29	163.66	143.99
11000	944.51	485.35	332.45	256.12	210.42	180.03	158.38
12000	1030.37	529.47	362.68	279.41	229.55	196.39	172.78
13000	1116.24	573.60	392.90	302.69	248.68	212.76	187.18
14000	1202.10	617.72	423.12	325.97	267.81	229.12	201.58
15000	1287.97	661.84	453.35	349.26	286.93	245.49	215.98
16000	1373.83	705.96	483.57	372.54	306.06	261.86	230.38
17000	1459.70	750.09	513.79	395.83	325.19	278.22	244.78
18000	1545.56	794.21	544.02	419.11	344.32	294.59	259.18
19000	1631.42	838.33	574.24	442.39	363.45	310.96	273.57
20000	1717.29	882.45	604.46	465.68	382.58	327.32	287.97
21000	1803.15	926.58	634.68	488.96	401.71	343.69	302.37
22000	1889.02	970.70	664.91	512.25	420.84	360.05	316.77
23000	1974.88	1014.82	695.13	535.53	439.97	376.42	331.17
24000	2060.75	1058.94	725.35	558.81	459.09	392.79	345.57
25000	2146.61	1103.07	755.58	582.10	478.22	409.15	359.97
26000	2232.47	1147.19	785.80	605.38	497.35	425.52	374.36
27000	2318.34	1191.31	816.02	628.67	516.48	441.88	388.76
28000	2404.20	1235.44	846.25	651.95	535.61	458.25	403.16
29000	2490.07	1279.56	876.47	675.23	554.74	474.62	417.56
30000	2575.93	1323.68	906.69	698.52	573.87	490.98	431.96
35000	3005.25	1544.29	1057.81	814.94	669.51	572.81	503.95
40000	3434.58	1764.91	1208.92	931.36	765.16	654.64	575.95
45000	3863.90	1985.52	1360.04	1047.78	860.80	736.47	647.94
50000	4293.22	2206.14	1511.15	1164.20	956.45	818.30	719.93
55000	4722.54	2426.75	1662.27	1280.62	1052.09	900.13	791.92
60000	5151.86	2647.36	1813.38	1397.04	1147.74	981.96	863.92
65000	5581.19	2867.98	1964.50	1513.45	1243.38	1063.79	935.91
70000	6010.51	3088.59	2115.61	1629.87	1339.03	1145.62	1007.90
75000	6439.83	3309.20	2266.73	1746.29	1434.67	1227.46	1079.90
80000	6869.15	3529.82	2417.84	1862.71	1530.32	1309.29	1151.89
85000	7298.48	3750.43	2568.96	1979.13	1625.96	1391.12	1223.88
90000	7727.80	3971.04	2720.08	2095.55	1721.61	1472.95	1295.88
95000	8157.12	4191.66	2871.19	2211.97	1817.25	1554.78	1367.87
100000	8586.44	4412.27	3022.31	2328.39	1912.90	1636.61	1439.86
200000	17172.88	8824.54	6044.61	4656.78	3825.79	3273.21	2879.73
300000	25759.32	13236.81	9066.92	6985.18	5738.69	4909.82	4319.59
400000	34345.76	17649.08	12089.22	9313.57	7651.58	6546.43	5759.45
500000	42932.21	22061.35	15111.53	11641.96	9564.48	8183.03	7199.32
1000000	85864.41	44122.70	30223.06	23283.92	19128.96	16366.07	14398.63

Amortization Amount	8 Years	9 Years	10 Years	15 Years	20 Years	25 Years	30 Years
25	0.32	0.29	0.27	0.21	0.17	0.15	0.14
50	0.65	0.59	0.54	0.41	0.35	0.31	0.29
100	1.29	1.18	1.09	0.82	0.69	0.62	0.57
200	2.59	2.36	2.18	1.64	1.38	1.24	1.14
300	3.88	3.54	3.26	2.46	2.07	1.85	1.71
400	5.17	4.72	4.35	3.28	2.77	2.47	2.29
500	6.46	5.89	5.44	4.10	3.46	3.09	2.86
600	7.76	7.07	6.53	4.92	4.15	3.71	3.43
700	9.05	8.25	7.62	5.74	4.84	4.32	4.00
800	10.34	9.43	8.71	6.56	5.53	4.94	4.57
900	11.64	10.61	9.79	7.38	6.22	5.56	5.14
1000	12.93	11.79	10.88	8.20	6.91	6.18	5.72
2000	25.86	23.58	21.76	16.41	13.83	12.35	11.43
3000	38.78	35.37	32.65	24.61	20.74	18.53	17.15
4000	51.71	47.16	43.53	32.81	27.65	24.71	22.86
5000	64.64	58.95	54.41	41.01	34.56	30.88	28.58
6000	77.57	70.74	65.29	49.22	41.48	37.06	34.29
7000	90.50	82.53	76.18	57.42	48.39	43.24	40.01
8000	103.43	94.32	87.06	65.62	55.30	49.41	45.73
9000	116.35	106.10	97.94	73.83	62.22	55.59	51.44
10000	129.28	117.89	108.82	82.03	69.13	61.77	57.16
11000	142.21	129.68	119.71	90.23	76.04	67.95	62.87
12000	155.14	141.47	130.59	98.43	82.95	74.12	68.59
13000	168.07	153.26	141.47	106.64	89.87	80.30	74.30
14000	181.00	165.05	152.35	114.84	96.78	86.48	80.02
15000	193.92	176.84	163.24	123.04	103.69	92.65	85.74
16000	206.85	188.63	174.12	131.24	110.61	98.83	91.45
17000	219.78	200.42	185.00	139.45	117.52	105.01	97.17
18000	232.71	212.21	195.88	147.65	124.43	111.18	102.88
19000	245.64	224.00	206.77	155.85	131.35	117.36	108.60
20000	258.57	235.79	217.65	164.06	138.26	123.54	114.31
21000	271.49	247.58	228.53	172.26	145.17	129.71	120.03
22000	284.42	259.37	239.41	180.46	152.08	135.89	125.75
23000	297.35	271.16	250.30	188.66	159.00	142.07	131.46
24000	310.28	282.95	261.18	196.87	165.91	148.24	137.18
25000	323.21	294.74	272.06	205.07	172.82	154.42	142.89
26000	336.14	306.52	282.94	213.27	179.74	160.60	148.61
27000	349.06	318.31	293.83	221.48	186.65	166.78	154.32
28000	361.99	330.10	304.71	229.68	193.56	172.95	160.04
29000	374.92	341.89	315.59	237.88	200.47	179.13	165.76
30000	387.85	353.68	326.47	246.08	207.39	185.31	171.47
35000	452.49	412.63	380.89	287.10	241.95	216.19	200.05
40000	517.13	471.58	435.30	328.11	276.52	247.07	228.63
45000	581.77	530.52	489.71	369.13	311.08	277.98	257.21
50000	646.42	589.47	544.12	410.14	345.65	308.84	285.79
55000	711.06	648.42	598.54	451.15	380.21	339.73	314.36
60000	775.70	707.37	652.95	492.17	414.77	370.61	342.94
65000	840.34	766.31	707.36	533.18	449.34	401.50	371.52
70000	904.98	825.26	761.77	574.20	483.90	432.38	400.10
75000	969.62	884.21	816.19	615.21	518.47	463.27	428.68
80000	1034.27	943.15	870.60	656.22	553.03	494.15	457.26
85000	1098.91	1002.10	925.01	697.24	587.60	525.03	485.84
90000	1163.55	1061.05	979.42	738.25	622.16	555.92	514.41
95000	1228.19	1120.00	1033.84	779.27	656.73	586.80	542.99
100000	1292.83	1178.94	1088.25	820.28	691.29	617.69	571.57
200000	2585.67	2357.88	2176.50	1640.56	1382.58	1235.37	1143.14
300000	3878.50	3536.83	3264.74	2460.84	2073.87	1853.06	1714.71
400000	5171.33	4715.77	4352.99	3281.12	2765.17	2470.75	2286.29
500000	6464.16	5894.71	5441.24	4101.41	3456.46	3088.44	2857.86
1000000	12928.33	11789.42	10882.48	8202.81	6912.91	6176.87	5715.71

5.75%

Amortization Amount	1 Year	2 Years	3 Years	4 Years	5 Years	6 Years	7 Years
25	2.15	1.10	0.76	0.58	0.48	0.41	0.36
50	4.30	2.21	1.51	1.17	0.96	0.82	0.72
100	8.59	4.42	3.03	2.33	1.92	1.64	1.45
200	17.18	8.84	6.06	4.67	3.84	3.28	2.89
300	25.78	13.25	9.08	7.00	5.76	4.93	4.34
400	34.37	17.67	12.11	9.34	7.67	6.57	5.78
500	42.96	22.09	15.14	11.67	9.59	8.21	7.23
600	51.55	26.51	18.17	14.00	11.51	9.85	8.67
700	60.14	30.92	21.19	16.34	13.43	11.50	10.12
800	68.74	35.34	24.22	18.67	15.35	13.14	11.57
900	77.33	39.76	27.25	21.01	17.27	14.78	13.01
1000	85.92	44.18	30.28	23.34	19.19	16.42	14.46
2000	171.84	88.36	60.56	46.68	38.37	32.85	28.91
3000	257.76	132.53	90.83	70.02	57.56	49.27	43.37
4000	343.68	176.71	121.11	93.36	76.74	65.69	57.83
5000	429.60	220.89	151.39	116.70	95.93	82.12	72.28
6000	515.52	265.07	181.67	140.04	115.11	98.54	86.74
7000	601.44	309.24	211.95	163.38	134.30	114.96	101.20
8000	687.36	353.42	242.23	186.72	153.48	131.39	115.65
9000	773.28	397.60	272.50	210.06	172.67	147.81	130.11
10000	859.20	441.78	302.78	233.40	191.85	164.23	144.57
11000	945.13	485.95	333.06	256.74	211.04	180.66	159.02
12000	1031.05	530.13	363.34	280.08	230.23	197.08	173.48
13000	1116.97	574.31	393.62	303.42	249.41	213.50	187.94
14000	1202.89	618.49	423.89	326.76	268.60	229.93	202.39
15000	1288.81	662.66	454.17	350.09	287.78	246.35	216.85
16000	1374.73	706.84	484.45	373.43	306.97	262.77	231.31
17000	1460.65	751.02	514.73	396.77	326.15	279.20	245.76
18000	1546.57	795.20	545.01	420.11	345.34	295.62	260.22
19000	1632.49	839.37	575.29	443.45	364.52	312.04	274.68
20000	1718.41	883.55	605.56	466.79	383.71	328.47	289.13
21000	1804.33	927.73	635.84	490.13	402.89	344.89	303.59
22000	1890.25	971.91	666.12	513.47	422.08	361.31	318.05
23000	1976.17	1016.08	696.40	536.81	441.26	377.74	332.50
24000	2062.09	1060.26	726.68	560.15	460.45	394.16	346.96
25000	2148.01	1104.44	756.95	583.49	479.64	410.58	361.42
26000	2233.93	1148.62	787.23	606.83	498.82	427.01	375.88
27000	2319.85	1192.80	817.51	630.17	518.01	443.43	390.33
28000	2405.77	1236.97	847.79	653.51	537.19	459.85	404.79
29000	2491.69	1281.15	878.07	676.85	556.38	476.28	419.25
30000	2577.61	1325.33	908.35	700.19	575.56	492.70	433.70
35000	3007.22	1546.22	1059.74	816.89	671.49	574.82	505.99
40000	3436.82	1767.10	1211.13	933.59	767.42	656.93	578.27
45000	3866.42	1987.99	1362.52	1050.28	863.34	739.05	650.55
50000	4296.02	2208.88	1513.91	1166.98	959.27	821.17	722.84
55000	4725.63	2429.77	1665.30	1283.68	1055.20	903.28	795.12
60000	5155.23	2650.66	1816.69	1400.38	1151.13	985.40	867.40
65000	5584.83	2871.54	1968.08	1517.08	1247.05	1067.52	939.69
70000	6014.43	3092.43	2119.47	1633.78	1342.98	1149.63	1011.97
75000	6444.04	3313.32	2270.86	1750.47	1438.91	1231.75	1084.25
80000	6873.64	3534.21	2422.26	1867.17	1534.83	1313.87	1156.54
85000	7303.24	3755.10	2573.65	1983.87	1630.76	1395.98	1228.82
90000	7732.84	3975.98	2725.04	2100.57	1726.69	1478.10	1301.11
95000	8162.45	4196.87	2876.43	2217.27	1822.62	1560.22	1373.39
100000	8592.05	4417.76	3027.82	2333.96	1918.54	1642.33	1445.67
200000	17184.10	8835.52	6055.64	4667.93	3837.08	3284.67	2891.35
300000	25776.14	13253.28	9083.46	7001.89	5755.63	4927.00	4337.02
400000	34368.19	17671.04	12111.28	9335.86	7674.17	6569.33	5782.69
500000	42960.24	22088.80	15139.10	11669.82	9592.71	8211.67	7228.37
1000000	85920.48	44177.60	30278.20	23339.65	19185.42	16423.33	14456.73

MONTHLY PAYMENT
NECESSARY TO AMORTIZE A LOAN **5.75%**

Amortization Amount	8 Years	9 Years	10 Years	15 Years	20 Years	25 Years	30 Years
25	0.32	0.30	0.27	0.21	0.17	0.16	0.14
50	0.65	0.59	0.55	0.41	0.35	0.31	0.29
100	1.30	1.18	1.09	0.83	0.70	0.63	0.58
200	2.60	2.37	2.19	1.65	1.40	1.25	1.16
300	3.90	3.55	3.28	2.48	2.09	1.88	1.74
400	5.19	4.74	4.38	3.31	2.79	2.50	2.32
500	6.49	5.92	5.47	4.13	3.49	3.13	2.90
600	7.79	7.11	6.57	4.96	4.19	3.75	3.48
700	9.09	8.29	7.66	5.79	4.89	4.38	4.05
800	10.39	9.48	8.75	6.61	5.59	5.00	4.63
900	11.69	10.66	· 9.85	7.44	6.28	5.63	5.21
1000	12.99	11.85	10.94	8.27	6.98	6.25	5.79
2000	25.97	23.70	21.89	16.54	13.96	12.50	11.59
3000	38.96	35.55	32.83	24.80	20.95	18.75	17.38
4000	51.95	47.40	43.77	33.07	27.93	25.00	23.17
5000	64.94	59.25	54.72	41.34	34.91	31.25	28.96
6000	77.92	71.10	65.66	49.61	41.89	37.50	34.76
7000	90.91	82.94	76.60	57.88	48.88	43.75	40.55
8000	103.90	94.79	87.55	66.14	55.86	50.00	46.34
9000	116.89	106.64	98.49	74.41	62.84	56.25	52.14
10000	129.87	118.49	109.43	82.68	69.82	62.50	57.93
11000	142.86	130.34	120.38	90.95	76.80	68.75	63.72
12000	155.85	142.19	131.32	99.21	83.79	75.00	69.51
13000	168.83	154.04	142.26	107.48	90.77	81.25	75.31
14000	181.82	165.89	153.20	115.75	97.75	87.50	81.10
15000	194.81	177.74	164.15	124.02	104.73	93.75	86.89
16000	207.80	189.59	175.09	132.29	111.72	100.00	92.68
17000	220.78	201.44	188.03	140.55	118.70	106.25	98.48
18000	233.77	213.29	196.98	148.82	125.68	112.50	104.27
19000	246.76	225.14	207.92	157.09	132.66	118.75	110.06
20000	259.75	236.99	218.86	165.36	139.64	125.00	115.86
21000	272.73	248.83	229.81	173.63	146.63	131.25	121.65
22000	285.72	260.68	240.75	181.89	153.61	137.50	127.44
23000	298.71	272.53	251.69	190.16	160.59	143.76	133.23
24000	311.69	284.38	262.64	198.43	167.57	150.01	139.03
25000	324.68	296.23	273.58	206.70	174.56	156.26	144.82
26000	337.67	308.08	284.52	214.97	181.54	162.51	150.61
27000	350.66	319.93	295.47	223.23	188.52	168.76	156.41
28000	363.64	331.78	306.41	231.50	195.50	175.01	162.20
29000	376.63	343.63	317.35	239.77	202.49	181.26	167.99
30000	389.62	355.48	328.30	248.04	209.47	187.51	173.78
35000	454.55	414.72	383.01	289.38	244.38	218.76	202.75
40000	519.49	473.97	437.73	330.72	279.29	250.01	231.71
45000	584.43	533.22	492.44	372.06	314.20	281.26	260.68
50000	649.36	592.46	547.16	413.39	349.11	312.51	289.64
55000	714.30	651.71	601.88	454.73	384.02	343.76	318.60
60000	779.24	710.96	656.59	496.07	418.93	375.01	347.57
65000	844.17	770.20	711.31	537.41	453.85	406.26	376.53
70000	909.11	829.45	766.02	578.75	488.76	437.52	405.50
75000	974.05	888.69	820.74	620.09	523.67	468.77	434.46
80000	1038.98	947.94	875.45	661.43	558.58	500.02	463.42
85000	1103.92	1007.19	930.17	702.77	593.49	531.27	492.39
90000	1168.86	1066.43	984.89	744.11	628.40	562.52	521.35
95000	1233.79	1125.68	1039.60	785.45	663.31	593.77	550.32
100000	1298.73	1184.93	1094.32	826.79	698.22	625.02	579.28
200000	2597.46	2369.85	2188.64	1653.58	1396.45	1250.04	1158.56
300000	3896.19	3554.78	3282.96	2480.37	2094.67	1875.07	1737.84
400000	5194.91	4739.70	4377.27	3307.16	2792.90	2500.09	2317.12
500000	6493.64	5924.63	5471.59	4133.95	3491.12	3125.11	2896.40
1000000	12987.28	11849.25	10943.18	8267.90	6982.24	6250.22	5792.80

5.875%

Amortization Amount	1 Year	2 Years	3 Years	4 Years	5 Years	6 Years	7 Years
25	2.15	1.11	0.76	0.58	0.48	0.41	0.36
50	4.30	2.21	1.52	1.17	0.96	0.82	0.73
100	8.60	4.42	3.03	2.34	1.92	1.65	1.45
200	17.20	8.85	6.07	4.68	3.85	3.30	2.90
300	25.79	13.27	9.10	7.02	5.77	4.94	4.35
400	34.39	17.69	12.13	9.36	7.70	6.59	5.81
500	42.99	22.12	15.17	11.70	9.62	8.24	7.26
600	51.59	26.54	18.20	14.04	11.55	9.89	8.71
700	60.18	30.96	21.23	16.38	13.47	11.54	10.16
800	68.78	35.39	24.27	18.72	15.39	13.18	11.61
900	77.38	39.81	27.30	21.06	17.32	14.83	13.06
1000	85.98	44.23	30.33	23.40	19.24	16.48	14.51
2000	171.95	88.47	60.67	46.79	38.48	32.96	29.03
3000	257.93	132.70	91.00	70.19	57.73	49.44	43.54
4000	343.91	176.93	121.33	93.58	76.97	65.92	58.06
5000	429.88	221.16	151.67	116.98	96.21	82.40	72.57
6000	515.86	265.40	182.00	140.37	115.45	98.88	87.09
7000	601.84	309.63	212.33	163.77	134.69	115.36	101.60
8000	687.81	353.86	242.67	187.16	153.94	131.85	116.12
9000	773.79	398.09	273.00	210.56	173.18	148.33	130.63
10000	859.77	442.33	303.33	233.95	192.42	164.81	145.15
11000	945.74	486.56	333.67	257.35	211.66	181.29	159.66
12000	1031.72	530.79	364.00	280.75	230.90	197.77	174.18
13000	1117.69	575.02	394.33	304.14	250.15	214.25	188.69
14000	1203.67	619.26	424.67	327.54	269.39	230.73	203.21
15000	1289.65	663.49	455.00	350.93	288.63	247.21	217.72
16000	1375.62	707.72	485.33	374.33	307.87	263.69	232.24
17000	1461.60	751.95	515.67	397.72	327.11	280.17	246.75
18000	1547.58	796.19	546.00	421.12	346.36	296.65	261.27
19000	1633.55	840.42	576.33	444.51	365.60	313.13	275.78
20000	1719.53	884.65	606.67	467.91	384.84	329.61	290.30
21000	1805.51	928.88	637.00	491.30	404.08	346.09	304.81
22000	1891.48	973.12	667.33	514.70	423.32	362.58	319.33
23000	1977.46	1017.35	697.67	538.10	442.57	379.06	333.84
24000	2063.44	1061.58	728.00	561.49	461.81	395.54	348.36
25000	2149.41	1105.81	758.33	584.89	481.05	412.02	362.87
26000	2235.39	1150.05	788.67	608.28	500.29	428.50	377.39
27000	2321.37	1194.28	819.00	631.68	519.53	444.98	391.90
28000	2407.34	1238.51	849.33	655.07	538.77	461.46	406.42
29000	2493.32	1282.74	879.67	678.47	558.02	477.94	420.93
30000	2579.30	1326.98	910.00	701.86	577.26	494.42	435.45
35000	3009.18	1548.14	1061.67	818.84	673.47	576.82	508.02
40000	3439.06	1769.30	1213.33	935.82	769.68	659.23	580.60
45000	3868.94	1990.46	1365.00	1052.79	865.89	741.63	653.17
50000	4298.83	2211.63	1516.67	1169.77	962.10	824.03	725.75
55000	4728.71	2432.79	1668.34	1286.75	1058.31	906.44	798.32
60000	5158.59	2653.95	1820.00	1403.73	1154.52	988.84	870.90
65000	5588.47	2875.11	1971.67	1520.70	1250.73	1071.24	943.47
70000	6018.36	3096.28	2123.34	1637.68	1346.94	1153.65	1016.05
75000	6448.24	3317.44	2275.00	1754.66	1443.15	1236.05	1088.62
80000	6878.12	3538.60	2426.67	1871.63	1539.36	1318.46	1161.20
85000	7308.01	3759.76	2578.34	1988.61	1635.57	1400.86	1233.77
90000	7737.89	3980.93	2730.00	2105.59	1731.78	1483.26	1306.35
95000	8167.77	4202.09	2881.67	2222.57	1827.99	1565.67	1378.92
100000	8597.65	4423.25	3033.34	2339.54	1924.20	1648.07	1451.49
200000	17195.31	8846.50	6066.67	4679.09	3848.39	3296.14	2902.99
300000	25792.96	13269.75	9100.01	7018.63	5772.59	4944.21	4354.48
400000	34390.61	17693.00	12133.35	9358.17	7696.78	6592.28	5805.98
500000	42988.27	22116.25	15166.69	11697.72	9620.98	8240.35	7257.47
1000000	85976.53	44232.51	30333.37	23395.44	19241.96	16480.69	14514.95

Amortization Amount	8 Years	9 Years	10 Years	15 Years	20 Years	25 Years	30 Years
25	0.33	0.30	0.28	0.21	0.18	0.16	0.15
50	0.85	0.60	0.55	0.42	0.35	0.32	0.29
100	1.30	1.19	1.10	0.83	0.71	0.63	0.59
200	2.61	2.38	2.20	1.67	1.41	1.26	1.17
300	3.91	3.57	3.30	2.50	2.12	1.90	1.76
400	5.22	4.76	4.40	3.33	2.82	2.53	2.35
500	6.52	5.95	5.50	4.17	3.53	3.16	2.94
600	7.83	7.15	6.60	5.00	4.23	3.79	3.52
700	9.13	8.34	7.70	5.83	4.94	4.43	4.11
800	10.44	9.53	8.80	6.67	5.64	5.06	4.70
900	11.74	10.72	9.90	7.50	6.35	5.69	5.28
1000	13.05	11.91	11.00	8.33	7.05	6.32	5.87
2000	26.09	23.82	22.01	16.67	14.10	12.65	11.74
3000	39.14	35.73	33.01	25.00	21.16	18.97	17.61
4000	52.19	47.64	44.02	33.33	28.21	25.30	23.48
5000	65.23	59.55	55.02	41.67	35.26	31.62	29.35
6000	78.28	71.46	66.02	50.00	42.31	37.94	35.22
7000	91.32	83.36	77.03	58.33	49.36	44.27	41.09
8000	104.37	95.27	88.03	66.67	56.42	50.59	46.96
9000	117.42	107.18	99.04	75.00	63.47	56.92	52.83
10000	130.46	119.09	110.04	83.33	70.52	63.24	58.70
11000	143.51	131.00	121.04	91.67	77.57	69.56	64.57
12000	156.56	142.91	132.05	100.00	84.62	75.89	70.44
13000	169.60	154.82	143.05	108.33	91.67	82.21	76.31
14000	182.65	166.73	154.06	116.67	98.73	88.54	82.18
15000	195.70	178.64	165.06	125.00	105.78	94.86	88.05
16000	208.74	190.55	176.06	133.33	112.83	101.18	93.92
17000	221.79	202.46	187.07	141.67	119.88	107.51	99.80
18000	234.83	214.37	198.07	150.00	126.93	113.83	105.67
19000	247.88	226.28	209.08	158.33	133.99	120.16	111.54
20000	260.93	238.18	220.08	166.66	141.04	126.48	117.41
21000	273.97	250.09	231.09	175.00	148.09	132.80	123.28
22000	287.02	262.00	242.09	183.33	155.14	139.13	129.15
23000	300.07	273.91	253.09	191.66	162.19	145.45	135.02
24000	313.11	285.82	264.10	200.00	169.25	151.77	140.89
25000	326.16	297.73	275.10	208.33	176.30	158.10	146.76
26000	339.21	309.64	286.11	216.66	183.35	164.42	152.63
27000	352.25	321.55	297.11	225.00	190.40	170.75	158.50
28000	365.30	333.46	308.11	233.33	197.45	177.07	164.37
29000	378.34	345.37	319.12	241.66	204.51	183.39	170.24
30000	391.39	357.28	330.12	250.00	211.56	189.72	176.11
35000	456.62	416.82	385.14	291.66	246.82	221.34	205.46
40000	521.86	476.37	440.16	333.33	282.08	252.96	234.81
45000	587.09	535.92	495.18	375.00	317.34	284.58	264.16
50000	652.32	595.46	550.20	416.66	352.60	316.20	293.52
55000	717.55	655.01	605.22	458.33	387.85	347.82	322.87
60000	782.78	714.55	660.24	499.99	423.11	379.44	352.22
65000	848.01	774.10	715.26	541.66	458.37	411.06	381.57
70000	913.25	833.65	770.28	583.33	493.63	442.68	410.92
75000	978.48	893.19	825.30	624.99	528.89	474.30	440.27
80000	1043.71	952.74	880.32	666.66	564.15	505.92	469.62
85000	1108.94	1012.28	935.34	708.33	599.41	537.54	498.98
90000	1174.17	1071.83	990.37	749.99	634.67	569.16	528.33
95000	1239.41	1131.38	1045.39	791.66	669.93	600.78	557.68
100000	1304.64	1190.92	1100.41	833.32	705.19	632.40	587.03
200000	2609.28	2381.85	2200.81	1666.65	1410.38	1264.79	1174.06
300000	3913.91	3572.77	3301.22	2499.97	2115.57	1897.19	1761.09
400000	5218.55	4763.69	4401.62	3333.29	2820.76	2529.58	2348.12
500000	6523.19	5954.62	5502.03	4166.62	3525.95	3161.98	2935.15
1000000	13046.38	11909.23	11004.06	8333.24	7051.90	6323.95	5870.31

6%

Amortization Amount	1 Year	2 Years	3 Years	4 Years	5 Years	6 Years	7 Years
25	2.15	1.11	0.76	0.59	0.48	0.41	0.36
50	4.30	2.21	1.52	1.17	0.96	0.83	0.73
100	8.60	4.43	3.04	2.35	1.93	1.65	1.46
200	17.21	8.86	6.08	4.69	3.86	3.31	2.91
300	25.81	13.29	9.12	7.04	5.79	4.96	4.37
400	34.41	17.71	12.16	9.38	7.72	6.62	5.83
500	43.02	22.14	15.19	11.73	9.65	8.27	7.29
600	51.62	26.57	18.23	14.07	11.58	9.92	8.74
700	60.22	31.00	21.27	16.42	13.51	11.58	10.20
800	68.83	35.43	24.31	18.76	15.44	13.23	11.66
900	77.43	39.86	27.35	21.11	17.37	14.88	13.12
1000	86.03	44.29	30.39	23.45	19.30	16.54	14.57
2000	172.07	88.57	60.78	46.90	38.60	33.08	29.15
3000	258.10	132.86	91.17	70.35	57.90	49.61	43.72
4000	344.13	177.15	121.55	93.79	77.19	66.15	58.29
5000	430.16	221.44	151.94	117.26	96.49	82.69	72.87
6000	516.20	265.72	182.33	140.71	115.79	99.23	87.44
7000	602.23	310.01	212.72	164.16	135.09	115.77	102.01
8000	688.26	354.30	243.11	187.61	154.39	132.31	116.59
9000	774.29	398.59	273.50	211.06	173.69	148.84	131.16
10000	860.33	442.87	303.89	234.51	192.99	165.38	145.73
11000	946.36	487.16	334.27	257.96	212.28	181.92	160.31
12000	1032.39	531.45	364.66	281.42	231.58	198.46	174.88
13000	1118.42	575.74	395.05	304.87	250.88	215.00	189.45
14000	1204.46	620.02	425.44	328.32	270.18	231.53	204.03
15000	1290.49	664.31	455.83	351.77	289.48	248.07	218.60
16000	1376.52	708.60	486.22	375.22	308.78	264.61	233.17
17000	1462.55	752.89	516.61	398.67	328.08	281.15	247.75
18000	1548.59	797.17	546.99	422.12	347.37	297.69	262.32
19000	1634.62	841.46	577.38	445.57	366.67	314.22	276.89
20000	1720.65	885.75	607.77	469.03	385.97	330.76	291.47
21000	1806.68	930.04	638.16	492.48	405.27	347.30	306.04
22000	1892.72	974.32	668.55	515.93	424.57	363.84	320.61
23000	1978.75	1018.61	698.94	539.38	443.87	380.38	335.19
24000	2064.78	1062.90	729.33	562.83	463.17	396.92	349.76
25000	2150.81	1107.19	759.71	586.28	482.46	413.45	364.33
26000	2236.85	1151.47	790.10	609.73	501.76	429.99	378.91
27000	2322.88	1195.76	820.49	633.18	521.06	446.53	393.48
28000	2408.91	1240.05	850.88	656.64	540.36	463.07	408.05
29000	2494.94	1284.34	881.27	680.09	559.66	479.61	422.62
30000	2580.98	1328.62	911.66	703.54	578.96	496.14	437.20
35000	3011.14	1550.06	1063.60	820.79	675.45	578.83	510.06
40000	3441.30	1771.50	1215.54	938.05	771.94	661.53	582.93
45000	3871.47	1992.93	1367.49	1055.31	868.44	744.22	655.80
50000	4301.63	2214.37	1519.43	1172.56	964.93	826.91	728.66
55000	4731.79	2435.81	1671.37	1289.82	1061.42	909.60	801.53
60000	5161.95	2657.25	1823.31	1407.08	1157.91	992.29	874.40
65000	5592.12	2878.68	1975.26	1524.33	1254.41	1074.98	947.26
70000	6022.28	3100.12	2127.20	1641.59	1350.90	1157.67	1020.13
75000	6452.44	3321.56	2279.14	1758.85	1447.39	1240.36	1093.00
80000	6882.61	3542.99	2431.09	1876.10	1543.89	1323.05	1165.86
85000	7312.77	3764.43	2583.03	1993.36	1640.38	1405.74	1238.73
90000	7742.93	3985.87	2734.97	2110.61	1736.87	1488.43	1311.59
95000	8173.10	4207.31	2886.91	2227.87	1833.36	1571.12	1384.46
100000	8603.26	4428.74	3038.86	2345.13	1929.86	1653.81	1457.33
200000	17206.52	8857.49	6077.72	4690.26	3859.71	3307.63	2914.65
300000	25809.77	13286.23	9116.57	7035.38	5789.57	4961.44	4371.98
400000	34413.03	17714.97	12155.43	9380.51	7719.43	6615.26	5829.31
500000	43016.29	22143.71	15194.29	11725.64	9649.29	8269.07	7286.64
1000000	86032.58	44287.43	30388.58	23451.28	19298.57	16538.14	14573.27

Amortization Amount	8 Years	9 Years	10 Years	15 Years	20 Years	25 Years	30 Years
25	0.33	0.30	0.28	0.21	0.18	0.16	0.15
50	0.66	0.60	0.55	0.42	0.36	0.32	0.30
100	1.31	1.20	1.11	0.84	0.71	0.64	0.59
200	2.62	2.39	2.21	1.68	1.42	1.28	1.19
300	3.93	3.59	3.32	2.52	2.14	1.92	1.78
400	5.24	4.79	4.43	3.36	2.85	2.56	2.38
500	6.55	5.98	5.53	4.20	3.56	3.20	2.97
600	7.86	7.18	6.64	5.04	4.27	3.84	3.57
700	9.17	8.38	7.75	5.88	4.99	4.48	4.16
800	10.48	9.58	8.85	6.72	5.70	5.12	4.76
900	11.80	10.77	9.96	7.56	6.41	5.76	5.35
1000	13.11	11.97	11.07	8.40	7.12	6.40	5.95
2000	26.21	23.94	22.13	16.80	14.24	12.80	11.90
3000	39.32	35.91	33.20	25.20	21.37	19.19	17.84
4000	52.42	47.88	44.26	33.60	28.49	25.59	23.79
5000	65.53	59.85	55.33	41.99	35.61	31.99	29.74
6000	78.63	71.82	66.39	50.39	42.73	38.39	35.69
7000	91.74	83.79	77.46	58.79	49.85	44.79	41.64
8000	104.84	95.75	88.52	67.19	56.98	51.18	47.59
9000	117.95	107.72	99.59	75.59	64.10	57.58	53.53
10000	131.06	119.69	110.65	83.99	71.22	63.98	59.48
11000	144.16	131.66	121.72	92.39	78.34	70.38	65.43
12000	157.27	143.63	132.78	100.79	85.46	76.78	71.38
13000	170.37	155.60	143.85	109.18	92.58	83.17	77.33
14000	183.48	167.57	154.91	117.58	99.71	89.57	83.28
15000	196.58	179.54	165.98	125.98	106.83	95.97	89.22
16000	209.69	191.51	177.04	134.38	113.95	102.37	95.17
17000	222.80	203.48	188.11	142.78	121.07	108.77	101.12
18000	235.90	215.45	199.17	151.18	128.19	115.17	107.07
19000	249.01	227.42	210.24	159.58	135.32	121.56	113.02
20000	262.11	239.39	221.30	167.98	142.44	127.96	118.96
21000	275.22	251.36	232.37	176.38	149.56	134.36	124.91
22000	288.32	263.33	243.43	184.77	156.68	140.76	130.86
23000	301.43	275.30	254.50	193.17	163.80	147.16	136.81
24000	314.53	287.26	265.56	201.57	170.93	153.55	142.76
25000	327.64	299.23	276.63	209.97	178.05	159.95	148.71
26000	340.75	311.20	287.69	218.37	185.17	166.35	154.65
27000	353.85	323.17	298.76	226.77	192.29	172.75	160.60
28000	366.96	335.14	309.82	235.17	199.41	179.15	166.55
29000	380.06	347.11	320.89	243.57	206.53	185.54	172.50
30000	393.17	359.08	331.95	251.96	213.66	191.94	178.45
35000	458.70	418.93	387.28	293.96	249.27	223.93	208.19
40000	524.22	478.77	442.60	335.95	284.88	255.92	237.93
45000	589.75	538.62	497.93	377.95	320.48	287.91	267.67
50000	655.28	598.47	553.25	419.94	356.09	319.90	297.41
55000	720.81	658.31	608.58	461.94	391.70	351.89	327.15
60000	786.34	718.16	663.91	503.93	427.31	383.88	356.89
65000	851.86	778.01	719.23	545.92	462.92	415.87	386.64
70000	917.39	837.86	774.56	587.92	498.53	447.86	416.38
75000	982.92	897.70	829.88	629.91	534.14	479.85	446.12
80000	1048.45	957.55	885.21	671.91	569.75	511.85	475.86
85000	1113.98	1017.40	940.53	713.90	605.36	543.84	505.60
90000	1179.50	1077.24	995.86	755.89	640.97	575.83	535.34
95000	1245.03	1137.09	1051.18	797.89	676.58	607.82	565.08
100000	1310.56	1196.94	1106.51	839.88	712.19	639.81	594.82
200000	2621.12	2393.87	2213.02	1679.77	1424.38	1279.61	1189.65
300000	3931.68	3590.81	3319.53	2519.65	2136.57	1919.42	1784.47
400000	5242.24	4787.74	4426.04	3359.54	2848.75	2559.23	2379.29
500000	6552.80	5984.68	5532.55	4199.41	3560.94	3199.03	2974.12
1000000	13105.60	11969.36	11065.10	8398.83	7121.88	6398.07	5948.23

6.125%

Amortization Amount	1 Year	2 Years	3 Years	4 Years	5 Years	6 Years	7 Years
25	2.15	1.11	0.76	0.59	0.48	0.41	0.37
50	4.30	2.22	1.52	1.18	0.97	0.83	0.73
100	8.61	4.43	3.04	2.35	1.94	1.66	1.46
200	17.22	8.87	6.09	4.70	3.87	3.32	2.93
300	25.83	13.30	9.13	7.05	5.81	4.98	4.39
400	34.44	17.74	12.18	9.40	7.74	6.64	5.85
500	43.04	22.17	15.22	11.75	9.68	8.30	7.32
600	51.65	26.61	18.27	14.10	11.61	9.96	8.78
700	60.26	31.04	21.31	16.46	13.55	11.62	10.24
800	68.87	35.47	24.36	18.81	15.48	13.28	11.71
900	77.48	39.91	27.40	21.16	17.42	14.94	13.17
1000	86.09	44.34	30.44	23.51	19.36	16.60	14.63
2000	172.18	88.68	60.89	47.01	38.71	33.19	29.26
3000	258.27	133.03	91.33	70.52	58.07	49.79	43.90
4000	344.35	177.37	121.78	94.03	77.42	66.38	58.53
5000	430.44	221.71	152.22	117.54	96.78	82.98	73.16
6000	516.53	266.05	182.66	141.04	116.13	99.57	87.79
7000	602.62	310.40	213.11	164.55	135.49	116.17	102.42
8000	688.71	354.74	243.55	188.06	154.84	132.77	117.05
9000	774.80	399.08	273.99	211.56	174.20	149.36	131.69
10000	860.89	443.42	304.44	235.07	193.55	165.96	146.32
11000	946.97	487.77	334.88	258.58	212.91	182.55	160.95
12000	1033.06	532.11	365.33	282.09	232.26	199.15	175.58
13000	1119.15	576.45	395.77	305.59	251.62	215.74	190.21
14000	1205.24	620.79	426.21	329.10	270.97	232.34	204.84
15000	1291.33	665.14	456.66	352.61	290.33	248.94	219.48
16000	1377.42	709.48	487.10	376.11	309.68	265.53	234.11
17000	1463.51	753.82	517.54	399.62	329.04	282.13	248.74
18000	1549.60	798.16	547.99	423.13	348.39	298.72	263.37
19000	1635.68	842.50	578.43	446.64	367.75	315.32	278.00
20000	1721.77	886.85	608.88	470.14	387.11	331.91	292.63
21000	1807.86	931.19	639.32	493.65	406.46	348.51	307.27
22000	1893.95	975.53	669.76	517.16	425.82	365.11	321.90
23000	1980.04	1019.87	700.21	540.66	445.17	381.70	336.53
24000	2066.13	1064.22	730.65	564.17	464.53	398.30	351.16
25000	2152.22	1108.56	761.10	587.68	483.88	414.89	365.79
26000	2238.30	1152.90	791.54	611.19	503.24	431.49	380.42
27000	2324.39	1197.24	821.98	634.69	522.59	448.08	395.06
28000	2410.48	1241.59	852.43	658.20	541.95	464.68	409.69
29000	2496.57	1285.93	882.87	681.71	561.30	481.27	424.32
30000	2582.66	1330.27	913.31	705.22	580.66	497.87	438.95
35000	3013.10	1551.98	1065.53	822.75	677.43	580.85	512.11
40000	3443.54	1773.69	1217.75	940.29	774.21	663.83	585.27
45000	3873.99	1995.41	1369.97	1057.82	870.99	746.81	658.43
50000	4304.43	2217.12	1522.19	1175.36	967.76	829.78	731.59
55000	4734.87	2438.83	1674.41	1292.89	1064.54	912.76	804.74
60000	5165.32	2660.54	1826.63	1410.43	1161.32	995.74	877.90
65000	5595.76	2882.25	1978.85	1527.97	1258.09	1078.72	951.06
70000	6026.20	3103.97	2131.07	1645.50	1354.87	1161.70	1024.22
75000	6456.65	3325.68	2283.29	1763.04	1451.64	1244.68	1097.38
80000	6887.09	3547.39	2435.51	1880.57	1548.42	1327.65	1170.54
85000	7317.53	3769.10	2587.72	1998.11	1645.20	1410.63	1243.70
90000	7747.98	3990.81	2739.94	2115.65	1741.97	1493.61	1316.85
95000	8178.42	4212.52	2892.16	2233.18	1838.75	1576.59	1390.01
100000	8608.86	4434.24	3044.38	2350.72	1935.53	1659.57	1463.17
200000	17217.73	8868.47	6088.76	4701.43	3871.05	3319.14	2926.34
300000	25826.59	13302.71	9133.14	7052.15	5806.58	4978.71	4389.51
400000	34435.45	17736.95	12177.53	9402.87	7742.10	6638.27	5852.68
500000	43044.31	22171.18	15221.91	11753.58	9677.63	8297.84	7315.85
1000000	86088.62	44342.37	30443.82	23507.17	19355.26	16595.68	14631.71

MONTHLY PAYMENT
NECESSARY TO AMORTIZE A LOAN — **6.125%**

Amortization Amount	8 Years	9 Years	10 Years	15 Years	20 Years	25 Years	30 Years
25	0.33	0.30	0.28	0.21	0.18	0.16	0.15
50	0.66	0.60	0.56	0.42	0.36	0.32	0.30
100	1.32	1.20	1.11	0.85	0.72	0.65	0.60
200	2.63	2.41	2.23	1.69	1.44	1.29	1.21
300	3.95	3.61	3.34	2.54	2.16	1.94	1.81
400	5.27	4.81	4.45	3.39	2.88	2.59	2.41
500	6.58	6.01	5.56	4.23	3.60	3.24	3.01
600	7.90	7.22	6.68	5.08	4.32	3.88	3.62
700	9.22	8.42	7.79	5.93	5.03	4.53	4.22
800	10.53	9.62	8.90	6.77	5.75	5.18	4.82
900	11.85	10.83	10.01	7.62	6.47	5.83	5.42
1000	13.16	12.03	11.13	8.46	7.19	6.47	6.03
2000	26.33	24.06	22.25	16.93	14.38	12.95	12.05
3000	39.49	36.09	33.38	25.39	21.58	19.42	18.08
4000	52.66	48.12	44.51	33.86	28.77	25.89	24.11
5000	65.82	60.15	55.63	42.32	35.96	32.36	30.13
6000	78.99	72.18	66.76	50.79	43.15	38.84	36.16
7000	92.15	84.21	77.88	59.25	50.35	45.31	42.19
8000	105.32	96.24	89.01	67.72	57.54	51.78	48.21
9000	118.48	108.27	100.14	76.18	64.73	58.25	54.24
10000	131.65	120.30	111.26	84.65	71.92	64.73	60.27
11000	144.81	132.33	122.39	93.11	79.11	71.20	66.29
12000	157.98	144.36	133.52	101.58	86.31	77.67	72.32
13000	171.14	156.39	144.64	110.04	93.50	84.14	78.35
14000	184.31	168.41	155.77	118.51	100.69	90.62	84.37
15000	197.47	180.44	166.89	126.97	107.88	97.09	90.40
16000	210.64	192.47	178.02	135.43	115.08	103.56	96.43
17000	223.80	204.50	189.15	143.90	122.27	110.03	102.45
18000	236.97	216.53	200.27	152.36	129.46	116.51	108.48
19000	250.13	228.56	211.40	160.83	136.65	122.98	114.50
20000	263.30	240.59	222.53	169.29	143.84	129.45	120.53
21000	276.46	252.62	233.65	177.76	151.04	135.92	126.56
22000	289.63	264.65	244.78	186.22	158.23	142.40	132.58
23000	302.79	276.68	255.91	194.69	165.42	148.87	138.61
24000	315.96	288.71	267.03	203.15	172.61	155.34	144.64
25000	329.12	300.74	278.16	211.62	179.80	161.81	150.66
26000	342.29	312.77	289.28	220.08	187.00	168.29	156.69
27000	355.45	324.80	300.41	228.55	194.19	174.76	162.72
28000	368.62	336.83	311.54	237.01	201.38	181.23	168.74
29000	381.78	348.86	322.66	245.48	208.57	187.70	174.77
30000	394.95	360.89	333.79	253.94	215.77	194.18	180.80
35000	460.77	421.04	389.42	296.26	251.73	226.54	210.93
40000	526.60	481.19	445.05	338.59	287.69	258.90	241.06
45000	592.42	541.33	500.68	380.91	323.65	291.26	271.20
50000	658.25	601.48	556.32	423.23	359.61	323.63	301.33
55000	724.07	661.63	611.95	465.56	395.57	355.99	331.46
60000	789.90	721.78	667.58	507.88	431.53	388.35	361.59
65000	855.72	781.93	723.21	550.20	467.49	420.72	391.73
70000	921.55	842.07	778.84	592.53	503.45	453.08	421.86
75000	987.37	902.22	834.47	634.85	539.41	485.44	451.99
80000	1053.20	962.37	890.10	677.17	575.38	517.80	482.13
85000	1119.02	1022.52	945.74	719.50	611.34	550.17	512.26
90000	1184.85	1082.67	1001.37	761.82	647.30	582.53	542.39
95000	1250.67	1142.82	1057.00	804.14	683.26	614.89	572.52
100000	1316.49	1202.96	1112.63	846.47	719.22	647.26	602.66
200000	2632.99	2405.93	2225.26	1692.93	1438.44	1294.51	1205.32
300000	3949.48	3608.89	3337.89	2539.40	2157.66	1941.77	1807.97
400000	5265.98	4811.85	4450.52	3385.87	2876.88	2589.02	2410.63
500000	6582.47	6014.82	5563.15	4232.34	3596.09	3236.28	3013.29
1000000	13164.95	12029.64	11126.31	8464.67	7192.19	6472.56	6026.58

37

6.25%

Amortization Amount	1 Year	2 Years	3 Years	4 Years	5 Years	6 Years	7 Years
25	2.15	1.11	0.76	0.59	0.49	0.42	0.37
50	4.31	2.22	1.52	1.18	0.97	0.83	0.73
100	8.61	4.44	3.05	2.36	1.94	1.67	1.47
200	17.23	8.88	6.10	4.71	3.88	3.33	2.94
300	25.84	13.32	9.15	7.07	5.82	5.00	4.41
400	34.46	17.76	12.20	9.43	7.76	6.66	5.88
500	43.07	22.20	15.25	11.78	9.71	8.33	7.35
600	51.69	26.64	18.30	14.14	11.65	9.99	8.81
700	60.30	31.08	21.35	16.49	13.59	11.66	10.28
800	68.92	35.52	24.40	18.85	15.53	13.32	11.75
900	77.53	39.96	27.45	21.21	17.47	14.99	13.22
1000	86.14	44.40	30.50	23.56	19.41	16.65	14.69
2000	172.29	88.79	61.00	47.13	38.82	33.31	29.38
3000	258.43	133.19	91.50	70.69	58.24	49.96	44.07
4000	344.58	177.59	122.00	94.25	77.65	66.61	58.76
5000	430.72	221.99	152.50	117.82	97.06	83.27	73.45
6000	516.87	266.38	182.99	141.38	116.47	99.92	88.14
7000	603.01	310.78	213.49	164.94	135.88	116.57	102.83
8000	689.16	355.18	243.99	188.50	155.30	133.23	117.52
9000	775.30	399.58	274.49	212.07	174.71	149.88	132.21
10000	861.45	443.97	304.99	235.63	194.12	166.53	146.90
11000	947.59	488.37	335.49	259.19	213.53	183.19	161.59
12000	1033.74	532.77	365.99	282.76	232.94	199.84	176.28
13000	1119.88	577.17	396.49	306.32	252.36	216.49	190.97
14000	1206.03	621.56	426.99	329.88	271.77	233.15	205.66
15000	1292.17	665.96	457.49	353.45	291.18	249.80	220.35
16000	1378.31	710.36	487.99	377.01	310.59	266.45	235.04
17000	1464.46	754.75	518.49	400.57	330.00	283.11	249.73
18000	1550.60	799.15	548.98	424.14	349.42	299.76	264.42
19000	1636.75	843.55	579.48	447.70	368.83	316.41	279.11
20000	1722.89	887.95	609.98	471.26	388.24	333.07	293.81
21000	1809.04	932.34	640.48	494.83	407.65	349.72	308.50
22000	1895.18	976.74	670.98	518.39	427.06	366.37	323.19
23000	1981.33	1021.14	701.48	541.95	446.48	383.03	337.88
24000	2067.47	1065.54	731.98	565.51	465.89	399.68	352.57
25000	2153.62	1109.93	762.48	589.08	485.30	416.33	367.26
26000	2239.76	1154.33	792.98	612.64	504.71	432.99	381.95
27000	2325.91	1198.73	823.48	636.20	524.12	449.64	396.64
28000	2412.05	1243.12	853.97	659.77	543.54	466.29	411.33
29000	2498.19	1287.52	884.47	683.33	562.95	482.95	426.02
30000	2584.34	1331.92	914.97	706.89	582.36	499.60	440.71
35000	3015.06	1553.91	1067.47	824.71	679.42	582.87	514.16
40000	3445.78	1775.89	1219.96	942.52	776.48	666.13	587.61
45000	3876.51	1997.88	1372.46	1060.34	873.54	749.40	661.06
50000	4307.23	2219.87	1524.95	1178.16	970.60	832.67	734.51
55000	4737.96	2441.85	1677.45	1295.97	1067.66	915.93	807.96
60000	5168.68	2663.84	1829.95	1413.79	1164.72	999.20	881.42
65000	5599.40	2885.83	1982.44	1531.60	1261.78	1082.47	954.87
70000	6030.13	3107.81	2134.94	1649.42	1358.84	1165.73	1028.32
75000	6460.85	3329.80	2287.43	1767.23	1455.90	1249.00	1101.77
80000	6891.57	3551.79	2439.93	1885.05	1552.96	1332.27	1175.22
85000	7322.30	3773.77	2592.42	2002.86	1650.02	1415.53	1248.67
90000	7753.02	3995.76	2744.92	2120.68	1747.08	1498.80	1322.12
95000	8183.74	4217.74	2897.41	2238.50	1844.14	1582.07	1395.57
100000	8614.47	4439.73	3049.91	2356.31	1941.20	1665.33	1469.03
200000	17228.93	8879.46	6099.82	4712.62	3882.40	3330.66	2938.05
300000	25843.40	13319.19	9149.73	7068.93	5823.60	4996.00	4407.08
400000	34457.86	17758.93	12199.64	9425.25	7764.81	6661.33	5876.10
500000	43072.33	22198.66	15249.54	11781.56	9706.01	8326.66	7345.13
1000000	86144.65	44397.31	30499.09	23563.11	19412.01	16653.32	14690.26

Amortization Amount	8 Years	9 Years	10 Years	15 Years	20 Years	25 Years	30 Years
25	0.33	0.30	0.28	0.21	0.18	0.16	0.15
50	0.66	0.60	0.56	0.43	0.36	0.33	0.31
100	1.32	1.21	1.12	0.85	0.73	0.65	0.61
200	2.64	2.42	2.24	1.71	1.45	1.31	1.22
300	3.97	3.63	3.36	2.56	2.18	1.96	1.83
400	5.29	4.84	4.48	3.41	2.91	2.62	2.44
500	6.61	6.05	5.59	4.27	3.63	3.27	3.05
600	7.93	7.25	6.71	5.12	4.36	3.93	3.66
700	9.26	8.46	7.83	5.97	5.08	4.58	4.27
800	10.58	9.67	8.95	6.82	5.81	5.24	4.88
900	11.90	10.88	10.07	7.68	6.54	5.89	5.49
1000	13.22	12.09	11.19	8.53	7.26	6.55	6.11
2000	26.45	24.18	22.38	17.06	14.53	13.09	12.21
3000	39.67	36.27	33.56	25.59	21.79	19.64	18.32
4000	52.90	48.36	44.75	34.12	29.05	26.19	24.42
5000	66.12	60.45	55.94	42.65	36.31	32.74	30.53
6000	79.35	72.54	67.13	51.18	43.58	39.28	36.63
7000	92.57	84.63	78.31	59.72	50.84	45.83	42.74
8000	105.80	96.72	89.50	68.25	58.10	52.38	48.84
9000	119.02	108.81	100.69	76.78	65.37	58.93	54.95
10000	132.24	120.90	111.88	85.31	72.63	65.47	61.05
11000	145.47	132.99	123.06	93.84	79.89	72.02	67.16
12000	158.69	145.08	134.25	102.37	87.15	78.57	73.26
13000	171.92	157.17	145.44	110.90	94.42	85.12	79.37
14000	185.14	169.26	156.63	119.43	101.68	91.66	85.47
15000	198.37	181.35	167.82	127.96	108.94	98.21	91.58
16000	211.59	193.44	179.00	136.49	116.20	104.76	97.69
17000	224.82	205.53	190.19	145.02	123.47	111.31	103.79
18000	238.04	217.62	201.38	153.55	130.73	117.85	109.90
19000	251.26	229.71	212.57	162.08	137.99	124.40	116.00
20000	264.49	241.80	223.75	170.62	145.26	130.95	122.11
21000	277.71	253.89	234.94	179.15	152.52	137.50	128.21
22000	290.94	265.98	246.13	187.68	159.78	144.04	134.32
23000	304.16	278.07	257.32	196.21	167.04	150.59	140.42
24000	317.39	290.16	268.50	204.74	174.31	157.14	146.53
25000	330.61	302.25	279.69	213.27	181.57	163.69	152.63
26000	343.84	314.34	290.88	221.80	188.83	170.23	158.74
27000	357.06	326.43	302.07	230.33	196.10	176.78	164.84
28000	370.28	338.52	313.26	238.86	203.36	183.33	170.95
29000	383.51	350.61	324.44	247.39	210.62	189.88	177.05
30000	396.73	362.70	335.63	255.92	217.88	196.42	183.16
35000	462.86	423.15	391.57	298.58	254.20	229.16	213.69
40000	528.98	483.60	447.51	341.23	290.51	261.90	244.21
45000	595.10	544.05	503.45	383.88	326.83	294.63	274.74
50000	661.22	604.50	559.38	426.54	363.14	327.37	305.27
55000	727.34	664.95	615.32	469.19	399.45	360.11	335.79
60000	793.47	725.40	671.26	511.85	435.77	392.84	366.32
65000	859.59	785.85	727.20	554.50	472.08	425.58	396.85
70000	925.71	846.30	783.14	597.15	508.40	458.32	427.37
75000	991.83	906.75	839.08	639.81	544.71	491.06	457.90
80000	1057.95	967.20	895.01	682.46	581.02	523.79	488.43
85000	1124.08	1027.66	950.95	725.11	617.34	556.53	518.95
90000	1190.20	1088.11	1006.89	767.77	653.65	589.27	549.48
95000	1256.32	1148.56	1062.83	810.42	689.97	622.00	580.01
100000	1322.44	1209.01	1118.77	853.08	726.28	654.74	610.53
200000	2644.89	2418.01	2237.54	1706.15	1452.56	1309.48	1221.07
300000	3967.33	3627.02	3356.30	2559.23	2178.84	1964.22	1831.60
400000	5289.77	4836.02	4475.07	3412.31	2905.12	2618.97	2442.13
500000	6612.21	6045.03	5593.84	4265.38	3631.41	3273.71	3052.66
1000000	13224.43	12090.06	11187.68	8530.76	7262.81	6547.42	6105.33

6.375%

Amortization Amount	1 Year	2 Years	3 Years	4 Years	5 Years	6 Years	7 Years
25	2.16	1.11	0.76	0.59	0.49	0.42	0.37
50	4.31	2.22	1.53	1.18	0.97	0.84	0.74
100	8.62	4.45	3.06	2.36	1.95	1.67	1.47
200	17.24	8.89	6.11	4.72	3.89	3.34	2.95
300	25.86	13.34	9.17	7.09	5.84	5.01	4.42
400	34.48	17.78	12.22	9.45	7.79	6.68	5.90
500	43.10	22.23	15.28	11.81	9.73	8.36	7.37
600	51.72	26.67	18.33	14.17	11.68	10.03	8.85
700	60.34	31.12	21.39	16.53	13.63	11.70	10.32
800	68.96	35.56	24.44	18.90	15.58	13.37	11.80
900	77.58	40.01	27.50	21.26	17.52	15.04	13.27
1000	86.20	44.45	30.55	23.62	19.47	16.71	14.75
2000	172.40	88.90	61.11	47.24	38.94	33.42	29.50
3000	258.60	133.36	91.66	70.86	58.41	50.13	44.25
4000	344.80	177.81	122.22	94.48	77.88	66.84	59.00
5000	431.00	222.26	152.77	118.10	97.34	83.56	73.74
6000	517.20	266.71	183.33	141.71	116.81	100.27	88.49
7000	603.40	311.17	213.88	165.33	136.28	116.98	103.24
8000	689.61	355.62	244.44	188.95	155.75	133.69	117.99
9000	775.81	400.07	274.99	212.57	175.22	150.40	132.74
10000	862.01	444.52	305.54	236.19	194.69	167.11	147.49
11000	948.21	488.98	336.10	259.81	214.16	183.82	162.24
12000	1034.41	533.43	366.65	283.43	233.63	200.53	176.99
13000	1120.61	577.88	397.21	307.05	253.09	217.24	191.74
14000	1206.81	622.33	427.76	330.67	272.56	233.95	206.48
15000	1293.01	666.78	458.32	354.29	292.03	250.67	221.23
16000	1379.21	711.24	488.87	377.91	311.50	267.38	235.98
17000	1465.41	755.69	519.42	401.52	330.97	284.09	250.73
18000	1551.61	800.14	549.98	425.14	350.44	300.80	265.48
19000	1637.81	844.59	580.53	448.76	369.91	317.51	280.23
20000	1724.01	889.05	611.09	472.38	389.38	334.22	294.98
21000	1810.21	933.50	641.64	496.00	408.85	350.93	309.73
22000	1896.41	977.95	672.20	519.62	428.31	367.64	324.48
23000	1982.62	1022.40	702.75	543.24	447.78	384.35	339.23
24000	2068.82	1066.85	733.31	566.86	467.25	401.07	353.97
25000	2155.02	1111.31	763.86	590.48	486.72	417.78	368.72
26000	2241.22	1155.76	794.41	614.10	506.19	434.49	383.47
27000	2327.42	1200.21	824.97	637.72	525.66	451.20	398.22
28000	2413.62	1244.66	855.52	661.34	545.13	467.91	412.97
29000	2499.82	1289.12	886.08	684.95	564.60	484.62	427.72
30000	2586.02	1333.57	916.63	708.57	584.07	501.33	442.47
35000	3017.02	1555.83	1069.40	826.67	681.41	584.89	516.21
40000	3448.03	1778.09	1222.18	944.76	778.75	668.44	589.96
45000	3879.03	2000.35	1374.95	1062.86	876.10	752.00	663.70
50000	4310.03	2222.61	1527.72	1180.96	973.44	835.55	737.45
55000	4741.04	2444.88	1680.49	1299.05	1070.79	919.11	811.19
60000	5172.04	2667.14	1833.26	1417.15	1168.13	1002.66	884.93
65000	5603.04	2889.40	1986.04	1535.24	1265.47	1086.22	958.68
70000	6034.05	3111.66	2138.81	1653.34	1362.82	1169.77	1032.42
75000	6465.05	3333.92	2291.58	1771.43	1460.16	1253.33	1106.17
80000	6896.05	3556.18	2444.35	1889.53	1557.51	1336.88	1179.91
85000	7327.06	3778.44	2597.12	2007.62	1654.85	1420.44	1253.66
90000	7758.06	4000.70	2749.90	2125.72	1752.20	1503.99	1327.40
95000	8189.06	4222.97	2902.67	2243.82	1849.54	1587.55	1401.15
100000	8620.07	4445.23	3055.44	2361.91	1946.88	1671.10	1474.89
200000	17240.14	8890.46	6110.88	4723.82	3893.77	3342.21	2949.78
300000	25860.20	13335.68	9166.32	7085.73	5840.65	5013.31	4424.67
400000	34480.27	17780.91	12221.76	9447.65	7787.54	6684.42	5899.57
500000	43100.34	22226.14	15277.20	11809.56	9734.42	8355.52	7374.46
1000000	86200.68	44452.28	30554.39	23619.11	19468.84	16711.05	14748.92

Amortization Amount	8 Years	9 Years	10 Years	15 Years	20 Years	25 Years	30 Years
25	0.33	0.30	0.28	0.21	0.18	0.17	0.15
50	0.66	0.61	0.56	0.43	0.37	0.33	0.31
100	1.33	1.22	1.12	0.86	0.73	0.66	0.62
200	2.66	2.43	2.25	1.72	1.47	1.32	1.24
300	3.99	3.65	3.37	2.58	2.20	1.99	1.86
400	5.31	4.86	4.50	3.44	2.93	2.65	2.47
500	6.64	6.08	5.62	4.30	3.67	3.31	3.09
600	7.97	7.29	6.75	5.16	4.40	3.97	3.71
700	9.30	8.51	7.87	6.02	5.13	4.64	4.33
800	10.63	9.72	9.00	6.88	5.87	5.30	4.95
900	11.96	10.94	10.12	7.74	6.60	5.96	5.57
1000	13.28	12.15	11.25	8.60	7.33	6.62	6.18
2000	26.57	24.30	22.50	17.19	14.67	13.25	12.37
3000	39.85	36.45	33.75	25.79	22.00	19.87	18.55
4000	53.14	48.60	45.00	34.39	29.34	26.49	24.74
5000	66.42	60.75	56.25	42.99	36.67	33.11	30.92
6000	79.70	72.90	67.50	51.58	44.00	39.74	37.11
7000	92.99	85.05	78.74	60.18	51.34	46.36	43.29
8000	106.27	97.21	89.99	68.78	58.67	52.98	49.48
9000	119.56	109.36	101.24	77.37	66.00	59.60	55.66
10000	132.84	121.51	112.49	85.97	73.34	66.23	61.84
11000	146.12	133.66	123.74	94.57	80.67	72.85	68.03
12000	159.41	145.81	134.99	103.17	88.01	79.47	74.21
13000	172.69	157.96	146.24	111.76	95.34	86.09	80.40
14000	185.98	170.11	157.49	120.36	102.67	92.72	86.58
15000	199.26	182.26	168.74	128.96	110.01	99.34	92.77
16000	212.54	194.41	179.99	137.55	117.34	105.96	98.95
17000	225.83	206.56	191.24	146.15	124.67	112.58	105.14
18000	239.11	218.71	202.49	154.75	132.01	119.21	111.32
19000	252.40	230.86	213.74	163.35	139.34	125.83	117.51
20000	265.68	243.01	224.98	171.94	146.68	132.45	123.69
21000	278.96	255.16	236.23	180.54	154.01	139.08	129.87
22000	292.25	267.31	247.48	189.14	161.34	145.70	136.06
23000	305.53	279.46	258.73	197.73	168.68	152.32	142.24
24000	318.82	291.62	269.98	206.33	176.01	158.94	148.43
25000	332.10	303.77	281.23	214.93	183.34	165.57	154.61
26000	345.39	315.92	292.48	223.52	190.68	172.19	160.80
27000	358.67	328.07	303.73	232.12	198.01	178.81	166.98
28000	371.95	340.22	314.98	240.72	205.35	185.43	173.17
29000	385.24	352.37	326.23	249.32	212.68	192.06	179.35
30000	398.52	364.52	337.48	257.91	220.01	198.68	185.53
35000	464.94	425.27	393.72	300.90	256.68	231.79	216.46
40000	531.36	486.03	449.97	343.88	293.35	264.91	247.38
45000	597.78	546.78	506.22	386.87	330.02	298.02	278.30
50000	664.20	607.53	562.46	429.86	366.69	331.13	309.22
55000	730.62	668.28	618.71	472.84	403.36	364.25	340.15
60000	797.04	729.04	674.95	515.83	440.03	397.36	371.07
65000	863.46	789.79	731.20	558.81	476.69	430.47	401.99
70000	929.88	850.54	787.45	601.80	513.36	463.59	432.91
75000	996.30	911.30	843.69	644.78	550.03	496.70	463.84
80000	1062.72	972.05	899.94	687.77	586.70	529.81	494.76
85000	1129.14	1032.80	956.18	730.75	623.37	562.92	525.68
90000	1195.56	1093.56	1012.43	773.74	660.04	596.04	556.60
95000	1261.98	1154.31	1068.68	816.73	696.71	629.15	587.53
100000	1328.40	1215.06	1124.92	859.71	733.38	662.26	618.45
200000	2656.81	2430.13	2249.84	1719.42	1466.75	1324.53	1236.90
300000	3985.21	3645.19	3374.77	2579.13	2200.13	1986.79	1855.34
400000	5313.62	4860.25	4499.69	3438.84	2933.50	2649.06	2473.79
500000	6642.02	6075.32	5624.61	4298.55	3666.88	3311.32	3092.24
1000000	13284.04	12150.64	11249.22	8597.11	7333.75	6622.65	6184.48

6.5%

MONTHLY PAYMENT
NECESSARY TO AMORTIZE A LOAN

Amortization Amount	1 Year	2 Years	3 Years	4 Years	5 Years	6 Years	7 Years
25	2.16	1.11	0.77	0.59	0.49	0.42	0.37
50	4.31	2.23	1.53	1.18	0.98	0.84	0.74
100	8.63	4.45	3.06	2.37	1.95	1.68	1.48
200	17.25	8.90	6.12	4.74	3.91	3.35	2.96
300	25.88	13.35	9.18	7.10	5.86	5.03	4.44
400	34.50	17.80	12.24	9.47	7.81	6.71	5.92
500	43.13	22.25	15.30	11.84	9.76	8.38	7.40
600	51.75	26.70	18.37	14.21	11.72	10.06	8.88
700	60.38	31.16	21.43	16.57	13.67	11.74	10.37
800	69.01	35.61	24.49	18.94	15.62	13.42	11.85
900	77.63	40.06	27.55	21.31	17.57	15.09	13.33
1000	86.26	44.51	30.61	23.68	19.53	16.77	14.81
2000	172.51	89.01	61.22	47.35	39.05	33.54	29.62
3000	258.77	133.52	91.83	71.03	58.58	50.31	44.42
4000	345.03	178.03	122.44	94.70	78.10	67.08	59.23
5000	431.28	222.54	153.05	118.38	97.63	83.84	74.04
6000	517.54	267.04	183.66	142.05	117.15	100.61	88.85
7000	603.80	311.55	214.27	165.73	136.68	117.38	103.65
8000	690.05	356.06	244.88	189.40	156.21	134.15	118.46
9000	776.31	400.57	275.49	213.08	175.73	150.92	133.27
10000	862.57	445.07	306.10	236.75	195.26	167.69	148.08
11000	948.82	489.58	336.71	260.43	214.78	184.46	162.88
12000	1035.08	534.09	367.32	284.10	234.31	201.23	177.69
13000	1121.34	578.59	397.93	307.78	253.83	218.00	192.50
14000	1207.59	623.10	428.54	331.45	273.36	234.76	207.31
15000	1293.85	667.61	459.15	355.13	292.89	251.53	222.12
16000	1380.11	712.12	489.76	378.80	312.41	268.30	236.92
17000	1466.36	756.62	520.37	402.48	331.94	285.07	251.73
18000	1552.62	801.13	550.98	426.15	351.46	301.84	266.54
19000	1638.88	845.64	581.58	449.83	370.99	318.61	281.35
20000	1725.13	890.15	612.19	473.50	390.51	335.38	296.15
21000	1811.39	934.65	642.80	497.18	410.04	352.15	310.96
22000	1897.65	979.16	673.41	520.85	429.57	368.92	325.77
23000	1983.90	1023.67	704.02	544.53	449.09	385.68	340.58
24000	2070.16	1068.17	734.63	568.20	468.62	402.45	355.38
25000	2156.42	1112.68	765.24	591.88	488.14	419.22	370.19
26000	2242.67	1157.19	795.85	615.55	507.67	435.99	385.00
27000	2328.93	1201.70	826.46	639.23	527.20	452.76	399.81
28000	2415.19	1246.20	857.07	662.90	546.72	469.53	414.62
29000	2501.44	1290.71	887.68	686.58	566.25	486.30	429.42
30000	2587.70	1335.22	918.29	710.25	585.77	503.07	444.23
35000	3018.98	1557.75	1071.34	828.63	683.40	586.91	518.27
40000	3450.27	1780.29	1224.39	947.01	781.03	670.75	592.31
45000	3881.55	2002.83	1377.44	1065.38	878.66	754.60	666.35
50000	4312.83	2225.36	1530.49	1183.76	976.29	838.44	740.38
55000	4744.12	2447.90	1683.54	1302.13	1073.92	922.29	814.42
60000	5175.40	2670.44	1836.58	1420.51	1171.54	1006.13	888.46
65000	5606.68	2892.97	1989.63	1538.89	1269.17	1089.98	962.50
70000	6037.97	3115.51	2142.68	1657.26	1366.80	1173.82	1036.54
75000	6469.25	3338.04	2295.73	1775.64	1464.43	1257.66	1110.58
80000	6900.54	3560.58	2448.78	1894.01	1562.06	1341.51	1184.61
85000	7331.82	3783.12	2601.83	2012.39	1659.69	1425.35	1258.65
90000	7763.10	4005.65	2754.88	2130.76	1757.32	1509.20	1332.69
95000	8194.39	4228.19	2907.92	2249.14	1854.95	1593.04	1406.73
100000	8625.67	4450.73	3060.97	2367.52	1952.57	1676.89	1480.77
200000	17251.34	8901.45	6121.95	4735.03	3905.15	3353.77	2961.54
300000	25877.01	13352.18	9182.92	7102.55	5857.72	5030.66	4442.31
400000	34502.68	17802.90	12243.89	9470.07	7810.30	6707.55	5923.07
500000	43128.35	22253.63	15304.87	11837.58	9762.87	8384.43	7403.84
1000000	86256.69	44507.25	30609.73	23675.16	19525.75	16768.87	14807.69

MONTHLY PAYMENT
NECESSARY TO AMORTIZE A LOAN

6.5%

Amortization Amount	8 Years	9 Years	10 Years	15 Years	20 Years	25 Years	30 Years
25	0.33	0.31	0.28	0.22	0.19	0.17	0.16
50	0.67	0.61	0.57	0.43	0.37	0.33	0.31
100	1.33	1.22	1.13	0.87	0.74	0.67	0.63
200	2.67	2.44	2.26	1.73	1.48	1.34	1.25
300	4.00	3.66	3.39	2.60	2.22	2.01	1.88
400	5.34	4.88	4.52	3.47	2.96	2.68	2.51
500	6.67	6.11	5.66	4.33	3.70	3.35	3.13
600	8.01	7.33	6.79	5.20	4.44	4.02	3.76
700	9.34	8.55	7.92	6.06	5.18	4.69	4.38
800	10.68	9.77	9.05	6.93	5.92	5.36	5.01
900	12.01	10.99	10.18	7.80	6.66	6.03	5.64
1000	13.34	12.21	11.31	8.66	7.41	6.70	6.26
2000	26.69	24.42	22.62	17.33	14.81	13.40	12.53
3000	40.03	36.63	33.93	25.99	22.22	20.09	18.79
4000	53.38	48.85	45.24	34.65	29.62	26.79	25.06
5000	66.72	61.06	56.55	43.32	37.03	33.49	31.32
6000	80.06	73.27	67.87	51.98	44.43	40.19	37.58
7000	93.41	85.48	79.18	60.65	51.84	46.89	43.85
8000	106.75	97.69	90.49	69.31	59.24	53.59	50.11
9000	120.09	109.90	101.80	77.97	66.65	60.28	56.38
10000	133.44	122.11	113.11	86.64	74.05	66.98	62.64
11000	146.78	134.32	124.42	95.30	81.46	73.68	68.90
12000	160.13	146.54	135.73	103.96	88.86	80.38	75.17
13000	173.47	158.75	147.04	112.63	96.27	87.08	81.43
14000	186.81	170.96	158.35	121.29	103.67	93.78	87.70
15000	200.16	183.17	169.66	129.96	111.08	100.47	93.96
16000	213.50	195.38	180.97	138.62	118.48	107.17	100.22
17000	226.84	207.59	192.29	147.28	125.89	113.87	106.49
18000	240.19	219.80	203.60	155.95	133.29	120.57	112.75
19000	253.53	232.02	214.91	164.61	140.70	127.27	119.02
20000	266.88	244.23	226.22	173.27	148.10	133.96	125.28
21000	280.22	256.44	237.53	181.94	155.51	140.66	131.54
22000	293.56	268.65	248.84	190.60	162.91	147.36	137.81
23000	306.91	280.86	260.15	199.26	170.32	154.06	144.07
24000	320.25	293.07	271.46	207.93	177.72	160.76	150.34
25000	333.59	305.28	282.77	216.59	185.13	167.46	156.60
26000	346.94	317.50	294.08	225.26	192.53	174.15	162.86
27000	360.28	329.71	305.40	233.92	199.94	180.85	169.13
28000	373.63	341.92	316.71	242.58	207.34	187.55	175.39
29000	386.97	354.13	328.02	251.25	214.75	194.25	181.66
30000	400.31	366.34	339.33	259.91	222.15	200.95	187.92
35000	467.03	427.40	395.88	303.23	259.18	234.44	219.24
40000	533.75	488.45	452.44	346.55	296.20	267.93	250.56
45000	600.47	549.51	508.99	389.87	333.23	301.42	281.88
50000	667.19	610.57	565.55	433.18	370.25	334.91	313.20
55000	733.91	671.62	622.10	476.50	407.28	368.40	344.52
60000	800.63	732.68	678.66	519.82	444.30	401.89	375.84
65000	867.35	793.74	735.21	563.14	481.33	435.39	407.16
70000	934.06	854.80	791.77	606.46	518.35	468.88	438.48
75000	1000.78	915.85	848.32	649.78	555.38	502.37	469.80
80000	1067.50	976.91	904.87	693.10	592.40	535.86	501.12
85000	1134.22	1037.97	961.43	736.41	629.43	569.35	532.44
90000	1200.94	1099.02	1017.98	779.73	666.45	602.84	563.76
95000	1267.66	1160.08	1074.54	823.05	703.48	636.33	595.08
100000	1334.38	1221.14	1131.09	866.37	740.50	669.82	626.40
200000	2668.76	2442.27	2262.19	1732.74	1481.00	1339.65	1252.80
300000	4003.13	3663.41	3393.28	2599.11	2221.50	2009.47	1879.21
400000	5337.51	4884.54	4524.37	3465.48	2962.00	2679.30	2505.61
500000	6671.89	6105.68	5655.47	4331.85	3702.50	3349.12	3132.01
1000000	13343.78	12211.36	11310.93	8663.69	7405.00	6698.24	6264.02

43

6.625%

Amortization Amount	1 Year	2 Years	3 Years	4 Years	5 Years	6 Years	7 Years
25	2.16	1.11	0.77	0.59	0.49	0.42	0.37
50	4.32	2.23	1.53	1.19	0.98	0.84	0.74
100	8.63	4.46	3.07	2.37	1.96	1.68	1.49
200	17.26	8.91	6.13	4.75	3.92	3.37	2.97
300	25.89	13.37	9.20	7.12	5.87	5.05	4.46
400	34.53	17.82	12.27	9.49	7.83	6.73	5.95
500	43.16	22.28	15.33	11.87	9.79	8.41	7.43
600	51.79	26.74	18.40	14.24	11.75	10.10	8.92
700	60.42	31.19	21.47	16.61	13.71	11.78	10.41
800	69.05	35.65	24.53	18.99	15.67	13.46	11.89
900	77.68	40.11	27.60	21.36	17.62	15.14	13.38
1000	86.31	44.56	30.67	23.73	19.58	16.83	14.87
2000	172.63	89.12	61.33	47.46	39.17	33.65	29.73
3000	258.94	133.69	92.00	71.19	58.75	50.48	44.60
4000	345.25	178.25	122.66	94.93	78.33	67.31	59.47
5000	431.56	222.81	153.33	118.66	97.92	84.13	74.33
6000	517.88	267.37	183.99	142.39	117.50	100.96	89.20
7000	604.19	311.94	214.66	166.12	137.08	117.79	104.07
8000	690.50	356.50	245.32	189.85	156.66	134.61	118.93
9000	776.81	401.06	275.99	213.58	176.24	151.44	133.80
10000	863.13	445.62	306.65	237.31	195.83	168.27	148.67
11000	949.44	490.18	337.32	261.04	215.41	185.09	163.53
12000	1035.75	534.75	367.98	284.78	234.99	201.92	178.40
13000	1122.07	579.31	398.65	308.51	254.58	218.75	193.27
14000	1208.38	623.87	429.31	332.24	274.16	235.57	208.13
15000	1294.69	668.43	459.98	355.97	293.74	252.40	223.00
16000	1381.00	713.00	490.64	379.70	313.32	269.23	237.87
17000	1467.32	757.56	521.31	403.43	332.91	286.06	252.73
18000	1553.63	802.12	551.97	427.16	352.49	302.88	267.60
19000	1639.94	846.68	582.64	450.89	372.07	319.71	282.46
20000	1726.25	891.24	613.30	474.63	391.65	336.54	297.33
21000	1812.57	935.81	643.97	498.36	411.24	353.36	312.20
22000	1898.88	980.37	674.63	522.09	430.82	370.19	327.06
23000	1985.19	1024.93	705.30	545.82	450.40	387.02	341.93
24000	2071.50	1069.49	735.96	569.55	469.99	403.84	356.80
25000	2157.82	1114.06	766.63	593.28	489.57	420.67	371.66
26000	2244.13	1158.62	797.29	617.01	509.15	437.50	386.53
27000	2330.44	1203.18	827.96	640.74	528.73	454.32	401.40
28000	2416.76	1247.74	858.62	664.48	548.32	471.15	416.26
29000	2503.07	1292.30	889.29	688.21	567.90	487.98	431.13
30000	2589.38	1336.87	919.95	711.94	587.48	504.80	446.00
35000	3020.94	1559.68	1073.28	830.59	685.40	588.94	520.33
40000	3452.51	1782.49	1226.60	949.25	783.31	673.07	594.66
45000	3884.07	2005.30	1379.93	1067.91	881.22	757.20	669.00
50000	4315.63	2228.11	1533.26	1186.56	979.14	841.34	743.33
55000	4747.20	2450.92	1686.58	1305.22	1077.05	925.47	817.66
60000	5178.76	2673.73	1839.91	1423.88	1174.96	1009.61	891.99
65000	5610.33	2896.55	1993.23	1542.53	1272.88	1093.74	966.33
70000	6041.89	3119.36	2146.56	1661.19	1370.79	1177.87	1040.66
75000	6473.45	3342.17	2299.88	1779.85	1468.70	1262.01	1114.99
80000	6905.02	3564.98	2453.21	1898.50	1566.62	1346.14	1189.33
85000	7336.58	3787.79	2606.53	2017.16	1664.53	1430.28	1263.66
90000	7768.14	4010.60	2759.86	2135.81	1762.44	1514.41	1337.99
95000	8199.71	4233.41	2913.18	2254.47	1860.36	1598.54	1412.32
100000	8631.27	4456.22	3066.51	2373.13	1958.27	1682.68	1486.66
200000	17262.54	8912.45	6133.02	4746.25	3916.54	3365.36	2973.31
300000	25893.81	13368.67	9199.53	7119.38	5874.82	5048.03	4459.97
400000	34525.08	17824.90	12266.04	9492.51	7833.09	6730.71	5946.63
500000	43156.35	22281.12	15332.55	11865.63	9791.36	8413.39	7433.28
1000000	86312.70	44562.24	30665.10	23731.27	19582.72	16826.78	14866.57

Amortization Amount	8 Years	9 Years	10 Years	15 Years	20 Years	25 Years	30 Years
25	0.34	0.31	0.28	0.22	0.19	0.17	0.16
50	0.67	0.61	0.57	0.44	0.37	0.34	0.32
100	1.34	1.23	1.14	0.87	0.75	0.68	0.63
200	2.68	2.45	2.27	1.75	1.50	1.35	1.27
300	4.02	3.68	3.41	2.62	2.24	2.03	1.90
400	5.36	4.91	4.55	3.49	2.99	2.71	2.54
500	6.70	6.14	5.69	4.37	3.74	3.39	3.17
600	8.04	7.36	6.82	5.24	4.49	4.06	3.81
700	9.38	8.59	7.96	6.11	5.23	4.74	4.44
800	10.72	9.82	9.10	6.98	5.98	5.42	5.08
900	12.06	11.05	10.24	7.86	6.73	6.10	5.71
1000	13.40	12.27	11.37	8.73	7.48	6.77	6.34
2000	26.81	24.54	22.75	17.46	14.95	13.55	12.69
3000	40.21	36.82	34.12	26.19	22.43	20.32	19.03
4000	53.61	49.09	45.49	34.92	29.91	27.10	25.38
5000	67.02	61.36	56.86	43.65	37.38	33.87	31.72
6000	80.42	73.63	68.24	52.38	44.86	40.65	38.06
7000	93.83	85.91	79.61	61.11	52.34	47.42	44.41
8000	107.23	98.18	90.98	69.84	59.81	54.19	50.75
9000	120.63	110.45	102.36	78.57	67.29	60.97	57.10
10000	134.04	122.72	113.73	87.31	74.77	67.74	63.44
11000	147.44	134.99	125.10	96.04	82.24	74.52	69.78
12000	160.84	147.27	136.47	104.77	89.72	81.29	76.13
13000	174.25	159.54	147.85	113.50	97.20	88.06	82.47
14000	187.65	171.81	159.22	122.23	104.67	94.84	88.82
15000	201.05	184.08	170.59	130.96	112.15	101.61	95.16
16000	214.46	196.36	181.96	139.69	119.63	108.39	101.50
17000	227.86	208.63	193.34	148.42	127.10	115.16	107.85
18000	241.27	220.90	204.71	157.15	134.58	121.94	114.19
19000	254.67	233.17	216.08	165.88	142.05	128.71	120.54
20000	268.07	245.44	227.46	174.61	149.53	135.48	126.88
21000	281.48	257.72	238.83	183.34	157.01	142.26	133.22
22000	294.88	269.99	250.20	192.07	164.48	149.03	139.57
23000	308.28	282.26	261.57	200.80	171.96	155.81	145.91
24000	321.69	294.53	272.95	209.53	179.44	162.58	152.26
25000	335.09	306.81	284.32	218.26	186.91	169.35	158.60
26000	348.49	319.08	295.69	226.99	194.39	176.13	164.94
27000	361.90	331.35	307.07	235.72	201.87	182.90	171.29
28000	375.30	343.62	318.44	244.45	209.34	189.68	177.63
29000	388.71	355.89	329.81	253.19	216.82	196.45	183.97
30000	402.11	368.17	341.18	261.92	224.30	203.23	190.32
35000	469.13	429.53	398.05	305.57	261.68	237.10	222.04
40000	536.15	490.89	454.91	349.22	299.06	270.97	253.76
45000	603.16	552.25	511.78	392.87	336.45	304.84	285.48
50000	670.18	613.61	568.64	436.53	373.83	338.71	317.20
55000	737.20	674.97	625.50	480.18	411.21	372.58	348.92
60000	804.22	736.33	682.37	523.83	448.59	406.45	380.64
65000	871.24	797.69	739.23	567.48	485.98	440.32	412.36
70000	938.26	859.06	796.10	611.14	523.36	474.19	444.08
75000	1005.27	920.42	852.96	654.79	560.74	508.06	475.80
80000	1072.29	981.78	909.82	698.44	598.13	541.94	507.52
85000	1139.31	1043.14	966.69	742.10	635.51	575.81	539.24
90000	1206.33	1104.50	1023.55	785.75	672.89	609.68	570.96
95000	1273.35	1165.86	1080.42	829.40	710.27	643.55	602.68
100000	1340.37	1227.22	1137.28	873.05	747.66	677.42	634.40
200000	2680.73	2454.45	2274.56	1746.11	1495.31	1354.84	1268.79
300000	4021.10	3681.67	3411.84	2619.16	2242.97	2032.26	1903.19
400000	5361.46	4908.89	4549.12	3492.21	2990.63	2709.68	2537.58
500000	6701.83	6136.11	5686.40	4365.26	3738.28	3387.09	3171.98
1000000	13403.65	12272.23	11372.80	8730.53	7476.57	6774.19	6343.96

45

6.75%

Amortization Amount	1 Year	2 Years	3 Years	4 Years	5 Years	6 Years	7 Years
25	2.16	1.12	0.77	0.59	0.49	0.42	0.37
50	4.32	2.23	1.54	1.19	0.98	0.84	0.75
100	8.64	4.46	3.07	2.38	1.96	1.69	1.49
200	17.27	8.92	6.14	4.76	3.93	3.38	2.99
300	25.91	13.39	9.22	7.14	5.89	5.07	4.48
400	34.55	17.85	12.29	9.51	7.86	6.75	5.97
500	43.18	22.31	15.36	11.89	9.82	8.44	7.46
600	51.82	26.77	18.43	14.27	11.78	10.13	8.96
700	60.46	31.23	21.50	16.65	13.75	11.82	10.45
800	69.09	35.69	24.58	19.03	15.71	13.51	11.94
900	77.73	40.16	27.65	21.41	17.68	15.20	13.43
1000	86.37	44.62	30.72	23.79	19.64	16.88	14.93
2000	172.74	89.23	61.44	47.57	39.28	33.77	29.85
3000	259.11	133.85	92.16	71.36	58.92	50.65	44.78
4000	345.47	178.47	122.88	95.15	78.56	67.54	59.70
5000	431.84	223.09	153.60	118.94	98.20	84.42	74.63
6000	518.21	267.70	184.32	142.72	117.84	101.31	89.55
7000	604.58	312.32	215.04	166.51	137.48	118.19	104.48
8000	690.95	356.94	245.76	190.30	157.12	135.08	119.40
9000	777.32	401.56	276.48	214.09	176.76	151.96	134.33
10000	863.69	446.17	307.21	237.87	196.40	168.85	149.26
11000	950.06	490.79	337.93	261.66	216.04	185.73	164.18
12000	1036.42	535.41	368.65	285.45	235.68	202.62	179.11
13000	1122.79	580.02	399.37	309.24	255.32	219.50	194.03
14000	1209.16	624.64	430.09	333.02	274.96	236.39	208.96
15000	1295.53	669.26	460.81	356.81	294.60	253.27	223.88
16000	1381.90	713.88	491.53	380.60	314.24	270.16	238.81
17000	1468.27	758.49	522.25	404.39	333.88	287.04	253.73
18000	1554.64	803.11	552.97	428.17	353.52	303.93	268.66
19000	1641.01	847.73	583.69	451.96	373.16	320.81	283.59
20000	1727.37	892.34	614.41	475.75	392.80	337.70	298.51
21000	1813.74	936.96	645.13	499.54	412.44	354.58	313.44
22000	1900.11	981.58	675.85	523.32	432.07	371.47	328.36
23000	1986.48	1026.20	706.57	547.11	451.71	388.35	343.29
24000	2072.85	1070.81	737.29	570.90	471.35	405.23	358.21
25000	2159.22	1115.43	768.01	594.69	490.99	422.12	373.14
26000	2245.59	1160.05	798.73	618.47	510.63	439.00	388.06
27000	2331.95	1204.67	829.45	642.26	530.27	455.89	402.99
28000	2418.32	1249.28	860.17	666.05	549.91	472.77	417.92
29000	2504.69	1293.90	890.89	689.84	569.55	489.66	432.84
30000	2591.06	1338.52	921.62	713.62	589.19	506.54	447.77
35000	3022.90	1561.60	1075.22	832.56	687.39	590.97	522.39
40000	3454.75	1784.69	1228.82	951.50	785.59	675.39	597.02
45000	3886.59	2007.78	1382.42	1070.43	883.79	759.81	671.65
50000	4318.43	2230.86	1536.03	1189.37	981.99	844.24	746.28
55000	4750.28	2453.95	1689.63	1308.31	1080.19	928.66	820.91
60000	5182.12	2677.03	1843.23	1427.25	1178.39	1013.09	895.53
65000	5613.97	2900.12	1996.83	1546.18	1276.58	1097.51	970.16
70000	6045.81	3123.21	2150.44	1665.12	1374.78	1181.93	1044.79
75000	6477.65	3346.29	2304.04	1784.06	1472.98	1266.36	1119.42
80000	6909.50	3569.38	2457.64	1902.99	1571.18	1350.78	1194.04
85000	7341.34	3792.47	2611.24	2021.93	1669.38	1435.21	1268.67
90000	7773.18	4015.55	2764.85	2140.87	1767.58	1519.63	1343.30
95000	8205.03	4238.64	2918.45	2259.81	1865.78	1604.05	1417.93
100000	8636.87	4461.72	3072.05	2378.74	1963.98	1688.48	1492.56
200000	17273.74	8923.45	6144.10	4757.49	3927.95	3376.96	2985.11
300000	25910.61	13385.17	9216.15	7136.23	5891.93	5065.43	4477.67
400000	34547.48	17846.90	12288.20	9514.97	7855.91	6753.91	5970.22
500000	43184.35	22308.62	15360.25	11893.71	9819.88	8442.39	7462.78
1000000	86368.70	44617.24	30720.51	23787.43	19639.77	16884.78	14925.56

46

Amortization Amount	8 Years	9 Years	10 Years	15 Years	20 Years	25 Years	30 Years
25	0.34	0.31	0.29	0.22	0.19	0.17	0.16
50	0.67	0.62	0.57	0.44	0.38	0.34	0.32
100	1.35	1.23	1.14	0.88	0.75	0.69	0.64
200	2.69	2.47	2.29	1.76	1.51	1.37	1.28
300	4.04	3.70	3.43	2.64	2.26	2.06	1.93
400	5.39	4.93	4.57	3.52	3.02	2.74	2.57
500	6.73	6.17	5.72	4.40	3.77	3.43	3.21
600	8.08	7.40	6.86	5.28	4.53	4.11	3.85
700	9.42	8.63	8.00	6.16	5.28	4.80	4.50
800	10.77	9.87	9.15	7.04	6.04	5.48	5.14
900	12.12	11.10	10.29	7.92	6.79	6.17	5.78
1000	13.46	12.33	11.43	8.80	7.55	6.85	6.42
2000	26.93	24.67	22.87	17.60	15.10	13.70	12.85
3000	40.39	37.00	34.30	26.39	22.65	20.55	19.27
4000	53.85	49.33	45.74	35.19	30.19	27.40	25.70
5000	67.32	61.67	57.17	43.99	37.74	34.25	32.12
6000	80.78	74.00	68.61	52.79	45.29	41.10	38.55
7000	94.25	86.33	80.04	61.58	52.84	47.95	44.97
8000	107.71	98.67	91.48	70.38	60.39	54.80	51.39
9000	121.17	111.00	102.91	79.18	67.94	61.65	57.82
10000	134.64	123.33	114.35	87.98	75.48	68.50	64.24
11000	148.10	135.67	125.78	96.77	83.03	75.36	70.67
12000	161.56	148.00	137.22	105.57	90.58	82.21	77.09
13000	175.03	160.33	148.65	114.37	98.13	89.06	83.52
14000	188.49	172.67	160.09	123.17	105.68	95.91	89.94
15000	201.95	185.00	171.52	131.96	113.23	102.76	96.36
16000	215.42	197.33	182.96	140.76	120.78	109.61	102.79
17000	228.88	209.67	194.39	149.56	128.32	116.46	109.21
18000	242.35	222.00	205.83	158.36	135.87	123.31	115.64
19000	255.81	234.33	217.26	167.15	143.42	130.16	122.06
20000	269.27	246.66	228.70	175.95	150.97	137.01	128.49
21000	282.74	259.00	240.13	184.75	158.52	143.86	134.91
22000	296.20	271.33	251.57	193.55	166.07	150.71	141.33
23000	309.66	283.66	263.00	202.34	173.61	157.56	147.76
24000	323.13	296.00	274.44	211.14	181.16	164.41	154.18
25000	336.59	308.33	285.87	219.94	188.71	171.26	160.61
26000	350.05	320.66	297.31	228.74	196.26	178.11	167.03
27000	363.52	333.00	308.74	237.54	203.81	184.96	173.46
28000	376.98	345.33	320.18	246.33	211.36	191.81	179.88
29000	390.45	357.66	331.61	255.13	218.90	198.66	186.30
30000	403.91	370.00	343.05	263.93	226.45	205.51	192.73
35000	471.23	431.66	400.22	307.92	264.20	239.77	224.85
40000	538.55	493.33	457.39	351.90	301.94	274.02	256.97
45000	605.86	555.00	514.57	395.89	339.68	308.27	289.09
50000	673.18	616.66	571.74	439.88	377.42	342.52	321.21
55000	740.50	678.33	628.92	483.87	415.16	376.78	353.34
60000	807.82	739.99	686.09	527.86	452.91	411.03	385.46
65000	875.14	801.66	743.26	571.84	490.65	445.28	417.58
70000	942.46	863.33	800.44	615.83	528.39	479.53	449.70
75000	1009.77	924.99	857.61	659.82	566.13	513.79	481.82
80000	1077.09	986.66	914.79	703.81	603.88	548.04	513.94
85000	1144.41	1048.33	971.96	747.80	641.62	582.29	546.06
90000	1211.73	1109.99	1029.14	791.78	679.36	616.54	578.18
95000	1279.05	1171.66	1086.31	835.77	717.10	650.80	610.31
100000	1346.36	1233.32	1143.48	879.76	754.84	685.05	642.43
200000	2692.73	2466.65	2286.97	1759.52	1509.69	1370.10	1284.86
300000	4039.09	3699.97	3430.45	2639.28	2264.53	2055.15	1927.28
400000	5385.46	4933.30	4573.94	3519.04	3019.38	2740.20	2569.71
500000	6731.82	6166.62	5717.42	4398.80	3774.22	3425.25	3212.14
1000000	13463.65	12333.24	11434.84	8797.61	7548.44	6850.50	6424.28

47

6.875%

Amortization Amount	1 Year	2 Years	3 Years	4 Years	5 Years	6 Years	7 Years
25	2.16	1.12	0.77	0.60	0.49	0.42	0.37
50	4.32	2.23	1.54	1.19	0.98	0.85	0.75
100	8.64	4.47	3.08	2.38	1.97	1.69	1.50
200	17.28	8.93	6.16	4.77	3.94	3.39	3.00
300	25.93	13.40	9.23	7.15	5.91	5.08	4.50
400	34.57	17.87	12.31	9.54	7.88	6.78	5.99
500	43.21	22.34	15.39	11.92	9.85	8.47	7.49
600	51.85	26.80	18.47	14.31	11.82	10.17	8.99
700	60.50	31.27	21.54	16.69	13.79	11.86	10.49
800	69.14	35.74	24.62	19.07	15.76	13.55	11.99
900	77.78	40.21	27.70	21.46	17.73	15.25	13.49
1000	86.42	44.67	30.78	23.84	19.70	16.94	14.98
2000	172.85	89.34	61.55	47.69	39.39	33.89	29.97
3000	259.27	134.02	92.33	71.53	59.09	50.83	44.95
4000	345.70	178.69	123.10	95.37	78.79	67.77	59.94
5000	432.12	223.36	153.88	119.22	98.48	84.71	74.92
6000	518.55	268.03	184.66	143.06	118.18	101.66	89.91
7000	604.97	312.71	215.43	166.91	137.88	118.60	104.89
8000	691.40	357.38	246.21	190.75	157.58	135.54	119.88
9000	777.82	402.05	276.98	214.59	177.27	152.49	134.86
10000	864.25	446.72	307.76	238.44	196.97	169.43	149.85
11000	950.67	491.39	338.54	262.28	216.67	186.37	164.83
12000	1037.10	536.07	369.31	286.12	236.36	203.31	179.82
13000	1123.52	580.74	400.09	309.97	256.06	220.26	194.80
14000	1209.95	625.41	430.86	333.81	275.76	237.20	209.79
15000	1296.37	670.08	481.64	357.65	295.45	254.14	224.77
16000	1382.80	714.76	492.42	381.50	315.15	271.09	239.75
17000	1469.22	759.43	523.19	405.34	334.85	288.03	254.74
18000	1555.64	804.10	553.97	429.19	354.54	304.97	269.72
19000	1642.07	848.77	584.74	453.03	374.24	321.91	284.71
20000	1728.49	893.45	615.52	476.87	393.94	338.86	299.69
21000	1814.92	938.12	646.29	500.72	413.63	355.80	314.68
22000	1901.34	982.79	677.07	524.56	433.33	372.74	329.66
23000	1987.77	1027.46	707.85	548.40	453.03	389.69	344.65
24000	2074.19	1072.13	738.62	572.25	472.73	406.63	359.63
25000	2160.62	1116.81	769.40	596.09	492.42	423.57	374.62
26000	2247.04	1161.48	800.17	619.93	512.12	440.51	389.60
27000	2333.47	1206.15	830.95	643.78	531.82	457.46	404.59
28000	2419.89	1250.82	861.73	667.62	551.51	474.40	419.57
29000	2506.32	1295.50	892.50	691.47	571.21	491.34	434.56
30000	2592.74	1340.17	923.28	715.31	590.91	508.29	449.54
35000	3024.86	1563.53	1077.16	834.53	689.39	593.00	524.46
40000	3456.99	1786.89	1231.04	953.75	787.88	677.71	599.39
45000	3889.11	2010.25	1384.92	1072.96	886.36	762.43	674.31
50000	4321.23	2233.61	1538.80	1192.18	984.84	847.14	749.23
55000	4753.36	2456.97	1692.68	1311.40	1083.33	931.86	824.16
60000	5185.48	2680.34	1846.56	1430.62	1181.81	1016.57	899.08
65000	5617.60	2903.70	2000.44	1549.84	1280.30	1101.29	974.00
70000	6049.73	3127.06	2154.32	1669.05	1378.78	1186.00	1048.93
75000	6481.85	3350.42	2308.20	1788.27	1477.27	1270.72	1123.85
80000	6913.98	3573.78	2462.08	1907.49	1575.75	1355.43	1198.77
85000	7346.10	3797.14	2615.96	2026.71	1674.24	1440.14	1273.70
90000	7778.22	4020.50	2769.84	2145.93	1772.72	1524.86	1348.62
95000	8210.35	4243.86	2923.71	2265.15	1871.20	1609.57	1423.54
100000	8642.47	4467.23	3077.59	2384.36	1969.69	1694.29	1498.47
200000	17284.94	8934.45	6155.19	4768.73	3939.38	3388.57	2996.93
300000	25927.41	13401.68	9232.78	7153.09	5909.07	5082.86	4495.40
400000	34569.88	17868.90	12310.38	9537.45	7878.75	6777.15	5993.86
500000	43212.35	22336.13	15387.97	11921.82	9848.44	8471.43	7492.33
1000000	86424.69	44672.25	30775.95	23843.64	19696.88	16942.87	14984.66

Amortization Amount	8 Years	9 Years	10 Years	15 Years	20 Years	25 Years	30 Years
25	0.34	0.31	0.29	0.22	0.19	0.17	0.16
50	0.68	0.62	0.57	0.44	0.38	0.35	0.33
100	1.35	1.24	1.15	0.89	0.76	0.69	0.65
200	2.70	2.48	2.30	1.77	1.52	1.39	1.30
300	4.06	3.72	3.45	2.66	2.29	2.08	1.95
400	5.41	4.96	4.60	3.55	3.05	2.77	2.60
500	6.76	6.20	5.75	4.43	3.81	3.46	3.25
600	8.11	7.44	6.90	5.32	4.57	4.16	3.90
700	9.47	8.68	8.05	6.21	5.33	4.85	4.55
800	10.82	9.92	9.20	7.09	6.10	5.54	5.20
900	12.17	11.15	10.35	7.98	6.86	6.23	5.85
1000	13.52	12.39	11.50	8.86	7.62	6.93	6.50
2000	27.05	24.79	22.99	17.73	15.24	13.85	13.01
3000	40.57	37.18	34.49	26.59	22.86	20.78	19.51
4000	54.10	49.58	45.99	35.46	30.48	27.71	26.02
5000	67.62	61.97	57.49	44.32	38.10	34.64	32.52
6000	81.14	74.37	68.98	53.19	45.72	41.56	39.03
7000	94.67	86.76	80.48	62.05	53.34	48.49	45.53
8000	108.19	99.16	91.98	70.92	60.96	55.42	52.04
9000	121.71	111.55	103.47	79.78	68.59	62.34	58.54
10000	135.24	123.94	114.97	88.65	76.21	69.27	65.05
11000	148.76	136.34	126.47	97.51	83.83	76.20	71.55
12000	162.29	148.73	137.96	106.38	91.45	83.13	78.06
13000	175.81	161.13	149.46	115.24	99.07	90.05	84.56
14000	189.33	173.52	160.96	124.11	106.69	96.98	91.07
15000	202.86	185.92	172.46	132.97	114.31	103.91	97.57
16000	216.38	198.31	183.95	141.84	121.93	110.83	104.08
17000	229.90	210.70	195.45	150.70	129.55	117.76	110.58
18000	243.43	223.10	206.95	159.57	137.17	124.69	117.09
19000	256.95	235.49	218.44	168.43	144.79	131.62	123.59
20000	270.48	247.89	229.94	177.30	152.41	138.54	130.10
21000	284.00	260.28	241.44	186.16	160.03	145.47	136.60
22000	297.52	272.68	252.93	195.03	167.65	152.40	143.11
23000	311.05	285.07	264.43	203.89	175.27	159.32	149.61
24000	324.57	297.47	275.93	212.76	182.89	166.25	156.12
25000	338.09	309.86	287.43	221.62	190.52	173.18	162.62
26000	351.62	322.25	298.92	230.49	198.14	180.11	169.13
27000	365.14	334.65	310.42	239.35	205.76	187.03	175.63
28000	378.67	347.04	321.92	248.22	213.38	193.96	182.14
29000	392.19	359.44	333.41	257.08	221.00	200.89	188.64
30000	405.71	371.83	344.91	265.95	228.62	207.81	195.15
35000	473.33	433.80	402.40	310.27	266.72	242.45	227.67
40000	540.95	495.78	459.88	354.60	304.82	277.09	260.20
45000	608.57	557.75	517.37	398.92	342.93	311.72	292.72
50000	676.19	619.72	574.85	443.25	381.03	346.36	325.25
55000	743.81	681.69	632.34	487.57	419.13	380.99	357.77
60000	811.43	743.66	689.82	531.90	457.24	415.63	390.30
65000	879.05	805.64	747.31	576.22	495.34	450.26	422.82
70000	946.66	867.61	804.79	620.55	533.44	484.90	455.35
75000	1014.28	929.58	862.28	664.87	571.55	519.54	487.87
80000	1081.90	991.55	919.76	709.19	609.65	554.17	520.40
85000	1149.52	1053.52	977.25	753.52	647.75	588.81	552.92
90000	1217.14	1115.50	1034.73	797.84	685.86	623.44	585.45
95000	1284.76	1177.47	1092.22	842.17	723.96	658.08	617.97
100000	1352.38	1239.44	1149.70	886.49	762.06	692.72	650.50
200000	2704.76	2478.88	2299.41	1772.99	1524.12	1385.43	1300.99
300000	4057.13	3718.32	3449.11	2659.48	2286.19	2078.15	1951.49
400000	5409.51	4957.76	4598.81	3545.97	3048.25	2770.86	2601.99
500000	6761.89	6197.20	5748.52	4432.47	3810.31	3463.58	3252.48
1000000	13523.78	12394.40	11497.04	8864.93	7620.62	6927.15	6504.97

7%

MONTHLY PAYMENT
NECESSARY TO AMORTIZE A LOAN

Amortization Amount	1 Year	2 Years	3 Years	4 Years	5 Years	6 Years	7 Years
25	2.16	1.12	0.77	0.60	0.49	0.43	0.38
50	4.32	2.24	1.54	1.19	0.99	0.85	0.75
100	8.65	4.47	3.08	2.39	1.98	1.70	1.50
200	17.30	8.95	6.17	4.78	3.95	3.40	3.01
300	25.94	13.42	9.25	7.17	5.93	5.10	4.51
400	34.59	17.89	12.33	9.56	7.90	6.80	6.02
500	43.24	22.36	15.42	11.95	9.88	8.50	7.52
600	51.89	26.84	18.50	14.34	11.85	10.20	9.03
700	60.54	31.31	21.58	16.73	13.83	11.90	10.53
800	69.18	35.78	24.67	19.12	15.80	13.60	12.04
900	77.83	40.25	27.75	21.51	17.78	15.30	13.54
1000	86.48	44.73	30.83	23.90	19.75	17.00	15.04
2000	172.96	89.45	61.66	47.80	39.51	34.00	30.09
3000	259.44	134.18	92.49	71.70	59.26	51.00	45.13
4000	345.92	178.91	123.33	95.60	79.02	68.00	60.18
5000	432.40	223.64	154.16	119.50	98.77	85.01	75.22
6000	518.88	268.36	184.99	143.40	118.52	102.01	90.26
7000	605.36	313.09	215.82	167.30	138.28	119.01	105.31
8000	691.85	357.82	246.65	191.20	158.03	136.01	120.35
9000	778.33	402.55	277.48	215.10	177.79	153.01	135.39
10000	864.81	447.27	308.31	239.00	197.54	170.01	150.44
11000	951.29	492.00	339.15	262.90	217.29	187.01	165.48
12000	1037.77	536.73	369.98	286.80	237.05	204.01	180.53
13000	1124.25	581.45	400.81	310.70	256.80	221.01	195.57
14000	1210.73	626.18	431.64	334.60	276.56	238.01	210.61
15000	1297.21	670.91	462.47	358.50	296.31	255.02	225.66
16000	1383.69	715.64	493.30	382.40	316.07	272.02	240.70
17000	1470.17	760.36	524.13	406.30	335.82	289.02	255.75
18000	1556.65	805.09	554.97	430.20	355.57	306.02	270.79
19000	1643.13	849.82	585.80	454.10	375.33	323.02	285.83
20000	1729.61	894.55	616.63	478.00	395.08	340.02	300.88
21000	1816.09	939.27	647.46	501.90	414.84	357.02	315.92
22000	1902.57	984.00	678.29	525.80	434.59	374.02	330.97
23000	1989.06	1028.73	709.12	549.70	454.34	391.02	346.01
24000	2075.54	1073.45	739.95	573.60	474.10	408.03	361.05
25000	2162.02	1118.18	770.79	597.50	493.85	425.03	376.10
26000	2248.50	1162.91	801.62	621.40	513.61	442.03	391.14
27000	2334.98	1207.64	832.45	645.30	533.36	459.03	406.18
28000	2421.46	1252.36	863.28	669.20	553.11	476.03	421.23
29000	2507.94	1297.09	894.11	693.10	572.87	493.03	436.27
30000	2594.42	1341.82	924.94	717.00	592.62	510.03	451.32
35000	3028.82	1565.45	1079.10	836.50	691.39	595.04	526.54
40000	3459.23	1789.09	1233.26	956.00	790.16	680.04	601.75
45000	3891.63	2012.73	1387.41	1075.50	888.93	765.05	676.97
50000	4324.03	2236.36	1541.57	1194.99	987.70	850.05	752.19
55000	4756.44	2460.00	1695.73	1314.49	1086.47	935.06	827.41
60000	5188.84	2683.64	1849.89	1433.99	1185.24	1020.06	902.63
65000	5621.24	2907.27	2004.04	1553.49	1284.01	1105.07	977.85
70000	6053.65	3130.91	2158.20	1672.99	1382.79	1190.07	1053.07
75000	6486.05	3354.55	2312.36	1792.49	1481.56	1275.08	1128.29
80000	6918.45	3578.18	2466.51	1911.99	1580.33	1360.08	1203.51
85000	7350.86	3801.82	2620.67	2031.49	1679.10	1445.09	1278.73
90000	7783.26	4025.46	2774.83	2150.99	1777.87	1530.09	1353.95
95000	8215.66	4249.09	2928.98	2270.49	1876.64	1615.10	1429.17
100000	8648.07	4472.73	3083.14	2389.99	1975.41	1700.11	1504.39
200000	17296.13	8945.46	6166.28	4779.98	3950.81	3400.21	3008.77
300000	25944.20	13418.19	9249.43	7169.97	5926.22	5100.32	4513.16
400000	34592.27	17890.91	12332.57	9559.96	7901.63	6800.42	6017.55
500000	43240.34	22363.64	15415.71	11949.95	9877.04	8500.53	7521.93
1000000	86480.67	44727.28	30831.42	23899.90	19754.07	17001.05	15043.87

Amortization Amount	8 Years	9 Years	10 Years	15 Years	20 Years	25 Years	30 Years
25	0.34	0.31	0.29	0.22	0.19	0.18	0.16
50	0.68	0.62	0.58	0.45	0.38	0.35	0.33
100	1.36	1.25	1.16	0.89	0.77	0.70	0.66
200	2.72	2.49	2.31	1.79	1.54	1.40	1.32
300	4.08	3.74	3.47	2.68	2.31.	2.10	1.98
400	5.43	4.98	4.62	3.57	3.08	2.80	2.63
500	6.79	6.23	5.78	4.47	3.85	3.50	3.29
600	8.15	7.47	6.94	5.36	4.62	4.20	3.95
700	9.51	8.72	8.09	6.25	5.39	4.90	4.61
800	10.87	9.96	9.25	7.15	6.15	5.60	5.27
900	12.23	11.21	10.40	8.04	6.92	6.30	5.93
1000	13.58	12.46	11.56	8.93	7.69	7.00	6.59
2000	27.17	24.91	23.12	17.86	15.39	14.01	13.17
3000	40.75	37.37	34.68	26.80	23.08	21.01	19.76
4000	54.34	49.82	46.24	35.73	30.77	28.02	26.34
5000	67.92	62.28	57.80	44.66	38.47	35.02	32.93
6000	81.50	74.73	69.36	53.59	46.16	42.02	39.52
7000	95.09	87.19	80.92	62.53	53.85	49.03	46.10
8000	108.67	99.65	92.48	71.46	61.54	56.03	52.69
9000	122.26	112.10	104.03	80.39	69.24	63.04	59.27
10000	135.84	124.56	115.59	89.32	76.93	70.04	65.86
11000	149.42	137.01	127.15	98.26	84.62	77.05	72.45
12000	163.01	149.47	138.71	107.19	92.32	84.05	79.03
13000	176.59	161.92	150.27	116.12	100.01	91.05	85.62
14000	190.18	174.38	161.83	125.05	107.70	98.06	92.20
15000	203.76	186.84	173.39	133.99	115.40	105.06	98.79
16000	217.34	199.29	184.95	142.92	123.09	112.07	105.38
17000	230.93	211.75	196.51	151.85	130.78	119.07	111.96
18000	244.51	224.20	208.07	160.78	138.48	126.07	118.55
19000	258.10	236.66	219.63	169.72	146.17	133.08	125.13
20000	271.68	249.11	231.19	178.65	153.86	140.08	131.72
21000	285.26	261.57	242.75	187.58	161.56	147.09	138.31
22000	298.85	274.03	254.31	196.51	169.25	154.09	144.89
23000	312.43	286.48	265.87	205.45	176.94	161.10	151.48
24000	326.02	298.94	277.43	214.38	184.63	168.10	158.06
25000	339.60	311.39	288.98	223.31	192.33	175.10	164.65
26000	353.18	323.85	300.54	232.24	200.02	182.11	171.24
27000	366.77	336.30	312.10	241.18	207.71	189.11	177.82
28000	380.35	348.76	323.66	250.11	215.41	196.12	184.41
29000	393.94	361.22	335.22	259.04	223.10	203.12	190.99
30000	407.52	373.67	346.78	267.97	230.79	210.12	197.58
35000	475.44	435.95	404.58	312.64	269.26	245.15	230.51
40000	543.36	498.23	462.38	357.30	307.72	280.17	263.44
45000	611.28	560.51	520.17	401.96	346.19	315.19	296.37
50000	679.20	622.79	577.97	446.62	384.66	350.21	329.30
55000	747.12	685.06	635.77	491.29	423.12	385.23	362.23
60000	815.04	747.34	693.56	535.95	461.59	420.25	395.16
65000	882.96	809.62	751.36	580.61	500.05	455.27	428.09
70000	950.88	871.90	809.16	625.27	538.52	490.29	461.02
75000	1018.80	934.18	866.95	669.94	576.98	525.31	493.95
80000	1086.72	996.46	924.75	714.60	615.45	560.33	526.88
85000	1154.64	1058.74	982.55	759.26	653.91	595.35	559.81
90000	1222.56	1121.01	1040.35	803.92	692.38	630.37	592.74
95000	1290.48	1183.29	1098.14	848.59	730.85	665.39	625.67
100000	1358.40	1245.57	1155.94	893.25	769.31	700.42	658.60
200000	2716.81	2491.14	2311.88	1786.50	1538.62	1400.83	1317.21
300000	4075.21	3736.71	3467.82	2679.75	2307.93	2101.25	1975.81
400000	5433.61	4982.28	4623.78	3573.00	3077.24	2801.66	2634.41
500000	6792.01	6227.85	5779.70	4466.25	3846.55	3502.08	3293.02
1000000	13584.03	12455.71	11559.40	8932.49	7693.11	7004.16	6586.03

7.125%

MONTHLY PAYMENT
NECESSARY TO AMORTIZE A LOAN

Amortization Amount	1 Year	2 Years	3 Years	4 Years	5 Years	6 Years	7 Years
25	2.16	1.12	0.77	0.60	0.50	0.43	0.38
50	4.33	2.24	1.54	1.20	0.99	0.85	0.76
100	8.65	4.48	3.09	2.40	1.98	1.71	1.51
200	17.31	8.96	6.18	4.79	3.96	3.41	3.02
300	25.96	13.43	9.27	7.19	5.94	5.12	4.53
400	34.61	17.91	12.35	9.58	7.92	6.82	6.04
500	43.27	22.39	15.44	11.98	9.91	8.53	7.55
600	51.92	26.87	18.53	14.37	11.89	10.24	9.06
700	60.58	31.35	21.62	16.77	13.87	11.94	10.57
800	69.23	35.83	24.71	19.16	15.85	13.65	12.08
900	77.88	40.30	27.80	21.56	17.83	15.35	13.59
1000	86.54	44.78	30.89	23.96	19.81	17.06	15.10
2000	173.07	89.56	61.77	47.91	39.62	34.12	30.21
3000	259.61	134.35	92.66	71.87	59.43	51.18	45.31
4000	346.15	179.13	123.55	95.82	79.25	68.24	60.41
5000	432.68	223.91	154.43	119.78	99.06	85.30	75.52
6000	519.22	268.69	185.32	143.74	118.87	102.36	90.62
7000	605.76	313.48	216.21	167.69	138.68	119.42	105.72
8000	692.29	358.26	247.10	191.65	158.49	136.47	120.83
9000	778.83	403.04	277.98	215.61	178.30	153.53	135.93
10000	865.37	447.82	308.87	239.56	198.11	170.59	151.03
11000	951.90	492.61	339.76	263.52	217.92	187.65	166.14
12000	1038.44	537.39	370.64	287.47	237.74	204.71	181.24
13000	1124.98	582.17	401.53	311.43	257.55	221.77	196.34
14000	1211.51	626.95	432.42	335.39	277.36	238.83	211.44
15000	1298.05	671.73	463.30	359.34	297.17	255.89	226.55
16000	1384.59	716.52	494.19	383.30	316.98	272.95	241.65
17000	1471.12	761.30	525.08	407.26	336.79	290.01	256.75
18000	1557.66	806.08	555.96	431.21	356.60	307.07	271.86
19000	1644.20	850.86	586.85	455.17	376.42	324.13	286.96
20000	1730.73	895.65	617.74	479.12	396.23	341.19	302.06
21000	1817.27	940.43	648.63	503.08	416.04	358.25	317.17
22000	1903.81	985.21	679.51	527.04	435.85	375.31	332.27
23000	1990.34	1029.99	710.40	550.99	455.66	392.36	347.37
24000	2076.88	1074.78	741.29	574.95	475.47	409.42	362.48
25000	2163.42	1119.56	772.17	598.91	495.28	426.48	377.58
26000	2249.95	1164.34	803.06	622.86	515.09	443.54	392.68
27000	2336.49	1209.12	833.95	646.82	534.91	460.60	407.79
28000	2423.03	1253.90	864.83	670.77	554.72	477.66	422.89
29000	2509.56	1298.69	895.72	694.73	574.53	494.72	437.99
30000	2596.10	1343.47	926.61	718.69	594.34	511.78	453.10
35000	3028.78	1567.38	1081.04	838.47	693.40	597.08	528.61
40000	3461.47	1791.29	1235.48	958.25	792.45	682.37	604.13
45000	3894.15	2015.20	1389.91	1078.03	891.51	767.67	679.64
50000	4326.83	2239.12	1544.35	1197.81	990.57	852.97	755.16
55000	4759.52	2463.03	1698.78	1317.59	1089.62	938.26	830.68
60000	5192.20	2686.94	1853.22	1437.37	1188.68	1023.56	906.19
65000	5624.88	2910.85	2007.65	1557.15	1287.74	1108.86	981.71
70000	6057.57	3134.76	2162.08	1676.93	1386.79	1194.15	1057.22
75000	6490.25	3358.67	2316.52	1796.72	1485.85	1279.45	1132.74
80000	6922.93	3582.59	2470.95	1916.50	1584.91	1364.75	1208.25
85000	7355.62	3806.50	2625.39	2036.28	1683.96	1450.04	1283.77
90000	7788.30	4030.41	2779.82	2156.06	1783.02	1535.34	1359.29
95000	8220.98	4254.32	2934.26	2275.84	1882.08	1620.64	1434.80
100000	8653.67	4478.23	3088.69	2395.62	1981.13	1705.93	1510.32
200000	17307.33	8956.46	6177.38	4791.24	3962.27	3411.86	3020.64
300000	25961.00	13434.70	9266.08	7186.86	5943.40	5117.80	4530.96
400000	34614.66	17912.93	12354.77	9582.49	7924.53	6823.73	6041.27
500000	43268.33	22391.16	15443.46	11978.11	9905.67	8529.66	7551.59
1000000	86536.65	44782.32	30886.92	23956.21	19811.34	17059.32	15103.18

Amortization Amount	8 Years	9 Years	10 Years	15 Years	20 Years	25 Years	30 Years
25	0.34	0.31	0.29	0.23	0.19	0.18	0.17
50	0.68	0.63	0.58	0.45	0.39	0.35	0.33
100	1.36	1.25	1.16	0.90	0.78	0.71	0.67
200	2.73	2.50	2.32	1.80	1.55	1.42	1.33
300	4.09	3.76	3.49	2.70	2.33	2.12	2.00
400	5.46	5.01	4.65	3.60	3.11	2.83	2.67
500	6.82	6.26	5.81	4.50	3.88	3.54	3.33
600	8.19	7.51	6.97	5.40	4.66	4.25	4.00
700	9.55	8.76	8.14	6.30	5.44	4.96	4.67
800	10.92	10.01	9.30	7.20	6.21	5.67	5.33
900	12.28	11.27	10.46	8.10	6.99	6.37	6.00
1000	13.64	12.52	11.62	9.00	7.77	7.08	6.67
2000	27.29	25.03	23.24	18.00	15.53	14.16	13.33
3000	40.93	37.55	34.87	27.00	23.30	21.24	20.00
4000	54.58	50.07	46.49	36.00	31.06	28.33	26.67
5000	68.22	62.59	58.11	45.00	38.83	35.41	33.34
6000	81.87	75.10	69.73	54.00	46.60	42.49	40.00
7000	95.51	87.62	81.35	63.00	54.36	49.57	46.67
8000	109.16	100.14	92.98	72.00	62.13	56.65	53.34
9000	122.80	112.65	104.60	81.00	69.89	63.73	60.01
10000	136.44	125.17	116.22	90.00	77.66	70.82	66.67
11000	150.09	137.69	127.84	99.00	85.42	77.90	73.34
12000	163.73	150.21	139.46	108.00	93.19	84.98	80.01
13000	177.38	162.72	151.09	117.00	100.96	92.06	86.68
14000	191.02	175.24	162.71	126.00	108.72	99.14	93.34
15000	204.67	187.76	174.33	135.00	116.49	106.22	100.01
16000	218.31	200.27	185.95	144.00	124.25	113.30	106.68
17000	231.95	212.79	197.57	153.01	132.02	120.39	113.35
18000	245.60	225.31	209.19	162.01	139.79	127.47	120.01
19000	259.24	237.83	220.82	171.01	147.55	134.55	126.68
20000	272.89	250.34	232.44	180.01	155.32	141.63	133.35
21000	286.53	262.86	244.06	189.01	163.08	148.71	140.02
22000	300.18	275.38	255.68	198.01	170.85	155.79	146.68
23000	313.82	287.89	267.30	207.01	178.62	162.87	153.35
24000	327.47	300.41	278.93	216.01	186.38	169.96	160.02
25000	341.11	312.93	290.55	225.01	194.15	177.04	166.69
26000	354.75	325.45	302.17	234.01	201.91	184.12	173.35
27000	368.40	337.96	313.79	243.01	209.68	191.20	180.02
28000	382.04	350.48	325.41	252.01	217.44	198.28	186.69
29000	395.69	363.00	337.04	261.01	225.21	205.36	193.36
30000	409.33	375.51	348.66	270.01	232.98	212.45	200.02
35000	477.55	438.10	406.77	315.01	271.81	247.85	233.36
40000	545.78	500.69	464.88	360.01	310.64	283.26	266.70
45000	614.00	563.27	522.99	405.01	349.47	318.67	300.04
50000	682.22	625.86	581.10	450.01	388.29	354.08	333.37
55000	750.44	688.44	639.21	495.02	427.12	389.48	366.71
60000	818.66	751.03	697.32	540.02	465.95	424.89	400.05
65000	886.89	813.62	755.43	585.02	504.78	460.30	433.38
70000	955.11	876.20	813.53	630.02	543.61	495.71	466.72
75000	1023.33	938.79	871.64	675.02	582.44	531.11	500.06
80000	1091.55	1001.37	929.75	720.02	621.27	566.52	533.40
85000	1159.77	1063.96	987.86	765.03	660.10	601.93	566.73
90000	1228.00	1126.54	1045.97	810.03	698.93	637.34	600.07
95000	1296.22	1189.13	1104.08	855.03	737.76	672.74	633.41
100000	1364.44	1251.72	1162.19	900.03	776.59	708.15	666.75
200000	2728.88	2503.43	2324.38	1800.06	1553.18	1416.30	1333.49
300000	4093.32	3755.15	3486.58	2700.09	2329.77	2124.45	2000.24
400000	5457.76	5006.86	4648.77	3600.12	3106.36	2832.60	2666.98
500000	6822.21	6258.58	5810.96	4500.15	3882.95	3540.75	3333.73
1000000	13644.41	12517.16	11621.92	9000.30	7765.89	7081.50	6667.46

7.25%

MONTHLY PAYMENT
NECESSARY TO AMORTIZE A LOAN

Amortization Amount	1 Year	2 Years	3 Years	4 Years	5 Years	6 Years	7 Years
25	2.16	1.12	0.77	0.60	0.50	0.43	0.38
50	4.33	2.24	1.55	1.20	0.99	0.86	0.76
100	8.66	4.48	3.09	2.40	1.99	1.71	1.52
200	17.32	8.97	6.19	4.80	3.97	3.42	3.03
300	25.98	13.45	9.28	7.20	5.96	5.14	4.55
400	34.64	17.93	12.38	9.61	7.95	6.85	6.07
500	43.30	22.42	15.47	12.01	9.93	8.56	7.58
600	51.96	26.90	18.57	14.41	11.92	10.27	9.10
700	60.61	31.39	21.66	16.81	13.91	11.98	10.61
800	69.27	35.87	24.75	19.21	15.89	13.69	12.13
900	77.93	40.35	27.85	21.61	17.88	15.41	13.65
1000	86.59	44.84	30.94	24.01	19.87	17.12	15.16
2000	173.19	89.67	61.88	48.03	39.74	34.24	30.33
3000	259.78	134.51	92.83	72.04	59.61	51.35	45.49
4000	346.37	179.35	123.77	96.05	79.47	68.47	60.65
5000	432.96	224.19	154.71	120.06	99.34	85.59	75.81
6000	519.56	269.02	185.65	144.08	119.21	102.71	90.98
7000	606.15	313.86	216.60	168.09	139.08	119.82	106.14
8000	692.74	358.70	247.54	192.10	158.95	136.94	121.30
9000	779.33	403.54	278.48	216.11	178.82	154.06	136.46
10000	865.93	448.37	309.42	240.13	198.69	171.18	151.63
11000	952.52	493.21	340.37	264.14	218.56	188.29	166.79
12000	1039.11	538.05	371.31	288.15	238.42	205.41	181.95
13000	1125.70	582.89	402.25	312.16	258.29	222.53	197.11
14000	1212.30	627.72	433.19	336.18	278.16	239.65	212.28
15000	1298.89	672.56	464.14	360.19	298.03	256.77	227.44
16000	1385.48	717.40	495.08	384.20	317.90	273.88	242.60
17000	1472.07	762.24	526.02	408.21	337.77	291.00	257.76
18000	1558.67	807.07	556.96	432.23	357.64	308.12	272.93
19000	1645.26	851.91	587.91	456.24	377.50	325.24	288.09
20000	1731.85	896.75	618.85	480.25	397.37	342.35	303.25
21000	1818.44	941.58	649.79	504.26	417.24	359.47	318.41
22000	1905.04	986.42	680.73	528.28	437.11	376.59	333.58
23000	1991.63	1031.26	711.68	552.29	456.98	393.71	348.74
24000	2078.22	1076.10	742.62	576.30	476.85	410.82	363.90
25000	2164.82	1120.93	773.56	600.31	496.72	427.94	379.07
26000	2251.41	1165.77	804.50	624.33	516.59	445.06	394.23
27000	2338.00	1210.61	835.45	648.34	536.45	462.18	409.39
28000	2424.59	1255.45	866.39	672.35	556.32	479.30	424.55
29000	2511.19	1300.28	897.33	696.36	576.19	496.41	439.72
30000	2597.78	1345.12	928.27	720.38	596.06	513.53	454.88
35000	3030.74	1569.31	1082.99	840.44	695.40	599.12	530.69
40000	3463.70	1793.49	1237.70	960.50	794.75	684.71	606.50
45000	3896.67	2017.68	1392.41	1080.57	894.09	770.30	682.32
50000	4329.63	2241.87	1547.12	1200.63	993.43	855.88	758.13
55000	4762.59	2466.06	1701.84	1320.69	1092.78	941.47	833.94
60000	5195.56	2690.24	1856.55	1440.75	1192.12	1027.06	909.76
65000	5628.52	2914.43	2011.26	1560.82	1291.46	1112.65	985.57
70000	6061.48	3138.62	2165.97	1680.88	1390.81	1198.24	1061.38
75000	6494.45	3362.80	2320.68	1800.94	1490.15	1283.83	1137.20
80000	6927.41	3586.99	2475.40	1921.01	1589.49	1369.42	1213.01
85000	7360.37	3811.18	2630.11	2041.07	1688.84	1455.00	1288.82
90000	7793.34	4035.36	2784.82	2161.13	1788.18	1540.59	1364.64
95000	8226.30	4259.55	2939.53	2281.20	1887.52	1626.18	1440.45
100000	8659.26	4483.74	3094.25	2401.26	1986.87	1711.77	1516.26
200000	17318.52	8967.47	6188.49	4802.52	3973.73	3423.54	3032.52
300000	25977.79	13451.21	9282.74	7203.77	5960.60	5135.31	4548.78
400000	34637.05	17934.95	12376.98	9605.03	7947.47	6847.08	6065.04
500000	43296.31	22418.69	15471.23	12006.29	9934.33	8558.84	7581.31
1000000	86592.62	44837.37	30942.46	24012.58	19868.67	17117.69	15162.61

Amortization Amount	8 Years	9 Years	10 Years	15 Years	20 Years	25 Years	30 Years
25	0.34	0.31	0.29	0.23	0.20	0.18	0.17
50	0.69	0.63	0.58	0.45	0.39	0.36	0.34
100	1.37	1.26	1.17	0.91	0.78	0.72	0.67
200	2.74	2.52	2.34	1.81	1.57	1.43	1.35
300	4.11	3.77	3.51	2.72	2.35	2.15	2.02
400	5.48	5.03	4.67	3.63	3.14	2.86	2.70
500	6.85	6.29	5.84	4.53	3.92	3.58	3.37
600	8.22	7.55	7.01	5.44	4.70	4.30	4.05
700	9.59	8.81	8.18	6.35	5.49	5.01	4.72
800	10.96	10.06	9.35	7.25	6.27	5.73	5.40
900	12.33	11.32	10.52	8.16	7.06	6.44	6.07
1000	13.70	12.58	11.68	9.07	7.84	7.16	6.75
2000	27.41	25.16	23.37	18.14	15.68	14.32	13.50
3000	41.11	37.74	35.05	27.21	23.52	21.48	20.25
4000	54.82	50.32	46.74	36.27	31.36	28.64	27.00
5000	68.52	62.89	58.42	45.34	39.19	35.80	33.75
6000	82.23	75.47	70.11	54.41	47.03	42.96	40.50
7000	95.93	88.05	81.79	63.48	54.87	50.11	47.24
8000	109.64	100.63	93.48	72.55	62.71	57.27	53.99
9000	123.34	113.21	105.16	81.62	70.55	64.43	60.74
10000	137.05	125.79	116.85	90.68	78.39	71.59	67.49
11000	150.75	138.37	128.53	99.75	86.23	78.75	74.24
12000	164.46	150.95	140.22	108.82	94.07	85.91	80.99
13000	178.16	163.52	151.90	117.89	101.91	93.07	87.74
14000	191.87	176.10	163.58	126.96	109.75	100.23	94.49
15000	205.57	188.68	175.27	136.03	117.58	107.39	101.24
16000	219.28	201.26	186.95	145.09	125.42	114.55	107.99
17000	232.98	213.84	198.64	154.16	133.26	121.71	114.74
18000	246.69	226.42	210.32	163.23	141.10	128.87	121.49
19000	260.39	239.00	222.01	172.30	148.94	136.02	128.24
20000	274.10	251.58	233.69	181.37	156.78	143.18	134.98
21000	287.80	264.15	245.38	190.44	164.62	150.34	141.73
22000	301.51	276.73	257.06	199.50	172.46	157.50	148.48
23000	315.21	289.31	268.75	208.57	180.30	164.66	155.23
24000	328.92	301.89	280.43	217.64	188.14	171.82	161.98
25000	342.62	314.47	292.12	226.71	195.97	178.98	168.73
26000	356.33	327.05	303.80	235.78	203.81	186.14	175.48
27000	370.03	339.63	315.48	244.85	211.65	193.30	182.23
28000	383.74	352.21	327.17	253.91	219.49	200.46	188.98
29000	397.44	364.78	338.85	262.98	227.33	207.62	195.73
30000	411.15	377.36	350.54	272.05	235.17	214.78	202.48
35000	479.67	440.26	408.96	317.39	274.36	250.57	236.22
40000	548.20	503.15	467.38	362.73	313.56	286.37	269.97
45000	616.72	566.04	525.81	408.08	352.75	322.16	303.72
50000	685.25	628.94	584.23	453.42	391.95	357.96	337.46
55000	753.77	691.83	642.65	498.76	431.14	393.76	371.21
60000	822.30	754.73	701.08	544.10	470.34	429.55	404.95
65000	890.82	817.62	759.50	589.44	509.53	465.35	438.70
70000	959.34	880.51	817.92	634.78	548.73	501.14	472.45
75000	1027.87	943.41	876.35	680.13	587.92	536.94	506.19
80000	1096.39	1006.30	934.77	725.47	627.12	572.73	539.94
85000	1164.92	1069.19	993.19	770.81	666.31	608.53	573.69
90000	1233.44	1132.09	1051.61	816.15	705.51	644.33	607.43
95000	1301.97	1194.98	1110.04	861.49	744.70	680.12	641.18
100000	1370.49	1257.88	1168.46	906.83	783.90	715.92	674.92
200000	2740.98	2515.75	2336.92	1813.67	1567.79	1431.84	1349.85
300000	4111.48	3773.63	3505.38	2720.50	2351.69	2147.76	2024.77
400000	5481.97	5031.50	4673.84	3627.34	3135.59	2863.67	2699.70
500000	6852.46	6289.38	5842.30	4534.17	3919.49	3579.59	3374.62
1000000	13704.92	12578.76	11684.61	9068.34	7838.97	7159.19	6749.24

7.375%

Amortization Amount	1 Year	2 Years	3 Years	4 Years	5 Years	6 Years	7 Years
25	2.17	1.12	0.77	0.60	0.50	0.43	0.38
50	4.33	2.24	1.55	1.20	1.00	0.86	0.76
100	8.66	4.49	3.10	2.41	1.99	1.72	1.52
200	17.33	8.98	6.20	4.81	3.99	3.44	3.04
300	25.99	13.47	9.30	7.22	5.98	5.15	4.57
400	34.66	17.96	12.40	9.63	7.97	6.87	6.09
500	43.32	22.45	15.50	12.03	9.96	8.59	7.61
600	51.99	26.94	18.60	14.44	11.96	10.31	9.13
700	60.65	31.42	21.70	16.85	13.95	12.02	10.66
800	69.32	35.91	24.80	19.26	15.94	13.74	12.18
900	77.98	40.40	27.90	21.66	17.93	15.46	13.70
1000	86.65	44.89	31.00	24.07	19.93	17.18	15.22
2000	173.30	89.78	62.00	48.14	39.85	34.35	30.44
3000	259.95	134.68	92.99	72.21	59.78	51.53	45.67
4000	346.59	179.57	123.99	96.28	79.70	68.70	60.89
5000	433.24	224.46	154.99	120.34	99.63	85.88	76.11
6000	519.89	269.35	185.99	144.41	119.56	103.06	91.33
7000	606.54	314.25	216.99	168.48	139.48	120.23	106.56
8000	693.19	359.14	247.98	192.55	159.41	137.41	121.78
9000	779.84	404.03	278.98	216.62	179.33	154.59	137.00
10000	866.49	448.92	309.98	240.69	199.26	171.76	152.22
11000	953.13	493.82	340.98	264.76	219.19	188.94	167.44
12000	1039.78	538.71	371.98	288.83	239.11	206.11	182.67
13000	1126.43	583.60	402.97	312.90	259.04	223.29	197.89
14000	1213.08	628.49	433.97	336.97	278.97	240.47	213.11
15000	1299.73	673.39	464.97	361.03	298.89	257.64	228.33
16000	1386.38	718.28	495.97	385.10	318.82	274.82	243.55
17000	1473.03	763.17	526.97	409.17	338.74	291.99	258.78
18000	1559.67	808.06	557.96	433.24	358.67	309.17	274.00
19000	1646.32	852.96	588.96	457.31	378.60	326.35	289.22
20000	1732.97	897.85	619.96	481.38	398.52	343.52	304.44
21000	1819.62	942.74	650.96	505.45	418.45	360.70	319.67
22000	1906.27	987.63	681.96	529.52	438.37	377.88	334.89
23000	1992.92	1032.53	712.95	553.59	458.30	395.05	350.11
24000	2079.57	1077.42	743.95	577.66	478.23	412.23	365.33
25000	2166.21	1122.31	774.95	601.72	498.15	429.40	380.55
26000	2252.86	1167.20	805.95	625.79	518.08	446.58	395.78
27000	2339.51	1212.10	836.95	649.86	538.00	463.76	411.00
28000	2426.16	1256.99	867.94	673.93	557.93	480.93	426.22
29000	2512.81	1301.88	898.94	698.00	577.86	498.11	441.44
30000	2599.46	1346.77	929.94	722.07	597.78	515.28	456.66
35000	3032.70	1571.24	1084.93	842.41	697.41	601.16	532.78
40000	3465.94	1795.70	1239.92	962.76	797.04	687.05	608.89
45000	3899.19	2020.16	1394.91	1083.10	896.67	772.93	685.00
50000	4332.43	2244.62	1549.90	1203.45	996.30	858.81	761.11
55000	4765.67	2469.08	1704.89	1323.79	1095.93	944.69	837.22
60000	5198.91	2693.55	1859.88	1444.14	1195.56	1030.57	913.33
65000	5632.16	2918.01	2014.87	1564.48	1295.19	1116.45	989.44
70000	6065.40	3142.47	2169.86	1684.83	1394.83	1202.33	1065.55
75000	6498.64	3366.93	2324.85	1805.17	1494.46	1288.21	1141.66
80000	6931.89	3591.39	2479.84	1925.52	1594.09	1374.09	1217.77
85000	7365.13	3815.86	2634.83	2045.86	1693.72	1459.97	1293.88
90000	7798.37	4040.32	2789.82	2166.21	1793.35	1545.85	1369.99
95000	8231.61	4264.78	2944.81	2286.55	1892.98	1631.73	1446.10
100000	8664.86	4489.24	3099.80	2406.90	1992.61	1717.61	1522.21
200000	17329.72	8978.49	6199.81	4813.80	3985.21	3435.23	3044.43
300000	25994.57	13467.73	9299.41	7220.70	5977.80	5152.84	4566.64
400000	34659.43	17956.97	12399.21	9627.60	7970.43	6870.46	6088.86
500000	43324.29	22446.22	15499.01	12034.50	9963.04	8588.07	7611.07
1000000	86648.58	44892.44	30998.03	24069.00	19926.07	17176.14	15222.15

Amortization Amount	8 Years	9 Years	10 Years	15 Years	20 Years	25 Years	30 Years
25	0.34	0.32	0.29	0.23	0.20	0.18	0.17
50	0.69	0.63	0.59	0.46	0.40	0.36	0.34
100	1.38	1.26	1.17	0.91	0.79	0.72	0.68
200	2.75	2.53	2.35	1.83	1.58	1.45	1.37
300	4.13	3.79	3.52	2.74	2.37	2.17	2.05
400	5.51	5.06	4.70	3.65	3.16	2.89	2.73
500	6.88	6.32	5.87	4.57	3.96	3.62	3.42
600	8.26	7.58	7.05	5.48	4.75	4.34	4.10
700	9.64	8.85	8.22	6.40	5.54	5.07	4.78
800	11.01	10.11	9.40	7.31	6.33	5.79	5.47
900	12.39	11.38	10.57	8.22	7.12	6.51	6.15
1000	13.77	12.64	11.75	9.14	7.91	7.24	6.83
2000	27.53	25.28	23.49	18.27	15.82	14.47	13.66
3000	41.30	37.92	35.24	27.41	23.74	21.71	20.49
4000	55.06	50.56	46.99	36.55	31.65	28.95	27.33
5000	68.83	63.20	58.74	45.68	39.56	36.19	34.16
6000	82.59	75.84	70.48	54.82	47.47	43.42	40.99
7000	96.36	88.48	82.23	63.96	55.39	50.66	47.82
8000	110.12	101.12	93.98	73.09	63.30	57.90	54.65
9000	123.89	113.76	105.73	82.23	71.21	65.13	61.48
10000	137.66	126.40	117.47	91.37	79.12	72.37	68.31
11000	151.42	139.05	129.22	100.50	87.04	79.61	75.15
12000	165.19	151.69	140.97	109.64	94.95	86.85	81.98
13000	178.95	164.33	152.72	118.78	102.86	94.08	88.81
14000	192.72	176.97	164.46	127.91	110.77	101.32	95.64
15000	206.48	189.61	176.21	137.05	118.69	108.56	102.47
16000	220.25	202.25	187.96	146.19	126.60	115.80	109.30
17000	234.01	214.89	199.71	155.32	134.51	123.03	116.13
18000	247.78	227.53	211.45	164.46	142.42	130.27	122.96
19000	261.55	240.17	223.20	173.60	150.33	137.51	129.80
20000	275.31	252.81	234.95	182.73	158.25	144.74	136.63
21000	289.08	265.45	246.70	191.87	166.16	151.98	143.46
22000	302.84	278.09	258.44	201.01	174.07	159.22	150.29
23000	316.61	290.73	270.19	210.14	181.98	166.46	157.12
24000	330.37	303.37	281.94	219.28	189.90	173.69	163.95
25000	344.14	316.01	293.69	228.42	197.81	180.93	170.78
26000	357.90	328.65	305.43	237.55	205.72	188.17	177.62
27000	371.67	341.29	317.18	246.69	213.63	195.40	184.45
28000	385.44	353.93	328.93	255.83	221.55	202.64	191.28
29000	399.20	366.57	340.68	264.96	229.46	209.88	198.11
30000	412.97	379.21	352.42	274.10	237.37	217.12	204.94
35000	481.79	442.42	411.16	319.78	276.93	253.30	239.10
40000	550.62	505.62	469.90	365.46	316.49	289.49	273.26
45000	619.45	568.82	528.64	411.15	356.06	325.67	307.41
50000	688.28	632.02	587.37	456.83	395.62	361.86	341.57
55000	757.11	695.23	646.11	502.51	435.18	398.05	375.73
60000	825.93	758.43	704.85	548.20	474.74	434.23	409.88
65000	894.76	821.63	763.58	593.88	514.30	470.42	444.04
70000	963.59	884.83	822.32	639.56	553.86	506.60	478.20
75000	1032.42	948.04	881.06	685.25	593.43	542.79	512.35
80000	1101.24	1011.24	939.80	730.93	632.99	578.98	546.51
85000	1170.07	1074.44	998.53	776.61	672.55	615.16	580.67
90000	1238.90	1137.64	1057.27	822.30	712.11	651.35	614.82
95000	1307.73	1200.85	1116.01	867.98	751.67	687.53	648.98
100000	1376.58	1264.05	1174.75	913.66	791.24	723.72	683.14
200000	2753.11	2528.10	2349.49	1827.32	1582.47	1447.44	1366.28
300000	4129.67	3792.15	3524.24	2740.99	2373.71	2171.16	2049.41
400000	5506.22	5056.20	4698.98	3654.65	3164.94	2894.88	2732.55
500000	6882.78	6320.25	5873.73	4568.31	3956.18	3618.60	3415.69
1000000	13765.55	12640.50	11747.46	9136.62	7912.35	7237.20	6831.38

7.5%

MONTHLY PAYMENT
NECESSARY TO AMORTIZE A LOAN

Amortization Amount	1 Year	2 Years	3 Years	4 Years	5 Years	6 Years	7 Years
25	2.17	1.12	0.78	0.60	0.50	0.43	0.38
50	4.34	2.25	1.55	1.21	1.00	0.86	0.76
100	8.67	4.49	3.11	2.41	2.00	1.72	1.53
200	17.34	8.99	6.21	4.83	4.00	3.45	3.06
300	26.01	13.48	9.32	7.24	6.00	5.17	4.58
400	34.68	17.98	12.42	9.65	7.99	6.89	6.11
500	43.35	22.47	15.53	12.06	9.99	8.62	7.64
600	52.02	26.97	18.63	14.48	11.99	10.34	9.17
700	60.69	31.46	21.74	16.89	13.99	12.06	10.70
800	69.36	35.96	24.84	19.30	15.99	13.79	12.23
900	78.03	40.45	27.95	21.71	17.99	15.51	13.75
1000	86.70	44.95	31.05	24.13	19.98	17.23	15.28
2000	173.41	89.90	62.11	48.25	39.97	34.47	30.56
3000	260.11	134.84	93.16	72.38	59.95	51.70	45.85
4000	346.82	179.79	124.21	96.50	79.93	68.94	61.13
5000	433.52	224.74	155.27	120.63	99.92	86.17	76.41
6000	520.23	269.69	186.32	144.75	119.90	103.41	91.69
7000	606.93	314.63	217.38	168.88	139.88	120.64	106.97
8000	693.64	359.58	248.43	193.00	159.87	137.88	122.25
9000	780.34	404.53	279.48	217.13	179.85	155.11	137.54
10000	867.05	449.48	310.54	241.25	199.84	172.35	152.82
11000	953.75	494.42	341.59	265.38	219.82	189.58	168.10
12000	1040.45	539.37	372.64	289.51	239.80	206.82	183.38
13000	1127.16	584.32	403.70	313.63	259.79	224.05	198.66
14000	1213.86	629.27	434.75	337.76	279.77	241.29	213.95
15000	1300.57	674.21	465.80	361.88	299.75	258.52	229.23
16000	1387.27	719.16	496.86	386.01	319.74	275.75	244.51
17000	1473.98	764.11	527.91	410.13	339.72	292.99	259.79
18000	1560.68	809.06	558.97	434.26	359.70	310.22	275.07
19000	1647.39	854.00	590.02	458.38	379.69	327.46	290.35
20000	1734.09	898.95	621.07	482.51	399.67	344.69	305.64
21000	1820.80	943.90	652.13	506.63	419.65	361.93	320.92
22000	1907.50	988.85	683.18	530.76	439.64	379.16	336.20
23000	1994.20	1033.79	714.23	554.89	459.62	396.40	351.48
24000	2080.91	1078.74	745.29	579.01	479.61	413.63	366.76
25000	2167.61	1123.69	776.34	603.14	499.59	430.87	382.04
26000	2254.32	1168.64	807.39	627.26	519.57	448.10	397.33
27000	2341.02	1213.58	838.45	651.39	539.56	465.34	412.61
28000	2427.73	1258.53	869.50	675.51	559.54	482.57	427.89
29000	2514.43	1303.48	900.56	699.64	579.52	499.81	443.17
30000	2601.14	1348.43	931.61	723.76	599.51	517.04	458.45
35000	3034.66	1573.16	1086.88	844.39	699.42	603.21	534.86
40000	3468.18	1797.90	1242.15	965.02	799.34	689.39	611.27
45000	3901.70	2022.64	1397.41	1085.65	899.26	775.56	687.68
50000	4335.23	2247.38	1552.68	1206.27	999.18	861.73	764.09
55000	4768.75	2472.11	1707.95	1326.90	1099.10	947.91	840.50
60000	5202.27	2696.85	1863.22	1447.53	1199.01	1034.08	916.91
65000	5635.79	2921.59	2018.49	1568.16	1298.93	1120.25	993.32
70000	6069.32	3146.33	2173.75	1688.78	1398.85	1206.43	1069.73
75000	6502.84	3371.06	2329.02	1809.41	1498.77	1292.60	1146.13
80000	6936.36	3595.80	2484.29	1930.04	1598.68	1378.77	1222.54
85000	7369.89	3820.54	2639.56	2050.66	1698.60	1464.95	1298.95
90000	7803.41	4045.28	2794.83	2171.29	1798.52	1551.12	1375.36
95000	8236.93	4270.01	2950.09	2291.92	1898.44	1637.30	1451.77
100000	8670.45	4494.75	3105.36	2412.55	1998.35	1723.47	1528.18
200000	17340.91	8989.50	6210.73	4825.09	3996.71	3446.94	3056.36
300000	26011.36	13484.25	9316.09	7237.64	5995.06	5170.41	4584.54
400000	34681.81	17979.01	12421.45	9650.19	7993.42	6893.87	6112.72
500000	43352.27	22473.76	15526.81	12062.73	9991.77	8617.34	7640.90
1000000	86704.53	44947.51	31053.63	24125.47	19983.55	17234.69	15281.79

MONTHLY PAYMENT
NECESSARY TO AMORTIZE A LOAN

7.5%

Amortization Amount	8 Years	9 Years	10 Years	15 Years	20 Years	25 Years	30 Years
25	0.35	0.32	0.30	0.23	0.20	0.18	0.17
50	0.69	0.64	0.59	0.46	0.40	0.37	0.35
100	1.38	1.27	1.18	0.92	0.80	0.73	0.69
200	2.77	2.54	2.36	1.84	1.60	1.46	1.38
300	4.15	3.81	3.54	2.76	2.40	2.19	2.07
400	5.53	5.08	4.72	3.68	3.19	2.93	2.77
500	6.91	6.35	5.91	4.60	3.99	3.66	3.46
600	8.30	7.62	7.09	5.52	4.79	4.39	4.15
700	9.68	8.89	8.27	6.44	5.59	5.12	4.84
800	11.06	10.16	9.45	7.36	6.39	5.85	5.53
900	12.44	11.43	10.63	8.28	7.19	6.58	6.22
1000	13.83	12.70	11.81	9.21	7.99	7.32	6.91
2000	27.65	25.40	23.62	18.41	15.97	14.63	13.83
3000	41.48	38.11	35.43	27.62	23.96	21.95	20.74
4000	55.31	50.81	47.24	36.82	31.94	29.26	27.66
5000	69.13	63.51	59.05	46.03	39.93	36.58	34.57
6000	82.96	76.21	70.86	55.23	47.92	43.89	41.48
7000	96.78	88.92	82.67	64.44	55.90	51.21	48.40
8000	110.61	101.62	94.48	73.64	63.89	58.52	55.31
9000	124.44	114.32	106.29	82.85	71.87	65.84	62.22
10000	138.26	127.02	118.10	92.05	79.86	73.16	69.14
11000	152.09	139.73	129.92	101.26	87.85	80.47	76.05
12000	165.92	152.43	141.73	110.46	95.83	87.79	82.97
13000	179.74	165.13	153.54	119.67	103.82	95.10	89.88
14000	193.57	177.83	165.35	128.87	111.80	102.42	96.79
15000	207.39	190.54	177.16	138.08	119.79	109.73	103.71
16000	221.22	203.24	188.97	147.28	127.78	117.05	110.62
17000	235.05	215.94	200.78	156.49	135.76	124.36	117.54
18000	248.87	228.64	212.59	165.69	143.75	131.68	124.45
19000	262.70	241.35	224.40	174.90	151.73	139.00	131.36
20000	276.53	254.05	236.21	184.10	159.72	146.31	138.28
21000	290.35	266.75	248.02	193.31	167.71	153.63	145.19
22000	304.18	279.45	259.83	202.51	175.69	160.94	152.10
23000	318.01	292.15	271.64	211.72	183.68	168.26	159.02
24000	331.83	304.86	283.45	220.92	191.66	175.57	165.93
25000	345.66	317.56	295.26	230.13	199.65	182.89	172.85
26000	359.48	330.26	307.07	239.33	207.64	190.20	179.76
27000	373.31	342.96	318.88	248.54	215.62	197.52	186.67
28000	387.14	355.67	330.69	257.74	223.61	204.84	193.59
29000	400.96	368.37	342.50	266.95	231.59	212.15	200.50
30000	414.79	381.07	354.31	276.15	239.58	219.47	207.42
35000	483.92	444.58	413.37	322.18	279.51	256.04	241.99
40000	553.05	508.10	472.42	368.21	319.44	292.62	276.55
45000	622.18	571.61	531.47	414.23	359.37	329.20	311.12
50000	691.32	635.12	590.52	460.26	399.30	365.78	345.69
55000	760.45	698.63	649.58	506.28	439.23	402.36	380.26
60000	829.58	762.14	708.63	552.31	479.16	438.93	414.83
65000	898.71	825.65	767.68	598.33	519.09	475.51	449.40
70000	967.84	889.17	826.73	644.36	559.02	512.09	483.97
75000	1036.97	952.68	885.78	690.39	598.95	548.67	518.54
80000	1106.11	1016.19	944.84	736.41	638.88	585.24	553.11
85000	1175.24	1079.70	1003.89	782.44	678.81	621.82	587.68
90000	1244.37	1143.21	1062.94	828.46	718.74	658.40	622.25
95000	1313.50	1206.73	1121.99	874.49	758.67	694.98	656.82
100000	1382.63	1270.24	1181.05	920.51	798.60	731.55	691.39
200000	2765.26	2540.48	2362.09	1841.03	1597.20	1463.11	1382.77
300000	4147.89	3810.71	3543.14	2761.54	2395.81	2194.66	2074.16
400000	5530.53	5080.95	4724.19	3682.05	3194.41	2926.22	2765.54
500000	6913.16	6351.19	5905.23	4602.57	3993.01	3657.77	3456.93
1000000	13826.31	12702.38	11810.47	9205.14	7986.02	7315.55	6913.86

7.625%

MONTHLY PAYMENT
NECESSARY TO AMORTIZE A LOAN

Amortization Amount	1 Year	2 Years	3 Years	4 Years	5 Years	6 Years	7 Years
25	2.17	1.13	0.78	0.60	0.50	0.43	0.38
50	4.34	2.25	1.56	1.21	1.00	0.86	0.77
100	8.68	4.50	3.11	2.42	2.00	1.73	1.53
200	17.35	9.00	6.22	4.84	4.01	3.46	3.07
300	26.03	13.50	9.33	7.25	6.01	5.19	4.60
400	34.70	18.00	12.44	9.67	8.02	6.92	6.14
500	43.38	22.50	15.55	12.09	10.02	8.65	7.67
600	52.06	27.00	18.67	14.51	12.02	10.38	9.20
700	60.73	31.50	21.78	16.93	14.03	12.11	10.74
800	69.41	36.00	24.89	19.35	16.03	13.83	12.27
900	78.08	40.50	28.00	21.76	18.04	15.56	13.81
1000	86.76	45.00	31.11	24.18	20.04	17.29	15.34
2000	173.52	90.01	62.22	48.36	40.08	34.59	30.68
3000	260.28	135.01	93.33	72.55	60.12	51.88	46.02
4000	347.04	180.01	124.44	96.73	80.16	69.17	61.37
5000	433.80	225.01	155.55	120.91	100.21	86.47	76.71
6000	520.56	270.02	186.66	145.09	120.25	103.76	92.05
7000	607.32	315.02	217.76	169.27	140.29	121.05	107.39
8000	694.08	360.02	248.87	193.46	160.33	138.35	122.73
9000	780.84	405.02	279.98	217.64	180.37	155.64	138.07
10000	867.60	450.03	311.09	241.82	200.41	172.93	153.42
11000	954.37	495.03	342.20	266.00	220.45	190.23	168.76
12000	1041.13	540.03	373.31	290.18	240.49	207.52	184.10
13000	1127.89	585.03	404.42	314.37	260.53	224.81	199.44
14000	1214.65	630.04	435.53	338.55	280.58	242.11	214.78
15000	1301.41	675.04	466.64	362.73	300.62	259.40	230.12
16000	1388.17	720.04	497.75	386.91	320.66	276.69	245.46
17000	1474.93	765.04	528.86	411.09	340.70	293.99	260.81
18000	1561.69	810.05	559.97	435.28	360.74	311.28	276.15
19000	1648.45	855.05	591.08	459.46	380.78	328.57	291.49
20000	1735.21	900.05	622.19	483.64	400.82	345.87	306.83
21000	1821.97	945.05	653.29	507.82	420.86	363.16	322.17
22000	1908.73	990.06	684.40	532.00	440.90	380.45	337.51
23000	1995.49	1035.06	715.51	556.19	460.95	397.75	352.86
24000	2082.25	1080.06	746.62	580.37	480.99	415.04	368.20
25000	2169.01	1125.07	777.73	604.55	501.03	432.33	383.54
26000	2255.77	1170.07	808.84	628.73	521.07	449.63	398.88
27000	2342.53	1215.07	839.95	652.91	541.11	466.92	414.22
28000	2429.29	1260.07	871.06	677.10	561.15	484.21	429.56
29000	2516.05	1305.08	902.17	701.28	581.19	501.51	444.90
30000	2602.81	1350.08	933.28	725.46	601.23	518.80	460.25
35000	3036.62	1575.09	1088.82	846.37	701.44	605.27	536.95
40000	3470.42	1800.10	1244.37	967.28	801.64	691.73	613.66
45000	3904.22	2025.12	1399.92	1088.19	901.85	778.20	690.37
50000	4338.02	2250.13	1555.48	1209.10	1002.05	864.67	767.08
55000	4771.83	2475.14	1711.01	1330.01	1102.26	951.13	843.78
60000	5205.63	2700.16	1866.56	1450.92	1202.47	1037.60	920.49
65000	5639.43	2925.17	2022.10	1571.83	1302.67	1124.07	997.20
70000	6073.23	3150.18	2177.65	1692.74	1402.88	1210.53	1073.91
75000	6507.04	3375.20	2333.19	1813.65	1503.08	1297.00	1150.62
80000	6940.84	3600.21	2488.74	1934.56	1603.29	1383.47	1227.32
85000	7374.64	3825.22	2644.29	2055.47	1703.49	1469.93	1304.03
90000	7808.44	4050.23	2799.83	2176.38	1803.70	1556.40	1380.74
95000	8242.25	4275.25	2955.38	2297.29	1903.90	1642.87	1457.45
100000	8676.05	4500.28	3110.93	2418.20	2004.11	1729.33	1534.15
200000	17352.09	9000.52	6221.85	4836.40	4008.22	3458.66	3068.31
300000	26028.14	13500.78	9332.78	7254.60	6012.33	5188.00	4602.46
400000	34704.19	18001.04	12443.70	9672.80	8016.44	6917.33	6136.62
500000	43380.24	22501.30	15554.63	12091.00	10020.55	8646.66	7670.77
1000000	86760.47	45002.60	31109.26	24181.99	20041.10	17293.32	15341.54

Amortization Amount	8 Years	9 Years	10 Years	15 Years	20 Years	25 Years	30 Years
25	0.35	0.32	0.30	0.23	0.20	0.18	0.17
50	0.69	0.64	0.59	0.46	0.40	0.37	0.35
100	1.39	1.28	1.19	0.93	0.81	0.74	0.70
200	2.78	2.55	2.37	1.85	1.61	1.48	1.40
300	4.17	3.83	3.56	2.78	2.42	2.22	2.10
400	5.55	5.11	4.75	3.71	3.22	2.96	2.80
500	6.94	6.38	5.94	4.64	4.03	3.70	3.50
600	8.33	7.66	7.12	5.56	4.84	4.44	4.20
700	9.72	8.94	8.31	6.49	5.64	5.18	4.90
800	11.11	10.21	9.50	7.42	6.45	5.92	5.60
900	12.50	11.49	10.69	8.35	7.25	6.65	6.30
1000	13.89	12.76	11.87	9.27	8.06	7.39	7.00
2000	27.77	25.53	23.75	18.55	16.12	14.79	13.99
3000	41.66	38.29	35.62	27.82	24.18	22.18	20.99
4000	55.55	51.06	47.49	37.10	32.24	29.58	27.99
5000	69.44	63.82	59.37	46.37	40.30	36.97	34.98
6000	83.32	76.59	71.24	55.64	48.36	44.37	41.98
7000	97.21	89.35	83.12	64.92	56.42	51.76	48.98
8000	111.10	102.12	94.99	74.19	64.48	59.15	55.97
9000	124.98	114.88	106.86	83.46	72.54	66.55	62.97
10000	138.87	127.64	118.74	92.74	80.60	73.94	69.97
11000	152.76	140.41	130.61	102.01	88.66	81.34	76.96
12000	166.65	153.17	142.48	111.29	96.72	88.73	83.96
13000	180.53	165.94	154.38	120.56	104.78	96.12	90.96
14000	194.42	178.70	166.23	129.83	112.84	103.52	97.95
15000	208.31	191.47	178.10	139.11	120.90	110.91	104.95
16000	222.20	204.23	189.98	148.38	128.96	118.31	111.95
17000	236.08	216.99	201.85	157.66	137.02	125.70	118.94
18000	249.97	229.76	213.73	166.93	145.08	133.10	125.94
19000	263.86	242.52	225.60	176.20	153.14	140.49	132.94
20000	277.74	255.29	237.47	185.48	161.20	147.88	139.93
21000	291.63	268.05	249.35	194.75	169.26	155.28	146.93
22000	305.52	280.82	261.22	204.03	177.32	162.67	153.93
23000	319.41	293.58	273.09	213.30	185.38	170.07	160.92
24000	333.29	306.35	284.97	222.57	193.44	177.46	167.92
25000	347.18	319.11	296.84	231.85	201.50	184.86	174.92
26000	361.07	331.87	308.71	241.12	209.56	192.25	181.91
27000	374.95	344.64	320.59	250.39	217.62	199.64	188.91
28000	388.84	357.40	332.46	259.67	225.68	207.04	195.91
29000	402.73	370.17	344.34	268.94	233.74	214.43	202.90
30000	416.62	382.93	356.21	278.22	241.80	221.83	209.90
35000	486.05	446.75	415.58	324.59	282.10	258.80	244.88
40000	555.49	510.58	474.95	370.96	322.40	295.77	279.87
45000	624.92	574.40	534.31	417.32	362.70	332.74	314.85
50000	694.36	638.22	593.68	463.69	403.00	369.71	349.83
55000	763.80	702.04	653.05	510.06	443.30	406.68	384.82
60000	833.23	765.86	712.42	556.43	483.60	443.65	419.80
65000	902.67	829.69	771.79	602.80	523.90	480.62	454.78
70000	972.10	893.51	831.15	649.17	564.20	517.60	489.77
75000	1041.54	957.33	890.52	695.54	604.50	554.57	524.75
80000	1110.98	1021.15	949.89	741.91	644.80	591.54	559.73
85000	1180.41	1084.97	1009.26	788.28	685.10	628.51	594.72
90000	1249.85	1148.80	1068.63	834.65	725.40	665.48	629.70
95000	1319.28	1212.62	1128.00	881.02	765.70	702.45	664.68
100000	1388.72	1276.44	1187.36	927.39	806.00	739.42	699.67
200000	2777.44	2552.88	2374.73	1854.78	1612.00	1478.84	1399.34
300000	4166.16	3829.32	3562.09	2782.17	2417.99	2218.27	2099.00
400000	5554.88	5105.76	4749.45	3709.55	3223.99	2957.69	2798.67
500000	6943.60	6382.20	5936.82	4636.94	4029.99	3697.11	3498.34
1000000	13887.20	12764.41	11873.63	9273.89	8059.98	7394.22	6996.68

7.75%

Amortization Amount	1 Year	2 Years	3 Years	4 Years	5 Years	6 Years	7 Years
25	2.17	1.13	0.78	0.61	0.50	0.43	0.39
50	4.34	2.25	1.56	1.21	1.00	0.87	0.77
100	8.68	4.51	3.12	2.42	2.01	1.74	1.54
200	17.36	9.01	6.23	4.85	4.02	3.47	3.08
300	26.04	13.52	9.35	7.27	6.03	5.21	4.62
400	34.73	18.02	12.47	9.70	8.04	6.94	6.16
500	43.41	22.53	15.58	12.12	10.05	8.68	7.70
600	52.09	27.03	18.70	14.54	12.06	10.41	9.24
700	60.77	31.54	21.82	16.97	14.07	12.15	10.78
800	69.45	36.05	24.93	19.39	16.08	13.88	12.32
900	78.13	40.55	28.05	21.81	18.09	15.62	13.86
1000	86.82	45.06	31.16	24.24	20.10	17.35	15.40
2000	173.63	90.12	62.33	48.48	40.20	34.70	30.80
3000	260.45	135.17	93.49	72.72	60.30	52.06	46.20
4000	347.27	180.23	124.66	96.95	80.39	69.41	61.61
5000	434.08	225.29	155.82	121.19	100.49	86.76	77.01
6000	520.90	270.35	186.99	145.43	120.59	104.11	92.41
7000	607.71	315.40	218.15	169.67	140.69	121.46	107.81
8000	694.53	360.46	249.32	193.91	160.79	138.82	123.21
9000	781.35	405.52	280.48	218.15	180.89	156.17	138.61
10000	868.16	450.58	311.65	242.39	200.99	173.52	154.01
11000	954.98	495.63	342.81	266.62	221.09	190.87	169.42
12000	1041.80	540.69	373.98	290.86	241.18	208.22	184.82
13000	1128.61	585.75	405.14	315.10	261.28	225.58	200.22
14000	1215.43	630.81	436.31	339.34	281.38	242.93	215.62
15000	1302.25	675.87	467.47	363.58	301.48	260.28	231.02
16000	1389.06	720.92	498.64	387.82	321.58	277.63	246.42
17000	1475.88	765.98	529.80	412.06	341.68	294.98	261.82
18000	1562.70	811.04	560.97	436.29	361.78	312.34	277.23
19000	1649.51	856.10	592.13	460.53	381.88	329.69	292.63
20000	1736.33	901.15	623.30	484.77	401.97	347.04	308.03
21000	1823.14	946.21	654.46	509.01	422.07	364.39	323.43
22000	1909.96	991.27	685.63	533.25	442.17	381.74	338.83
23000	1996.78	1036.33	716.79	557.49	462.27	399.10	354.23
24000	2083.59	1081.38	747.96	581.73	482.37	416.45	369.63
25000	2170.41	1126.44	779.12	605.96	502.47	433.80	385.04
26000	2257.23	1171.50	810.29	630.20	522.57	451.15	400.44
27000	2344.04	1216.56	841.45	654.44	542.67	468.51	415.84
28000	2430.86	1261.62	872.62	678.68	562.76	485.86	431.24
29000	2517.68	1306.67	903.78	702.92	582.86	503.21	446.64
30000	2604.49	1351.73	934.95	727.16	602.96	520.56	462.04
35000	3038.57	1577.02	1090.77	848.35	703.45	607.32	539.05
40000	3472.66	1802.31	1246.60	969.54	803.95	694.08	616.06
45000	3906.74	2027.60	1402.42	1090.74	904.44	780.84	693.06
50000	4340.82	2252.89	1558.25	1211.93	1004.94	867.60	770.07
55000	4774.90	2478.17	1714.07	1333.12	1105.43	954.36	847.08
60000	5208.98	2703.46	1869.90	1454.31	1205.92	1041.12	924.08
65000	5643.07	2928.75	2025.72	1575.51	1306.42	1127.88	1001.09
70000	6077.15	3154.04	2181.54	1696.70	1406.91	1214.64	1078.10
75000	6511.23	3379.33	2337.37	1817.89	1507.40	1301.40	1155.11
80000	6945.31	3604.62	2493.19	1939.09	1607.90	1388.16	1232.11
85000	7379.39	3829.91	2649.02	2060.28	1708.39	1474.92	1309.12
90000	7813.48	4055.19	2804.84	2181.47	1808.88	1561.68	1386.13
95000	8247.56	4280.48	2960.67	2302.66	1909.38	1648.44	1463.13
100000	8681.64	4505.77	3116.49	2423.86	2009.87	1735.20	1540.14
200000	17363.28	9011.54	6232.99	4847.71	4019.74	3470.41	3080.28
300000	26044.90	13517.31	9349.48	7271.57	6029.61	5205.61	4620.42
400000	34726.56	18023.08	12465.97	9695.43	8039.48	6940.82	6160.56
500000	43408.20	22528.85	15582.46	12119.28	10049.36	8676.02	7700.70
1000000	86816.41	45057.71	31164.93	24238.57	20098.71	17352.04	15401.40

MONTHLY PAYMENT
NECESSARY TO AMORTIZE A LOAN
7.75%

Amortization Amount	8 Years	9 Years	10 Years	15 Years	20 Years	25 Years	30 Years
25	0.35	0.32	0.30	0.23	0.20	0.19	0.18
50	0.70	0.64	0.60	0.47	0.41	0.37	0.35
100	1.39	1.28	1.19	0.93	0.81	0.75	0.71
200	2.79	2.57	2.39	1.87	1.63	1.49	1.42
300	4.18	3.85	3.58	2.80	2.44	2.24	2.12
400	5.58	5.13	4.77	3.74	3.25	2.99	2.83
500	6.97	6.41	5.97	4.67	4.07	3.74	3.54
600	8.37	7.70	7.16	5.61	4.88	4.48	4.25
700	9.76	8.98	8.36	6.54	5.69	5.23	4.96
800	11.16	10.26	9.55	7.47	6.51	5.98	5.66
900	12.55	11.54	10.74	8.41	7.32	6.73	6.37
1000	13.95	12.83	11.94	9.34	8.13	7.47	7.08
2000	27.90	25.65	23.87	18.69	16.27	14.95	14.16
3000	41.84	38.48	35.81	28.03	24.40	22.42	21.24
4000	55.79	51.31	47.75	37.37	32.54	29.89	28.32
5000	69.74	64.13	59.68	46.71	40.67	37.37	35.40
6000	83.69	76.96	71.62	56.06	48.81	44.84	42.48
7000	97.64	89.79	83.56	65.40	56.94	52.31	49.56
8000	111.59	102.61	95.50	74.74	65.07	59.79	56.64
9000	125.53	115.44	107.43	84.09	73.21	67.26	63.72
10000	139.48	128.27	119.37	93.43	81.34	74.73	70.80
11000	153.43	141.09	131.31	102.77	89.48	82.21	77.88
12000	167.38	153.92	143.24	112.11	97.61	89.68	84.96
13000	181.33	166.75	155.18	121.46	105.74	97.15	92.04
14000	195.27	179.57	167.12	130.80	113.88	104.62	99.12
15000	209.22	192.40	179.05	140.14	122.01	112.10	106.20
16000	223.17	205.23	190.99	149.49	130.15	119.57	113.28
17000	237.12	218.05	202.93	158.83	138.28	127.04	120.36
18000	251.07	230.88	214.87	168.17	146.42	134.52	127.44
19000	265.02	243.71	226.80	177.51	154.55	141.99	134.52
20000	278.96	256.53	238.74	186.86	162.68	149.46	141.60
21000	292.91	269.36	250.68	196.20	170.82	156.94	148.68
22000	306.86	282.18	262.61	205.54	178.95	164.41	155.76
23000	320.81	295.01	274.55	214.89	187.09	171.88	162.84
24000	334.76	307.84	286.49	224.23	195.22	179.36	169.92
25000	348.71	320.66	298.42	233.57	203.36	186.83	177.00
26000	362.65	333.49	310.36	242.91	211.49	194.30	184.08
27000	376.60	346.32	322.30	252.26	219.62	201.78	191.16
28000	390.55	359.14	334.23	261.60	227.76	209.25	198.24
29000	404.50	371.97	346.17	270.94	235.89	216.72	205.32
30000	418.45	384.80	358.11	280.29	244.03	224.20	212.39
35000	488.19	448.93	417.79	327.00	284.70	261.56	247.79
40000	557.93	513.06	477.48	373.71	325.37	298.93	283.19
45000	627.67	577.20	537.16	420.43	366.04	336.29	318.59
50000	697.41	641.33	596.85	467.14	406.71	373.66	353.99
55000	767.15	705.46	656.53	513.86	447.38	411.03	389.39
60000	836.89	769.59	716.22	560.57	488.05	448.39	424.79
65000	906.63	833.73	775.90	607.29	528.72	485.76	460.19
70000	976.37	897.86	835.59	654.00	569.40	523.12	495.59
75000	046.12	961.99	895.27	700.72	610.07	560.49	530.99
80000	1115.86	1026.13	954.96	747.43	650.74	597.86	566.39
85000	1185.60	1090.26	1014.64	794.14	691.41	635.22	601.79
90000	1255.34	1154.39	1074.33	840.86	732.08	672.59	637.18
95000	1325.08	1218.53	1134.01	887.57	772.75	709.95	672.58
100000	1394.82	1282.66	1193.70	934.29	813.42	747.32	707.98
200000	2789.64	2565.32	2387.39	1868.57	1626.85	1494.64	1415.97
300000	4184.46	3847.97	3581.09	2802.86	2440.27	2241.96	2123.95
400000	5579.29	5130.63	4774.78	3737.15	3253.69	2989.28	2831.93
500000	6974.11	6413.29	5968.48	4671.44	4067.11	3736.61	3539.92
1000000	13948.21	12826.58	11936.96	9342.87	8134.23	7473.21	7079.83

63

7.875%

NECESSARY TO AMORTIZE A LOAN

MONTHLY PAYMENT

Amortization Amount	1 Year	2 Years	3 Years	4 Years	5 Years	6 Years	7 Years
25	2.17	1.13	0.78	0.61	0.50	0.44	0.39
50	4.34	2.26	1.56	1.21	1.01	0.87	0.77
100	8.69	4.51	3.12	2.43	2.02	1.74	1.55
200	17.37	9.02	6.24	4.86	4.03	3.48	3.09
300	26.06	13.53	9.37	7.29	6.05	5.22	4.64
400	34.75	18.05	12.49	9.72	8.06	6.96	6.18
500	43.44	22.56	15.61	12.15	10.08	8.71	7.73
600	52.12	27.07	18.73	14.58	12.09	10.45	9.28
700	60.81	31.58	21.85	17.01	14.11	12.19	10.82
800	69.50	36.09	24.98	19.44	16.13	13.93	12.37
900	78.19	40.60	28.10	21.87	18.14	15.67	13.92
1000	86.87	45.11	31.22	24.30	20.16	17.41	15.46
2000	173.74	90.23	62.44	48.59	40.31	34.82	30.92
3000	260.62	135.34	93.66	72.89	60.47	52.23	46.38
4000	347.49	180.45	124.88	97.18	80.63	69.64	61.85
5000	434.36	225.56	156.10	121.48	100.78	87.05	77.31
6000	521.23	270.68	187.32	145.77	120.94	104.47	92.77
7000	608.11	315.79	218.54	170.07	141.09	121.88	108.23
8000	694.98	360.90	249.76	194.36	161.25	139.29	123.69
9000	781.85	406.02	280.99	218.66	181.41	156.70	139.15
10000	868.72	451.13	312.21	242.95	201.56	174.11	154.61
11000	955.60	496.24	343.43	267.25	221.72	191.52	170.08
12000	1042.47	541.35	374.65	291.54	241.88	208.93	185.54
13000	1129.34	586.47	405.87	315.84	262.03	226.34	201.00
14000	1216.21	631.58	437.09	340.13	282.19	243.75	216.46
15000	1303.09	676.69	468.31	364.43	302.35	261.16	231.92
16000	1389.96	721.81	499.53	388.72	322.50	278.57	247.38
17000	1476.83	766.92	530.75	413.02	342.66	295.98	262.84
18000	1563.70	812.03	561.97	437.31	362.82	313.40	278.30
19000	1650.57	857.14	593.19	461.61	382.97	330.81	293.77
20000	1737.45	902.26	624.41	485.90	403.13	348.22	309.23
21000	1824.32	947.37	655.63	510.20	423.28	365.63	324.69
22000	1911.19	992.48	686.85	534.49	443.44	383.04	340.15
23000	1998.06	1037.59	718.07	558.79	463.60	400.45	355.61
24000	2084.94	1082.71	749.29	583.08	483.75	417.86	371.07
25000	2171.81	1127.82	780.52	607.38	503.91	435.27	386.53
26000	2258.68	1172.93	811.74	631.67	524.07	452.68	402.00
27000	2345.55	1218.05	842.96	655.97	544.22	470.09	417.46
28000	2432.43	1263.16	874.18	680.27	564.38	487.50	432.92
29000	2519.30	1308.27	905.40	704.56	584.54	504.91	448.38
30000	2606.17	1353.38	936.62	728.86	604.69	522.33	463.84
35000	3040.53	1578.95	1092.72	850.33	705.47	609.38	541.15
40000	3474.89	1804.51	1248.82	971.81	806.26	696.43	618.45
45000	3909.26	2030.08	1404.93	1093.28	907.04	783.49	695.76
50000	4343.62	2255.64	1561.03	1214.76	1007.82	870.54	773.07
55000	4777.98	2481.21	1717.13	1336.24	1108.60	957.60	850.38
60000	5212.34	2706.77	1873.24	1457.71	1209.38	1044.65	927.68
65000	5646.70	2932.33	2029.34	1579.19	1310.17	1131.71	1004.99
70000	6081.06	3157.90	2185.44	1700.66	1410.95	1218.76	1082.30
75000	6515.43	3383.46	2341.55	1822.14	1511.73	1305.81	1159.60
80000	6949.79	3609.03	2497.65	1943.62	1612.51	1392.87	1236.91
85000	7384.15	3834.59	2653.75	2065.09	1713.29	1479.92	1314.22
90000	7818.51	4060.15	2809.86	2186.57	1814.08	1566.98	1391.52
95000	8252.87	4285.72	2965.96	2308.04	1914.86	1654.03	1468.83
100000	8687.23	4511.28	3122.06	2429.52	2015.64	1741.09	1546.14
200000	17374.47	9022.56	6244.12	4859.04	4031.28	3482.17	3092.27
300000	26061.70	13533.85	9366.19	7288.56	6046.92	5223.26	4638.41
400000	34748.94	18045.13	12488.25	9718.08	8062.56	6964.34	6184.55
500000	43436.17	22556.41	15610.31	12147.60	10078.20	8705.43	7730.69
1000000	86872.34	45112.82	31220.62	24295.19	20156.40	17410.85	15461.37

Amortization Amount	8 Years	9 Years	10 Years	15 Years	20 Years	25 Years	30 Years
25	0.35	0.32	0.30	0.24	0.21	0.19	0.18
50	0.70	0.64	0.60	0.47	0.41	0.38	0.36
100	1.40	1.29	1.20	0.94	0.82	0.76	0.72
200	2.80	2.58	2.40	1.88	1.64	1.51	1.43
300	4.20	3.87	3.60	2.82	2.46	2.27	2.15
400	5.60	5.16	4.80	3.76	3.28	3.02	2.87
500	7.00	6.44	6.00	4.71	4.10	3.78	3.58
600	8.41	7.73	7.20	5.65	4.93	4.53	4.30
700	9.81	9.02	8.40	6.59	5.75	5.29	5.01
800	11.21	10.31	9.60	7.53	6.57	6.04	5.73
900	12.61	11.60	10.80	8.47	7.39	6.80	6.45
1000	14.01	12.89	12.00	9.41	8.21	7.55	7.16
2000	28.02	25.78	24.00	18.82	16.42	15.11	14.33
3000	42.03	38.67	36.00	28.24	24.63	22.66	21.49
4000	56.04	51.56	48.00	37.65	32.84	30.21	28.65
5000	70.05	64.44	60.00	47.06	41.04	37.76	35.82
6000	84.06	77.33	72.00	56.47	49.25	45.32	42.98
7000	98.07	90.22	84.00	65.88	57.46	52.87	50.14
8000	112.07	103.11	96.00	75.30	65.67	60.42	57.31
9000	126.08	116.00	108.00	84.71	73.88	67.97	64.47
10000	140.09	128.89	120.00	94.12	82.09	75.53	71.63
11000	154.10	141.78	132.00	103.53	90.30	83.08	78.80
12000	168.11	154.67	144.01	112.95	98.51	90.63	85.96
13000	182.12	167.56	156.01	122.36	106.71	98.18	93.12
14000	196.13	180.44	168.01	131.77	114.92	105.74	100.29
15000	210.14	193.33	180.01	141.18	123.13	113.29	107.45
16000	224.15	206.22	192.01	150.59	131.34	120.84	114.61
17000	238.16	219.11	204.01	160.01	139.55	128.39	121.78
18000	252.17	232.00	216.01	169.42	147.76	135.95	128.94
19000	266.18	244.89	228.01	178.83	155.97	143.50	136.10
20000	280.19	257.78	240.01	188.24	164.18	151.05	143.27
21000	294.20	270.67	252.01	197.65	172.38	158.60	150.43
22000	308.21	283.56	264.01	207.07	180.59	166.16	157.59
23000	322.22	296.44	276.01	216.48	188.80	173.71	164.76
24000	336.22	309.33	288.01	225.89	197.01	181.26	171.92
25000	350.23	322.22	300.01	235.30	205.22	188.81	179.08
26000	364.24	335.11	312.01	244.71	213.43	196.37	186.25
27000	378.25	348.00	324.01	254.13	221.64	203.92	193.41
28000	392.26	360.89	336.01	263.54	229.85	211.47	200.57
29000	406.27	373.78	348.01	272.95	238.05	219.02	207.74
30000	420.28	386.67	360.01	282.36	246.26	226.58	214.90
35000	490.33	451.11	420.02	329.42	287.31	264.34	250.72
40000	560.37	515.56	480.02	376.48	328.35	302.10	286.53
45000	630.42	580.00	540.02	423.54	369.39	339.86	322.35
50000	700.47	644.44	600.02	470.60	410.44	377.63	358.17
55000	770.51	708.89	660.02	517.66	451.48	415.39	393.98
60000	840.56	773.33	720.03	564.73	492.53	453.15	429.80
65000	910.61	837.78	780.03	611.79	533.57	490.91	465.62
70000	980.65	902.22	840.03	658.85	574.61	528.68	501.43
75000	1050.70	966.67	900.03	705.91	615.66	566.44	537.25
80000	1120.75	1031.11	960.04	752.97	656.70	604.20	573.06
85000	1190.79	1095.56	1020.04	800.03	697.74	641.96	608.88
90000	1260.84	1160.00	1080.04	847.09	738.79	679.73	644.70
95000	1330.89	1224.44	1140.04	894.15	779.83	717.49	680.51
100000	1400.94	1288.89	1200.04	941.21	820.88	755.25	716.33
200000	2801.87	2577.78	2400.09	1882.42	1641.75	1510.50	1432.66
300000	4202.81	3866.67	3600.13	2823.63	2462.63	2265.75	2148.99
400000	5603.74	5155.56	4800.18	3764.83	3283.50	3021.01	2865.32
500000	7004.68	6444.45	6000.22	4706.04	4104.38	3776.26	3581.66
1000000	14009.35	12888.89	12000.45	9412.08	8208.76	7552.52	7163.31

8%
MONTHLY PAYMENT
NECESSARY TO AMORTIZE A LOAN

Amortization Amount	1 Year	2 Years	3 Years	4 Years	5 Years	6 Years	7 Years
25	2.17	1.13	0.78	0.61	0.51	0.44	0.39
50	4.35	2.26	1.56	1.22	1.01	0.87	0.78
100	8.69	4.52	3.13	2.44	2.02	1.75	1.55
200	17.39	9.03	6.26	4.87	4.04	3.49	3.10
300	26.08	13.55	9.38	7.31	6.06	5.24	4.66
400	34.77	18.07	12.51	9.74	8.09	6.99	6.21
500	43.46	22.58	15.64	12.18	10.11	8.73	7.76
600	52.16	27.10	18.77	14.61	12.13	10.48	9.31
700	60.85	31.62	21.89	17.05	14.15	12.23	10.87
800	69.54	36.13	25.02	19.48	16.17	13.98	12.42
900	78.24	40.65	28.15	21.92	18.19	15.72	13.97
1000	86.93	45.17	31.28	24.35	20.21	17.47	15.52
2000	173.86	90.34	62.55	48.70	40.43	34.94	31.04
3000	260.78	135.50	93.83	73.06	60.64	52.41	46.56
4000	347.71	180.67	125.11	97.41	80.86	69.88	62.09
5000	434.64	225.84	156.38	121.76	101.07	87.35	77.61
6000	521.57	271.01	187.66	146.11	121.28	104.82	93.13
7000	608.50	316.18	218.93	170.46	141.50	122.29	108.65
8000	695.43	361.34	250.21	194.81	161.71	139.76	124.17
9000	782.35	406.51	281.49	219.17	181.93	157.23	139.69
10000	869.28	451.68	312.76	243.52	202.14	174.70	155.21
11000	956.21	496.85	344.04	267.87	222.36	192.17	170.74
12000	1043.14	542.02	375.32	292.22	242.57	209.64	186.26
13000	1130.07	587.18	406.59	316.57	262.78	227.11	201.78
14000	1217.00	632.35	437.87	340.93	283.00	244.58	217.30
15000	1303.92	677.52	469.15	365.28	303.21	262.05	232.82
16000	1390.85	722.69	500.42	389.63	323.43	279.52	248.34
17000	1477.78	767.86	531.70	413.98	343.64	296.99	263.86
18000	1564.71	813.02	562.97	438.33	363.85	314.46	279.39
19000	1651.64	858.19	594.25	462.69	384.07	331.93	294.91
20000	1738.57	903.36	625.53	487.04	404.28	349.40	310.43
21000	1825.49	948.53	656.80	511.39	424.50	366.86	325.95
22000	1912.42	993.69	688.08	535.74	444.71	384.33	341.47
23000	1999.35	1038.86	719.36	560.09	464.93	401.80	356.99
24000	2086.28	1084.03	750.63	584.44	485.14	419.27	372.51
25000	2173.21	1129.20	781.91	608.80	505.35	436.74	388.04
26000	2260.13	1174.37	813.19	633.15	525.57	454.21	403.56
27000	2347.06	1219.53	844.46	657.50	545.78	471.68	419.08
28000	2433.99	1264.70	875.74	681.85	566.00	489.15	434.60
29000	2520.92	1309.87	907.01	706.20	586.21	506.62	450.12
30000	2607.85	1355.04	938.29	730.56	606.42	524.09	465.64
35000	3042.49	1580.88	1094.67	852.32	707.50	611.44	543.25
40000	3477.13	1806.72	1251.05	974.07	808.57	698.79	620.86
45000	3911.77	2032.56	1407.44	1095.83	909.64	786.14	698.46
50000	4346.41	2258.40	1563.82	1217.59	1010.71	873.49	776.07
55000	4781.05	2484.24	1720.20	1339.35	1111.78	960.84	853.68
60000	5215.70	2710.08	1876.58	1461.11	1212.85	1048.19	931.29
65000	5650.34	2935.92	2032.96	1582.87	1313.92	1135.53	1008.89
70000	6084.98	3161.76	2189.34	1704.63	1414.99	1222.88	1086.50
75000	6519.62	3387.60	2345.73	1826.39	1516.06	1310.23	1164.11
80000	6954.26	3613.44	2502.11	1948.15	1617.13	1397.58	1241.72
85000	7388.90	3839.28	2658.49	2069.91	1718.20	1484.93	1319.32
90000	7823.54	4065.12	2814.87	2191.67	1819.27	1572.28	1396.93
95000	8258.18	4290.96	2971.25	2313.43	1920.34	1659.63	1474.54
100000	8692.83	4516.79	3127.64	2435.19	2021.42	1746.98	1552.14
200000	17385.65	9033.59	6255.27	4870.37	4042.83	3493.95	3104.29
300000	26078.48	13550.38	9382.91	7305.56	6064.25	5240.93	4656.43
400000	34771.30	18067.18	12510.54	9740.75	8085.66	6987.90	6208.58
500000	43464.13	22583.97	15638.18	12175.93	10107.08	8734.88	7760.72
1000000	86928.26	45167.95	31276.35	24351.87	20214.16	17469.75	15521.44

Amortization Amount	8 Years	9 Years	10 Years	15 Years	20 Years	25 Years	30 Years
25	0.35	0.32	0.30	0.24	0.21	0.19	0.18
50	0.70	0.65	0.60	0.47	0.41	0.38	0.36
100	1.41	1.30	1.21	0.95	0.83	0.76	0.72
200	2.81	2.59	2.41	1.90	1.66	1.53	1.45
300	4.22	3.89	3.62	2.84	2.49	2.29	2.17
400	5.63	5.18	4.83	3.79	3.31	3.05	2.90
500	7.04	6.48	6.03	4.74	4.14	3.82	3.62
600	8.44	7.77	7.24	5.69	4.97	4.58	4.35
700	9.85	9.07	8.44	6.64	5.80	5.34	5.07
800	11.26	10.36	9.65	7.59	6.63	6.11	5.80
900	12.66	11.66	10.86	8.53	7.46	6.87	6.52
1000	14.07	12.95	12.06	9.48	8.28	7.63	7.25
2000	28.14	25.90	24.13	18.96	16.57	15.26	14.49
3000	42.21	38.85	36.19	28.44	24.85	22.90	21.74
4000	56.28	51.81	48.26	37.93	33.13	30.53	28.99
5000	70.35	64.76	60.32	47.41	41.42	38.16	36.24
6000	84.42	77.71	72.38	56.89	49.70	45.79	43.48
7000	98.49	90.66	84.45	66.37	57.99	53.42	50.73
8000	112.56	103.61	96.51	75.85	66.27	61.06	57.98
9000	126.64	116.56	108.58	85.33	74.55	68.69	65.22
10000	140.71	129.51	120.64	94.82	82.84	76.32	72.47
11000	154.78	142.46	132.70	104.30	91.12	83.95	79.72
12000	168.85	155.42	144.77	113.78	99.40	91.59	86.97
13000	182.92	168.37	156.83	123.26	107.69	99.22	94.21
14000	196.99	181.32	168.90	132.74	115.97	106.85	101.46
15000	211.06	194.27	180.96	142.22	124.25	114.48	108.71
16000	225.13	207.22	193.03	151.70	132.54	122.11	115.95
17000	239.20	220.17	205.09	161.19	140.82	129.75	123.20
18000	253.27	233.12	217.15	170.67	149.10	137.38	130.45
19000	267.34	246.08	229.22	180.15	157.39	145.01	137.70
20000	281.41	259.03	241.28	189.63	165.67	152.64	144.94
21000	295.48	271.98	253.35	199.11	173.96	160.27	152.19
22000	309.55	284.93	265.41	208.59	182.24	167.91	159.44
23000	323.62	297.88	277.47	218.08	190.52	175.54	166.68
24000	337.69	310.83	289.54	227.56	198.81	183.17	173.93
25000	351.77	323.78	301.60	237.04	207.09	190.80	181.18
26000	365.84	336.73	313.67	246.52	215.37	198.44	188.42
27000	379.91	349.69	325.73	256.00	223.66	206.07	195.67
28000	393.98	362.64	337.79	265.48	231.94	213.70	202.92
29000	408.05	375.59	349.86	274.96	240.22	221.33	210.17
30000	422.12	388.54	361.92	284.45	248.51	228.96	217.41
35000	492.47	453.30	422.24	331.85	289.93	267.12	253.65
40000	562.82	518.05	482.56	379.26	331.34	305.29	289.88
45000	633.18	582.81	542.88	426.67	372.76	343.45	326.12
50000	703.53	647.57	603.20	474.08	414.18	381.61	362.36
55000	773.88	712.32	663.52	521.48	455.60	419.77	398.59
60000	844.24	777.08	723.85	568.89	497.01	457.93	434.83
65000	914.59	841.84	784.17	616.30	538.43	496.09	471.06
70000	984.94	906.59	844.49	663.71	579.85	534.25	507.30
75000	1055.30	971.35	904.81	711.11	621.27	572.41	543.53
80000	1125.65	1036.11	965.13	758.52	662.69	610.57	579.77
85000	1196.00	1100.86	1025.45	805.93	704.10	648.73	616.00
90000	1266.36	1165.62	1085.77	853.34	745.52	686.89	652.24
95000	1336.71	1230.38	1146.09	900.75	786.94	725.05	688.48
100000	1407.06	1295.13	1206.41	948.15	828.36	763.21	724.71
200000	2814.12	2590.27	2412.82	1896.31	1656.71	1526.43	1449.42
300000	4221.18	3885.40	3619.23	2844.46	2485.07	2289.64	2174.13
400000	5628.24	5180.54	4825.64	3792.61	3313.43	3052.85	2898.84
500000	7035.31	6475.67	6032.05	4740.76	4141.79	3816.07	3623.56
1000000	14070.61	12951.35	12064.09	9481.53	8283.57	7632.13	7247.11

8.125%

MONTHLY PAYMENT
NECESSARY TO AMORTIZE A LOAN

Amortization Amount	1 Year	2 Years	3 Years	4 Years	5 Years	6 Years	7 Years
25	2.17	1.13	0.78	0.61	0.51	0.44	0.39
50	4.35	2.26	1.57	1.22	1.01	0.88	0.78
100	8.70	4.52	3.13	2.44	2.03	1.75	1.56
200	17.40	9.04	6.27	4.88	4.05	3.51	3.12
300	26.10	13.57	9.40	7.32	6.08	5.26	4.67
400	34.79	18.09	12.53	9.76	8.11	7.01	6.23
500	43.49	22.61	15.67	12.20	10.14	8.76	7.79
600	52.19	27.13	18.80	14.65	12.18	10.52	9.35
700	60.89	31.66	21.93	17.09	14.19	12.27	10.91
800	69.59	36.18	25.07	19.53	16.22	14.02	12.47
900	78.29	40.70	28.20	21.97	18.24	15.78	14.02
1000	86.98	45.22	31.33	24.41	20.27	17.53	15.58
2000	173.97	90.45	62.66	48.82	40.54	35.06	31.16
3000	260.95	135.67	94.00	73.23	60.82	52.59	46.74
4000	347.94	180.89	125.33	97.63	81.09	70.11	62.33
5000	434.92	226.12	156.66	122.04	101.36	87.64	77.91
6000	521.91	271.34	187.99	146.45	121.63	105.17	93.49
7000	608.89	316.56	219.32	170.86	141.90	122.70	109.07
8000	695.87	361.78	250.66	195.27	162.18	140.23	124.65
9000	782.86	407.01	281.99	219.68	182.45	157.76	140.23
10000	869.84	452.23	313.32	244.09	202.72	175.29	155.82
11000	956.83	497.45	344.65	268.49	222.99	192.82	171.40
12000	1043.81	542.68	375.99	292.90	243.26	210.34	186.98
13000	1130.79	587.90	407.32	317.31	263.54	227.87	202.56
14000	1217.78	633.12	438.65	341.72	283.81	245.40	218.14
15000	1304.76	678.35	469.98	366.13	304.08	262.93	233.72
16000	1391.75	723.57	501.31	390.54	324.35	280.46	249.31
17000	1478.73	768.79	532.65	414.95	344.62	297.99	264.89
18000	1565.72	814.02	563.98	439.35	364.90	315.52	280.47
19000	1652.70	859.24	595.31	463.76	385.17	333.05	296.05
20000	1739.68	904.46	626.64	488.17	405.44	350.57	311.63
21000	1826.67	949.68	657.97	512.58	425.71	368.10	327.21
22000	1913.65	994.91	689.31	536.99	445.98	385.63	342.80
23000	2000.64	1040.13	720.64	561.40	466.26	403.16	358.38
24000	2087.62	1085.35	751.97	585.81	486.53	420.69	373.96
25000	2174.60	1130.58	783.30	610.21	506.80	438.22	389.54
26000	2261.59	1175.80	814.63	634.62	527.07	455.75	405.12
27000	2348.57	1221.02	845.97	659.03	547.34	473.28	420.70
28000	2435.56	1266.25	877.30	683.44	567.62	490.80	436.29
29000	2522.54	1311.47	908.63	707.85	587.89	508.33	451.87
30000	2609.53	1356.69	939.96	732.26	608.16	525.86	467.45
35000	3044.45	1582.81	1096.62	854.30	709.52	613.51	545.36
40000	3479.37	1808.92	1253.28	976.34	810.88	701.15	623.26
45000	3914.29	2035.04	1409.95	1098.39	912.24	788.79	701.17
50000	4349.21	2261.15	1566.61	1220.43	1013.60	876.44	779.08
55000	4784.13	2487.27	1723.27	1342.47	1114.96	964.08	856.99
60000	5219.05	2713.39	1879.93	1464.52	1216.32	1051.72	934.90
65000	5653.97	2939.50	2036.59	1586.56	1317.68	1139.37	1012.81
70000	6088.89	3165.62	2193.25	1708.60	1419.04	1227.01	1090.71
75000	6523.81	3391.73	2349.91	1830.64	1520.40	1314.66	1168.62
80000	6958.73	3617.85	2506.57	1952.69	1621.76	1402.30	1246.53
85000	7393.65	3843.96	2663.23	2074.73	1723.12	1489.94	1324.44
90000	7828.58	4070.08	2819.89	2196.77	1824.48	1577.59	1402.35
95000	8263.50	4296.19	2976.55	2318.82	1925.84	1665.23	1480.25
100000	8698.42	4522.31	3133.21	2440.86	2027.20	1752.87	1558.16
200000	17396.83	9044.62	6266.42	4881.72	4054.40	3505.75	3116.32
300000	26095.25	13566.93	9399.63	7322.58	6081.60	5258.62	4674.49
400000	34793.67	18089.24	12532.85	9763.44	8108.79	7011.50	6232.65
500000	43492.08	22611.54	15666.06	12204.30	10135.99	8764.37	7790.81
1000000	86984.17	45223.09	31332.12	24408.60	20271.99	17528.74	15581.62

68

MONTHLY PAYMENT
NECESSARY TO AMORTIZE A LOAN

8.125%

Amortization Amount	8 Years	9 Years	10 Years	15 Years	20 Years	25 Years	30 Years
25	0.35	0.33	0.30	0.24	0.21	0.19	0.18
50	0.71	0.65	0.61	0.48	0.42	0.39	0.37
100	1.41	1.30	1.21	0.96	0.84	0.77	0.73
200	2.83	2.60	2.43	1.91	1.67	1.54	1.47
300	4.24	3.90	3.64	2.87	2.51	2.31	2.20
400	5.65	5.21	4.85	3.82	3.34	3.08	2.93
500	7.07	6.51	6.06	4.78	4.18	3.86	3.67
600	8.48	7.81	7.28	5.73	5.02	4.63	4.40
700	9.89	9.11	8.49	6.69	5.85	5.40	5.13
800	11.31	10.41	9.70	7.64	6.69	6.17	5.86
900	12.72	11.71	10.92	8.60	7.52	6.94	6.60
1000	14.13	13.01	12.13	9.55	8.36	7.71	7.33
2000	28.26	26.03	24.26	19.10	16.72	15.42	14.66
3000	42.40	39.04	36.38	28.65	25.08	23.14	21.99
4000	56.53	52.06	48.51	38.20	33.43	30.85	29.32
5000	70.66	65.07	60.64	47.76	41.79	38.56	36.66
6000	84.79	78.08	72.77	57.31	50.15	46.27	43.99
7000	98.92	91.10	84.90	66.86	58.51	53.98	51.32
8000	113.06	104.11	97.02	76.41	66.87	61.70	58.65
9000	127.19	117.13	109.15	85.96	75.23	69.41	65.98
10000	141.32	130.14	121.28	95.51	83.59	77.12	73.31
11000	155.45	143.15	133.41	105.06	91.95	84.83	80.64
12000	169.58	156.17	145.53	114.61	100.30	92.54	87.97
13000	183.72	169.18	157.66	124.17	108.66	100.26	95.31
14000	197.85	182.20	169.79	133.72	117.02	107.97	102.64
15000	211.98	195.21	181.92	143.27	125.38	115.68	109.97
16000	226.11	208.22	194.05	152.82	133.74	123.39	117.30
17000	240.24	221.24	206.17	162.37	142.10	131.11	124.63
18000	254.38	234.25	218.30	171.92	150.46	138.82	131.96
19000	268.51	247.26	230.43	181.47	158.81	146.53	139.29
20000	282.64	260.28	242.56	191.02	167.17	154.24	146.62
21000	296.77	273.29	254.69	200.58	175.53	161.95	153.96
22000	310.90	286.31	266.81	210.13	183.89	169.67	161.29
23000	325.04	299.32	278.94	219.68	192.25	177.38	168.62
24000	339.17	312.33	291.07	229.23	200.61	185.09	175.95
25000	353.30	325.35	303.20	238.78	208.97	192.80	183.28
26000	367.43	338.36	315.33	248.33	217.33	200.51	190.61
27000	381.56	351.38	327.45	257.88	225.68	208.23	197.94
28000	395.70	364.39	339.58	267.43	234.04	215.94	205.27
29000	409.83	377.40	351.71	276.98	242.40	223.65	212.61
30000	423.96	390.42	363.84	286.54	250.76	231.36	219.94
35000	494.62	455.49	424.48	334.29	292.55	269.92	256.59
40000	565.28	520.56	485.12	382.05	334.35	308.48	293.25
45000	635.94	585.63	545.76	429.80	376.14	347.04	329.91
50000	706.60	650.70	606.39	477.56	417.93	385.60	366.56
55000	777.26	715.77	667.03	525.32	459.73	424.16	403.22
60000	847.92	780.84	727.67	573.07	501.52	462.72	439.87
65000	918.58	845.91	788.31	620.83	543.31	501.28	476.53
70000	989.24	910.98	848.95	668.58	585.11	539.84	513.19
75000	1059.90	976.05	909.59	716.34	626.90	578.40	549.84
80000	1130.56	1041.12	970.23	764.10	668.69	616.96	586.50
85000	1201.22	1106.18	1030.87	811.85	710.49	655.53	623.15
90000	1271.88	1171.25	1091.51	859.61	752.28	694.09	659.81
95000	1342.54	1236.32	1152.15	907.36	794.07	732.65	696.47
100000	1413.20	1301.39	1212.79	955.12	835.87	771.21	733.12
200000	2826.40	2602.79	2425.58	1910.24	1671.73	1542.41	1466.24
300000	4239.60	3904.18	3638.37	2865.36	2507.60	2313.62	2199.37
400000	5652.80	5205.58	4851.16	3820.48	3343.47	3084.82	2932.49
500000	7066.00	6506.97	6063.95	4775.60	4179.33	3856.03	3665.61
1000000	14132.00	13013.94	12127.89	9551.20	8358.67	7712.06	7331.22

8.25%

Amortization Amount	1 Year	2 Years	3 Years	4 Years	5 Years	6 Years	7 Years
25	2.18	1.13	0.78	0.61	0.51	0.44	0.39
50	4.35	2.26	1.57	1.22	1.02	0.88	0.78
100	8.70	4.53	3.14	2.45	2.03	1.76	1.56
200	17.41	9.06	6.28	4.89	4.07	3.52	3.13
300	26.11	13.58	9.42	7.34	6.10	5.28	4.69
400	34.82	18.11	12.56	9.79	8.13	7.04	6.26
500	43.52	22.64	15.69	12.23	10.16	8.79	7.82
600	52.22	27.17	18.83	14.68	12.20	10.55	9.39
700	60.93	31.69	21.97	17.13	14.23	12.31	10.95
800	69.63	36.22	25.11	19.57	16.26	14.07	12.51
900	78.34	40.75	28.25	22.02	18.30	15.83	14.08
1000	87.04	45.28	31.39	24.47	20.33	17.59	15.64
2000	174.08	90.56	62.78	48.93	40.66	35.18	31.28
3000	261.12	135.83	94.16	73.40	60.99	52.76	46.93
4000	348.16	181.11	125.55	97.86	81.32	70.35	62.57
5000	435.20	226.39	156.94	122.33	101.65	87.94	78.21
6000	522.24	271.67	188.33	146.79	121.98	105.53	93.85
7000	609.28	316.95	219.72	171.26	142.31	123.11	109.49
8000	696.32	362.23	251.10	195.72	162.64	140.70	125.14
9000	783.36	407.50	282.49	220.19	182.97	158.29	140.78
10000	870.40	452.78	313.88	244.65	203.30	175.88	156.42
11000	957.44	498.06	345.27	269.12	223.63	193.47	172.06
12000	1044.48	543.34	376.65	293.58	243.96	211.05	187.70
13000	1131.52	588.62	408.04	318.05	264.29	228.64	203.34
14000	1218.56	633.90	439.43	342.52	284.62	246.23	218.99
15000	1305.60	679.17	470.82	366.98	304.95	263.82	234.63
16000	1392.64	724.45	502.21	391.45	325.28	281.41	250.27
17000	1479.68	769.73	533.59	415.91	345.61	298.99	265.91
18000	1566.72	815.01	564.98	440.38	365.94	316.58	281.55
19000	1653.76	860.29	596.37	464.84	386.27	334.17	297.20
20000	1740.80	905.56	627.76	489.31	406.60	351.76	312.84
21000	1827.84	950.84	659.15	513.77	426.93	369.34	328.48
22000	1914.88	996.12	690.53	538.24	447.26	386.93	344.12
23000	2001.92	1041.40	721.92	562.70	467.59	404.52	359.76
24000	2088.96	1086.68	753.31	587.17	487.92	422.11	375.41
25000	2176.00	1131.96	784.70	611.63	508.25	439.70	391.05
26000	2263.04	1177.23	816.09	636.10	528.58	457.28	406.69
27000	2350.08	1222.51	847.47	660.57	548.91	474.87	422.33
28000	2437.12	1267.79	878.86	685.03	569.24	492.46	437.97
29000	2524.16	1313.07	910.25	709.50	589.57	510.05	453.62
30000	2611.20	1358.35	941.64	733.96	609.90	527.63	469.26
35000	3046.40	1584.74	1098.58	856.29	711.55	615.57	547.47
40000	3481.60	1811.13	1255.52	978.62	813.20	703.51	625.68
45000	3916.80	2037.52	1412.46	1100.94	914.84	791.45	703.89
50000	4352.00	2263.91	1569.40	1223.27	1016.49	879.39	782.10
55000	4787.20	2490.30	1726.34	1345.60	1118.14	967.33	860.31
60000	5222.40	2716.69	1883.27	1467.92	1219.79	1055.27	938.51
65000	5657.60	2943.09	2040.21	1590.25	1321.44	1143.21	1016.72
70000	6092.81	3169.48	2197.15	1712.58	1423.09	1231.15	1094.93
75000	6528.01	3395.87	2354.09	1834.90	1524.74	1319.09	1173.14
80000	6963.21	3622.26	2511.03	1957.23	1626.39	1407.03	1251.35
85000	7398.41	3848.65	2667.97	2079.56	1728.04	1494.96	1329.56
90000	7833.61	4075.04	2824.91	2201.88	1829.69	1582.90	1407.77
95000	8268.81	4301.43	2981.85	2324.21	1931.34	1670.84	1485.98
100000	8704.01	4527.82	3138.79	2446.54	2032.99	1758.78	1564.19
200000	17408.01	9055.65	6277.58	4893.08	4065.98	3517.56	3128.38
300000	26112.02	13583.47	9416.37	7339.61	6098.96	5276.35	4692.57
400000	34816.03	18111.30	12555.16	9786.15	8131.95	7035.13	6256.76
500000	43520.04	22639.12	15693.95	12232.69	10164.94	8793.91	7820.95
1000000	87040.07	45278.24	31387.91	24465.38	20329.88	17587.82	15641.91

Amortization Amount	8 Years	9 Years	10 Years	15 Years	20 Years	25 Years	30 Years
25	0.35	0.33	0.30	0.24	0.21	0.19	0.19
50	0.71	0.65	0.61	0.48	0.42	0.39	0.37
100	1.42	1.31	1.22	0.96	0.84	0.78	0.74
200	2.84	2.62	2.44	1.92	1.69	1.56	1.48
300	4.26	3.92	3.66	2.89	2.53	2.34	2.22
400	5.68	5.23	4.88	3.85	3.37	3.12	2.97
500	7.10	6.54	6.10	4.81	4.22	3.90	3.71
600	8.52	7.85	7.32	5.77	5.06	4.68	4.45
700	9.94	9.15	8.53	6.73	5.90	5.45	5.19
800	11.35	10.46	9.75	7.70	6.75	6.23	5.93
900	12.77	11.77	10.97	8.66	7.59	7.01	6.67
1000	14.19	13.08	12.19	9.62	8.43	7.79	7.42
2000	28.39	26.15	24.38	19.24	16.87	15.58	14.83
3000	42.58	39.23	36.58	28.86	25.30	23.38	22.25
4000	56.77	52.31	48.77	38.48	33.74	31.17	29.66
5000	70.96	65.38	60.96	48.11	42.17	38.96	37.08
6000	85.16	78.46	73.15	57.73	50.60	46.75	44.49
7000	99.35	91.54	85.34	67.35	59.04	54.55	51.91
8000	113.55	104.61	97.53	76.97	67.47	62.34	59.33
9000	127.74	117.69	109.73	86.59	75.91	70.13	66.74
10000	141.94	130.77	121.92	96.21	84.34	77.92	74.16
11000	156.13	143.84	134.11	105.83	92.77	85.72	81.57
12000	170.32	156.92	146.30	115.45	101.21	93.51	88.99
13000	184.52	170.00	158.49	125.07	109.64	101.30	96.40
14000	198.71	183.07	170.69	134.70	118.08	109.09	103.82
15000	212.90	196.15	182.88	144.32	126.51	116.88	111.23
16000	227.10	209.23	195.07	153.94	134.94	124.68	118.65
17000	241.29	222.30	207.26	163.56	143.38	132.47	126.07
18000	255.48	235.38	219.45	173.18	151.81	140.26	133.48
19000	269.68	248.46	231.65	182.80	160.25	148.05	140.90
20000	283.87	261.53	243.84	192.42	168.68	155.85	148.31
21000	298.06	274.61	256.03	202.04	177.11	163.64	155.73
22000	312.26	287.69	268.22	211.66	185.55	171.43	163.14
23000	326.45	300.76	280.41	221.29	193.98	179.22	170.56
24000	340.64	313.84	292.60	230.91	202.42	187.01	177.98
25000	354.84	326.92	304.80	240.53	210.85	194.81	185.39
26000	369.03	339.99	316.99	250.15	219.28	202.60	192.81
27000	383.22	353.07	329.18	259.77	227.72	210.39	200.22
28000	397.42	366.15	341.37	269.39	236.15	218.18	207.64
29000	411.61	379.22	353.56	279.01	244.59	225.98	215.05
30000	425.81	392.30	365.76	288.63	253.02	233.77	222.47
35000	496.77	457.68	426.71	336.74	295.19	272.73	259.55
40000	567.74	523.07	487.67	384.84	337.36	311.69	296.63
45000	638.71	588.45	548.63	432.95	379.53	350.65	333.70
50000	709.68	653.83	609.59	481.06	421.70	389.61	370.78
55000	780.64	719.22	670.55	529.16	463.87	428.58	407.86
60000	851.61	784.60	731.51	577.27	506.04	467.54	444.94
65000	922.58	849.98	792.47	625.37	548.21	506.50	482.02
70000	993.55	915.37	853.43	673.48	590.38	545.46	519.10
75000	1064.51	980.75	914.39	721.58	632.55	584.42	556.17
80000	1135.48	1046.13	975.35	769.69	674.72	623.38	593.25
85000	1206.45	1111.52	1036.31	817.79	716.89	662.34	630.33
90000	1277.42	1176.90	1097.27	865.90	759.06	701.31	667.41
95000	1348.38	1242.28	1158.23	914.00	801.23	740.27	704.49
100000	1419.35	1307.67	1219.18	962.11	843.40	779.23	741.56
200000	2838.70	2615.33	2438.37	1924.22	1686.81	1558.46	1483.13
300000	4258.05	3923.00	3657.55	2886.33	2530.21	2337.69	2224.69
400000	5677.40	5230.67	4876.74	3848.44	3373.61	3116.92	2966.26
500000	7096.75	6538.34	6095.92	4810.55	4217.02	3896.14	3707.82
1000000	14193.51	13076.67	12191.85	9621.10	8434.04	7792.29	7415.65

8.375%

Amortization Amount	1 Year	2 Years	3 Years	4 Years	5 Years	6 Years	7 Years
25	2.18	1.13	0.79	0.61	0.51	0.44	0.39
50	4.35	2.27	1.57	1.23	1.02	0.88	0.79
100	8.71	4.53	3.14	2.45	2.04	1.76	1.57
200	17.42	9.07	6.29	4.90	4.08	3.53	3.14
300	26.13	13.60	9.43	7.36	6.12	5.29	4.71
400	34.84	18.13	12.58	9.81	8.16	7.06	6.28
500	43.55	22.67	15.72	12.26	10.19	8.82	7.85
600	52.26	27.20	18.87	14.71	12.23	10.59	9.42
700	60.97	31.73	22.01	17.17	14.27	12.35	10.99
800	69.68	36.27	25.15	19.62	16.31	14.12	12.56
900	78.39	40.80	28.30	22.07	18.35	15.88	14.13
1000	87.10	45.33	31.44	24.52	20.39	17.65	15.70
2000	174.19	90.67	62.89	49.04	40.78	35.29	31.40
3000	261.29	136.00	94.33	73.57	61.16	52.94	47.11
4000	348.38	181.33	125.77	98.09	81.55	70.59	62.81
5000	435.48	226.67	157.22	122.61	101.94	88.23	78.51
6000	522.58	272.00	188.66	147.13	122.33	105.88	94.21
7000	609.67	317.33	220.11	171.66	142.71	123.53	109.92
8000	696.77	362.67	251.55	196.18	163.10	141.18	125.62
9000	783.86	408.00	282.99	220.70	183.49	158.82	141.32
10000	870.96	453.33	314.44	245.22	203.88	176.47	157.02
11000	958.05	498.67	345.88	269.74	224.27	194.12	172.73
12000	1045.15	544.00	377.32	294.27	244.65	211.76	188.43
13000	1132.25	589.33	408.77	318.79	265.04	229.41	204.13
14000	1219.34	634.67	440.21	343.31	285.43	247.06	219.83
15000	1306.44	680.00	471.66	367.83	305.82	264.70	235.53
16000	1393.54	725.33	503.10	392.36	326.21	282.35	251.24
17000	1480.63	770.67	534.54	416.88	346.59	300.00	266.94
18000	1567.73	816.00	565.99	441.40	366.98	317.65	282.64
19000	1654.82	861.33	597.43	465.92	387.37	335.29	298.34
20000	1741.92	906.67	628.87	490.44	407.76	352.94	314.05
21000	1829.02	952.00	660.32	514.97	428.14	370.59	329.75
22000	1916.11	997.33	691.76	539.49	448.53	388.23	345.45
23000	2003.21	1042.67	723.21	564.01	468.92	405.88	361.15
24000	2090.30	1088.00	754.65	588.53	489.31	423.53	376.86
25000	2177.40	1133.34	786.09	613.06	509.70	441.17	392.56
26000	2264.50	1178.67	817.54	637.58	530.08	458.82	408.26
27000	2351.59	1224.00	848.98	662.10	550.47	476.47	423.96
28000	2438.69	1269.34	880.42	686.62	570.86	494.12	439.66
29000	2525.78	1314.67	911.87	711.14	591.25	511.76	455.37
30000	2612.88	1360.00	943.31	735.67	611.64	529.41	471.07
35000	3048.36	1586.67	1100.53	858.28	713.57	617.64	549.58
40000	3483.84	1813.34	1257.75	980.89	815.51	705.88	628.09
45000	3919.32	2040.00	1414.97	1103.50	917.45	794.11	706.60
50000	4354.80	2266.67	1572.19	1226.11	1019.39	882.35	785.12
55000	4790.28	2493.34	1729.41	1348.72	1121.33	970.58	863.63
60000	5225.76	2720.00	1886.62	1471.33	1223.27	1058.82	942.14
65000	5661.24	2946.67	2043.84	1593.94	1325.21	1147.05	1020.65
70000	6096.72	3173.34	2201.06	1716.55	1427.15	1235.29	1099.16
75000	6532.20	3400.01	2358.28	1839.17	1529.09	1323.52	1177.67
80000	6967.68	3626.67	2515.50	1961.78	1631.03	1411.76	1256.18
85000	7403.16	3853.34	2672.72	2084.39	1732.97	1499.99	1334.70
90000	7838.64	4080.01	2829.94	2207.00	1834.91	1588.23	1413.21
95000	8274.12	4306.67	2987.15	2329.61	1936.85	1676.46	1491.72
100000	8709.60	4533.34	3144.37	2452.22	2038.79	1764.70	1570.23
200000	17419.19	9066.68	6288.75	4904.44	4077.57	3529.40	3140.46
300000	26128.79	13600.02	9433.12	7356.66	6116.36	5294.10	4710.69
400000	34838.39	18133.36	12577.49	9808.88	8155.14	7058.79	6280.92
500000	43547.98	22666.70	15721.87	12261.10	10193.93	8823.49	7851.15
1000000	87095.97	45333.41	31443.74	24522.21	20387.85	17646.99	15702.30

Amortization Amount	8 Years	9 Years	10 Years	15 Years	20 Years	25 Years	30 Years
25	0.36	0.33	0.31	0.24	0.21	0.20	0.19
50	0.71	0.66	0.61	0.48	0.43	0.39	0.38
100	1.43	1.31	1.23	0.97	0.85	0.79	0.75
200	2.85	2.63	2.45	1.94	1.70	1.57	1.50
300	4.28	3.94	3.68	2.91	2.55	2.36	2.25
400	5.70	5.26	4.90	3.88	3.40	3.15	3.00
500	7.13	6.57	6.13	4.85	4.25	3.94	3.75
600	8.55	7.88	7.35	5.81	5.11	4.72	4.50
700	9.98	9.20	8.58	6.78	5.96	5.51	5.25
800	11.40	10.51	9.80	7.75	6.81	6.30	6.00
900	12.83	11.83	11.03	8.72	7.66	7.09	6.75
1000	14.26	13.14	12.26	9.69	8.51	7.87	7.50
2000	28.51	26.28	24.51	19.38	17.02	15.75	15.00
3000	42.77	39.42	36.77	29.07	25.53	23.62	22.50
4000	57.02	52.56	49.02	38.76	34.04	31.49	30.00
5000	71.28	65.70	61.28	48.46	42.55	39.36	37.50
6000	85.53	78.84	73.54	58.15	51.06	47.24	45.00
7000	99.79	91.98	85.79	67.84	59.57	55.11	52.50
8000	114.04	105.12	98.05	77.53	68.08	62.98	60.00
9000	128.30	118.26	110.30	87.22	76.59	70.86	67.50
10000	142.55	131.40	122.56	96.91	85.10	78.73	75.00
11000	156.81	144.54	134.82	106.60	93.61	86.60	82.50
12000	171.06	157.67	147.07	116.29	102.12	94.47	90.00
13000	185.32	170.81	159.33	125.99	110.63	102.35	97.50
14000	199.57	183.95	171.58	135.68	119.14	110.22	105.01
15000	213.83	197.09	183.84	145.37	127.65	118.09	112.51
16000	228.08	210.23	196.10	155.06	136.15	125.97	120.01
17000	242.34	223.37	208.35	164.75	144.66	133.84	127.51
18000	256.59	236.51	220.61	174.44	153.17	141.71	135.01
19000	270.85	249.65	232.86	184.13	161.68	149.58	142.51
20000	285.10	262.79	245.12	193.82	170.19	157.46	150.01
21000	299.36	275.93	257.38	203.52	178.70	165.33	157.51
22000	313.61	289.07	269.63	213.21	187.21	173.20	165.01
23000	327.87	302.21	281.89	222.90	195.72	181.07	172.51
24000	342.12	315.35	294.14	232.59	204.23	188.95	180.01
25000	356.38	328.49	306.40	242.28	212.74	196.82	187.51
26000	370.63	341.63	318.66	251.97	221.25	204.69	195.01
27000	384.89	354.77	330.91	261.66	229.76	212.57	202.51
28000	399.14	367.91	343.17	271.35	238.27	220.44	210.01
29000	413.40	381.05	355.42	281.05	246.78	228.31	217.51
30000	427.65	394.19	367.68	290.74	255.29	236.18	225.01
35000	498.93	459.88	428.96	339.19	297.84	275.55	262.51
40000	570.21	525.58	490.24	387.65	340.39	314.91	300.01
45000	641.48	591.28	551.52	436.11	382.94	354.28	337.52
50000	712.76	656.98	612.80	484.56	425.48	393.64	375.02
55000	784.03	722.68	674.08	533.02	468.03	433.00	412.52
60000	855.31	788.37	735.36	581.47	510.58	472.37	450.02
65000	926.58	854.07	796.64	629.93	553.13	511.73	487.52
70000	997.86	919.77	857.92	678.39	595.68	551.10	525.03
75000	1069.14	985.47	919.20	726.84	638.23	590.46	562.53
80000	1140.41	1051.16	980.48	775.30	680.77	629.83	600.03
85000	1211.69	1116.86	1041.76	823.75	723.32	669.19	637.53
90000	1282.96	1182.56	1103.04	872.21	765.87	708.55	675.03
95000	1354.24	1248.26	1164.32	920.67	808.42	747.92	712.54
100000	1425.51	1313.96	1225.60	969.12	850.97	787.28	750.04
200000	2851.03	2627.91	2451.19	1938.25	1701.94	1574.56	1500.07
300000	4276.54	3941.87	3676.79	2907.37	2552.90	2361.84	2250.11
400000	5702.06	5255.82	4902.39	3876.49	3403.87	3149.13	3000.15
500000	7127.57	6569.78	6127.98	4845.61	4254.84	3936.41	3750.19
1000000	14255.14	13139.55	12255.96	9691.23	8509.68	7872.81	7500.37

8.5%

MONTHLY PAYMENT
NECESSARY TO AMORTIZE A LOAN

Amortization Amount	1 Year	2 Years	3 Years	4 Years	5 Years	6 Years	7 Years
25	2.18	1.13	0.79	0.61	0.51	0.44	0.39
50	4.36	2.27	1.57	1.23	1.02	0.89	0.79
100	8.72	4.54	3.15	2.46	2.04	1.77	1.58
200	17.43	9.08	6.30	4.92	4.09	3.54	3.15
300	26.15	13.62	9.45	7.37	6.13	5.31	4.73
400	34.86	18.16	12.60	9.83	8.18	7.08	6.31
500	43.58	22.69	15.75	12.29	10.22	8.85	7.88
600	52.29	27.23	18.90	14.75	12.27	10.62	9.46
700	61.01	31.77	22.05	17.21	14.31	12.39	11.03
800	69.72	36.31	25.20	19.66	16.36	14.16	12.61
900	78.44	40.85	28.35	22.12	18.40	15.94	14.19
1000	87.15	45.39	31.50	24.58	20.45	17.71	15.76
2000	174.30	90.78	63.00	49.16	40.89	35.41	31.53
3000	261.46	136.17	94.50	73.74	61.34	53.12	47.29
4000	348.61	181.55	126.00	98.32	81.78	70.82	63.05
5000	435.76	226.94	157.50	122.90	102.23	88.53	78.81
6000	522.91	272.33	189.00	147.47	122.68	106.24	94.58
7000	610.06	317.72	220.50	172.05	143.12	123.94	110.34
8000	697.21	363.11	252.00	196.63	163.57	141.65	126.10
9000	784.37	408.50	283.50	221.21	184.01	159.36	141.87
10000	871.52	453.89	315.00	245.79	204.46	177.06	157.63
11000	958.67	499.27	346.50	270.37	224.90	194.77	173.39
12000	1045.82	544.66	378.00	294.95	245.35	212.47	189.15
13000	1132.97	590.05	409.49	319.53	265.80	230.18	204.92
14000	1220.13	635.44	440.99	344.11	286.24	247.89	220.68
15000	1307.28	680.83	472.49	368.69	306.69	265.59	236.44
16000	1394.43	726.22	503.99	393.27	327.13	283.30	252.20
17000	1481.58	771.61	535.49	417.84	347.58	301.01	267.97
18000	1568.73	816.99	566.99	442.42	368.03	318.71	283.73
19000	1655.89	862.38	598.49	467.00	388.47	336.42	299.49
20000	1743.04	907.77	629.99	491.58	408.92	354.12	315.26
21000	1830.19	953.16	661.49	516.16	429.36	371.83	331.02
22000	1917.34	998.55	692.99	540.74	449.81	389.54	346.78
23000	2004.49	1043.94	724.49	565.32	470.26	407.24	362.54
24000	2091.64	1089.33	755.99	589.90	490.70	424.95	378.31
25000	2178.80	1134.71	787.49	614.48	511.15	442.66	394.07
26000	2265.95	1180.10	818.99	639.06	531.59	460.36	409.83
27000	2353.10	1225.49	850.49	663.64	552.04	478.07	425.60
28000	2440.25	1270.88	881.99	688.21	572.48	495.77	441.36
29000	2527.40	1316.27	913.49	712.79	592.93	513.48	457.12
30000	2614.56	1361.66	944.99	737.37	613.38	531.19	472.88
35000	3050.31	1588.60	1102.49	860.27	715.61	619.72	551.70
40000	3486.07	1815.54	1259.98	983.16	817.84	708.25	630.51
45000	3921.83	2042.49	1417.48	1106.06	920.06	796.78	709.33
50000	4357.59	2269.43	1574.98	1228.95	1022.29	885.31	788.14
55000	4793.35	2496.37	1732.48	1351.85	1124.52	973.84	866.95
60000	5229.11	2723.32	1889.98	1474.75	1226.75	1062.37	945.77
65000	5664.87	2950.26	2047.47	1597.64	1328.98	1150.91	1024.58
70000	6100.63	3177.20	2204.97	1720.54	1431.21	1239.44	1103.40
75000	6536.39	3404.14	2362.47	1843.43	1533.44	1327.97	1182.21
80000	6972.15	3631.09	2519.97	1966.33	1635.67	1416.50	1261.02
85000	7407.91	3858.03	2677.47	2089.22	1737.90	1505.03	1339.84
90000	7843.67	4084.97	2834.96	2212.12	1840.13	1593.56	1418.65
95000	8279.43	4311.92	2992.46	2335.01	1942.36	1682.09	1497.47
100000	8715.19	4538.86	3149.96	2457.91	2044.59	1770.62	1576.28
200000	17430.37	9077.72	6299.92	4915.82	4089.18	3541.25	3152.56
300000	26145.56	13616.58	9449.88	7373.73	6133.77	5311.87	4728.84
400000	34860.74	18155.43	12599.84	9831.64	8178.36	7082.50	6305.12
500000	43575.93	22694.29	15749.80	12289.54	10222.94	8853.12	7881.40
1000000	87151.86	45388.58	31499.59	24579.09	20445.89	17706.24	15762.80

Amortization Amount	8 Years	9 Years	10 Years	15 Years	20 Years	25 Years	30 Years
25	0.36	0.33	0.31	0.24	0.21	0.20	0.19
50	0.72	0.66	0.62	0.49	0.43	0.40	0.38
100	1.43	1.32	1.23	0.98	0.86	0.80	0.76
200	2.86	2.64	2.46	1.95	1.72	1.59	1.52
300	4.30	3.96	3.70	2.93	2.58	2.39	2.28
400	5.73	5.28	4.93	3.90	3.43	3.18	3.03
500	7.16	6.60	6.16	4.88	4.29	3.98	3.79
600	8.59	7.92	7.39	5.86	5.15	4.77	4.55
700	10.02	9.24	8.62	6.83	6.01	5.57	5.31
800	11.45	10.56	9.86	7.81	6.87	6.36	6.07
900	12.89	11.88	11.09	8.79	7.73	7.16	6.83
1000	14.32	13.20	12.32	9.76	8.59	7.95	7.59
2000	28.63	26.41	24.64	19.52	17.17	15.91	15.17
3000	42.95	39.61	36.96	29.28	25.76	23.86	22.76
4000	57.27	52.81	49.28	39.05	34.34	31.81	30.34
5000	71.58	66.01	61.60	48.81	42.93	39.77	37.93
6000	85.90	79.22	73.92	58.57	51.51	47.72	45.51
7000	100.22	92.42	86.24	68.33	60.10	55.68	53.10
8000	114.54	105.62	98.56	78.09	68.68	63.63	60.68
9000	128.85	118.82	110.88	87.85	77.27	71.58	68.27
10000	143.17	132.03	123.20	97.62	85.86	79.54	75.85
11000	157.49	145.23	135.52	107.38	94.44	87.49	83.44
12000	171.80	158.43	147.84	117.14	103.03	95.44	91.02
13000	186.12	171.63	160.16	126.90	111.61	103.40	98.61
14000	200.44	184.84	172.48	136.66	120.20	111.35	106.20
15000	214.75	198.04	184.80	146.42	128.78	119.30	113.78
16000	229.07	211.24	197.12	156.19	137.37	127.26	121.37
17000	243.39	224.44	209.44	165.95	145.96	135.21	128.95
18000	257.70	237.65	221.76	175.71	154.54	143.17	136.54
19000	272.02	250.85	234.08	185.47	163.13	151.12	144.12
20000	286.34	264.05	246.40	195.23	171.71	159.07	151.71
21000	300.65	277.25	258.72	204.99	180.30	167.03	159.29
22000	314.97	290.46	271.05	214.75	188.88	174.98	166.88
23000	329.29	303.66	283.37	224.52	197.47	182.93	174.46
24000	343.61	316.86	295.69	234.28	206.05	190.89	182.05
25000	357.92	330.06	308.01	244.04	214.64	198.84	189.63
26000	372.24	343.27	320.33	253.80	223.22	206.79	197.22
27000	386.56	356.47	332.65	263.56	231.81	214.75	204.81
28000	400.87	369.67	344.97	273.32	240.40	222.70	212.39
29000	415.19	382.87	357.29	283.09	248.98	230.66	219.98
30000	429.51	396.08	369.61	292.85	257.57	238.61	227.56
35000	501.09	462.09	431.21	341.66	300.50	278.38	265.49
40000	572.68	528.10	492.81	390.46	343.42	318.15	303.42
45000	644.26	594.12	554.41	439.27	386.35	357.91	341.34
50000	715.84	660.13	616.01	488.08	429.28	397.68	379.27
55000	787.43	726.14	677.61	536.89	472.21	437.45	417.20
60000	859.01	792.15	739.21	585.69	515.14	477.22	455.12
65000	930.60	858.17	800.82	634.50	558.06	516.99	493.05
70000	1002.18	924.18	862.42	683.31	600.99	556.75	530.98
75000	1073.77	990.19	924.02	732.12	643.92	596.52	568.90
80000	1145.35	1056.21	985.62	780.93	686.85	636.29	606.83
85000	1216.94	1122.22	1047.22	829.73	729.78	676.06	644.76
90000	1288.52	1188.23	1108.82	878.54	772.70	715.83	682.69
95000	1360.10	1254.24	1170.42	927.35	815.63	755.60	720.61
100000	1431.69	1320.26	1232.02	976.16	858.56	795.36	758.54
200000	2863.38	2640.51	2464.05	1952.32	1717.12	1590.73	1517.08
300000	4295.07	3960.77	3696.07	2928.47	2575.68	2386.09	2275.62
400000	5726.76	5281.03	4928.09	3904.63	3434.24	3181.45	3034.16
500000	7158.45	6601.28	6160.12	4880.79	4292.80	3976.82	3792.70
1000000	14316.89	13202.56	12320.23	9761.58	8585.59	7953.64	7585.39

8.625%

MONTHLY PAYMENT
NECESSARY TO AMORTIZE A LOAN

Amortization Amount	1 Year	2 Years	3 Years	4 Years	5 Years	6 Years	7 Years
25	2.18	1.14	0.79	0.62	0.51	0.44	0.40
50	4.36	2.27	1.58	1.23	1.03	0.89	0.79
100	8.72	4.54	3.16	2.46	2.05	1.78	1.58
200	17.44	9.09	6.31	4.93	4.10	3.55	3.16
300	26.16	13.63	9.47	7.39	6.15	5.33	4.75
400	34.88	18.18	12.62	9.85	8.20	7.11	6.33
500	43.60	22.72	15.78	12.32	10.25	8.88	7.91
600	52.32	27.27	18.93	14.78	12.30	10.66	9.49
700	61.05	31.81	22.09	17.25	14.35	12.44	11.08
800	69.77	36.36	25.24	19.71	16.40	14.21	12.66
900	78.49	40.90	28.40	22.17	18.45	15.99	14.24
1000	87.21	45.44	31.56	24.64	20.50	17.77	15.82
2000	174.42	90.89	63.11	49.27	41.01	35.53	31.65
3000	261.62	136.33	94.67	73.91	61.51	53.30	47.47
4000	348.83	181.78	126.22	98.54	82.02	71.06	63.29
5000	436.04	227.22	157.78	123.18	102.52	88.83	79.12
6000	523.25	272.66	189.33	147.82	123.02	106.59	94.94
7000	610.45	318.11	220.89	172.45	143.53	124.36	110.76
8000	697.66	363.55	252.44	197.09	164.03	142.12	126.59
9000	784.87	408.99	284.00	221.72	184.54	159.89	142.41
10000	872.08	454.44	315.55	246.36	205.04	177.66	158.23
11000	959.29	499.88	347.11	271.00	225.54	195.42	174.06
12000	1046.49	545.33	378.67	295.63	246.05	213.19	189.88
13000	1133.70	590.77	410.22	320.27	266.55	230.95	205.70
14000	1220.91	636.21	441.78	344.90	287.06	248.72	221.53
15000	1308.12	681.66	473.33	369.54	307.56	266.48	237.35
16000	1395.32	727.10	504.89	394.18	328.06	284.25	253.17
17000	1482.53	772.54	536.44	418.81	348.57	302.01	269.00
18000	1569.74	817.99	568.00	443.45	369.07	319.78	284.82
19000	1656.95	863.43	599.55	468.08	389.58	337.55	300.64
20000	1744.15	908.88	631.11	492.72	410.08	355.31	316.47
21000	1831.36	954.32	662.67	517.36	430.58	373.08	332.29
22000	1918.57	999.76	694.22	541.99	451.09	390.84	348.11
23000	2005.78	1045.21	725.78	566.63	471.59	408.61	363.94
24000	2092.99	1090.65	757.33	591.26	492.10	426.37	379.76
25000	2180.19	1136.09	788.89	615.90	512.60	444.14	395.59
26000	2267.40	1181.54	820.44	640.54	533.10	461.91	411.41
27000	2354.61	1226.98	852.00	665.17	553.61	479.67	427.23
28000	2441.82	1272.43	883.55	689.81	574.11	497.44	443.06
29000	2529.02	1317.87	915.11	714.44	594.62	515.20	458.88
30000	2616.23	1363.31	946.66	739.08	615.12	532.97	474.70
35000	3052.27	1590.53	1104.44	862.26	717.64	621.80	553.82
40000	3488.31	1817.75	1262.22	985.44	820.16	710.62	632.94
45000	3924.35	2044.97	1420.00	1108.62	922.68	799.45	712.05
50000	4360.39	2272.19	1577.77	1231.80	1025.20	888.28	791.17
55000	4796.43	2499.41	1735.55	1354.98	1127.72	977.11	870.29
60000	5232.46	2726.63	1893.33	1478.16	1230.24	1065.93	949.40
65000	5668.50	2953.85	2051.11	1601.34	1332.76	1154.76	1028.52
70000	6104.54	3181.06	2208.88	1724.52	1435.28	1243.59	1107.64
75000	6540.58	3408.28	2366.66	1847.70	1537.80	1332.42	1186.76
80000	6976.62	3635.50	2524.44	1970.88	1640.32	1421.25	1265.87
85000	7412.66	3862.72	2682.22	2094.06	1742.84	1510.07	1344.99
90000	7848.70	4089.94	2839.99	2217.24	1845.36	1598.90	1424.11
95000	8284.73	4317.16	2997.77	2340.42	1947.88	1687.73	1503.22
100000	8720.77	4544.38	3155.55	2463.60	2050.40	1776.56	1582.34
200000	17441.55	9088.75	6311.10	4927.20	4100.80	3553.12	3164.69
300000	26162.32	13633.13	9466.65	7390.81	6151.20	5329.67	4747.02
400000	34883.09	18177.51	12622.19	9854.41	8201.60	7106.23	6329.36
500000	43603.87	22721.89	15777.74	12318.01	10252.00	8882.79	7911.70
1000000	87207.74	45443.77	31555.48	24636.02	20503.99	17765.58	15823.41

Amortization Amount	8 Years	9 Years	10 Years	15 Years	20 Years	25 Years	30 Years
25	0.36	0.33	0.31	0.25	0.22	0.20	0.19
50	0.72	0.66	0.62	0.49	0.43	0.40	0.38
100	1.44	1.33	1.24	0.98	0.87	0.80	0.77
200	2.88	2.65	2.48	1.97	1.73	1.61	1.53
300	4.31	3.98	3.72	2.95	2.60	2.41	2.30
400	5.75	5.31	4.95	3.93	3.46	3.21	3.07
500	7.19	6.63	6.19	4.92	4.33	4.02	3.84
600	8.63	7.96	7.43	5.90	5.20	4.82	4.60
700	10.07	9.29	8.67	6.88	6.06	5.62	5.37
800	11.50	10.61	9.91	7.87	6.93	6.43	6.14
900	12.94	11.94	11.15	8.85	7.80	7.23	6.90
1000	14.38	13.27	12.38	9.83	8.66	8.03	7.67
2000	28.76	26.53	24.77	19.66	17.32	16.07	15.34
3000	43.14	39.80	37.15	29.50	25.99	24.10	23.01
4000	57.52	53.06	49.54	39.33	34.65	32.14	30.68
5000	71.89	66.33	61.92	49.16	43.31	40.17	38.35
6000	86.27	79.59	74.31	58.99	51.97	48.21	46.02
7000	100.65	92.86	86.69	68.83	60.63	56.24	53.69
8000	115.03	106.13	99.08	78.66	69.29	64.28	61.37
9000	129.41	119.39	111.46	88.49	77.96	72.31	69.04
10000	143.79	132.66	123.85	98.32	86.62	80.35	76.71
11000	158.17	145.92	136.23	108.15	95.28	88.38	84.38
12000	172.55	159.19	148.62	117.99	103.94	96.42	92.05
13000	186.92	172.45	161.00	127.82	112.60	104.45	99.72
14000	201.30	185.72	173.39	137.65	121.26	112.49	107.39
15000	215.68	198.99	185.77	147.48	129.93	120.52	115.06
16000	230.06	212.25	198.15	157.31	138.59	128.56	122.73
17000	244.44	225.52	210.54	167.15	147.25	136.59	130.40
18000	258.82	238.78	222.92	176.98	155.91	144.63	138.07
19000	273.20	252.05	235.31	186.81	164.57	152.66	145.74
20000	287.58	265.31	247.69	196.64	173.24	160.69	153.41
21000	301.95	278.58	260.08	206.48	181.90	168.73	161.08
22000	316.33	291.85	272.46	216.31	190.56	176.76	168.76
23000	330.71	305.11	284.85	226.14	199.22	184.80	176.43
24000	345.09	318.38	297.23	235.97	207.88	192.83	184.10
25000	359.47	331.64	309.62	245.80	216.54	200.87	191.77
26000	373.85	344.91	322.00	255.64	225.21	208.90	199.44
27000	388.23	358.17	334.39	265.47	233.87	216.94	207.11
28000	402.61	371.44	346.77	275.30	242.53	224.97	214.78
29000	416.98	384.71	359.16	285.13	251.19	233.01	222.45
30000	431.36	397.97	371.54	294.96	259.85	241.04	230.12
35000	503.26	464.30	433.46	344.13	303.16	281.22	268.47
40000	575.15	530.63	495.39	393.29	346.47	321.39	306.83
45000	647.04	596.96	557.31	442.45	389.78	361.56	345.18
50000	718.94	663.29	619.23	491.61	433.09	401.74	383.54
55000	790.83	729.61	681.16	540.77	476.40	441.91	421.89
60000	862.73	795.94	743.08	589.93	519.71	482.08	460.24
65000	934.62	862.27	805.00	639.09	563.02	522.26	498.60
70000	1006.51	928.60	866.93	688.25	606.32	562.43	536.95
75000	1078.41	994.93	928.85	737.41	649.63	602.61	575.30
80000	1150.30	1061.26	990.77	786.57	692.94	642.78	613.66
85000	1222.20	1127.59	1052.70	835.73	736.25	682.95	652.01
90000	1294.09	1193.91	1114.62	884.89	779.56	723.13	690.36
95000	1365.98	1260.24	1176.54	934.05	822.87	763.30	728.72
100000	1437.88	1326.57	1238.47	983.22	866.18	803.47	767.07
200000	2875.75	2653.14	2476.93	1966.43	1732.35	1606.95	1534.14
300000	4313.63	3979.72	3715.40	2949.65	2598.53	2410.42	2301.21
400000	5751.50	5306.29	4953.86	3932.86	3464.71	3213.90	3068.28
500000	7189.39	6632.86	6192.33	4916.08	4330.89	4017.37	3835.35
1000000	14378.77	13265.72	12384.66	9832.15	8661.77	8034.75	7670.70

8.75%

Amortization Amount	1 Year	2 Years	3 Years	4 Years	5 Years	6 Years	7 Years
25	2.18	1.14	0.79	0.62	0.51	0.45	0.40
50	4.36	2.27	1.58	1.23	1.03	0.89	0.79
100	8.73	4.55	3.16	2.47	2.06	1.78	1.59
200	17.45	9.10	6.32	4.94	4.11	3.57	3.18
300	26.18	13.65	9.48	7.41	6.17	5.35	4.77
400	34.91	18.20	12.64	9.88	8.22	7.13	6.35
500	43.63	22.75	15.81	12.35	10.28	8.91	7.94
600	52.36	27.30	18.97	14.82	12.34	10.70	9.53
700	61.08	31.85	22.13	17.29	14.39	12.48	11.12
800	69.81	36.40	25.29	19.75	16.45	14.26	12.71
900	78.54	40.95	28.45	22.22	18.51	16.04	14.30
1000	87.26	45.50	31.61	24.69	20.56	17.83	15.88
2000	174.53	91.00	63.22	49.39	41.12	35.65	31.77
3000	261.79	136.50	94.83	74.08	61.69	53.48	47.65
4000	349.05	182.00	126.45	98.77	82.25	71.30	63.54
5000	436.32	227.49	158.06	123.47	102.81	89.13	79.42
6000	523.58	272.99	189.67	148.16	123.37	106.95	95.30
7000	610.85	318.49	221.28	172.85	143.94	124.78	111.19
8000	698.11	363.99	252.89	197.54	164.50	142.60	127.07
9000	785.37	409.49	284.50	222.24	185.06	160.43	142.96
10000	872.64	454.99	316.11	246.93	205.62	178.25	158.84
11000	959.90	500.49	347.73	271.62	226.18	196.08	174.73
12000	1047.16	545.99	379.34	296.32	246.75	213.90	190.61
13000	1134.43	591.49	410.95	321.01	267.31	231.73	206.49
14000	1221.69	636.99	442.56	345.70	287.87	249.55	222.38
15000	1308.95	682.48	474.17	370.40	308.43	267.38	238.26
16000	1396.22	727.98	505.78	395.09	328.99	285.20	254.15
17000	1483.48	773.48	537.39	419.78	349.56	303.03	270.03
18000	1570.74	818.98	569.01	444.47	370.12	320.85	285.91
19000	1658.01	864.48	600.62	469.17	390.68	338.68	301.80
20000	1745.27	909.98	632.23	493.86	411.24	356.50	317.68
21000	1832.54	955.48	663.84	518.55	431.81	374.33	333.57
22000	1919.80	1000.98	695.45	543.25	452.37	392.15	349.45
23000	2007.06	1046.48	727.06	567.94	472.93	409.98	365.33
24000	2094.33	1091.98	758.67	592.63	493.49	427.80	381.22
25000	2181.59	1137.47	790.29	617.33	514.05	445.63	397.10
26000	2268.85	1182.97	821.90	642.02	534.62	463.45	412.99
27000	2356.12	1228.47	853.51	666.71	555.18	481.28	428.87
28000	2443.38	1273.97	885.12	691.40	575.74	499.10	444.76
29000	2530.64	1319.47	916.73	716.10	596.30	516.93	460.64
30000	2617.91	1364.97	948.34	740.79	616.87	534.75	476.52
35000	3054.23	1592.46	1106.40	864.26	719.68	623.88	555.94
40000	3490.54	1819.96	1264.46	987.72	822.49	713.00	635.36
45000	3926.86	2047.45	1422.51	1111.19	925.30	802.13	714.79
50000	4363.18	2274.95	1580.57	1234.65	1028.11	891.25	794.21
55000	4799.50	2502.44	1738.63	1358.12	1130.92	980.38	873.63
60000	5235.82	2729.94	1896.68	1481.58	1233.73	1069.50	953.05
65000	5672.13	2957.43	2054.74	1605.05	1336.54	1158.63	1032.47
70000	6108.45	3184.93	2212.80	1728.51	1439.35	1247.75	1111.89
75000	6544.77	3412.42	2370.86	1851.98	1542.16	1336.88	1191.31
80000	6981.09	3639.92	2528.91	1975.44	1644.97	1426.00	1270.73
85000	7417.41	3867.41	2686.97	2098.91	1747.78	1515.13	1350.15
90000	7853.72	4094.91	2845.03	2222.37	1850.60	1604.25	1429.57
95000	8290.04	4322.40	3003.08	2345.84	1953.41	1693.38	1508.99
100000	8726.36	4549.90	3161.14	2469.30	2056.22	1782.50	1588.41
200000	17452.72	9099.80	6322.28	4938.60	4112.43	3565.00	3176.82
300000	26179.08	13649.69	9483.42	7407.90	6168.65	5347.50	4765.23
400000	34905.44	18199.59	12644.56	9877.20	8224.87	7130.00	6353.65
500000	43631.80	22749.49	15805.70	12346.50	10281.09	8912.50	7942.06
1000000	87263.61	45498.98	31611.40	24693.01	20562.17	17825.01	15884.11

Amortization Amount	8 Years	9 Years	10 Years	15 Years	20 Years	25 Years	30 Years
25	0.36	0.33	0.31	0.25	0.22	0.20	0.19
50	0.72	0.67	0.62	0.50	0.44	0.41	0.39
100	1.44	1.33	1.24	0.99	0.87	0.81	0.78
200	2.89	2.67	2.49	1.98	1.75	1.62	1.55
300	4.33	4.00	3.73	2.97	2.62	2.43	2.33
400	5.78	5.33	4.98	3.96	3.50	3.25	3.10
500	7.22	6.66	6.22	4.95	4.37	4.06	3.88
600	8.66	8.00	7.47	5.94	5.24	4.87	4.65
700	10.11	9.33	8.71	6.93	6.12	5.68	5.43
800	11.55	10.66	9.96	7.92	6.99	6.49	6.21
900	13.00	12.00	11.20	8.91	7.86	7.30	6.98
1000	14.44	13.33	12.45	9.90	8.74	8.12	7.76
2000	28.88	26.66	24.90	19.81	17.48	16.23	15.51
3000	43.32	39.99	37.35	29.71	26.21	24.35	23.27
4000	57.76	53.32	49.80	39.61	34.95	32.46	31.03
5000	72.20	66.65	62.25	49.51	43.69	40.58	38.78
6000	86.64	79.97	74.70	59.42	52.43	48.70	46.54
7000	101.09	93.30	87.14	69.32	61.17	56.81	54.29
8000	115.53	106.63	99.59	79.22	69.91	64.93	62.05
9000	129.97	119.96	112.04	89.13	78.64	73.05	69.81
10000	144.41	133.29	124.49	99.03	87.38	81.16	77.56
11000	158.85	146.62	136.94	108.93	96.12	89.28	85.32
12000	173.29	159.95	149.39	118.84	104.86	97.39	93.08
13000	187.73	173.28	161.84	128.74	113.60	105.51	100.83
14000	202.17	186.61	174.29	138.64	122.34	113.63	108.59
15000	216.61	199.94	186.74	148.54	131.07	121.74	116.34
16000	231.05	213.26	199.19	158.45	139.81	129.86	124.10
17000	245.49	226.59	211.64	168.35	148.55	137.97	131.86
18000	259.93	239.92	224.09	178.25	157.29	146.09	139.61
19000	274.37	253.25	236.54	188.16	166.03	154.21	147.37
20000	288.82	266.58	248.98	198.06	174.76	162.32	155.13
21000	303.26	279.91	261.43	207.96	183.50	170.44	162.88
22000	317.70	293.24	273.88	217.86	192.24	178.56	170.64
23000	332.14	306.57	286.33	227.77	200.98	186.67	178.39
24000	346.58	319.90	298.78	237.67	209.72	194.79	186.15
25000	361.02	333.23	311.23	247.57	218.46	202.90	193.91
26000	375.46	346.55	323.68	257.48	227.19	211.02	201.66
27000	389.90	359.88	336.13	267.38	235.93	219.14	209.42
28000	404.34	373.21	348.58	277.28	244.67	227.25	217.18
29000	418.78	386.54	361.03	287.19	253.41	235.37	224.93
30000	433.22	399.87	373.48	297.09	262.15	243.48	232.69
35000	505.43	466.52	435.72	346.60	305.84	284.06	271.47
40000	577.63	533.16	497.97	396.12	349.53	324.65	310.25
45000	649.83	599.81	560.22	445.63	393.22	365.23	349.03
50000	722.04	666.45	622.46	495.15	436.91	405.81	387.82
55000	794.24	733.10	684.71	544.66	480.60	446.39	426.60
60000	866.65	799.74	746.95	594.18	524.29	486.97	465.38
65000	938.65	866.39	809.20	643.69	567.98	527.55	504.16
70000	1010.85	933.03	871.45	693.21	611.68	568.13	542.94
75000	1083.06	999.68	933.69	742.72	655.37	608.71	581.72
80000	1155.26	1066.32	995.94	792.24	699.06	649.29	620.50
85000	1227.47	1132.97	1058.19	841.75	742.75	689.87	659.29
90000	1299.67	1199.61	1120.43	891.27	786.44	730.45	698.07
95000	1371.87	1266.26	1182.68	940.78	830.13	771.03	736.85
100000	1444.08	1332.90	1244.92	990.29	873.82	811.61	775.63
200000	2888.15	2665.80	2489.85	1980.59	1747.64	1623.23	1551.26
300000	4332.23	3998.70	3734.77	2970.88	2621.47	2434.84	2326.89
400000	5776.31	5331.60	4979.70	3961.18	3495.29	3246.46	3102.52
500000	7220.39	6664.51	6224.62	4951.47	4369.11	4058.07	3878.15
1000000	14440.77	13329.01	12449.24	9902.94	8738.22	8116.14	7756.30

8.875%

MONTHLY PAYMENT
NECESSARY TO AMORTIZE A LOAN

Amortization Amount	1 Year	2 Years	3 Years	4 Years	5 Years	6 Years	7 Years
25	2.18	1.14	0.79	0.62	0.52	0.45	0.40
50	4.37	2.28	1.58	1.24	1.03	0.89	0.80
100	8.73	4.56	3.17	2.48	2.06	1.79	1.59
200	17.48	9.11	6.33	4.95	4.12	3.58	3.19
300	26.20	13.67	9.50	7.43	6.19	5.37	4.78
400	34.93	18.22	12.67	9.90	8.25	7.15	6.38
500	43.66	22.78	15.83	12.38	10.31	8.94	7.97
600	52.39	27.33	19.00	14.85	12.37	10.73	9.57
700	61.12	31.89	22.17	17.33	14.43	12.52	11.16
800	69.86	36.44	25.33	19.80	16.50	14.31	12.76
900	78.59	41.00	28.50	22.28	18.56	16.10	14.35
1000	87.32	45.55	31.67	24.75	20.62	17.88	15.94
2000	174.64	91.11	63.33	49.50	41.24	35.77	31.89
3000	261.96	136.66	95.00	74.25	61.86	53.65	47.83
4000	349.28	182.22	126.67	99.00	82.48	71.54	63.78
5000	436.60	227.77	158.34	123.75	103.10	89.42	79.72
6000	523.92	273.33	190.00	148.50	123.72	107.31	95.67
7000	611.24	318.88	221.67	173.25	144.34	125.19	111.61
8000	698.56	364.43	253.34	198.00	164.96	143.08	127.56
9000	785.88	409.99	285.01	222.75	185.58	160.96	143.50
10000	873.19	455.54	316.67	247.50	206.20	178.85	159.45
11000	960.51	501.10	348.34	272.25	226.82	196.73	175.39
12000	1047.83	546.65	380.01	297.00	247.44	214.61	191.34
13000	1135.15	592.20	411.68	321.75	268.07	232.50	207.28
14000	1222.47	637.76	443.34	346.50	288.69	250.38	223.23
15000	1309.79	683.31	475.01	371.25	309.31	268.27	239.17
16000	1397.11	728.87	506.68	396.00	329.93	286.15	255.12
17000	1484.43	774.42	538.35	420.75	350.55	304.04	271.06
18000	1571.75	819.98	570.01	445.50	371.17	321.92	287.01
19000	1659.07	865.53	601.68	470.25	391.79	339.81	302.95
20000	1746.39	911.08	633.35	495.00	412.41	357.69	318.90
21000	1833.71	956.64	665.01	519.75	433.03	375.57	334.84
22000	1921.03	1002.19	696.68	544.50	453.65	393.46	350.79
23000	2008.35	1047.75	728.35	569.25	474.27	411.34	366.73
24000	2095.67	1093.30	760.02	594.00	494.89	429.23	382.68
25000	2182.99	1138.85	791.68	618.75	515.51	447.11	398.62
26000	2270.31	1184.41	823.35	643.50	536.13	465.00	414.57
27000	2357.63	1229.96	855.02	668.25	556.75	482.88	430.51
28000	2444.95	1275.52	886.69	693.00	577.37	500.77	446.46
29000	2532.26	1321.07	918.35	717.75	597.99	518.65	462.40
30000	2619.58	1366.63	950.02	742.50	618.61	536.54	478.35
35000	3056.18	1594.40	1108.36	866.25	721.71	625.96	558.07
40000	3492.78	1822.17	1266.69	990.00	824.82	715.38	637.80
45000	3929.38	2049.94	1425.03	1113.75	927.92	804.80	717.52
50000	4365.97	2277.71	1583.37	1237.50	1031.02	894.23	797.25
55000	4802.57	2505.48	1741.70	1361.25	1134.12	983.65	876.97
60000	5239.17	2733.25	1900.04	1485.00	1237.22	1073.07	956.70
65000	5675.77	2961.02	2058.38	1608.75	1340.33	1162.49	1036.42
70000	6112.36	3188.79	2216.72	1732.50	1443.43	1251.92	1116.14
75000	6548.96	3416.56	2375.05	1856.25	1546.53	1341.34	1195.87
80000	6985.56	3644.34	2533.39	1980.00	1649.63	1430.76	1275.59
85000	7422.16	3872.11	2691.73	2103.75	1752.74	1520.18	1355.32
90000	7858.75	4099.88	2850.06	2227.50	1855.84	1609.61	1435.04
95000	8295.35	4327.65	3008.40	2351.25	1958.94	1699.03	1514.77
100000	8731.95	4555.42	3166.74	2475.00	2062.04	1788.45	1594.49
200000	17463.89	9110.84	6333.47	4950.01	4124.08	3576.90	3188.99
300000	26195.84	13666.26	9500.21	7425.01	6186.12	5365.36	4783.48
400000	34927.79	18221.68	12666.94	9900.02	8248.17	7153.81	6377.97
500000	43659.74	22777.10	15833.68	12375.02	10310.21	8942.26	7972.46
1000000	87319.47	45554.19	31667.36	24750.04	20620.42	17884.52	15944.93

MONTHLY PAYMENT
NECESSARY TO AMORTIZE A LOAN **8.875%**

Amortization Amount	8 Years	9 Years	10 Years	15 Years	20 Years	25 Years	30 Years
25	0.36	0.33	0.31	0.25	0.22	0.20	0.20
50	0.73	0.67	0.63	0.50	0.44	0.41	0.39
100	1.45	1.34	1.25	1.00	0.88	0.82	0.78
200	2.90	2.68	2.50	1.99	1.76	1.64	1.57
300	4.35	4.02	3.75	2.99	2.64	2.46	2.35
400	5.80	5.36	5.01	3.99	3.53	3.28	3.14
500	7.25	6.70	6.26	4.99	4.41	4.10	3.92
600	8.70	8.04	7.51	5.98	5.29	4.92	4.71
700	10.15	9.37	8.76	6.98	6.17	5.74	5.49
800	11.60	10.71	10.01	7.98	7.05	6.56	6.27
900	13.05	12.05	11.26	8.98	7.93	7.38	7.06
1000	14.50	13.39	12.51	9.97	8.81	8.20	7.84
2000	29.01	26.78	25.03	19.95	17.63	16.40	15.68
3000	43.51	40.18	37.54	29.92	26.44	24.59	23.53
4000	58.01	53.57	50.06	39.90	35.26	32.79	31.37
5000	72.51	66.96	62.57	49.87	44.07	40.99	39.21
6000	87.02	80.35	75.08	59.84	52.89	49.19	47.05
7000	101.52	93.75	87.60	69.82	61.70	57.38	54.90
8000	116.02	107.14	100.11	79.79	70.52	65.58	62.74
9000	130.53	120.53	112.63	89.77	79.33	73.78	70.58
10000	145.03	133.92	125.14	99.74	88.15	81.98	78.42
11000	159.53	147.32	137.65	109.71	96.96	90.18	86.26
12000	174.03	160.71	150.17	119.69	105.78	98.37	94.11
13000	188.54	174.10	162.68	129.66	114.59	106.57	101.95
14000	203.04	187.49	175.20	139.64	123.41	114.77	109.79
15000	217.54	200.89	187.71	149.61	132.22	122.97	117.63
16000	232.05	214.28	200.22	159.58	141.04	131.17	125.47
17000	246.55	227.67	212.74	169.56	149.85	139.36	133.32
18000	261.05	241.06	225.25	179.53	158.67	147.56	141.16
19000	275.55	254.46	237.77	189.51	167.48	155.76	149.00
20000	290.06	267.85	250.28	199.48	176.30	163.96	156.84
21000	304.56	281.24	262.79	209.45	185.11	172.15	164.69
22000	319.06	294.63	275.31	219.43	193.93	180.35	172.53
23000	333.57	308.03	287.82	229.40	202.74	188.55	180.37
24000	348.07	321.42	300.34	239.37	211.56	196.75	188.21
25000	362.57	334.81	312.85	249.35	220.37	204.95	196.05
26000	377.08	348.20	325.36	259.32	229.19	213.14	203.90
27000	391.58	361.60	337.88	269.30	238.00	221.34	211.74
28000	406.08	374.99	350.39	279.27	246.82	229.54	219.58
29000	420.58	388.38	362.91	289.24	255.63	237.74	227.42
30000	435.09	401.77	375.42	299.22	264.45	245.93	235.27
35000	507.60	468.74	437.99	349.09	308.52	286.92	274.48
40000	580.12	535.70	500.56	398.96	352.60	327.91	313.69
45000	652.63	602.66	563.13	448.83	396.67	368.90	352.90
50000	725.14	669.62	625.70	498.70	440.75	409.89	392.11
55000	797.66	736.58	688.27	548.57	484.82	450.88	431.32
60000	870.17	803.55	750.84	598.44	528.90	491.87	470.53
65000	942.69	870.51	813.41	648.31	572.97	532.86	509.74
70000	1015.20	937.47	875.98	698.18	617.04	573.85	548.95
75000	1087.72	1004.43	938.55	748.05	661.12	614.84	588.16
80000	1160.23	1071.40	1001.12	797.92	705.19	655.83	627.37
85000	1232.75	1138.36	1063.69	847.79	749.27	696.81	666.59
90000	1305.26	1205.32	1126.26	897.66	793.34	737.80	705.80
95000	1377.77	1272.28	1188.83	947.53	837.42	778.79	745.01
100000	1450.29	1339.24	1251.40	997.40	881.49	819.78	784.22
200000	2900.58	2678.49	2502.79	1994.79	1762.99	1639.56	1568.44
300000	4350.87	4017.73	3754.19	2992.19	2644.48	2459.35	2352.65
400000	5801.16	5356.98	5005.59	3989.58	3525.97	3279.13	3136.87
500000	7251.45	6696.22	6256.99	4986.98	4407.46	4098.91	3921.09
1000000	14502.89	13392.44	12513.97	9973.96	8814.93	8197.82	7842.18

81

9%

Amortization Amount	1 Year	2 Years	3 Years	4 Years	5 Years	6 Years	7 Years
25	2.18	1.14	0.79	0.62	0.52	0.45	0.40
50	4.37	2.28	1.59	1.24	1.03	0.90	0.80
100	8.74	4.56	3.17	2.48	2.07	1.79	1.60
200	17.48	9.12	6.34	4.96	4.14	3.59	3.20
300	26.21	13.68	9.52	7.44	6.20	5.38	4.80
400	34.95	18.24	12.69	9.92	8.27	7.18	6.40
500	43.69	22.80	15.86	12.40	10.34	8.97	8.00
600	52.43	27.37	19.03	14.88	12.41	10.77	9.60
700	61.16	31.93	22.21	17.36	14.48	12.56	11.20
800	69.90	36.49	25.38	19.85	16.54	14.36	12.80
900	78.64	41.05	28.55	22.33	18.61	16.15	14.41
1000	87.38	45.61	31.72	24.81	20.68	17.94	16.01
2000	174.75	91.22	63.45	49.61	41.36	35.89	32.01
3000	262.13	136.83	95.17	74.42	62.04	53.83	48.02
4000	349.50	182.44	126.89	99.23	82.71	71.78	64.02
5000	436.88	228.05	158.62	124.04	103.39	89.72	80.03
6000	524.25	273.66	190.34	148.84	124.07	107.66	96.04
7000	611.63	319.27	222.06	173.65	144.75	125.61	112.04
8000	699.00	364.88	253.79	198.46	165.43	143.55	128.05
9000	786.38	410.48	285.51	223.26	186.11	161.50	144.05
10000	873.75	456.09	317.23	248.07	206.79	179.44	160.06
11000	961.13	501.70	348.96	272.88	227.47	197.39	176.06
12000	1048.50	547.31	380.68	297.69	248.14	215.33	192.07
13000	1135.88	592.92	412.40	322.49	268.82	233.27	208.08
14000	1223.25	638.53	444.13	347.30	289.50	251.22	224.08
15000	1310.63	684.14	475.85	372.11	310.18	269.16	240.09
16000	1398.01	729.75	507.57	396.91	330.86	287.11	256.09
17000	1485.38	775.36	539.30	421.72	351.54	305.05	272.10
18000	1572.76	820.97	571.02	446.53	372.22	322.99	288.11
19000	1660.13	866.58	602.74	471.34	392.90	340.94	304.11
20000	1747.51	912.19	634.47	496.14	413.57	358.88	320.12
21000	1834.88	957.80	666.19	520.95	434.25	376.83	336.12
22000	1922.26	1003.41	697.91	545.76	454.93	394.77	352.13
23000	2009.63	1049.02	729.64	570.56	475.61	412.71	368.13
24000	2097.01	1094.63	761.36	595.37	496.29	430.66	384.14
25000	2184.38	1140.24	793.08	620.18	516.97	448.60	400.15
26000	2271.76	1185.84	824.81	644.99	537.65	466.55	416.15
27000	2359.13	1231.45	856.53	669.79	558.33	484.49	432.16
28000	2446.51	1277.06	888.25	694.60	579.00	502.44	448.16
29000	2533.88	1322.67	919.98	719.41	599.68	520.38	464.17
30000	2621.26	1368.28	951.70	744.21	620.36	538.32	480.18
35000	3058.14	1596.33	1110.32	868.25	723.76	628.04	560.20
40000	3495.01	1824.38	1268.93	992.28	827.15	717.77	640.23
45000	3931.89	2052.42	1427.55	1116.32	930.54	807.49	720.26
50000	4368.77	2280.47	1586.17	1240.36	1033.94	897.21	800.29
55000	4805.64	2508.52	1744.78	1364.39	1137.33	986.93	880.32
60000	5242.52	2736.57	1903.40	1488.43	1240.72	1076.65	960.35
65000	5679.40	2964.61	2062.02	1612.46	1344.12	1166.37	1040.38
70000	6116.27	3192.66	2220.63	1736.50	1447.51	1256.09	1120.41
75000	6553.15	3420.71	2379.25	1860.53	1550.90	1345.81	1200.44
80000	6990.03	3648.75	2537.87	1984.57	1654.30	1435.53	1280.47
85000	7426.90	3876.80	2696.48	2108.61	1757.69	1525.25	1360.50
90000	7863.78	4104.85	2855.10	2232.64	1861.09	1614.97	1440.53
95000	8300.66	4332.89	3013.72	2356.68	1964.48	1704.69	1520.56
100000	8737.53	4560.94	3172.33	2480.71	2067.87	1794.41	1600.58
200000	17475.07	9121.88	6344.67	4961.42	4135.75	3588.83	3201.17
300000	26212.60	13682.83	9517.00	7442.14	6203.62	5383.24	4801.75
400000	34950.13	18243.77	12689.34	9922.85	8271.49	7177.65	6402.34
500000	43687.66	22804.71	15861.67	12403.56	10339.36	8972.06	8002.92
1000000	87375.33	45609.42	31723.34	24807.12	20678.73	17944.13	16005.84

Amortization Amount	8 Years	9 Years	10 Years	15 Years	20 Years	25 Years	30 Years
25	0.36	0.34	0.31	0.25	0.22	0.21	0.20
50	0.73	0.67	0.63	0.50	0.44	0.41	0.40
100	1.46	1.35	1.28	1.00	0.89	0.83	0.79
200	2.91	2.69	2.52	2.01	1.78	1.66	1.59
300	4.37	4.04	3.77	3.01	2.67	2.48	2.38
400	5.83	5.38	5.03	4.02	3.56	3.31	3.17
500	7.28	6.73	6.29	5.02	4.45	4.14	3.96
600	8.74	8.07	7.55	6.03	5.34	4.97	4.76
700	10.20	9.42	8.81	7.03	6.22	5.80	5.55
800	11.65	10.76	10.06	8.04	7.11	6.62	6.34
900	13.11	12.11	11.32	9.04	8.00	7.45	7.14
1000	14.57	13.46	12.58	10.05	8.89	8.28	7.93
2000	29.13	26.91	25.16	20.09	17.78	16.56	15.86
3000	43.70	40.37	37.74	30.14	26.68	24.84	23.78
4000	58.26	53.82	50.32	40.18	35.57	33.12	31.71
5000	72.83	67.28	62.89	50.23	44.46	41.40	39.64
6000	87.39	80.74	75.47	60.27	53.35	49.68	47.57
7000	101.96	94.19	88.05	70.32	62.24	57.96	55.50
8000	116.52	107.65	100.63	80.36	71.14	66.24	63.43
9000	131.09	121.10	113.21	90.41	80.03	74.52	71.35
10000	145.65	134.56	125.79	100.45	88.92	82.80	79.28
11000	160.22	148.02	138.37	110.50	97.81	91.08	87.21
12000	174.78	161.47	150.95	120.54	106.70	99.36	95.14
13000	189.35	174.93	163.53	130.59	115.59	107.64	103.07
14000	203.91	188.38	176.10	140.63	124.49	115.92	111.00
15000	218.48	201.84	188.68	150.68	133.38	124.20	118.92
16000	233.04	215.30	201.26	160.72	142.27	132.48	126.85
17000	247.61	228.75	213.84	170.77	151.16	140.76	134.78
18000	262.17	242.21	226.42	180.81	160.05	149.04	142.71
19000	276.74	255.66	239.00	190.86	168.95	157.32	150.64
20000	291.30	269.12	251.58	200.90	177.84	165.60	158.57
21000	305.87	282.58	264.16	210.95	186.73	173.88	166.49
22000	320.43	296.03	276.73	220.99	195.62	182.16	174.42
23000	335.00	309.49	289.31	231.04	204.51	190.43	182.35
24000	349.56	322.94	301.89	241.08	213.41	198.71	190.28
25000	364.13	336.40	314.47	251.13	222.30	206.99	198.21
26000	378.69	349.86	327.05	261.17	231.19	215.27	206.14
27000	393.26	363.31	339.63	271.22	240.08	223.55	214.06
28000	407.82	376.77	352.21	281.27	248.97	231.83	221.99
29000	422.39	390.22	364.79	291.31	257.86	240.11	229.92
30000	436.95	403.68	377.37	301.36	266.76	248.39	237.85
35000	509.78	470.96	440.26	351.58	311.22	289.79	277.49
40000	582.61	538.24	503.15	401.81	355.68	331.19	317.13
45000	655.43	605.52	566.05	452.03	400.14	372.59	356.77
50000	728.26	672.80	628.94	502.26	444.59	413.99	396.42
55000	801.08	740.08	691.84	552.49	489.05	455.39	436.06
60000	873.91	807.36	754.73	602.71	533.51	496.79	475.70
65000	946.73	874.64	817.63	652.94	577.97	538.19	515.34
70000	1019.56	941.92	880.52	703.16	622.43	579.58	554.98
75000	1092.39	1009.20	943.41	753.39	666.89	620.98	594.62
80000	1165.21	1076.48	1006.31	803.62	711.35	662.38	634.27
85000	1238.04	1143.76	1069.20	853.84	755.81	703.78	673.91
90000	1310.86	1211.04	1132.10	904.07	800.27	745.18	713.55
95000	1383.69	1278.32	1194.99	954.29	844.73	786.58	753.19
100000	1456.51	1345.60	1257.89	1004.52	889.19	827.98	792.83
200000	2913.03	2691.20	2515.77	2009.04	1778.38	1655.95	1585.67
300000	4369.54	4036.80	3773.66	3013.56	2667.57	2483.93	2378.50
400000	5826.05	5382.40	5031.54	4018.08	3556.76	3311.91	3171.33
500000	7282.57	6728.00	6289.43	5022.59	4445.95	4139.89	3964.16
1000000	14565.14	13456.01	12578.86	10045.19	8891.89	8279.77	7928.33

9.125%

MONTHLY PAYMENT
NECESSARY TO AMORTIZE A LOAN

Amortization Amount	1 Year	2 Years	3 Years	4 Years	5 Years	6 Years	7 Years
25	2.19	1.14	0.79	0.62	0.52	0.45	0.40
50	4.37	2.28	1.59	1.24	1.04	0.90	0.80
100	8.74	4.57	3.18	2.49	2.07	1.80	1.61
200	17.49	9.13	6.36	4.97	4.15	3.60	3.21
300	26.23	13.70	9.53	7.46	6.22	5.40	4.82
400	34.97	18.27	12.71	9.95	8.29	7.20	6.43
500	43.72	22.83	15.89	12.43	10.37	9.00	8.03
600	52.46	27.40	19.07	14.92	12.44	10.80	9.64
700	61.20	31.97	22.25	17.40	14.52	12.60	11.25
800	69.94	36.53	25.42	19.89	16.59	14.40	12.85
900	78.69	41.10	28.60	22.38	18.66	16.20	14.46
1000	87.43	45.66	31.78	24.86	20.74	18.00	16.07
2000	174.86	91.33	63.56	49.73	41.47	36.01	32.13
3000	262.29	136.99	95.34	74.59	62.21	54.01	48.20
4000	349.72	182.66	127.12	99.46	82.95	72.02	64.27
5000	437.16	228.32	158.90	124.32	103.69	90.02	80.33
6000	524.59	273.99	190.68	149.19	124.42	108.02	96.40
7000	612.02	319.65	222.46	174.05	145.16	126.03	112.47
8000	699.45	365.32	254.23	198.91	165.90	144.03	128.53
9000	786.88	410.98	286.01	223.78	186.63	162.03	144.60
10000	874.31	456.65	317.79	248.64	207.37	180.04	160.67
11000	961.74	502.31	349.57	273.51	228.11	198.04	176.74
12000	1049.17	547.98	381.35	298.37	248.85	216.05	192.80
13000	1136.61	593.64	413.13	323.24	269.58	234.05	208.87
14000	1224.04	639.31	444.91	348.10	290.32	252.05	224.94
15000	1311.47	684.97	476.69	372.96	311.06	270.06	241.00
16000	1398.90	730.63	508.47	397.83	331.79	288.06	257.07
17000	1486.33	776.30	540.25	422.69	352.53	306.06	273.14
18000	1573.76	821.96	572.03	447.56	373.27	324.07	289.20
19000	1661.19	867.63	603.81	472.42	394.01	342.07	305.27
20000	1748.62	913.29	635.59	497.29	414.74	360.08	321.34
21000	1836.05	958.96	667.37	522.15	435.48	378.08	337.40
22000	1923.49	1004.62	699.15	547.01	456.22	396.08	353.47
23000	2010.92	1050.29	730.93	571.88	476.95	414.09	369.54
24000	2098.35	1095.95	762.70	596.74	497.69	432.09	385.60
25000	2185.78	1141.62	794.48	621.61	518.43	450.10	401.67
26000	2273.21	1187.28	826.26	646.47	539.16	468.10	417.74
27000	2360.64	1232.95	858.04	671.33	559.90	486.10	433.81
28000	2448.07	1278.61	889.82	696.20	580.64	504.11	449.87
29000	2535.50	1324.28	921.60	721.06	601.38	522.11	465.94
30000	2622.94	1369.94	953.38	745.93	622.11	540.11	482.01
35000	3060.09	1598.26	1112.28	870.25	725.80	630.13	562.34
40000	3497.25	1826.59	1271.17	994.57	829.48	720.15	642.67
45000	3934.40	2054.91	1430.07	1118.89	933.17	810.17	723.01
50000	4371.56	2283.23	1588.97	1243.21	1036.86	900.19	803.34
55000	4808.71	2511.56	1747.86	1367.53	1140.54	990.21	883.68
60000	5245.87	2739.88	1906.76	1491.86	1244.23	1080.23	964.01
65000	5683.03	2968.20	2065.66	1616.18	1347.91	1170.25	1044.35
70000	6120.18	3196.53	2224.56	1740.50	1451.60	1260.27	1124.68
75000	6557.34	3424.85	2383.45	1864.82	1555.28	1350.29	1205.01
80000	6994.49	3653.17	2542.35	1989.14	1658.97	1440.31	1285.35
85000	7431.65	3881.50	2701.25	2113.46	1762.65	1530.32	1365.68
90000	7868.81	4109.82	2860.14	2237.78	1866.34	1620.34	1446.02
95000	8305.96	4338.14	3019.04	2362.10	1970.03	1710.36	1526.35
100000	8743.12	4566.47	3177.94	2486.43	2073.71	1800.38	1606.69
200000	17486.23	9132.93	6355.87	4972.85	4147.42	3600.76	3213.37
300000	26229.35	13699.40	9533.81	7459.28	6221.13	5401.14	4820.06
400000	34972.47	18265.86	12711.74	9945.70	8294.84	7201.53	6426.75
500000	43715.59	22832.33	15889.68	12432.13	10368.56	9001.91	8033.43
1000000	87431.17	45664.66	31779.36	24864.26	20737.11	18003.81	16066.87

Amortization Amount	8 Years	9 Years	10 Years	15 Years	20 Years	25 Years	30 Years
25	0.37	0.34	0.32	0.25	0.22	0.21	0.20
50	0.73	0.68	0.63	0.51	0.45	0.42	0.40
100	1.46	1.35	1.28	1.01	0.90	0.84	0.80
200	2.93	2.70	2.53	2.02	1.79	1.67	1.60
300	4.39	4.06	3.79	3.03	2.69	2.51	2.40
400	5.85	5.41	5.06	4.05	3.59	3.34	3.21
500	7.31	6.76	6.32	5.06	4.48	4.18	4.01
600	8.78	8.11	7.59	6.07	5.38	5.02	4.81
700	10.24	9.46	8.85	7.08	6.28	5.85	5.61
800	11.70	10.82	10.12	8.09	7.18	6.69	6.41
900	13.16	12.17	11.38	9.10	8.07	7.53	7.21
1000	14.63	13.52	12.64	10.12	8.97	8.36	8.01
2000	29.25	27.04	25.29	20.23	17.94	16.72	16.03
3000	43.88	40.56	37.93	30.35	26.91	25.09	24.04
4000	58.51	54.08	50.58	40.47	35.88	33.45	32.06
5000	73.14	67.60	63.22	50.58	44.85	41.81	40.07
6000	87.76	81.12	75.86	60.70	53.81	50.17	48.09
7000	102.39	94.64	88.51	70.82	62.78	58.53	56.10
8000	117.02	108.16	101.15	80.93	71.75	66.90	64.12
9000	131.65	121.68	113.80	91.05	80.72	75.26	72.13
10000	146.27	135.20	126.44	101.17	89.69	83.62	80.15
11000	160.90	148.72	139.08	111.28	98.66	91.98	88.16
12000	175.53	162.24	151.73	121.40	107.63	100.34	96.18
13000	190.16	175.76	164.37	131.52	116.60	108.71	104.19
14000	204.78	189.28	177.01	141.63	125.57	117.07	112.21
15000	219.41	202.80	189.66	151.75	134.54	125.43	120.22
16000	234.04	216.32	202.30	161.87	143.51	133.79	128.24
17000	248.67	229.84	214.95	171.98	152.48	142.15	136.25
18000	263.29	243.35	227.59	182.10	161.44	150.52	144.27
19000	277.92	256.87	240.23	192.22	170.41	158.88	152.28
20000	292.55	270.39	252.88	202.33	179.38	167.24	160.29
21000	307.18	283.91	265.52	212.45	188.35	175.60	168.31
22000	321.80	297.43	278.17	222.57	197.32	183.96	176.32
23000	336.43	310.95	290.81	232.68	206.29	192.33	184.34
24000	351.06	324.47	303.45	242.80	215.26	200.69	192.35
25000	365.69	337.99	316.10	252.92	224.23	209.05	200.37
26000	380.31	351.51	328.74	263.03	233.20	217.41	208.38
27000	394.94	365.03	341.39	273.15	242.17	225.77	216.40
28000	409.57	378.55	354.03	283.27	251.14	234.14	224.41
29000	424.20	392.07	366.67	293.38	260.10	242.50	232.43
30000	438.82	405.59	379.32	303.50	269.07	250.86	240.44
35000	511.96	473.19	442.54	354.08	313.92	292.67	280.52
40000	585.10	540.79	505.76	404.67	358.76	334.48	320.59
45000	658.24	608.39	568.98	455.25	403.61	376.29	360.66
50000	731.37	675.99	632.19	505.83	448.46	418.10	400.74
55000	804.51	743.58	695.41	556.41	493.30	459.91	440.81
60000	877.65	811.18	758.63	607.00	538.15	501.72	480.88
65000	950.79	878.78	821.85	657.58	582.99	543.53	520.96
70000	1023.92	946.38	885.07	708.16	627.84	585.34	561.03
75000	1097.06	1013.98	948.29	758.75	672.68	627.15	601.11
80000	1170.20	1081.58	1011.51	809.33	717.53	668.96	641.18
85000	1243.34	1149.18	1074.73	859.91	762.38	710.77	681.25
90000	1316.47	1216.77	1137.95	910.50	807.22	752.58	721.33
95000	1389.61	1284.37	1201.17	961.08	852.07	794.39	761.40
100000	1462.75	1351.97	1264.39	1011.66	896.91	836.20	801.47
200000	2925.50	2703.94	2528.78	2023.33	1793.82	1672.40	1602.95
300000	4388.25	4055.91	3793.17	3034.99	2690.74	2508.60	2404.42
400000	5851.00	5407.89	5057.56	4046.65	3587.65	3344.80	3205.90
500000	7313.75	6759.86	6321.95	5058.32	4484.56	4181.00	4007.37
1000000	14627.50	13519.71	12643.89	10116.64	8969.12	8362.00	8014.74

9.25%

Amortization Amount	1 Year	2 Years	3 Years	4 Years	5 Years	6 Years	7 Years
25	2.19	1.14	0.80	0.62	0.52	0.45	0.40
50	4.37	2.29	1.59	1.25	1.04	0.90	0.81
100	8.75	4.57	3.18	2.49	2.08	1.81	1.61
200	17.50	9.14	6.37	4.98	4.16	3.81	3.23
300	26.25	13.72	9.55	7.48	6.24	5.42	4.84
400	34.99	18.29	12.73	9.97	8.32	7.23	6.45
500	43.74	22.86	15.92	12.46	10.40	9.03	8.06
600	52.49	27.43	19.10	14.95	12.48	10.84	9.68
700	61.24	32.00	22.28	17.45	14.56	12.64	11.29
800	69.99	36.58	25.47	19.94	16.64	14.45	12.90
900	78.74	41.15	28.65	22.43	18.72	16.26	14.52
1000	87.49	45.72	31.84	24.92	20.80	18.06	16.13
2000	174.97	91.44	63.67	49.84	41.59	36.13	32.26
3000	262.46	137.16	95.51	74.76	62.39	54.19	48.38
4000	349.95	182.88	127.34	99.69	83.18	72.25	64.51
5000	437.44	228.60	159.18	124.61	103.98	90.32	80.64
6000	524.92	274.32	191.01	149.53	124.77	108.38	96.77
7000	612.41	320.04	222.85	174.45	145.57	126.45	112.90
8000	699.90	365.76	254.68	199.37	166.36	144.51	129.02
9000	787.38	411.48	286.52	224.29	187.16	162.57	145.15
10000	874.87	457.20	318.35	249.21	207.96	180.64	161.28
11000	962.36	502.92	350.19	274.14	228.75	198.70	177.41
12000	1049.84	548.64	382.02	299.06	249.55	216.76	193.54
13000	1137.33	594.36	413.86	323.98	270.34	234.83	209.66
14000	1224.82	640.08	445.70	348.90	291.14	252.89	225.79
15000	1312.31	685.80	477.53	373.82	311.93	270.95	241.92
16000	1399.79	731.52	509.37	398.74	332.73	289.02	258.05
17000	1487.28	777.24	541.20	423.66	353.52	307.08	274.18
18000	1574.77	822.96	573.04	448.59	374.32	325.14	290.30
19000	1662.25	868.68	604.87	473.51	395.12	343.21	306.43
20000	1749.74	914.40	636.71	498.43	415.91	361.27	322.56
21000	1837.23	960.12	668.54	523.35	436.71	379.34	338.69
22000	1924.71	1005.84	700.38	548.27	457.50	397.40	354.82
23000	2012.20	1051.56	732.21	573.19	478.30	415.46	370.94
24000	2099.69	1097.28	764.05	598.11	499.09	433.53	387.07
25000	2187.18	1143.00	795.89	623.04	519.89	451.59	403.20
26000	2274.66	1188.72	827.72	647.96	540.68	469.65	419.33
27000	2362.15	1234.44	859.56	672.88	561.48	487.72	435.46
28000	2449.64	1280.16	891.39	697.80	582.28	505.78	451.58
29000	2537.12	1325.88	923.23	722.72	603.07	523.84	467.71
30000	2624.61	1371.60	955.06	747.64	623.87	541.91	483.84
35000	3062.05	1600.20	1114.24	872.25	727.84	632.23	564.48
40000	3499.48	1828.80	1273.42	996.86	831.82	722.54	645.12
45000	3936.92	2057.40	1432.59	1121.46	935.80	812.86	725.76
50000	4374.35	2286.00	1591.77	1246.07	1039.78	903.18	806.40
55000	4811.79	2514.59	1750.95	1370.68	1143.76	993.50	887.04
60000	5249.22	2743.19	1910.12	1495.29	1247.73	1083.82	967.68
65000	5686.66	2971.79	2069.30	1619.89	1351.71	1174.13	1048.32
70000	6124.09	3200.39	2228.48	1744.50	1455.69	1264.45	1128.96
75000	6561.53	3428.99	2387.66	1869.11	1559.67	1354.77	1209.60
80000	6998.96	3657.59	2546.83	1993.72	1663.65	1445.09	1290.24
85000	7436.40	3886.19	2706.01	2118.32	1767.62	1535.41	1370.88
90000	7873.83	4114.79	2865.19	2242.93	1871.60	1625.72	1451.52
95000	8311.27	4343.39	3024.36	2367.54	1975.58	1716.04	1532.16
100000	8748.70	4571.99	3183.54	2492.14	2079.56	1806.36	1612.80
200000	17497.40	9143.98	6367.08	4984.29	4159.11	3612.72	3225.60
300000	26246.10	13715.97	9550.62	7476.43	6238.67	5419.08	4838.40
400000	34994.81	18287.96	12734.16	9968.58	8318.23	7225.44	6451.20
500000	43743.51	22859.95	15917.70	12460.72	10397.78	9031.79	8064.00
1000000	87487.01	45719.91	31835.41	24921.44	20795.56	18063.59	16127.99

Amortization Amount	8 Years	9 Years	10 Years	15 Years	20 Years	25 Years	30 Years
25	0.37	0.34	0.32	0.25	0.23	0.21	0.20
50	0.73	0.68	0.64	0.51	0.45	0.42	0.41
100	1.47	1.36	1.27	1.02	0.90	0.84	0.81
200	2.94	2.72	2.54	2.04	1.81	1.69	1.62
300	4.41	4.08	3.81	3.06	2.71	2.53	2.43
400	5.88	5.43	5.08	4.08	3.62	3.38	3.24
500	7.34	6.79	6.35	5.09	4.52	4.22	4.05
600	8.81	8.15	7.63	6.11	5.43	5.07	4.86
700	10.28	9.51	8.90	7.13	6.33	5.91	5.67
800	11.75	10.87	10.17	8.15	7.24	6.76	6.48
900	13.22	12.23	11.44	9.17	8.14	7.60	7.29
1000	14.69	13.58	12.71	10.19	9.05	8.44	8.10
2000	29.38	27.17	25.42	20.38	18.09	16.89	16.20
3000	44.07	40.75	38.13	30.56	27.14	25.33	24.30
4000	58.76	54.33	50.84	40.75	36.19	33.78	32.41
5000	73.45	67.92	63.55	50.94	45.23	42.22	40.51
6000	88.14	81.50	76.25	61.13	54.28	50.67	48.61
7000	102.83	95.08	88.96	71.32	63.33	59.11	56.71
8000	117.52	108.67	101.67	81.51	72.37	67.56	64.81
9000	132.21	122.25	114.38	91.69	81.42	76.00	72.91
10000	146.90	135.84	127.09	101.88	90.47	84.44	81.01
11000	161.59	149.42	139.80	112.07	99.51	92.89	89.12
12000	176.28	163.00	152.51	122.26	108.56	101.33	97.22
13000	190.97	176.59	165.22	132.45	117.61	109.78	105.32
14000	205.66	190.17	177.93	142.64	126.65	118.22	113.42
15000	220.35	203.75	190.64	152.82	135.70	126.67	121.52
16000	235.04	217.34	203.35	163.01	144.75	135.11	129.62
17000	249.73	230.92	216.05	173.20	153.79	143.56	137.72
18000	264.42	244.50	228.76	183.39	162.84	152.00	145.83
19000	279.11	258.09	241.47	193.58	171.89	160.45	153.93
20000	293.80	271.67	254.18	203.77	180.93	168.89	162.03
21000	308.49	285.25	266.89	213.95	189.98	177.33	170.13
22000	323.18	298.84	279.60	224.14	199.03	185.78	178.23
23000	337.87	312.42	292.31	234.33	208.07	194.22	186.33
24000	352.56	326.01	305.02	244.52	217.12	202.67	194.43
25000	367.25	339.59	317.73	254.71	226.16	211.11	202.54
26000	381.94	353.17	330.44	264.90	235.21	219.56	210.64
27000	396.63	366.76	343.15	275.08	244.26	228.00	218.74
28000	411.32	380.34	355.85	285.27	253.30	236.45	226.84
29000	426.01	393.92	368.56	295.46	262.35	244.89	234.94
30000	440.70	407.51	381.27	305.65	271.40	253.33	243.04
35000	514.15	475.42	444.82	356.59	316.63	295.56	283.55
40000	587.60	543.34	508.36	407.53	361.86	337.78	324.06
45000	661.05	611.26	571.91	458.47	407.10	380.00	364.56
50000	734.50	679.18	635.45	509.41	452.33	422.22	405.07
55000	807.95	747.10	699.00	560.36	497.56	464.45	445.58
60000	881.40	815.01	762.54	611.30	542.80	506.67	486.09
65000	954.85	882.93	826.09	662.24	588.03	548.89	526.59
70000	1028.30	950.85	889.64	713.18	633.26	591.11	567.10
75000	1101.75	1018.77	953.18	764.12	678.49	633.34	607.61
80000	1175.20	1086.68	1016.73	815.06	723.73	675.56	648.11
85000	1248.65	1154.60	1080.27	866.01	768.96	717.78	688.62
90000	1322.10	1222.52	1143.82	916.95	814.19	760.00	729.13
95000	1395.55	1290.44	1207.36	967.89	859.43	802.23	769.63
100000	1469.00	1358.36	1270.91	1018.83	904.66	844.45	810.14
200000	2938.00	2716.71	2541.82	2037.66	1809.32	1688.90	1620.28
300000	4407.00	4075.07	3812.72	3056.49	2713.98	2533.35	2430.43
400000	5875.99	5433.42	5083.63	4075.32	3618.64	3377.80	3240.57
500000	7344.99	6791.78	6354.54	5094.15	4523.30	4222.25	4050.71
1000000	14689.98	13583.55	12709.08	10188.30	9046.60	8444.50	8101.42

9.375%

Amortization Amount	1 Year	2 Years	3 Years	4 Years	5 Years	6 Years	7 Years
25	2.19	1.14	0.80	0.62	0.52	0.45	0.40
50	4.38	2.29	1.59	1.25	1.04	0.91	0.81
100	8.75	4.58	3.19	2.50	2.09	1.81	1.62
200	17.51	9.16	6.38	5.00	4.17	3.62	3.24
300	26.26	13.73	9.57	7.49	6.26	5.44	4.86
400	35.02	18.31	12.76	9.99	8.34	7.25	6.48
500	43.77	22.89	15.95	12.49	10.43	9.06	8.09
600	52.53	27.47	19.13	14.99	12.51	10.87	9.71
700	61.28	32.04	22.32	17.49	14.60	12.69	11.33
800	70.03	36.62	25.51	19.98	16.68	14.50	12.95
900	78.79	41.20	28.70	22.48	18.77	16.31	14.57
1000	87.54	45.78	31.89	24.98	20.85	18.12	16.19
2000	175.09	91.55	63.78	49.96	41.71	36.25	32.38
3000	262.63	137.33	95.67	74.94	62.56	54.37	48.57
4000	350.17	183.10	127.57	99.91	83.42	72.49	64.76
5000	437.71	228.88	159.46	124.89	104.27	90.62	80.95
6000	525.26	274.65	191.35	149.87	125.12	108.74	97.14
7000	612.80	320.43	223.24	174.85	145.98	126.86	113.32
8000	700.34	366.20	255.13	199.83	166.83	144.99	129.51
9000	787.89	411.98	287.02	224.81	187.69	163.11	145.70
10000	875.43	457.75	318.91	249.79	208.54	181.23	161.89
11000	962.97	503.53	350.81	274.77	229.39	199.36	178.08
12000	1050.51	549.30	382.70	299.74	250.25	217.48	194.27
13000	1138.06	595.08	414.59	324.72	271.10	235.60	210.46
14000	1225.60	640.85	446.48	349.70	291.96	253.73	226.65
15000	1313.14	686.63	478.37	374.68	312.81	271.85	242.84
16000	1400.69	732.40	510.26	399.66	333.67	289.98	259.03
17000	1488.23	778.18	542.16	424.64	354.52	308.10	275.22
18000	1575.77	823.95	574.05	449.62	375.37	326.22	291.41
19000	1663.31	869.73	605.94	474.59	396.23	344.35	307.60
20000	1750.86	915.50	637.83	499.57	417.08	362.47	323.78
21000	1838.40	961.28	669.72	524.55	437.94	380.59	339.97
22000	1925.94	1007.05	701.61	549.53	458.79	398.72	356.16
23000	2013.49	1052.83	733.51	574.51	479.64	416.84	372.35
24000	2101.03	1098.60	765.40	599.49	500.50	434.96	388.54
25000	2188.57	1144.38	797.29	624.47	521.35	453.09	404.73
26000	2276.11	1190.15	829.18	649.45	542.21	471.21	420.92
27000	2363.66	1235.93	861.07	674.42	563.06	489.33	437.11
28000	2451.20	1281.70	892.96	699.40	583.91	507.46	453.30
29000	2538.74	1327.48	924.85	724.38	604.77	525.58	469.49
30000	2626.29	1373.26	956.74	749.36	625.62	543.70	485.68
35000	3064.00	1602.13	1116.20	874.25	729.89	634.32	566.62
40000	3501.71	1831.01	1275.66	999.15	834.16	724.94	647.57
45000	3939.43	2059.88	1435.12	1124.04	938.43	815.56	728.51
50000	4377.14	2288.76	1594.57	1248.93	1042.70	906.17	809.46
55000	4814.86	2517.63	1754.03	1373.83	1146.97	996.79	890.41
60000	5252.57	2746.51	1913.49	1498.72	1251.24	1087.41	971.35
65000	5690.28	2975.39	2072.95	1623.61	1355.52	1178.02	1052.30
70000	6128.00	3204.26	2232.40	1748.51	1459.79	1268.64	1133.25
75000	6565.71	3433.14	2391.86	1873.40	1564.06	1359.26	1214.19
80000	7003.43	3662.01	2551.32	1998.29	1668.33	1449.88	1295.14
85000	7441.14	3890.89	2710.78	2123.19	1772.60	1540.49	1376.08
90000	7878.86	4119.77	2870.23	2248.08	1876.87	1631.11	1457.03
95000	8316.57	4348.64	3029.69	2372.97	1981.14	1721.73	1537.98
100000	8754.28	4577.52	3189.15	2497.87	2085.41	1812.35	1618.92
200000	17508.57	9155.03	6378.30	4995.74	4170.82	3624.69	3237.84
300000	26262.85	13732.55	9567.45	7493.60	6256.22	5437.04	4856.77
400000	35017.14	18310.07	12756.59	9991.47	8341.63	7249.38	6475.69
500000	43771.42	22887.58	15945.74	12489.34	10427.04	9061.73	8094.61
1000000	87542.84	45775.17	31891.49	24978.68	20854.08	18123.45	16189.22

Amortization Amount	8 Years	9 Years	10 Years	15 Years	20 Years	25 Years	30 Years
25	0.37	0.34	0.32	0.26	0.23	0.21	0.20
50	0.74	0.68	0.64	0.51	0.46	0.43	0.41
100	1.48	1.36	1.28	1.03	0.91	0.85	0.82
200	2.95	2.73	2.55	2.05	1.82	1.71	1.64
300	4.43	4.09	3.83	3.08	2.74	2.56	2.46
400	5.90	5.46	5.11	4.10	3.65	3.41	3.28
500	7.38	6.82	6.39	5.13	4.56	4.26	4.09
600	8.85	8.19	7.66	6.16	5.47	5.12	4.91
700	10.33	9.55	8.94	7.18	6.39	5.97	5.73
800	11.80	10.92	10.22	8.21	7.30	6.82	6.55
900	13.28	12.28	11.50	9.23	8.21	7.67	7.37
1000	14.75	13.65	12.77	10.26	9.12	8.53	8.19
2000	29.51	27.30	25.55	20.52	18.25	17.05	16.38
3000	44.26	40.94	38.32	30.78	27.37	25.58	24.57
4000	59.01	54.59	51.10	41.04	36.50	34.11	32.75
5000	73.76	68.24	63.87	51.30	45.62	42.64	40.94
6000	88.52	81.89	76.65	61.56	54.75	51.16	49.13
7000	103.27	95.53	89.42	71.82	63.87	59.69	57.32
8000	118.02	109.18	102.20	82.08	72.99	68.22	65.51
9000	132.77	122.83	114.97	92.34	82.12	76.75	73.70
10000	147.53	136.48	127.74	102.60	91.24	85.27	81.88
11000	162.28	150.12	140.52	112.86	100.37	93.80	90.07
12000	177.03	163.77	153.29	123.12	109.49	102.33	98.26
13000	191.78	177.42	166.07	133.38	118.62	110.85	106.45
14000	206.54	191.07	178.84	143.64	127.74	119.38	114.64
15000	221.29	204.71	191.62	153.90	136.86	127.91	122.83
16000	236.04	218.36	204.39	164.16	145.99	136.44	131.01
17000	250.79	232.01	217.17	174.42	155.11	144.96	139.20
18000	265.55	245.66	229.94	184.68	164.24	153.49	147.39
19000	280.30	259.30	242.71	194.94	173.36	162.02	155.58
20000	295.05	272.95	255.49	205.20	182.49	170.55	163.77
21000	309.80	286.60	268.26	215.46	191.61	179.07	171.96
22000	324.56	300.25	281.04	225.72	200.74	187.60	180.14
23000	339.31	313.89	293.81	235.98	209.86	196.13	188.33
24000	354.06	327.54	306.59	246.24	218.98	204.65	196.52
25000	368.81	341.19	319.36	256.50	228.11	213.18	204.71
26000	383.57	354.84	332.14	266.76	237.23	221.71	212.90
27000	398.32	368.48	344.91	277.02	246.36	230.24	221.09
28000	413.07	382.13	357.68	287.28	255.48	238.76	229.27
29000	427.83	395.78	370.46	297.55	264.61	247.29	237.46
30000	442.58	409.43	383.23	307.81	273.73	255.82	245.65
35000	516.34	477.66	447.10	359.11	319.35	298.45	286.59
40000	590.10	545.90	510.98	410.41	364.97	341.09	327.53
45000	663.87	614.14	574.85	461.71	410.59	383.73	368.48
50000	737.63	682.38	638.72	513.01	456.22	426.36	409.42
55000	811.39	750.61	702.59	564.31	501.84	469.00	450.36
60000	885.16	818.85	766.47	615.61	547.46	511.64	491.30
65000	958.92	887.09	830.34	666.91	593.08	554.27	532.24
70000	1032.68	955.33	894.21	718.21	638.70	596.91	573.18
75000	1106.44	1023.56	958.08	769.51	684.32	639.54	614.13
80000	1180.21	1091.80	1021.95	820.81	729.95	682.18	655.07
85000	1253.97	1160.04	1085.83	872.11	775.57	724.82	696.01
90000	1327.73	1228.28	1149.70	923.42	821.19	767.45	736.95
95000	1401.50	1296.52	1213.57	974.72	866.81	810.09	777.89
100000	1475.26	1364.75	1277.44	1026.02	912.43	852.73	818.84
200000	2950.52	2729.51	2554.88	2052.03	1824.87	1705.45	1637.67
300000	4425.78	4094.26	3832.33	3078.05	2737.30	2558.18	2456.51
400000	5901.04	5459.01	5109.77	4104.07	3649.73	3410.90	3275.34
500000	7376.29	6823.77	6387.21	5130.09	4562.16	4263.63	4094.18
1000000	14752.59	13647.53	12774.42	10260.17	9124.33	8527.26	8188.35

9.5%

Amortization Amount	1 Year	2 Years	3 Years	4 Years	5 Years	6 Years	7 Years
25	2.19	1.15	0.80	0.63	0.52	0.45	0.41
50	4.38	2.29	1.60	1.25	1.05	0.91	0.81
100	8.76	4.58	3.19	2.50	2.09	1.82	1.63
200	17.52	9.17	6.39	5.01	4.18	3.64	3.25
300	26.28	13.75	9.58	7.51	6.27	5.46	4.88
400	35.04	18.33	12.78	10.01	8.37	7.27	6.50
500	43.80	22.92	15.97	12.52	10.46	9.09	8.13
600	52.56	27.50	19.17	15.02	12.55	10.91	9.75
700	61.32	32.08	22.36	17.53	14.64	12.73	11.38
800	70.08	36.66	25.56	20.03	16.73	14.55	13.00
900	78.84	41.25	28.75	22.53	18.82	16.37	14.63
1000	87.60	45.83	31.95	25.04	20.91	18.18	16.25
2000	175.20	91.66	63.90	50.07	41.83	36.37	32.50
3000	262.80	137.49	95.84	75.11	62.74	54.55	48.75
4000	350.39	183.32	127.79	100.14	83.65	72.73	65.00
5000	437.99	229.15	159.74	125.18	104.56	90.92	81.25
6000	525.59	274.98	191.69	150.22	125.48	109.10	97.50
7000	613.19	320.81	223.63	175.25	146.39	127.28	113.75
8000	700.79	366.64	255.58	200.29	167.30	145.47	130.00
9000	788.39	412.47	287.53	225.32	188.21	163.65	146.25
10000	875.99	458.30	319.48	250.36	209.13	181.83	162.51
11000	963.59	504.13	351.42	275.40	230.04	200.02	178.76
12000	1051.18	549.97	383.37	300.43	250.95	218.20	195.01
13000	1138.78	595.80	415.32	325.47	271.86	236.38	211.26
14000	1226.38	641.63	447.27	350.50	292.78	254.57	227.51
15000	1313.98	687.46	479.21	375.54	313.69	272.75	243.76
16000	1401.58	733.29	511.16	400.58	334.60	290.93	260.01
17000	1489.18	779.12	543.11	425.61	355.52	309.12	276.28
18000	1576.78	824.95	575.06	450.65	376.43	327.30	292.51
19000	1664.37	870.78	607.00	475.68	397.34	345.48	308.76
20000	1751.97	916.61	638.95	500.72	418.25	363.67	325.01
21000	1839.57	962.44	670.90	525.76	439.17	381.85	341.26
22000	1927.17	1008.27	702.85	550.79	460.08	400.03	357.51
23000	2014.77	1054.10	734.79	575.83	480.99	418.22	373.76
24000	2102.37	1099.93	766.74	600.86	501.90	436.40	390.01
25000	2189.97	1145.76	798.69	625.90	522.82	454.58	406.26
26000	2277.57	1191.59	830.64	650.93	543.73	472.77	422.51
27000	2365.16	1237.42	862.59	675.97	564.64	490.95	438.76
28000	2452.76	1283.25	894.53	701.01	585.55	509.14	455.02
29000	2540.36	1329.08	926.48	726.04	606.47	527.32	471.27
30000	2627.96	1374.91	958.43	751.08	627.38	545.50	487.52
35000	3065.95	1604.07	1118.17	876.26	731.94	636.42	568.77
40000	3503.95	1833.22	1277.90	1001.44	836.51	727.34	650.02
45000	3941.94	2062.37	1437.64	1126.62	941.07	818.25	731.27
50000	4379.93	2291.52	1597.38	1251.80	1045.63	909.17	812.53
55000	4817.93	2520.67	1757.12	1376.98	1150.20	1000.09	893.78
60000	5255.92	2749.83	1916.86	1502.16	1254.76	1091.00	975.03
65000	5693.91	2978.98	2076.59	1627.34	1359.32	1181.92	1056.29
70000	6131.91	3208.13	2236.33	1752.52	1463.89	1272.84	1137.54
75000	6569.90	3437.28	2396.07	1877.70	1568.45	1363.75	1218.79
80000	7007.89	3666.44	2555.81	2002.88	1673.01	1454.67	1300.04
85000	7445.89	3895.59	2715.55	2128.06	1777.58	1545.59	1381.30
90000	7883.88	4124.74	2875.28	2253.24	1882.14	1636.51	1462.55
95000	8321.87	4353.89	3035.02	2378.42	1986.70	1727.42	1543.80
100000	8759.87	4583.04	3194.76	2503.60	2091.27	1818.34	1625.06
200000	17519.73	9166.09	6389.52	5007.19	4182.53	3636.68	3250.11
300000	26279.60	13749.13	9584.28	7510.79	6273.80	5455.02	4875.17
400000	35039.47	18332.18	12779.04	10014.38	8365.07	7273.36	6500.22
500000	43799.33	22915.22	15973.80	12517.98	10456.33	9091.70	8125.28
1000000	87598.67	45830.44	31947.60	25035.96	20912.67	18183.40	16250.55

Amortization Amount	8 Years	9 Years	10 Years	15 Years	20 Years	25 Years	30 Years
25	0.37	0.34	0.32	0.26	0.23	0.22	0.21
50	0.74	0.69	0.64	0.52	0.46	0.43	0.41
100	1.48	1.37	1.28	1.03	0.92	0.86	0.83
200	2.96	2.74	2.57	2.07	1.84	1.72	1.66
300	4.44	4.11	3.85	3.10	2.76	2.58	2.48
400	5.93	5.48	5.14	4.13	3.68	3.44	3.31
500	7.41	6.86	6.42	5.17	4.60	4.31	4.14
600	8.89	8.23	7.70	6.20	5.52	5.17	4.97
700	10.37	9.60	8.99	7.23	6.44	6.03	5.79
800	11.85	10.97	10.27	8.27	7.36	6.89	6.62
900	13.33	12.34	11.56	9.30	8.28	7.75	7.45
1000	14.82	13.71	12.84	10.33	9.20	8.61	8.28
2000	29.63	27.42	25.68	20.66	18.40	17.22	16.55
3000	44.45	41.13	38.52	31.00	27.61	25.83	24.83
4000	59.26	54.85	51.36	41.33	36.81	34.44	33.10
5000	74.08	68.56	64.20	51.66	46.01	43.05	41.38
6000	88.89	82.27	77.04	61.99	55.21	51.66	49.65
7000	103.71	95.98	89.88	72.33	64.42	60.27	57.93
8000	118.52	109.69	102.72	82.66	73.62	68.88	66.20
9000	133.34	123.40	115.56	92.99	82.82	77.49	74.48
10000	148.15	137.12	128.40	103.32	92.02	86.10	82.76
11000	162.97	150.83	141.24	113.65	101.23	94.71	91.03
12000	177.78	164.54	154.08	123.99	110.43	103.32	99.31
13000	192.60	178.25	166.92	134.32	119.63	111.93	107.58
14000	207.41	191.96	179.76	144.65	128.83	120.54	115.86
15000	222.23	205.67	192.60	154.98	138.03	129.15	124.13
16000	237.04	219.39	205.44	165.32	147.24	137.76	132.41
17000	251.86	233.10	218.28	175.65	156.44	146.37	140.68
18000	266.68	246.81	231.12	185.98	165.64	154.98	148.96
19000	281.49	260.52	243.96	196.31	174.84	163.60	157.24
20000	296.31	274.23	256.80	206.65	184.05	172.21	165.51
21000	311.12	287.94	269.64	216.98	193.25	180.82	173.79
22000	325.94	301.66	282.48	227.31	202.45	189.43	182.06
23000	340.75	315.37	295.32	237.64	211.65	198.04	190.34
24000	355.57	329.08	308.16	247.97	220.86	206.65	198.61
25000	370.38	342.79	321.00	258.31	230.06	215.26	206.89
26000	385.20	356.50	333.84	268.64	239.26	223.87	215.16
27000	400.01	370.21	346.68	278.97	248.46	232.48	223.44
28000	414.83	383.93	359.52	289.30	257.66	241.09	231.72
29000	429.64	397.64	372.36	299.64	266.87	249.70	239.99
30000	444.46	411.35	385.20	309.97	276.07	258.31	248.27
35000	518.54	479.91	449.40	361.63	322.08	301.36	289.64
40000	592.61	548.47	513.60	413.29	368.09	344.41	331.02
45000	666.69	617.02	577.80	464.95	414.10	387.46	372.40
50000	740.77	685.58	642.00	516.61	460.12	430.51	413.78
55000	814.84	754.14	706.20	568.27	506.13	473.57	455.15
60000	888.92	822.70	770.39	619.94	552.14	516.62	496.53
65000	963.00	891.26	834.59	671.60	598.15	559.67	537.91
70000	1037.07	959.82	898.79	723.26	644.16	602.72	579.29
75000	1111.15	1028.37	962.99	774.92	690.17	645.77	620.67
80000	1185.22	1096.93	1027.19	826.58	736.18	688.82	662.04
85000	1259.30	1165.49	1091.39	878.24	782.20	731.87	703.42
90000	1333.38	1234.05	1155.59	929.90	828.21	774.92	744.80
95000	1407.45	1302.61	1219.79	981.56	874.22	817.98	786.18
100000	1481.53	1371.16	1283.99	1033.23	920.23	861.03	827.55
200000	2963.06	2742.33	2567.98	2066.45	1840.46	1722.06	1655.11
300000	4444.59	4113.49	3851.97	3099.68	2760.69	2583.08	2482.66
400000	5926.12	5484.66	5135.97	4132.90	3680.92	3444.11	3310.22
500000	7407.66	6855.82	6419.96	5166.13	4601.15	4305.14	4137.77
1000000	14815.31	13711.64	12839.91	10332.26	9202.31	8610.28	8275.54

9.625%

Amortization Amount	1 Year	2 Years	3 Years	4 Years	5 Years	6 Years	7 Years
25	2.19	1.15	0.80	0.63	0.52	0.46	0.41
50	4.38	2.29	1.60	1.25	1.05	0.91	0.82
100	8.77	4.59	3.20	2.51	2.10	1.82	1.63
200	17.53	9.18	6.40	5.02	4.19	3.65	3.26
300	26.30	13.77	9.60	7.53	6.29	5.47	4.89
400	35.06	18.35	12.80	10.04	8.39	7.30	6.52
500	43.83	22.94	16.00	12.55	10.49	9.12	8.16
600	52.59	27.53	19.20	15.06	12.58	10.95	9.79
700	61.36	32.12	22.40	17.57	14.68	12.77	11.42
800	70.12	36.71	25.60	20.07	16.78	14.59	13.05
900	78.89	41.30	28.80	22.58	18.87	16.42	14.68
1000	87.65	45.89	32.00	25.09	20.97	18.24	16.31
2000	175.31	91.77	64.01	50.19	41.94	36.49	32.62
3000	262.96	137.66	96.01	75.28	62.91	54.73	48.94
4000	350.62	183.54	128.01	100.37	83.89	72.97	65.25
5000	438.27	229.43	160.02	125.47	104.86	91.22	81.56
6000	525.93	275.31	192.02	150.56	125.83	109.46	97.87
7000	613.58	321.20	224.03	175.65	146.80	127.70	114.18
8000	701.24	367.09	256.03	200.75	167.77	145.95	130.50
9000	788.89	412.97	288.03	225.84	188.74	164.19	146.81
10000	876.54	458.86	320.04	250.93	209.71	182.43	163.12
11000	964.20	504.74	352.04	276.03	230.68	200.68	179.43
12000	1051.85	550.63	384.04	301.12	251.66	218.92	195.74
13000	1139.51	596.51	416.05	326.21	272.63	237.16	212.06
14000	1227.16	642.40	448.05	351.31	293.60	255.41	228.37
15000	1314.82	688.29	480.06	376.40	314.57	273.65	244.68
16000	1402.47	734.17	512.06	401.49	335.54	291.89	260.99
17000	1490.13	780.06	544.06	426.59	356.51	310.14	277.30
18000	1577.78	825.94	576.07	451.68	377.48	328.38	293.62
19000	1665.44	871.83	608.07	476.77	398.46	346.63	309.93
20000	1753.09	917.71	640.07	501.87	419.43	364.87	326.24
21000	1840.74	963.60	672.08	526.96	440.40	383.11	342.55
22000	1928.40	1009.49	704.08	552.05	461.37	401.36	358.86
23000	2016.05	1055.37	736.09	577.15	482.34	419.60	375.18
24000	2103.71	1101.26	768.09	602.24	503.31	437.84	391.49
25000	2191.36	1147.14	800.09	627.33	524.28	456.09	407.80
26000	2279.02	1193.03	832.10	652.43	545.25	474.33	424.11
27000	2366.67	1238.91	864.10	677.52	566.23	492.57	440.42
28000	2454.33	1284.80	896.10	702.61	587.20	510.82	456.74
29000	2541.98	1330.69	928.11	727.71	608.17	529.06	473.05
30000	2629.63	1376.57	960.11	752.80	629.14	547.30	489.36
35000	3067.91	1606.00	1120.13	878.27	734.00	638.52	570.92
40000	3506.18	1835.43	1280.15	1003.73	838.85	729.74	652.48
45000	3944.45	2064.86	1440.17	1129.20	943.71	820.95	734.04
50000	4382.72	2294.29	1600.19	1254.66	1048.57	912.17	815.60
55000	4821.00	2523.72	1760.21	1380.13	1153.42	1003.39	897.16
60000	5259.27	2753.14	1920.22	1505.60	1258.28	1094.61	978.72
65000	5697.54	2982.57	2080.24	1631.06	1363.14	1185.82	1060.28
70000	6135.81	3212.00	2240.26	1756.53	1467.99	1277.04	1141.84
75000	6574.09	3441.43	2400.28	1882.00	1572.85	1368.26	1223.40
80000	7012.36	3670.86	2560.30	2007.46	1677.71	1459.47	1304.96
85000	7450.63	3900.29	2720.32	2132.93	1782.56	1550.69	1386.52
90000	7888.90	4129.72	2880.34	2258.40	1887.42	1641.91	1468.08
95000	8327.18	4359.14	3040.35	2383.86	1992.28	1733.13	1549.64
100000	8765.45	4588.57	3200.37	2509.33	2097.13	1824.34	1631.20
200000	17530.90	9177.15	6400.75	5018.66	4194.27	3648.69	3262.40
300000	26296.34	13765.72	9601.12	7527.99	6291.40	5473.03	4893.60
400000	35061.79	18354.29	12801.49	10037.32	8388.53	7297.37	6524.79
500000	43827.24	22942.87	16001.87	12546.65	10485.66	9121.72	8155.99
1000000	87654.48	45885.73	32003.74	25093.30	20971.33	18243.43	16311.99

Amortization Amount	8 Years	9 Years	10 Years	15 Years	20 Years	25 Years	30 Years
25	0.37	0.34	0.32	0.26	0.23	0.22	0.21
50	0.74	0.69	0.65	0.52	0.46	0.43	0.42
100	1.49	1.38	1.29	1.04	0.93	0.87	0.84
200	2.98	2.76	2.58	2.08	1.86	1.74	1.67
300	4.46	4.13	3.87	3.12	2.78	2.61	2.51
400	5.95	5.51	5.16	4.16	3.71	3.48	3.35
500	7.44	6.89	6.45	5.20	4.64	4.35	4.18
600	8.93	8.27	7.74	6.24	5.57	5.22	5.02
700	10.41	9.64	9.03	7.28	6.50	6.09	5.85
800	11.90	11.02	10.32	8.32	7.42	6.95	6.69
900	13.39	12.40	11.61	9.36	8.35	7.82	7.53
1000	14.88	13.78	12.91	10.40	9.28	8.69	8.36
2000	29.76	27.55	25.81	20.81	18.56	17.39	18.73
3000	44.63	41.33	38.72	31.21	27.84	26.08	25.09
4000	59.51	55.10	51.62	41.62	37.12	34.77	33.45
5000	74.39	68.88	64.53	52.02	46.40	43.47	41.81
6000	89.27	82.66	77.43	62.43	55.68	52.16	50.18
7000	104.15	96.43	90.34	72.83	64.96	60.85	58.54
8000	119.03	110.21	103.24	83.24	74.24	69.55	66.90
9000	133.90	123.98	116.15	93.64	83.52	78.24	75.27
10000	148.78	137.76	129.06	104.05	92.81	86.94	83.63
11000	163.66	151.53	141.96	114.45	102.09	95.63	91.99
12000	178.54	165.31	154.87	124.85	111.37	104.32	100.36
13000	193.42	179.09	167.77	135.26	120.65	113.02	108.72
14000	208.29	192.86	180.68	145.66	129.93	121.71	117.08
15000	223.17	206.64	193.58	156.07	139.21	130.40	125.44
16000	238.05	220.41	206.49	166.47	148.49	139.10	133.81
17000	252.93	234.19	219.39	176.88	157.77	147.79	142.17
18000	267.81	247.97	232.30	187.28	167.05	156.48	150.53
19000	282.68	261.74	245.21	197.69	176.33	165.18	158.90
20000	297.56	275.52	258.11	208.09	185.61	173.87	167.26
21000	312.44	289.29	271.02	218.50	194.89	182.56	175.62
22000	327.32	303.07	283.92	228.90	204.17	191.26	183.99
23000	342.20	316.85	296.83	239.30	213.45	199.95	192.35
24000	357.08	330.62	309.73	249.71	222.73	208.65	200.71
25000	371.95	344.40	322.64	260.11	232.01	217.34	209.07
26000	386.83	358.17	335.54	270.52	241.29	226.03	217.44
27000	401.71	371.95	348.45	280.92	250.57	234.73	225.80
28000	416.59	385.72	361.36	291.33	259.85	243.42	234.16
29000	431.47	399.50	374.26	301.73	269.14	252.11	242.53
30000	446.34	413.28	387.17	312.14	278.42	260.81	250.89
35000	520.74	482.16	451.69	364.16	324.82	304.27	292.70
40000	595.13	551.04	516.22	416.18	371.22	347.74	334.52
45000	669.52	619.92	580.75	468.21	417.62	391.21	376.33
50000	743.91	688.79	645.28	520.23	464.03	434.68	418.15
55000	818.30	757.67	709.81	572.25	510.43	478.15	459.96
60000	892.69	826.55	774.33	624.27	556.83	521.61	501.78
65000	967.08	895.43	838.86	676.30	603.23	565.08	543.59
70000	1041.47	964.31	903.39	728.32	649.64	608.55	585.41
75000	1115.86	1033.19	967.92	780.34	696.04	652.02	627.22
80000	1190.25	1102.07	1032.44	832.36	742.44	695.48	669.04
85000	1264.64	1170.95	1096.97	884.39	788.84	738.95	710.85
90000	1339.03	1239.83	1161.50	936.41	835.25	782.42	752.67
95000	1413.42	1308.71	1226.03	988.43	881.65	825.89	794.48
100000	1487.82	1377.59	1290.56	1040.46	928.05	869.36	836.30
200000	2975.63	2755.18	2581.11	2080.91	1856.11	1738.71	1672.59
300000	4463.45	4132.77	3871.67	3121.37	2784.16	2608.07	2508.89
400000	5951.26	5510.36	5162.22	4161.82	3712.21	3477.42	3345.19
500000	7439.08	6887.95	6452.78	5202.28	4640.26	4346.78	4181.49
1000000	14878.15	13775.89	12905.55	10404.56	9280.53	8693.55	8362.97

9.75%

Amortization Amount	1 Year	2 Years	3 Years	4 Years	5 Years	6 Years	7 Years
25	2.19	1.15	0.80	0.63	0.53	0.46	0.41
50	4.39	2.30	1.60	1.26	1.05	0.92	0.82
100	8.77	4.59	3.21	2.52	2.10	1.83	1.64
200	17.54	9.19	6.41	5.03	4.21	3.66	3.27
300	26.31	13.78	9.62	7.55	6.31	5.49	4.91
400	35.08	18.38	12.82	10.06	8.41	7.32	6.55
500	43.86	22.97	16.03	12.58	10.52	9.15	8.19
600	52.63	27.56	19.24	15.09	12.62	10.98	9.82
700	61.40	32.16	22.44	17.61	14.72	12.81	11.46
800	70.17	36.75	25.65	20.12	16.82	14.64	13.10
900	78.94	41.35	28.85	22.64	18.93	16.47	14.74
1000	87.71	45.94	32.06	25.15	21.03	18.30	16.37
2000	175.42	91.88	64.12	50.30	42.06	36.61	32.75
3000	263.13	137.82	96.18	75.45	63.09	54.91	49.12
4000	350.84	183.76	128.24	100.60	84.12	73.21	65.49
5000	438.55	229.71	160.30	125.75	105.15	91.52	81.87
6000	526.26	275.65	192.36	150.90	126.18	109.82	98.24
7000	613.97	321.59	224.42	176.05	147.21	128.12	114.61
8000	701.68	367.53	256.48	201.21	168.24	146.43	130.99
9000	789.39	413.47	288.54	226.36	189.27	164.73	147.36
10000	877.10	459.41	320.60	251.51	210.30	183.04	163.74
11000	964.81	505.35	352.66	276.66	231.33	201.34	180.11
12000	1052.52	551.29	384.72	301.81	252.36	219.64	196.48
13000	1140.23	597.23	416.78	326.96	273.39	237.95	212.86
14000	1227.94	643.17	448.84	352.11	294.42	256.25	229.23
15000	1315.65	689.12	480.90	377.28	315.45	274.55	245.60
16000	1403.36	735.06	512.96	402.41	336.48	292.86	261.98
17000	1491.07	781.00	545.02	427.56	357.51	311.16	278.35
18000	1578.79	826.94	577.08	452.71	378.54	329.46	294.72
19000	1666.50	872.88	609.14	477.86	399.57	347.77	311.10
20000	1754.21	918.82	641.20	503.01	420.60	366.07	327.47
21000	1841.92	964.76	673.26	528.16	441.63	384.37	343.84
22000	1929.63	1010.70	705.32	553.31	462.66	402.68	360.22
23000	2017.34	1056.64	737.38	578.47	483.69	420.98	376.59
24000	2105.05	1102.58	769.44	603.62	504.72	439.29	392.96
25000	2192.76	1148.53	801.50	628.77	525.75	457.59	409.34
26000	2280.47	1194.47	833.56	653.92	546.78	475.89	425.71
27000	2368.18	1240.41	865.62	679.07	567.81	494.20	442.09
28000	2455.89	1286.35	897.68	704.22	588.84	512.50	458.46
29000	2543.60	1332.29	929.74	729.37	609.87	530.80	474.83
30000	2631.31	1378.23	961.80	754.52	630.90	549.11	491.21
35000	3069.86	1607.94	1122.10	880.27	736.05	640.62	573.07
40000	3508.41	1837.64	1282.40	1006.03	841.20	732.14	654.94
45000	3946.96	2067.35	1442.70	1131.78	946.35	823.66	736.81
50000	4385.51	2297.05	1603.00	1257.53	1051.50	915.18	818.68
55000	4824.07	2526.76	1763.29	1383.29	1156.65	1006.70	900.54
60000	5262.62	2756.46	1923.59	1509.04	1261.80	1098.21	982.41
65000	5701.17	2986.17	2083.89	1634.79	1366.95	1189.73	1064.28
70000	6139.72	3215.87	2244.19	1760.54	1472.10	1281.25	1146.15
75000	6578.27	3445.58	2404.49	1886.30	1577.25	1372.77	1228.01
80000	7016.82	3675.28	2564.79	2012.05	1682.40	1464.28	1309.88
85000	7455.37	3904.99	2725.09	2137.81	1787.55	1555.80	1391.75
90000	7893.93	4134.69	2885.39	2263.56	1892.70	1647.32	1473.62
95000	8332.48	4364.40	3045.69	2389.31	1997.85	1738.84	1555.48
100000	8771.03	4594.10	3205.99	2515.07	2103.00	1830.35	1637.35
200000	17542.06	9188.21	6411.98	5030.14	4206.01	3660.71	3274.70
300000	26313.09	13782.31	9617.97	7545.20	6309.01	5491.06	4912.06
400000	35084.12	18376.41	12823.96	10060.27	8412.02	7321.42	6549.41
500000	43855.15	22970.52	16029.95	12575.34	10515.02	9151.77	8186.76
1000000	87710.29	45941.03	32059.91	25150.68	21030.05	18303.55	16373.52

MONTHLY PAYMENT
NECESSARY TO AMORTIZE A LOAN **9.75%**

Amortization Amount	8 Years	9 Years	10 Years	15 Years	20 Years	25 Years	30 Years
25	0.37	0.35	0.32	0.26	0.23	0.22	0.21
50	0.75	0.69	0.65	0.52	0.47	0.44	0.42
100	1.49	1.38	1.30	1.05	0.94	0.88	0.85
200	2.99	2.77	2.59	2.10	1.87	1.76	1.69
300	4.48	4.15	3.89	3.14	2.81	2.63	2.54
400	5.98	5.54	5.19	4.19	3.74	3.51	3.38
500	7.47	6.92	6.49	5.24	4.68	4.39	4.23
600	8.96	8.30	7.78	6.29	5.62	5.27	5.07
700	10.46	9.69	9.08	7.33	6.55	6.14	5.92
800	11.95	11.07	10.38	8.38	7.49	7.02	6.76
900	13.45	12.46	11.67	9.43	8.42	7.90	7.61
1000	14.94	13.84	12.97	10.48	9.36	8.78	8.45
2000	29.88	27.68	25.94	20.95	18.72	17.55	16.90
3000	44.82	41.52	38.91	31.43	28.08	26.33	25.35
4000	59.76	55.36	51.86	41.91	37.44	35.11	33.80
5000	74.71	69.20	64.86	52.39	46.79	43.89	42.25
6000	89.65	83.04	77.83	62.86	56.15	52.66	50.70
7000	104.59	96.88	90.80	73.34	65.51	61.44	59.15
8000	119.53	110.72	103.77	83.82	74.87	70.22	67.61
9000	134.47	124.56	116.74	94.29	84.23	78.99	76.06
10000	149.41	138.40	129.71	104.77	93.59	87.77	84.51
11000	164.35	152.24	142.68	115.25	102.95	96.55	92.96
12000	179.29	166.08	155.66	125.72	112.31	105.32	101.41
13000	194.23	179.92	168.63	136.20	121.67	114.10	109.86
14000	209.18	193.76	181.60	146.68	131.03	122.88	118.31
15000	224.12	207.60	194.57	157.16	140.38	131.66	126.76
16000	239.06	221.44	207.54	167.63	149.74	140.43	135.21
17000	254.00	235.28	220.51	178.11	159.10	149.21	143.66
18000	268.94	249.12	233.48	188.59	168.46	157.99	152.11
19000	283.88	262.97	246.46	199.06	177.82	166.76	160.56
20000	298.82	276.81	259.43	209.54	187.18	175.54	169.01
21000	313.76	290.65	272.40	220.02	196.54	184.32	177.46
22000	328.70	304.49	285.37	230.50	205.90	193.10	185.91
23000	343.65	318.33	298.34	240.97	215.26	201.87	194.36
24000	358.59	332.17	311.31	251.45	224.62	210.65	202.82
25000	373.53	346.01	324.28	261.93	233.97	219.43	211.27
26000	388.47	359.85	337.25	272.40	243.33	228.20	219.72
27000	403.41	373.69	350.23	282.88	252.69	236.98	228.17
28000	418.35	387.53	363.20	293.36	262.05	245.76	236.62
29000	433.29	401.37	376.17	303.83	271.41	254.54	245.07
30000	448.23	415.21	389.14	314.31	280.77	263.31	253.52
35000	522.94	484.41	454.00	366.70	327.56	307.20	295.77
40000	597.64	553.61	518.85	419.08	374.36	351.08	338.03
45000	672.35	622.81	583.71	471.47	421.15	394.97	380.28
50000	747.06	692.01	648.57	523.85	467.95	438.85	422.53
55000	821.76	761.21	713.42	576.24	514.74	482.74	464.79
60000	896.47	830.42	778.28	628.62	561.54	526.62	507.04
65000	971.17	899.62	843.14	681.01	608.33	570.51	549.29
70000	1045.88	968.82	907.99	733.39	655.13	614.40	591.54
75000	1120.58	1038.02	972.85	785.78	701.92	658.28	633.80
80000	1195.29	1107.22	1037.71	838.17	748.72	702.17	676.05
85000	1269.99	1176.42	1102.56	890.55	795.51	746.05	718.30
90000	1344.70	1245.62	1167.42	942.94	842.31	789.94	760.56
95000	1419.41	1314.83	1232.28	995.32	889.10	833.82	802.81
100000	1494.11	1384.03	1297.13	1047.71	935.90	877.71	845.06
200000	2988.22	2768.05	2594.27	2095.41	1871.80	1755.42	1690.13
300000	4482.33	4152.08	3891.40	3143.12	2807.70	2633.12	2535.19
400000	5976.45	5536.11	5188.54	4190.83	3743.60	3510.83	3380.26
500000	7470.56	6920.14	6485.67	5238.53	4679.50	4388.54	4225.32
1000000	14941.11	13840.27	12971.34	10477.07	9358.99	8777.08	8450.64

9.875%

Amortization Amount	1 Year	2 Years	3 Years	4 Years	5 Years	6 Years	7 Years
25	2.19	1.15	0.80	0.63	0.53	0.48	0.41
50	4.39	2.30	1.61	1.26	1.05	0.92	0.82
100	8.78	4.60	3.21	2.52	2.11	1.84	1.64
200	17.55	9.20	6.42	5.04	4.22	3.67	3.29
300	26.33	13.80	9.63	7.56	6.33	5.51	4.93
400	35.11	18.40	12.85	10.08	8.44	7.35	6.57
500	43.88	23.00	16.06	12.60	10.54	9.18	8.22
600	52.66	27.60	19.27	15.12	12.65	11.02	9.86
700	61.44	32.20	22.48	17.65	14.76	12.85	11.50
800	70.21	36.80	25.69	20.17	16.87	14.69	13.15
900	78.99	41.40	28.90	22.69	18.98	16.53	14.79
1000	87.77	46.00	32.12	25.21	21.09	18.36	16.44
2000	175.53	91.99	64.23	50.42	42.18	36.73	32.87
3000	263.30	137.99	96.35	75.62	63.27	55.09	49.31
4000	351.06	183.99	128.46	100.83	84.36	73.46	65.74
5000	438.83	229.98	160.58	126.04	105.44	91.82	82.18
6000	526.60	275.98	192.70	151.25	126.53	110.18	98.61
7000	614.36	321.97	224.81	176.46	147.62	128.55	115.05
8000	702.13	367.97	256.93	201.66	168.71	146.91	131.48
9000	789.89	413.97	289.05	226.87	189.80	165.27	147.92
10000	877.66	459.96	321.16	252.08	210.89	183.64	164.35
11000	965.43	505.96	353.28	277.29	231.98	202.00	180.79
12000	1053.19	551.96	385.39	302.50	253.07	220.37	197.22
13000	1140.96	597.95	417.51	327.71	274.15	238.73	213.66
14000	1228.73	643.95	449.63	352.91	295.24	257.09	230.09
15000	1316.49	689.95	481.74	378.12	316.33	275.46	246.53
16000	1404.26	735.94	513.86	403.33	337.42	293.82	262.96
17000	1492.02	781.94	545.97	428.54	358.51	312.18	279.40
18000	1579.79	827.93	578.09	453.75	379.60	330.55	295.83
19000	1667.56	873.93	610.21	478.95	400.69	348.91	312.27
20000	1755.32	919.93	642.32	504.16	421.78	367.28	328.70
21000	1843.09	965.92	674.44	529.37	442.87	385.64	345.14
22000	1930.85	1011.92	706.55	554.58	463.95	404.00	361.57
23000	2018.62	1057.92	738.67	579.79	485.04	422.37	378.01
24000	2106.39	1103.91	770.79	604.99	506.13	440.73	394.44
25000	2194.15	1149.91	802.90	630.20	527.22	459.09	410.88
26000	2281.92	1195.90	835.02	655.41	548.31	477.46	427.31
27000	2369.68	1241.90	867.14	680.62	569.40	495.82	443.75
28000	2457.45	1287.90	899.25	705.83	590.49	514.19	460.18
29000	2545.22	1333.89	931.37	731.04	611.58	532.55	476.62
30000	2632.98	1379.89	963.48	756.24	632.67	550.91	493.05
35000	3071.81	1609.87	1124.06	882.28	738.11	642.73	575.23
40000	3510.64	1839.85	1284.64	1008.32	843.55	734.55	657.41
45000	3949.47	2069.84	1445.23	1134.37	949.00	826.37	739.58
50000	4388.30	2299.82	1605.81	1260.41	1054.44	918.19	821.76
55000	4827.13	2529.80	1766.39	1386.45	1159.89	1010.01	903.93
60000	5265.97	2759.78	1926.97	1512.49	1265.33	1101.83	986.11
65000	5704.80	2989.76	2087.55	1638.53	1370.77	1193.64	1068.29
70000	6143.63	3219.74	2248.13	1764.57	1476.22	1285.46	1150.46
75000	6582.46	3449.73	2408.71	1890.61	1581.66	1377.28	1232.64
80000	7021.29	3679.71	2569.29	2016.65	1687.11	1469.10	1314.81
85000	7460.12	3909.69	2729.87	2142.69	1792.55	1560.92	1396.99
90000	7898.95	4139.67	2890.45	2268.73	1898.00	1652.74	1479.16
95000	8337.78	4369.65	3051.03	2394.77	2003.44	1744.56	1561.34
100000	8776.61	4599.63	3211.61	2520.81	2108.88	1836.38	1643.52
200000	17553.22	9199.27	6423.22	5041.62	4217.77	3672.75	3287.03
300000	26329.83	13798.90	9634.83	7562.43	6326.65	5509.13	4930.55
400000	35106.44	18398.54	12846.44	10083.25	8435.54	7345.50	6574.07
500000	43883.04	22998.17	16058.06	12604.06	10544.42	9181.88	8217.58
1000000	87766.09	45996.34	32116.11	25208.11	21088.84	18363.75	16435.16

Amortization Amount	8 Years	9 Years	10 Years	15 Years	20 Years	25 Years	30 Years
25	0.38	0.35	0.33	0.26	0.24	0.22	0.21
50	0.75	0.70	0.65	0.53	0.47	0.44	0.43
100	1.50	1.39	1.30	1.05	0.94	0.89	0.85
200	3.00	2.78	2.61	2.11	1.89	1.77	1.71
300	4.50	4.17	3.91	3.16	2.83	2.66	2.56
400	6.00	5.56	5.21	4.22	3.78	3.54	3.42
500	7.50	6.95	6.52	5.27	4.72	4.43	4.27
600	9.00	8.34	7.82	6.33	5.66	5.32	5.12
700	10.50	9.73	9.13	7.38	6.61	6.20	5.98
800	12.00	11.12	10.43	8.44	7.55	7.09	6.83
900	13.50	12.51	11.73	9.49	8.49	7.97	7.68
1000	15.00	13.90	13.04	10.55	9.44	8.86	8.54
2000	30.01	27.81	26.07	21.10	18.88	17.72	17.08
3000	45.01	41.71	39.11	31.65	28.31	26.58	25.62
4000	60.02	55.62	52.15	42.20	37.75	35.44	34.15
5000	75.02	69.52	65.19	52.75	47.19	44.30	42.69
6000	90.03	83.43	78.22	63.30	56.63	53.17	51.23
7000	105.03	97.33	91.26	73.85	66.06	62.03	59.77
8000	120.03	111.24	104.30	84.40	75.50	70.89	68.31
9000	135.04	125.14	117.34	94.95	84.94	79.75	76.85
10000	150.04	139.05	130.37	105.50	94.38	88.61	85.39
11000	165.05	152.95	143.41	116.05	103.81	97.47	93.92
12000	180.05	166.86	156.45	126.60	113.25	106.33	102.46
13000	195.05	180.76	169.48	137.15	122.69	115.19	111.00
14000	210.06	194.67	182.52	147.70	132.13	124.05	119.54
15000	225.06	208.57	195.56	158.25	141.57	132.91	128.08
16000	240.07	222.48	208.60	168.80	151.00	141.77	136.62
17000	255.07	236.38	221.63	179.35	160.44	150.63	145.16
18000	270.08	250.29	234.67	189.90	169.88	159.50	153.69
19000	285.08	264.19	247.71	200.45	179.32	168.36	162.23
20000	300.08	278.10	260.75	211.00	188.75	177.22	170.77
21000	315.09	292.00	273.78	221.55	198.19	186.08	179.31
22000	330.09	305.91	286.82	232.10	207.63	194.94	187.85
23000	345.10	319.81	299.86	242.64	217.07	203.80	196.39
24000	360.10	333.71	312.89	253.19	226.50	212.66	204.93
25000	375.10	347.62	325.93	263.74	235.94	221.52	213.46
26000	390.11	361.52	338.97	274.29	245.38	230.38	222.00
27000	405.11	375.43	352.01	284.84	254.82	239.24	230.54
28000	420.12	389.33	365.04	295.39	264.26	248.10	239.08
29000	435.12	403.24	378.08	305.94	273.69	256.96	247.62
30000	450.13	417.14	391.12	316.49	283.13	265.83	256.16
35000	525.15	486.67	456.30	369.24	330.32	310.13	298.85
40000	600.17	556.19	521.49	421.99	377.51	354.43	341.54
45000	675.19	625.72	586.68	474.74	424.70	398.74	384.23
50000	750.21	695.24	651.86	527.49	471.89	443.04	426.93
55000	825.23	764.76	717.05	580.24	519.07	487.35	469.62
60000	900.25	834.29	782.24	632.99	566.26	531.65	512.31
65000	975.27	903.81	847.42	685.74	613.45	575.96	555.01
70000	1050.29	973.34	912.61	738.48	660.64	620.26	597.70
75000	1125.31	1042.86	977.80	791.23	707.83	664.56	640.39
80000	1200.34	1112.38	1042.98	843.98	755.02	708.87	683.08
85000	1275.36	1181.91	1108.17	896.73	802.20	753.17	725.78
90000	1350.38	1251.43	1173.36	949.48	849.39	797.48	768.47
95000	1425.40	1320.95	1238.54	1002.23	896.58	841.78	811.16
100000	1500.42	1390.48	1303.73	1054.98	943.77	886.09	853.85
200000	3000.84	2780.96	2607.46	2109.96	1887.54	1772.17	1707.71
300000	4501.26	4171.44	3911.18	3164.93	2831.31	2658.26	2561.56
400000	6001.68	5561.91	5214.91	4219.91	3775.08	3544.34	3415.42
500000	7502.10	6952.39	6518.64	5274.89	4718.85	4430.43	4269.27
1000000	15004.19	13904.79	13037.28	10549.78	9437.70	8860.85	8538.55

10%

Amortization Amount	1 Year	2 Years	3 Years	4 Years	5 Years	6 Years	7 Years
25	2.20	1.15	0.80	0.63	0.53	0.46	0.41
50	4.39	2.30	1.61	1.26	1.06	0.92	0.82
100	8.78	4.61	3.22	2.53	2.11	1.84	1.65
200	17.56	9.21	6.43	5.05	4.23	3.68	3.30
300	26.35	13.82	9.65	7.58	6.34	5.53	4.95
400	35.13	18.42	12.87	10.11	8.46	7.37	6.60
500	43.91	23.03	16.09	12.63	10.57	9.21	8.25
600	52.69	27.63	19.30	15.16	12.69	11.05	9.90
700	61.48	32.24	22.52	17.69	14.80	12.90	11.55
800	70.26	36.84	25.74	20.21	16.92	14.74	13.20
900	79.04	41.45	28.96	22.74	19.03	16.58	14.85
1000	87.82	46.05	32.17	25.27	21.15	18.42	16.50
2000	175.64	92.10	64.34	50.53	42.30	36.85	32.99
3000	263.47	138.15	96.52	75.80	63.44	55.27	49.49
4000	351.29	184.21	128.69	101.06	84.59	73.70	65.99
5000	439.11	230.26	160.86	126.33	105.74	92.12	82.48
6000	526.93	276.31	193.03	151.59	126.89	110.54	98.98
7000	614.75	322.36	225.21	176.86	148.03	128.97	115.48
8000	702.58	368.41	257.38	202.12	169.18	147.39	131.98
9000	790.40	414.46	289.55	227.39	190.33	165.82	148.47
10000	878.22	460.52	321.72	252.66	211.48	184.24	164.97
11000	966.04	506.57	353.90	277.92	232.62	202.66	181.47
12000	1053.86	552.62	386.07	303.19	253.77	221.09	197.96
13000	1141.68	598.67	418.24	328.45	274.92	239.51	214.46
14000	1229.51	644.72	450.41	353.72	296.07	257.94	230.96
15000	1317.33	690.77	482.59	378.98	317.22	276.36	247.45
16000	1405.15	736.83	514.76	404.25	338.36	294.78	263.95
17000	1492.97	782.88	546.93	429.52	359.51	313.21	280.45
18000	1580.79	828.93	579.10	454.78	380.66	331.63	296.94
19000	1668.62	874.98	611.27	480.05	401.81	350.06	313.44
20000	1756.44	921.03	643.45	505.31	422.95	368.48	329.94
21000	1844.26	967.08	675.62	530.58	444.10	386.90	346.43
22000	1932.08	1013.14	707.79	555.84	465.25	405.33	362.93
23000	2019.90	1059.19	739.96	581.11	486.40	423.75	379.43
24000	2107.73	1105.24	772.14	606.37	507.54	442.18	395.93
25000	2195.55	1151.29	804.31	631.64	528.69	460.60	412.42
26000	2283.37	1197.34	836.48	656.91	549.84	479.03	428.92
27000	2371.19	1243.39	868.65	682.17	570.99	497.45	445.42
28000	2459.01	1289.45	900.83	707.44	592.14	515.87	461.91
29000	2546.83	1335.50	933.00	732.70	613.28	534.30	478.41
30000	2634.66	1381.55	965.17	757.97	634.43	552.72	494.91
35000	3073.77	1611.81	1126.03	884.30	740.17	644.84	577.39
40000	3512.88	1842.07	1286.89	1010.62	845.91	736.96	659.88
45000	3951.98	2072.32	1447.76	1136.95	951.65	829.08	742.36
50000	4391.09	2302.58	1608.62	1263.28	1057.38	921.20	824.85
55000	4830.20	2532.84	1769.48	1389.61	1163.12	1013.32	907.33
60000	5269.31	2763.10	1930.34	1515.94	1268.86	1105.44	989.81
65000	5708.42	2993.36	2091.20	1642.26	1374.60	1197.56	1072.30
70000	6147.53	3223.62	2252.06	1768.59	1480.34	1289.68	1154.78
75000	6586.64	3453.87	2412.93	1894.92	1586.08	1381.80	1237.27
80000	7025.75	3684.13	2573.79	2021.25	1691.82	1473.92	1319.75
85000	7464.86	3914.39	2734.65	2147.58	1797.55	1566.04	1402.24
90000	7903.97	4144.65	2895.51	2273.90	1903.29	1658.16	1484.72
95000	8343.08	4374.91	3056.37	2400.23	2009.03	1750.28	1567.21
100000	8782.19	4605.17	3217.23	2526.56	2114.77	1842.40	1649.69
200000	17564.38	9210.33	6434.47	5053.12	4229.54	3684.81	3299.38
300000	26346.56	13815.50	9651.70	7579.68	6344.31	5527.21	4949.07
400000	35128.75	18420.67	12868.94	10106.24	8459.08	7369.62	6598.76
500000	43910.94	23025.83	16086.17	12632.80	10573.85	9212.02	8248.45
1000000	87821.88	46051.66	32172.35	25265.60	21147.70	18424.04	16496.90

MONTHLY PAYMENT
NECESSARY TO AMORTIZE A LOAN
10%

Amortization Amount	8 Years	9 Years	10 Years	15 Years	20 Years	25 Years	30 Years
25	0.38	0.35	0.33	0.27	0.24	0.22	0.22
50	0.75	0.70	0.66	0.53	0.48	0.45	0.43
100	1.51	1.40	1.31	1.06	0.95	0.89	0.86
200	3.01	2.79	2.62	2.12	1.90	1.79	1.73
300	4.52	4.19	3.93	3.19	2.85	2.68	2.59
400	6.03	5.59	5.24	4.25	3.81	3.58	3.45
500	7.53	6.98	6.55	5.31	4.76	4.47	4.31
600	9.04	8.38	7.86	6.37	5.71	5.37	5.18
700	10.55	9.78	9.17	7.44	6.66	6.26	6.04
800	12.05	11.18	10.48	8.50	7.61	7.16	6.90
900	13.56	12.57	11.79	9.56	8.56	8.05	7.76
1000	15.07	13.97	13.10	10.62	9.52	8.94	8.63
2000	30.13	27.94	26.21	21.25	19.03	17.89	17.25
3000	45.20	41.91	39.31	31.87	28.55	26.83	25.88
4000	60.27	55.88	52.41	42.49	38.07	35.78	34.51
5000	75.34	69.85	65.52	53.11	47.58	44.72	43.13
6000	90.40	83.82	78.62	63.74	57.10	53.67	51.76
7000	105.47	97.79	91.72	74.36	66.62	62.61	60.39
8000	120.54	111.76	104.83	84.98	76.13	71.56	69.01
9000	135.61	125.72	117.93	95.60	85.65	80.50	77.64
10000	150.67	139.69	131.03	106.23	95.17	89.45	86.27
11000	165.74	153.66	144.14	116.85	104.68	98.39	94.89
12000	180.81	167.63	157.24	127.47	114.20	107.34	103.52
13000	195.88	181.60	170.34	138.10	123.72	116.28	112.15
14000	210.94	195.57	183.45	148.72	133.23	125.23	120.77
15000	226.01	209.54	196.55	159.34	142.75	134.17	129.40
16000	241.08	223.51	209.65	169.96	152.27	143.12	138.03
17000	256.15	237.48	222.76	180.59	161.78	152.06	146.65
18000	271.21	251.45	235.86	191.21	171.30	161.01	155.28
19000	286.28	265.42	248.96	201.83	180.82	169.95	163.91
20000	301.35	279.39	262.07	212.45	190.33	178.90	172.53
21000	316.42	293.36	275.17	223.08	199.85	187.84	181.16
22000	331.48	307.33	288.27	233.70	209.37	196.79	189.79
23000	346.55	321.30	301.38	244.32	218.88	205.73	198.41
24000	361.62	335.27	314.48	254.94	228.40	214.68	207.04
25000	376.68	349.24	327.58	265.57	237.92	223.62	215.67
26000	391.75	363.21	340.69	276.19	247.43	232.57	224.29
27000	406.82	377.17	353.79	286.81	256.95	241.51	232.92
28000	421.89	391.14	366.89	297.44	266.47	250.46	241.55
29000	436.95	405.11	380.00	308.06	275.98	259.40	250.17
30000	452.02	419.08	393.10	318.68	285.50	268.35	258.80
35000	527.36	488.93	458.62	371.79	333.08	313.07	301.93
40000	602.70	558.78	524.13	424.91	380.67	357.79	345.07
45000	678.03	628.62	589.65	478.02	428.25	402.52	388.20
50000	753.37	698.47	655.17	531.13	475.83	447.24	431.33
55000	828.71	768.32	720.69	584.25	523.42	491.97	474.47
60000	904.04	838.17	786.20	637.36	571.00	536.69	517.60
65000	979.38	908.01	851.72	690.48	618.58	581.42	560.73
70000	1054.72	977.86	917.24	743.59	666.17	626.14	603.87
75000	1130.05	1047.71	982.75	796.70	713.75	670.87	647.00
80000	1205.39	1117.55	1048.27	849.82	761.33	715.59	690.13
85000	1280.73	1187.40	1113.79	902.93	808.91	760.31	733.27
90000	1356.07	1257.25	1179.30	956.04	856.50	805.04	776.40
95000	1431.40	1327.10	1244.82	1009.16	904.08	849.76	819.53
100000	1506.74	1396.94	1310.34	1062.27	951.66	894.49	862.67
200000	3013.48	2793.89	2620.67	2124.54	1903.33	1788.97	1725.34
300000	4520.22	4190.83	3931.01	3186.81	2854.99	2683.46	2588.00
400000	6026.96	5587.77	5241.35	4249.08	3806.66	3577.95	3450.67
500000	7533.70	6984.72	6551.68	5311.35	4758.32	4472.44	4313.34
1000000	15067.39	13969.43	13103.37	10622.70	9516.64	8944.87	8626.68

10.125%

Amortization Amount	1 Year	2 Years	3 Years	4 Years	5 Years	6 Years	7 Years
25	2.20	1.15	0.81	0.63	0.53	0.46	0.41
50	4.39	2.31	1.61	1.27	1.06	0.92	0.83
100	8.79	4.61	3.22	2.53	2.12	1.85	1.66
200	17.58	9.22	6.45	5.06	4.24	3.70	3.31
300	26.36	13.83	9.67	7.60	6.36	5.55	4.97
400	35.15	18.44	12.89	10.13	8.48	7.39	6.62
500	43.94	23.05	16.11	12.66	10.60	9.24	8.28
600	52.73	27.66	19.34	15.19	12.72	11.09	9.94
700	61.51	32.27	22.56	17.73	14.84	12.94	11.59
800	70.30	36.89	25.78	20.26	16.97	14.79	13.25
900	79.09	41.50	29.01	22.79	19.09	16.64	14.90
1000	87.88	46.11	32.23	25.32	21.21	18.48	16.56
2000	175.76	92.21	64.46	50.65	42.41	36.97	33.12
3000	263.63	138.32	96.69	75.97	63.62	55.45	49.68
4000	351.51	184.43	128.91	101.29	84.83	73.94	66.23
5000	439.39	230.53	161.14	126.62	106.03	92.42	82.79
6000	527.27	276.64	193.37	151.94	127.24	110.91	99.35
7000	615.14	322.75	225.60	177.26	148.45	129.39	115.91
8000	703.02	368.86	257.83	202.59	169.65	147.88	132.47
9000	790.90	414.96	290.06	227.91	190.86	166.36	149.03
10000	878.78	461.07	322.29	253.23	212.07	184.84	165.59
11000	966.65	507.18	354.51	278.55	233.27	203.33	182.15
12000	1054.53	553.28	386.74	303.88	254.48	221.81	198.70
13000	1142.41	599.39	418.97	329.20	275.69	240.30	215.26
14000	1230.29	645.50	451.20	354.52	296.89	258.78	231.82
15000	1318.16	691.60	483.43	379.85	318.10	277.27	248.38
16000	1406.04	737.71	515.66	405.17	339.31	295.75	264.94
17000	1493.92	783.82	547.89	430.49	360.51	314.24	281.50
18000	1581.80	829.93	580.11	455.82	381.72	332.72	298.06
19000	1669.68	876.03	612.34	481.14	402.93	351.20	314.62
20000	1757.55	922.14	644.57	506.46	424.13	369.69	331.17
21000	1845.43	968.25	676.80	531.79	445.34	388.17	347.73
22000	1933.31	1014.35	709.03	557.11	466.55	406.66	364.29
23000	2021.19	1060.46	741.26	582.43	487.75	425.14	380.85
24000	2109.06	1106.57	773.49	607.76	508.96	443.63	397.41
25000	2196.94	1152.67	805.72	633.08	530.17	462.11	413.97
26000	2284.82	1198.78	837.94	658.40	551.37	480.59	430.53
27000	2372.70	1244.89	870.17	683.72	572.58	499.08	447.09
28000	2460.57	1291.00	902.40	709.05	593.79	517.56	463.64
29000	2548.45	1337.10	934.63	734.37	614.99	536.05	480.20
30000	2636.33	1383.21	966.86	759.69	636.20	554.53	496.76
35000	3075.72	1613.74	1128.00	886.31	742.23	646.95	579.56
40000	3515.11	1844.28	1289.14	1012.93	848.26	739.38	662.35
45000	3954.49	2074.81	1450.29	1139.54	954.30	831.80	745.14
50000	4393.88	2305.35	1611.43	1266.16	1060.33	924.22	827.94
55000	4833.27	2535.88	1772.57	1392.77	1166.36	1016.64	910.73
60000	5272.66	2766.42	1933.72	1519.39	1272.40	1109.06	993.52
65000	5712.05	2996.95	2094.86	1646.00	1378.43	1201.49	1076.32
70000	6151.44	3227.49	2256.00	1772.62	1484.46	1293.91	1159.11
75000	6590.82	3458.02	2417.15	1899.23	1590.50	1386.33	1241.91
80000	7030.21	3688.56	2578.29	2025.85	1696.53	1478.75	1324.70
85000	7469.60	3919.09	2739.43	2152.47	1802.56	1571.18	1407.49
90000	7908.99	4149.63	2900.57	2279.08	1908.60	1663.60	1490.29
95000	8348.38	4380.16	3061.72	2405.70	2014.63	1756.02	1573.08
100000	8787.77	4610.70	3222.86	2532.31	2120.66	1848.44	1655.87
200000	17575.53	9221.40	6445.72	5064.63	4241.32	3696.88	3311.75
300000	26363.30	13832.10	9668.58	7596.94	6361.99	5545.32	4967.62
400000	35151.07	18442.80	12891.44	10129.25	8482.65	7393.77	6623.50
500000	43938.83	23053.50	16114.31	12661.56	10603.31	9242.21	8279.37
1000000	87877.66	46107.00	32228.61	25323.13	21206.62	18484.42	16558.75

Amortization Amount	8 Years	9 Years	10 Years	15 Years	20 Years	25 Years	30 Years
25	0.38	0.35	0.33	0.27	0.24	0.23	0.22
50	0.76	0.70	0.66	0.53	0.48	0.45	0.44
100	1.51	1.40	1.32	1.07	0.96	0.90	0.87
200	3.03	2.81	2.63	2.14	1.92	1.81	1.74
300	4.54	4.21	3.95	3.21	2.88	2.71	2.61
400	6.05	5.61	5.27	4.28	3.84	3.61	3.49
500	7.57	7.02	6.58	5.35	4.80	4.51	4.36
600	9.08	8.42	7.90	6.42	5.76	5.42	5.23
700	10.59	9.82	9.22	7.49	6.72	6.32	6.10
800	12.10	11.23	10.54	8.56	7.68	7.22	6.97
900	13.62	12.63	11.85	9.63	8.64	8.13	7.84
1000	15.13	14.03	13.17	10.70	9.60	9.03	8.72
2000	30.26	28.07	26.34	21.39	19.19	18.06	17.43
3000	45.39	42.10	39.51	32.09	28.79	27.09	26.15
4000	60.52	56.14	52.68	42.78	38.38	36.12	34.86
5000	75.65	70.17	65.85	53.48	47.98	45.15	43.58
6000	90.78	84.21	79.02	64.17	57.57	54.17	52.29
7000	105.91	98.24	92.19	74.87	67.17	63.20	61.01
8000	121.05	112.27	105.36	85.57	76.77	72.23	69.72
9000	136.18	126.31	118.53	96.26	86.36	81.26	78.44
10000	151.31	140.34	131.70	106.96	95.96	90.29	87.15
11000	166.44	154.38	144.87	117.65	105.55	99.32	95.87
12000	181.57	168.41	158.04	128.35	115.15	108.35	104.58
13000	196.70	182.44	171.20	139.05	124.75	117.38	113.30
14000	211.83	196.48	184.37	149.74	134.34	126.41	122.01
15000	226.96	210.51	197.54	160.44	143.94	135.44	130.73
16000	242.09	224.55	210.71	171.13	153.53	144.47	139.44
17000	257.22	238.58	223.88	181.83	163.13	153.50	148.16
18000	272.35	252.62	237.05	192.52	172.72	162.52	156.87
19000	287.48	266.65	250.22	203.22	182.32	171.55	165.59
20000	302.61	280.68	263.39	213.92	191.92	180.58	174.30
21000	317.74	294.72	276.56	224.61	201.51	189.61	183.02
22000	332.88	308.75	289.73	235.31	211.11	198.64	191.73
23000	348.01	322.79	302.90	246.00	220.70	207.67	200.45
24000	363.14	336.82	316.07	256.70	230.30	216.70	209.16
25000	378.27	350.86	329.24	267.40	239.90	225.73	217.88
26000	393.40	364.89	342.41	278.09	249.49	234.76	226.59
27000	408.53	378.92	355.58	288.79	259.09	243.79	235.31
28000	423.66	392.96	368.75	299.48	268.68	252.82	244.02
29000	438.79	406.99	381.92	310.18	278.28	261.84	252.74
30000	453.92	421.03	395.09	320.87	287.87	270.87	261.45
35000	529.57	491.20	460.94	374.35	335.85	316.02	305.03
40000	605.23	561.37	526.78	427.83	383.83	361.17	348.60
45000	680.88	631.54	592.63	481.31	431.81	406.31	392.18
50000	756.54	701.71	658.48	534.79	479.79	451.46	435.75
55000	832.19	771.88	724.33	588.27	527.77	496.60	479.33
60000	907.84	842.05	790.18	641.75	575.75	541.75	522.90
65000	983.50	912.22	856.02	695.23	623.73	586.89	566.48
70000	1059.15	982.40	921.87	748.71	671.71	632.04	610.05
75000	1134.80	1052.57	987.72	802.19	719.69	677.18	653.63
80000	1210.46	1122.74	1053.57	855.67	767.67	722.33	697.20
85000	1286.11	1192.91	1119.42	909.14	815.64	767.48	740.78
90000	1361.76	1263.08	1185.26	962.62	863.62	812.62	784.35
95000	1437.42	1333.25	1251.11	1016.10	911.60	857.77	827.93
100000	1513.07	1403.42	1316.96	1069.58	959.58	902.91	871.50
200000	3026.14	2806.84	2633.92	2139.16	1919.16	1805.83	1743.01
300000	4539.21	4210.26	3950.88	3208.75	2878.75	2708.74	2614.51
400000	6052.28	5613.69	5267.84	4278.33	3838.33	3611.65	3486.02
500000	7565.35	7017.11	6584.80	5347.91	4797.91	4514.56	4357.52
1000000	15130.71	14034.22	13169.60	10695.82	9595.82	9029.13	8715.04

10.25%

Amortization Amount	1 Year	2 Years	3 Years	4 Years	5 Years	6 Years	7 Years
25	2.20	1.15	0.81	0.63	0.53	0.46	0.42
50	4.40	2.31	1.61	1.27	1.06	0.93	0.83
100	8.79	4.62	3.23	2.54	2.13	1.85	1.66
200	17.59	9.23	6.46	5.08	4.25	3.71	3.32
300	26.38	13.85	9.69	7.61	6.38	5.56	4.99
400	35.17	18.46	12.91	10.15	8.51	7.42	6.65
500	43.97	23.08	16.14	12.69	10.63	9.27	8.31
600	52.76	27.70	19.37	15.23	12.76	11.13	9.97
700	61.55	32.31	22.60	17.77	14.89	12.98	11.63
800	70.35	36.93	25.83	20.30	17.01	14.84	13.30
900	79.14	41.55	29.06	22.84	19.14	16.69	14.96
1000	87.93	46.16	32.28	25.38	21.27	18.54	16.62
2000	175.87	92.32	64.57	50.76	42.53	37.09	33.24
3000	263.80	138.49	96.85	76.14	63.80	55.63	49.86
4000	351.73	184.65	129.14	101.52	85.06	74.18	66.48
5000	439.67	230.81	161.42	126.90	106.33	92.72	83.10
6000	527.60	276.97	193.71	152.28	127.59	111.27	99.72
7000	615.53	323.14	225.99	177.66	148.86	129.81	116.34
8000	703.47	369.30	258.28	203.05	170.12	148.36	132.97
9000	791.40	415.46	290.56	228.43	191.39	166.90	149.59
10000	879.33	461.62	322.85	253.81	212.66	185.45	166.21
11000	967.27	507.79	355.13	279.19	233.92	203.99	182.83
12000	1055.20	553.95	387.42	304.57	255.19	222.54	199.45
13000	1143.13	600.11	419.70	329.95	276.45	241.08	216.07
14000	1231.07	646.27	451.99	355.33	297.72	259.63	232.69
15000	1319.00	692.44	484.27	380.71	318.98	278.17	249.31
16000	1406.94	738.60	516.56	406.09	340.25	296.72	265.93
17000	1494.87	784.76	548.84	431.47	361.52	315.26	282.55
18000	1582.80	830.92	581.13	456.85	382.78	333.81	299.17
19000	1670.74	877.08	613.41	482.23	404.05	352.35	315.79
20000	1758.67	923.25	645.70	507.61	425.31	370.90	332.41
21000	1846.60	969.41	677.98	532.99	446.58	389.44	349.03
22000	1934.54	1015.57	710.27	558.38	467.84	407.99	365.66
23000	2022.47	1061.73	742.55	583.76	489.11	426.53	382.28
24000	2110.40	1107.90	774.84	609.14	510.37	445.08	398.90
25000	2198.34	1154.06	807.12	634.52	531.64	463.62	415.52
26000	2286.27	1200.22	839.41	659.90	552.91	482.17	432.14
27000	2374.20	1246.38	871.69	685.28	574.17	500.71	448.76
28000	2462.14	1292.55	903.98	710.66	595.44	519.26	465.38
29000	2550.07	1338.71	936.26	736.04	616.70	537.80	482.00
30000	2638.00	1384.87	968.55	761.42	637.97	556.35	498.62
35000	3077.67	1615.68	1129.97	888.32	744.30	649.07	581.72
40000	3517.34	1846.49	1291.40	1015.23	850.62	741.79	664.83
45000	3957.00	2077.31	1452.82	1142.13	956.95	834.52	747.93
50000	4396.67	2308.12	1614.25	1269.04	1063.28	927.24	831.03
55000	4836.34	2538.93	1775.67	1395.94	1169.61	1019.97	914.14
60000	5276.01	2769.74	1937.09	1522.84	1275.94	1112.69	997.24
65000	5715.67	3000.55	2098.52	1649.75	1382.27	1205.42	1080.34
70000	6155.34	3231.36	2259.94	1776.65	1488.59	1298.14	1163.45
75000	6595.01	3462.18	2421.37	1903.55	1594.92	1390.87	1246.55
80000	7034.68	3692.99	2582.79	2030.46	1701.25	1483.59	1329.66
85000	7474.34	3923.80	2744.22	2157.36	1807.58	1576.31	1412.76
90000	7914.01	4154.61	2905.64	2284.26	1913.91	1669.04	1495.86
95000	8353.68	4385.42	3067.07	2411.17	2020.23	1761.76	1578.97
100000	8793.34	4616.23	3228.49	2538.07	2126.56	1854.49	1662.07
200000	17586.69	9232.47	6456.98	5076.14	4253.12	3708.97	3324.14
300000	26380.03	13848.70	9685.47	7614.21	6379.69	5563.46	4986.21
400000	35173.38	18464.94	12913.96	10152.28	8506.25	7417.95	6648.28
500000	43966.72	23081.17	16142.45	12690.35	10632.81	9272.44	8310.34
1000000	87933.44	46162.35	32284.91	25380.71	21265.62	18544.87	16620.69

MONTHLY PAYMENT
NECESSARY TO AMORTIZE A LOAN
10.25%

Amortization Amount	8 Years	9 Years	10 Years	15 Years	20 Years	25 Years	30 Years
25	0.38	0.35	0.33	0.27	0.24	0.23	0.22
50	0.76	0.70	0.66	0.54	0.48	0.46	0.44
100	1.52	1.41	1.32	1.08	0.97	0.91	0.88
200	3.04	2.82	2.65	2.15	1.94	1.82	1.76
300	4.56	4.23	3.97	3.23	2.90	2.73	2.64
400	6.08	5.64	5.29	4.31	3.87	3.65	3.52
500	7.60	7.05	6.62	5.38	4.84	4.56	4.40
600	9.12	8.46	7.94	6.46	5.81	5.47	5.28
700	10.64	9.87	9.27	7.54	6.77	6.38	6.16
800	12.16	11.28	10.59	8.62	7.74	7.29	7.04
900	13.67	12.69	11.91	9.69	8.71	8.20	7.92
1000	15.19	14.10	13.24	10.77	9.68	9.11	8.80
2000	30.39	28.20	26.47	21.54	19.35	18.23	17.61
3000	45.58	42.30	39.71	32.31	29.03	27.34	26.41
4000	60.78	56.40	52.94	43.08	38.70	36.45	35.21
5000	75.97	70.50	66.18	53.85	48.38	45.57	44.02
6000	91.16	84.59	79.42	64.61	58.05	54.68	52.82
7000	106.36	98.69	92.65	75.38	67.73	63.80	61.63
8000	121.55	112.79	105.89	86.15	77.40	72.91	70.43
9000	136.75	126.89	119.12	96.92	87.08	82.02	79.23
10000	151.94	140.99	132.36	107.69	96.75	91.14	88.04
11000	167.14	155.09	145.60	118.46	106.43	100.25	96.84
12000	182.33	169.19	158.83	129.23	116.10	109.36	105.64
13000	197.52	183.29	172.07	140.00	125.78	118.48	114.45
14000	212.72	197.39	185.30	150.77	135.45	127.59	123.25
15000	227.91	211.49	198.54	161.54	145.13	136.70	132.05
16000	243.11	225.59	211.78	172.31	154.80	145.82	140.86
17000	258.30	239.69	225.01	183.08	164.48	154.93	149.66
18000	273.49	253.78	238.25	193.84	174.15	164.05	158.47
19000	288.69	267.88	251.48	204.61	183.83	173.16	167.27
20000	303.88	281.98	264.72	215.38	193.50	182.27	176.07
21000	319.08	296.08	277.96	226.15	203.18	191.39	184.88
22000	334.27	310.18	291.19	236.92	212.86	200.50	193.68
23000	349.47	324.28	304.43	247.69	222.53	209.61	202.48
24000	364.66	338.38	317.66	258.46	232.21	218.73	211.29
25000	379.85	352.48	330.90	269.23	241.88	227.84	220.09
26000	395.05	366.58	344.14	280.00	251.56	236.95	228.89
27000	410.24	380.68	357.37	290.77	261.23	246.07	237.70
28000	425.44	394.78	370.61	301.54	270.91	255.18	246.50
29000	440.63	408.87	383.84	312.31	280.58	264.30	255.30
30000	455.82	422.97	397.08	323.07	290.26	273.41	264.11
35000	531.79	493.47	463.26	376.92	338.63	318.98	308.13
40000	607.77	563.97	529.44	430.77	387.01	364.54	352.14
45000	683.74	634.46	595.62	484.61	435.39	410.11	396.16
50000	759.71	704.96	661.80	538.46	483.76	455.68	440.18
55000	835.68	775.45	727.98	592.30	532.14	501.25	484.20
60000	911.65	845.95	794.16	646.15	580.51	546.82	528.22
65000	987.62	916.44	860.34	699.99	628.89	592.39	572.23
70000	1063.59	986.94	926.52	753.84	677.27	637.95	616.25
75000	1139.56	1057.43	992.70	807.69	725.64	683.52	660.27
80000	1215.53	1127.93	1058.88	861.53	774.02	729.09	704.29
85000	1291.50	1198.43	1125.06	915.38	822.39	774.66	748.31
90000	1367.47	1268.92	1191.24	969.22	870.77	820.23	792.33
95000	1443.44	1339.42	1257.42	1023.07	919.15	865.79	836.34
100000	1519.41	1409.91	1323.60	1076.91	967.52	911.36	880.36
200000	3038.83	2819.83	2647.20	2153.83	1935.05	1822.72	1760.72
300000	4558.24	4229.74	3970.79	3230.74	2902.57	2734.09	2641.08
400000	6077.66	5639.65	5294.39	4307.66	3870.09	3645.45	3521.45
500000	7597.07	7049.56	6617.99	5384.57	4837.62	4556.81	4401.81
1000000	15194.14	14099.13	13235.98	10769.15	9675.23	9113.62	8803.61

103

10.375%

Amortization Amount	1 Year	2 Years	3 Years	4 Years	5 Years	6 Years	7 Years
25	2.20	1.16	0.81	0.64	0.53	0.47	0.42
50	4.40	2.31	1.62	1.27	1.07	0.93	0.83
100	8.80	4.62	3.23	2.54	2.13	1.86	1.67
200	17.60	9.24	6.47	5.09	4.26	3.72	3.34
300	26.40	13.87	9.70	7.63	6.40	5.58	5.00
400	35.20	18.49	12.94	10.18	8.53	7.44	6.67
500	43.99	23.11	16.17	12.72	10.66	9.30	8.34
600	52.79	27.73	19.40	15.26	12.79	11.16	10.01
700	61.59	32.35	22.64	17.81	14.93	13.02	11.68
800	70.39	36.97	25.87	20.35	17.06	14.88	13.35
900	79.19	41.60	29.11	22.89	19.19	16.74	15.01
1000	87.99	46.22	32.34	25.44	21.32	18.61	16.68
2000	175.98	92.44	64.68	50.88	42.65	37.21	33.37
3000	263.97	138.65	97.02	76.32	63.97	55.82	50.05
4000	351.96	184.87	129.36	101.75	85.30	74.42	66.73
5000	439.95	231.09	161.71	127.19	106.62	93.03	83.41
6000	527.94	277.31	194.05	152.63	127.95	111.63	100.10
7000	615.92	323.52	226.39	178.07	149.27	130.24	116.78
8000	703.91	369.74	258.73	203.51	170.60	148.84	133.46
9000	791.90	415.96	291.07	228.95	191.92	167.45	150.14
10000	879.89	462.18	323.41	254.38	213.25	186.05	166.83
11000	967.88	508.39	355.75	279.82	234.57	204.66	183.51
12000	1055.87	554.61	388.09	305.26	255.90	223.26	200.19
13000	1143.86	600.83	420.44	330.70	277.22	241.87	216.88
14000	1231.85	647.05	452.78	356.14	298.55	260.48	233.56
15000	1319.84	693.27	485.12	381.58	319.87	279.08	250.24
16000	1407.83	739.48	517.46	407.01	341.19	297.69	266.92
17000	1495.82	785.70	549.80	432.45	362.52	316.29	283.61
18000	1583.81	831.92	582.14	457.89	383.84	334.90	300.29
19000	1671.79	878.14	614.48	483.33	405.17	353.50	316.97
20000	1759.78	924.35	646.82	508.77	426.49	372.11	333.65
21000	1847.77	970.57	679.17	534.21	447.82	390.71	350.34
22000	1935.76	1016.79	711.51	559.64	469.14	409.32	367.02
23000	2023.75	1063.01	743.85	585.08	490.47	427.92	383.70
24000	2111.74	1109.22	776.19	610.52	511.79	446.53	400.39
25000	2199.73	1155.44	808.53	635.96	533.12	465.14	417.07
26000	2287.72	1201.66	840.87	661.40	554.44	483.74	433.75
27000	2375.71	1247.88	873.21	686.84	575.77	502.35	450.43
28000	2463.70	1294.10	905.55	712.27	597.09	520.95	467.12
29000	2551.69	1340.31	937.90	737.71	618.42	539.56	483.80
30000	2639.68	1386.53	970.24	763.15	639.74	558.16	500.48
35000	3079.62	1617.62	1131.94	890.34	746.36	651.19	583.90
40000	3519.57	1848.71	1293.65	1017.53	852.99	744.22	667.31
45000	3959.51	2079.80	1455.36	1144.73	959.61	837.24	750.72
50000	4399.46	2310.89	1617.06	1271.92	1066.23	930.27	834.14
55000	4839.41	2541.97	1778.77	1399.11	1172.86	1023.30	917.55
60000	5279.35	2773.06	1940.47	1526.30	1279.48	1116.32	1000.96
65000	5719.30	3004.15	2102.18	1653.49	1386.10	1209.35	1084.38
70000	6159.24	3235.24	2263.89	1780.68	1492.73	1302.38	1167.79
75000	6599.19	3466.33	2425.59	1907.88	1599.35	1395.41	1251.20
80000	7039.14	3697.42	2587.30	2035.07	1705.97	1488.43	1334.62
85000	7479.08	3928.50	2749.00	2162.26	1812.60	1581.46	1418.03
90000	7919.03	4159.59	2910.71	2289.45	1919.22	1674.49	1501.45
95000	8358.97	4390.68	3072.42	2416.64	2025.84	1767.51	1584.86
100000	8798.92	4621.77	3234.12	2543.83	2132.47	1860.54	1668.27
200000	17597.84	9243.54	6468.25	5087.67	4264.94	3721.08	3336.55
300000	26396.76	13865.31	9702.37	7631.50	6397.40	5581.62	5004.82
400000	35195.68	18487.08	12936.49	10175.34	8529.87	7442.17	6673.09
500000	43994.60	23108.85	16170.62	12719.17	10662.34	9302.71	8341.37
1000000	87989.21	46217.70	32341.23	25438.34	21324.68	18605.41	16682.73

Amortization Amount	8 Years	9 Years	10 Years	15 Years	20 Years	25 Years	30 Years
25	0.38	0.35	0.33	0.27	0.24	0.23	0.22
50	0.76	0.71	0.67	0.54	0.49	0.46	0.44
100	1.53	1.42	1.33	1.08	0.98	0.92	0.89
200	3.05	2.83	2.66	2.17	1.95	1.84	1.78
300	4.58	4.25	3.99	3.25	2.93	2.76	2.67
400	6.10	5.67	5.32	4.34	3.90	3.68	3.56
500	7.63	7.08	6.65	5.42	4.88	4.60	4.45
600	9.15	8.50	7.98	6.51	5.85	5.52	5.34
700	10.68	9.91	9.31	7.59	6.83	6.44	6.22
800	12.21	11.33	10.64	8.67	7.80	7.36	7.11
900	13.73	12.75	11.97	9.76	8.78	8.28	8.00
1000	15.26	14.16	13.30	10.84	9.75	9.20	8.89
2000	30.52	28.33	26.61	21.69	19.51	18.40	17.78
3000	45.77	42.49	39.91	32.53	29.26	27.60	26.68
4000	61.03	56.66	53.21	43.37	39.02	36.79	35.57
5000	76.29	70.82	66.51	54.21	48.77	45.99	44.46
6000	91.55	84.99	79.82	65.06	58.53	55.19	53.35
7000	106.80	99.15	93.12	75.90	68.28	64.39	62.25
8000	122.06	113.31	106.42	86.74	78.04	73.59	71.14
9000	137.32	127.48	119.72	97.58	87.79	82.79	80.03
10000	152.58	141.64	133.03	108.43	97.55	91.98	88.92
11000	167.83	155.81	146.33	119.27	107.30	101.18	97.82
12000	183.09	169.97	159.63	130.11	117.06	110.38	106.71
13000	198.35	184.13	172.93	140.95	126.81	119.58	115.60
14000	213.61	198.30	186.24	151.80	136.57	128.78	124.49
15000	228.87	212.46	199.54	162.64	146.32	137.98	133.39
16000	244.12	226.63	212.84	173.48	156.08	147.17	142.28
17000	259.38	240.79	226.14	184.33	165.83	156.37	151.17
18000	274.64	254.96	239.45	195.17	175.59	165.57	160.06
19000	289.90	269.12	252.75	206.01	185.34	174.77	168.96
20000	305.15	283.28	266.05	216.85	195.10	183.97	177.85
21000	320.41	297.45	279.35	227.70	204.85	193.17	186.74
22000	335.67	311.61	292.66	238.54	214.61	202.36	195.63
23000	350.93	325.78	305.96	249.38	224.36	211.56	204.53
24000	366.18	339.94	319.26	260.22	234.12	220.76	213.42
25000	381.44	354.10	332.56	271.07	243.87	229.96	222.31
26000	396.70	368.27	345.87	281.91	253.63	239.16	231.20
27000	411.96	382.43	359.17	292.75	263.38	248.36	240.09
28000	427.22	396.60	372.47	303.59	273.14	257.55	248.99
29000	442.47	410.76	385.77	314.44	282.89	266.75	257.88
30000	457.73	424.93	399.08	325.28	292.65	275.95	266.77
35000	534.02	495.75	465.59	379.49	341.42	321.94	311.23
40000	610.31	566.57	532.10	433.71	390.19	367.93	355.70
45000	686.60	637.39	598.61	487.92	438.97	413.93	400.16
50000	762.88	708.21	665.13	542.13	487.74	459.92	444.62
55000	839.17	779.03	731.64	596.35	536.52	505.91	489.08
60000	915.46	849.85	798.15	650.56	585.29	551.90	533.54
65000	991.75	920.67	864.66	704.77	634.07	597.89	578.01
70000	1068.04	991.49	931.18	758.99	682.84	643.88	622.47
75000	1144.33	1062.31	997.69	813.20	731.62	689.88	666.93
80000	1220.61	1133.13	1064.20	867.41	780.39	735.87	711.39
85000	1296.90	1203.95	1130.71	921.63	829.16	781.86	755.85
90000	1373.19	1274.78	1197.23	975.84	877.94	827.85	800.32
95000	1449.48	1345.60	1263.74	1030.05	926.71	873.84	844.78
100000	1525.77	1416.42	1330.25	1084.27	975.49	919.83	889.24
200000	3051.54	2832.83	2660.50	2168.54	1950.97	1839.67	1778.48
300000	4577.31	4249.25	3990.75	3252.80	2926.46	2759.50	2667.72
400000	6103.07	5665.67	5321.00	4337.07	3901.95	3679.34	3556.96
500000	7628.84	7082.09	6651.25	5421.34	4877.43	4599.17	4446.20
1000000	15257.69	14164.17	13302.50	10842.68	9754.87	9198.35	8892.40

10.5%

Amortization Amount	1 Year	2 Years	3 Years	4 Years	5 Years	6 Years	7 Years
25	2.20	1.16	0.81	0.64	0.53	0.47	0.42
50	4.40	2.31	1.62	1.27	1.07	0.93	0.84
100	8.80	4.63	3.24	2.55	2.14	1.87	1.67
200	17.61	9.25	6.48	5.10	4.28	3.73	3.35
300	26.41	13.88	9.72	7.65	6.42	5.60	5.02
400	35.22	18.51	12.96	10.20	8.55	7.47	6.70
500	44.02	23.14	16.20	12.75	10.69	9.33	8.37
600	52.83	27.78	19.44	15.30	12.83	11.20	10.05
700	61.63	32.39	22.68	17.85	14.97	13.07	11.72
800	70.44	37.02	25.92	20.40	17.11	14.93	13.40
900	79.24	41.65	29.16	22.95	19.25	16.80	15.07
1000	88.04	46.27	32.40	25.50	21.38	18.67	16.74
2000	176.09	92.55	64.80	50.99	42.77	37.33	33.49
3000	264.13	138.82	97.19	76.49	64.15	56.00	50.23
4000	352.18	185.09	129.59	101.98	85.54	74.66	66.98
5000	440.22	231.37	161.99	127.48	106.92	93.33	83.72
6000	528.27	277.64	194.39	152.98	128.30	112.00	100.47
7000	616.31	323.91	226.78	178.47	149.69	130.66	117.21
8000	704.36	370.18	259.18	203.97	171.07	149.33	133.96
9000	792.40	416.46	291.58	229.46	192.45	167.99	150.70
10000	880.45	462.73	323.98	254.96	213.84	186.66	167.45
11000	968.49	509.00	356.37	280.46	235.22	205.33	184.19
12000	1056.54	555.28	388.77	305.95	256.61	223.99	200.94
13000	1144.58	601.55	421.17	331.45	277.99	242.66	217.68
14000	1232.63	647.82	453.57	356.94	299.37	261.32	234.43
15000	1320.67	694.10	485.96	382.44	320.76	279.99	251.17
16000	1408.72	740.37	518.36	407.94	342.14	298.66	267.92
17000	1496.76	786.64	550.76	433.43	363.52	317.32	284.66
18000	1584.81	832.92	583.16	458.93	384.91	335.99	301.41
19000	1672.85	879.19	615.55	484.42	406.29	354.65	318.15
20000	1760.90	925.46	647.95	509.92	427.68	373.32	334.90
21000	1848.94	971.73	680.35	535.42	449.06	391.99	351.64
22000	1936.99	1018.01	712.75	560.91	470.44	410.65	368.39
23000	2025.03	1064.28	745.14	586.41	491.83	429.32	385.13
24000	2113.08	1110.55	777.54	611.90	513.21	447.98	401.88
25000	2201.12	1156.83	809.94	637.40	534.60	466.65	418.62
26000	2289.17	1203.10	842.34	662.90	555.98	485.32	435.37
27000	2377.21	1249.37	874.73	688.39	577.36	503.98	452.11
28000	2465.26	1295.65	907.13	713.89	598.75	522.65	468.86
29000	2553.30	1341.92	939.53	739.38	620.13	541.32	485.60
30000	2641.35	1388.19	971.93	764.88	641.51	559.98	502.35
35000	3081.57	1619.56	1133.92	892.36	748.43	653.31	586.07
40000	3521.80	1850.92	1295.90	1019.84	855.35	746.64	669.80
45000	3962.02	2082.29	1457.89	1147.32	962.27	839.97	753.52
50000	4402.25	2313.65	1619.88	1274.80	1069.19	933.30	837.24
55000	4842.47	2545.02	1781.87	1402.28	1176.11	1026.63	920.97
60000	5282.70	2776.38	1943.86	1529.76	1283.03	1119.96	1004.69
65000	5722.92	3007.75	2105.84	1657.24	1389.95	1213.29	1088.42
70000	6163.15	3239.12	2267.83	1784.72	1496.87	1306.62	1172.14
75000	6603.37	3470.48	2429.82	1912.20	1603.79	1399.95	1255.87
80000	7043.60	3701.85	2591.81	2039.68	1710.70	1493.28	1339.59
85000	7483.82	3933.21	2753.80	2167.16	1817.62	1586.61	1423.31
90000	7924.05	4164.58	2915.78	2294.64	1924.54	1679.94	1507.04
95000	8364.27	4395.94	3077.77	2422.12	2031.46	1773.27	1590.76
100000	8804.50	4627.31	3239.76	2549.60	2138.38	1866.60	1674.49
200000	17608.99	9254.61	6479.52	5099.20	4276.76	3733.21	3348.98
300000	26413.49	13881.92	9719.28	7648.81	6415.14	5599.81	5023.46
400000	35217.99	18509.23	12959.04	10198.41	8553.52	7466.42	6697.95
500000	44022.48	23136.54	16198.80	12748.01	10691.90	9333.02	8372.44
1000000	88044.96	46273.07	32397.59	25496.02	21383.80	18666.04	16744.88

Amortization Amount	8 Years	9 Years	10 Years	15 Years	20 Years	25 Years	30 Years
25	0.38	0.36	0.33	0.27	0.25	0.23	0.22
50	0.77	0.71	0.67	0.55	0.49	0.46	0.45
100	1.53	1.42	1.34	1.09	0.98	0.93	0.90
200	3.06	2.85	2.67	2.18	1.97	1.86	1.80
300	4.60	4.27	4.01	3.27	2.95	2.78	2.69
400	6.13	5.69	5.35	4.37	3.93	3.71	3.59
500	7.66	7.11	6.68	5.46	4.92	4.64	4.49
600	9.19	8.54	8.02	6.55	5.90	5.57	5.39
700	10.72	9.96	9.36	7.64	6.88	6.50	6.29
800	12.26	11.38	10.70	8.73	7.87	7.43	7.19
900	13.79	12.81	12.03	9.82	8.85	8.35	8.08
1000	15.32	14.23	13.37	10.92	9.83	9.28	8.98
2000	30.64	28.46	26.74	21.83	19.67	18.57	17.96
3000	45.96	42.69	40.11	32.75	29.50	27.85	26.94
4000	61.29	56.92	53.48	43.67	39.34	37.13	35.93
5000	76.61	71.15	66.85	54.58	49.17	46.42	44.91
6000	91.93	85.38	80.22	65.50	59.01	55.70	53.89
7000	107.25	99.61	93.58	76.41	68.84	64.98	62.87
8000	122.57	113.83	106.95	87.33	78.68	74.27	71.85
9000	137.89	128.06	120.32	98.25	88.51	83.55	80.83
10000	153.21	142.29	133.69	109.16	98.35	92.83	89.81
11000	168.53	156.52	147.06	120.08	108.18	102.12	98.80
12000	183.86	170.75	160.43	131.00	118.02	111.40	107.78
13000	199.18	184.98	173.80	141.91	127.85	120.68	116.76
14000	214.50	199.21	187.17	152.83	137.69	129.97	125.74
15000	229.82	213.44	200.54	163.75	147.52	139.25	134.72
16000	245.14	227.67	213.91	174.66	157.36	148.53	143.70
17000	260.46	241.90	227.28	185.58	167.19	157.82	152.68
18000	275.78	256.13	240.65	196.50	177.03	167.10	161.67
19000	291.11	270.36	254.01	207.41	186.86	176.38	170.65
20000	306.43	284.59	267.38	218.33	196.69	185.67	179.63
21000	321.75	298.82	280.75	229.24	206.53	194.95	188.61
22000	337.07	313.05	294.12	240.16	216.36	204.23	197.59
23000	352.39	327.28	307.49	251.08	226.20	213.52	206.57
24000	367.71	341.50	320.86	261.99	236.03	222.80	215.55
25000	383.03	355.73	334.23	272.91	245.87	232.08	224.54
26000	398.36	369.96	347.60	283.83	255.70	241.37	233.52
27000	413.68	384.19	360.97	294.74	265.54	250.65	242.50
28000	429.00	398.42	374.34	305.66	275.37	259.93	251.48
29000	444.32	412.65	387.71	316.58	285.21	269.22	260.46
30000	459.64	426.88	401.08	327.49	295.04	278.50	269.44
35000	536.25	498.03	467.92	382.07	344.22	324.92	314.35
40000	612.85	569.17	534.77	436.66	393.39	371.33	359.26
45000	689.46	640.32	601.61	491.24	442.56	417.75	404.16
50000	766.07	711.47	668.46	545.82	491.74	464.16	449.07
55000	842.67	782.61	735.30	600.40	540.91	510.58	493.98
60000	919.28	853.76	802.15	654.98	590.08	557.00	538.88
65000	995.89	924.91	869.00	709.57	639.26	603.41	583.79
70000	1072.49	996.05	935.84	764.15	688.43	649.83	628.70
75000	1149.10	1067.20	1002.69	818.73	737.61	696.25	673.61
80000	1225.71	1138.35	1069.53	873.31	786.78	742.66	718.51
85000	1302.31	1209.49	1136.38	927.89	835.95	789.08	763.42
90000	1378.92	1280.64	1203.23	982.48	885.13	835.50	808.33
95000	1455.53	1351.79	1270.07	1037.06	934.30	881.91	853.23
100000	1532.14	1422.93	1336.92	1091.64	983.47	928.33	898.14
200000	3064.27	2845.87	2673.83	2183.28	1966.95	1856.66	1796.28
300000	4596.41	4268.80	4010.75	3274.92	2950.42	2784.99	2694.42
400000	6128.54	5691.74	5347.67	4366.56	3933.89	3713.32	3592.56
500000	7660.68	7114.67	6684.59	5458.20	4917.37	4641.65	4490.70
1000000	15321.35	14229.35	13369.17	10916.40	9834.73	9283.30	8981.40

10.625%

MONTHLY PAYMENT
NECESSARY TO AMORTIZE A LOAN

Amortization Amount	1 Year	2 Years	3 Years	4 Years	5 Years	6 Years	7 Years
25	2.20	1.16	0.81	0.64	0.54	0.47	0.42
50	4.41	2.32	1.62	1.28	1.07	0.94	0.84
100	8.81	4.63	3.25	2.56	2.14	1.87	1.68
200	17.62	9.27	6.49	5.11	4.29	3.75	3.36
300	26.43	13.90	9.74	7.67	6.43	5.62	5.04
400	35.24	18.53	12.98	10.22	8.58	7.49	6.72
500	44.05	23.16	16.23	12.78	10.72	9.36	8.40
600	52.86	27.80	19.47	15.33	12.87	11.24	10.08
700	61.67	32.43	22.72	17.89	15.01	13.11	11.76
800	70.48	37.06	25.96	20.44	17.15	14.98	13.45
900	79.29	41.70	29.21	23.00	19.30	16.85	15.13
1000	88.10	46.33	32.45	25.55	21.44	18.73	16.81
2000	176.20	92.66	64.91	51.11	42.89	37.45	33.61
3000	264.30	138.99	97.36	76.66	64.33	56.18	50.42
4000	352.40	185.31	129.82	102.21	85.77	74.91	67.23
5000	440.50	231.64	162.27	127.77	107.21	93.63	84.04
6000	528.60	277.97	194.72	153.32	128.66	112.36	100.84
7000	616.71	324.30	227.18	178.88	150.10	131.09	117.65
8000	704.81	370.63	259.63	204.43	171.54	149.81	134.46
9000	792.91	416.96	292.09	229.98	192.99	168.54	151.26
10000	881.01	463.28	324.54	255.54	214.43	187.27	168.07
11000	969.11	509.61	356.99	281.09	235.87	205.99	184.88
12000	1057.21	555.94	389.45	306.64	257.32	224.72	201.69
13000	1145.31	602.27	421.90	332.20	278.76	243.45	218.49
14000	1233.41	648.60	454.36	357.75	300.20	262.17	235.30
15000	1321.51	694.93	486.81	383.31	321.64	280.90	252.11
16000	1409.61	741.26	519.26	408.86	343.09	299.63	268.91
17000	1497.71	787.58	551.72	434.41	364.53	318.35	285.72
18000	1585.81	833.91	584.17	459.97	385.97	337.08	302.53
19000	1673.91	880.24	616.63	485.52	407.42	355.81	319.34
20000	1762.01	926.57	649.08	511.07	428.86	374.53	336.14
21000	1850.12	972.90	681.53	536.63	450.30	393.26	352.95
22000	1938.22	1019.23	713.99	562.18	471.75	411.99	369.76
23000	2026.32	1065.55	746.44	587.74	493.19	430.72	386.56
24000	2114.42	1111.88	778.90	613.29	514.63	449.44	403.37
25000	2202.52	1158.21	811.35	638.84	536.07	468.17	420.18
26000	2290.62	1204.54	843.80	664.40	557.52	486.90	436.99
27000	2378.72	1250.87	876.26	689.95	578.96	505.62	453.79
28000	2466.82	1297.20	908.71	715.50	600.40	524.35	470.60
29000	2554.92	1343.53	941.17	741.06	621.85	543.08	487.41
30000	2643.02	1389.85	973.62	766.61	643.29	561.80	504.21
35000	3083.53	1621.50	1135.89	894.38	750.50	655.44	588.25
40000	3524.03	1853.14	1298.16	1022.15	857.72	749.07	672.28
45000	3964.53	2084.78	1460.43	1149.92	964.93	842.70	756.32
50000	4405.04	2316.42	1622.70	1277.69	1072.15	936.34	840.36
55000	4845.54	2548.07	1784.97	1405.46	1179.36	1029.97	924.39
60000	5286.04	2779.71	1947.24	1533.22	1286.58	1123.60	1008.43
65000	5726.55	3011.35	2109.51	1660.99	1393.79	1217.24	1092.46
70000	6167.05	3242.99	2271.78	1788.76	1501.01	1310.87	1176.50
75000	6607.55	3474.63	2434.05	1916.53	1608.22	1404.51	1260.53
80000	7048.06	3706.28	2596.32	2044.30	1715.44	1498.14	1344.57
85000	7488.56	3937.92	2758.59	2172.07	1822.65	1591.77	1428.61
90000	7929.06	4169.56	2920.86	2299.84	1929.87	1685.41	1512.64
95000	8369.57	4401.20	3083.13	2427.61	2037.08	1779.04	1596.68
100000	8810.07	4632.85	3245.40	2555.37	2144.30	1872.67	1680.71
200000	17620.14	9265.69	6490.80	5110.75	4288.60	3745.35	3361.42
300000	26430.21	13898.54	9736.19	7666.12	6432.90	5618.02	5042.14
400000	35240.29	18531.38	12981.59	10221.50	8577.20	7490.70	6722.85
500000	44050.36	23164.23	16226.99	12776.87	10721.50	9363.37	8403.56
1000000	88100.72	46328.46	32453.98	25553.75	21443.00	18726.75	16807.12

Amortization Amount	8 Years	9 Years	10 Years	15 Years	20 Years	25 Years	30 Years
25	0.38	0.36	0.34	0.27	0.25	0.23	0.23
50	0.77	0.71	0.67	0.55	0.50	0.47	0.45
100	1.54	1.43	1.34	1.10	0.99	0.94	0.91
200	3.08	2.86	2.69	2.20	1.98	1.87	1.81
300	4.62	4.29	4.03	3.30	2.97	2.81	2.72
400	6.15	5.72	5.37	4.40	3.97	3.75	3.63
500	7.69	7.15	6.72	5.50	4.96	4.68	4.54
600	9.23	8.58	8.06	6.59	5.95	5.62	5.44
700	10.77	10.01	9.41	7.69	6.94	6.56	6.35
800	12.31	11.44	10.75	8.79	7.93	7.49	7.26
900	13.85	12.87	12.09	9.89	8.92	8.43	8.16
1000	15.39	14.29	13.44	10.99	9.91	9.37	9.07
2000	30.77	28.59	26.87	21.98	19.83	18.74	18.14
3000	46.16	42.88	40.31	32.97	29.74	28.11	27.21
4000	61.54	57.18	53.74	43.96	39.66	37.47	36.28
5000	76.93	71.47	67.18	54.95	49.57	46.84	45.35
6000	92.31	85.77	80.62	65.94	59.49	56.21	54.42
7000	107.70	100.06	94.05	76.93	69.40	65.58	63.49
8000	123.08	114.36	107.49	87.92	79.32	74.95	72.56
9000	138.47	128.65	120.92	98.91	89.23	84.32	81.64
10000	153.85	142.95	134.36	109.90	99.15	93.68	90.71
11000	169.24	157.24	147.80	120.89	109.06	103.05	99.78
12000	184.62	171.54	161.23	131.88	118.98	112.42	108.85
13000	200.01	185.83	174.67	142.87	128.89	121.79	117.92
14000	215.39	200.13	188.10	153.86	138.81	131.16	126.99
15000	230.78	214.42	201.54	164.85	148.72	140.53	136.06
16000	246.16	228.71	214.98	175.85	158.64	149.90	145.13
17000	261.55	243.01	228.41	186.84	168.55	159.26	154.20
18000	276.93	257.30	241.85	197.83	178.47	168.63	163.27
19000	292.32	271.60	255.28	208.82	188.38	178.00	172.34
20000	307.70	285.89	268.72	219.81	198.30	187.37	181.41
21000	323.09	300.19	282.16	230.80	208.21	196.74	190.48
22000	338.47	314.48	295.59	241.79	218.13	206.11	199.55
23000	353.86	328.78	309.03	252.78	228.04	215.47	208.62
24000	369.24	343.07	322.46	263.77	237.96	224.84	217.69
25000	384.63	357.37	335.90	274.76	247.87	234.21	226.77
26000	400.01	371.66	349.34	285.75	257.79	243.58	235.84
27000	415.40	385.96	362.77	296.74	267.70	252.95	244.91
28000	430.78	400.25	376.21	307.73	277.61	262.32	253.98
29000	446.17	414.54	389.64	318.72	287.53	271.69	263.05
30000	461.55	428.84	403.08	329.71	297.44	281.05	272.12
35000	538.48	500.31	470.26	384.66	347.02	327.90	317.47
40000	615.41	571.79	537.44	439.61	396.59	374.74	362.82
45000	692.33	643.26	604.62	494.56	446.17	421.58	408.18
50000	769.26	714.73	671.80	549.52	495.74	468.42	453.53
55000	846.18	786.21	738.98	604.47	545.32	515.27	498.88
60000	923.11	857.68	806.16	659.42	594.89	562.11	544.24
65000	1000.03	929.15	873.34	714.37	644.46	608.95	589.59
70000	1076.96	1000.63	940.52	769.32	694.04	655.79	634.94
75000	1153.88	1072.10	1007.70	824.27	743.61	702.64	680.30
80000	1230.81	1143.57	1074.88	879.23	793.19	749.48	725.65
85000	1307.74	1215.05	1142.06	934.18	842.76	796.32	771.00
90000	1384.66	1286.52	1209.24	989.13	892.33	843.16	816.35
95000	1461.59	1357.99	1276.42	1044.08	941.91	890.00	861.71
100000	1538.51	1429.47	1343.60	1099.03	991.48	936.85	907.06
200000	3077.03	2858.93	2687.20	2198.07	1982.96	1873.69	1814.12
300000	4615.54	4288.40	4030.80	3297.10	2974.45	2810.54	2721.18
400000	6154.05	5717.86	5374.39	4396.13	3965.93	3747.39	3628.24
500000	7692.57	7147.33	6717.99	5495.16	4957.41	4684.24	4535.30
1000000	15385.13	14294.65	13435.99	10990.33	9914.82	9368.47	9070.60

10.75%

MONTHLY PAYMENT
NECESSARY TO AMORTIZE A LOAN

Amortization Amount	1 Year	2 Years	3 Years	4 Years	5 Years	6 Years	7 Years
25	2.20	1.16	0.81	0.64	0.54	0.47	0.42
50	4.41	2.32	1.63	1.28	1.08	0.94	0.84
100	8.82	4.64	3.25	2.56	2.15	1.88	1.69
200	17.63	9.28	6.50	5.12	4.30	3.76	3.37
300	26.45	13.92	9.75	7.68	6.45	5.64	5.06
400	35.26	18.55	13.00	10.24	8.60	7.52	6.75
500	44.08	23.19	16.26	12.81	10.75	9.39	8.43
600	52.89	27.83	19.51	15.37	12.90	11.27	10.12
700	61.71	32.47	22.76	17.93	15.05	13.15	11.81
800	70.53	37.11	26.01	20.49	17.20	15.03	13.50
900	79.34	41.75	29.26	23.05	19.35	16.91	15.18
1000	88.16	46.38	32.51	25.61	21.50	18.79	16.87
2000	176.31	92.77	65.02	51.22	43.00	37.58	33.74
3000	264.47	139.15	97.53	76.83	64.51	56.36	50.61
4000	352.63	185.54	130.04	102.45	86.01	75.15	67.48
5000	440.78	231.92	162.55	128.06	107.51	93.94	84.35
6000	528.94	278.30	195.06	153.67	129.01	112.73	101.22
7000	617.10	324.69	227.57	179.28	150.52	131.51	118.09
8000	705.25	371.07	260.08	204.89	172.02	150.30	134.96
9000	793.41	417.45	292.59	230.50	193.52	169.09	151.83
10000	881.56	463.84	325.10	256.12	215.02	187.88	168.69
11000	969.72	510.22	357.61	281.73	236.52	206.66	185.56
12000	1057.88	556.61	390.12	307.34	258.03	225.45	202.43
13000	1146.03	602.99	422.64	332.95	279.53	244.24	219.30
14000	1234.19	649.37	455.15	358.56	301.03	263.03	236.17
15000	1322.35	695.76	487.66	384.17	322.53	281.81	253.04
16000	1410.50	742.14	520.17	409.78	344.04	300.60	269.91
17000	1498.66	788.53	552.68	435.40	365.54	319.39	286.78
18000	1586.82	834.91	585.19	461.01	387.04	338.18	303.65
19000	1674.97	881.29	617.70	486.62	408.54	356.96	320.52
20000	1763.13	927.68	650.21	512.23	430.05	375.75	337.39
21000	1851.29	974.06	682.72	537.84	451.55	394.54	354.26
22000	1939.44	1020.44	715.23	563.45	473.05	413.33	371.13
23000	2027.60	1066.83	747.74	589.07	494.55	432.11	388.00
24000	2115.75	1113.21	780.25	614.68	516.05	450.90	404.87
25000	2203.91	1159.60	812.76	640.29	537.56	469.69	421.74
26000	2292.07	1205.98	845.27	665.90	559.06	488.48	438.61
27000	2380.22	1252.36	877.78	691.51	580.56	507.26	455.48
28000	2468.38	1298.75	910.29	717.12	602.06	526.05	472.35
29000	2556.54	1345.13	942.80	742.73	623.57	544.84	489.21
30000	2644.69	1391.52	975.31	768.35	645.07	563.63	506.08
35000	3085.48	1623.43	1137.86	896.40	752.58	657.56	590.43
40000	3526.26	1855.35	1300.42	1024.46	860.09	751.50	674.78
45000	3967.04	2087.27	1462.97	1152.52	967.60	845.44	759.13
50000	4407.82	2319.19	1625.52	1280.58	1075.11	939.38	843.47
55000	4848.61	2551.11	1788.07	1408.63	1182.62	1033.31	927.82
60000	5289.39	2783.03	1950.62	1536.69	1290.14	1127.25	1012.17
65000	5730.17	3014.95	2113.18	1664.75	1397.65	1221.19	1096.52
70000	6170.95	3246.87	2275.73	1792.81	1505.16	1315.13	1180.86
75000	6611.73	3478.79	2438.28	1920.86	1612.67	1409.07	1265.21
80000	7052.52	3710.71	2600.83	2048.92	1720.18	1503.00	1349.56
85000	7493.30	3942.63	2763.38	2176.98	1827.69	1596.94	1433.90
90000	7934.08	4174.55	2925.94	2305.04	1935.20	1690.88	1518.25
95000	8374.86	4406.47	3088.49	2433.09	2042.71	1784.82	1602.60
100000	8815.65	4638.38	3251.04	2561.15	2150.23	1878.75	1686.95
200000	17631.29	9276.77	6502.08	5122.30	4300.45	3757.51	3373.89
300000	26446.94	13915.15	9753.12	7683.46	6450.68	5636.26	5060.84
400000	35262.58	18553.54	13004.16	10244.61	8600.90	7515.02	6747.79
500000	44078.23	23191.92	16255.20	12805.76	10751.13	9393.77	8434.73
1000000	88156.46	46383.85	32510.40	25611.52	21502.26	18787.54	16869.46

110

Amortization Amount	8 Years	9 Years	10 Years	15 Years	20 Years	25 Years	30 Years
25	0.39	0.36	0.34	0.28	0.25	0.24	0.23
50	0.77	0.72	0.68	0.55	0.50	0.47	0.46
100	1.54	1.44	1.35	1.11	1.00	0.95	0.92
200	3.09	2.87	2.70	2.21	2.00	1.89	1.83
300	4.63	4.31	4.05	3.32	3.00	2.84	2.75
400	6.18	5.74	5.40	4.43	4.00	3.78	3.66
500	7.72	7.18	6.75	5.53	5.00	4.73	4.58
600	9.27	8.62	8.10	6.64	6.00	5.67	5.50
700	10.81	10.05	9.45	7.75	7.00	6.62	6.41
800	12.36	11.49	10.80	8.85	8.00	7.56	7.33
900	13.90	12.92	12.15	9.96	9.00	8.51	8.24
1000	15.45	14.36	13.50	11.06	10.00	9.45	9.16
2000	30.90	28.72	27.01	22.13	19.99	18.91	18.32
3000	46.35	43.08	40.51	33.19	29.99	28.36	27.48
4000	61.80	57.44	54.01	44.26	39.98	37.82	36.64
5000	77.25	71.80	67.51	55.32	49.98	47.27	45.80
6000	92.69	86.16	81.02	66.39	59.97	56.72	54.96
7000	108.14	100.52	94.52	77.45	69.97	66.18	64.12
8000	123.59	114.88	108.02	88.52	79.96	75.63	73.28
9000	139.04	129.24	121.53	99.58	89.96	85.08	82.44
10000	154.49	143.60	135.03	110.64	99.95	94.54	91.60
11000	169.94	157.96	148.53	121.71	109.95	103.99	100.76
12000	185.39	172.32	162.04	132.77	119.94	113.45	109.92
13000	200.84	186.68	175.54	143.84	129.94	122.90	119.08
14000	216.29	201.04	189.04	154.90	139.93	132.35	128.24
15000	231.74	215.40	202.54	165.97	149.93	141.81	137.40
16000	247.18	229.76	216.05	177.03	159.92	151.26	146.56
17000	262.63	244.12	229.55	188.10	169.92	160.72	155.72
18000	278.08	258.48	243.05	199.16	179.91	170.17	164.88
19000	293.53	272.84	256.56	210.22	189.91	179.62	174.04
20000	308.98	287.20	270.06	221.29	199.90	189.08	183.20
21000	324.43	301.56	283.56	232.35	209.90	198.53	192.36
22000	339.88	315.92	297.06	243.42	219.89	207.99	201.52
23000	355.33	330.28	310.57	254.48	229.89	217.44	210.68
24000	370.78	344.64	324.07	265.55	239.88	226.89	219.84
25000	386.23	359.00	337.57	276.61	249.88	236.35	229.00
26000	401.67	373.36	351.08	287.68	259.87	245.80	238.16
27000	417.12	387.72	364.58	298.74	269.87	255.25	247.32
28000	432.57	402.08	378.08	309.80	279.86	264.71	256.48
29000	448.02	416.44	391.59	320.87	289.86	274.16	265.64
30000	463.47	430.80	405.09	331.93	299.85	283.62	274.80
35000	540.72	502.60	472.60	387.26	349.83	330.89	320.60
40000	617.96	574.40	540.12	442.58	399.81	378.15	366.40
45000	695.21	646.20	607.63	497.90	449.78	425.42	412.20
50000	772.45	718.00	675.15	553.22	499.76	472.69	458.00
55000	849.70	789.80	742.66	608.54	549.73	519.96	503.80
60000	926.94	861.61	810.18	663.87	599.71	567.23	549.60
65000	1004.19	933.41	877.69	719.19	649.68	614.50	595.40
70000	1081.43	1005.21	945.21	774.51	699.66	661.77	641.20
75000	1158.68	1077.01	1012.72	829.83	749.63	709.04	687.00
80000	1235.92	1148.81	1080.24	885.16	799.61	756.31	732.80
85000	1313.17	1220.61	1147.75	940.48	849.59	803.58	778.60
90000	1390.41	1292.41	1215.26	995.80	899.56	850.85	824.40
95000	1467.66	1364.21	1282.78	1051.12	949.54	898.12	870.20
100000	1544.90	1436.01	1350.29	1106.44	999.51	945.39	916.00
200000	3089.81	2872.02	2700.59	2212.89	1999.03	1890.77	1832.00
300000	4634.71	4308.03	4050.88	3319.33	2998.54	2836.16	2748.00
400000	6179.61	5744.04	5401.18	4425.78	3998.05	3781.55	3664.00
500000	7724.51	7180.05	6751.47	5532.22	4997.56	4726.93	4580.00
1000000	15449.03	14360.09	13502.94	11064.45	9995.13	9453.86	9160.00

10.875%

MONTHLY PAYMENT
NECESSARY TO AMORTIZE A LOAN

Amortization Amount	1 Year	2 Years	3 Years	4 Years	5 Years	6 Years	7 Years
25	2.21	1.16	0.81	0.64	0.54	0.47	0.42
50	4.41	2.32	1.63	1.28	1.08	0.94	0.85
100	8.82	4.64	3.26	2.57	2.16	1.88	1.69
200	17.64	9.29	6.51	5.13	4.31	3.77	3.39
300	26.46	13.93	9.77	7.70	6.47	5.65	5.08
400	35.28	18.58	13.03	10.27	8.62	7.54	6.77
500	44.11	23.22	16.28	12.83	10.78	9.42	8.47
600	52.93	27.86	19.54	15.40	12.94	11.31	10.16
700	61.75	32.51	22.80	17.97	15.09	13.19	11.85
800	70.57	37.15	26.05	20.54	17.25	15.08	13.55
900	79.39	41.80	29.31	23.10	19.41	16.96	15.24
1000	88.21	46.44	32.57	25.67	21.56	18.85	16.93
2000	176.42	92.88	65.13	51.34	43.12	37.70	33.86
3000	264.64	139.32	97.70	77.01	64.68	56.55	50.80
4000	352.85	185.76	130.27	102.68	86.25	75.39	67.73
5000	441.06	232.20	162.83	128.35	107.81	94.24	84.66
6000	529.27	278.64	195.40	154.02	129.37	113.09	101.59
7000	617.49	325.07	227.97	179.69	150.93	131.94	118.52
8000	705.70	371.51	260.53	205.35	172.49	150.79	135.46
9000	793.91	417.95	293.10	231.02	194.05	169.64	152.39
10000	882.12	464.39	325.67	256.69	215.62	188.48	169.32
11000	970.33	510.83	358.24	282.36	237.18	207.33	186.25
12000	1058.55	557.27	390.80	308.03	258.74	226.18	203.18
13000	1146.76	603.71	423.37	333.70	280.30	245.03	220.11
14000	1234.97	650.15	455.94	359.37	301.86	263.88	237.05
15000	1323.18	696.59	488.50	385.04	323.42	282.73	253.98
16000	1411.40	743.03	521.07	410.71	344.99	301.57	270.91
17000	1499.61	789.47	553.64	436.38	366.55	320.42	287.84
18000	1587.82	835.91	586.20	462.05	388.11	339.27	304.77
19000	1676.03	882.35	618.77	487.72	409.67	358.12	321.71
20000	1764.24	928.79	651.34	513.39	431.23	376.97	338.64
21000	1852.46	975.22	683.90	539.06	452.79	395.82	355.57
22000	1940.67	1021.66	716.47	564.73	474.35	414.67	372.50
23000	2028.88	1068.10	749.04	590.40	495.92	433.51	389.43
24000	2117.09	1114.54	781.60	616.06	517.48	452.36	406.37
25000	2205.30	1160.98	814.17	641.73	539.04	471.21	423.30
26000	2293.52	1207.42	846.74	667.40	560.60	490.06	440.23
27000	2381.73	1253.86	879.30	693.07	582.16	508.91	457.16
28000	2469.94	1300.30	911.87	718.74	603.72	527.76	474.09
29000	2558.15	1346.74	944.44	744.41	625.29	546.60	491.03
30000	2646.37	1393.18	977.01	770.08	646.85	565.45	507.96
35000	3087.43	1625.37	1139.84	898.43	754.66	659.69	592.62
40000	3528.49	1857.57	1302.67	1026.77	862.46	753.94	677.28
45000	3969.55	2089.77	1465.51	1155.12	970.27	848.18	761.94
50000	4410.61	2321.96	1628.34	1283.47	1078.08	942.42	846.60
55000	4851.67	2554.16	1791.18	1411.81	1185.89	1036.66	931.25
60000	5292.73	2786.36	1954.01	1540.16	1293.69	1130.91	1015.91
65000	5733.79	3018.55	2116.84	1668.51	1401.50	1225.15	1100.57
70000	6174.85	3250.75	2279.68	1796.85	1509.31	1319.39	1185.23
75000	6615.91	3482.94	2442.51	1925.20	1617.12	1413.63	1269.89
80000	7056.98	3715.14	2605.35	2053.55	1724.93	1507.87	1354.55
85000	7498.04	3947.34	2768.18	2181.89	1832.73	1602.12	1439.21
90000	7939.10	4179.53	2931.02	2310.24	1940.54	1696.36	1523.87
95000	8380.16	4411.73	3093.85	2438.59	2048.35	1790.60	1608.53
100000	8821.22	4643.93	3256.68	2566.94	2156.16	1884.84	1693.19
200000	17642.44	9287.85	6513.37	5133.87	4312.32	3769.68	3386.38
300000	26463.66	13931.78	9770.05	7700.81	6468.47	5654.53	5079.57
400000	35284.88	18575.70	13026.74	10267.74	8624.63	7539.37	6772.76
500000	44106.10	23219.63	16283.42	12834.68	10780.79	9424.21	8465.95
1000000	88212.19	46439.25	32566.84	25669.35	21561.58	18848.42	16931.91

112

Amortization Amount	8 Years	9 Years	10 Years	15 Years	20 Years	25 Years	30 Years
25	0.39	0.36	0.34	0.28	0.25	0.24	0.23
50	0.78	0.72	0.68	0.56	0.50	0.48	0.46
100	1.55	1.44	1.36	1.11	1.01	0.95	0.92
200	3.10	2.89	2.71	2.23	2.02	1.91	1.85
300	4.65	4.33	4.07	3.34	3.02	2.86	2.77
400	6.21	5.77	5.43	4.46	4.03	3.82	3.70
500	7.76	7.21	6.79	5.57	5.04	4.77	4.62
600	9.31	8.66	8.14	6.68	6.05	5.72	5.55
700	10.86	10.10	9.50	7.80	7.05	6.68	6.47
800	12.41	11.54	10.86	8.91	8.06	7.63	7.40
900	13.96	12.98	12.21	10.02	9.07	8.59	8.32
1000	15.51	14.43	13.57	11.14	10.08	9.54	9.25
2000	31.03	28.85	27.14	22.28	20.15	19.08	18.50
3000	46.54	43.28	40.71	33.42	30.23	28.62	27.75
4000	62.05	57.70	54.28	44.56	40.30	38.16	37.00
5000	77.57	72.13	67.85	55.69	50.38	47.70	46.25
6000	93.08	86.55	81.42	66.83	60.45	57.24	55.50
7000	108.59	100.98	94.99	77.97	70.53	66.78	64.75
8000	124.10	115.41	108.56	89.11	80.61	76.32	74.00
9000	139.62	129.83	122.13	100.25	90.68	85.86	83.25
10000	155.13	144.26	135.70	111.39	100.76	95.39	92.50
11000	170.64	158.68	149.27	122.53	110.83	104.93	101.75
12000	186.16	173.11	162.84	133.67	120.91	114.47	111.00
13000	201.67	187.53	176.41	144.80	130.98	124.01	120.24
14000	217.18	201.96	189.98	155.94	141.06	133.55	129.49
15000	232.70	216.38	203.55	167.08	151.13	143.09	138.74
16000	248.21	230.81	217.12	178.22	161.21	152.63	147.99
17000	263.72	245.24	230.69	189.36	171.29	162.17	157.24
18000	279.23	259.66	244.26	200.50	181.36	171.71	166.49
19000	294.75	274.09	257.83	211.64	191.44	181.25	175.74
20000	310.26	288.51	271.40	222.78	201.51	190.79	184.99
21000	325.77	302.94	284.97	233.91	211.59	200.33	194.24
22000	341.29	317.36	298.54	245.05	221.66	209.87	203.49
23000	356.80	331.79	312.11	256.19	231.74	219.41	212.74
24000	372.31	346.22	325.68	267.33	241.82	228.95	221.99
25000	387.83	360.64	339.25	278.47	251.89	238.49	231.24
26000	403.34	375.07	352.82	289.61	261.97	248.03	240.49
27000	418.85	389.49	366.39	300.75	272.04	257.57	249.74
28000	434.37	403.92	379.96	311.89	282.12	267.11	258.99
29000	449.88	418.34	393.53	323.02	292.19	276.64	268.24
30000	465.39	432.77	407.10	334.16	302.27	286.18	277.49
35000	542.96	504.90	474.95	389.86	352.65	333.88	323.74
40000	620.52	577.03	542.80	445.55	403.03	381.58	369.98
45000	698.09	649.15	610.65	501.24	453.40	429.28	416.23
50000	775.65	721.28	678.50	556.94	503.78	476.97	462.48
55000	853.22	793.41	746.35	612.63	554.16	524.67	508.73
60000	930.78	865.54	814.20	668.33	604.54	572.37	554.98
65000	1008.35	937.67	882.05	724.02	654.92	620.07	601.22
70000	1085.91	1009.80	949.90	779.71	705.30	667.76	647.47
75000	1163.48	1081.92	1017.75	835.41	755.67	715.46	693.72
80000	1241.04	1154.05	1085.60	891.10	806.05	763.16	739.97
85000	1318.61	1226.18	1153.45	946.79	856.43	810.86	786.22
90000	1396.17	1298.31	1221.30	1002.49	906.81	858.55	832.46
95000	1473.74	1370.44	1289.15	1058.18	957.19	906.25	878.71
100000	1551.30	1442.57	1357.00	1113.88	1007.57	953.95	924.96
200000	3102.61	2885.13	2714.01	2227.75	2015.13	1907.89	1849.92
300000	4653.91	4327.70	4071.01	3341.63	3022.70	2861.84	2774.88
400000	6205.22	5770.26	5428.02	4455.50	4030.26	3815.79	3699.84
500000	7756.52	7212.83	6785.02	5569.38	5037.83	4769.74	4624.80
1000000	15513.04	14425.66	13570.04	11138.76	10075.66	9539.47	9249.60

11%

MONTHLY PAYMENT
NECESSARY TO AMORTIZE A LOAN

Amortization Amount	1 Year	2 Years	3 Years	4 Years	5 Years	6 Years	7 Years
25	2.21	1.16	0.82	0.64	0.54	0.47	0.42
50	4.41	2.32	1.63	1.29	1.08	0.95	0.85
100	8.83	4.65	3.26	2.57	2.16	1.89	1.70
200	17.65	9.30	6.52	5.15	4.32	3.78	3.40
300	26.48	13.95	9.79	7.72	6.49	5.67	5.10
400	35.31	18.60	13.05	10.29	8.65	7.56	6.80
500	44.13	23.25	16.31	12.86	10.81	9.45	8.50
600	52.96	27.90	19.57	15.44	12.97	11.35	10.20
700	61.79	32.55	22.84	18.01	15.13	13.24	11.90
800	70.61	37.20	26.10	20.58	17.30	15.13	13.60
900	79.44	41.85	29.36	23.15	19.46	17.02	15.30
1000	88.27	46.49	32.62	25.73	21.62	18.91	16.99
2000	176.54	92.99	65.25	51.45	43.24	37.82	33.99
3000	264.80	139.48	97.87	77.18	64.86	56.73	50.98
4000	353.07	185.98	130.49	102.91	86.48	75.64	67.98
5000	441.34	232.47	163.12	128.64	108.10	94.55	84.97
6000	529.61	278.97	195.74	154.36	129.73	113.46	101.97
7000	617.88	325.46	228.36	180.09	151.35	132.37	118.96
8000	706.14	371.96	260.99	205.82	172.97	151.28	135.96
9000	794.41	418.45	293.61	231.55	194.59	170.18	152.95
10000	882.68	464.95	326.23	257.27	216.21	189.09	169.94
11000	970.95	511.44	358.86	283.00	237.83	208.00	186.94
12000	1059.22	557.94	391.48	308.73	259.45	226.91	203.93
13000	1147.48	604.43	424.10	334.45	281.07	245.82	220.93
14000	1235.75	650.93	456.73	360.18	302.69	264.73	237.92
15000	1324.02	697.42	489.35	385.91	324.31	283.64	254.92
16000	1412.29	743.91	521.97	411.64	345.94	302.55	271.91
17000	1500.55	790.41	554.60	437.36	367.56	321.46	288.91
18000	1588.82	836.90	587.22	463.09	389.18	340.37	305.90
19000	1677.09	883.40	619.84	488.82	410.80	359.28	322.89
20000	1765.36	929.89	652.47	514.54	432.42	378.19	339.89
21000	1853.63	976.39	685.09	540.27	454.04	397.10	356.88
22000	1941.89	1022.88	717.71	566.00	475.66	416.01	373.88
23000	2030.16	1069.38	750.34	591.73	497.28	434.92	390.87
24000	2118.43	1115.87	782.96	617.45	518.90	453.83	407.87
25000	2206.70	1162.37	815.58	643.18	540.52	472.73	424.86
26000	2294.97	1208.86	848.21	668.91	562.15	491.64	441.86
27000	2383.23	1255.36	880.83	694.64	583.77	510.55	458.85
28000	2471.50	1301.85	913.45	720.36	605.39	529.46	475.84
29000	2559.77	1348.35	946.08	746.09	627.01	548.37	492.84
30000	2648.04	1394.84	978.70	771.82	648.63	567.28	509.83
35000	3089.38	1627.31	1141.82	900.45	756.73	661.83	594.81
40000	3530.72	1859.79	1304.93	1029.09	864.84	756.38	679.78
45000	3972.06	2092.26	1468.05	1157.73	972.94	850.92	764.75
50000	4413.40	2324.73	1631.17	1286.36	1081.05	945.47	849.72
55000	4854.74	2557.21	1794.28	1415.00	1189.15	1040.02	934.69
60000	5296.08	2789.68	1957.40	1543.63	1297.26	1134.56	1019.67
65000	5737.41	3022.15	2120.52	1672.27	1405.36	1229.11	1104.64
70000	6178.75	3254.63	2283.63	1800.91	1513.47	1323.66	1189.61
75000	6620.09	3487.10	2446.75	1929.54	1621.57	1418.20	1274.58
80000	7061.43	3719.57	2609.87	2058.18	1729.68	1512.75	1359.56
85000	7502.77	3952.05	2772.98	2186.81	1837.78	1607.30	1444.53
90000	7944.11	4184.52	2936.10	2315.45	1945.89	1701.84	1529.50
95000	8385.45	4416.99	3099.22	2444.09	2053.99	1796.39	1614.47
100000	8826.79	4649.47	3262.33	2572.72	2162.10	1890.94	1699.45
200000	17653.58	9298.93	6524.66	5145.44	4324.19	3781.88	3398.89
300000	26480.34	13948.40	9787.00	7718.17	6486.29	5672.81	5098.34
400000	35307.17	18597.87	13049.33	10290.89	8648.39	7563.75	6797.78
500000	44133.96	23247.34	16311.66	12863.61	10810.49	9454.69	8497.23
1000000	88267.92	46494.67	32623.32	25727.22	21620.97	18909.38	16994.45

Amortization Amount	8 Years	9 Years	10 Years	15 Years	20 Years	25 Years	30 Years
25	0.39	0.36	0.34	0.28	0.25	0.24	0.23
50	0.78	0.72	0.68	0.56	0.51	0.48	0.47
100	1.56	1.45	1.36	1.12	1.02	0.96	0.93
200	3.12	2.90	2.73	2.24	2.03	1.93	1.87
300	4.67	4.35	4.09	3.36	3.05	2.89	2.80
400	6.23	5.80	5.45	4.49	4.06	3.85	3.74
500	7.79	7.25	6.82	5.61	5.08	4.81	4.67
600	9.35	8.69	8.18	6.73	6.09	5.78	5.60
700	10.90	10.14	9.55	7.85	7.11	6.74	6.54
800	12.46	11.59	10.91	8.97	8.13	7.70	7.47
900	14.02	13.04	12.27	10.09	9.14	8.66	8.41
1000	15.58	14.49	13.64	11.21	10.16	9.63	9.34
2000	31.15	28.98	27.27	22.43	20.31	19.25	18.68
3000	46.73	43.47	40.91	33.64	30.47	28.88	28.02
4000	62.31	57.97	54.55	44.85	40.63	38.50	37.36
5000	77.89	72.46	68.19	56.07	50.78	48.13	46.70
6000	93.46	86.95	81.82	67.28	60.94	57.75	56.04
7000	109.04	101.44	95.46	78.49	71.09	67.38	65.38
8000	124.62	115.93	109.10	89.71	81.25	77.00	74.72
9000	140.19	130.42	122.74	100.92	91.41	86.63	84.05
10000	155.77	144.91	136.37	112.13	101.56	96.25	93.39
11000	171.35	159.40	150.01	123.35	111.72	105.88	102.73
12000	186.93	173.90	163.65	134.56	121.88	115.50	112.07
13000	202.50	188.39	177.28	145.77	132.03	125.13	121.41
14000	218.08	202.88	190.92	156.99	142.19	134.75	130.75
15000	233.66	217.37	204.56	168.20	152.35	144.38	140.09
16000	249.23	231.86	218.20	179.41	162.50	154.00	149.43
17000	264.81	246.35	231.83	190.63	172.66	163.63	158.77
18000	280.39	260.84	245.47	201.84	182.82	173.26	168.11
19000	295.97	275.34	259.11	213.05	192.97	182.88	177.45
20000	311.54	289.83	272.75	224.27	203.13	192.51	186.79
21000	327.12	304.32	286.38	235.48	213.28	202.13	196.13
22000	342.70	318.81	300.02	246.69	223.44	211.76	205.47
23000	358.27	333.30	313.66	257.91	233.60	221.38	214.81
24000	373.85	347.79	327.29	269.12	243.75	231.01	224.15
25000	389.43	362.28	340.93	280.33	253.91	240.63	233.48
26000	405.01	376.78	354.57	291.55	264.07	250.26	242.82
27000	420.58	391.27	368.21	302.76	274.22	259.88	252.16
28000	436.16	405.76	381.84	313.97	284.38	269.51	261.50
29000	451.74	420.25	395.48	325.18	294.54	279.13	270.84
30000	467.31	434.74	409.12	336.40	304.69	288.76	280.18
35000	545.20	507.20	477.31	392.46	355.47	336.89	326.88
40000	623.09	579.65	545.49	448.53	406.26	385.01	373.58
45000	700.97	652.11	613.68	504.60	457.04	433.14	420.27
50000	778.86	724.57	681.86	560.66	507.82	481.26	466.97
55000	856.74	797.02	750.05	616.73	558.60	529.39	513.67
60000	934.63	869.48	818.24	672.80	609.38	577.52	560.36
65000	1012.52	941.94	886.42	728.86	660.17	625.64	607.06
70000	1090.40	1014.39	954.61	784.93	710.95	673.77	653.76
75000	1168.29	1086.85	1022.80	841.00	761.73	721.90	700.45
80000	1246.17	1159.31	1090.98	897.06	812.51	770.02	747.15
85000	1324.06	1231.76	1159.17	953.13	863.29	818.15	793.85
90000	1401.94	1304.22	1227.36	1009.19	914.08	866.28	840.54
95000	1479.83	1376.68	1295.54	1065.26	964.86	914.40	887.24
100000	1557.72	1449.13	1363.73	1121.33	1015.64	962.53	933.94
200000	3115.43	2898.27	2727.46	2242.65	2031.28	1925.06	1867.88
300000	4673.15	4347.40	4091.19	3363.98	3046.92	2887.59	2801.81
400000	6230.87	5796.54	5454.91	4485.31	4062.56	3850.12	3735.75
500000	7788.58	7245.67	6818.64	5606.63	5078.20	4812.65	4669.69
1000000	15577.16	14491.35	13637.29	11213.27	10156.40	9625.29	9339.38

11.125%

MONTHLY PAYMENT
NECESSARY TO AMORTIZE A LOAN

Amortization Amount	1 Year	2 Years	3 Years	4 Years	5 Years	6 Years	7 Years
25	2.21	1.16	0.82	0.64	0.54	0.47	0.43
50	4.42	2.33	1.63	1.29	1.08	0.95	0.85
100	8.83	4.66	3.27	2.58	2.17	1.90	1.71
200	17.66	9.31	6.54	5.16	4.34	3.79	3.41
300	26.50	13.97	9.80	7.74	6.50	5.69	5.12
400	35.33	18.62	13.07	10.31	8.67	7.59	6.82
500	44.16	23.28	16.34	12.89	10.84	9.49	8.53
600	52.99	27.93	19.61	15.47	13.01	11.38	10.23
700	61.83	32.59	22.88	18.05	15.18	13.28	11.94
800	70.66	37.24	26.14	20.63	17.34	15.18	13.65
900	79.49	41.90	29.41	23.21	19.51	17.07	15.35
1000	88.32	46.55	32.68	25.79	21.68	18.97	17.06
2000	176.65	93.10	65.36	51.57	43.36	37.94	34.11
3000	264.97	139.65	98.04	77.36	65.04	56.91	51.17
4000	353.29	186.20	130.72	103.14	86.72	75.88	68.23
5000	441.62	232.75	163.40	128.93	108.40	94.85	85.29
6000	529.94	279.30	196.08	154.71	130.08	113.82	102.34
7000	618.27	325.85	228.76	180.50	151.76	132.79	119.40
8000	706.59	372.40	261.44	206.28	173.44	151.76	136.46
9000	794.91	418.95	294.12	232.07	195.12	170.73	153.51
10000	883.24	465.50	326.80	257.85	216.80	189.70	170.57
11000	971.56	512.05	359.48	283.64	238.48	208.67	187.63
12000	1059.88	558.60	392.16	309.42	260.17	227.65	204.69
13000	1148.21	605.15	424.84	335.21	281.85	246.62	221.74
14000	1236.53	651.70	457.52	360.99	303.53	265.59	238.80
15000	1324.85	698.25	490.20	386.78	325.21	284.56	255.86
16000	1413.18	744.80	522.88	412.56	346.89	303.53	272.91
17000	1501.50	791.35	555.56	438.35	368.57	322.50	289.97
18000	1589.83	837.90	588.24	464.13	390.25	341.47	307.03
19000	1678.15	884.45	620.92	489.92	411.93	360.44	324.08
20000	1766.47	931.00	653.60	515.70	433.61	379.41	341.14
21000	1854.80	977.55	686.28	541.49	455.29	398.38	358.20
22000	1943.12	1024.10	718.96	567.27	476.97	417.35	375.26
23000	2031.44	1070.65	751.64	593.06	498.65	436.32	392.31
24000	2119.77	1117.20	784.32	618.84	520.33	455.29	409.37
25000	2208.09	1163.75	817.00	644.63	542.01	474.26	426.43
26000	2296.41	1210.30	849.68	670.41	563.69	493.23	443.48
27000	2384.74	1256.85	882.36	696.20	585.37	512.20	460.54
28000	2473.06	1303.40	915.04	721.98	607.05	531.17	477.60
29000	2561.39	1349.95	947.72	747.77	628.73	550.14	494.66
30000	2649.71	1396.50	980.39	773.55	650.41	569.11	511.71
35000	3091.33	1629.25	1143.79	902.48	758.82	663.96	597.00
40000	3532.95	1862.00	1307.19	1031.41	867.22	758.82	682.28
45000	3974.56	2094.75	1470.59	1160.33	975.62	853.67	767.57
50000	4416.18	2327.50	1633.99	1289.26	1084.02	948.52	852.85
55000	4857.80	2560.26	1797.39	1418.18	1192.42	1043.37	938.14
60000	5299.42	2793.01	1960.79	1547.11	1300.83	1138.23	1023.43
65000	5741.04	3025.76	2124.19	1676.03	1409.23	1233.08	1108.71
70000	6182.65	3258.51	2287.59	1804.96	1517.63	1327.93	1194.00
75000	6624.27	3491.26	2450.99	1933.89	1626.03	1422.78	1279.28
80000	7065.89	3724.01	2614.39	2062.81	1734.43	1517.63	1364.57
85000	7507.51	3956.76	2777.79	2191.74	1842.84	1612.49	1449.85
90000	7949.13	4189.51	2941.18	2320.66	1951.24	1707.34	1535.14
95000	8390.75	4422.26	3104.58	2449.59	2059.64	1802.19	1620.42
100000	8832.36	4655.01	3267.98	2578.51	2168.04	1897.04	1705.71
200000	17664.73	9310.02	6535.97	5157.03	4336.09	3794.08	3411.42
300000	26497.09	13965.03	9803.95	7735.54	6504.13	5691.12	5117.13
400000	35329.45	18620.04	13071.93	10314.06	8672.17	7588.17	6822.84
500000	44161.82	23275.05	16339.92	12892.57	10840.21	9485.21	8528.55
1000000	88323.64	46550.10	32679.83	25785.15	21680.43	18970.42	17057.09

116

Amortization Amount	8 Years	9 Years	10 Years	15 Years	20 Years	25 Years	30 Years
25	0.39	0.36	0.34	0.28	0.26	0.24	0.24
50	0.78	0.73	0.69	0.56	0.51	0.49	0.47
100	1.56	1.46	1.37	1.13	1.02	0.97	0.94
200	3.13	2.91	2.74	2.26	2.05	1.94	1.89
300	4.69	4.37	4.11	3.39	3.07	2.91	2.83
400	6.26	5.82	5.48	4.52	4.09	3.88	3.77
500	7.82	7.28	6.85	5.64	5.12	4.86	4.71
600	9.38	8.73	8.22	6.77	6.14	5.83	5.66
700	10.95	10.19	9.59	7.90	7.17	6.80	6.60
800	12.51	11.65	10.96	9.03	8.19	7.77	7.54
900	14.08	13.10	12.33	10.16	9.21	8.74	8.49
1000	15.64	14.56	13.70	11.29	10.24	9.71	9.43
2000	31.28	29.11	27.41	22.58	20.47	19.42	18.86
3000	46.92	43.67	41.11	33.86	30.71	29.13	28.29
4000	62.57	58.23	54.82	45.15	40.95	38.85	37.72
5000	78.21	72.79	68.52	56.44	51.19	48.56	47.15
6000	93.85	87.34	82.23	67.73	61.42	58.27	56.58
7000	109.49	101.90	95.93	79.02	71.66	67.98	66.01
8000	125.13	116.46	109.64	90.30	81.90	77.69	75.43
9000	140.77	131.01	123.34	101.59	92.14	87.40	84.86
10000	156.41	145.57	137.05	112.88	102.37	97.11	94.29
11000	172.06	160.13	150.75	124.17	112.61	106.82	103.72
12000	187.70	174.69	164.46	135.46	122.85	116.54	113.15
13000	203.34	189.24	178.16	146.74	133.09	126.25	122.58
14000	218.98	203.80	191.87	158.03	143.32	135.96	132.01
15000	234.62	218.36	205.57	169.32	153.56	145.67	141.44
16000	250.26	232.91	219.27	180.61	163.80	155.38	150.87
17000	265.90	247.47	232.98	191.90	174.03	165.09	160.30
18000	281.55	262.03	246.68	203.18	184.27	174.80	169.73
19000	297.19	276.59	260.39	214.47	194.51	184.52	179.16
20000	312.83	291.14	274.09	225.76	204.75	194.23	188.59
21000	328.47	305.70	287.80	237.05	214.98	203.94	198.02
22000	344.11	320.26	301.50	248.34	225.22	213.65	207.45
23000	359.75	334.81	315.21	259.62	235.46	223.36	216.87
24000	375.39	349.37	328.91	270.91	245.70	233.07	226.30
25000	391.04	363.93	342.62	282.20	255.93	242.78	235.73
26000	408.68	378.49	356.32	293.49	266.17	252.49	245.16
27000	422.32	393.04	370.03	304.78	276.41	262.21	254.59
28000	437.96	407.60	383.73	316.06	286.65	271.92	264.02
29000	453.60	422.16	397.44	327.35	296.88	281.63	273.45
30000	469.24	436.72	411.14	338.64	307.12	291.34	282.88
35000	547.45	509.50	479.66	395.08	358.31	339.90	330.03
40000	625.66	582.29	548.19	451.52	409.49	388.45	377.17
45000	703.86	655.07	616.71	507.96	460.68	437.01	424.32
50000	782.07	727.86	685.23	564.40	511.87	485.57	471.47
55000	860.28	800.64	753.76	620.84	563.05	534.12	518.61
60000	938.48	873.43	822.28	677.28	614.24	582.68	565.76
65000	1016.69	946.22	890.80	733.72	665.43	631.24	612.91
70000	1094.90	1019.00	959.33	790.16	716.61	679.79	660.05
75000	1173.11	1091.79	1027.85	846.60	767.80	728.35	707.20
80000	1251.31	1164.57	1096.37	903.04	818.99	776.91	754.35
85000	1329.52	1237.36	1164.90	959.48	870.17	825.46	801.49
90000	1407.73	1310.15	1233.42	1015.92	921.36	874.02	848.64
95000	1485.93	1382.93	1301.94	1072.36	972.55	922.58	895.79
100000	1564.14	1455.72	1370.47	1128.80	1023.73	971.13	942.93
200000	3128.28	2911.43	2740.93	2257.59	2047.47	1942.26	1885.87
300000	4692.42	4367.15	4111.40	3386.39	3071.20	2913.40	2828.80
400000	6256.56	5822.87	5481.87	4515.19	4094.94	3884.53	3771.74
500000	7820.70	7278.59	6852.34	5643.98	5118.67	4855.66	4714.67
1000000	15641.40	14557.17	13704.67	11287.97	10237.35	9711.32	9429.35

Amortization Amount	1 Year	2 Years	3 Years	4 Years	5 Years	6 Years	7 Years
25	2.21	1.17	0.82	0.65	0.54	0.48	0.43
50	4.42	2.33	1.64	1.29	1.09	0.95	0.86
100	8.84	4.66	3.27	2.58	2.17	1.90	1.71
200	17.68	9.32	6.55	5.17	4.35	3.81	3.42
300	26.51	13.98	9.82	7.75	6.52	5.71	5.14
400	35.35	18.64	13.09	10.34	8.70	7.61	6.85
500	44.19	23.30	16.37	12.92	10.87	9.52	8.56
600	53.03	27.96	19.64	15.51	13.04	11.42	10.27
700	61.87	32.62	22.92	18.09	15.22	13.32	11.98
800	70.70	37.28	26.19	20.67	17.39	15.23	13.70
900	79.54	41.94	29.46	23.26	19.57	17.13	15.41
1000	88.38	46.61	32.74	25.84	21.74	19.03	17.12
2000	176.76	93.21	65.47	51.69	43.48	38.06	34.24
3000	265.14	139.82	98.21	77.53	65.22	57.09	51.36
4000	353.52	186.42	130.95	103.37	86.96	76.13	68.48
5000	441.90	233.03	163.68	129.22	108.70	95.16	85.60
6000	530.28	279.63	196.42	155.06	130.44	114.19	102.72
7000	618.66	326.24	229.15	180.90	152.18	133.22	119.84
8000	707.03	372.84	261.89	206.74	173.92	152.25	136.96
9000	795.41	419.45	294.63	232.59	195.66	171.28	154.08
10000	883.79	466.06	327.36	258.43	217.40	190.32	171.20
11000	972.17	512.66	360.10	284.27	239.14	209.35	188.32
12000	1060.55	559.27	392.84	310.12	260.88	228.38	205.44
13000	1148.93	605.87	425.57	335.96	282.62	247.41	222.56
14000	1237.31	652.48	458.31	361.80	304.36	266.44	239.68
15000	1325.69	699.08	491.05	387.65	326.10	285.47	256.80
16000	1414.07	745.69	523.78	413.49	347.84	304.50	273.92
17000	1502.45	792.29	556.52	439.33	369.58	323.54	291.04
18000	1590.83	838.90	589.25	465.18	391.32	342.57	308.16
19000	1679.21	885.51	621.99	491.02	413.06	361.60	325.28
20000	1787.59	932.11	654.73	516.86	434.80	380.63	342.40
21000	1855.97	978.72	687.46	542.71	456.54	399.66	359.52
22000	1944.35	1025.32	720.20	568.55	478.28	418.69	376.64
23000	2032.72	1071.93	752.94	594.39	500.02	437.73	393.76
24000	2121.10	1118.53	785.67	620.23	521.76	456.76	410.88
25000	2209.48	1165.14	818.41	646.08	543.50	475.79	428.00
26000	2297.86	1211.74	851.15	671.92	565.24	494.82	445.12
27000	2386.24	1258.35	883.88	697.76	586.98	513.85	462.24
28000	2474.62	1304.96	916.62	723.61	608.72	532.88	479.36
29000	2563.00	1351.56	949.35	749.45	630.46	551.91	496.48
30000	2651.38	1398.17	982.09	775.29	652.20	570.95	513.59
35000	3093.28	1631.19	1145.77	904.51	760.90	666.10	599.19
40000	3535.17	1864.22	1309.45	1033.72	869.60	761.26	684.79
45000	3977.07	2097.25	1473.14	1162.94	978.30	856.42	770.39
50000	4418.97	2330.28	1636.82	1292.16	1087.00	951.58	855.99
55000	4860.86	2563.30	1800.50	1421.37	1195.70	1046.73	941.59
60000	5302.76	2796.33	1964.18	1550.59	1304.40	1141.89	1027.19
65000	5744.66	3029.36	2127.86	1679.80	1413.10	1237.05	1112.79
70000	6186.55	3262.39	2291.55	1809.02	1521.80	1332.21	1198.39
75000	6628.45	3495.42	2455.23	1938.23	1630.50	1427.37	1283.99
80000	7070.35	3728.44	2618.91	2067.45	1739.20	1522.52	1369.59
85000	7512.24	3961.47	2782.59	2196.66	1847.90	1617.68	1455.19
90000	7954.14	4194.50	2946.27	2325.88	1956.60	1712.84	1540.78
95000	8396.04	4427.53	3109.96	2455.10	2065.30	1808.00	1626.38
100000	8837.93	4660.55	3273.64	2584.31	2174.00	1903.15	1711.98
200000	17675.87	9321.11	6547.27	5168.62	4347.99	3806.31	3423.97
300000	26513.80	13981.66	9820.91	7752.94	6521.99	5709.46	5135.95
400000	35351.74	18642.22	13094.55	10337.25	8695.98	7612.62	6847.93
500000	44189.67	23302.77	16368.19	12921.56	10869.98	9515.77	8559.92
1000000	88379.35	46605.54	32736.37	25843.12	21739.95	19031.54	17119.83

Amortization Amount	8 Years	9 Years	10 Years	15 Years	20 Years	25 Years	30 Years
25	0.39	0.37	0.34	0.28	0.26	0.24	0.24
50	0.79	0.73	0.69	0.57	0.52	0.49	0.48
100	1.57	1.46	1.38	1.14	1.03	0.98	0.95
200	3.14	2.92	2.75	2.27	2.06	1.96	1.90
300	4.71	4.39	4.13	3.41	3.10	2.94	2.86
400	6.28	5.85	5.51	4.55	4.13	3.92	3.81
500	7.85	7.31	6.89	5.68	5.16	4.90	4.76
600	9.42	8.77	8.26	6.82	6.19	5.88	5.71
700	10.99	10.24	9.64	7.95	7.22	6.86	6.66
800	12.56	11.70	11.02	9.09	8.25	7.84	7.62
900	14.14	13.16	12.39	10.23	9.29	8.82	8.57
1000	15.71	14.62	13.77	11.36	10.32	9.80	9.52
2000	31.41	29.25	27.54	22.73	20.64	19.60	19.04
3000	47.12	43.87	41.32	34.09	30.96	29.39	28.56
4000	62.82	58.49	55.09	45.45	41.27	39.19	38.08
5000	78.53	73.12	68.86	56.81	51.59	48.99	47.60
6000	94.23	87.74	82.63	68.18	61.91	58.79	57.12
7000	109.94	102.36	96.41	79.54	72.23	68.58	66.64
8000	125.65	116.98	110.18	90.90	82.55	78.38	76.16
9000	141.35	131.61	123.95	102.27	92.87	88.18	85.68
10000	157.06	146.23	137.72	113.63	103.19	97.98	95.19
11000	172.76	160.85	151.49	124.99	113.50	107.77	104.71
12000	188.47	175.48	165.27	136.35	123.82	117.57	114.23
13000	204.17	190.10	179.04	147.72	134.14	127.37	123.75
14000	219.88	204.72	192.81	159.08	144.46	137.17	133.27
15000	235.59	219.35	206.58	170.44	154.78	146.96	142.79
16000	251.29	233.97	220.36	181.81	165.10	156.76	152.31
17000	267.00	248.59	234.13	193.17	175.41	166.56	161.83
18000	282.70	263.22	247.90	204.53	185.73	176.36	171.35
19000	298.41	277.84	261.67	215.89	196.05	186.15	180.87
20000	314.12	292.46	275.44	227.26	206.37	195.95	190.39
21000	329.82	307.09	289.22	238.62	216.69	205.75	199.91
22000	345.53	321.71	302.99	249.98	227.01	215.55	209.43
23000	361.23	336.33	316.76	261.35	237.33	225.34	218.95
24000	376.94	350.95	330.53	272.71	247.64	235.14	228.47
25000	392.64	365.58	344.30	284.07	257.96	244.94	237.99
26000	408.35	380.20	358.08	295.43	268.28	254.74	247.51
27000	424.06	394.82	371.85	306.80	278.60	264.53	257.03
28000	439.76	409.45	385.62	318.16	288.92	274.33	266.55
29000	455.47	424.07	399.39	329.52	299.24	284.13	276.07
30000	471.17	438.69	413.17	340.89	309.56	293.93	285.58
35000	549.70	511.81	482.03	397.70	361.15	342.91	333.18
40000	628.23	584.92	550.89	454.51	412.74	391.90	380.78
45000	706.76	658.04	619.75	511.33	464.33	440.89	428.38
50000	785.29	731.16	688.61	568.14	515.93	489.88	475.97
55000	863.82	804.27	757.47	624.96	567.52	538.87	523.57
60000	942.35	877.39	826.33	681.77	619.11	587.85	571.17
65000	1020.87	950.50	895.19	738.59	670.70	636.84	618.77
70000	1099.40	1023.62	964.05	795.40	722.30	685.83	666.36
75000	1177.93	1096.73	1032.91	852.21	773.89	734.82	713.96
80000	1256.46	1169.85	1101.78	909.03	825.48	783.80	761.56
85000	1334.99	1242.97	1170.64	965.84	877.07	832.79	809.16
90000	1413.52	1316.08	1239.50	1022.66	928.67	881.78	856.75
95000	1492.05	1389.20	1308.36	1079.47	980.26	930.77	904.35
100000	1570.58	1462.31	1377.22	1136.29	1031.85	979.75	951.95
200000	3141.15	2924.62	2754.44	2272.57	2063.70	1959.51	1903.90
300000	4711.73	4386.94	4131.66	3408.86	3095.55	2939.26	2855.85
400000	6282.30	5849.25	5508.88	4545.14	4127.40	3919.02	3807.80
500000	7852.88	7311.56	6886.10	5681.43	5159.26	4898.77	4759.75
1000000	15705.75	14623.12	13772.20	11362.86	10318.51	9797.55	9519.49

11.375%

Amortization Amount	1 Year	2 Years	3 Years	4 Years	5 Years	6 Years	7 Years
25	2.21	1.17	0.82	0.65	0.54	0.48	0.43
50	4.42	2.33	1.64	1.30	1.09	0.95	0.86
100	8.84	4.67	3.28	2.59	2.18	1.91	1.72
200	17.69	9.33	6.56	5.18	4.36	3.82	3.44
300	26.53	14.00	9.84	7.77	6.54	5.73	5.15
400	35.37	18.66	13.12	10.36	8.72	7.64	6.87
500	44.22	23.33	16.40	12.95	10.90	9.55	8.59
600	53.06	28.00	19.68	15.54	13.08	11.46	10.31
700	61.90	32.66	22.96	18.13	15.26	13.36	12.03
800	70.75	37.33	26.23	20.72	17.44	15.27	13.75
900	79.59	41.99	29.51	23.31	19.62	17.18	15.46
1000	88.44	46.66	32.79	25.90	21.80	19.09	17.18
2000	176.87	93.32	65.59	51.80	43.60	38.19	34.37
3000	265.31	139.98	98.38	77.70	65.40	57.28	51.55
4000	353.74	186.64	131.17	103.60	87.20	76.37	68.73
5000	442.18	233.30	163.96	129.51	109.00	95.46	85.91
6000	530.61	279.97	196.76	155.41	130.80	114.56	103.10
7000	619.05	326.63	229.55	181.31	152.60	133.65	120.28
8000	707.48	373.29	262.34	207.21	174.40	152.74	137.46
9000	795.92	419.95	295.14	233.11	196.20	171.83	154.64
10000	884.35	466.61	327.93	259.01	218.00	190.93	171.83
11000	972.79	513.27	360.72	284.91	239.79	210.02	189.01
12000	1061.22	559.93	393.52	310.81	261.59	229.11	206.19
13000	1149.66	606.59	426.31	336.71	283.39	248.21	223.37
14000	1238.09	653.25	459.10	362.62	305.19	267.30	240.56
15000	1326.53	699.91	491.89	388.52	326.99	286.39	257.74
16000	1414.96	746.58	524.69	414.42	348.79	305.48	274.92
17000	1503.40	793.24	557.48	440.32	370.59	324.58	292.11
18000	1591.83	839.90	590.27	466.22	392.39	343.67	309.29
19000	1680.27	886.56	623.07	492.12	414.19	362.76	326.47
20000	1768.70	933.22	655.86	518.02	435.99	381.85	343.65
21000	1857.14	979.88	688.65	543.92	457.79	400.95	360.84
22000	1945.57	1026.54	721.44	569.82	479.59	420.04	378.02
23000	2034.01	1073.20	754.24	595.73	501.39	439.13	395.20
24000	2122.44	1119.86	787.03	621.63	523.19	458.23	412.38
25000	2210.88	1166.52	819.82	647.53	544.99	477.32	429.57
26000	2299.31	1213.19	852.62	673.43	566.79	496.41	446.75
27000	2387.75	1259.85	885.41	699.33	588.59	515.50	463.93
28000	2476.18	1306.51	918.20	725.23	610.39	534.60	481.11
29000	2564.62	1353.17	951.00	751.13	632.19	553.69	498.30
30000	2653.05	1399.83	983.79	777.03	653.99	572.78	515.48
35000	3095.23	1633.13	1147.75	906.54	762.98	668.25	601.39
40000	3537.40	1866.44	1311.72	1036.05	871.98	763.71	687.31
45000	3979.58	2099.74	1475.68	1165.55	980.98	859.17	773.22
50000	4421.75	2333.05	1639.65	1295.06	1089.98	954.64	859.13
55000	4863.93	2566.35	1803.61	1424.56	1198.97	1050.10	945.05
60000	5306.10	2799.66	1967.58	1554.07	1307.97	1145.56	1030.96
65000	5748.28	3032.96	2131.54	1683.57	1416.97	1241.03	1116.87
70000	6190.45	3266.27	2295.51	1813.08	1525.97	1336.49	1202.79
75000	6632.63	3499.57	2459.47	1942.59	1634.97	1431.96	1288.70
80000	7074.80	3732.88	2623.44	2072.09	1743.96	1527.42	1374.61
85000	7516.98	3966.18	2787.40	2201.60	1852.96	1622.88	1460.53
90000	7959.15	4199.49	2951.36	2331.10	1961.96	1718.35	1546.44
95000	8401.33	4432.79	3115.33	2460.61	2070.96	1813.81	1632.35
100000	8843.50	4666.10	3279.29	2590.11	2179.95	1909.27	1718.27
200000	17687.01	9332.20	6558.59	5180.23	4359.91	3818.55	3436.53
300000	26530.51	13998.30	9837.88	7770.34	6539.86	5727.82	5154.80
400000	35374.02	18664.40	13117.18	10360.45	8719.82	7637.10	6873.07
500000	44217.52	23330.49	16396.47	12950.57	10899.77	9546.37	8591.33
1000000	88435.05	46660.99	32792.94	25901.14	21799.54	19092.75	17182.67

Amortization Amount	8 Years	9 Years	10 Years	15 Years	20 Years	25 Years	30 Years
25	0.39	0.37	0.35	0.29	0.26	0.25	0.24
50	0.79	0.73	0.69	0.57	0.52	0.49	0.48
100	1.58	1.47	1.38	1.14	1.04	0.99	0.96
200	3.15	2.94	2.77	2.29	2.08	1.98	1.92
300	4.73	4.41	4.15	3.43	3.12	2.97	2.88
400	6.31	5.88	5.54	4.58	4.16	3.95	3.84
500	7.89	7.34	6.92	5.72	5.20	4.94	4.80
600	9.46	8.81	8.30	6.86	6.24	5.93	5.77
700	11.04	10.28	9.69	8.01	7.28	6.92	6.73
800	12.62	11.75	11.07	9.15	8.32	7.91	7.69
900	14.19	13.22	12.46	10.29	9.36	8.90	8.65
1000	15.77	14.69	13.84	11.44	10.40	9.88	9.61
2000	31.54	29.38	27.68	22.88	20.80	19.77	19.22
3000	47.31	44.07	41.52	34.31	31.20	29.65	28.83
4000	63.08	58.76	55.36	45.75	41.60	39.54	38.44
5000	78.85	73.45	69.20	57.19	52.00	49.42	48.05
6000	94.62	88.14	83.04	68.63	62.40	59.30	57.66
7000	110.39	102.82	96.88	80.07	72.80	69.19	67.27
8000	126.16	117.51	110.72	91.50	83.20	79.07	76.88
9000	141.93	132.20	124.56	102.94	93.60	88.96	86.49
10000	157.70	146.89	138.40	114.38	104.00	98.84	96.10
11000	173.47	161.58	152.24	125.82	114.40	108.72	105.71
12000	189.24	176.27	166.08	137.26	124.80	118.61	115.32
13000	205.01	190.96	179.92	148.69	135.20	128.49	124.93
14000	220.78	205.65	193.76	160.13	145.60	138.38	134.54
15000	236.55	220.34	207.60	171.57	156.00	148.26	144.15
16000	252.32	235.03	221.44	183.01	166.40	158.14	153.76
17000	268.09	249.72	235.28	194.44	176.80	168.03	163.37
18000	283.86	264.41	249.12	205.88	187.20	177.91	172.98
19000	299.63	279.09	262.96	217.32	197.60	187.80	182.59
20000	315.40	293.78	276.80	228.76	208.00	197.68	192.20
21000	331.17	308.47	290.64	240.20	218.40	207.56	201.81
22000	346.94	323.16	304.48	251.63	228.80	217.45	211.42
23000	362.72	337.85	318.32	263.07	239.20	227.33	221.03
24000	378.49	352.54	332.16	274.51	249.60	237.22	230.64
25000	394.26	367.23	346.00	285.95	270.00	247.10	240.25
26000	410.03	381.92	359.84	297.39	270.40	256.98	249.86
27000	425.80	396.61	373.68	308.82	280.80	266.87	259.46
28000	441.57	411.30	387.52	320.26	291.20	276.75	269.07
29000	457.34	425.99	401.36	331.70	301.60	286.64	278.68
30000	473.11	440.68	415.20	343.14	312.00	296.52	288.29
35000	551.96	514.12	484.40	400.33	364.00	345.94	336.34
40000	630.81	587.57	553.59	457.52	416.00	395.36	384.39
45000	709.66	661.01	622.79	514.71	467.99	444.78	432.44
50000	788.51	734.46	691.99	571.90	519.99	494.20	480.49
55000	867.36	807.91	761.19	629.09	571.99	543.62	528.54
60000	946.21	881.35	830.39	686.28	623.99	593.04	576.59
65000	1025.06	954.80	899.59	743.47	675.99	642.46	624.64
70000	1103.92	1028.24	968.79	800.66	727.99	691.88	672.69
75000	1182.77	1101.69	1037.99	857.85	779.99	741.30	720.74
80000	1261.62	1175.14	1107.19	915.03	831.99	790.72	768.78
85000	1340.47	1248.58	1176.39	972.22	883.99	840.14	816.83
90000	1419.32	1322.03	1245.59	1029.41	935.99	889.56	864.88
95000	1498.17	1395.47	1314.79	1086.60	987.99	938.98	912.93
100000	1577.02	1488.92	1383.99	1143.79	1039.98	988.40	960.98
200000	3154.04	2937.84	2767.97	2287.59	2079.98	1976.80	1921.96
300000	4731.07	4406.76	4151.96	3431.38	3119.96	2965.19	2882.94
400000	6308.09	5875.68	5535.94	4575.17	4159.95	3953.59	3843.92
500000	7885.11	7344.60	6919.93	5718.97	5199.94	4941.99	4804.91
1000000	15770.22	14689.20	13839.86	11437.94	10399.88	9883.98	9609.81

11.5%

MONTHLY PAYMENT
NECESSARY TO AMORTIZE A LOAN

Amortization Amount	1 Year	2 Years	3 Years	4 Years	5 Years	6 Years	7 Years
25	2.21	1.17	0.82	0.65	0.55	0.48	0.43
50	4.42	2.34	1.64	1.30	1.09	0.96	0.86
100	8.85	4.67	3.28	2.60	2.19	1.92	1.72
200	17.70	9.34	6.57	5.19	4.37	3.83	3.45
300	26.55	14.01	9.85	7.79	6.56	5.75	5.17
400	35.40	18.69	13.14	10.38	8.74	7.66	6.90
500	44.25	23.36	16.42	12.98	10.93	9.58	8.62
600	53.09	28.03	19.71	15.58	13.12	11.49	10.35
700	61.94	32.70	22.99	18.17	15.30	13.41	12.07
800	70.79	37.37	26.28	20.77	17.49	15.32	13.80
900	79.64	42.04	29.56	23.36	19.67	17.24	15.52
1000	88.49	46.72	32.85	25.96	21.86	19.15	17.25
2000	176.98	93.43	65.70	51.92	43.72	38.31	34.49
3000	265.47	140.15	98.55	77.88	65.58	57.46	51.74
4000	353.96	186.87	131.40	103.84	87.44	76.62	68.98
5000	442.45	233.58	164.25	129.80	109.30	95.77	86.23
6000	530.94	280.30	197.10	155.76	131.16	114.92	103.47
7000	619.44	327.02	229.95	181.71	153.01	134.08	120.72
8000	707.93	373.73	262.80	207.67	174.87	153.23	137.96
9000	796.42	420.45	295.65	233.63	196.73	172.39	155.21
10000	884.91	467.16	328.50	259.59	218.59	191.54	172.46
11000	973.40	513.88	361.34	285.55	240.45	210.69	189.70
12000	1061.89	560.60	394.19	311.51	262.31	229.85	206.95
13000	1150.38	607.31	427.04	337.47	284.17	249.00	224.19
14000	1238.87	654.03	459.89	363.43	306.03	268.16	241.44
15000	1327.36	700.75	492.74	389.39	327.89	287.31	258.68
16000	1415.85	747.46	525.59	415.35	349.75	306.46	275.93
17000	1504.34	794.18	558.44	441.31	371.61	325.62	293.18
18000	1592.83	840.90	591.29	467.27	393.47	344.77	310.42
19000	1681.32	887.61	624.14	493.22	415.32	363.93	327.67
20000	1769.81	934.33	656.99	519.18	437.18	383.08	344.91
21000	1858.31	981.05	689.84	545.14	459.04	402.23	362.16
22000	1946.80	1027.76	722.69	571.10	480.90	421.39	379.40
23000	2035.29	1074.48	755.54	597.06	502.76	440.54	396.65
24000	2123.78	1121.19	788.39	623.02	524.62	459.70	413.89
25000	2212.27	1167.91	821.24	648.98	546.48	478.85	431.14
26000	2300.76	1214.63	854.09	674.94	568.34	498.00	448.39
27000	2389.25	1261.34	886.94	700.90	590.20	517.16	465.63
28000	2477.74	1308.06	919.79	726.86	612.06	536.31	482.88
29000	2566.23	1354.78	952.64	752.82	633.92	555.47	500.12
30000	2654.72	1401.49	985.49	778.78	655.78	574.62	517.37
35000	3097.18	1635.08	1149.73	908.57	765.07	670.39	603.60
40000	3539.63	1868.66	1313.98	1038.37	874.37	766.16	689.82
45000	3982.08	2102.24	1478.23	1168.16	983.66	861.93	776.05
50000	4424.54	2335.82	1642.48	1297.96	1092.96	957.70	862.28
55000	4866.99	2569.40	1806.72	1427.76	1202.26	1053.47	948.51
60000	5309.44	2802.99	1970.97	1557.55	1311.55	1149.24	1034.74
65000	5751.90	3036.57	2135.22	1687.35	1420.85	1245.01	1120.96
70000	6194.35	3270.15	2299.47	1817.14	1530.14	1340.78	1207.19
75000	6636.81	3503.73	2463.72	1946.94	1639.44	1436.55	1293.42
80000	7079.26	3737.32	2627.96	2076.74	1748.74	1532.32	1379.65
85000	7521.71	3970.90	2792.21	2206.53	1858.03	1628.09	1465.88
90000	7964.17	4204.48	2956.46	2336.33	1967.33	1723.86	1552.10
95000	8406.62	4438.06	3120.71	2466.12	2076.62	1819.63	1638.33
100000	8849.07	4671.65	3284.95	2595.92	2185.92	1915.40	1724.56
200000	17698.15	9343.29	6569.91	5191.84	4371.84	3830.81	3449.12
300000	26547.22	14014.94	9854.86	7787.76	6557.76	5746.21	5173.68
400000	35396.30	18686.58	13139.82	10383.68	8743.68	7661.61	6898.24
500000	44245.37	23358.23	16424.77	12979.60	10929.60	9577.02	8622.80
1000000	88490.74	46716.45	32849.54	25959.20	21859.19	19154.04	17245.60

Amortization Amount	8 Years	9 Years	10 Years	15 Years	20 Years	25 Years	30 Years
25	0.40	0.37	0.35	0.29	0.26	0.25	0.24
50	0.79	0.74	0.70	0.58	0.52	0.50	0.49
100	1.58	1.48	1.39	1.15	1.05	1.00	0.97
200	3.17	2.95	2.78	2.30	2.10	1.99	1.94
300	4.75	4.43	4.17	3.45	3.14	2.99	2.91
400	6.33	5.90	5.56	4.61	4.19	3.99	3.88
500	7.92	7.38	6.95	5.76	5.24	4.99	4.85
600	9.50	8.85	8.34	6.91	6.29	5.98	5.82
700	11.08	10.33	9.74	8.06	7.34	6.98	6.79
800	12.67	11.80	11.13	9.21	8.39	7.98	7.76
900	14.25	13.28	12.52	10.36	9.43	8.97	8.73
1000	15.83	14.76	13.91	11.51	10.48	9.97	9.70
2000	31.67	29.51	27.82	23.03	20.96	19.94	19.40
3000	47.50	44.27	41.72	34.54	31.44	29.91	29.10
4000	63.34	59.02	55.63	46.05	41.93	39.88	38.80
5000	79.17	73.78	69.54	57.57	52.41	49.85	48.50
6000	95.01	88.53	83.45	69.08	62.89	59.82	58.20
7000	110.84	103.29	97.35	80.59	73.37	69.79	67.90
8000	126.68	118.04	111.26	92.11	83.85	79.76	77.60
9000	142.51	132.80	125.17	103.62	94.33	89.74	87.30
10000	158.35	147.55	139.08	115.13	104.81	99.71	97.00
11000	174.18	162.31	152.98	126.65	115.30	109.68	106.70
12000	190.02	177.06	166.89	138.16	125.78	119.65	116.40
13000	205.85	191.82	180.80	149.67	136.26	129.62	126.10
14000	221.69	206.58	194.71	161.18	146.74	139.59	135.80
15000	237.52	221.33	208.62	172.70	157.22	149.56	145.50
16000	253.36	236.09	222.52	184.21	167.70	159.53	155.20
17000	269.19	250.84	236.43	195.72	178.18	169.50	164.91
18000	285.03	265.60	250.34	207.24	188.67	179.47	174.61
19000	300.86	280.35	264.25	218.75	199.15	189.44	184.31
20000	316.70	295.11	278.15	230.26	209.63	199.41	194.01
21000	332.53	309.86	292.06	241.78	220.11	209.38	203.71
22000	348.37	324.62	305.97	253.29	230.59	219.35	213.41
23000	364.20	339.37	319.88	264.80	241.07	229.32	223.11
24000	380.04	354.13	333.78	276.32	251.55	239.29	232.81
25000	395.87	368.89	347.69	287.83	262.04	249.27	242.51
26000	411.70	383.64	361.60	299.34	272.52	259.24	252.21
27000	427.54	398.40	375.51	310.86	283.00	269.21	261.91
28000	443.37	413.15	389.41	322.37	293.48	279.18	271.61
29000	459.21	427.91	403.32	333.88	303.96	289.15	281.31
30000	475.04	442.66	417.23	345.40	314.44	299.12	291.01
35000	554.22	516.44	486.77	402.96	366.85	348.97	339.51
40000	633.39	590.22	556.31	460.53	419.26	398.82	388.01
45000	712.57	663.99	625.85	518.09	471.67	448.68	436.51
50000	791.74	737.77	695.38	575.66	524.07	498.53	485.02
55000	870.91	811.55	764.92	633.23	576.48	548.38	533.52
60000	950.09	885.32	834.46	690.79	628.89	598.24	582.02
65000	1029.26	959.10	904.00	748.36	681.29	648.09	630.52
70000	1108.44	1032.88	973.54	805.92	733.70	697.94	679.02
75000	1187.61	1106.66	1043.08	863.49	786.11	747.80	727.52
80000	1266.78	1180.43	1112.61	921.06	838.52	797.65	776.02
85000	1345.96	1254.21	1182.15	978.62	890.92	847.50	824.53
90000	1425.13	1327.99	1251.69	1036.19	943.33	897.35	873.03
95000	1504.31	1401.76	1321.23	1093.75	995.74	947.21	921.53
100000	1583.48	1475.54	1390.77	1151.32	1048.15	997.06	970.03
200000	3166.96	2951.08	2781.53	2302.64	2096.29	1994.12	1940.06
300000	4750.44	4426.62	4172.30	3453.96	3144.44	2991.18	2910.09
400000	6333.92	5902.16	5563.07	4605.28	4192.58	3988.24	3880.12
500000	7917.40	7377.70	6953.83	5756.60	5240.73	4985.30	4850.15
1000000	15834.80	14755.40	13907.67	11513.20	10481.46	9970.61	9700.30

11.625%

Amortization Amount	1 Year	2 Years	3 Years	4 Years	5 Years	6 Years	7 Years
25	2.21	1.17	0.82	0.65	0.55	0.48	0.43
50	4.43	2.34	1.65	1.30	1.10	0.96	0.87
100	8.85	4.68	3.29	2.60	2.19	1.92	1.73
200	17.71	9.35	6.58	5.20	4.38	3.84	3.46
300	26.56	14.03	9.87	7.81	6.58	5.76	5.19
400	35.42	18.71	13.16	10.41	8.77	7.69	6.92
500	44.27	23.39	16.45	13.01	10.96	9.61	8.65
600	53.13	28.06	19.74	15.61	13.15	11.53	10.39
700	61.98	32.74	23.03	18.21	15.34	13.45	12.12
800	70.84	37.42	26.32	20.81	17.54	15.37	13.85
900	79.69	42.09	29.62	23.42	19.73	17.29	15.58
1000	88.55	46.77	32.91	26.02	21.92	19.22	17.31
2000	177.09	93.54	65.81	52.03	43.84	38.43	34.62
3000	265.64	140.32	98.72	78.05	65.76	57.65	51.93
4000	354.19	187.09	131.62	104.07	87.68	76.86	69.23
5000	442.73	233.86	164.53	130.09	109.59	96.08	86.54
6000	531.28	280.63	197.44	156.10	131.51	115.29	103.85
7000	619.83	327.40	230.34	182.12	153.43	134.51	121.16
8000	708.37	374.18	263.25	208.14	175.35	153.72	138.47
9000	796.92	420.95	296.16	234.16	197.27	172.94	155.78
10000	885.46	467.72	329.06	260.17	219.19	192.15	173.09
11000	974.01	514.49	361.97	286.19	241.11	211.37	190.40
12000	1062.56	561.26	394.87	312.21	263.03	230.58	207.70
13000	1151.10	608.04	427.78	338.23	284.95	249.80	225.01
14000	1239.65	654.81	460.69	364.24	306.86	269.02	242.32
15000	1328.20	701.58	493.59	390.26	328.78	288.23	259.63
16000	1416.74	748.35	526.50	416.28	350.70	307.45	276.94
17000	1505.29	795.12	559.40	442.29	372.62	326.66	294.25
18000	1593.84	841.89	592.31	468.31	394.54	345.88	311.56
19000	1682.38	888.67	625.22	494.33	416.46	365.09	328.86
20000	1770.93	935.44	658.12	520.35	438.38	384.31	346.17
21000	1859.48	982.21	691.03	546.36	460.30	403.52	363.48
22000	1948.02	1028.98	723.94	572.38	482.22	422.74	380.79
23000	2036.57	1075.75	756.84	598.40	504.13	441.95	398.10
24000	2125.11	1122.53	789.75	624.42	526.05	461.17	415.41
25000	2213.66	1169.30	822.65	650.43	547.97	480.39	432.72
26000	2302.21	1216.07	855.56	676.45	569.89	499.60	450.02
27000	2390.75	1262.84	888.47	702.47	591.81	518.82	467.33
28000	2479.30	1309.61	921.37	728.48	613.73	538.03	484.64
29000	2567.85	1356.39	954.28	754.50	635.65	557.25	501.95
30000	2656.39	1403.16	987.19	780.52	657.57	576.46	519.26
35000	3099.13	1637.02	1151.72	910.61	767.16	672.54	605.80
40000	3541.86	1870.88	1316.25	1040.69	876.76	768.62	692.35
45000	3984.59	2104.74	1480.78	1170.78	986.35	864.69	778.89
50000	4427.32	2338.60	1645.31	1300.87	1095.95	960.77	865.43
55000	4870.05	2572.46	1809.84	1430.95	1205.54	1056.85	951.98
60000	5312.79	2806.32	1974.37	1561.04	1315.13	1152.92	1038.52
65000	5755.52	3040.18	2138.90	1691.13	1424.73	1249.00	1125.06
70000	6198.25	3274.03	2303.43	1821.21	1534.32	1345.08	1211.60
75000	6640.98	3507.89	2467.96	1951.30	1643.92	1441.16	1298.15
80000	7083.71	3741.75	2632.49	2081.39	1753.51	1537.23	1384.69
85000	7526.45	3975.61	2797.02	2211.47	1863.11	1633.31	1471.23
90000	7969.18	4209.47	2961.56	2341.56	1972.70	1729.39	1557.78
95000	8411.91	4443.33	3126.09	2471.64	2082.30	1825.46	1644.32
100000	8854.64	4677.19	3290.62	2601.73	2191.89	1921.54	1730.86
200000	17709.29	9354.39	6581.23	5203.46	4383.78	3843.08	3461.73
300000	26563.93	14031.58	9871.85	7805.19	6575.67	5764.62	5192.59
400000	35418.57	18708.77	13162.47	10406.93	8767.57	7686.16	6923.45
500000	44273.22	23385.96	16453.08	13008.66	10959.46	9607.70	8654.32
1000000	88546.43	46771.93	32906.17	26017.32	21918.91	19215.40	17308.64

Amortization Amount	8 Years	9 Years	10 Years	15 Years	20 Years	25 Years	30 Years
25	0.40	0.37	0.35	0.29	0.26	0.25	0.24
50	0.79	0.74	0.70	0.58	0.53	0.50	0.49
100	1.59	1.48	1.40	1.16	1.06	1.01	0.98
200	3.18	2.96	2.80	2.32	2.11	2.01	1.96
300	4.77	4.45	4.19	3.48	3.17	3.02	2.94
400	6.36	5.93	5.59	4.64	4.23	4.02	3.92
500	7.95	7.41	6.99	5.79	5.28	5.03	4.90
600	9.54	8.89	8.39	6.95	6.34	6.03	5.87
700	11.13	10.38	9.78	8.11	7.39	7.04	6.85
800	12.72	11.86	11.18	9.27	8.45	8.05	7.83
900	14.31	13.34	12.58	10.43	9.51	9.05	8.81
1000	15.90	14.82	13.98	11.59	10.56	10.06	9.79
2000	31.80	29.64	27.95	23.18	21.13	20.11	19.58
3000	47.70	44.47	41.93	34.77	31.69	30.17	29.37
4000	63.60	59.29	55.90	46.35	42.25	40.23	39.16
5000	79.50	74.11	69.88	57.94	52.82	50.29	48.95
6000	95.40	88.93	83.85	69.53	63.38	60.34	58.75
7000	111.30	103.75	97.83	81.12	73.94	70.40	68.54
8000	127.20	118.57	111.80	92.71	84.51	80.46	78.33
9000	143.10	133.40	125.78	104.30	95.07	90.52	88.12
10000	158.99	148.22	139.76	115.89	105.63	100.57	97.91
11000	174.89	163.04	153.73	127.48	116.20	110.63	107.70
12000	190.79	177.86	167.71	139.06	126.76	120.69	117.49
13000	206.69	192.68	181.68	150.65	137.32	130.75	127.28
14000	222.59	207.50	195.66	162.24	147.89	140.80	137.07
15000	238.49	222.33	209.63	173.83	158.45	150.86	146.86
16000	254.39	237.15	223.61	185.42	169.01	160.92	156.66
17000	270.29	251.97	237.59	197.01	179.57	170.98	166.45
18000	286.19	266.79	251.56	208.60	190.14	181.03	176.24
19000	302.09	281.61	265.54	220.18	200.70	191.09	186.03
20000	317.99	296.43	279.51	231.77	211.28	201.15	195.82
21000	333.89	311.26	293.49	243.36	221.83	211.21	205.61
22000	349.79	326.08	307.46	254.95	232.39	221.26	215.40
23000	365.69	340.90	321.44	266.54	242.95	231.32	225.19
24000	381.59	355.72	335.41	278.13	253.52	241.38	234.98
25000	397.49	370.54	349.39	289.72	264.08	251.44	244.77
26000	413.39	385.37	363.37	301.30	274.64	261.49	254.58
27000	429.29	400.19	377.34	312.89	285.21	271.55	264.36
28000	445.19	415.01	391.32	324.48	295.77	281.61	274.15
29000	461.09	429.83	405.29	336.07	306.33	291.67	283.94
30000	476.98	444.65	419.27	347.66	316.90	301.72	293.73
35000	556.48	518.76	489.15	405.60	369.71	352.01	342.68
40000	635.98	592.87	559.02	463.55	422.53	402.30	391.64
45000	715.48	666.98	628.90	521.49	475.35	452.58	440.59
50000	794.97	741.09	698.78	579.43	528.16	502.87	489.55
55000	874.47	815.20	768.66	637.38	580.98	553.16	538.50
60000	953.97	889.30	838.54	695.32	633.79	603.45	587.46
65000	1033.47	963.41	908.41	753.26	686.61	653.73	636.41
70000	1112.96	1037.52	978.29	811.21	739.43	704.02	685.37
75000	1192.46	1111.63	1048.17	869.15	792.24	754.31	734.32
80000	1271.96	1185.74	1118.05	927.09	845.06	804.59	783.28
85000	1351.46	1259.85	1187.93	985.04	897.87	854.88	832.23
90000	1430.95	1333.96	1257.81	1042.98	950.69	905.17	881.19
95000	1510.45	1408.06	1327.68	1100.92	1003.51	955.46	930.14
100000	1589.95	1482.17	1397.56	1158.87	1056.32	1005.74	979.10
200000	3179.90	2964.35	2795.12	2317.73	2112.65	2011.48	1958.19
300000	4769.85	4446.52	4192.68	3476.60	3168.97	3017.23	2937.29
400000	6359.79	5928.69	5590.24	4635.46	4225.29	4022.97	3916.38
500000	7949.74	7410.87	6987.81	5794.33	5281.62	5028.71	4895.48
1000000	15899.49	14821.73	13975.61	11588.65	10563.23	10057.42	9790.96

11.75%

Amortization Amount	1 Year	2 Years	3 Years	4 Years	5 Years	6 Years	7 Years
25	2.22	1.17	0.82	0.65	0.55	0.48	0.43
50	4.43	2.34	1.65	1.30	1.10	0.96	0.87
100	8.86	4.68	3.30	2.61	2.20	1.93	1.74
200	17.72	9.37	6.59	5.22	4.40	3.86	3.47
300	26.58	14.05	9.89	7.82	6.59	5.78	5.21
400	35.44	18.73	13.19	10.43	8.79	7.71	6.95
500	44.30	23.41	16.48	13.04	10.99	9.64	8.69
600	53.16	28.10	19.78	15.65	13.19	11.57	10.42
700	62.02	32.78	23.07	18.25	15.39	13.49	12.16
800	70.88	37.46	26.37	20.86	17.58	15.42	13.90
900	79.74	42.14	29.67	23.47	19.78	17.35	15.63
1000	88.60	46.83	32.96	26.08	21.98	19.28	17.37
2000	177.20	93.65	65.93	52.15	43.96	38.55	34.74
3000	265.81	140.48	98.89	78.23	65.94	57.83	52.12
4000	354.41	187.31	131.85	104.30	87.91	77.11	69.49
5000	443.01	234.14	164.81	130.38	109.89	96.38	86.86
6000	531.61	280.96	197.78	156.45	131.87	115.66	104.23
7000	620.21	327.79	230.74	182.53	153.85	134.94	121.60
8000	708.82	374.62	263.70	208.60	175.83	154.21	138.97
9000	797.42	421.45	296.67	234.68	197.81	173.49	156.35
10000	886.02	468.27	329.63	260.75	219.79	192.77	173.72
11000	974.62	515.10	362.59	286.83	241.77	212.05	191.09
12000	1063.23	561.93	395.55	312.91	263.74	231.32	208.46
13000	1151.83	608.76	428.52	338.98	285.72	250.60	225.83
14000	1240.43	655.58	461.48	365.06	307.70	269.88	243.20
15000	1329.03	702.41	494.44	391.13	329.68	289.15	260.58
16000	1417.63	749.24	527.41	417.21	351.66	308.43	277.95
17000	1506.24	796.07	560.37	443.28	373.64	327.71	295.32
18000	1594.84	842.89	593.33	469.36	395.62	346.98	312.69
19000	1683.44	889.72	626.29	495.43	417.60	366.26	330.06
20000	1772.04	936.55	659.26	521.51	439.57	385.54	347.44
21000	1860.64	983.38	692.22	547.59	461.55	404.81	364.81
22000	1949.25	1030.20	725.18	573.66	483.53	424.09	382.18
23000	2037.85	1077.03	758.15	599.74	505.51	443.37	399.55
24000	2126.45	1123.86	791.11	625.81	527.49	462.64	416.92
25000	2215.05	1170.69	824.07	651.89	549.47	481.92	434.29
26000	2303.65	1217.51	857.03	677.96	571.45	501.20	451.67
27000	2392.26	1264.34	890.00	704.04	593.42	520.48	469.04
28000	2480.86	1311.17	922.96	730.11	615.40	539.75	486.41
29000	2569.46	1357.99	955.92	756.19	637.38	559.03	503.78
30000	2658.06	1404.82	988.88	782.28	659.36	578.31	521.15
35000	3101.07	1638.96	1153.70	912.64	769.25	674.69	608.01
40000	3544.08	1873.10	1318.51	1043.02	879.15	771.07	694.87
45000	3987.09	2107.23	1483.33	1173.40	989.04	867.46	781.73
50000	4430.11	2341.37	1648.14	1303.77	1098.93	963.84	868.59
55000	4873.12	2575.51	1812.96	1434.15	1208.83	1060.23	955.45
60000	5316.13	2809.64	1977.77	1564.53	1318.72	1156.61	1042.31
65000	5759.14	3043.78	2142.58	1694.91	1428.62	1253.00	1129.16
70000	6202.15	3277.92	2307.40	1825.28	1538.51	1349.38	1216.02
75000	6645.16	3512.06	2472.21	1955.66	1648.40	1445.76	1302.88
80000	7088.17	3746.19	2637.03	2086.04	1758.30	1542.15	1389.74
85000	7531.18	3980.33	2801.84	2216.42	1868.19	1638.53	1476.60
90000	7974.19	4214.47	2966.65	2346.79	1978.08	1734.92	1563.46
95000	8417.20	4448.60	3131.47	2477.17	2087.98	1831.30	1650.32
100000	8860.21	4682.74	3296.28	2607.55	2197.87	1927.69	1737.18
200000	17720.42	9365.48	6592.57	5215.10	4395.74	3855.37	3474.35
300000	26580.63	14048.22	9888.85	7822.64	6593.61	5783.06	5211.53
400000	35440.84	18730.96	13185.13	10430.19	8791.48	7710.74	6948.71
500000	44301.05	23413.71	16481.41	13037.74	10989.35	9638.43	8685.88
1000000	88602.11	46827.41	32962.83	26075.48	21978.70	19276.86	17371.77

126

MONTHLY PAYMENT
NECESSARY TO AMORTIZE A LOAN
11.75%

Amortization Amount	8 Years	9 Years	10 Years	15 Years	20 Years	25 Years	30 Years
25	0.40	0.37	0.35	0.29	0.27	0.25	0.25
50	0.80	0.74	0.70	0.58	0.53	0.51	0.49
100	1.60	1.49	1.40	1.17	1.06	1.01	0.99
200	3.19	2.98	2.81	2.33	2.13	2.03	1.98
300	4.79	4.47	4.21	3.50	3.19	3.04	2.96
400	6.39	5.96	5.62	4.67	4.26	4.06	3.95
500	7.98	7.44	7.02	5.83	5.32	5.07	4.94
600	9.58	8.93	8.43	7.00	6.39	6.09	5.93
700	11.18	10.42	9.83	8.16	7.45	7.10	6.92
800	12.77	11.91	11.23	9.33	8.52	8.12	7.91
900	14.37	13.40	12.64	10.50	9.58	9.13	8.89
1000	15.96	14.89	14.04	11.66	10.65	10.14	9.88
2000	31.93	29.78	28.09	23.33	21.29	20.29	19.76
3000	47.89	44.66	42.13	34.99	31.94	30.43	29.65
4000	63.86	59.55	56.17	46.66	42.58	40.58	39.53
5000	79.82	74.44	70.22	58.32	53.23	50.72	49.41
6000	95.79	89.33	84.26	69.99	63.87	60.87	59.29
7000	111.75	104.22	98.31	81.65	74.52	71.01	69.17
8000	127.71	119.11	112.35	93.31	85.16	81.16	79.05
9000	143.68	133.99	126.39	104.98	95.81	91.30	88.94
10000	159.64	148.88	140.44	116.64	106.45	101.44	98.82
11000	175.61	163.77	154.48	128.31	117.10	111.59	108.70
12000	191.57	178.66	168.52	139.97	127.74	121.73	118.58
13000	207.54	193.55	182.57	151.64	138.39	131.88	128.46
14000	223.50	208.43	196.61	163.30	149.03	142.02	138.34
15000	239.46	223.32	210.66	174.96	159.68	152.17	148.23
16000	255.43	238.21	224.70	186.63	170.32	162.31	158.11
17000	271.39	253.10	238.74	198.29	180.97	172.46	167.99
18000	287.36	267.99	252.79	209.96	191.61	182.60	177.87
19000	303.32	282.88	266.83	221.62	202.26	192.74	187.75
20000	319.29	297.76	280.87	233.29	212.90	202.89	197.64
21000	335.25	312.65	294.92	244.95	223.55	213.03	207.52
22000	351.21	327.54	308.96	256.61	234.19	223.18	217.40
23000	367.18	342.43	323.00	268.28	244.84	233.32	227.28
24000	383.14	357.32	337.05	279.94	255.48	243.47	237.16
25000	399.11	372.20	351.09	291.61	266.13	253.61	247.04
26000	415.07	387.09	365.14	303.27	276.78	263.76	256.93
27000	431.04	401.98	379.18	314.94	287.42	273.90	266.81
28000	447.00	416.87	393.22	326.60	298.07	284.04	276.69
29000	462.96	431.76	407.27	338.26	308.71	294.19	286.57
30000	478.93	446.65	421.31	349.93	319.36	304.33	296.45
35000	558.75	521.09	491.53	408.25	372.58	355.06	345.86
40000	638.57	595.53	561.75	466.57	425.81	405.78	395.27
45000	718.39	669.97	631.97	524.89	479.03	456.50	444.68
50000	798.21	744.41	702.18	583.21	532.26	507.22	494.09
55000	878.04	818.85	772.40	641.54	585.49	557.94	543.50
60000	957.86	893.29	842.62	699.86	638.71	608.67	592.91
65000	1037.68	967.73	912.84	758.18	691.94	659.39	642.32
70000	1117.50	1042.17	983.06	816.50	745.16	710.11	691.72
75000	1197.32	1116.61	1053.28	874.82	798.39	760.83	741.13
80000	1277.14	1191.06	1123.50	933.14	851.62	811.55	790.54
85000	1356.96	1265.50	1193.71	991.46	904.84	862.28	839.95
90000	1436.79	1339.94	1263.93	1049.79	958.07	913.00	889.36
95000	1516.61	1414.38	1334.15	1108.11	1011.29	963.72	938.77
100000	1596.43	1488.82	1404.37	1166.43	1064.52	1014.44	988.18
200000	3192.86	2977.64	2808.74	2332.86	2129.04	2028.89	1976.35
300000	4789.09	4466.46	4213.11	3499.29	3193.56	3043.33	2964.53
400000	6385.72	5955.28	5617.48	4665.71	4258.08	4057.77	3952.71
500000	7982.14	7444.09	7021.85	5832.14	5322.60	5072.22	4940.89
1000000	15964.29	14888.19	14043.69	11664.28	10645.21	10144.43	9881.77

11.875%

Amortization Amount	1 Year	2 Years	3 Years	4 Years	5 Years	6 Years	7 Years
25	2.22	1.17	0.83	0.65	0.55	0.48	0.44
50	4.43	2.34	1.65	1.31	1.10	0.97	0.87
100	8.87	4.69	3.30	2.61	2.20	1.93	1.74
200	17.73	9.38	6.60	5.23	4.41	3.87	3.49
300	26.60	14.06	9.91	7.84	6.61	5.80	5.23
400	35.46	18.75	13.21	10.45	8.82	7.74	6.97
500	44.33	23.44	16.51	13.07	11.02	9.67	8.72
600	53.19	28.13	19.81	15.68	13.22	11.60	10.46
700	62.06	32.82	23.11	18.29	15.43	13.54	12.20
800	70.93	37.51	26.42	20.91	17.63	15.47	13.95
900	79.79	42.19	29.72	23.52	19.83	17.40	15.69
1000	88.66	46.88	33.02	26.13	22.04	19.34	17.43
2000	177.32	93.77	66.04	52.27	44.08	38.68	34.87
3000	265.97	140.65	99.06	78.40	66.12	58.02	52.30
4000	354.63	187.53	132.08	104.53	88.15	77.35	69.74
5000	443.29	234.41	165.10	130.67	110.19	96.69	87.17
6000	531.95	281.30	198.12	156.80	132.23	116.03	104.61
7000	620.60	328.18	231.14	182.94	154.27	135.37	122.04
8000	709.26	375.06	264.16	209.07	176.31	154.71	139.48
9000	797.92	421.95	297.18	235.20	198.35	174.05	156.91
10000	886.58	468.83	330.20	261.34	220.39	193.38	174.35
11000	975.24	515.71	363.21	287.47	242.42	212.72	191.78
12000	1063.89	562.59	396.23	313.60	264.46	232.06	209.22
13000	1152.55	609.48	429.25	339.74	286.50	251.40	226.65
14000	1241.21	656.36	462.27	365.87	308.54	270.74	244.09
15000	1329.87	703.24	495.29	392.01	330.58	290.08	261.52
16000	1418.52	750.13	528.31	418.14	352.62	309.41	278.96
17000	1507.18	797.01	561.33	444.27	374.66	328.75	296.39
18000	1595.84	843.89	594.35	470.41	396.69	348.09	313.83
19000	1684.50	890.78	627.37	496.54	418.73	367.43	331.26
20000	1773.16	937.66	660.39	522.67	440.77	386.77	348.70
21000	1861.81	984.54	693.41	548.81	462.81	406.11	366.13
22000	1950.47	1031.42	726.43	574.94	484.85	425.44	383.57
23000	2039.13	1078.31	759.45	601.07	506.89	444.78	401.00
24000	2127.79	1125.19	792.47	627.21	528.93	464.12	418.44
25000	2216.44	1172.07	825.49	653.34	550.96	483.46	435.87
26000	2305.10	1218.96	858.51	679.48	573.00	502.80	453.31
27000	2393.76	1265.84	891.53	705.61	595.04	522.14	470.74
28000	2482.42	1312.72	924.55	731.74	617.08	541.47	488.18
29000	2571.08	1359.60	957.57	757.88	639.12	560.81	505.61
30000	2659.73	1406.49	990.59	784.01	661.16	580.15	523.05
35000	3103.02	1640.90	1155.68	914.68	771.35	676.84	610.22
40000	3546.31	1875.32	1320.78	1045.35	881.54	773.54	697.40
45000	3989.60	2109.73	1485.88	1176.02	991.73	870.23	784.57
50000	4432.89	2344.15	1650.98	1306.68	1101.93	966.92	871.75
55000	4876.18	2578.56	1816.07	1437.35	1212.12	1063.61	958.92
60000	5319.47	2812.97	1981.17	1568.02	1322.31	1160.30	1046.10
65000	5762.76	3047.39	2146.27	1698.69	1432.51	1257.00	1133.27
70000	6206.04	3281.80	2311.37	1829.36	1542.70	1353.69	1220.45
75000	6649.33	3516.22	2476.46	1960.03	1652.89	1450.38	1307.62
80000	7092.62	3750.63	2641.56	2090.69	1763.08	1547.07	1394.80
85000	7535.91	3985.05	2806.66	2221.36	1873.28	1643.76	1481.97
90000	7979.20	4219.46	2971.76	2352.03	1983.47	1740.45	1569.15
95000	8422.49	4453.88	3136.85	2482.70	2093.66	1837.15	1656.32
100000	8865.78	4688.29	3301.95	2613.37	2203.85	1933.84	1743.50
200000	17731.56	9376.58	6603.90	5226.74	4407.71	3867.68	3487.00
300000	26597.33	14064.87	9905.85	7840.11	6611.56	5801.52	5230.50
400000	35463.11	18753.16	13207.81	10453.47	8815.42	7735.35	6974.00
500000	44328.89	23441.45	16509.76	13066.84	11019.27	9669.19	8717.50
1000000	88657.78	46882.91	33019.52	26133.69	22038.54	19338.39	17434.99

Amortization Amount	8 Years	9 Years	10 Years	15 Years	20 Years	25 Years	30 Years
25	0.40	0.37	0.35	0.29	0.27	0.26	0.25
50	0.80	0.75	0.71	0.59	0.54	0.51	0.50
100	1.60	1.50	1.41	1.17	1.07	1.02	1.00
200	3.21	2.99	2.82	2.35	2.15	2.05	1.99
300	4.81	4.49	4.23	3.52	3.22	3.07	2.99
400	6.41	5.98	5.64	4.70	4.29	4.09	3.99
500	8.01	7.48	7.06	5.87	5.36	5.12	4.99
600	9.62	8.97	8.47	7.04	6.44	6.14	5.98
700	11.22	10.47	9.88	8.22	7.51	7.16	6.98
800	12.82	11.96	11.29	9.39	8.58	8.19	7.98
900	14.43	13.46	12.70	10.57	9.65	9.21	8.98
1000	16.03	14.95	14.11	11.74	10.73	10.23	9.97
2000	32.06	29.91	28.22	23.48	21.45	20.46	19.95
3000	48.09	44.86	42.34	35.22	32.18	30.69	29.92
4000	64.12	59.82	56.45	46.96	42.91	40.93	39.89
5000	80.15	74.77	70.56	58.70	53.64	51.16	49.86
6000	96.18	89.73	84.67	70.44	64.36	61.39	59.84
7000	112.20	104.68	98.78	82.18	75.09	71.62	69.81
8000	128.23	119.64	112.90	93.92	85.82	81.85	79.78
9000	144.26	134.59	127.01	105.66	96.55	92.08	89.75
10000	160.29	149.55	141.12	117.40	107.27	102.32	99.73
11000	176.32	164.50	155.23	129.14	118.00	112.55	109.70
12000	192.35	179.46	169.34	140.88	128.73	122.78	119.67
13000	208.38	194.41	183.45	152.62	139.46	133.01	129.65
14000	224.41	209.37	197.57	164.36	150.18	143.24	139.62
15000	240.44	224.32	211.68	176.10	160.91	153.47	149.59
16000	256.47	239.28	225.79	187.84	171.64	163.71	159.56
17000	272.50	254.23	239.90	199.58	182.37	173.94	169.54
18000	288.53	269.19	254.01	211.32	193.09	184.17	179.51
19000	304.55	284.14	268.13	223.06	203.82	194.40	189.48
20000	320.58	299.10	282.24	234.80	214.55	204.63	199.45
21000	336.61	314.05	296.35	246.54	225.27	214.86	209.43
22000	352.64	329.00	310.46	258.28	236.00	225.10	219.40
23000	368.67	343.96	324.57	270.02	246.73	235.33	229.37
24000	384.70	358.91	338.69	281.76	257.46	245.56	239.35
25000	400.73	373.87	352.80	293.50	268.18	255.79	249.32
26000	416.76	388.82	366.91	305.24	278.91	266.02	259.29
27000	432.79	403.78	381.02	316.98	289.64	276.25	269.26
28000	448.82	418.73	395.13	328.72	300.37	286.49	279.24
29000	464.85	433.69	409.25	340.46	311.09	296.72	289.21
30000	480.88	448.64	423.36	352.20	321.82	306.95	299.18
35000	561.02	523.42	493.92	410.90	375.46	358.11	349.05
40000	641.17	598.19	564.48	469.60	429.10	409.26	398.91
45000	721.31	672.96	635.04	528.30	482.73	460.42	448.77
50000	801.46	747.74	705.60	587.01	536.37	511.58	498.64
55000	881.61	822.51	776.16	645.71	590.01	562.74	548.50
60000	961.75	897.29	846.71	704.41	643.64	613.90	598.36
65000	1041.90	972.06	917.27	763.11	697.28	665.06	648.23
70000	1122.04	1046.83	987.83	821.81	750.92	716.21	698.09
75000	1202.19	1121.61	1058.39	880.51	804.55	767.37	747.96
80000	1282.34	1196.38	1128.95	939.21	858.19	818.53	797.82
85000	1362.48	1271.16	1199.51	997.91	911.83	869.69	847.68
90000	1442.63	1345.93	1270.07	1056.61	965.46	920.85	897.55
95000	1522.77	1420.70	1340.63	1115.31	1019.10	972.00	947.41
100000	1602.92	1495.48	1411.19	1174.01	1072.74	1023.16	997.27
200000	3205.84	2990.95	2822.38	2348.02	2145.48	2046.32	1994.55
300000	4808.76	4486.43	4233.57	3522.03	3218.21	3069.49	2991.82
400000	6411.68	5981.91	5644.77	4696.04	4290.95	4092.65	3989.10
500000	8014.60	7477.38	7055.96	5870.05	5363.69	5115.81	4986.37
1000000	16029.20	14954.77	14111.91	11740.10	10727.38	10231.62	9972.75

12%

MONTHLY PAYMENT
NECESSARY TO AMORTIZE A LOAN

Amortization Amount	1 Year	2 Years	3 Years	4 Years	5 Years	6 Years	7 Years
25	2.22	1.17	0.83	0.65	0.55	0.48	0.44
50	4.44	2.35	1.65	1.31	1.10	0.97	0.87
100	8.87	4.69	3.31	2.62	2.21	1.94	1.75
200	17.74	9.39	6.62	5.24	4.42	3.88	3.50
300	26.61	14.08	9.92	7.86	6.63	5.82	5.25
400	35.49	18.78	13.23	10.48	8.84	7.76	7.00
500	44.36	23.47	16.54	13.10	11.05	9.70	8.75
600	53.23	28.16	19.85	15.72	13.26	11.64	10.50
700	62.10	32.86	23.15	18.33	15.47	13.58	12.25
800	70.97	37.55	26.46	20.95	17.68	15.52	14.00
900	79.84	42.24	29.77	23.57	19.89	17.46	15.75
1000	88.71	46.94	33.08	26.19	22.10	19.40	17.50
2000	177.43	93.88	66.15	52.38	44.20	38.80	35.00
3000	266.14	140.82	99.23	78.58	66.30	58.20	52.49
4000	354.85	187.75	132.30	104.77	88.39	77.60	69.99
5000	443.57	234.69	165.38	130.96	110.49	97.00	87.49
6000	532.28	281.63	198.46	157.15	132.59	116.40	104.99
7000	620.99	328.57	231.53	183.34	154.69	135.80	122.49
8000	709.71	375.51	264.61	209.54	176.79	155.20	139.99
9000	798.42	422.45	297.69	235.73	198.89	174.60	157.48
10000	887.13	469.38	330.76	261.92	220.98	194.00	174.98
11000	975.85	516.32	363.84	288.11	243.08	213.40	192.48
12000	1064.56	563.26	396.91	314.30	265.18	232.80	209.98
13000	1153.27	610.20	429.99	340.50	287.28	252.20	227.48
14000	1241.99	657.14	463.07	366.69	309.38	271.60	244.98
15000	1330.70	704.08	496.14	392.88	331.48	291.00	262.47
16000	1419.42	751.01	529.22	419.07	353.58	310.40	279.97
17000	1508.13	797.95	562.30	445.26	375.67	329.80	297.47
18000	1596.84	844.89	595.37	471.45	397.77	349.20	314.97
19000	1685.56	891.83	628.45	497.65	419.87	368.60	332.47
20000	1774.27	938.77	661.52	523.84	441.97	388.00	349.97
21000	1862.98	985.71	694.60	550.03	464.07	407.40	367.46
22000	1951.70	1032.65	727.68	576.22	486.17	426.80	384.96
23000	2040.41	1079.58	760.75	602.41	508.26	446.20	402.46
24000	2129.12	1126.52	793.83	628.61	530.36	465.60	419.96
25000	2217.84	1173.46	826.91	654.80	552.46	485.00	437.46
26000	2306.55	1220.40	859.98	680.99	574.56	504.40	454.96
27000	2395.26	1267.34	893.06	707.18	596.66	523.80	472.45
28000	2483.98	1314.28	926.13	733.37	618.76	543.20	489.95
29000	2572.69	1361.21	959.21	759.57	640.86	562.60	507.45
30000	2661.40	1408.15	992.29	785.76	662.95	582.00	524.95
35000	3104.97	1642.84	1157.67	916.72	773.45	679.00	612.44
40000	3548.54	1877.54	1323.05	1047.68	883.94	776.00	699.93
45000	3992.10	2112.23	1488.43	1178.64	994.43	873.00	787.42
50000	4435.67	2346.92	1653.81	1309.60	1104.92	970.00	874.92
55000	4879.24	2581.61	1819.19	1440.56	1215.42	1067.00	962.41
60000	5322.81	2816.30	1984.57	1571.52	1325.91	1164.00	1049.90
65000	5766.37	3051.00	2149.96	1702.48	1436.40	1261.00	1137.39
70000	6209.94	3285.69	2315.34	1833.44	1546.89	1358.00	1224.88
75000	6653.51	3520.38	2480.72	1964.40	1657.38	1455.00	1312.37
80000	7097.08	3755.07	2646.10	2095.36	1767.88	1552.00	1399.87
85000	7540.64	3989.77	2811.48	2226.32	1878.37	1649.00	1487.36
90000	7984.21	4224.46	2976.86	2357.27	1988.86	1746.00	1574.85
95000	8427.78	4459.15	3142.24	2488.23	2099.35	1843.00	1662.34
100000	8871.34	4693.84	3307.62	2619.19	2209.85	1940.00	1749.83
200000	17742.69	9387.68	6615.25	5238.39	4419.69	3880.00	3499.66
300000	26614.03	14081.52	9922.87	7857.58	6629.54	5820.00	5249.49
400000	35485.38	18775.37	13230.49	10476.98	8839.38	7760.00	6999.33
500000	44356.72	23469.21	16538.12	13095.97	11049.23	9700.00	8749.16
1000000	88713.44	46938.42	33076.23	26191.94	22098.46	19400.00	17498.32

Amortization Amount	8 Years	9 Years	10 Years	15 Years	20 Years	25 Years	30 Years
25	0.40	0.38	0.35	0.30	0.27	0.26	0.25
50	0.80	0.75	0.71	0.59	0.54	0.52	0.50
100	1.61	1.50	1.42	1.18	1.08	1.03	1.01
200	3.22	3.00	2.84	2.36	2.16	2.06	2.01
300	4.83	4.51	4.25	3.54	3.24	3.10	3.02
400	6.44	6.01	5.67	4.73	4.32	4.13	4.03
500	8.05	7.51	7.09	5.91	5.40	5.16	5.03
600	9.66	9.01	8.51	7.09	6.49	6.19	6.04
700	11.27	10.52	9.93	8.27	7.57	7.22	7.04
800	12.88	12.02	11.34	9.45	8.65	8.26	8.05
900	14.48	13.52	12.76	10.63	9.73	9.29	9.06
1000	16.09	15.02	14.18	11.82	10.81	10.32	10.06
2000	32.19	30.04	28.36	23.63	21.62	20.64	20.13
3000	48.28	45.06	42.54	35.45	32.43	30.96	30.19
4000	64.38	60.09	56.72	47.26	43.24	41.28	40.26
5000	80.47	75.11	70.90	59.08	54.05	51.59	50.32
6000	96.57	90.13	85.08	70.90	64.86	61.91	60.38
7000	112.66	105.15	99.26	82.71	75.67	72.23	70.45
8000	128.75	120.17	113.44	94.53	86.48	82.55	80.51
9000	144.85	135.19	127.62	106.34	97.29	92.87	90.57
10000	160.94	150.21	141.80	118.16	108.10	103.19	100.64
11000	177.04	165.24	155.98	129.98	118.91	113.51	110.70
12000	193.13	180.26	170.16	141.79	129.72	123.83	120.77
13000	209.22	195.28	184.34	153.61	140.53	134.15	130.83
14000	225.32	210.30	198.52	165.43	151.34	144.47	140.89
15000	241.41	225.32	212.70	177.24	162.15	154.78	150.96
16000	257.51	240.34	226.88	189.06	172.96	165.10	161.02
17000	273.60	255.37	241.06	200.87	183.77	175.42	171.09
18000	289.70	270.39	255.24	212.69	194.58	185.74	181.15
19000	305.79	285.41	269.43	224.51	205.39	196.06	191.21
20000	321.88	300.43	283.61	236.32	216.19	206.38	201.28
21000	337.98	315.45	297.79	248.14	227.00	216.70	211.34
22000	354.07	330.47	311.97	259.95	237.81	227.02	221.41
23000	370.17	345.49	326.15	271.77	248.62	237.34	231.47
24000	386.26	360.52	340.33	283.59	259.43	247.66	241.53
25000	402.36	375.54	354.51	295.40	270.24	257.97	251.60
26000	418.45	390.56	368.69	307.22	281.05	268.29	261.66
27000	434.54	405.58	382.87	319.03	291.86	278.61	271.72
28000	450.64	420.60	397.05	330.85	302.67	288.93	281.79
29000	466.73	435.62	411.23	342.67	313.48	299.25	291.85
30000	482.83	450.64	425.41	354.48	324.29	309.57	301.92
35000	563.30	525.75	496.31	413.56	378.34	361.16	352.24
40000	643.77	600.86	567.21	472.64	432.39	412.76	402.55
45000	724.24	675.97	638.11	531.72	486.44	464.35	452.87
50000	804.71	751.07	709.01	590.80	540.49	515.95	503.19
55000	885.18	826.18	779.91	649.89	594.54	567.54	553.51
60000	965.65	901.29	850.82	708.97	648.58	619.14	603.83
65000	1046.12	976.40	921.72	768.05	702.63	670.73	654.15
70000	1126.60	1051.50	992.62	827.13	756.68	722.33	704.47
75000	1207.07	1126.61	1063.52	886.21	810.73	773.92	754.79
80000	1287.54	1201.72	1134.42	945.29	864.78	825.52	805.11
85000	1368.01	1276.83	1205.32	1004.37	918.83	877.11	855.43
90000	1448.48	1351.93	1276.22	1063.45	972.88	928.71	905.75
95000	1528.95	1427.04	1347.13	1122.53	1026.93	980.30	956.07
100000	1609.42	1502.15	1418.03	1181.61	1080.97	1031.90	1006.39
200000	3218.85	3004.29	2836.05	2363.22	2161.95	2063.80	2012.77
300000	4828.27	4506.44	4254.08	3544.83	3242.92	3095.70	3019.16
400000	6437.69	6008.59	5672.10	4726.44	4323.90	4127.60	4025.55
500000	8047.11	7510.74	7090.13	5908.05	5404.87	5159.50	5031.94
1000000	16094.23	15021.47	14180.27	11816.10	10809.74	10319.00	10063.87

12.125%

MONTHLY PAYMENT
NECESSARY TO AMORTIZE A LOAN

Amortization Amount	1 Year	2 Years	3 Years	4 Years	5 Years	6 Years	7 Years
25	2.22	1.17	0.83	0.66	0.55	0.49	0.44
50	4.44	2.35	1.66	1.31	1.11	0.97	0.88
100	8.88	4.70	3.31	2.63	2.22	1.95	1.76
200	17.75	9.40	6.63	5.25	4.43	3.89	3.51
300	26.63	14.10	9.94	7.88	6.65	5.84	5.27
400	35.51	18.80	13.25	10.50	8.86	7.78	7.02
500	44.38	23.50	16.57	13.13	11.08	9.73	8.78
600	53.26	28.20	19.88	15.75	13.30	11.68	10.54
700	62.14	32.90	23.19	18.38	15.51	13.62	12.29
800	71.02	37.60	26.51	21.00	17.73	15.57	14.05
900	79.89	42.29	29.82	23.63	19.94	17.52	15.81
1000	88.77	46.99	33.13	26.25	22.16	19.46	17.56
2000	177.54	93.99	66.27	52.50	44.32	38.92	35.12
3000	266.31	140.98	99.40	78.75	66.48	58.39	52.69
4000	355.08	187.98	132.53	105.00	88.63	77.85	70.25
5000	443.85	234.97	165.66	131.25	110.79	97.31	87.81
6000	532.61	281.96	198.80	157.50	132.95	116.77	105.37
7000	621.38	328.96	231.93	183.75	155.11	136.23	122.93
8000	710.15	375.95	265.06	210.00	177.27	155.69	140.49
9000	798.92	422.95	298.20	236.25	199.43	175.16	158.06
10000	887.69	469.94	331.33	262.50	221.58	194.62	175.62
11000	976.46	516.93	364.46	288.75	243.74	214.08	193.18
12000	1065.23	563.93	397.60	315.00	265.90	233.54	210.74
13000	1154.00	610.92	430.73	341.25	288.06	253.00	228.30
14000	1242.77	657.92	463.86	367.50	310.22	272.46	245.86
15000	1331.54	704.91	496.99	393.75	332.38	291.93	263.43
16000	1420.31	751.90	530.13	420.00	354.53	311.39	280.99
17000	1509.07	798.90	563.26	446.25	376.69	330.85	298.55
18000	1597.84	845.89	596.39	472.50	398.85	350.31	316.11
19000	1686.61	892.88	629.53	498.75	421.01	369.77	333.67
20000	1775.38	939.88	662.66	525.00	443.17	389.23	351.23
21000	1864.15	986.87	695.79	551.26	465.33	408.70	368.80
22000	1952.92	1033.87	728.93	577.51	487.49	428.16	386.36
23000	2041.69	1080.86	762.06	603.76	509.64	447.62	403.92
24000	2130.46	1127.85	795.19	630.01	531.80	467.08	421.48
25000	2219.23	1174.85	828.32	656.26	553.96	486.54	439.04
26000	2308.00	1221.84	861.46	682.51	576.12	506.00	456.61
27000	2396.77	1268.84	894.59	708.76	598.28	525.47	474.17
28000	2485.53	1315.83	927.72	735.01	620.44	544.93	491.73
29000	2574.30	1362.82	960.86	761.26	642.59	564.39	509.29
30000	2663.07	1409.82	993.99	787.51	664.75	583.85	526.85
35000	3106.92	1644.79	1159.65	918.76	775.55	681.16	614.66
40000	3550.76	1879.76	1325.32	1050.01	886.34	778.47	702.47
45000	3994.61	2114.73	1490.98	1181.26	997.13	875.78	790.28
50000	4438.45	2349.70	1656.65	1312.51	1107.92	973.08	878.09
55000	4882.30	2584.67	1822.31	1443.76	1218.71	1070.39	965.90
60000	5326.15	2819.64	1987.98	1575.01	1329.51	1167.70	1053.70
65000	5769.99	3054.61	2153.64	1706.27	1440.30	1265.01	1141.51
70000	6213.84	3289.58	2319.31	1837.52	1551.09	1362.32	1229.32
75000	6657.68	3524.55	2484.97	1968.77	1661.88	1459.63	1317.13
80000	7101.53	3759.51	2650.64	2100.02	1772.67	1556.94	1404.94
85000	7545.37	3994.48	2816.30	2231.27	1883.47	1654.24	1492.75
90000	7989.22	4229.45	2981.97	2362.52	1994.26	1751.55	1580.56
95000	8433.06	4464.42	3147.63	2493.77	2105.05	1848.86	1668.36
100000	8876.91	4699.39	3313.30	2625.02	2215.84	1946.17	1756.17
200000	17753.82	9398.79	6626.60	5250.05	4431.69	3892.34	3512.35
300000	26630.73	14098.18	9939.89	7875.07	6647.53	5838.51	5268.52
400000	35507.64	18797.57	13253.19	10500.10	8863.37	7784.68	7024.69
500000	44384.55	23496.97	16566.49	13125.12	11079.22	9730.85	8780.87
1000000	88769.09	46993.94	33132.98	26250.25	22158.43	19461.69	17561.74

Amortization Amount	8 Years	9 Years	10 Years	15 Years	20 Years	25 Years	30 Years
25	0.40	0.38	0.36	0.30	0.27	0.26	0.25
50	0.81	0.75	0.71	0.59	0.54	0.52	0.51
100	1.62	1.51	1.42	1.19	1.09	1.04	1.02
200	3.23	3.02	2.85	2.38	2.18	2.08	2.03
300	4.85	4.53	4.27	3.57	3.27	3.12	3.05
400	6.46	6.04	5.70	4.76	4.36	4.16	4.06
500	8.08	7.54	7.12	5.95	5.45	5.20	5.08
600	9.70	9.05	8.55	7.14	6.54	6.24	6.09
700	11.31	10.56	9.97	8.32	7.62	7.28	7.11
800	12.93	12.07	11.40	9.51	8.71	8.33	8.12
900	14.54	13.58	12.82	10.70	9.80	9.37	9.14
1000	16.16	15.09	14.25	11.89	10.89	10.41	10.16
2000	32.32	30.18	28.50	23.78	21.78	20.81	20.31
3000	48.48	45.26	42.75	35.68	32.68	31.22	30.47
4000	64.64	60.35	57.00	47.57	43.57	41.63	40.62
5000	80.80	75.44	71.24	59.46	54.46	52.03	50.78
6000	96.96	90.53	85.49	71.35	65.35	62.44	60.93
7000	113.12	105.62	99.74	83.25	76.25	72.85	71.09
8000	129.27	120.71	113.99	95.14	87.14	83.25	81.24
9000	145.43	135.79	128.24	107.03	98.03	93.66	91.40
10000	161.59	150.88	142.49	118.92	108.92	104.07	101.55
11000	177.75	165.97	156.74	130.81	119.82	114.47	111.71
12000	193.91	181.06	170.99	142.71	130.71	124.88	121.86
13000	210.07	196.15	185.23	154.60	141.60	135.29	132.02
14000	226.23	211.24	199.48	166.49	152.49	145.69	142.17
15000	242.39	226.32	213.73	178.38	163.38	156.10	152.33
16000	258.55	241.41	227.98	190.28	174.28	166.50	162.48
17000	274.71	256.50	242.23	202.17	185.17	176.91	172.64
18000	290.87	271.59	256.48	214.06	196.06	187.32	182.79
19000	307.03	286.68	270.73	225.95	206.95	197.72	192.95
20000	323.19	301.77	284.98	237.85	217.85	208.13	203.10
21000	339.35	316.85	299.22	249.74	228.74	218.54	213.26
22000	355.51	331.94	313.47	261.63	239.63	228.94	223.41
23000	371.67	347.03	327.72	273.52	250.52	239.35	233.57
24000	387.82	362.12	341.97	285.41	261.42	249.76	243.72
25000	403.98	377.21	356.22	297.31	272.31	260.16	253.88
26000	420.14	392.30	370.47	309.20	283.20	270.57	264.03
27000	436.30	407.38	384.72	321.09	294.09	280.98	274.19
28000	452.46	422.47	398.97	332.98	304.98	291.38	284.34
29000	468.62	437.56	413.21	344.88	315.88	301.79	294.50
30000	484.78	452.65	427.46	356.77	326.77	312.20	304.65
35000	565.58	528.09	498.71	416.23	381.23	364.23	355.43
40000	646.37	603.53	569.95	475.69	435.69	416.26	406.21
45000	727.17	678.97	641.19	535.15	490.15	468.29	456.98
50000	807.97	754.42	712.44	594.61	544.61	520.33	507.76
55000	888.76	829.86	783.68	654.07	599.08	572.36	558.53
60000	969.56	905.30	854.93	713.54	653.54	624.39	609.31
65000	1050.36	980.74	926.17	773.00	708.00	676.43	660.08
70000	1131.16	1056.18	997.41	832.46	762.46	728.46	710.86
75000	1211.95	1131.62	1068.66	891.92	816.92	780.49	761.64
80000	1292.75	1207.06	1139.90	951.38	871.38	832.52	812.41
85000	1373.55	1282.51	1211.14	1010.84	925.85	884.56	863.19
90000	1454.34	1357.95	1282.39	1070.30	980.31	936.59	913.96
95000	1535.14	1433.39	1353.63	1129.77	1034.77	988.62	964.74
100000	1615.94	1508.83	1424.88	1189.23	1089.23	1040.65	1015.51
200000	3231.87	3017.66	2849.75	2378.45	2178.46	2081.31	2031.03
300000	4847.81	4526.49	4274.63	3567.68	3267.69	3121.96	3046.54
400000	6463.74	6035.32	5699.50	4756.91	4356.92	4162.62	4062.06
500000	8079.68	7544.15	7124.38	5946.14	5446.15	5203.27	5077.57
1000000	16159.36	15088.30	14248.76	11892.27	10892.30	10406.55	10155.15

133

12.25%

Amortization Amount	1 Year	2 Years	3 Years	4 Years	5 Years	6 Years	7 Years
25	2.22	1.18	0.83	0.66	0.56	0.49	0.44
50	4.44	2.35	1.66	1.32	1.11	0.98	0.88
100	8.88	4.70	3.32	2.63	2.22	1.95	1.76
200	17.76	9.41	6.64	5.26	4.44	3.90	3.53
300	26.65	14.11	9.96	7.89	6.67	5.86	5.29
400	35.53	18.82	13.28	10.52	8.89	7.81	7.05
500	44.41	23.52	16.59	13.15	11.11	9.76	8.81
600	53.29	28.23	19.91	15.79	13.33	11.71	10.58
700	62.18	32.93	23.23	18.42	15.55	13.67	12.34
800	71.06	37.64	26.55	21.05	17.77	15.62	14.10
900	79.94	42.34	29.87	23.68	20.00	17.57	15.86
1000	88.82	47.05	33.19	26.31	22.22	19.52	17.63
2000	177.65	94.10	66.38	52.62	44.44	39.05	35.25
3000	266.47	141.15	99.57	78.93	66.66	58.57	52.88
4000	355.30	188.20	132.76	105.23	88.87	78.09	70.50
5000	444.12	235.25	165.95	131.54	111.09	97.62	88.13
6000	532.95	282.30	199.14	157.85	133.31	117.14	105.75
7000	621.77	329.35	232.33	184.16	155.53	136.66	123.38
8000	710.60	376.40	265.52	210.47	177.75	156.19	141.00
9000	799.42	423.45	298.71	236.78	199.97	175.71	158.63
10000	888.25	470.49	331.90	263.09	222.18	195.23	176.25
11000	977.07	517.54	365.09	289.39	244.40	214.76	193.88
12000	1065.90	564.59	398.28	315.70	266.62	234.28	211.50
13000	1154.72	611.64	431.47	342.01	288.84	253.81	229.13
14000	1243.55	658.69	464.66	368.32	311.06	273.33	246.75
15000	1332.37	705.74	497.85	394.63	333.28	292.85	264.38
16000	1421.20	752.79	531.04	420.94	355.50	312.38	282.00
17000	1510.02	799.84	564.23	447.25	377.71	331.90	299.63
18000	1598.85	846.89	597.42	473.55	399.93	351.42	317.25
19000	1687.67	893.94	630.61	499.86	422.15	370.95	334.88
20000	1776.49	940.99	663.80	526.17	444.37	390.47	352.50
21000	1865.32	988.04	696.98	552.48	466.59	409.99	370.13
22000	1954.14	1035.09	730.17	578.79	488.81	429.52	387.76
23000	2042.97	1082.14	763.36	605.10	511.02	449.04	405.38
24000	2131.79	1129.19	796.55	631.41	533.24	468.56	423.01
25000	2220.62	1176.24	829.74	657.71	555.46	488.09	440.63
26000	2309.44	1223.29	862.93	684.02	577.68	507.61	458.26
27000	2398.27	1270.34	896.12	710.33	599.90	527.13	475.88
28000	2487.09	1317.39	929.31	736.64	622.12	546.66	493.51
29000	2575.92	1364.43	962.50	762.95	644.34	566.18	511.13
30000	2664.74	1411.48	995.69	789.26	666.55	585.70	528.76
35000	3108.87	1646.73	1161.64	920.80	777.65	683.32	616.88
40000	3552.99	1881.98	1327.59	1052.34	888.74	780.94	705.01
45000	3997.11	2117.23	1493.54	1183.89	999.83	878.56	793.14
50000	4441.24	2352.47	1659.49	1315.43	1110.92	976.17	881.26
55000	4885.36	2587.72	1825.44	1446.97	1222.02	1073.79	969.39
60000	5329.48	2822.97	1991.39	1578.52	1333.11	1171.41	1057.51
65000	5773.61	3058.22	2157.33	1710.06	1444.20	1269.03	1145.64
70000	6217.73	3293.46	2323.28	1841.60	1555.29	1366.64	1233.77
75000	6661.86	3528.71	2489.23	1973.14	1666.39	1464.26	1321.89
80000	7105.98	3763.96	2655.18	2104.69	1777.48	1561.88	1410.02
85000	7550.10	3999.20	2821.13	2236.23	1888.57	1659.49	1498.15
90000	7994.23	4234.45	2987.08	2367.77	1999.66	1757.11	1586.27
95000	8438.35	4469.70	3153.03	2499.32	2110.76	1854.73	1674.40
100000	8882.47	4704.95	3318.98	2630.86	2221.85	1952.35	1762.52
200000	17764.95	9409.89	6637.95	5261.72	4443.70	3904.69	3525.05
300000	26647.42	14114.84	9956.93	7892.58	6665.54	5857.04	5287.57
400000	35529.90	18819.79	13275.90	10523.44	8887.39	7809.39	7050.10
500000	44412.37	23524.73	16594.88	13154.30	11109.24	9761.73	8812.62
1000000	88824.74	47049.47	33189.76	26308.60	22218.48	19523.47	17625.25

Amortization Amount	8 Years	9 Years	10 Years	15 Years	20 Years	25 Years	30 Years
25	0.41	0.38	0.36	0.30	0.27	0.26	0.26
50	0.81	0.76	0.72	0.60	0.55	0.52	0.51
100	1.62	1.52	1.43	1.20	1.10	1.05	1.02
200	3.24	3.03	2.86	2.39	2.20	2.10	2.05
300	4.87	4.55	4.30	3.59	3.29	3.15	3.07
400	6.49	6.06	5.73	4.79	4.39	4.20	4.10
500	8.11	7.58	7.16	5.98	5.49	5.25	5.12
600	9.73	9.09	8.59	7.18	6.59	6.30	6.15
700	11.36	10.61	10.02	8.38	7.88	7.35	7.17
800	12.98	12.12	11.45	9.57	8.78	8.40	8.20
900	14.60	13.64	12.89	10.77	9.88	9.44	9.22
1000	16.22	15.16	14.32	11.97	10.98	10.49	10.25
2000	32.45	30.31	28.63	23.94	21.95	20.99	20.49
3000	48.67	45.47	42.95	35.91	32.93	31.48	30.74
4000	64.90	60.62	57.27	47.87	43.90	41.98	40.99
5000	81.12	75.78	71.59	59.84	54.88	52.47	51.23
6000	97.35	90.93	85.90	71.81	65.85	62.97	61.48
7000	113.57	106.09	100.22	83.78	76.83	73.46	71.73
8000	129.80	121.24	114.54	95.75	87.80	83.95	81.97
9000	146.02	136.40	128.86	107.72	98.78	94.45	92.22
10000	162.25	151.55	143.17	119.69	109.75	104.94	102.47
11000	178.47	166.71	157.49	131.65	120.73	115.44	112.71
12000	194.70	181.86	171.81	143.62	131.70	125.93	122.96
13000	210.92	197.02	186.13	155.59	142.68	136.43	133.21
14000	227.14	212.17	200.44	167.56	153.65	146.92	143.45
15000	243.37	227.33	214.76	179.53	164.63	157.41	153.70
16000	259.59	242.48	229.08	191.50	175.60	167.91	163.95
17000	275.82	257.64	243.40	203.47	186.58	178.40	174.19
18000	292.04	272.79	257.71	215.44	197.55	188.90	184.44
19000	308.27	287.95	272.03	227.40	208.53	199.39	194.68
20000	324.49	303.11	286.35	239.37	219.50	209.89	204.93
21000	340.72	318.26	300.67	251.34	230.48	220.38	215.18
22000	356.94	333.42	314.98	263.31	241.45	230.87	225.42
23000	373.17	348.57	329.30	275.28	252.43	241.37	235.67
24000	389.39	363.73	343.62	287.25	263.40	251.86	245.92
25000	405.62	378.88	357.93	299.22	274.38	262.36	256.16
26000	421.84	394.04	372.25	311.18	285.35	272.85	266.41
27000	438.06	409.19	386.57	323.15	296.33	283.35	276.66
28000	454.29	424.35	400.89	335.12	307.30	293.84	286.90
29000	470.51	439.50	415.20	347.09	318.28	304.33	297.15
30000	486.74	454.66	429.52	359.06	329.25	314.83	307.40
35000	567.86	530.43	501.11	418.90	384.13	367.30	358.63
40000	648.98	606.21	572.70	478.74	439.00	419.77	409.86
45000	730.11	681.99	644.28	538.59	493.88	472.24	461.10
50000	811.23	757.76	715.87	598.43	548.75	524.71	512.33
55000	892.35	833.54	787.46	658.27	603.63	577.18	563.56
60000	973.48	909.32	859.04	718.12	658.50	629.66	614.79
65000	1054.60	985.09	930.63	777.96	713.38	682.13	666.03
70000	1135.72	1060.87	1002.22	837.80	768.25	734.60	717.26
75000	1216.85	1136.64	1073.80	897.65	823.13	787.07	768.49
80000	1297.97	1212.42	1145.39	957.49	878.00	839.54	819.73
85000	1379.09	1288.20	1216.98	1017.33	932.88	892.01	870.96
90000	1460.21	1363.97	1288.57	1077.18	987.75	944.48	922.19
95000	1541.34	1439.75	1360.15	1137.02	1042.63	996.96	973.42
100000	1622.46	1515.53	1431.74	1196.86	1097.50	1049.43	1024.66
200000	3244.92	3031.05	2863.48	2393.72	2195.01	2098.85	2049.31
300000	4867.38	4546.58	4295.22	3590.59	3292.51	3148.28	3073.97
400000	6489.84	6062.10	5726.96	4787.45	4390.02	4197.71	4098.63
500000	8112.30	7577.63	7158.69	5984.31	5487.52	5247.14	5123.28
1000000	16224.61	15155.26	14317.39	11968.62	10975.04	10494.27	10246.57

135

12.375%

Amortization Amount	1 Year	2 Years	3 Years	4 Years	5 Years	6 Years	7 Years
25	2.22	1.18	0.83	0.66	0.56	0.49	0.44
50	4.44	2.36	1.66	1.32	1.11	0.98	0.88
100	8.89	4.71	3.32	2.64	2.23	1.96	1.77
200	17.78	9.42	6.65	5.27	4.46	3.92	3.54
300	26.66	14.13	9.97	7.91	6.68	5.88	5.31
400	35.55	18.84	13.30	10.55	8.91	7.83	7.08
500	44.44	23.55	16.62	13.18	11.14	9.79	8.84
600	53.33	28.26	19.95	15.82	13.37	11.75	10.61
700	62.22	32.97	23.27	18.46	15.60	13.71	12.38
800	71.10	37.68	26.60	21.09	17.82	15.67	14.15
900	79.99	42.39	29.92	23.73	20.05	17.63	15.92
1000	88.88	47.11	33.25	26.37	22.28	19.59	17.69
2000	177.76	94.21	66.49	52.73	44.56	39.17	35.38
3000	266.64	141.32	99.74	79.10	66.84	58.76	53.07
4000	355.52	188.42	132.99	105.47	89.11	78.34	70.76
5000	444.40	235.53	166.23	131.83	111.39	97.93	88.44
6000	533.28	282.63	199.48	158.20	133.67	117.51	106.13
7000	622.16	329.74	232.73	184.57	155.95	137.10	123.82
8000	711.04	376.84	265.97	210.94	178.23	156.68	141.51
9000	799.92	423.95	299.22	237.30	200.51	176.27	159.20
10000	888.80	471.05	332.47	263.67	222.79	195.85	176.89
11000	977.68	518.16	365.71	290.04	245.08	215.44	194.58
12000	1066.56	565.26	398.96	316.40	267.34	235.02	212.27
13000	1155.44	612.37	432.21	342.77	289.62	254.61	229.96
14000	1244.33	659.47	465.45	369.14	311.90	274.19	247.64
15000	1333.21	706.58	498.70	395.50	334.18	293.78	265.33
16000	1422.09	753.68	531.95	421.87	356.46	313.37	283.02
17000	1510.97	800.79	565.19	448.24	378.74	332.95	300.71
18000	1599.85	847.89	598.44	474.61	401.01	352.54	318.40
19000	1688.73	895.00	631.68	500.97	423.29	372.12	336.09
20000	1777.61	942.10	664.93	527.34	445.57	391.71	353.78
21000	1866.49	989.21	698.18	553.71	467.85	411.29	371.47
22000	1955.37	1036.31	731.42	580.07	490.13	430.88	389.15
23000	2044.25	1083.42	764.67	606.44	512.41	450.46	406.84
24000	2133.13	1130.52	797.92	632.81	534.69	470.05	424.53
25000	2222.01	1177.63	831.16	659.17	556.96	489.63	442.22
26000	2310.89	1224.73	864.41	685.54	579.24	509.22	459.91
27000	2399.77	1271.84	897.66	711.91	601.52	528.80	477.60
28000	2488.65	1318.94	930.90	738.28	623.80	548.39	495.29
29000	2577.53	1366.05	964.15	764.64	646.08	567.97	512.98
30000	2666.41	1413.15	997.40	791.01	668.36	587.56	530.67
35000	3110.81	1648.68	1163.63	922.84	779.75	685.49	619.11
40000	3555.22	1884.20	1329.86	1054.68	891.14	783.41	707.55
45000	3999.62	2119.73	1496.10	1186.51	1002.54	881.34	796.00
50000	4444.02	2355.25	1662.33	1318.35	1113.93	979.27	884.44
55000	4888.42	2590.78	1828.56	1450.18	1225.32	1077.19	972.89
60000	5332.82	2826.30	1994.79	1582.02	1336.71	1175.12	1061.33
65000	5777.22	3061.83	2161.03	1713.85	1448.11	1273.05	1149.78
70000	6221.63	3297.35	2327.26	1845.69	1559.50	1370.97	1238.22
75000	6666.03	3532.88	2493.49	1977.52	1670.89	1468.90	1326.66
80000	7110.43	3768.40	2659.73	2109.36	1782.29	1566.83	1415.11
85000	7554.83	4003.93	2825.96	2241.19	1893.68	1664.75	1503.55
90000	7999.23	4239.45	2992.19	2373.03	2005.07	1762.68	1592.00
95000	8443.64	4474.98	3158.42	2504.86	2116.47	1860.61	1680.44
100000	8888.04	4710.50	3324.66	2636.70	2227.86	1958.53	1768.89
200000	17776.08	9421.00	6649.31	5273.40	4455.72	3917.06	3537.77
300000	26664.11	14131.50	9973.97	7910.10	6683.57	5875.60	5306.66
400000	35552.15	18842.00	13298.63	10546.80	8911.43	7834.13	7075.54
500000	44440.19	23552.50	16623.28	13183.50	11139.29	9792.66	8844.43
1000000	88880.38	47105.01	33246.57	26367.00	22278.58	19585.32	17688.86

Amortization Amount	8 Years	9 Years	10 Years	15 Years	20 Years	25 Years	30 Years
25	0.41	0.38	0.36	0.30	0.28	0.26	0.26
50	0.81	0.76	0.72	0.60	0.55	0.53	0.52
100	1.63	1.52	1.44	1.20	1.11	1.08	1.03
200	3.26	3.04	2.88	2.41	2.21	2.12	2.07
300	4.89	4.57	4.32	3.61	3.32	3.17	3.10
400	6.52	6.09	5.75	4.82	4.42	4.23	4.14
500	8.14	7.61	7.19	6.02	5.53	5.29	5.17
600	9.77	9.13	8.63	7.23	6.63	6.35	6.20
700	11.40	10.66	10.07	8.43	7.74	7.41	7.24
800	13.03	12.18	11.51	9.64	8.85	8.47	8.27
900	14.66	13.70	12.95	10.84	9.95	9.52	9.30
1000	16.29	15.22	14.39	12.05	11.06	10.58	10.34
2000	32.58	30.44	28.77	24.09	22.12	21.16	20.68
3000	48.87	45.67	43.16	36.14	33.17	31.75	31.01
4000	65.16	60.89	57.54	48.18	44.23	42.33	41.35
5000	81.45	76.11	71.93	60.23	55.29	52.91	51.69
6000	97.74	91.33	86.32	72.27	66.35	63.49	62.03
7000	114.03	106.56	100.70	84.32	77.41	74.08	72.37
8000	130.32	121.78	115.09	96.36	88.46	84.66	82.71
9000	146.61	137.00	129.48	108.41	99.52	95.24	93.04
10000	162.90	152.22	143.86	120.45	110.58	105.82	103.38
11000	179.19	167.45	158.25	132.50	121.64	116.40	113.72
12000	195.48	182.67	172.63	144.54	132.70	126.99	124.06
13000	211.77	197.89	187.02	156.59	143.75	137.57	134.40
14000	228.06	213.11	201.41	168.63	154.81	148.15	144.73
15000	244.35	228.33	215.79	180.68	165.87	158.73	155.07
16000	260.64	243.56	230.18	192.72	176.93	169.31	165.41
17000	276.93	258.78	244.56	204.77	187.99	179.90	175.75
18000	293.22	274.00	258.95	216.81	199.04	190.48	186.09
19000	309.51	289.22	273.34	228.86	210.10	201.06	196.42
20000	325.80	304.45	287.72	240.90	221.16	211.64	206.76
21000	342.09	319.67	302.11	252.95	232.22	222.23	217.10
22000	358.38	334.89	316.50	264.99	243.28	232.81	227.44
23000	374.67	350.11	330.88	277.04	254.33	243.39	237.78
24000	390.96	365.34	345.27	289.08	265.39	253.97	248.12
25000	407.25	380.56	359.65	301.13	276.45	264.55	258.45
26000	423.54	395.78	374.04	313.17	287.51	275.14	268.79
27000	439.83	411.00	388.43	325.22	298.57	285.72	279.13
28000	456.12	426.23	402.81	337.26	309.62	296.30	289.47
29000	472.41	441.45	417.20	349.31	320.68	306.88	299.81
30000	488.70	456.67	431.58	361.35	331.74	317.46	310.14
35000	570.15	532.78	503.52	421.58	387.03	370.38	361.83
40000	651.60	608.89	575.45	481.81	442.32	423.29	413.53
45000	733.05	685.00	647.38	542.03	497.61	476.20	465.22
50000	814.50	761.12	719.31	602.26	552.90	529.11	516.91
55000	895.95	837.23	791.24	662.48	608.19	582.02	568.60
60000	977.40	913.34	863.17	722.71	663.48	634.93	620.29
65000	1058.85	989.45	935.10	782.93	718.77	687.84	671.98
70000	1140.30	1065.56	1007.03	843.16	774.06	740.75	723.67
75000	1221.75	1141.67	1078.96	903.39	829.35	793.66	775.36
80000	1303.20	1217.79	1150.89	963.61	884.64	846.57	827.05
85000	1384.65	1293.90	1222.82	1023.84	939.93	899.48	878.74
90000	1466.10	1370.01	1294.75	1084.06	995.22	952.39	930.43
95000	1547.55	1446.12	1366.68	1144.29	1050.51	1005.31	982.12
100000	1629.00	1522.23	1438.62	1204.52	1105.80	1058.22	1033.81
200000	3257.99	3044.47	2877.23	2409.03	2211.59	2116.43	2067.63
300000	4886.99	4566.70	4315.85	3613.55	3317.39	3174.65	3101.44
400000	6515.98	6088.93	5754.46	4818.06	4423.19	4232.87	4135.25
500000	8144.98	7611.16	7193.08	6022.58	5528.98	5291.08	5169.06
1000000	16289.96	15222.33	14386.15	12045.15	11057.97	10582.17	10338.13

12.5%

Amortization Amount	1 Year	2 Years	3 Years	4 Years	5 Years	6 Years	7 Years
25	2.22	1.18	0.83	0.66	0.56	0.49	0.44
50	4.45	2.36	1.67	1.32	1.12	0.98	0.89
100	8.89	4.72	3.33	2.64	2.23	1.96	1.78
200	17.79	9.43	6.66	5.29	4.47	3.93	3.55
300	26.68	14.15	9.99	7.93	6.70	5.89	5.33
400	35.57	18.86	13.32	10.57	8.94	7.86	7.10
500	44.47	23.58	16.65	13.21	11.17	9.82	8.88
600	53.36	28.30	19.98	15.86	13.40	11.79	10.65
700	62.26	33.01	23.31	18.50	15.64	13.75	12.43
800	71.15	37.73	26.64	21.14	17.87	15.72	14.20
900	80.04	42.44	29.97	23.78	20.10	17.68	15.98
1000	88.94	47.16	33.30	26.43	22.34	19.65	17.75
2000	177.87	94.32	66.61	52.85	44.68	39.29	35.51
3000	266.81	141.48	99.91	79.28	67.02	58.94	53.26
4000	355.74	188.64	133.21	105.70	89.35	78.59	71.01
5000	444.68	235.80	166.52	132.13	111.69	98.24	88.76
6000	533.62	282.96	199.82	158.55	134.03	117.88	106.52
7000	622.55	330.12	233.12	184.98	156.37	137.53	124.27
8000	711.49	377.28	266.43	211.40	178.71	157.18	142.02
9000	800.42	424.45	299.73	237.83	201.05	176.83	159.77
10000	889.36	471.61	333.03	264.25	223.39	196.47	177.53
11000	978.30	518.77	366.34	290.68	245.73	216.12	195.28
12000	1067.23	565.93	399.64	317.11	268.06	235.77	213.03
13000	1156.17	613.09	432.94	343.53	290.40	255.41	230.78
14000	1245.10	660.25	466.25	369.96	312.74	275.06	248.54
15000	1334.04	707.41	499.55	396.38	335.08	294.71	266.29
16000	1422.98	754.57	532.85	422.81	357.42	314.36	284.04
17000	1511.91	801.73	566.16	449.23	379.76	334.00	301.79
18000	1600.85	848.89	599.46	475.66	402.10	353.65	319.55
19000	1689.78	896.05	632.76	502.08	424.44	373.30	337.30
20000	1778.72	943.21	666.07	528.51	446.77	392.95	355.05
21000	1867.66	990.37	699.37	554.93	469.11	412.59	372.80
22000	1956.59	1037.53	732.67	581.36	491.45	432.24	390.56
23000	2045.53	1084.69	765.98	607.79	513.79	451.89	408.31
24000	2134.46	1131.85	799.28	634.21	536.13	471.53	426.06
25000	2223.40	1179.01	832.59	660.64	558.47	491.18	443.81
26000	2312.34	1226.17	865.89	687.06	580.81	510.83	461.57
27000	2401.27	1273.34	899.19	713.49	603.15	530.48	479.32
28000	2490.21	1320.50	932.50	739.91	625.48	550.12	497.07
29000	2579.14	1367.66	965.80	766.34	647.82	569.77	514.82
30000	2668.08	1414.82	999.10	792.76	670.16	589.42	532.58
35000	3112.76	1650.62	1165.62	924.89	781.86	687.65	621.34
40000	3557.44	1886.42	1332.14	1057.02	893.55	785.89	710.10
45000	4002.12	2122.23	1498.65	1189.14	1005.24	884.13	798.87
50000	4446.80	2358.03	1665.17	1321.27	1116.94	982.36	887.63
55000	4891.48	2593.83	1831.69	1453.40	1228.63	1080.60	976.39
60000	5336.16	2829.63	1998.20	1585.53	1340.32	1178.84	1065.15
65000	5780.84	3065.44	2164.72	1717.65	1452.02	1277.07	1153.92
70000	6225.52	3301.24	2331.24	1849.78	1563.71	1375.31	1242.68
75000	6670.20	3537.04	2497.76	1981.91	1675.41	1473.54	1331.44
80000	7114.88	3772.84	2664.27	2114.04	1787.10	1571.78	1420.21
85000	7559.56	4008.65	2830.79	2246.16	1898.79	1670.02	1508.97
90000	8004.24	4244.45	2997.31	2378.29	2010.49	1768.25	1597.73
95000	8448.92	4480.25	3163.82	2510.42	2122.18	1866.49	1686.49
100000	8893.60	4716.06	3330.34	2642.54	2233.87	1964.73	1775.26
200000	17787.20	9432.11	6660.68	5285.09	4467.75	3929.45	3550.51
300000	26680.80	14148.17	9991.02	7927.63	6701.62	5894.18	5325.77
400000	35574.40	18864.22	13321.36	10570.18	8935.50	7858.90	7101.03
500000	44468.00	23580.28	16651.70	13212.72	11169.37	9823.63	8876.28
1000000	88936.01	47160.56	33303.40	26425.44	22338.75	19647.25	17752.56

Amortization Amount	8 Years	9 Years	10 Years	15 Years	20 Years	25 Years	30 Years
25	0.41	0.38	0.38	0.30	0.28	0.27	0.26
50	0.82	0.76	0.72	0.61	0.56	0.53	0.52
100	1.64	1.53	1.45	1.21	1.11	1.07	1.04
200	3.27	3.06	2.89	2.42	2.23	2.13	2.09
300	4.91	4.59	4.34	3.64	3.34	3.20	3.13
400	6.54	6.12	5.78	4.85	4.46	4.27	4.17
500	8.18	7.64	7.23	6.06	5.57	5.34	5.21
600	9.81	9.17	8.67	7.27	6.68	6.40	6.26
700	11.45	10.70	10.12	8.49	7.80	7.47	7.30
800	13.08	12.23	11.56	9.70	8.91	8.54	8.34
900	14.72	13.76	13.01	10.91	10.03	9.60	9.39
1000	16.36	15.29	14.46	12.12	11.14	10.67	10.43
2000	32.71	30.58	28.91	24.24	22.28	21.34	20.86
3000	49.07	45.87	43.37	36.37	33.42	32.01	31.29
4000	65.42	61.16	57.82	48.49	44.56	42.68	41.72
5000	81.78	76.45	72.28	60.61	55.71	53.35	52.15
6000	98.13	91.74	86.73	72.73	66.85	64.02	62.58
7000	114.49	107.03	101.19	84.85	77.99	74.69	73.01
8000	130.84	122.32	115.64	96.97	89.13	85.36	83.44
9000	147.20	137.61	130.10	109.10	100.27	96.03	93.87
10000	163.55	152.90	144.55	121.22	111.41	106.70	104.30
11000	179.91	168.18	159.01	133.34	122.55	117.37	114.73
12000	196.27	183.47	173.46	145.46	133.69	128.04	125.16
13000	212.62	198.76	187.92	157.58	144.83	138.71	135.59
14000	228.98	214.05	202.37	169.71	155.98	149.38	146.02
15000	245.33	229.34	216.83	181.83	167.12	160.05	156.45
16000	261.69	244.63	231.28	193.95	178.26	170.72	166.88
17000	278.04	259.92	245.74	206.07	189.40	181.39	177.31
18000	294.40	275.21	260.19	218.19	200.54	192.06	187.74
19000	310.75	290.50	274.65	230.32	211.68	202.73	198.17
20000	327.11	305.79	289.10	242.44	222.82	213.40	208.60
21000	343.46	321.08	303.56	254.56	233.96	224.07	219.03
22000	359.82	336.37	318.01	266.68	245.10	234.74	229.46
23000	376.17	351.66	332.47	278.80	256.24	245.42	239.89
24000	392.53	366.95	346.92	290.92	267.39	256.09	250.32
25000	408.89	382.24	361.38	303.05	278.53	266.76	260.75
26000	425.24	397.53	375.83	315.17	289.67	277.43	271.18
27000	441.60	412.82	390.29	327.29	300.81	288.10	281.61
28000	457.95	428.11	404.74	339.41	311.95	298.77	292.03
29000	474.31	443.40	419.20	351.53	323.09	309.44	302.46
30000	490.66	458.69	433.65	363.66	334.23	320.11	312.89
35000	572.44	535.13	505.93	424.26	389.94	373.46	365.04
40000	654.22	611.58	578.20	484.87	445.64	426.81	417.19
45000	735.99	688.03	650.48	545.48	501.35	480.16	469.34
50000	817.77	764.48	722.75	606.09	557.05	533.51	521.49
55000	899.55	840.92	795.03	666.70	612.76	586.86	573.64
60000	981.33	917.37	867.30	727.31	668.46	640.21	625.79
65000	1063.10	993.82	939.58	787.92	724.17	693.56	677.94
70000	1144.88	1070.27	1011.85	848.53	779.88	746.92	730.09
75000	1226.66	1146.71	1084.13	909.14	835.58	800.27	782.24
80000	1308.43	1223.16	1156.40	969.75	891.29	853.62	834.39
85000	1390.21	1299.61	1228.68	1030.36	946.99	906.97	886.53
90000	1471.99	1376.06	1300.95	1090.97	1002.70	960.32	938.68
95000	1553.77	1452.51	1373.23	1151.58	1058.40	1013.67	990.83
100000	1635.54	1528.95	1445.50	1212.19	1114.11	1067.02	1042.98
200000	3271.08	3057.91	2891.01	2424.37	2228.22	2134.05	2085.96
300000	4906.63	4586.86	4336.51	3636.56	3342.32	3201.07	3128.95
400000	6542.17	6115.81	5782.02	4848.74	4456.43	4268.09	4171.93
500000	8177.71	7644.76	7227.52	6060.93	5570.54	5335.11	5214.91
1000000	16355.42	15289.53	14455.05	12121.85	11141.08	10670.23	10429.82

12.625%

Amortization Amount	1 Year	2 Years	3 Years	4 Years	5 Years	6 Years	7 Years
25	2.22	1.18	0.83	0.66	0.56	0.49	0.45
50	4.45	2.36	1.67	1.32	1.12	0.99	0.89
100	8.90	4.72	3.34	2.85	2.24	1.97	1.78
200	17.80	9.44	6.67	5.30	4.48	3.94	3.56
300	26.70	14.16	10.01	7.95	6.72	5.91	5.34
400	35.60	18.89	13.34	10.59	8.96	7.88	7.13
500	44.50	23.61	16.68	13.24	11.20	9.85	8.91
600	53.39	28.33	20.02	15.89	13.44	11.83	10.69
700	62.29	33.05	23.35	18.54	15.68	13.80	12.47
800	71.19	37.77	26.69	21.19	17.92	15.77	14.25
900	80.09	42.49	30.02	23.84	20.16	17.74	16.03
1000	88.99	47.22	33.36	26.48	22.40	19.71	17.82
2000	177.98	94.43	66.72	52.97	44.80	39.42	35.63
3000	266.97	141.65	100.08	79.45	67.20	59.13	53.45
4000	355.97	188.86	133.44	105.94	89.60	78.84	71.27
5000	444.96	236.08	166.80	132.42	111.99	98.55	89.08
6000	533.95	283.30	200.16	158.90	134.39	118.26	106.90
7000	622.94	330.51	233.52	185.39	156.79	137.96	124.71
8000	711.93	377.73	266.88	211.87	179.19	157.67	142.53
9000	800.92	424.95	300.24	238.36	201.59	177.38	160.35
10000	889.92	472.16	333.60	264.84	223.99	197.09	178.16
11000	978.91	519.38	366.96	291.32	246.39	216.80	195.98
12000	1067.90	566.59	400.32	317.81	268.79	236.51	213.80
13000	1156.89	613.81	433.68	344.29	291.19	256.22	231.61
14000	1245.88	661.03	467.04	370.78	313.59	275.93	249.43
15000	1334.87	708.24	500.40	397.26	335.98	295.64	267.25
16000	1423.87	755.46	533.76	423.74	358.38	315.35	285.06
17000	1512.86	802.67	567.12	450.23	380.78	335.06	302.88
18000	1601.85	849.89	600.48	476.71	403.18	354.77	320.69
19000	1690.84	897.11	633.85	503.19	425.58	374.48	338.51
20000	1779.83	944.32	667.21	529.68	447.98	394.19	356.33
21000	1868.82	991.54	700.57	556.16	470.38	413.89	374.14
22000	1957.82	1038.75	733.93	582.65	492.78	433.60	391.96
23000	2046.81	1085.97	767.29	609.13	515.18	453.31	409.78
24000	2135.80	1133.19	800.65	635.61	537.58	473.02	427.59
25000	2224.79	1180.40	834.01	662.10	559.97	492.73	445.41
26000	2313.78	1227.62	867.37	688.58	582.37	512.44	463.23
27000	2402.77	1274.84	900.73	715.07	604.77	532.15	481.04
28000	2491.77	1322.05	934.09	741.55	627.17	551.86	498.86
29000	2580.76	1369.27	967.45	768.03	649.57	571.57	516.67
30000	2669.75	1416.48	1000.81	794.52	671.97	591.28	534.49
35000	3114.71	1652.56	1167.61	926.94	783.96	689.82	623.57
40000	3559.67	1888.64	1334.41	1059.36	895.96	788.37	712.65
45000	4004.62	2124.73	1501.21	1191.78	1007.95	886.92	801.74
50000	4449.58	2360.81	1668.01	1324.20	1119.95	985.46	890.82
55000	4894.54	2596.89	1834.81	1456.62	1231.94	1084.01	979.90
60000	5339.50	2832.97	2001.62	1589.04	1343.94	1182.56	1068.98
65000	5784.46	3069.05	2168.42	1721.46	1455.93	1281.10	1158.06
70000	6229.41	3305.13	2335.22	1853.88	1567.93	1379.65	1247.15
75000	6674.37	3541.21	2502.02	1986.30	1679.92	1478.20	1336.23
80000	7119.33	3777.29	2668.82	2118.71	1791.92	1576.74	1425.31
85000	7564.29	4013.37	2835.62	2251.13	1903.91	1675.29	1514.39
90000	8009.25	4249.45	3002.42	2383.55	2015.91	1773.83	1603.47
95000	8454.20	4485.53	3169.23	2515.97	2127.90	1872.38	1692.55
100000	8899.16	4721.61	3336.03	2648.39	2239.90	1970.93	1781.64
200000	17798.33	9443.22	6672.05	5296.79	4479.80	3941.85	3563.27
300000	26697.49	14164.84	10008.08	7945.18	6719.69	5912.78	5344.91
400000	35596.65	18886.45	13344.11	10593.57	8959.59	7883.71	7126.55
500000	44495.81	23608.06	16680.13	13241.97	11199.49	9854.63	8908.18
1000000	88991.63	47216.12	33360.27	26483.93	22398.98	19709.27	17816.36

Amortization Amount	8 Years	9 Years	10 Years	15 Years	20 Years	25 Years	30 Years
25	0.41	0.38	0.36	0.30	0.28	0.27	0.26
50	0.82	0.77	0.73	0.61	0.56	0.54	0.53
100	1.64	1.54	1.45	1.22	1.12	1.08	1.05
200	3.28	3.07	2.90	2.44	2.24	2.15	2.10
300	4.93	4.61	4.36	3.66	3.37	3.23	3.16
400	6.57	6.14	5.81	4.88	4.49	4.30	4.21
500	8.21	7.68	7.26	6.10	5.61	5.38	5.26
600	9.85	9.21	8.71	7.32	6.73	6.46	6.31
700	11.49	10.75	10.17	8.54	7.86	7.53	7.37
800	13.14	12.29	11.62	9.76	8.98	8.61	8.42
900	14.78	13.82	13.07	10.98	10.10	9.68	9.47
1000	16.42	15.36	14.52	12.20	11.22	10.76	10.52
2000	32.84	30.71	29.05	24.40	22.45	21.52	21.04
3000	49.26	46.07	43.57	36.60	33.67	32.28	31.56
4000	65.68	61.43	58.10	48.79	44.90	43.03	42.09
5000	82.10	76.78	72.62	60.99	56.12	53.79	52.61
6000	98.53	92.14	87.14	73.19	67.35	64.55	63.13
7000	114.95	107.50	101.67	85.39	78.57	75.31	73.65
8000	131.37	122.85	116.19	97.59	89.79	86.07	84.17
9000	147.79	138.21	130.72	109.79	101.02	96.83	94.69
10000	164.21	153.57	145.24	121.99	112.24	107.58	105.22
11000	180.63	168.93	159.76	134.19	123.47	118.34	115.74
12000	197.05	184.28	174.29	146.38	134.69	129.10	126.26
13000	213.47	199.64	188.81	158.58	145.92	139.86	136.78
14000	229.89	215.00	203.34	170.78	157.14	150.62	147.30
15000	246.31	230.35	217.86	182.98	168.37	161.38	157.82
16000	262.74	245.71	232.39	195.18	179.59	172.14	168.35
17000	279.16	261.07	246.91	207.38	190.81	182.89	178.87
18000	295.58	276.42	261.43	219.58	202.04	193.65	189.39
19000	312.00	291.78	275.96	231.78	213.26	204.41	199.91
20000	328.42	307.14	290.48	243.97	224.49	215.17	210.43
21000	344.84	322.49	305.01	256.17	235.71	225.93	220.95
22000	361.26	337.85	319.53	268.37	246.94	236.69	231.48
23000	377.68	353.21	334.05	280.57	258.16	247.44	242.00
24000	394.10	368.56	348.58	292.77	269.38	258.20	252.52
25000	410.52	383.92	363.10	304.97	280.61	268.96	263.04
26000	426.95	399.28	377.63	317.17	291.83	279.72	273.56
27000	443.37	414.63	392.15	329.37	303.06	290.48	284.08
28000	459.79	429.99	406.67	341.56	314.28	301.24	294.61
29000	476.21	445.35	421.20	353.76	325.51	312.00	305.13
30000	492.63	460.71	435.72	365.96	336.73	322.75	315.65
35000	574.73	537.49	508.34	426.96	392.85	376.55	368.26
40000	656.84	614.27	580.96	487.95	448.97	430.34	420.87
45000	738.94	691.06	653.58	548.94	505.10	484.13	473.47
50000	821.05	767.84	726.20	609.94	561.22	537.92	526.08
55000	903.15	844.63	798.82	670.93	617.34	591.71	578.69
60000	985.26	921.41	871.44	731.92	673.46	645.51	631.30
65000	1067.36	998.19	944.07	792.92	729.58	699.30	683.91
70000	1149.47	1074.98	1016.69	853.91	785.71	753.09	736.52
75000	1231.57	1151.76	1089.31	914.90	841.83	806.88	789.12
80000	1313.68	1228.55	1161.93	975.90	897.95	860.68	841.73
85000	1395.78	1305.33	1234.55	1036.89	954.07	914.47	894.34
90000	1477.89	1382.12	1307.17	1097.89	1010.19	968.26	946.95
95000	1559.99	1458.90	1379.79	1158.88	1066.32	1022.05	999.56
100000	1642.10	1535.68	1452.41	1219.87	1122.44	1075.85	1052.16
200000	3284.20	3071.37	2904.82	2439.75	2244.87	2151.69	2104.33
300000	4926.30	4607.05	4357.22	3659.62	3367.31	3227.54	3156.49
400000	6568.40	6142.74	5809.63	4879.49	4489.75	4303.38	4208.66
500000	8210.50	7678.42	7262.04	6099.36	5612.19	5379.23	5260.82
1000000	16421.00	15356.85	14524.08	12198.73	11224.37	10758.45	10521.65

12.75%

MONTHLY PAYMENT
NECESSARY TO AMORTIZE A LOAN

Amortization Amount	1 Year	2 Years	3 Years	4 Years	5 Years	6 Years	7 Years
25	2.23	1.18	0.84	0.66	0.56	0.49	0.45
50	4.45	2.36	1.67	1.33	1.12	0.99	0.89
100	8.90	4.73	3.34	2.65	2.25	1.98	1.79
200	17.81	9.45	6.68	5.31	4.49	3.95	3.58
300	26.71	14.18	10.03	7.96	6.74	5.93	5.36
400	35.62	18.91	13.37	10.62	8.98	7.91	7.15
500	44.52	23.64	16.71	13.27	11.23	9.89	8.94
600	53.43	28.36	20.05	15.93	13.48	11.86	10.73
700	62.33	33.09	23.39	18.58	15.72	13.84	12.52
800	71.24	37.82	26.73	21.23	17.97	15.82	14.30
900	80.14	42.54	30.08	23.89	20.21	17.79	16.09
1000	89.05	47.27	33.42	26.54	22.46	19.77	17.88
2000	178.09	94.54	66.83	53.08	44.92	39.54	35.76
3000	267.14	141.82	100.25	79.63	67.38	59.31	53.64
4000	356.19	189.09	133.67	106.17	89.84	79.09	71.52
5000	445.24	236.36	167.09	132.71	112.30	98.86	89.40
6000	534.28	283.63	200.50	159.25	134.76	118.63	107.28
7000	623.33	330.90	233.92	185.80	157.21	138.40	125.16
8000	712.38	378.17	267.34	212.34	179.67	158.17	143.04
9000	801.43	425.45	300.75	238.88	202.13	177.94	160.92
10000	890.47	472.72	334.17	265.42	224.59	197.71	178.80
11000	979.52	519.99	367.59	291.97	247.05	217.48	196.68
12000	1068.57	567.26	401.01	318.51	269.51	237.26	214.56
13000	1157.61	614.53	434.42	345.05	291.97	257.03	232.44
14000	1246.66	661.80	467.84	371.59	314.43	276.80	250.32
15000	1335.71	709.08	501.26	398.14	336.89	296.57	268.20
16000	1424.76	756.35	534.67	424.68	359.35	316.34	286.08
17000	1513.80	803.62	568.09	451.22	381.81	336.11	303.96
18000	1602.85	850.89	601.51	477.76	404.27	355.88	321.84
19000	1691.90	898.16	634.93	504.31	426.73	375.66	339.72
20000	1780.94	945.43	668.34	530.85	449.19	395.43	357.61
21000	1869.99	992.71	701.76	557.39	471.64	415.20	375.49
22000	1959.04	1039.98	735.18	583.93	494.10	434.97	393.37
23000	2048.09	1087.25	768.59	610.48	516.56	454.74	411.25
24000	2137.13	1134.52	802.01	637.02	539.02	474.51	429.13
25000	2226.18	1181.79	835.43	663.56	561.48	494.28	447.01
26000	2315.23	1229.06	868.85	690.10	583.94	514.06	464.89
27000	2404.28	1276.34	902.26	716.65	606.40	533.83	482.77
28000	2493.32	1323.61	935.68	743.19	628.86	553.60	500.65
29000	2582.37	1370.88	969.10	769.73	651.32	573.37	518.53
30000	2671.42	1418.15	1002.51	796.27	673.78	593.14	536.41
35000	3116.65	1654.51	1169.60	928.99	786.07	692.00	625.81
40000	3561.89	1890.87	1336.69	1061.70	898.37	790.85	715.21
45000	4007.13	2127.23	1503.77	1194.41	1010.67	889.71	804.61
50000	4452.36	2363.58	1670.86	1327.12	1122.96	988.57	894.01
55000	4897.60	2599.94	1837.94	1459.84	1235.26	1087.42	983.41
60000	5342.83	2836.30	2005.03	1592.55	1347.56	1186.28	1072.82
65000	5788.07	3072.66	2172.12	1725.26	1459.85	1285.14	1162.22
70000	6233.31	3309.02	2339.20	1857.97	1572.15	1384.00	1251.62
75000	6678.54	3545.38	2506.29	1990.69	1684.45	1482.85	1341.02
80000	7123.78	3781.74	2673.37	2123.40	1796.74	1581.71	1430.42
85000	7569.02	4018.09	2840.46	2256.11	1909.04	1680.57	1519.82
90000	8014.25	4254.45	3007.54	2388.82	2021.34	1779.42	1609.22
95000	8459.49	4490.81	3174.63	2521.53	2133.63	1878.28	1698.62
100000	8904.72	4727.17	3341.72	2654.25	2245.93	1977.14	1788.03
200000	17809.45	9454.34	6683.43	5308.49	4491.86	3954.27	3576.05
300000	26714.17	14181.51	10025.15	7962.74	6737.78	5931.41	5364.07
400000	35618.90	18908.68	13366.86	10616.98	8983.71	7908.54	7152.10
500000	44523.62	23635.85	16708.58	13271.24	11229.64	9885.68	8940.13
1000000	89047.24	47271.70	33417.16	26542.47	22459.28	19771.36	17880.26

142

Amortization Amount	8 Years	9 Years	10 Years	15 Years	20 Years	25 Years	30 Years
25	0.41	0.39	0.36	0.31	0.28	0.27	0.27
50	0.82	0.77	0.73	0.61	0.57	0.54	0.53
100	1.65	1.54	1.46	1.23	1.13	1.08	1.06
200	3.30	3.08	2.92	2.46	2.26	2.17	2.12
300	4.95	4.63	4.38	3.68	3.39	3.25	3.18
400	6.59	6.17	5.84	4.91	4.52	4.34	4.25
500	8.24	7.71	7.30	6.14	5.65	5.42	5.31
600	9.89	9.25	8.76	7.37	6.78	6.51	6.37
700	11.54	10.80	10.22	8.59	7.92	7.59	7.43
800	13.19	12.34	11.67	9.82	9.05	8.68	8.49
900	14.84	13.88	13.13	11.05	10.18	9.76	9.55
1000	16.49	15.42	14.59	12.28	11.31	10.85	10.61
2000	32.97	30.85	29.19	24.55	22.62	21.69	21.23
3000	49.46	46.27	43.78	36.83	33.92	32.54	31.84
4000	65.95	61.70	58.37	49.10	45.23	43.38	42.45
5000	82.43	77.12	72.97	61.38	56.54	54.23	53.07
6000	98.92	92.55	87.56	73.65	67.85	65.08	63.68
7000	115.41	107.97	102.15	85.93	79.15	75.93	74.30
8000	131.89	123.39	116.75	98.21	90.46	86.77	84.91
9000	148.38	138.82	131.34	110.48	101.77	97.62	95.52
10000	164.87	154.24	145.93	122.76	113.08	108.47	106.14
11000	181.35	169.67	160.53	135.03	124.39	119.32	116.75
12000	197.84	185.09	175.12	147.31	135.69	130.16	127.36
13000	214.33	200.52	189.71	159.59	147.00	141.01	137.98
14000	230.81	215.94	204.31	171.86	158.31	151.86	148.59
15000	247.30	231.36	218.90	184.14	169.62	162.70	159.20
16000	263.79	246.79	233.49	196.41	180.93	173.55	169.82
17000	280.27	262.21	248.09	208.69	192.23	184.40	180.43
18000	296.76	277.64	262.68	220.96	203.54	195.24	191.04
19000	313.25	293.06	277.27	233.24	214.85	206.09	201.66
20000	329.73	308.49	291.86	245.52	226.16	216.94	212.27
21000	346.22	323.91	306.46	257.79	237.46	227.78	222.89
22000	362.71	339.33	321.05	270.07	248.77	238.63	233.50
23000	379.19	354.76	335.64	282.34	260.08	249.48	244.11
24000	395.68	370.18	350.24	294.62	271.39	260.32	254.73
25000	412.17	385.61	364.83	306.89	282.70	271.17	265.34
26000	428.65	401.03	379.42	319.17	294.00	282.02	275.95
27000	445.14	416.46	394.02	331.45	305.31	292.86	286.57
28000	461.63	431.88	408.61	343.72	316.62	303.71	297.18
29000	478.11	447.30	423.20	356.00	327.93	314.56	307.79
30000	494.60	462.73	437.80	368.27	339.24	325.41	318.41
35000	577.03	539.85	510.76	429.65	395.77	379.64	371.48
40000	659.47	616.97	583.73	491.03	452.31	433.87	424.54
45000	741.90	694.09	656.70	552.41	508.85	488.11	477.61
50000	824.33	771.21	729.66	613.79	565.39	542.34	530.68
55000	906.77	848.34	802.63	675.17	621.93	596.58	583.75
60000	989.20	925.46	875.59	736.55	678.47	650.81	636.82
65000	1071.63	1002.58	948.56	797.93	735.01	705.04	689.88
70000	1154.07	1079.70	1021.53	859.30	791.55	759.28	742.95
75000	1236.50	1156.82	1094.49	920.68	848.05	813.51	796.02
80000	1318.93	1233.94	1167.46	982.06	904.63	867.75	849.09
85000	1401.37	1311.06	1240.43	1043.44	961.17	921.98	902.16
90000	1483.80	1388.19	1313.39	1104.82	1017.71	976.22	955.22
95000	1566.23	1465.31	1386.36	1166.20	1074.24	1030.45	1008.29
100000	1648.67	1542.43	1459.32	1227.58	1130.78	1084.68	1061.36
200000	3297.34	3084.86	2918.65	2455.15	2261.57	2169.37	2122.72
300000	4946.00	4627.29	4377.97	3682.73	3392.35	3254.05	3184.08
400000	6594.67	6169.71	5837.30	4910.31	4523.14	4338.74	4245.44
500000	8243.34	7712.14	7296.62	6137.89	5653.92	5423.42	5306.80
1000000	16486.68	15424.28	14593.24	12275.77	11307.84	10846.84	10613.60

12.875%

MONTHLY PAYMENT
NECESSARY TO AMORTIZE A LOAN

Amortization Amount	1 Year	2 Years	3 Years	4 Years	5 Years	6 Years	7 Years
25	2.23	1.18	0.84	0.67	0.56	0.50	0.45
50	4.46	2.37	1.67	1.33	1.13	0.99	0.90
100	8.91	4.73	3.35	2.66	2.25	1.98	1.79
200	17.82	9.47	6.69	5.32	4.50	3.97	3.59
300	26.73	14.20	10.04	7.98	6.76	5.95	5.38
400	35.64	18.93	13.39	10.64	9.01	7.93	7.18
500	44.55	23.66	16.74	13.30	11.26	9.92	8.97
600	53.46	28.40	20.08	15.96	13.51	11.90	10.77
700	62.37	33.13	23.43	18.62	15.76	13.88	12.56
800	71.28	37.86	26.78	21.28	18.02	15.87	14.36
900	80.19	42.59	30.13	23.94	20.27	17.85	16.15
1000	89.10	47.33	33.47	26.60	22.52	19.83	17.94
2000	178.21	94.65	66.95	53.20	45.04	39.67	35.89
3000	267.31	141.98	100.42	79.80	67.56	59.50	53.83
4000	356.41	189.31	133.90	106.40	90.08	79.33	71.78
5000	445.51	236.64	167.37	133.01	112.60	99.17	89.72
6000	534.62	283.96	200.84	159.61	135.12	119.00	107.67
7000	623.72	331.29	234.32	186.21	157.64	138.83	125.61
8000	712.82	378.62	267.79	212.81	180.16	158.67	143.55
9000	801.93	425.95	301.27	239.41	202.68	178.50	161.50
10000	891.03	473.27	334.74	266.01	225.20	198.34	179.44
11000	980.13	520.60	368.21	292.61	247.72	218.17	197.39
12000	1069.23	567.93	401.69	319.21	270.24	238.00	215.33
13000	1158.34	615.25	435.16	345.81	292.76	257.84	233.28
14000	1247.44	662.58	468.64	372.41	315.27	277.67	251.22
15000	1336.54	709.91	502.11	399.01	337.79	297.50	269.16
16000	1425.65	757.24	535.59	425.62	360.31	317.34	287.11
17000	1514.75	804.56	569.06	452.22	382.83	337.17	305.05
18000	1603.85	851.89	602.53	478.82	405.35	357.00	323.00
19000	1692.95	899.22	636.01	505.42	427.87	376.84	340.94
20000	1782.06	946.55	669.48	532.02	450.39	396.67	358.88
21000	1871.16	993.87	702.96	558.62	472.91	416.50	376.83
22000	1960.26	1041.20	736.43	585.22	495.43	436.34	394.77
23000	2049.37	1088.53	769.90	611.82	517.95	456.17	412.72
24000	2138.47	1135.85	803.38	638.43	540.47	476.00	430.66
25000	2227.57	1183.18	836.85	665.03	562.99	495.84	448.61
26000	2316.67	1230.51	870.33	691.63	585.51	515.67	466.55
27000	2405.78	1277.84	903.80	718.23	608.03	535.51	484.49
28000	2494.88	1325.16	937.27	744.83	630.55	555.34	502.44
29000	2583.98	1372.49	970.75	771.43	653.07	575.17	520.38
30000	2673.09	1419.82	1004.22	798.03	675.59	595.01	538.33
35000	3118.60	1656.46	1171.59	931.04	788.19	694.17	628.05
40000	3564.11	1893.09	1338.96	1064.04	900.79	793.34	717.77
45000	4009.63	2129.73	1506.33	1197.05	1013.38	892.51	807.49
50000	4455.14	2366.36	1673.70	1330.05	1125.98	991.68	897.21
55000	4900.66	2603.00	1841.07	1463.06	1238.58	1090.84	986.93
60000	5346.17	2839.64	2008.45	1596.06	1351.18	1190.01	1076.65
65000	5791.68	3076.27	2175.82	1729.07	1463.78	1289.18	1166.38
70000	6237.20	3312.91	2343.19	1862.07	1576.37	1388.35	1256.10
75000	6682.71	3549.55	2510.56	1995.08	1688.97	1487.51	1345.82
80000	7128.23	3786.18	2677.93	2128.08	1801.57	1586.68	1435.54
85000	7573.74	4022.82	2845.30	2261.09	1914.17	1685.85	1525.26
90000	8019.26	4259.46	3012.67	2394.10	2026.77	1785.02	1614.98
95000	8464.77	4496.09	3180.04	2527.10	2139.37	1884.19	1704.70
100000	8910.28	4732.73	3347.41	2660.11	2251.96	1983.35	1794.42
200000	17820.57	9465.46	6694.82	5320.21	4503.93	3966.71	3588.85
300000	26730.85	14198.19	10042.23	7980.32	6755.89	5950.06	5383.27
400000	35641.14	18930.91	13389.63	10640.42	9007.85	7933.41	7177.70
500000	44551.42	23663.64	16737.04	13300.53	11259.82	9916.77	8972.12
1000000	89102.85	47327.29	33474.09	26601.06	22519.64	19833.53	17944.25

Amortization Amount	8 Years	9 Years	10 Years	15 Years	20 Years	25 Years	30 Years
25	0.41	0.39	0.37	0.31	0.28	0.27	0.27
50	0.83	0.77	0.73	0.62	0.57	0.55	0.54
100	1.66	1.55	1.47	1.24	1.14	1.09	1.07
200	3.31	3.10	2.93	2.47	2.28	2.19	2.14
300	4.97	4.65	4.40	3.71	3.42	3.28	3.21
400	6.62	6.20	5.87	4.94	4.56	4.37	4.28
500	8.28	7.75	7.33	6.18	5.70	5.47	5.35
600	9.93	9.30	8.80	7.41	6.83	6.56	6.42
700	11.59	10.84	10.26	8.65	7.97	7.65	7.49
800	13.24	12.39	11.73	9.88	9.11	8.75	8.56
900	14.90	13.94	13.20	11.12	10.25	9.84	9.64
1000	16.55	15.49	14.66	12.35	11.39	10.94	10.71
2000	33.10	30.98	29.33	24.71	22.78	21.87	21.41
3000	49.66	46.48	43.99	37.06	34.17	32.81	32.12
4000	66.21	61.97	58.65	49.41	45.57	43.74	42.82
5000	82.76	77.46	73.31	61.76	56.96	54.68	53.53
6000	99.31	92.95	87.98	74.12	68.35	65.61	64.23
7000	115.87	108.44	102.64	86.47	79.74	76.55	74.94
8000	132.42	123.93	117.30	98.82	91.13	87.48	85.65
9000	148.97	139.43	131.96	111.18	102.52	98.42	96.35
10000	165.52	154.92	146.63	123.53	113.91	109.35	107.06
11000	182.08	170.41	161.29	135.88	125.31	120.29	117.76
12000	198.63	185.90	175.95	148.24	136.70	131.22	128.47
13000	215.18	201.39	190.61	160.59	148.09	142.16	139.17
14000	231.73	216.89	205.28	172.94	159.48	153.10	149.88
15000	248.29	232.38	219.94	185.29	170.87	164.03	160.59
16000	264.84	247.87	234.60	197.65	182.26	174.97	171.29
17000	281.39	263.36	249.26	210.00	193.66	185.90	182.00
18000	297.94	278.85	263.93	222.35	205.05	196.84	192.70
19000	314.50	294.35	278.59	234.71	216.44	207.77	203.41
20000	331.05	309.84	293.25	247.06	227.83	218.71	214.11
21000	347.60	325.33	307.91	259.41	239.22	229.64	224.82
22000	364.15	340.82	322.58	271.77	250.61	240.58	235.53
23000	380.71	356.31	337.24	284.12	262.00	251.51	246.23
24000	397.26	371.80	351.90	296.47	273.40	262.45	256.94
25000	413.81	387.30	366.56	308.82	284.79	273.38	267.64
26000	430.36	402.79	381.23	321.18	296.18	284.32	278.35
27000	446.92	418.28	395.89	333.53	307.57	295.26	289.05
28000	463.47	433.77	410.55	345.88	318.96	306.19	299.76
29000	480.02	449.26	425.21	358.24	330.35	317.13	310.46
30000	496.57	464.76	439.88	370.59	341.74	328.06	321.17
35000	579.34	542.21	513.19	432.35	398.70	382.74	374.70
40000	662.10	619.67	586.50	494.12	455.66	437.42	428.23
45000	744.86	697.13	659.81	555.88	512.62	492.09	481.76
50000	827.62	774.59	733.13	617.65	569.57	546.77	535.28
55000	910.39	852.05	806.44	679.41	626.53	601.45	588.81
60000	993.15	929.51	879.75	741.18	683.49	656.12	642.34
65000	1075.91	1006.97	953.06	802.94	740.45	710.80	695.87
70000	1158.67	1084.43	1026.38	864.71	797.40	765.48	749.40
75000	1241.43	1161.89	1099.69	926.47	854.36	820.15	802.93
80000	1324.20	1239.35	1173.00	988.24	911.32	874.83	856.45
85000	1406.96	1316.81	1246.32	1050.00	968.28	929.51	909.98
90000	1489.72	1394.27	1319.63	1111.77	1025.23	984.18	963.51
95000	1572.48	1471.73	1392.94	1173.53	1082.19	1038.86	1017.04
100000	1655.25	1549.18	1466.25	1235.30	1139.15	1093.54	1070.57
200000	3310.49	3098.37	2932.51	2470.60	2278.30	2187.08	2141.14
300000	4965.74	4647.55	4398.76	3705.90	3417.45	3280.61	3211.71
400000	6620.99	6196.74	5865.01	4941.20	4556.60	4374.15	4282.27
500000	8276.23	7745.92	7331.27	6176.49	5695.74	5467.69	5352.84
1000000	16552.46	15491.84	14662.54	12352.99	11391.49	10935.38	10705.68

13%
MONTHLY PAYMENT
NECESSARY TO AMORTIZE A LOAN

Amortization Amount	1 Year	2 Years	3 Years	4 Years	5 Years	6 Years	7 Years
25	2.23	1.18	0.84	0.67	0.56	0.50	0.45
50	4.46	2.37	1.68	1.33	1.13	0.99	0.90
100	8.92	4.74	3.35	2.67	2.26	1.99	1.80
200	17.83	9.48	6.71	5.33	4.52	3.98	3.60
300	26.75	14.21	10.06	8.00	6.77	5.97	5.40
400	35.66	18.95	13.41	10.66	9.03	7.96	7.20
500	44.58	23.69	16.77	13.33	11.29	9.95	9.00
600	53.50	28.43	20.12	16.00	13.55	11.94	10.80
700	62.41	33.17	23.47	18.66	15.81	13.93	12.61
800	71.33	37.91	26.82	21.33	18.06	15.92	14.41
900	80.24	42.64	30.18	23.99	20.32	17.91	16.21
1000	89.16	47.38	33.53	26.66	22.58	19.90	18.01
2000	178.32	94.77	67.06	53.32	45.16	39.79	36.02
3000	267.48	142.15	100.59	79.98	67.74	59.69	54.02
4000	356.63	189.53	134.12	106.64	90.32	79.58	72.03
5000	445.79	236.91	167.66	133.30	112.90	99.48	90.04
6000	534.95	284.30	201.19	159.96	135.48	119.37	108.05
7000	624.11	331.68	234.72	186.62	158.06	139.27	126.06
8000	713.27	379.06	268.25	213.28	180.64	159.17	144.07
9000	802.43	426.45	301.78	239.94	203.22	179.06	162.07
10000	891.58	473.83	335.31	266.60	225.80	198.96	180.08
11000	980.74	521.21	368.84	293.26	248.38	218.85	198.09
12000	1069.90	568.59	402.37	319.92	270.96	238.75	216.10
13000	1159.06	615.98	435.90	346.58	293.54	258.65	234.11
14000	1248.22	663.36	469.43	373.24	316.12	278.54	252.12
15000	1337.38	710.74	502.97	399.90	338.70	298.44	270.12
16000	1426.54	758.13	536.50	426.56	361.28	318.33	288.13
17000	1515.69	805.51	570.03	453.21	383.86	338.23	306.14
18000	1604.85	852.89	603.56	479.87	406.44	358.12	324.15
19000	1694.01	900.27	637.09	506.53	429.02	378.02	342.16
20000	1783.17	947.66	670.62	533.19	451.60	397.92	360.17
21000	1872.33	995.04	704.15	559.85	474.18	417.81	378.17
22000	1961.49	1042.42	737.68	586.51	496.76	437.71	396.18
23000	2050.64	1089.81	771.21	613.17	519.34	457.60	414.19
24000	2139.80	1137.19	804.74	639.83	541.92	477.50	432.20
25000	2228.96	1184.57	838.28	666.49	564.50	497.39	450.21
26000	2318.12	1231.95	871.81	693.15	587.08	517.29	468.22
27000	2407.28	1279.34	905.34	719.81	609.66	537.19	486.22
28000	2496.44	1326.72	938.87	746.47	632.24	557.08	504.23
29000	2585.59	1374.10	972.40	773.13	654.82	576.98	522.24
30000	2674.75	1421.49	1005.93	799.79	677.40	596.87	540.25
35000	3120.55	1658.40	1173.59	933.09	790.30	696.35	630.29
40000	3566.34	1895.32	1341.24	1066.39	903.20	795.83	720.33
45000	4012.13	2132.23	1508.90	1199.69	1016.10	895.31	810.37
50000	4457.92	2369.14	1676.55	1332.98	1129.00	994.79	900.42
55000	4903.71	2606.06	1844.21	1466.28	1241.90	1094.27	990.46
60000	5349.51	2842.97	2011.86	1599.58	1354.80	1193.75	1080.50
65000	5795.30	3079.89	2179.52	1732.88	1467.70	1293.23	1170.54
70000	6241.09	3316.80	2347.17	1866.18	1580.60	1392.70	1260.58
75000	6686.88	3553.72	2514.83	1999.48	1693.50	1492.18	1350.62
80000	7132.68	3790.63	2682.48	2132.78	1806.40	1591.66	1440.67
85000	7578.47	4027.55	2850.14	2266.07	1919.31	1691.14	1530.71
90000	8024.26	4264.46	3017.79	2399.37	2032.21	1790.62	1620.75
95000	8470.05	4501.37	3185.45	2532.67	2145.11	1890.10	1710.79
100000	8915.84	4738.29	3353.10	2665.97	2258.01	1989.58	1800.83
200000	17831.69	9476.58	6706.21	5331.94	4516.01	3979.16	3601.67
300000	26747.53	14214.86	10059.31	7997.91	6774.02	5968.73	5402.50
400000	35663.38	18953.15	13412.42	10663.88	9032.02	7958.31	7203.33
500000	44579.22	23691.44	16765.52	13329.85	11290.03	9947.89	9004.16
1000000	89158.44	47382.88	33531.04	26659.69	22580.06	19895.78	18008.33

Amortization Amount	8 Years	9 Years	10 Years	15 Years	20 Years	25 Years	30 Years
25	0.42	0.39	0.37	0.31	0.29	0.28	0.27
50	0.83	0.78	0.74	0.62	0.57	0.55	0.54
100	1.66	1.56	1.47	1.24	1.15	1.10	1.08
200	3.32	3.11	2.95	2.49	2.30	2.20	2.16
300	4.99	4.67	4.42	3.73	3.44	3.31	3.24
400	6.65	6.22	5.89	4.97	4.59	4.41	4.32
500	8.31	7.78	7.37	6.22	5.74	5.51	5.40
600	9.97	9.34	8.84	7.46	6.89	6.61	6.48
700	11.63	10.89	10.31	8.70	8.03	7.72	7.56
800	13.29	12.45	11.79	9.94	9.18	8.82	8.64
900	14.96	14.00	13.26	11.19	10.33	9.92	9.72
1000	16.62	15.56	14.73	12.43	11.48	11.02	10.80
2000	33.24	31.12	29.46	24.86	22.95	22.05	21.60
3000	49.86	46.68	44.20	37.29	34.43	33.07	32.39
4000	66.47	62.24	58.93	49.72	45.90	44.10	43.19
5000	83.09	77.80	73.66	62.15	57.38	55.12	53.99
6000	99.71	93.36	88.39	74.58	68.85	66.14	64.79
7000	116.33	108.92	103.12	87.01	80.33	77.17	75.59
8000	132.95	124.48	117.86	99.44	91.80	88.19	86.38
9000	149.57	140.04	132.59	111.87	103.28	99.22	97.18
10000	166.18	155.60	147.32	124.30	114.75	110.24	107.98
11000	182.80	171.15	162.05	136.73	126.23	121.26	118.78
12000	199.42	186.71	176.78	149.16	137.70	132.29	129.57
13000	216.04	202.27	191.52	161.59	149.18	143.31	140.37
14000	232.66	217.83	206.25	174.03	160.65	154.34	151.17
15000	249.28	233.39	220.98	186.46	172.13	165.36	161.97
16000	265.89	248.95	235.71	198.89	183.60	176.39	172.77
17000	282.51	264.51	250.44	211.32	195.08	187.41	183.56
18000	299.13	280.07	265.18	223.75	206.56	198.43	194.36
19000	315.75	295.63	279.91	236.18	218.03	209.46	205.16
20000	332.37	311.19	294.64	248.61	229.51	220.48	215.96
21000	348.99	326.75	309.37	261.04	240.98	231.51	226.76
22000	365.60	342.31	324.10	273.47	252.46	242.53	237.55
23000	382.22	357.87	338.84	285.90	263.93	253.55	248.35
24000	398.84	373.43	353.57	298.33	275.41	264.58	259.15
25000	415.46	388.99	368.30	310.76	286.88	275.60	269.95
26000	432.08	404.55	383.03	323.19	298.36	286.63	280.74
27000	448.70	420.11	397.76	335.62	309.83	297.65	291.54
28000	465.31	435.67	412.49	348.05	321.31	308.67	302.34
29000	481.93	451.23	427.23	360.48	332.78	319.70	313.14
30000	498.55	466.79	441.96	372.91	344.26	330.72	323.94
35000	581.64	544.58	515.62	435.06	401.64	385.84	377.93
40000	664.73	622.38	589.28	497.21	459.01	440.96	431.92
45000	747.83	700.18	662.94	559.37	516.39	496.08	485.90
50000	830.92	777.98	736.60	621.52	573.77	551.20	539.89
55000	914.01	855.77	810.26	683.67	631.14	606.32	593.88
60000	997.10	933.57	883.92	745.82	688.52	661.44	647.87
65000	1080.19	1011.37	957.58	807.97	745.89	716.56	701.86
70000	1163.29	1089.17	1031.24	870.13	803.27	771.69	755.85
75000	1246.38	1166.96	1104.90	932.28	860.65	826.81	809.84
80000	1329.47	1244.76	1178.56	994.43	918.02	881.93	863.83
85000	1412.56	1322.56	1252.22	1056.58	975.40	937.05	917.82
90000	1495.65	1400.36	1325.88	1118.73	1032.78	992.17	971.81
95000	1578.74	1478.15	1399.54	1180.89	1090.15	1047.29	1025.80
100000	1661.84	1555.95	1473.20	1243.04	1147.53	1102.41	1079.79
200000	3323.67	3111.90	2946.39	2486.07	2295.06	2204.81	2159.58
300000	4985.51	4667.86	4419.59	3729.11	3442.59	3307.22	3239.37
400000	6647.34	6223.81	5892.78	4972.15	4590.12	4409.63	4319.15
500000	8309.18	7779.76	7365.98	6215.19	5737.65	5512.04	5398.94
1000000	16618.36	15559.52	14731.96	12430.37	11475.30	11024.07	10797.88

13.125%

Amortization Amount	1 Year	2 Years	3 Years	4 Years	5 Years	6 Years	7 Years
25	2.23	1.19	0.84	0.67	0.57	0.50	0.45
50	4.46	2.37	1.68	1.34	1.13	1.00	0.90
100	8.92	4.74	3.36	2.67	2.26	2.00	1.81
200	17.84	9.49	6.72	5.34	4.53	3.99	3.61
300	26.76	14.23	10.08	8.02	6.79	5.99	5.42
400	35.69	18.98	13.44	10.69	9.06	7.98	7.23
500	44.61	23.72	16.79	13.36	11.32	9.98	9.04
600	53.53	28.46	20.15	16.03	13.58	11.97	10.84
700	62.45	33.21	23.51	18.70	15.85	13.97	12.65
800	71.37	37.95	26.87	21.37	18.11	15.97	14.46
900	80.29	42.69	30.23	24.05	20.38	17.96	16.27
1000	89.21	47.44	33.59	26.72	22.64	19.96	18.07
2000	178.43	94.88	67.18	53.44	45.28	39.92	36.15
3000	267.64	142.32	100.76	80.16	67.92	59.87	54.22
4000	356.86	189.75	134.35	106.87	90.56	79.83	72.29
5000	446.07	237.19	167.94	133.59	113.20	99.79	90.36
6000	535.28	284.63	201.53	160.31	135.84	119.75	108.44
7000	624.50	332.07	235.12	187.03	158.48	139.71	126.51
8000	713.71	379.51	268.70	213.75	181.12	159.66	144.58
9000	802.93	426.95	302.29	240.47	203.76	179.62	162.65
10000	892.14	474.38	335.88	267.18	226.41	199.58	180.73
11000	981.35	521.82	369.47	293.90	249.05	219.54	198.80
12000	1070.57	569.26	403.06	320.62	271.69	239.50	216.87
13000	1159.78	616.70	436.64	347.34	294.33	259.46	234.94
14000	1249.00	664.14	470.23	374.06	316.97	279.41	253.02
15000	1338.21	711.58	503.82	400.78	339.61	299.37	271.09
16000	1427.42	759.02	537.41	427.49	362.25	319.33	289.16
17000	1516.64	806.45	571.00	454.21	384.89	339.29	307.23
18000	1605.85	853.89	604.58	480.93	407.53	359.25	325.31
19000	1695.07	901.33	638.17	507.65	430.17	379.20	343.38
20000	1784.28	948.77	671.76	534.37	452.81	399.16	361.45
21000	1873.49	996.21	705.35	561.09	475.45	419.12	379.52
22000	1962.71	1043.65	738.94	587.80	498.09	439.08	397.60
23000	2051.92	1091.09	772.52	614.52	520.73	459.04	415.67
24000	2141.14	1138.52	806.11	641.24	543.37	478.99	433.74
25000	2230.35	1185.96	839.70	667.96	566.01	498.95	451.81
26000	2319.56	1233.40	873.29	694.68	588.65	518.91	469.89
27000	2408.78	1280.84	906.88	721.40	611.29	538.87	487.96
28000	2497.99	1328.28	940.46	748.11	633.94	558.83	506.03
29000	2587.21	1375.72	974.05	774.83	656.58	578.79	524.10
30000	2676.42	1423.15	1007.64	801.55	679.22	598.74	542.18
35000	3122.49	1660.35	1175.58	935.14	792.42	698.53	632.54
40000	3568.56	1897.54	1343.52	1068.73	905.62	798.32	722.90
45000	4014.63	2134.73	1511.46	1202.33	1018.82	898.11	813.26
50000	4460.70	2371.92	1679.40	1335.92	1132.03	997.91	903.63
55000	4906.77	2609.12	1847.34	1469.51	1245.23	1097.70	993.99
60000	5352.84	2846.31	2015.28	1603.10	1358.43	1197.49	1084.35
65000	5798.91	3083.50	2183.22	1736.69	1471.64	1297.28	1174.71
70000	6244.98	3320.69	2351.16	1870.29	1584.84	1397.07	1265.08
75000	6691.05	3557.89	2519.10	2003.88	1698.04	1496.86	1355.44
80000	7137.12	3795.08	2687.04	2137.47	1811.24	1596.65	1445.80
85000	7583.19	4032.27	2854.98	2271.06	1924.45	1696.44	1536.16
90000	8029.26	4269.46	3022.92	2404.65	2037.65	1796.23	1626.53
95000	8475.33	4506.66	3190.86	2538.24	2150.85	1896.02	1716.89
100000	8921.40	4743.85	3358.80	2671.84	2264.05	1995.81	1807.25
200000	17842.81	9487.70	6717.60	5343.67	4528.11	3991.62	3614.50
300000	26764.21	14231.55	10076.41	8015.51	6792.16	5987.43	5421.75
400000	35685.61	18975.40	13435.21	10687.35	9056.22	7983.24	7229.00
500000	44607.02	23719.25	16794.01	13359.18	11320.27	9978.06	9036.25
1000000	89214.03	47438.49	33588.02	26718.37	22640.54	19958.11	18072.50

Amortization Amount	8 Years	9 Years	10 Years	15 Years	20 Years	25 Years	30 Years
25	0.42	0.39	0.37	0.31	0.29	0.28	0.27
50	0.83	0.78	0.74	0.63	0.58	0.56	0.54
100	1.67	1.56	1.48	1.25	1.16	1.11	1.09
200	3.34	3.13	2.96	2.50	2.31	2.22	2.18
300	5.01	4.69	4.44	3.75	3.47	3.33	3.27
400	6.67	6.25	5.92	5.00	4.62	4.45	4.36
500	8.34	7.81	7.40	6.25	5.78	5.56	5.45
600	10.01	9.38	8.88	7.50	6.94	6.67	6.53
700	11.68	10.94	10.36	8.76	8.09	7.78	7.62
800	13.35	12.50	11.84	10.01	9.25	8.89	8.71
900	15.02	14.06	13.32	11.26	10.40	10.00	9.80
1000	16.68	15.63	14.80	12.51	11.56	11.11	10.89
2000	33.37	31.25	29.60	25.02	23.12	22.23	21.78
3000	50.05	46.88	44.40	37.52	34.68	33.34	32.67
4000	66.74	62.51	59.21	50.03	46.24	44.45	43.56
5000	83.42	78.14	74.01	62.54	57.80	55.56	54.45
6000	100.11	93.76	88.81	75.05	69.36	66.68	65.34
7000	116.79	109.39	103.61	87.56	80.92	77.79	76.23
8000	133.47	125.02	118.41	100.06	92.47	88.90	87.12
9000	150.16	140.65	133.21	112.57	104.03	100.02	98.01
10000	166.84	156.27	148.02	125.08	115.59	111.13	108.90
11000	183.53	171.90	162.82	137.59	127.15	122.24	119.79
12000	200.21	187.53	177.62	150.10	138.71	133.36	130.68
13000	216.90	203.16	192.42	162.60	150.27	144.47	141.57
14000	233.58	218.78	207.22	175.11	161.83	155.58	152.46
15000	250.27	234.41	222.02	187.62	173.39	166.69	163.35
16000	266.95	250.04	236.82	200.13	184.95	177.81	174.24
17000	283.63	265.66	251.63	212.63	196.51	188.92	185.13
18000	300.32	281.29	266.43	225.14	208.07	200.03	196.02
19000	317.00	296.92	281.23	237.65	219.63	211.15	206.91
20000	333.69	312.55	296.03	250.16	231.19	222.26	217.80
21000	350.37	328.17	310.83	262.67	242.75	233.37	228.69
22000	367.06	343.80	325.63	275.17	254.30	244.48	239.58
23000	383.74	359.43	340.43	287.68	265.86	255.60	250.47
24000	400.42	375.06	355.24	300.19	277.42	266.71	261.36
25000	417.11	390.68	370.04	312.70	288.98	277.82	272.26
26000	433.79	406.31	384.84	325.21	300.54	288.94	283.15
27000	450.48	421.94	399.64	337.71	312.10	300.05	294.04
28000	467.16	437.57	414.44	350.22	323.66	311.16	304.93
29000	483.85	453.19	429.24	362.73	335.22	322.27	315.82
30000	500.53	468.82	444.05	375.24	346.78	333.39	326.71
35000	583.95	546.96	518.05	437.78	404.58	388.95	381.16
40000	667.37	625.09	592.06	500.32	462.37	444.52	435.61
45000	750.80	703.23	666.07	562.86	520.17	500.08	490.06
50000	834.22	781.37	740.08	625.40	577.96	555.65	544.51
55000	917.64	859.50	814.08	687.94	635.76	611.21	598.96
60000	1001.06	937.64	888.09	750.48	693.56	666.78	653.41
65000	1084.48	1015.78	962.10	813.01	751.35	722.34	707.86
70000	1167.91	1093.91	1036.11	875.55	809.15	777.90	762.31
75000	1251.33	1172.05	1110.11	938.09	866.95	833.47	816.77
80000	1334.75	1250.19	1184.12	1000.63	924.74	889.03	871.22
85000	1418.17	1328.32	1258.13	1063.17	982.54	944.60	925.67
90000	1501.59	1406.46	1332.14	1125.71	1040.34	1000.16	980.12
95000	1585.01	1484.60	1406.14	1188.25	1098.13	1055.73	1034.57
100000	1668.44	1562.73	1480.15	1250.79	1155.93	1111.29	1089.02
200000	3336.87	3125.46	2960.30	2501.58	2311.86	2222.58	2178.04
300000	5005.31	4688.20	4440.46	3752.38	3467.79	3333.88	3267.06
400000	6673.74	6250.93	5920.61	5003.17	4623.72	4445.17	4356.08
500000	8342.18	7813.66	7400.76	6253.96	5779.65	5556.46	5445.10
1000000	16684.36	15627.32	14801.52	12507.92	11559.29	11112.92	10890.20

13.25%

MONTHLY PAYMENT
NECESSARY TO AMORTIZE A LOAN

Amortization Amount	1 Year	2 Years	3 Years	4 Years	5 Years	6 Years	7 Years
25	2.23	1.19	0.84	0.67	0.57	0.50	0.45
50	4.46	2.37	1.68	1.34	1.14	1.00	0.91
100	8.93	4.75	3.36	2.68	2.27	2.00	1.81
200	17.85	9.50	6.73	5.36	4.54	4.00	3.63
300	26.78	14.25	10.09	8.03	6.81	6.01	5.44
400	35.71	19.00	13.46	10.71	9.08	8.01	7.25
500	44.63	23.75	16.82	13.39	11.35	10.01	9.07
600	53.56	28.50	20.19	16.07	13.62	12.01	10.88
700	62.49	33.25	23.55	18.74	15.89	14.01	12.70
800	71.42	38.00	26.92	21.42	18.16	16.02	14.51
900	80.34	42.74	30.28	24.10	20.43	18.02	16.32
1000	89.27	47.49	33.65	26.78	22.70	20.02	18.14
2000	178.54	94.99	67.29	53.55	45.40	40.04	36.27
3000	267.81	142.48	100.94	80.33	68.10	60.06	54.41
4000	357.08	189.98	134.58	107.11	90.80	80.08	72.55
5000	446.35	237.47	168.23	133.89	113.51	100.10	90.68
6000	535.62	284.96	201.87	160.66	136.21	120.12	108.82
7000	624.89	332.46	235.52	187.44	158.91	140.14	126.96
8000	714.16	379.95	269.16	214.22	181.61	160.16	145.09
9000	803.43	427.45	302.81	240.99	204.31	180.18	163.23
10000	892.70	474.94	336.45	267.77	227.01	200.21	181.37
11000	981.97	522.44	370.10	294.55	249.71	220.23	199.50
12000	1071.24	569.93	403.74	321.33	272.41	240.25	217.64
13000	1160.50	617.42	437.39	348.10	295.11	260.27	235.78
14000	1249.77	664.92	471.03	374.88	317.82	280.29	253.91
15000	1339.04	712.41	504.68	401.66	340.52	300.31	272.05
16000	1428.31	759.91	538.32	428.43	363.22	320.33	290.19
17000	1517.58	807.40	571.97	455.21	385.92	340.35	308.33
18000	1606.85	854.89	605.61	481.99	408.62	360.37	326.46
19000	1696.12	902.39	639.26	508.76	431.32	380.39	344.60
20000	1785.39	949.88	672.90	535.54	454.02	400.41	362.74
21000	1874.66	997.38	706.55	562.32	476.72	420.43	380.87
22000	1963.93	1044.87	740.19	589.10	499.42	440.45	399.01
23000	2053.20	1092.36	773.84	615.87	522.13	460.47	417.15
24000	2142.47	1139.86	807.48	642.65	544.83	480.49	435.28
25000	2231.74	1187.35	841.13	669.43	567.53	500.51	453.42
26000	2321.01	1234.85	874.77	696.20	590.23	520.53	471.56
27000	2410.28	1282.34	908.42	722.98	612.93	540.55	489.69
28000	2499.55	1329.84	942.06	749.76	635.63	560.57	507.83
29000	2588.82	1377.33	975.71	776.54	658.33	580.60	525.97
30000	2678.09	1424.82	1009.35	803.31	681.03	600.62	544.10
35000	3124.44	1662.29	1177.58	937.20	794.54	700.72	634.79
40000	3570.78	1899.76	1345.80	1071.08	908.04	800.82	725.47
45000	4017.13	2137.23	1514.03	1204.97	1021.55	900.92	816.15
50000	4463.48	2374.71	1682.25	1338.85	1135.05	1001.03	906.84
55000	4909.83	2612.18	1850.48	1472.74	1248.56	1101.13	997.52
60000	5356.18	2849.65	2018.70	1606.63	1362.07	1201.23	1088.21
65000	5802.52	3087.12	2186.93	1740.51	1475.57	1301.33	1178.89
70000	6248.87	3324.59	2355.15	1874.40	1589.08	1401.44	1269.57
75000	6695.22	3562.06	2523.38	2008.28	1702.58	1501.54	1360.26
80000	7141.57	3799.53	2691.60	2142.17	1816.09	1601.64	1450.94
85000	7587.92	4037.00	2859.83	2276.05	1929.59	1701.74	1541.63
90000	8034.27	4274.47	3028.05	2409.94	2043.10	1801.85	1632.31
95000	8480.61	4511.94	3196.28	2543.82	2156.60	1901.95	1722.99
100000	8926.96	4749.41	3364.50	2677.71	2270.11	2002.05	1813.68
200000	17853.92	9498.82	8729.01	5355.42	4540.22	4004.10	3627.35
300000	26780.88	14248.23	10093.51	8033.13	6810.33	6006.16	5441.03
400000	35707.84	18997.64	13458.01	10710.84	9080.44	8008.21	7254.71
500000	44634.81	23747.06	16822.52	13388.55	11350.55	10010.26	9068.38
1000000	89269.61	47494.11	33645.03	26777.09	22701.09	20020.52	18136.77

150

Amortization Amount	8 Years	9 Years	10 Years	15 Years	20 Years	25 Years	30 Years
25	0.42	0.39	0.37	0.31	0.29	0.28	0.27
50	0.84	0.78	0.74	0.63	0.58	0.56	0.55
100	1.68	1.57	1.49	1.26	1.16	1.12	1.10
200	3.35	3.14	2.97	2.52	2.33	2.24	2.20
300	5.03	4.71	4.46	3.78	3.49	3.36	3.29
400	6.70	6.28	5.95	5.03	4.66	4.48	4.39
500	8.38	7.85	7.44	6.29	5.82	5.60	5.49
600	10.05	9.42	8.92	7.55	6.99	6.72	6.59
700	11.73	10.99	10.41	8.81	8.15	7.84	7.69
800	13.40	12.56	11.90	10.07	9.31	8.96	8.79
900	15.08	14.13	13.38	11.33	10.48	10.08	9.88
1000	16.75	15.70	14.87	12.59	11.64	11.20	10.98
2000	33.50	31.39	29.74	25.17	23.29	22.40	21.97
3000	50.25	47.09	44.61	37.76	34.93	33.61	32.95
4000	67.00	62.78	59.48	50.34	46.57	44.81	43.93
5000	83.75	78.48	74.36	62.93	58.22	56.01	54.91
6000	100.50	94.17	89.23	75.51	69.86	67.21	65.90
7000	117.25	109.87	104.10	88.10	81.50	78.41	76.88
8000	134.00	125.56	118.97	100.69	93.15	89.62	87.86
9000	150.75	141.26	133.84	113.27	104.79	100.82	98.84
10000	167.50	156.95	148.71	125.86	116.43	112.02	109.83
11000	184.26	172.65	163.58	138.44	128.08	123.22	120.81
12000	201.01	188.34	178.45	151.03	139.72	134.42	131.79
13000	217.76	204.04	193.33	163.61	151.36	145.62	142.77
14000	234.51	219.73	208.20	176.20	163.01	156.83	153.76
15000	251.26	235.43	223.07	188.78	174.65	168.03	164.74
16000	268.01	251.12	237.94	201.37	186.30	179.23	175.72
17000	284.76	266.82	252.81	213.96	197.94	190.43	186.70
18000	301.51	282.51	267.68	226.54	209.58	201.63	197.69
19000	318.26	298.21	282.55	239.13	221.23	212.84	208.67
20000	335.01	313.90	297.42	251.71	232.87	224.04	219.65
21000	351.76	329.60	312.30	264.30	244.51	235.24	230.64
22000	368.51	345.30	327.17	276.88	256.16	246.44	241.62
23000	385.26	360.99	342.04	289.47	267.80	257.64	252.60
24000	402.01	376.69	356.91	302.06	279.44	268.85	263.58
25000	418.76	392.38	371.78	314.64	291.09	280.05	274.57
26000	435.51	408.08	386.65	327.23	302.73	291.25	285.55
27000	452.26	423.77	401.52	339.81	314.37	302.45	296.53
28000	469.01	439.47	416.39	352.40	326.02	313.65	307.51
29000	485.76	455.16	431.26	364.98	337.66	324.86	318.50
30000	502.51	470.86	446.14	377.57	349.30	336.06	329.48
35000	586.27	549.33	520.49	440.50	407.52	392.07	384.39
40000	670.02	627.81	594.85	503.43	465.74	448.08	439.31
45000	753.77	706.29	669.20	566.35	523.96	504.09	494.22
50000	837.52	784.76	743.56	629.28	582.17	560.10	549.13
55000	921.28	863.24	817.92	692.21	640.39	616.11	604.04
60000	1005.03	941.71	892.27	755.14	698.61	672.11	658.96
65000	1088.78	1020.19	966.63	818.07	756.82	728.12	713.87
70000	1172.53	1098.67	1040.98	880.99	815.04	784.13	768.78
75000	1256.29	1177.14	1115.34	943.92	873.26	840.14	823.70
80000	1340.04	1255.62	1189.70	1006.85	931.48	896.15	878.61
85000	1423.79	1334.10	1264.05	1069.78	989.69	952.16	933.52
90000	1507.54	1412.57	1338.41	1132.71	1047.91	1008.17	988.44
95000	1591.29	1491.05	1412.76	1195.64	1106.13	1064.18	1043.35
100000	1675.05	1569.52	1487.12	1258.56	1164.34	1120.19	1098.26
200000	3350.09	3139.05	2974.24	2517.13	2328.69	2240.38	2196.53
300000	5025.14	4708.57	4461.36	3775.69	3493.03	3360.57	3294.79
400000	6700.19	6278.10	5948.48	5034.25	4657.38	4480.76	4393.05
500000	8375.24	7847.62	7435.60	6292.82	5821.72	5600.96	5491.32
1000000	16750.47	15695.24	14871.20	12585.64	11643.45	11201.91	10982.63

13.375%

Amortization Amount	1 Year	2 Years	3 Years	4 Years	5 Years	6 Years	7 Years
25	2.23	1.19	0.84	0.67	0.57	0.50	0.46
50	4.47	2.38	1.69	1.34	1.14	1.00	0.91
100	8.93	4.75	3.37	2.68	2.28	2.01	1.82
200	17.87	9.51	6.74	5.37	4.55	4.02	3.64
300	26.80	14.26	10.11	8.05	6.83	6.02	5.46
400	35.73	19.02	13.48	10.73	9.10	8.03	7.28
500	44.66	23.77	16.85	13.42	11.38	10.04	9.10
600	53.60	28.53	20.22	16.10	13.66	12.05	10.92
700	62.53	33.28	23.59	18.79	15.93	14.06	12.74
800	71.46	38.04	26.96	21.47	18.21	16.07	14.56
900	80.39	42.79	30.33	24.15	20.49	18.07	16.38
1000	89.33	47.55	33.70	26.84	22.76	20.08	18.20
2000	178.65	95.10	67.40	53.67	45.52	40.17	36.40
3000	267.98	142.65	101.11	80.51	68.29	60.25	54.60
4000	357.30	190.20	134.81	107.34	91.05	80.33	72.80
5000	446.63	237.75	168.51	134.18	113.81	100.42	91.01
6000	535.95	285.30	202.21	161.02	138.57	120.50	109.21
7000	625.28	332.85	235.91	187.85	159.33	140.58	127.41
8000	714.60	380.40	269.62	214.69	182.09	160.66	145.61
9000	803.93	427.95	303.32	241.52	204.86	180.75	163.81
10000	893.25	475.50	337.02	268.36	227.62	200.83	182.01
11000	982.58	523.05	370.72	295.19	250.38	220.91	200.21
12000	1071.90	570.60	404.42	322.03	273.14	241.00	218.41
13000	1161.23	618.15	438.13	348.87	295.90	261.08	236.61
14000	1250.55	665.70	471.83	375.70	318.66	281.16	254.82
15000	1339.88	713.25	505.53	402.54	341.43	301.25	273.02
16000	1429.20	760.80	539.23	429.37	364.19	321.33	291.22
17000	1518.53	808.35	572.94	456.21	386.95	341.41	309.42
18000	1607.85	855.90	606.64	483.05	409.71	361.49	327.62
19000	1697.18	903.45	640.34	509.88	432.47	381.58	345.82
20000	1786.50	950.99	674.04	536.72	455.23	401.66	364.02
21000	1875.83	998.54	707.74	563.55	478.00	421.74	382.22
22000	1965.15	1046.09	741.45	590.39	500.76	441.83	400.42
23000	2054.48	1093.64	775.15	617.22	523.52	461.91	418.63
24000	2143.80	1141.19	808.85	644.06	546.28	481.99	436.83
25000	2233.13	1188.74	842.55	670.90	569.04	502.08	455.03
26000	2322.45	1236.29	876.25	697.73	591.80	522.16	473.23
27000	2411.78	1283.84	909.96	724.57	614.57	542.24	491.43
28000	2501.11	1331.39	943.66	751.40	637.33	562.32	509.63
29000	2590.43	1378.94	977.36	778.24	660.09	582.41	527.83
30000	2679.76	1426.49	1011.06	805.08	682.85	602.49	546.03
35000	3126.38	1664.24	1179.57	939.26	796.66	702.91	637.04
40000	3573.01	1901.99	1348.08	1073.43	910.47	803.32	728.05
45000	4019.63	2139.74	1516.59	1207.61	1024.28	903.74	819.05
50000	4466.26	2377.49	1685.10	1341.79	1138.09	1004.15	910.06
55000	4912.89	2615.24	1853.61	1475.97	1251.89	1104.57	1001.06
60000	5359.51	2852.98	2022.12	1610.15	1365.70	1204.98	1092.07
65000	5806.14	3090.73	2190.63	1744.33	1479.51	1305.40	1183.07
70000	6252.76	3328.48	2359.14	1878.51	1593.32	1405.81	1274.08
75000	6699.39	3566.23	2527.66	2012.69	1707.13	1506.23	1365.08
80000	7146.01	3803.98	2696.17	2146.87	1820.94	1606.64	1456.09
85000	7592.64	4041.73	2864.68	2281.05	1934.74	1707.06	1547.10
90000	8039.27	4279.48	3033.19	2415.23	2048.55	1807.47	1638.10
95000	8485.89	4517.23	3201.70	2549.41	2162.36	1907.89	1729.11
100000	8932.52	4754.97	3370.21	2683.59	2276.17	2008.30	1820.11
200000	17865.04	9509.95	6740.41	5367.17	4552.34	4016.60	3640.23
300000	26797.56	14264.92	10110.62	8050.76	6828.51	6024.90	5460.34
400000	35730.07	19019.90	13480.83	10734.35	9104.68	8033.20	7280.45
500000	44662.59	23774.87	16851.04	13417.93	11380.85	10041.50	9100.56
1000000	89325.18	47549.74	33702.07	26835.86	22761.70	20083.00	18201.13

Amortization Amount	8 Years	9 Years	10 Years	15 Years	20 Years	25 Years	30 Years
25	0.42	0.39	0.37	0.32	0.29	0.28	0.28
50	0.84	0.79	0.75	0.63	0.59	0.56	0.55
100	1.68	1.58	1.49	1.27	1.17	1.13	1.11
200	3.36	3.15	2.99	2.53	2.35	2.26	2.22
300	5.05	4.73	4.48	3.80	3.52	3.39	3.32
400	6.73	6.31	5.98	5.07	4.69	4.52	4.43
500	8.41	7.88	7.47	6.33	5.86	5.65	5.54
600	10.09	9.46	8.96	7.60	7.04	6.77	6.65
700	11.77	11.03	10.46	8.86	8.21	7.90	7.75
800	13.45	12.61	11.95	10.13	9.38	9.03	8.86
900	15.14	14.19	13.45	11.40	10.55	10.16	9.97
1000	16.82	15.76	14.94	12.66	11.73	11.29	11.08
2000	33.63	31.53	29.88	25.33	23.46	22.58	22.15
3000	50.45	47.29	44.82	37.99	35.18	33.87	33.23
4000	67.27	63.05	59.76	50.65	46.91	45.16	44.30
5000	84.08	78.82	74.71	63.32	58.64	56.46	55.38
6000	100.90	94.58	89.65	75.98	70.37	67.75	66.45
7000	117.72	110.34	104.59	88.64	82.09	79.04	77.53
8000	134.53	126.11	119.53	101.31	93.82	90.33	88.60
9000	151.35	141.87	134.47	113.97	105.55	101.62	99.68
10000	168.17	157.63	149.41	126.64	117.28	112.91	110.75
11000	184.98	173.40	164.35	139.30	129.01	124.20	121.83
12000	201.80	189.16	179.29	151.96	140.73	135.49	132.90
13000	218.62	204.92	194.23	164.63	152.46	146.78	143.98
14000	235.43	220.69	209.17	177.29	164.19	158.07	155.05
15000	252.25	236.45	224.12	189.95	175.92	169.37	166.13
16000	269.07	252.21	239.06	202.62	187.64	180.66	177.20
17000	285.88	267.98	254.00	215.28	199.37	191.95	188.28
18000	302.70	283.74	268.94	227.94	211.10	203.24	199.35
19000	319.52	299.50	283.88	240.61	222.83	214.53	210.43
20000	336.33	315.27	298.82	253.27	234.56	225.82	221.50
21000	353.15	331.03	313.76	265.93	246.28	237.11	232.58
22000	369.97	346.79	328.70	278.60	258.01	248.40	243.65
23000	386.78	362.58	343.64	291.26	289.74	259.69	254.73
24000	403.60	378.32	358.58	303.92	281.47	270.99	265.80
25000	420.42	394.08	373.53	316.59	293.19	282.28	276.88
26000	437.23	409.85	388.47	329.25	304.92	293.57	287.95
27000	454.05	425.61	403.41	341.91	316.65	304.86	299.03
28000	470.87	441.37	418.35	354.58	328.38	316.15	310.10
29000	487.68	457.14	433.29	367.24	340.11	327.44	321.18
30000	504.50	472.90	448.23	379.91	351.83	338.73	332.26
35000	588.58	551.71	522.94	443.22	410.47	395.19	387.63
40000	672.67	630.53	597.64	506.54	469.11	451.64	443.01
45000	756.75	709.35	672.35	569.86	527.75	508.10	498.38
50000	840.83	788.16	747.05	633.18	586.39	564.55	553.76
55000	924.92	866.98	821.76	696.49	645.03	621.01	609.13
60000	1009.00	945.80	896.46	759.81	703.67	677.46	664.51
65000	1093.08	1024.61	971.17	823.13	762.30	733.92	719.89
70000	1177.17	1103.43	1045.87	886.45	820.94	790.37	775.26
75000	1261.25	1182.25	1120.58	949.76	879.58	846.83	830.64
80000	1345.33	1261.06	1195.28	1013.08	938.22	903.28	886.01
85000	1429.42	1339.88	1269.99	1076.40	996.86	959.74	941.39
90000	1513.50	1418.69	1344.69	1139.72	1055.50	1016.19	996.77
95000	1597.59	1497.51	1419.40	1203.03	1114.14	1072.65	1052.14
100000	1681.67	1576.33	1494.10	1266.35	1172.78	1129.10	1107.52
200000	3363.34	3152.66	2988.20	2532.70	2345.55	2258.21	2215.03
300000	5045.01	4728.98	4482.31	3799.05	3518.33	3387.31	3322.55
400000	6726.67	6305.31	5976.41	5065.41	4691.11	4516.42	4430.07
500000	8408.34	7881.64	7470.51	6331.76	5863.88	5645.52	5537.59
1000000	16816.68	15763.28	14941.02	12663.51	11727.77	11291.05	11075.17

13.5%

MONTHLY PAYMENT
NECESSARY TO AMORTIZE A LOAN

Amortization Amount	1 Year	2 Years	3 Years	4 Years	5 Years	6 Years	7 Years
25	2.23	1.19	0.84	0.67	0.57	0.50	0.46
50	4.47	2.38	1.69	1.34	1.14	1.01	0.91
100	8.94	4.76	3.38	2.69	2.28	2.01	1.83
200	17.88	9.52	6.75	5.38	4.56	4.03	3.65
300	26.81	14.28	10.13	8.07	6.85	6.04	5.48
400	35.75	19.04	13.50	10.76	9.13	8.06	7.31
500	44.69	23.80	16.88	13.45	11.41	10.07	9.13
600	53.63	28.56	20.26	16.14	13.69	12.09	10.96
700	62.57	33.32	23.63	18.83	15.98	14.10	12.79
800	71.50	38.08	27.01	21.52	18.26	16.12	14.61
900	80.44	42.84	30.38	24.21	20.54	18.13	16.44
1000	89.38	47.61	33.76	26.89	22.82	20.15	18.27
2000	178.76	95.21	67.52	53.79	45.64	40.29	36.53
3000	268.14	142.82	101.28	80.68	68.47	60.44	54.80
4000	357.52	190.42	135.04	107.58	91.29	80.58	73.06
5000	446.90	238.03	168.80	134.47	114.11	100.73	91.33
6000	536.28	285.63	202.55	161.37	136.93	120.87	109.59
7000	625.67	333.24	236.31	188.26	159.76	141.02	127.86
8000	715.05	380.84	270.07	215.16	182.58	161.16	146.12
9000	804.43	428.45	303.83	242.05	205.40	181.31	164.39
10000	893.81	476.05	337.59	268.95	228.22	201.46	182.66
11000	983.19	523.66	371.35	295.84	251.05	221.60	200.92
12000	1072.57	571.26	405.11	322.74	273.87	241.75	219.19
13000	1161.95	618.87	438.87	349.63	296.69	261.89	237.45
14000	1251.33	666.48	472.63	376.53	319.51	282.04	255.72
15000	1340.71	714.08	506.39	403.42	342.34	302.18	273.98
16000	1430.09	761.69	540.15	430.31	365.16	322.33	292.25
17000	1519.47	809.29	573.91	457.21	387.98	342.47	310.51
18000	1608.85	856.90	607.66	484.10	410.80	362.62	328.78
19000	1698.23	904.50	641.42	511.00	433.63	382.77	347.05
20000	1787.61	952.11	675.18	537.89	456.45	402.91	365.31
21000	1877.00	999.71	708.94	564.79	479.27	423.06	383.58
22000	1966.38	1047.32	742.70	591.68	502.09	443.20	401.84
23000	2055.76	1094.92	776.46	618.58	524.91	463.35	420.11
24000	2145.14	1142.53	810.22	645.47	547.74	483.49	438.37
25000	2234.52	1190.13	843.98	672.37	570.56	503.64	456.64
26000	2323.90	1237.74	877.74	699.26	593.38	523.78	474.91
27000	2413.28	1285.35	911.50	726.16	616.20	543.93	493.17
28000	2502.66	1332.95	945.26	753.05	639.03	564.08	511.44
29000	2592.04	1380.56	979.02	779.95	661.85	584.22	529.70
30000	2681.42	1428.16	1012.77	806.84	684.67	604.37	547.97
35000	3128.33	1666.19	1181.57	941.31	798.78	705.09	639.30
40000	3575.23	1904.22	1350.37	1075.79	912.90	805.82	730.62
45000	4022.13	2142.24	1519.16	1210.26	1027.01	906.55	821.95
50000	4469.04	2380.27	1687.96	1344.73	1141.12	1007.28	913.28
55000	4915.94	2618.30	1856.75	1479.21	1255.23	1108.01	1004.61
60000	5362.84	2856.32	2025.55	1613.68	1369.34	1208.73	1095.93
65000	5809.75	3094.35	2194.34	1748.15	1483.45	1309.46	1187.26
70000	6256.65	3332.38	2363.14	1882.63	1597.57	1410.19	1278.59
75000	6703.56	3570.40	2531.94	2017.10	1711.68	1510.92	1369.92
80000	7150.46	3808.43	2700.73	2151.57	1825.79	1611.65	1461.25
85000	7597.36	4046.46	2869.53	2286.05	1939.90	1712.37	1552.57
90000	8044.27	4284.48	3038.32	2420.52	2054.01	1813.10	1643.90
95000	8491.17	4522.51	3207.12	2554.99	2168.13	1913.83	1735.23
100000	8938.07	4760.54	3375.91	2689.47	2282.24	2014.56	1826.56
200000	17876.15	9521.08	6751.83	5378.94	4564.48	4029.11	3653.12
300000	26814.22	14281.61	10127.74	8068.40	6846.71	6043.67	5479.67
400000	35752.30	19042.15	13503.66	10757.87	9128.95	8058.23	7306.23
500000	44690.37	23802.69	16879.57	13447.34	11411.19	10072.78	9132.79
1000000	89380.75	47605.38	33759.14	26894.68	22822.38	20145.57	18265.58

Amortization Amount	8 Years	9 Years	10 Years	15 Years	20 Years	25 Years	30 Years
25	0.42	0.40	0.38	0.32	0.30	0.28	0.28
50	0.84	0.79	0.75	0.64	0.59	0.57	0.56
100	1.69	1.58	1.50	1.27	1.18	1.14	1.12
200	3.38	3.17	3.00	2.55	2.36	2.28	2.23
300	5.06	4.75	4.50	3.82	3.54	3.41	3.35
400	6.75	6.33	6.00	5.10	4.72	4.55	4.47
500	8.44	7.92	7.51	6.37	5.91	5.69	5.58
600	10.13	9.50	9.01	7.64	7.09	6.83	6.70
700	11.82	11.08	10.51	8.92	8.27	7.97	7.82
800	13.51	12.67	12.01	10.19	9.45	9.10	8.93
900	15.19	14.25	13.51	11.47	10.63	10.24	10.05
1000	16.88	15.83	15.01	12.74	11.81	11.38	11.17
2000	33.77	31.66	30.02	25.48	23.62	22.76	22.34
3000	50.65	47.49	45.03	38.22	35.44	34.14	33.50
4000	67.53	63.33	60.04	50.97	47.25	45.52	44.67
5000	84.42	79.16	75.05	63.71	59.06	56.90	55.84
6000	101.30	94.99	90.07	76.45	70.87	68.28	67.01
7000	118.18	110.82	105.08	89.19	82.69	79.66	78.17
8000	135.06	126.65	120.09	101.93	94.50	91.04	89.34
9000	151.95	142.48	135.10	114.67	106.31	102.42	100.51
10000	168.83	158.31	150.11	127.42	118.12	113.80	111.68
11000	185.71	174.15	165.12	140.16	129.93	125.18	122.85
12000	202.60	189.98	180.13	152.90	141.75	136.56	134.01
13000	219.48	205.81	195.14	165.64	153.56	147.94	145.18
14000	236.36	221.64	210.15	178.38	165.37	159.32	156.35
15000	253.25	237.47	225.16	191.12	177.18	170.70	167.52
16000	270.13	253.30	240.18	203.86	189.00	182.09	178.69
17000	287.01	269.13	255.19	216.61	200.81	193.47	189.85
18000	303.89	284.97	270.20	229.35	212.62	204.85	201.02
19000	320.78	300.80	285.21	242.09	224.43	216.23	212.19
20000	337.66	316.63	300.22	254.83	236.25	227.61	223.36
21000	354.54	332.46	315.23	267.57	248.06	238.99	234.52
22000	371.43	348.29	330.24	280.31	259.87	250.37	245.69
23000	388.31	364.12	345.25	293.06	271.68	261.75	256.86
24000	405.19	379.95	360.26	305.80	283.49	273.13	268.03
25000	422.08	395.79	375.27	318.54	295.31	284.51	279.20
26000	438.96	411.62	390.28	331.28	307.12	295.89	290.36
27000	455.84	427.45	405.30	344.02	318.93	307.27	301.53
28000	472.72	443.28	420.31	356.76	330.74	318.65	312.70
29000	489.61	459.11	435.32	369.51	342.56	330.03	323.87
30000	506.49	474.94	450.33	382.25	354.37	341.41	335.03
35000	590.91	554.10	525.38	445.95	413.43	398.31	390.87
40000	675.32	633.26	600.44	509.66	472.49	455.21	446.71
45000	759.74	712.41	675.49	573.37	531.55	512.11	502.55
50000	844.15	791.57	750.55	637.08	590.61	569.02	558.39
55000	928.57	870.73	825.60	700.79	649.67	625.92	614.23
60000	1012.98	949.89	900.66	764.49	708.74	682.82	670.07
65000	1097.40	1029.04	975.71	828.20	767.80	739.72	725.91
70000	1181.81	1108.20	1050.77	891.91	826.86	796.62	781.75
75000	1266.23	1187.36	1125.82	955.62	885.92	853.52	837.59
80000	1350.64	1266.51	1200.88	1019.32	944.98	910.43	893.43
85000	1435.06	1345.67	1275.93	1083.03	1004.04	967.33	949.26
90000	1519.47	1424.83	1350.99	1146.74	1063.10	1024.23	1005.10
95000	1603.89	1503.99	1426.04	1210.45	1122.16	1081.13	1060.94
100000	1688.30	1583.14	1501.10	1274.16	1181.23	1138.03	1116.78
200000	3376.60	3166.29	3002.19	2548.31	2362.45	2276.06	2233.56
300000	5064.90	4749.43	4503.29	3822.47	3543.68	3414.10	3350.35
400000	6753.20	6332.57	6004.38	5096.62	4724.90	4552.13	4467.13
500000	8441.50	7915.72	7505.48	6370.78	5906.13	5690.16	5583.91
1000000	16883.01	15831.43	15010.96	12741.55	11812.25	11380.32	11167.82

13.625%

Amortization Amount	1 Year	2 Years	3 Years	4 Years	5 Years	6 Years	7 Years
25	2.24	1.19	0.85	0.67	0.57	0.51	0.46
50	4.47	2.38	1.69	1.35	1.14	1.01	0.92
100	8.94	4.77	3.38	2.70	2.29	2.02	1.83
200	17.89	9.53	6.76	5.39	4.58	4.04	3.67
300	26.83	14.30	10.14	8.09	6.86	6.06	5.50
400	35.77	19.06	13.53	10.78	9.15	8.08	7.33
500	44.72	23.83	16.91	13.48	11.44	10.10	9.17
600	53.66	28.60	20.29	16.17	13.73	12.12	11.00
700	62.61	33.36	23.67	18.87	16.02	14.15	12.83
800	71.55	38.13	27.05	21.56	18.31	16.17	14.66
900	80.49	42.89	30.43	24.26	20.59	18.19	16.50
1000	89.44	47.66	33.82	26.95	22.88	20.21	18.33
2000	178.87	95.32	67.63	53.91	45.77	40.42	36.66
3000	268.31	142.98	101.45	80.86	68.65	60.62	54.99
4000	357.75	190.64	135.26	107.81	91.53	80.83	73.32
5000	447.18	238.31	169.08	134.77	114.42	101.04	91.65
6000	536.62	285.97	202.90	161.72	137.30	121.25	109.98
7000	626.05	333.63	236.71	188.67	160.18	141.46	128.31
8000	715.49	381.29	270.53	215.63	183.06	161.67	146.64
9000	804.93	428.95	304.35	242.58	205.95	181.87	164.97
10000	894.36	476.61	338.16	269.54	228.83	202.08	183.30
11000	983.80	524.27	371.98	296.49	251.71	222.29	201.63
12000	1073.24	571.93	405.79	323.44	274.60	242.50	219.96
13000	1162.67	619.59	439.61	350.40	297.48	262.71	238.29
14000	1252.11	667.25	473.43	377.35	320.36	282.91	256.62
15000	1341.54	714.92	507.24	404.30	343.25	303.12	274.95
16000	1430.98	762.58	541.06	431.26	366.13	323.33	293.28
17000	1520.42	810.24	574.88	458.21	389.01	343.54	311.61
18000	1609.85	857.90	608.69	485.16	411.90	363.75	329.94
19000	1699.29	905.56	642.51	512.12	434.78	383.96	348.27
20000	1788.73	953.22	676.32	539.07	457.66	404.16	366.60
21000	1878.16	1000.88	710.14	566.02	480.55	424.37	384.93
22000	1967.60	1048.54	743.96	592.98	503.43	444.58	403.26
23000	2057.04	1096.20	777.77	619.93	526.31	464.79	421.59
24000	2146.47	1143.86	811.59	646.88	549.19	485.00	439.92
25000	2235.91	1191.53	845.41	673.84	572.08	505.21	458.25
26000	2325.34	1239.19	879.22	700.79	594.96	525.41	476.58
27000	2414.78	1286.85	913.04	727.75	617.84	545.62	494.91
28000	2504.22	1334.51	946.85	754.70	640.73	565.83	513.24
29000	2593.65	1382.17	980.67	781.65	663.61	586.04	531.57
30000	2683.09	1429.83	1014.49	808.61	686.49	606.25	549.90
35000	3130.27	1668.14	1183.57	943.37	800.91	707.29	641.55
40000	3577.45	1906.44	1352.65	1078.14	915.32	808.33	733.20
45000	4024.63	2144.75	1521.73	1212.91	1029.74	909.37	824.86
50000	4471.82	2383.05	1690.81	1347.68	1144.16	1010.41	916.51
55000	4919.00	2621.36	1859.89	1482.44	1258.57	1111.45	1008.16
60000	5366.18	2859.66	2028.97	1617.21	1372.99	1212.49	1099.81
65000	5813.36	3097.97	2198.06	1751.98	1487.40	1313.53	1191.46
70000	6260.54	3336.27	2367.14	1886.75	1601.82	1414.57	1283.11
75000	6707.72	3574.58	2536.22	2021.52	1716.23	1515.62	1374.76
80000	7154.90	3812.88	2705.30	2156.28	1830.65	1616.66	1466.41
85000	7602.09	4051.19	2874.38	2291.05	1945.06	1717.70	1558.06
90000	8049.27	4289.49	3043.46	2425.82	2059.48	1818.74	1649.71
95000	8496.45	4527.80	3212.54	2560.59	2173.90	1919.78	1741.36
100000	8943.63	4766.10	3381.62	2695.35	2288.31	2020.82	1833.01
200000	17887.26	9532.21	6763.25	5390.71	4576.62	4041.64	3666.02
300000	26830.89	14298.31	10144.87	8086.06	6864.93	6062.46	5499.04
400000	35774.52	19064.41	13526.49	10781.42	9153.24	8083.28	7332.05
500000	44718.15	23830.52	16908.12	13476.77	11441.55	10104.10	9165.06
1000000	89436.30	47661.03	33816.24	26953.54	22883.11	20208.21	18330.12

Amortization Amount	8 Years	9 Years	10 Years	15 Years	20 Years	25 Years	30 Years
25	0.42	0.40	0.38	0.32	0.30	0.29	0.28
50	0.85	0.79	0.75	0.64	0.59	0.57	0.56
100	1.69	1.59	1.51	1.28	1.19	1.15	1.13
200	3.39	3.18	3.02	2.56	2.38	2.29	2.25
300	5.08	4.77	4.52	3.85	3.57	3.44	3.38
400	6.78	6.36	6.03	5.13	4.76	4.59	4.50
500	8.47	7.95	7.54	6.41	5.95	5.73	5.63
600	10.17	9.54	9.05	7.69	7.14	6.88	6.76
700	11.86	11.13	10.56	8.97	8.33	8.03	7.88
800	13.56	12.72	12.06	10.26	9.52	9.18	9.01
900	15.25	14.31	13.57	11.54	10.71	10.32	10.13
1000	16.95	15.90	15.08	12.82	11.90	11.47	11.26
2000	33.90	31.80	30.16	25.64	23.79	22.94	22.52
3000	50.85	47.70	45.24	38.46	35.69	34.41	33.78
4000	67.80	63.60	60.32	51.28	47.59	45.88	45.04
5000	84.75	79.50	75.41	64.10	59.48	57.35	56.30
6000	101.70	95.40	90.49	76.92	71.38	68.82	67.56
7000	118.65	111.30	105.57	89.74	83.28	80.29	78.82
8000	135.60	127.20	120.65	102.56	95.18	91.76	90.08
9000	152.54	143.10	135.73	115.38	107.07	103.23	101.35
10000	169.49	159.00	150.81	128.20	118.97	114.70	112.61
11000	186.44	174.90	165.89	141.02	130.87	126.17	123.87
12000	203.39	190.80	180.97	153.84	142.76	137.64	135.13
13000	220.34	206.70	196.05	166.66	154.66	149.11	146.39
14000	237.29	222.60	211.13	179.48	166.56	160.58	157.65
15000	254.24	238.50	226.22	192.30	178.45	172.05	168.91
16000	271.19	254.40	241.30	205.12	190.35	183.52	180.17
17000	288.14	270.29	256.38	217.94	202.25	194.99	191.43
18000	305.09	286.19	271.46	230.76	214.14	206.46	202.69
19000	322.04	302.09	286.54	243.58	226.04	217.92	213.95
20000	338.99	317.99	301.62	256.40	237.94	229.39	225.21
21000	355.94	333.89	316.70	269.21	249.83	240.86	236.47
22000	372.89	349.79	331.78	282.03	261.73	252.33	247.73
23000	389.84	365.69	346.86	294.85	273.63	263.80	258.99
24000	406.79	381.59	361.94	307.67	285.53	275.27	270.25
25000	423.74	397.49	377.03	320.49	297.42	286.74	281.51
26000	440.69	413.39	392.11	333.31	309.32	298.21	292.77
27000	457.63	429.29	407.19	346.13	321.22	309.68	304.04
28000	474.58	445.19	422.27	358.95	333.11	321.15	315.30
29000	491.53	461.09	437.35	371.77	345.01	332.62	326.56
30000	508.48	476.99	452.43	384.59	356.91	344.09	337.82
35000	593.23	556.49	527.84	448.69	416.39	401.44	394.12
40000	677.98	635.99	603.24	512.79	475.88	458.79	450.42
45000	762.72	715.49	678.65	576.89	535.36	516.14	506.73
50000	847.47	794.99	754.05	640.99	594.84	573.49	563.03
55000	932.22	874.48	829.46	705.09	654.33	630.84	619.33
60000	1016.97	953.98	904.86	769.19	713.81	688.18	675.63
65000	1101.71	1033.48	980.27	833.28	773.30	745.53	731.94
70000	1186.46	1112.98	1055.67	897.38	832.78	802.88	788.24
75000	1271.21	1192.48	1131.08	961.48	892.27	860.23	844.54
80000	1355.95	1271.98	1206.48	1025.58	951.75	917.58	900.85
85000	1440.70	1351.47	1281.89	1089.68	1011.24	974.93	957.15
90000	1525.45	1430.97	1357.29	1153.78	1070.72	1032.28	1013.45
95000	1610.20	1510.47	1432.70	1217.88	1130.20	1089.62	1069.75
100000	1694.94	1589.97	1508.10	1281.98	1189.69	1146.97	1126.06
200000	3389.89	3179.94	3016.21	2563.95	2379.38	2293.95	2252.11
300000	5084.83	4769.91	4524.31	3845.93	3569.07	3440.92	3378.17
400000	6779.77	6359.88	6032.41	5127.90	4758.76	4587.89	4504.23
500000	8474.72	7949.85	7540.52	6409.88	5948.45	5734.87	5630.28
1000000	16949.43	15899.70	15081.03	12819.75	11896.89	11469.74	11260.57

13.75%

Amortization Amount	1 Year	2 Years	3 Years	4 Years	5 Years	6 Years	7 Years
25	2.24	1.19	0.85	0.68	0.57	0.51	0.46
50	4.47	2.39	1.69	1.35	1.15	1.01	0.92
100	8.95	4.77	3.39	2.70	2.29	2.03	1.84
200	17.90	9.54	6.77	5.40	4.59	4.05	3.68
300	26.85	14.32	10.16	8.10	6.88	6.08	5.52
400	35.80	19.09	13.55	10.80	9.18	8.11	7.36
500	44.75	23.86	16.94	13.51	11.47	10.14	9.20
600	53.70	28.63	20.32	16.21	13.77	12.16	11.04
700	62.64	33.40	23.71	18.91	16.06	14.19	12.88
800	71.59	38.17	27.10	21.61	18.36	16.22	14.72
900	80.54	42.95	30.49	24.31	20.65	18.24	16.56
1000	89.49	47.72	33.87	27.01	22.94	20.27	18.39
2000	178.98	95.43	67.75	54.02	45.89	40.54	36.79
3000	268.48	143.15	101.62	81.04	68.83	60.81	55.18
4000	357.97	190.87	135.49	108.05	91.78	81.08	73.58
5000	447.46	238.58	169.37	135.06	114.72	101.35	91.97
6000	536.95	286.30	203.24	162.07	137.66	121.63	110.37
7000	626.44	334.02	237.11	189.09	160.61	141.90	128.76
8000	715.93	381.73	270.99	216.10	183.55	162.17	147.16
9000	805.43	429.45	304.86	243.11	206.50	182.44	165.55
10000	894.92	477.17	338.73	270.12	229.44	202.71	183.95
11000	984.41	524.88	372.61	297.14	252.38	222.98	202.34
12000	1073.90	572.60	406.48	324.15	275.33	243.25	220.74
13000	1163.39	620.32	440.35	351.16	298.27	263.52	239.13
14000	1252.89	668.03	474.23	378.17	321.21	283.79	257.53
15000	1342.38	715.75	508.10	405.19	344.16	304.06	275.92
16000	1431.87	763.47	541.97	432.20	367.10	324.33	294.32
17000	1521.36	811.18	575.85	459.21	390.05	344.61	312.71
18000	1610.85	858.90	609.72	486.22	412.99	364.88	331.11
19000	1700.35	906.62	643.59	513.24	435.93	385.15	349.50
20000	1789.84	954.33	677.47	540.25	458.88	405.42	367.90
21000	1879.33	1002.05	711.34	567.26	481.82	425.69	386.29
22000	1968.82	1049.77	745.21	594.27	504.77	445.96	404.68
23000	2058.31	1097.48	779.09	621.29	527.71	466.23	423.08
24000	2147.80	1145.20	812.96	648.30	550.65	486.50	441.47
25000	2237.30	1192.92	846.83	675.31	573.60	506.77	459.87
26000	2326.79	1240.63	880.71	702.32	596.54	527.04	478.26
27000	2416.28	1288.35	914.58	729.34	619.49	547.31	496.66
28000	2505.77	1336.07	948.45	756.35	642.43	567.59	515.05
29000	2595.26	1383.78	982.33	783.36	665.37	587.86	533.45
30000	2684.76	1431.50	1016.20	810.37	688.32	608.13	551.84
35000	3132.21	1670.08	1185.57	945.44	803.04	709.48	643.82
40000	3579.67	1908.67	1354.93	1080.50	917.76	810.84	735.79
45000	4027.13	2147.25	1524.30	1215.56	1032.48	912.19	827.76
50000	4474.59	2385.83	1693.67	1350.62	1147.20	1013.55	919.74
55000	4922.05	2624.42	1863.03	1485.68	1261.91	1114.90	1011.71
60000	5369.51	2863.00	2032.40	1620.75	1376.63	1216.26	1103.69
65000	5816.97	3101.59	2201.77	1755.81	1491.35	1317.61	1195.66
70000	6264.43	3340.17	2371.14	1890.87	1606.07	1418.96	1287.63
75000	6711.89	3578.75	2540.50	2025.93	1720.79	1520.32	1379.61
80000	7159.35	3817.34	2709.87	2161.00	1835.51	1621.67	1471.58
85000	7606.81	4055.92	2879.24	2296.06	1950.23	1723.03	1563.55
90000	8054.27	4294.50	3048.60	2431.12	2064.95	1824.38	1655.53
95000	8501.73	4533.09	3217.97	2566.18	2179.67	1925.74	1747.50
100000	8949.19	4771.67	3387.34	2701.24	2294.39	2027.09	1839.48
200000	17898.37	9543.34	6774.67	5402.49	4588.78	4054.18	3678.95
300000	26847.56	14315.01	10162.01	8103.73	6883.17	6081.28	5518.43
400000	35796.74	19086.68	13549.34	10804.98	9177.56	8108.37	7357.90
500000	44745.93	23858.35	16936.68	13506.22	11471.95	10135.46	9197.38
1000000	89491.85	47716.70	33873.36	27012.45	22943.91	20270.92	18394.76

Amortization Amount	8 Years	9 Years	10 Years	15 Years	20 Years	25 Years	30 Years
25	0.43	0.40	0.38	0.32	0.30	0.29	0.28
50	0.85	0.80	0.76	0.64	0.60	0.58	0.57
100	1.70	1.60	1.52	1.29	1.20	1.16	1.14
200	3.40	3.19	3.03	2.58	2.40	2.31	2.27
300	5.10	4.79	4.55	3.87	3.59	3.47	3.41
400	6.81	6.39	6.06	5.16	4.79	4.62	4.54
500	8.51	7.98	7.58	6.45	5.99	5.78	5.68
600	10.21	9.58	9.09	7.74	7.19	6.94	6.81
700	11.91	11.18	10.61	9.03	8.39	8.09	7.95
800	13.61	12.77	12.12	10.32	9.59	9.25	9.08
900	15.31	14.37	13.64	11.61	10.78	10.40	10.22
1000	17.02	15.97	15.15	12.90	11.98	11.56	11.35
2000	34.03	31.94	30.30	25.80	23.96	23.12	22.71
3000	51.05	47.90	45.45	38.69	35.95	34.68	34.06
4000	68.06	63.87	60.60	51.59	47.93	46.24	45.41
5000	85.08	79.84	75.76	64.49	59.91	57.80	56.77
6000	102.10	95.81	90.91	77.39	71.89	69.36	68.12
7000	119.11	111.78	106.06	90.29	83.87	80.91	79.47
8000	136.13	127.74	121.21	103.18	95.85	92.47	90.83
9000	153.14	143.71	136.36	116.08	107.84	104.03	102.18
10000	170.16	159.68	151.51	128.98	119.82	115.59	113.53
11000	187.18	175.65	166.66	141.88	131.80	127.15	124.89
12000	204.19	191.62	181.81	154.78	143.78	138.71	136.24
13000	221.21	207.59	196.97	167.68	155.76	150.27	147.59
14000	238.22	223.55	212.12	180.57	167.74	161.83	158.95
15000	255.24	239.52	227.27	193.47	179.73	173.39	170.30
16000	272.26	255.49	242.42	206.37	191.71	184.95	181.65
17000	289.27	271.46	257.57	219.27	203.69	196.51	193.01
18000	306.29	287.43	272.72	232.17	215.67	208.07	204.36
19000	323.30	303.39	287.87	245.06	227.65	219.63	215.71
20000	340.32	319.36	303.02	257.96	239.63	231.19	227.07
21000	357.34	335.33	318.18	270.86	251.62	242.74	238.42
22000	374.35	351.30	333.33	283.76	263.60	254.30	249.78
23000	391.37	367.27	348.48	296.66	275.58	265.86	261.13
24000	408.38	383.23	363.63	309.55	287.56	277.42	272.48
25000	425.40	399.20	378.78	322.45	299.54	288.98	283.84
26000	442.41	415.17	393.93	335.35	311.52	300.54	295.19
27000	459.43	431.14	409.08	348.25	323.51	312.10	306.54
28000	476.45	447.11	424.23	361.15	335.49	323.66	317.90
29000	493.46	463.07	439.39	374.05	347.47	335.22	329.25
30000	510.48	479.04	454.54	386.94	359.45	346.78	340.60
35000	595.56	558.88	530.29	451.43	419.36	404.57	397.37
40000	680.64	638.72	606.05	515.92	479.27	462.37	454.14
45000	765.72	718.56	681.81	580.42	539.18	520.17	510.90
50000	850.80	798.40	757.56	644.91	599.08	577.96	567.67
55000	935.88	878.24	833.32	709.40	658.99	635.76	624.44
60000	1020.96	958.09	909.07	773.89	718.90	693.56	681.20
65000	1106.04	1037.93	984.83	838.38	778.81	751.35	737.97
70000	1191.12	1117.77	1060.59	902.87	838.72	809.15	794.74
75000	1276.20	1197.61	1136.34	967.36	898.63	866.95	851.51
80000	1361.28	1277.45	1212.10	1031.85	958.54	924.74	908.27
85000	1446.36	1357.29	1287.85	1096.34	1018.44	982.54	965.04
90000	1531.44	1437.13	1363.61	1160.83	1078.35	1040.34	1021.81
95000	1616.52	1516.97	1439.37	1225.32	1138.26	1098.13	1078.57
100000	1701.60	1596.81	1515.12	1289.81	1198.17	1155.93	1135.34
200000	3403.19	3193.62	3030.25	2579.62	2396.34	2311.86	2270.68
300000	5104.79	4790.43	4545.37	3869.43	3594.51	3467.78	3406.02
400000	6806.38	6387.24	6060.49	5159.24	4792.68	4623.71	4541.37
500000	8507.98	7984.04	7575.62	6449.06	5990.85	5779.64	5676.71
1000000	17015.96	15968.09	15151.23	12898.11	11981.69	11559.28	11353.42

13.875%

MONTHLY PAYMENT
NECESSARY TO AMORTIZE A LOAN

Amortization Amount	1 Year	2 Years	3 Years	4 Years	5 Years	6 Years	7 Years
25	2.24	1.19	0.85	0.68	0.58	0.51	0.46
50	4.48	2.39	1.70	1.35	1.15	1.02	0.92
100	8.95	4.78	3.39	2.71	2.30	2.03	1.85
200	17.91	9.55	6.79	5.41	4.60	4.07	3.69
300	26.86	14.33	10.18	8.12	6.90	6.10	5.54
400	35.82	19.11	13.57	10.83	9.20	8.13	7.38
500	44.77	23.89	16.97	13.54	11.50	10.17	9.23
600	53.73	28.66	20.36	16.24	13.80	12.20	11.08
700	62.68	33.44	23.75	18.95	16.10	14.23	12.92
800	71.64	38.22	27.14	21.66	18.40	16.27	14.77
900	80.59	43.00	30.54	24.36	20.70	18.30	16.61
1000	89.55	47.77	33.93	27.07	23.00	20.33	18.46
2000	179.09	95.54	67.86	54.14	46.01	40.67	36.92
3000	268.64	143.32	101.79	81.21	69.01	61.00	55.38
4000	358.19	191.09	135.72	108.29	92.02	81.33	73.84
5000	447.74	238.86	169.65	135.36	115.02	101.67	92.30
6000	537.28	286.63	203.58	162.43	138.03	122.00	110.76
7000	626.83	334.41	237.51	189.50	161.03	142.34	129.22
8000	716.38	382.18	271.44	216.57	184.04	162.67	147.68
9000	805.93	429.95	305.37	243.64	207.04	183.00	166.14
10000	895.47	477.72	339.31	270.71	230.05	203.34	184.59
11000	985.02	525.50	373.24	297.79	253.05	223.67	203.05
12000	1074.57	573.27	407.17	324.86	276.06	244.00	221.51
13000	1164.12	621.04	441.10	351.93	299.06	264.34	239.97
14000	1253.66	668.81	475.03	379.00	322.07	284.67	258.43
15000	1343.21	716.59	508.96	406.07	345.07	305.01	276.89
16000	1432.76	764.36	542.89	433.14	368.08	325.34	295.35
17000	1522.31	812.13	576.82	460.21	391.08	345.67	313.81
18000	1611.85	859.90	610.75	487.29	414.09	366.01	332.27
19000	1701.40	907.67	644.68	514.36	437.09	386.34	350.73
20000	1790.95	955.45	678.61	541.43	460.10	406.67	369.19
21000	1880.50	1003.22	712.54	568.50	483.10	427.01	387.65
22000	1970.04	1050.99	746.47	595.57	506.10	447.34	406.11
23000	2059.59	1098.76	780.40	622.64	529.11	467.68	424.57
24000	2149.14	1146.54	814.33	649.71	552.11	488.01	443.03
25000	2238.68	1194.31	848.26	676.79	575.12	508.34	461.49
26000	2328.23	1242.08	882.19	703.86	598.12	528.68	479.95
27000	2417.78	1289.85	916.12	730.93	621.13	549.01	498.41
28000	2507.33	1337.63	950.05	758.00	644.13	569.34	516.87
29000	2596.87	1385.40	983.98	785.07	667.14	589.68	535.33
30000	2686.42	1433.17	1017.92	812.14	690.14	610.01	553.78
35000	3134.16	1672.03	1187.57	947.50	805.17	711.68	646.08
40000	3581.90	1910.89	1357.22	1082.86	920.19	813.35	738.38
45000	4029.63	2149.76	1526.87	1218.21	1035.21	915.02	830.68
50000	4477.37	2388.62	1696.53	1353.57	1150.24	1016.69	922.97
55000	4925.11	2627.48	1866.18	1488.93	1265.26	1118.35	1015.27
60000	5372.84	2866.34	2035.83	1624.28	1380.29	1220.02	1107.57
65000	5820.58	3105.20	2205.48	1759.64	1495.31	1321.69	1199.87
70000	6268.32	3344.07	2375.14	1895.00	1610.33	1423.36	1292.16
75000	6716.05	3582.93	2544.79	2030.36	1725.36	1525.03	1384.46
80000	7163.79	3821.79	2714.44	2165.71	1840.38	1626.70	1476.76
85000	7611.53	4060.65	2884.09	2301.07	1955.40	1728.37	1569.06
90000	8059.27	4299.51	3053.75	2436.43	2070.43	1830.03	1661.35
95000	8507.00	4538.37	3223.40	2571.78	2185.45	1931.70	1753.65
100000	8954.74	4777.24	3393.05	2707.14	2300.48	2033.37	1845.95
200000	17909.48	9554.47	6786.10	5414.28	4600.95	4066.74	3691.90
300000	26864.22	14331.71	10179.15	8121.42	6901.43	6100.12	5537.85
400000	35818.96	19108.95	13572.21	10828.56	9201.91	8133.49	7383.79
500000	44773.70	23886.18	16965.26	13535.70	11502.38	10166.86	9229.74
1000000	89547.39	47772.37	33930.52	27071.40	23004.76	20333.72	18459.49

160

Amortization Amount	8 Years	9 Years	10 Years	15 Years	20 Years	25 Years	30 Years
25	0.43	0.40	0.38	0.32	0.30	0.29	0.29
50	0.85	0.80	0.76	0.65	0.60	0.58	0.57
100	1.71	1.60	1.52	1.30	1.21	1.16	1.14
200	3.42	3.21	3.04	2.60	2.41	2.33	2.29
300	5.12	4.81	4.57	3.89	3.62	3.49	3.43
400	6.83	6.41	6.09	5.19	4.83	4.66	4.58
500	8.54	8.02	7.61	6.49	6.03	5.82	5.72
600	10.25	9.62	9.13	7.79	7.24	6.99	6.87
700	11.96	11.23	10.66	9.08	8.45	8.15	8.01
800	13.67	12.83	12.18	10.38	9.65	9.32	9.16
900	15.37	14.43	13.70	11.68	10.86	10.48	10.30
1000	17.08	16.04	15.22	12.98	12.07	11.65	11.45
2000	34.17	32.07	30.44	25.95	24.13	23.30	22.89
3000	51.25	48.11	45.66	38.93	36.20	34.95	34.34
4000	68.33	64.15	60.89	51.91	48.27	46.60	45.79
5000	85.41	80.18	76.11	64.88	60.33	58.24	57.23
6000	102.50	96.22	91.33	77.86	72.40	69.89	68.68
7000	119.58	112.26	106.55	90.84	84.47	81.54	80.12
8000	136.66	128.29	121.77	103.81	96.53	93.19	91.57
9000	153.74	144.33	136.99	116.79	108.60	104.84	103.02
10000	170.83	160.37	152.22	129.77	120.67	116.49	114.46
11000	187.91	176.40	167.44	142.74	132.73	128.14	125.91
12000	204.99	192.44	182.66	155.72	144.80	139.79	137.36
13000	222.07	208.48	197.88	168.70	156.87	151.44	148.80
14000	239.16	224.51	213.10	181.67	168.93	163.09	160.25
15000	256.24	240.55	228.32	194.65	181.00	174.73	171.70
16000	273.32	256.59	243.54	207.63	193.07	186.38	183.14
17000	290.40	272.62	258.77	220.60	205.13	198.03	194.59
18000	307.49	288.66	273.99	233.58	217.20	209.68	206.03
19000	324.57	304.70	289.21	246.56	229.27	221.33	217.48
20000	341.65	320.73	304.43	259.53	241.33	232.98	228.93
21000	358.73	336.77	319.65	272.51	253.40	244.63	240.37
22000	375.82	352.81	334.87	285.49	265.47	256.28	251.82
23000	392.90	368.84	350.10	298.46	277.53	267.93	263.27
24000	409.98	384.88	365.32	311.44	289.60	279.58	274.71
25000	427.06	400.91	380.54	324.42	301.67	291.22	286.16
26000	444.15	416.95	395.76	337.39	313.73	302.87	297.61
27000	461.23	432.99	410.98	350.37	325.80	314.52	309.05
28000	478.31	449.02	426.20	363.35	337.87	326.17	320.50
29000	495.40	465.06	441.43	376.32	349.93	337.82	331.94
30000	512.48	481.10	456.65	389.30	362.00	349.47	343.39
35000	597.89	561.28	532.75	454.18	422.33	407.71	400.62
40000	683.30	641.46	608.86	519.07	482.67	465.96	457.85
45000	768.72	721.65	684.97	583.95	543.00	524.20	515.09
50000	854.13	801.83	761.08	648.83	603.33	582.45	572.32
55000	939.54	882.01	837.19	713.71	663.67	640.69	629.55
60000	1024.96	962.20	913.29	778.60	724.00	698.94	686.78
65000	1110.37	1042.38	989.40	843.48	784.33	757.18	744.01
70000	1195.78	1122.56	1065.51	908.36	844.67	815.43	801.25
75000	1281.19	1202.74	1141.62	973.25	905.00	873.67	858.48
80000	1366.61	1282.93	1217.72	1038.13	965.33	931.92	915.71
85000	1452.02	1363.11	1293.83	1103.01	1025.67	990.16	972.94
90000	1537.43	1443.29	1369.94	1167.90	1086.00	1048.41	1030.17
95000	1622.85	1523.48	1446.05	1232.78	1146.33	1106.65	1087.40
100000	1708.26	1603.66	1522.16	1297.66	1206.67	1164.90	1144.64
200000	3416.52	3207.32	3044.31	2595.33	2413.33	2329.79	2289.27
300000	5124.78	4810.98	4566.47	3892.99	3620.00	3494.69	3433.91
400000	6833.04	6414.64	6088.62	5190.65	4826.66	4659.58	4578.54
500000	8541.30	8018.30	7610.78	6488.31	6033.33	5824.48	5723.18
1000000	17082.59	16036.59	15221.55	12976.63	12066.65	11648.96	11446.36

14%

MONTHLY PAYMENT
NECESSARY TO AMORTIZE A LOAN

Amortization Amount	1 Year	2 Years	3 Years	4 Years	5 Years	6 Years	7 Years
25	2.24	1.20	0.85	0.68	0.58	0.51	0.46
50	4.48	2.39	1.70	1.36	1.15	1.02	0.93
100	8.96	4.78	3.40	2.71	2.31	2.04	1.85
200	17.92	9.57	6.80	5.43	4.61	4.08	3.70
300	26.88	14.35	10.20	8.14	6.92	6.12	5.56
400	35.84	19.13	13.60	10.85	9.23	8.16	7.41
500	44.80	23.91	16.99	13.57	11.53	10.20	9.26
600	53.76	28.70	20.39	16.28	13.84	12.24	11.11
700	62.72	33.48	23.79	18.99	16.15	14.28	12.97
800	71.68	38.26	27.19	21.70	18.45	16.32	14.82
900	80.64	43.05	30.59	24.42	20.76	18.36	16.67
1000	89.60	47.83	33.99	27.13	23.07	20.40	18.52
2000	179.21	95.66	67.98	54.26	46.13	40.79	37.05
3000	268.81	143.48	101.96	81.39	69.20	61.19	55.57
4000	358.41	191.31	135.95	108.52	92.26	81.59	74.10
5000	448.01	239.14	169.94	135.65	115.33	101.98	92.62
6000	537.62	286.97	203.93	162.78	138.39	122.38	111.15
7000	627.22	334.80	237.91	189.91	161.46	142.78	129.67
8000	716.82	382.62	271.90	217.04	184.53	163.17	148.19
9000	806.43	430.45	305.89	244.17	207.59	183.57	166.72
10000	896.03	478.28	339.88	271.30	230.66	203.97	185.24
11000	985.63	526.11	373.86	298.43	253.72	224.36	203.77
12000	1075.24	573.94	407.85	325.56	276.79	244.76	222.29
13000	1164.84	621.76	441.84	352.70	299.85	265.16	240.82
14000	1254.44	669.59	475.83	379.83	322.92	285.55	259.34
15000	1344.04	717.42	509.82	406.96	345.99	305.95	277.86
16000	1433.65	765.25	543.80	434.09	369.05	326.35	296.39
17000	1523.25	813.08	577.79	461.22	392.12	346.74	314.91
18000	1612.85	860.90	611.78	488.35	415.18	367.14	333.44
19000	1702.46	908.73	645.77	515.48	438.25	387.54	351.96
20000	1792.06	956.56	679.75	542.61	461.31	407.93	370.49
21000	1881.66	1004.39	713.74	569.74	484.38	428.33	389.01
22000	1971.26	1052.22	747.73	596.87	507.45	448.72	407.53
23000	2060.87	1100.05	781.72	624.00	530.51	469.12	426.06
24000	2150.47	1147.87	815.70	651.13	553.58	489.52	444.58
25000	2240.07	1195.70	849.69	678.26	576.64	509.91	463.11
26000	2329.68	1243.53	883.68	705.39	599.71	530.31	481.63
27000	2419.28	1291.36	917.67	732.52	622.77	550.71	500.16
28000	2508.88	1339.19	951.66	759.65	645.84	571.10	518.68
29000	2598.48	1387.01	985.64	786.78	668.90	591.50	537.20
30000	2688.09	1434.84	1019.63	813.91	691.97	611.90	555.73
35000	3136.10	1673.98	1189.57	949.56	807.30	713.88	648.35
40000	3584.12	1913.12	1359.51	1085.22	922.63	815.86	740.97
45000	4032.13	2152.26	1529.45	1220.87	1037.96	917.85	833.59
50000	4480.15	2391.40	1699.38	1356.52	1153.28	1019.83	926.22
55000	4928.16	2630.54	1869.32	1492.17	1268.61	1121.81	1018.84
60000	5376.18	2869.68	2039.26	1627.82	1383.94	1223.80	1111.46
65000	5824.19	3108.82	2209.20	1763.48	1499.27	1325.78	1204.08
70000	6272.20	3347.96	2379.14	1899.13	1614.60	1427.76	1296.70
75000	6720.22	3587.10	2549.08	2034.78	1729.93	1529.74	1389.32
80000	7168.23	3826.24	2719.02	2170.43	1845.25	1631.73	1481.94
85000	7616.25	4065.38	2888.95	2306.08	1960.58	1733.71	1574.57
90000	8064.26	4304.52	3058.89	2441.74	2075.91	1835.69	1667.19
95000	8512.28	4543.66	3228.83	2577.39	2191.24	1937.68	1759.81
100000	8960.29	4782.81	3398.77	2713.04	2306.57	2039.66	1852.43
200000	17920.58	9565.61	6797.54	5426.08	4613.14	4079.32	3704.86
300000	26880.88	14348.42	10196.31	8139.12	6919.71	6118.98	5557.29
400000	35841.17	19131.22	13595.08	10852.16	9226.27	8158.64	7409.72
500000	44801.46	23914.03	16993.85	13565.20	11532.84	10198.30	9262.15
1000000	89602.92	47828.05	33987.70	27130.40	23065.68	20396.59	18524.30

Amortization Amount	8 Years	9 Years	10 Years	15 Years	20 Years	25 Years	30 Years
25	0.43	0.40	0.38	0.33	0.30	0.29	0.29
50	0.86	0.81	0.76	0.65	0.61	0.59	0.58
100	1.71	1.61	1.53	1.31	1.22	1.17	1.15
200	3.43	3.22	3.06	2.61	2.43	2.35	2.31
300	5.14	4.83	4.59	3.92	3.65	3.52	3.46
400	6.86	6.44	6.12	5.22	4.86	4.70	4.62
500	8.57	8.05	7.65	6.53	6.08	5.87	5.77
600	10.29	9.66	9.18	7.83	7.29	7.04	6.92
700	12.00	11.27	10.70	9.14	8.51	8.22	8.08
800	13.72	12.88	12.23	10.44	9.72	9.39	9.23
900	15.43	14.49	13.76	11.75	10.94	10.56	10.39
1000	17.15	16.11	15.29	13.06	12.15	11.74	11.54
2000	34.30	32.21	30.58	26.11	24.30	23.48	23.08
3000	51.45	48.32	45.88	39.17	36.46	35.22	34.62
4000	68.60	64.42	61.17	52.22	48.61	46.96	46.16
5000	85.75	80.53	76.46	65.28	60.76	58.69	57.70
6000	102.90	96.63	91.75	78.33	72.91	70.43	69.24
7000	120.05	112.74	107.04	91.39	85.06	82.17	80.78
8000	137.19	128.84	122.34	104.44	97.21	93.91	92.32
9000	154.34	144.95	137.63	117.50	109.37	105.65	103.85
10000	171.49	161.05	152.92	130.55	121.52	117.39	115.39
11000	188.64	177.16	168.21	143.61	133.67	129.13	126.93
12000	205.79	193.26	183.50	156.66	145.82	140.87	138.47
13000	222.94	209.37	198.80	169.72	157.97	152.60	150.01
14000	240.09	225.47	214.09	182.77	170.12	164.34	161.55
15000	257.24	241.58	229.38	195.83	182.28	176.08	173.09
16000	274.39	257.68	244.67	208.88	194.43	187.82	184.63
17000	291.54	273.79	259.96	221.94	206.58	199.56	196.17
18000	308.69	289.89	275.26	235.00	218.73	211.30	207.71
19000	325.84	306.00	290.55	248.05	230.88	223.04	219.25
20000	342.99	322.10	305.84	261.11	243.04	234.78	230.79
21000	360.14	338.21	321.13	274.16	255.19	246.51	242.33
22000	377.29	354.31	336.42	287.22	267.34	258.25	253.87
23000	394.43	370.42	351.72	300.27	279.49	269.99	265.41
24000	411.58	386.53	367.01	313.33	291.64	281.73	276.95
25000	428.73	402.63	382.30	326.38	303.79	293.47	288.48
26000	445.88	418.74	397.59	339.44	315.95	305.21	300.02
27000	463.03	434.84	412.88	352.49	328.10	316.95	311.56
28000	480.18	450.95	428.18	365.55	340.25	328.69	323.10
29000	497.33	467.05	443.47	378.60	352.40	340.42	334.64
30000	514.48	483.16	458.78	391.66	364.55	352.16	346.18
35000	600.23	563.68	535.22	456.94	425.31	410.86	403.88
40000	685.97	644.21	611.68	522.21	486.07	469.55	461.58
45000	771.72	724.73	688.14	587.49	546.83	528.24	519.27
50000	857.47	805.26	764.60	652.76	607.59	586.94	576.97
55000	943.21	885.79	841.06	718.04	668.35	645.63	634.67
60000	1028.96	966.31	917.52	783.32	729.11	704.33	692.36
65000	1114.71	1046.84	993.98	848.59	789.86	763.02	750.06
70000	1200.45	1127.36	1070.44	913.87	850.62	821.71	807.76
75000	1286.20	1207.89	1146.90	979.15	911.38	880.41	865.45
80000	1371.95	1288.42	1223.36	1044.42	972.14	939.10	923.15
85000	1457.69	1368.94	1299.82	1109.70	1032.90	997.80	980.85
90000	1543.44	1449.47	1376.28	1174.98	1093.66	1056.49	1038.55
95000	1629.19	1530.00	1452.74	1240.25	1154.42	1115.18	1096.24
100000	1714.93	1610.52	1529.20	1305.53	1215.18	1173.88	1153.94
200000	3429.87	3221.04	3058.40	2611.06	2430.35	2347.75	2307.88
300000	5144.80	4831.56	4587.60	3916.59	3645.53	3521.63	3461.82
400000	6859.73	6442.08	6116.80	5222.12	4860.70	4695.51	4615.76
500000	8574.67	8052.61	7646.00	6527.65	6075.88	5869.38	5769.70
1000000	17149.33	16105.21	15292.00	13055.30	12151.76	11738.76	11539.40

14.125%

Amortization Amount	1 Year	2 Years	3 Years	4 Years	5 Years	6 Years	7 Years
25	2.24	1.20	0.85	0.68	0.58	0.51	0.46
50	4.48	2.39	1.70	1.36	1.16	1.02	0.93
100	8.97	4.79	3.40	2.72	2.31	2.05	1.86
200	17.93	9.58	6.81	5.44	4.63	4.09	3.72
300	26.90	14.37	10.21	8.16	6.94	6.14	5.58
400	35.86	19.15	13.62	10.88	9.25	8.18	7.44
500	44.83	23.94	17.02	13.59	11.56	10.23	9.29
600	53.80	28.73	20.43	16.31	13.88	12.28	11.15
700	62.76	33.52	23.83	19.03	16.19	14.32	13.01
800	71.73	38.31	27.24	21.75	18.50	16.37	14.87
900	80.69	43.10	30.64	24.47	20.81	18.41	16.73
1000	89.66	47.88	34.04	27.19	23.13	20.46	18.59
2000	179.32	95.77	68.09	54.38	46.25	40.92	37.18
3000	268.98	143.65	102.13	81.57	69.38	61.38	55.77
4000	358.63	191.53	136.18	108.76	92.51	81.84	74.36
5000	448.29	239.42	170.22	135.95	115.63	102.30	92.95
6000	537.95	287.30	204.27	163.14	138.76	122.76	111.54
7000	627.61	335.19	238.31	190.33	161.89	143.22	130.12
8000	717.27	383.07	272.36	217.52	185.01	163.68	148.71
9000	806.93	430.95	306.40	244.70	208.14	184.14	167.30
10000	896.58	478.84	340.45	271.89	231.27	204.60	185.89
11000	986.24	526.72	374.49	299.08	254.39	225.05	204.48
12000	1075.90	574.60	408.54	326.27	277.52	245.51	223.07
13000	1165.56	622.49	442.58	353.46	300.65	265.97	241.66
14000	1255.22	670.37	476.63	380.65	323.77	286.43	260.25
15000	1344.88	718.26	510.67	407.84	346.90	306.89	278.84
16000	1434.54	766.14	544.72	435.03	370.03	327.35	297.43
17000	1524.19	814.02	578.76	462.22	393.15	347.81	316.02
18000	1613.85	861.91	612.81	489.41	416.28	368.27	334.61
19000	1703.51	909.79	646.85	516.60	439.41	388.73	353.20
20000	1793.17	957.67	680.90	543.79	462.53	409.19	371.78
21000	1882.83	1005.56	714.94	570.98	485.66	429.65	390.37
22000	1972.49	1053.44	748.99	598.17	508.79	450.11	408.96
23000	2062.14	1101.33	783.03	625.36	531.91	470.57	427.55
24000	2151.80	1149.21	817.08	652.55	555.04	491.03	446.14
25000	2241.46	1197.09	851.12	679.74	578.17	511.49	464.73
26000	2331.12	1244.98	885.17	706.93	601.29	531.95	483.32
27000	2420.78	1292.86	919.21	734.11	624.42	552.41	501.91
28000	2510.44	1340.74	953.26	761.30	647.55	572.87	520.50
29000	2600.10	1388.63	987.30	788.49	670.67	593.33	539.09
30000	2689.75	1436.51	1021.35	815.68	693.80	613.79	557.68
35000	3138.05	1675.93	1191.57	951.63	809.43	716.08	650.62
40000	3586.34	1915.35	1361.80	1087.58	925.07	818.38	743.57
45000	4034.63	2154.77	1532.02	1223.52	1040.70	920.68	836.51
50000	4482.92	2394.19	1702.25	1359.47	1156.33	1022.98	929.46
55000	4931.21	2633.61	1872.47	1495.42	1271.97	1125.27	1022.41
60000	5379.51	2873.02	2042.69	1631.37	1387.60	1227.57	1115.35
65000	5827.80	3112.44	2212.92	1767.31	1503.23	1329.87	1208.30
70000	6276.09	3351.86	2383.14	1903.26	1618.87	1432.17	1301.24
75000	6724.38	3591.28	2553.37	2039.21	1734.50	1534.47	1394.19
80000	7172.68	3830.70	2723.59	2175.16	1850.13	1636.76	1487.14
85000	7620.97	4070.12	2893.82	2311.10	1965.77	1739.06	1580.08
90000	8069.26	4309.54	3064.04	2447.05	2081.40	1841.36	1673.03
95000	8517.55	4548.96	3234.27	2583.00	2197.03	1943.66	1765.98
100000	8965.84	4788.37	3404.49	2718.94	2312.67	2045.95	1858.92
200000	17931.69	9576.75	6808.98	5437.89	4625.33	4091.91	3717.84
300000	26897.53	14365.12	10213.47	8156.83	6938.00	6137.86	5576.76
400000	35863.38	19153.50	13617.96	10875.78	9250.67	8183.82	7435.69
500000	44829.22	23941.87	17022.46	13594.72	11563.33	10229.77	9294.61
1000000	89658.45	47883.75	34044.91	27189.44	23126.67	20459.54	18589.21

MONTHLY PAYMENT
NECESSARY TO AMORTIZE A LOAN **14.125%**

Amortization Amount	8 Years	9 Years	10 Years	15 Years	20 Years	25 Years	30 Years
25	0.43	0.40	0.38	0.33	0.31	0.30	0.29
50	0.86	0.81	0.77	0.66	0.61	0.59	0.58
100	1.72	1.62	1.54	1.31	1.22	1.18	1.16
200	3.44	3.23	3.07	2.63	2.45	2.37	2.33
300	5.16	4.85	4.61	3.94	3.67	3.55	3.49
400	6.89	6.47	6.15	5.25	4.89	4.73	4.65
500	8.61	8.09	7.68	6.57	6.12	5.91	5.82
600	10.33	9.70	9.22	7.88	7.34	7.10	6.98
700	12.05	11.32	10.75	9.19	8.57	8.28	8.14
800	13.77	12.94	12.29	10.51	9.79	9.46	9.31
900	15.49	14.56	13.83	11.82	11.01	10.65	10.47
1000	17.22	16.17	15.36	13.13	12.24	11.83	11.63
2000	34.43	32.35	30.73	26.27	24.47	23.66	23.27
3000	51.65	48.52	46.09	39.40	36.71	35.49	34.90
4000	68.86	64.70	61.45	52.54	48.95	47.31	46.53
5000	86.08	80.87	76.81	65.67	61.19	59.14	58.16
6000	103.30	97.04	92.18	78.80	73.42	70.97	69.80
7000	120.51	113.22	107.54	91.94	85.66	82.80	81.43
8000	137.73	129.39	122.90	105.07	97.90	94.63	93.06
9000	154.95	145.57	138.26	118.21	110.13	106.46	104.69
10000	172.16	161.74	153.63	131.34	122.37	118.29	116.33
11000	189.38	177.91	168.99	144.48	134.61	130.12	127.96
12000	206.59	194.09	184.35	157.61	146.84	141.94	139.59
13000	223.81	210.26	199.71	170.74	159.08	153.77	151.22
14000	241.03	226.44	215.08	183.88	171.32	165.60	162.86
15000	258.24	242.61	230.44	197.01	183.56	177.43	174.49
16000	275.46	258.78	245.80	210.15	195.79	189.26	186.12
17000	292.67	274.96	261.16	223.28	208.03	201.09	197.75
18000	309.89	291.13	276.53	236.41	220.27	212.92	209.39
19000	327.11	307.30	291.89	249.55	232.50	224.75	221.02
20000	344.32	323.48	307.25	262.68	244.74	236.57	232.65
21000	361.54	339.65	322.61	275.82	256.98	248.40	244.28
22000	378.76	355.83	337.98	288.95	269.21	260.23	255.92
23000	395.97	372.00	353.34	302.08	281.45	272.06	267.55
24000	413.19	388.17	368.70	315.22	293.69	283.89	279.18
25000	430.40	404.35	384.06	328.35	305.93	295.72	290.81
26000	447.62	420.52	399.43	341.49	318.16	307.55	302.45
27000	464.84	436.70	414.79	354.62	330.40	319.37	314.08
28000	482.05	452.87	430.15	367.76	342.64	331.20	325.71
29000	499.27	469.04	445.51	380.89	354.87	343.03	337.34
30000	516.49	485.22	460.88	394.02	367.11	354.86	348.98
35000	602.57	566.09	537.69	459.69	428.30	414.00	407.14
40000	688.65	646.96	614.50	525.36	489.48	473.15	465.30
45000	774.73	727.83	691.32	591.04	550.67	532.29	523.46
50000	860.81	808.70	768.13	656.71	611.85	591.43	581.63
55000	946.89	889.57	844.94	722.38	673.04	650.58	639.79
60000	1032.97	970.44	921.75	788.05	734.22	709.72	697.95
65000	1119.05	1051.31	998.57	853.72	795.41	768.87	756.11
70000	1205.13	1132.18	1075.38	919.39	856.59	828.01	814.28
75000	1291.21	1213.05	1152.19	985.06	917.78	887.15	872.44
80000	1377.29	1293.92	1229.01	1050.73	978.96	946.30	930.60
85000	1463.37	1374.79	1305.82	1116.40	1040.15	1005.44	988.76
90000	1549.46	1455.65	1382.63	1182.07	1101.33	1064.58	1046.93
95000	1635.54	1536.52	1459.45	1247.74	1162.52	1123.73	1105.09
100000	1721.62	1617.39	1536.26	1313.41	1223.70	1182.87	1163.25
200000	3443.23	3234.79	3072.52	2626.82	2447.40	2365.74	2326.51
300000	5164.85	4852.18	4608.77	3940.24	3671.11	3548.61	3489.76
400000	6886.47	6469.58	6145.03	5253.65	4894.81	4731.48	4653.01
500000	8608.09	8086.97	7681.29	6567.06	6118.51	5914.35	5816.26
1000000	17216.17	16173.94	15362.58	13134.12	12237.02	11828.70	11632.53

14.25%

Amortization Amount	1 Year	2 Years	3 Years	4 Years	5 Years	6 Years	7 Years
25	2.24	1.20	0.85	0.68	0.58	0.51	0.47
50	4.49	2.40	1.71	1.36	1.16	1.03	0.93
100	8.97	4.79	3.41	2.72	2.32	2.05	1.87
200	17.94	9.59	6.82	5.45	4.64	4.10	3.73
300	26.91	14.38	10.23	8.17	6.96	6.16	5.60
400	35.89	19.18	13.64	10.90	9.28	8.21	7.46
500	44.86	23.97	17.05	13.62	11.59	10.26	9.33
600	53.83	28.76	20.46	16.35	13.91	12.31	11.19
700	62.80	33.56	23.87	19.07	16.23	14.37	13.06
800	71.77	38.35	27.28	21.80	18.55	16.42	14.92
900	80.74	43.15	30.69	24.52	20.87	18.47	16.79
1000	89.71	47.94	34.10	27.25	23.19	20.52	18.65
2000	179.43	95.88	68.20	54.50	46.38	41.05	37.31
3000	269.14	143.82	102.31	81.75	69.56	61.57	55.96
4000	358.86	191.76	136.41	108.99	92.75	82.09	74.62
5000	448.57	239.70	170.51	136.24	115.94	102.61	93.27
6000	538.28	287.64	204.61	163.49	139.13	123.14	111.93
7000	628.00	335.58	238.72	190.74	162.31	143.66	130.58
8000	717.71	383.52	272.82	217.99	185.50	164.18	149.23
9000	807.43	431.46	306.92	245.24	208.69	184.70	167.89
10000	897.14	479.39	341.02	272.49	231.88	205.23	186.54
11000	986.85	527.33	375.12	299.73	255.06	225.75	205.20
12000	1076.57	575.27	409.23	326.98	278.25	246.27	223.85
13000	1166.28	623.21	443.33	354.23	301.44	266.79	242.50
14000	1256.00	671.15	477.43	381.48	324.63	287.32	261.16
15000	1345.71	719.09	511.53	408.73	347.82	307.84	279.81
16000	1435.42	767.03	545.63	435.98	371.00	328.36	298.47
17000	1525.14	814.97	579.74	463.23	394.19	348.88	317.12
18000	1614.85	862.91	613.84	490.47	417.38	369.41	335.78
19000	1704.57	910.85	647.94	517.72	440.57	389.93	354.43
20000	1794.28	958.79	682.04	544.97	463.75	410.45	373.08
21000	1883.99	1006.73	716.15	572.22	486.94	430.97	391.74
22000	1973.71	1054.67	750.25	599.47	510.13	451.50	410.39
23000	2063.42	1102.61	784.35	626.72	533.32	472.02	429.05
24000	2153.14	1150.55	818.45	653.96	556.50	492.54	447.70
25000	2242.85	1198.49	852.55	681.21	579.69	513.06	466.36
26000	2332.56	1246.43	886.66	708.46	602.88	533.59	485.01
27000	2422.28	1294.37	920.76	735.71	626.07	554.11	503.66
28000	2511.99	1342.30	954.86	762.96	649.26	574.63	522.32
29000	2601.70	1390.24	988.96	790.21	672.44	595.15	540.97
30000	2691.42	1438.18	1023.06	817.46	695.63	615.68	559.63
35000	3139.99	1677.88	1193.58	953.70	811.57	718.29	652.90
40000	3588.56	1917.58	1364.09	1089.94	927.51	820.90	746.17
45000	4037.13	2157.28	1534.60	1226.18	1043.45	923.52	839.44
50000	4485.70	2396.97	1705.11	1362.43	1159.39	1026.13	932.71
55000	4934.27	2636.67	1875.62	1498.67	1275.32	1128.74	1025.98
60000	5382.84	2876.37	2046.13	1634.91	1391.26	1231.35	1119.25
65000	5831.41	3116.06	2216.64	1771.15	1507.20	1333.97	1212.52
70000	6279.98	3355.76	2387.15	1907.40	1623.14	1436.58	1305.79
75000	6728.55	3595.46	2557.66	2043.64	1739.08	1539.19	1399.07
80000	7177.12	3835.16	2728.17	2179.88	1855.02	1641.80	1492.34
85000	7625.69	4074.85	2898.68	2316.13	1970.96	1744.42	1585.61
90000	8074.26	4314.55	3069.19	2452.37	2086.89	1847.03	1678.88
95000	8522.83	4554.25	3239.70	2588.61	2202.83	1949.64	1772.15
100000	8971.40	4793.95	3410.21	2724.85	2318.77	2052.26	1865.42
200000	17942.79	9587.89	6820.43	5449.71	4637.54	4104.51	3730.84
300000	26914.19	14381.84	10230.64	8174.56	6956.31	6156.77	5596.26
400000	35885.59	19175.78	13640.86	10899.41	9275.08	8209.02	7461.68
500000	44856.98	23969.73	17051.07	13624.27	11593.85	10261.28	9327.11
1000000	89713.96	47939.45	34102.15	27248.53	23187.71	20522.56	18654.21

Amortization Amount	8 Years	9 Years	10 Years	15 Years	20 Years	25 Years	30 Years
25	0.43	0.41	0.39	0.33	0.31	0.30	0.29
50	0.86	0.81	0.77	0.66	0.62	0.60	0.59
100	1.73	1.62	1.54	1.32	1.23	1.19	1.17
200	3.46	3.25	3.09	2.64	2.46	2.38	2.35
300	5.18	4.87	4.63	3.96	3.70	3.58	3.52
400	6.91	6.50	6.17	5.29	4.93	4.77	4.69
500	8.64	8.12	7.72	6.61	6.16	5.96	5.86
600	10.37	9.75	9.26	7.93	7.39	7.15	7.04
700	12.10	11.37	10.80	9.25	8.63	8.34	8.21
800	13.83	12.99	12.35	10.57	9.86	9.53	9.38
900	15.55	14.62	13.89	11.89	11.09	10.73	10.55
1000	17.28	16.24	15.43	13.21	12.32	11.92	11.73
2000	34.57	32.49	30.87	26.43	24.64	23.84	23.45
3000	51.85	48.73	46.30	39.64	36.97	35.76	35.18
4000	69.13	64.97	61.73	52.85	49.29	47.67	46.90
5000	86.42	81.21	77.17	66.07	61.61	59.59	58.63
6000	103.70	97.46	92.60	79.28	73.93	71.51	70.35
7000	120.98	113.70	108.03	92.49	86.26	83.43	82.08
8000	138.26	129.94	123.47	105.70	98.58	95.35	93.81
9000	155.55	146.19	138.90	118.92	110.90	107.27	105.53
10000	172.83	162.43	154.33	132.13	123.22	119.19	117.26
11000	190.11	178.67	169.77	145.34	135.55	131.11	128.98
12000	207.40	194.91	185.20	158.56	147.87	143.02	140.71
13000	224.68	211.16	200.63	171.77	160.19	154.94	152.43
14000	241.96	227.40	216.07	184.98	172.51	166.86	164.16
15000	259.25	243.64	231.50	198.20	184.84	178.78	175.89
16000	276.53	259.88	246.93	211.41	197.16	190.70	187.61
17000	293.81	276.13	262.37	224.62	209.48	202.62	199.34
18000	311.10	292.37	277.80	237.84	221.80	214.54	211.06
19000	328.38	308.61	293.23	251.05	234.13	226.46	222.79
20000	345.66	324.86	308.67	264.26	246.45	238.37	234.51
21000	362.95	341.10	324.10	277.48	258.77	250.29	246.24
22000	380.23	357.34	339.53	290.69	271.09	262.21	257.97
23000	397.51	373.58	354.97	303.90	283.42	274.13	269.69
24000	414.79	389.83	370.40	317.11	295.74	286.05	281.42
25000	432.08	406.07	385.83	330.33	308.06	297.97	293.14
26000	449.36	422.31	401.27	343.54	320.38	309.89	304.87
27000	466.64	438.56	416.70	356.75	332.71	321.81	316.60
28000	483.93	454.80	432.13	369.97	345.03	333.72	328.32
29000	501.21	471.04	447.57	383.18	357.35	345.64	340.05
30000	518.49	487.28	463.00	396.39	369.67	357.56	351.77
35000	604.91	568.50	540.16	462.46	431.28	417.16	410.40
40000	691.32	649.71	617.33	528.52	492.90	476.75	469.03
45000	777.74	730.93	694.50	594.59	554.51	536.34	527.66
50000	864.16	812.14	771.66	660.65	616.12	595.94	586.29
55000	950.57	893.35	848.83	726.72	677.73	655.53	644.92
60000	1036.99	974.57	926.00	792.79	739.35	715.12	703.54
65000	1123.40	1055.78	1003.16	858.85	800.96	774.72	762.17
70000	1209.82	1137.00	1080.33	924.92	862.57	834.31	820.80
75000	1296.23	1218.21	1157.50	990.98	924.18	893.91	879.43
80000	1382.65	1299.42	1234.66	1057.05	985.79	953.50	938.06
85000	1469.06	1380.64	1311.83	1123.11	1047.41	1013.09	996.69
90000	1555.48	1461.85	1389.00	1189.18	1109.02	1072.69	1055.32
95000	1641.90	1543.07	1466.16	1255.24	1170.63	1132.28	1113.95
100000	1728.31	1624.28	1543.33	1321.31	1232.24	1191.87	1172.57
200000	3456.62	3248.56	3086.66	2642.62	2464.49	2383.75	2345.15
300000	5184.94	4872.84	4629.98	3963.93	3696.73	3575.62	3517.72
400000	6913.25	6497.12	6173.31	5285.24	4928.97	4767.50	4690.30
500000	8641.56	8121.40	7716.64	6606.55	6161.21	5959.37	5862.87
1000000	17283.12	16242.79	15433.28	13213.10	12322.43	11918.75	11725.74

14.375%

Amortization Amount	1 Year	2 Years	3 Years	4 Years	5 Years	6 Years	7 Years
25	2.24	1.20	0.85	0.68	0.58	0.51	0.47
50	4.49	2.40	1.71	1.37	1.16	1.03	0.94
100	8.98	4.80	3.42	2.73	2.32	2.06	1.87
200	17.95	9.60	6.83	5.46	4.85	4.12	3.74
300	26.93	14.40	10.25	8.19	6.97	6.18	5.62
400	35.91	19.20	13.66	10.92	9.30	8.23	7.49
500	44.88	24.00	17.08	13.65	11.62	10.29	9.36
600	53.86	28.80	20.50	16.38	13.95	12.35	11.23
700	62.84	33.60	23.91	19.12	16.27	14.41	13.10
800	71.82	38.40	27.33	21.85	18.60	16.47	14.98
900	80.79	43.20	30.74	24.58	20.92	18.53	16.85
1000	89.77	48.00	34.16	27.31	23.25	20.59	18.72
2000	179.54	95.99	68.32	54.62	46.50	41.17	37.44
3000	269.31	143.99	102.48	81.92	69.75	61.76	56.16
4000	359.08	191.98	136.64	109.23	93.00	82.34	74.88
5000	448.85	239.98	170.80	136.54	116.24	102.93	93.60
6000	538.62	287.97	204.96	163.85	139.49	123.51	112.32
7000	628.39	335.97	239.12	191.15	162.74	144.10	131.04
8000	718.16	383.96	273.28	218.46	185.99	164.69	149.75
9000	807.93	431.96	307.43	245.77	209.24	185.27	168.47
10000	897.69	479.95	341.59	273.08	232.49	205.86	187.19
11000	987.46	527.95	375.75	300.38	255.74	226.44	205.91
12000	1077.23	575.94	409.91	327.69	278.99	247.03	224.63
13000	1167.00	623.94	444.07	355.00	302.23	267.61	243.35
14000	1256.77	671.93	478.23	382.31	325.48	288.20	262.07
15000	1346.54	719.93	512.39	409.62	348.73	308.78	280.79
16000	1436.31	767.92	546.55	436.92	371.98	329.37	299.51
17000	1526.08	815.92	580.71	464.23	395.23	349.96	318.23
18000	1615.85	863.91	614.87	491.54	418.48	370.54	336.95
19000	1705.62	911.91	649.03	518.85	441.73	391.13	355.67
20000	1795.39	959.90	683.19	546.15	464.98	411.71	374.39
21000	1885.16	1007.90	717.35	573.46	488.23	432.30	393.11
22000	1974.93	1055.89	751.51	600.77	511.47	452.88	411.82
23000	2064.70	1103.88	785.67	628.08	534.72	473.47	430.54
24000	2154.47	1151.88	819.83	655.38	557.97	494.06	449.26
25000	2244.24	1199.88	853.99	682.69	581.22	514.64	467.98
26000	2334.01	1247.87	888.14	710.00	604.47	535.23	486.70
27000	2423.78	1295.87	922.30	737.31	627.72	555.81	505.42
28000	2513.55	1343.86	956.46	764.61	650.97	576.40	524.14
29000	2603.31	1391.86	990.62	791.92	674.22	596.98	542.86
30000	2693.08	1439.86	1024.78	819.23	697.46	617.57	561.58
35000	3141.93	1679.83	1195.58	955.77	813.71	720.50	655.18
40000	3590.78	1919.81	1366.38	1092.31	929.95	823.43	748.77
45000	4039.63	2159.78	1537.17	1228.85	1046.20	926.35	842.37
50000	4488.47	2399.76	1707.97	1365.38	1162.44	1029.28	935.96
55000	4937.32	2639.73	1878.77	1501.92	1278.68	1132.21	1029.56
60000	5386.17	2879.71	2049.57	1638.46	1394.93	1235.14	1123.18
65000	5835.02	3119.69	2220.36	1775.00	1511.17	1338.07	1216.75
70000	6283.86	3359.66	2391.16	1911.54	1627.42	1441.00	1310.35
75000	6732.71	3599.64	2561.96	2048.08	1743.66	1543.92	1403.95
80000	7181.56	3839.61	2732.75	2184.61	1859.90	1646.85	1497.54
85000	7630.41	4079.59	2903.55	2321.15	1976.15	1749.78	1591.14
90000	8079.25	4319.57	3074.35	2457.69	2092.39	1852.71	1684.74
95000	8528.10	4559.54	3245.14	2594.23	2208.64	1955.64	1778.33
100000	8976.95	4799.52	3415.94	2730.77	2324.88	2058.57	1871.93
200000	17953.89	9599.03	6831.88	5461.53	4649.76	4117.13	3743.86
300000	26930.84	14398.55	10247.83	8192.30	6974.64	6175.70	5615.79
400000	35907.79	19198.07	13663.77	10923.07	9299.52	8234.26	7487.72
500000	44884.74	23997.58	17079.71	13653.83	11624.41	10292.83	9359.65
1000000	89769.47	47995.17	34159.42	27307.67	23248.81	20585.66	18719.30

Amortization Amount	8 Years	9 Years	10 Years	15 Years	20 Years	25 Years	30 Years
25	0.43	0.41	0.39	0.33	0.31	0.30	0.30
50	0.87	0.82	0.78	0.66	0.62	0.60	0.59
100	1.74	1.63	1.55	1.33	1.24	1.20	1.18
200	3.47	3.26	3.10	2.66	2.48	2.40	2.36
300	5.21	4.89	4.65	3.99	3.72	3.60	3.55
400	6.94	6.52	6.20	5.32	4.96	4.80	4.73
500	8.68	8.16	7.75	6.65	6.20	6.00	5.91
600	10.41	9.79	9.30	7.98	7.44	7.21	7.09
700	12.15	11.42	10.85	9.30	8.69	8.41	8.27
800	13.88	13.05	12.40	10.63	9.93	9.61	9.46
900	15.62	14.68	13.95	11.96	11.17	10.81	10.64
1000	17.35	16.31	15.50	13.29	12.41	12.01	11.82
2000	34.70	32.62	31.01	26.58	24.82	24.02	23.64
3000	52.05	48.94	46.51	39.88	37.22	36.03	35.46
4000	69.40	65.25	62.02	53.17	49.63	48.04	47.28
5000	86.75	81.56	77.52	66.46	62.04	60.04	59.10
6000	104.10	97.87	93.02	79.75	74.45	72.05	70.91
7000	121.45	114.18	108.53	93.05	86.86	84.06	82.73
8000	138.80	130.49	124.03	106.34	99.26	96.07	94.55
9000	156.15	146.81	139.54	119.63	111.67	108.08	106.37
10000	173.50	163.12	155.04	132.92	124.08	120.09	118.19
11000	190.85	179.43	170.55	146.21	136.49	132.10	130.01
12000	208.20	195.74	186.05	159.51	148.90	144.11	141.83
13000	225.55	212.05	201.55	172.80	161.30	156.12	153.65
14000	242.90	228.36	217.06	186.09	173.71	168.12	165.47
15000	260.25	244.68	232.56	199.38	186.12	180.13	177.29
16000	277.60	260.99	248.07	212.68	198.53	192.14	189.10
17000	294.95	277.30	263.57	225.97	210.94	204.15	200.92
18000	312.30	293.61	279.07	239.26	223.34	216.16	212.74
19000	329.65	309.92	294.58	252.55	235.75	228.17	224.56
20000	347.00	326.24	310.08	265.84	248.16	240.18	236.38
21000	364.35	342.55	325.59	279.14	260.57	252.19	248.20
22000	381.70	358.86	341.09	292.43	272.98	264.20	260.02
23000	399.05	375.17	356.59	305.72	285.38	276.21	271.84
24000	416.40	391.48	372.10	319.01	297.79	288.21	283.66
25000	433.75	407.79	387.60	332.31	310.20	300.22	295.48
26000	451.10	424.11	403.11	345.60	322.61	312.23	307.30
27000	468.45	440.42	418.61	358.89	335.02	324.24	319.11
28000	485.80	456.73	434.11	372.18	347.42	336.25	330.93
29000	503.15	473.04	449.62	385.47	359.83	348.26	342.75
30000	520.50	489.35	465.12	398.77	372.24	360.27	354.57
35000	607.26	570.91	542.64	465.23	434.28	420.31	413.67
40000	694.01	652.47	620.16	531.69	496.32	480.36	472.76
45000	780.76	734.03	697.68	598.15	558.36	540.40	531.86
50000	867.51	815.59	775.21	664.61	620.40	600.45	590.95
55000	954.26	897.15	852.73	731.07	682.44	660.49	650.05
60000	1041.01	978.71	930.25	797.53	744.48	720.54	709.14
65000	1127.76	1060.26	1007.77	863.99	806.52	780.58	768.24
70000	1214.51	1141.82	1085.29	930.46	868.56	840.62	827.33
75000	1301.26	1223.38	1162.81	996.92	930.60	900.67	886.43
80000	1388.01	1304.94	1240.33	1063.38	992.64	960.71	945.52
85000	1474.76	1386.50	1317.85	1129.84	1054.68	1020.76	1004.62
90000	1561.51	1468.06	1395.37	1196.30	1116.72	1080.80	1063.71
95000	1648.27	1549.62	1472.89	1262.76	1178.76	1140.85	1122.81
100000	1735.02	1631.18	1550.41	1329.22	1240.80	1200.89	1181.90
200000	3470.03	3262.35	3100.82	2658.45	2481.60	2401.78	2363.81
300000	5205.05	4893.53	4651.23	3987.67	3722.39	3602.68	3545.71
400000	6940.07	6524.70	6201.64	5316.89	4963.19	4803.57	4727.62
500000	8675.08	8155.88	7752.05	6646.11	6203.99	6004.46	5909.52
1000000	17350.16	16311.75	15504.10	13292.23	12407.98	12008.92	11819.04

14.5%

Amortization Amount	1 Year	2 Years	3 Years	4 Years	5 Years	6 Years	7 Years
25	2.25	1.20	0.86	0.68	0.58	0.52	0.47
50	4.49	2.40	1.71	1.37	1.17	1.03	0.94
100	8.98	4.81	3.42	2.74	2.33	2.06	1.88
200	17.96	9.61	6.84	5.47	4.66	4.13	3.76
300	26.95	14.42	10.27	8.21	6.99	6.19	5.64
400	35.93	19.22	13.69	10.95	9.32	8.26	7.51
500	44.91	24.03	17.11	13.68	11.65	10.32	9.39
600	53.89	28.83	20.53	16.42	13.99	12.39	11.27
700	62.88	33.64	23.95	19.16	16.32	14.45	13.15
800	71.86	38.44	27.37	21.89	18.65	16.52	15.03
900	80.84	43.25	30.80	24.63	20.98	18.58	16.91
1000	89.82	48.05	34.22	27.37	23.31	20.65	18.78
2000	179.65	96.10	68.43	54.73	46.62	41.30	37.57
3000	269.47	144.15	102.65	82.10	69.93	61.95	56.35
4000	359.30	192.20	136.87	109.47	93.24	82.60	75.14
5000	449.12	240.25	171.08	136.83	116.55	103.24	93.92
6000	538.95	288.31	205.30	164.20	139.86	123.89	112.71
7000	628.77	336.36	239.52	191.57	163.17	144.54	131.49
8000	718.60	384.41	273.73	218.93	186.48	165.19	150.28
9000	808.42	432.46	307.95	246.30	209.79	185.84	169.06
10000	898.25	480.51	342.17	273.67	233.10	206.49	187.84
11000	988.07	528.56	376.38	301.04	256.41	227.14	206.63
12000	1077.90	576.61	410.60	328.40	279.72	247.79	225.41
13000	1167.72	624.66	444.82	355.77	303.03	268.43	244.20
14000	1257.55	672.71	479.03	383.14	326.34	289.08	262.98
15000	1347.37	720.76	513.25	410.50	349.65	309.73	281.77
16000	1437.20	768.81	547.47	437.87	372.96	330.38	300.55
17000	1527.02	816.87	581.68	465.24	396.27	351.03	319.34
18000	1616.85	864.92	615.90	492.60	419.58	371.68	338.12
19000	1706.67	912.97	650.12	519.97	442.89	392.33	356.91
20000	1796.50	961.02	684.33	547.34	466.20	412.98	375.69
21000	1886.32	1009.07	718.55	574.70	489.51	433.63	394.47
22000	1976.15	1057.12	752.77	602.07	512.82	454.27	413.26
23000	2065.97	1105.17	786.98	629.44	536.13	474.92	432.04
24000	2155.80	1153.22	821.20	656.80	559.44	495.57	450.83
25000	2245.62	1201.27	855.42	684.17	582.75	516.22	469.61
26000	2335.45	1249.32	889.63	711.54	606.06	536.87	488.40
27000	2425.27	1297.37	923.85	738.90	629.37	557.52	507.18
28000	2515.10	1345.43	958.07	766.27	652.68	578.17	525.97
29000	2604.92	1393.48	992.28	793.64	675.99	598.82	544.75
30000	2694.75	1441.53	1026.50	821.01	699.30	619.47	563.53
35000	3143.87	1681.78	1197.58	957.84	815.85	722.71	657.46
40000	3593.00	1922.04	1368.67	1094.67	932.40	825.95	751.38
45000	4042.12	2162.29	1539.75	1231.51	1048.95	929.20	845.30
50000	4491.25	2402.54	1710.84	1368.34	1165.50	1032.44	939.22
55000	4940.37	2642.80	1881.92	1505.18	1282.05	1135.69	1033.15
60000	5389.50	2883.05	2053.00	1642.01	1398.60	1238.93	1127.07
65000	5838.62	3123.31	2224.09	1778.84	1515.15	1342.17	1220.99
70000	6287.75	3363.56	2395.17	1915.68	1631.70	1445.42	1314.91
75000	6736.87	3603.82	2566.25	2052.51	1748.25	1548.66	1408.84
80000	7186.00	3844.07	2737.34	2189.35	1864.80	1651.91	1502.76
85000	7635.12	4084.33	2908.42	2326.18	1981.35	1755.15	1596.68
90000	8084.25	4324.58	3079.50	2463.02	2097.90	1858.40	1690.60
95000	8533.37	4564.83	3250.59	2599.85	2214.45	1961.64	1784.53
100000	8982.50	4805.09	3421.67	2736.68	2331.00	2064.88	1878.45
200000	17964.99	9610.18	6843.34	5473.37	4662.00	4129.77	3756.90
300000	26947.49	14415.27	10265.01	8210.05	6992.99	6194.85	5635.34
400000	35929.99	19220.36	13686.69	10946.74	9323.99	8259.54	7513.79
500000	44912.49	24025.45	17108.36	13683.42	11654.99	10324.42	9392.24
1000000	89824.97	48050.89	34216.71	27366.85	23309.98	20648.84	18784.48

MONTHLY PAYMENT
NECESSARY TO AMORTIZE A LOAN
14.5%

Amortization Amount	8 Years	9 Years	10 Years	15 Years	20 Years	25 Years	30 Years
25	0.44	0.41	0.39	0.33	0.31	0.30	0.30
50	0.87	0.82	0.78	0.67	0.62	0.60	0.60
100	1.74	1.64	1.56	1.34	1.25	1.21	1.19
200	3.48	3.28	3.12	2.67	2.50	2.42	2.38
300	5.23	4.91	4.67	4.01	3.75	3.63	3.57
400	6.97	6.55	6.23	5.35	5.00	4.84	4.76
500	8.71	8.19	7.79	6.69	6.25	6.05	5.96
600	10.45	9.83	9.35	8.02	7.50	7.26	7.15
700	12.19	11.47	10.90	9.36	8.75	8.47	8.34
800	13.93	13.10	12.46	10.70	9.99	9.68	9.53
900	15.68	14.74	14.02	12.03	11.24	10.89	10.72
1000	17.42	16.38	15.58	13.37	12.49	12.10	11.91
2000	34.83	32.76	31.15	26.74	24.99	24.20	23.82
3000	52.25	49.14	46.73	40.11	37.48	36.30	35.74
4000	69.67	65.52	62.30	53.49	49.97	48.40	47.65
5000	87.09	81.90	77.88	66.86	62.47	60.50	59.56
6000	104.50	98.28	93.45	80.23	74.96	72.60	71.47
7000	121.92	114.67	109.03	93.60	87.46	84.69	83.39
8000	139.34	131.05	124.60	106.97	99.95	96.79	95.30
9000	156.76	147.43	140.18	120.34	112.44	108.89	107.21
10000	174.17	163.81	155.75	133.72	124.94	120.99	119.12
11000	191.59	180.19	171.33	147.09	137.43	133.09	131.04
12000	209.01	196.57	186.90	160.46	149.92	145.19	142.95
13000	226.43	212.95	202.48	173.83	162.42	157.29	154.86
14000	243.84	229.33	218.05	187.20	174.91	169.39	166.77
15000	261.26	245.71	233.63	200.57	187.41	181.49	178.69
16000	278.68	262.09	249.20	213.94	199.90	193.59	190.60
17000	296.09	278.47	264.78	227.32	212.39	205.69	202.51
18000	313.51	294.85	280.35	240.69	224.89	217.79	214.42
19000	330.93	311.24	295.93	254.06	237.38	229.88	226.34
20000	348.35	327.62	311.50	267.43	249.87	241.98	238.25
21000	365.76	344.00	327.08	280.80	262.37	254.08	250.16
22000	383.18	360.38	342.65	294.17	274.86	266.18	262.07
23000	400.60	376.76	358.23	307.54	287.35	278.28	273.99
24000	418.02	393.14	373.80	320.92	299.85	290.38	285.90
25000	435.43	409.52	389.38	334.29	312.34	302.48	297.81
26000	452.85	425.90	404.95	347.66	324.84	314.58	309.72
27000	470.27	442.28	420.53	361.03	337.33	326.68	321.64
28000	487.68	458.66	436.10	374.40	349.82	338.78	333.55
29000	505.10	475.04	451.68	387.77	362.32	350.88	345.46
30000	522.52	491.42	467.25	401.15	374.81	362.98	357.37
35000	609.61	573.33	545.13	468.00	437.28	423.47	416.93
40000	696.69	655.23	623.00	534.86	499.75	483.97	476.50
45000	783.78	737.14	700.88	601.72	562.22	544.46	536.06
50000	870.87	819.04	778.75	668.58	624.68	604.96	595.62
55000	957.95	900.95	856.63	735.43	687.15	665.46	655.18
60000	1045.04	982.85	934.50	802.29	749.62	725.95	714.75
65000	1132.13	1064.75	1012.38	869.15	812.09	786.45	774.31
70000	1219.21	1146.66	1090.25	936.01	874.56	846.94	833.87
75000	1306.30	1228.56	1168.13	1002.86	937.03	907.44	893.43
80000	1393.38	1310.47	1246.00	1069.72	999.49	967.94	952.99
85000	1480.47	1392.37	1323.88	1136.58	1061.96	1028.43	1012.56
90000	1567.56	1474.27	1401.75	1203.44	1124.43	1088.93	1072.12
95000	1654.64	1556.18	1479.63	1270.29	1186.90	1149.42	1131.68
100000	1741.73	1638.08	1557.50	1337.15	1249.37	1209.92	1191.24
200000	3483.46	3276.17	3115.01	2674.30	2498.73	2419.84	2382.48
300000	5225.19	4914.25	4672.51	4011.45	3748.10	3629.76	3573.73
400000	6966.92	6552.33	6230.02	5348.60	4997.47	4839.68	4764.97
500000	8708.66	8190.41	7787.52	6685.75	6246.84	6049.60	5956.21
1000000	17417.31	16380.83	15575.05	13371.50	12493.67	12099.21	11912.42

14.625%

Amortization Amount	1 Year	2 Years	3 Years	4 Years	5 Years	6 Years	7 Years
25	2.25	1.20	0.86	0.69	0.58	0.52	0.47
50	4.49	2.41	1.71	1.37	1.17	1.04	0.94
100	8.99	4.81	3.43	2.74	2.34	2.07	1.88
200	17.98	9.62	6.85	5.49	4.67	4.14	3.77
300	26.96	14.43	10.28	8.23	7.01	6.21	5.65
400	35.95	19.24	13.71	10.97	9.35	8.28	7.54
500	44.94	24.05	17.14	13.71	11.69	10.36	9.42
600	53.93	28.86	20.56	16.46	14.02	12.43	11.31
700	62.92	33.67	23.99	19.20	16.36	14.50	13.19
800	71.90	38.49	27.42	21.94	18.70	16.57	15.08
900	80.89	43.30	30.85	24.68	21.03	18.64	16.96
1000	89.88	48.11	34.27	27.43	23.37	20.71	18.85
2000	179.76	96.21	68.55	54.85	46.74	41.42	37.70
3000	269.64	144.32	102.82	82.28	70.11	62.14	56.55
4000	359.52	192.43	137.10	109.70	93.48	82.85	75.40
5000	449.40	240.53	171.37	137.13	116.86	103.56	94.25
6000	539.28	288.64	205.64	164.56	140.23	124.27	113.10
7000	629.16	336.75	239.92	191.98	163.60	144.98	131.95
8000	719.04	384.85	274.19	219.41	186.97	165.70	150.80
9000	808.92	432.96	308.47	246.83	210.34	186.41	169.65
10000	898.80	481.07	342.74	274.26	233.71	207.12	188.50
11000	988.69	529.17	377.01	301.69	257.08	227.83	207.35
12000	1078.57	577.28	411.29	329.11	280.45	248.55	226.20
13000	1168.45	625.39	445.56	356.54	303.83	269.26	245.05
14000	1258.33	673.49	479.84	383.96	327.20	289.97	263.90
15000	1348.21	721.60	514.11	411.39	350.57	310.68	282.75
16000	1438.09	769.71	548.38	438.82	373.94	331.39	301.60
17000	1527.97	817.81	582.66	466.24	397.31	352.11	320.45
18000	1617.85	865.92	616.93	493.67	420.68	372.82	339.30
19000	1707.73	914.03	651.21	521.10	444.05	393.53	358.15
20000	1797.61	962.13	685.48	548.52	467.42	414.24	376.99
21000	1887.49	1010.24	719.75	575.95	490.80	434.95	395.84
22000	1977.37	1058.35	754.03	603.37	514.17	455.67	414.69
23000	2067.25	1106.45	788.30	630.80	537.54	476.38	433.54
24000	2157.13	1154.56	822.58	658.23	560.91	497.09	452.39
25000	2247.01	1202.67	856.85	685.65	584.28	517.80	471.24
26000	2336.89	1250.77	891.12	713.08	607.65	538.51	490.09
27000	2426.77	1298.88	925.40	740.50	631.02	559.23	508.94
28000	2516.65	1346.99	959.67	767.93	654.39	579.94	527.79
29000	2606.53	1395.09	993.95	795.36	677.76	600.65	546.64
30000	2696.41	1443.20	1028.22	822.78	701.14	621.36	565.49
35000	3145.82	1683.73	1199.59	959.91	817.99	724.92	659.74
40000	3595.22	1924.27	1370.96	1097.04	934.85	828.48	753.99
45000	4044.62	2164.80	1542.33	1234.17	1051.70	932.04	848.24
50000	4494.02	2405.33	1713.70	1371.30	1168.56	1035.60	942.49
55000	4943.43	2645.86	1885.07	1508.43	1285.42	1139.16	1036.74
60000	5392.83	2886.40	2056.44	1645.56	1402.27	1242.73	1130.98
65000	5842.23	3126.93	2227.81	1782.69	1519.13	1346.29	1225.23
70000	6291.63	3367.48	2399.18	1919.82	1635.98	1449.85	1319.48
75000	6741.03	3608.00	2570.55	2056.96	1752.84	1553.41	1413.73
80000	7190.44	3848.53	2741.92	2194.09	1869.70	1656.97	1507.98
85000	7639.84	4089.06	2913.29	2331.22	1986.55	1760.53	1602.23
90000	8089.24	4329.60	3084.66	2468.35	2103.41	1864.09	1696.48
95000	8538.64	4570.13	3256.03	2605.48	2220.26	1967.65	1790.73
100000	8988.05	4810.66	3427.40	2742.61	2337.12	2071.21	1884.97
200000	17976.09	9621.33	6854.81	5485.21	4674.24	4142.42	3769.95
300000	26964.14	14431.99	10282.21	8227.82	7011.36	6213.63	5654.92
400000	35952.19	19242.65	13709.61	10970.43	9348.48	8284.84	7539.90
500000	44940.23	24053.32	17137.02	13713.03	11685.60	10356.04	9424.87
1000000	89880.46	48106.63	34274.04	27426.07	23371.20	20712.09	18849.74

MONTHLY PAYMENT
NECESSARY TO AMORTIZE A LOAN **14.625%**

Amortization Amount	8 Years	9 Years	10 Years	15 Years	20 Years	25 Years	30 Years
25	0.44	0.41	0.39	0.34	0.31	0.30	0.30
50	0.87	0.82	0.78	0.67	0.63	0.61	0.60
100	1.75	1.65	1.56	1.35	1.26	1.22	1.20
200	3.50	3.29	3.13	2.69	2.52	2.44	2.40
300	5.25	4.94	4.69	4.04	3.77	3.66	3.60
400	6.99	6.58	6.26	5.38	5.03	4.88	4.80
500	8.74	8.23	7.82	6.73	6.29	6.09	6.00
600	10.49	9.87	9.39	8.07	7.55	7.31	7.20
700	12.24	11.52	10.95	9.42	8.81	8.53	8.40
800	13.99	13.16	12.52	10.76	10.06	9.75	9.60
900	15.74	14.81	14.08	12.11	11.32	10.97	10.81
1000	17.48	16.45	15.65	13.45	12.58	12.19	12.01
2000	34.97	32.90	31.29	26.90	25.16	24.38	24.01
3000	52.45	49.35	46.94	40.35	37.74	36.57	36.02
4000	69.94	65.80	62.58	53.80	50.32	48.76	48.02
5000	87.42	82.25	78.23	67.25	62.90	60.95	60.03
6000	104.91	98.70	93.88	80.71	75.48	73.14	72.04
7000	122.39	115.15	109.52	94.16	88.06	85.33	84.04
8000	139.88	131.60	125.17	107.61	100.64	97.52	96.05
9000	157.36	148.05	140.82	121.06	113.22	109.71	108.05
10000	174.85	164.50	156.46	134.51	125.80	121.90	120.06
11000	192.33	180.95	172.11	147.96	138.37	134.09	132.06
12000	209.81	197.40	187.75	161.41	150.95	146.28	144.07
13000	227.30	213.85	203.40	174.86	163.53	158.46	156.08
14000	244.78	230.30	219.05	188.31	176.11	170.65	168.08
15000	262.27	246.75	234.69	201.76	188.69	182.84	180.09
16000	279.75	263.20	250.34	215.21	201.27	195.03	192.09
17000	297.24	279.65	265.98	228.67	213.85	207.22	204.10
18000	314.72	296.10	281.63	242.12	226.43	219.41	216.11
19000	332.21	312.55	297.28	255.57	239.01	231.60	228.11
20000	349.69	329.00	312.92	269.02	251.59	243.79	240.12
21000	367.18	345.45	328.57	282.47	264.17	255.98	252.12
22000	384.66	361.90	344.21	295.92	276.75	268.17	264.13
23000	402.14	378.35	359.86	309.37	289.33	280.36	276.14
24000	419.63	394.80	375.51	322.82	301.91	292.55	288.14
25000	437.11	411.25	391.15	336.27	314.49	304.74	300.15
26000	454.60	427.70	406.80	349.72	327.07	316.93	312.15
27000	472.08	444.15	422.45	363.18	339.65	329.12	324.16
28000	489.57	460.60	438.09	376.63	352.23	341.31	336.16
29000	507.05	477.05	453.74	390.08	364.81	353.50	348.17
30000	524.54	493.50	469.38	403.53	377.39	365.69	360.18
35000	611.96	575.75	547.61	470.78	440.28	426.64	420.21
40000	699.38	658.00	625.84	538.04	503.18	487.58	480.23
45000	786.81	740.25	704.08	605.29	566.08	548.53	540.26
50000	874.23	822.50	782.31	672.55	628.98	609.48	600.29
55000	961.65	904.75	860.54	739.80	691.87	670.43	660.32
60000	1049.07	987.00	938.77	807.06	754.77	731.38	720.35
65000	1136.50	1069.25	1017.00	874.31	817.67	792.32	780.38
70000	1223.92	1151.50	1095.23	941.56	880.57	853.27	840.41
75000	1311.34	1233.75	1173.46	1008.82	943.46	914.22	900.44
80000	1398.76	1316.00	1251.69	1076.07	1006.36	975.17	960.47
85000	1486.19	1398.25	1329.92	1143.33	1069.26	1036.12	1020.50
90000	1573.61	1480.50	1408.15	1210.58	1132.16	1097.06	1080.53
95000	1661.03	1562.75	1486.38	1277.84	1195.05	1158.01	1140.56
100000	1748.46	1645.01	1564.61	1345.09	1257.95	1218.96	1200.59
200000	3496.91	3290.01	3129.22	2690.19	2515.90	2437.92	2401.17
300000	5245.37	4935.01	4693.83	4035.28	3773.85	3656.88	3601.76
400000	6993.82	6580.01	6258.45	5380.37	5031.80	4875.84	4802.35
500000	8742.28	8225.01	7823.06	6725.46	6289.76	6094.80	6002.94
1000000	17484.56	16450.01	15646.11	13450.93	12579.51	12189.61	12005.87

14.75%

Amortization Amount	1 Year	2 Years	3 Years	4 Years	5 Years	6 Years	7 Years
25	2.25	1.20	0.86	0.69	0.59	0.52	0.47
50	4.50	2.41	1.72	1.37	1.17	1.04	0.95
100	8.99	4.82	3.43	2.75	2.34	2.08	1.89
200	17.99	9.63	6.87	5.50	4.69	4.16	3.78
300	26.98	14.45	10.30	8.25	7.03	6.23	5.67
400	35.97	19.26	13.73	10.99	9.37	8.31	7.57
500	44.97	24.08	17.17	13.74	11.72	10.39	9.46
600	53.96	28.90	20.60	16.49	14.06	12.47	11.35
700	62.96	33.71	24.03	19.24	16.40	14.54	13.24
800	71.95	38.53	27.47	21.99	18.75	16.62	15.13
900	80.94	43.35	30.90	24.74	21.09	18.70	17.02
1000	89.94	48.16	34.33	27.49	23.43	20.78	18.92
2000	179.87	96.32	68.66	54.97	46.86	41.55	37.83
3000	269.81	144.49	102.99	82.46	70.30	62.33	56.75
4000	359.74	192.65	137.33	109.94	93.73	83.10	75.66
5000	449.68	240.81	171.66	137.43	117.16	103.88	94.58
6000	539.62	288.97	205.99	164.91	140.59	124.65	113.49
7000	629.55	337.14	240.32	192.40	164.03	145.43	132.41
8000	719.49	385.30	274.65	219.88	187.46	166.20	151.32
9000	809.42	433.46	308.98	247.37	210.89	186.98	170.24
10000	899.36	481.62	343.31	274.85	234.32	207.75	189.15
11000	989.30	529.79	377.65	302.34	257.76	228.53	208.07
12000	1079.23	577.95	411.98	329.82	281.19	249.30	226.98
13000	1169.17	626.11	446.31	357.31	304.62	270.08	245.90
14000	1259.10	674.27	480.64	384.79	328.05	290.86	264.81
15000	1349.04	722.44	514.97	412.28	351.49	311.63	283.73
16000	1438.98	770.60	549.30	439.77	374.92	332.41	302.64
17000	1528.91	818.76	583.63	467.25	398.35	353.18	321.56
18000	1618.85	866.92	617.96	494.74	421.78	373.96	340.47
19000	1708.78	915.09	652.30	522.22	445.22	394.73	359.39
20000	1798.72	963.25	686.63	549.71	468.65	415.51	378.30
21000	1888.65	1011.41	720.96	577.19	492.08	436.28	397.22
22000	1978.59	1059.57	755.29	604.68	515.51	457.06	416.13
23000	2068.53	1107.73	789.62	632.16	538.95	477.83	435.05
24000	2158.46	1155.90	823.95	659.65	562.38	498.61	453.96
25000	2248.40	1204.06	858.28	687.13	585.81	519.39	472.88
26000	2338.33	1252.22	892.62	714.62	609.24	540.16	491.79
27000	2428.27	1300.38	926.95	742.10	632.68	560.94	510.71
28000	2518.21	1348.55	961.28	769.59	656.11	581.71	529.62
29000	2608.14	1396.71	995.61	797.07	679.54	602.49	548.54
30000	2698.08	1444.87	1029.94	824.56	702.97	623.26	567.45
35000	3147.76	1685.68	1201.60	961.99	820.14	727.14	662.03
40000	3597.44	1926.50	1373.26	1099.41	937.30	831.02	756.60
45000	4047.12	2167.31	1544.91	1236.84	1054.46	934.89	851.18
50000	4496.80	2408.12	1716.57	1374.27	1171.62	1038.77	945.75
55000	4946.48	2648.93	1888.23	1511.69	1288.79	1142.65	1040.33
60000	5396.16	2889.74	2059.88	1649.12	1405.95	1246.52	1134.91
65000	5845.84	3130.55	2231.54	1786.55	1523.11	1350.40	1229.48
70000	6295.52	3371.37	2403.20	1923.97	1640.27	1454.28	1324.06
75000	6745.20	3612.18	2574.85	2061.40	1757.44	1558.16	1418.63
80000	7194.88	3852.99	2746.51	2198.83	1874.60	1662.03	1513.21
85000	7644.56	4093.80	2918.17	2336.25	1991.76	1765.91	1607.78
90000	8094.24	4334.61	3089.82	2473.68	2108.92	1869.79	1702.36
95000	8543.91	4575.43	3261.48	2611.11	2226.09	1973.66	1796.93
100000	8993.59	4816.24	3433.14	2748.53	2343.25	2077.54	1891.51
200000	17987.19	9632.48	6866.28	5497.07	4686.50	4155.08	3783.02
300000	26980.76	14448.71	10299.42	8245.60	7029.75	6232.62	5674.53
400000	35974.38	19264.95	13732.56	10994.14	9372.99	8310.17	7566.04
500000	44967.97	24081.19	17165.69	13742.67	11716.24	10387.71	9457.55
1000000	89935.95	48162.38	34331.39	27485.34	23432.49	20775.42	18915.10

174

Amortization Amount	8 Years	9 Years	10 Years	15 Years	20 Years	25 Years	30 Years
25	0.44	0.41	0.39	0.34	0.32	0.31	0.30
50	0.88	0.83	0.79	0.68	0.63	0.61	0.60
100	1.76	1.65	1.57	1.35	1.27	1.23	1.21
200	3.51	3.30	3.14	2.71	2.53	2.46	2.42
300	5.27	4.96	4.72	4.06	3.80	3.68	3.63
400	7.02	6.61	6.29	5.41	5.07	4.91	4.84
500	8.78	8.26	7.86	6.77	6.33	6.14	6.05
600	10.53	9.91	9.43	8.12	7.60	7.37	7.26
700	12.29	11.56	11.00	9.47	8.87	8.60	8.47
800	14.04	13.22	12.57	10.82	10.13	9.82	9.68
900	15.80	14.87	14.15	12.18	11.40	11.05	10.89
1000	17.55	16.52	15.72	13.53	12.67	12.28	12.10
2000	35.10	33.04	31.43	27.06	25.33	24.56	24.20
3000	52.66	49.56	47.15	40.59	38.00	36.84	36.30
4000	70.21	66.08	62.87	54.12	50.66	49.12	48.40
5000	87.76	82.60	78.59	67.65	63.33	61.40	60.50
6000	105.31	99.12	94.30	81.18	75.99	73.68	72.60
7000	122.86	115.64	110.02	94.71	88.66	85.96	84.70
8000	140.42	132.15	125.74	108.24	101.32	98.24	96.80
9000	157.97	148.67	141.46	121.77	113.99	110.52	108.89
10000	175.52	165.19	157.17	135.30	126.65	122.80	120.99
11000	193.07	181.71	172.89	148.84	139.32	135.08	133.09
12000	210.62	198.23	188.61	162.37	151.99	147.36	145.19
13000	228.17	214.75	204.32	175.90	164.65	159.64	157.29
14000	245.73	231.27	220.04	189.43	177.32	171.92	169.39
15000	263.28	247.79	235.76	202.96	189.98	184.20	181.49
16000	280.83	264.31	251.48	216.49	202.65	196.48	193.59
17000	298.38	280.83	267.19	230.02	215.31	208.76	205.69
18000	315.93	297.35	282.91	243.55	227.98	221.04	217.79
19000	333.49	313.87	298.63	257.08	240.64	233.32	229.89
20000	351.04	330.39	314.35	270.61	253.31	245.60	241.99
21000	368.59	346.91	330.06	284.14	265.98	257.88	254.09
22000	386.14	363.42	345.78	297.67	278.64	270.16	266.19
23000	403.69	379.94	361.50	311.20	291.31	282.44	278.29
24000	421.25	396.46	377.22	324.73	303.97	294.72	290.39
25000	438.80	412.98	392.93	338.26	316.64	307.00	302.49
26000	456.35	429.50	408.65	351.79	329.30	319.28	314.58
27000	473.90	446.02	424.37	365.32	341.97	331.56	326.68
28000	491.45	462.54	440.08	378.85	354.63	343.84	338.78
29000	509.01	479.06	455.80	392.38	367.30	356.12	350.88
30000	526.56	495.58	471.52	405.91	379.96	368.40	362.98
35000	614.32	578.18	550.11	473.57	443.29	429.80	423.48
40000	702.08	660.77	628.69	541.22	506.62	491.20	483.98
45000	789.84	743.37	707.28	608.87	569.95	552.61	544.47
50000	877.60	825.97	785.87	676.52	633.27	614.01	604.97
55000	965.36	908.56	864.45	744.18	696.60	675.41	665.47
60000	1053.11	991.16	943.04	811.83	759.93	736.81	725.96
65000	1140.87	1073.76	1021.62	879.48	823.26	798.21	786.46
70000	1228.63	1156.35	1100.21	947.13	886.58	859.61	846.96
75000	1316.39	1238.95	1178.80	1014.79	949.91	921.01	907.46
80000	1404.15	1321.54	1257.38	1082.44	1013.24	982.41	967.95
85000	1491.91	1404.14	1335.97	1150.09	1076.57	1043.81	1028.45
90000	1579.67	1486.74	1414.56	1217.74	1139.89	1105.21	1088.95
95000	1667.43	1569.33	1493.14	1285.40	1203.22	1166.61	1149.44
100000	1755.19	1651.93	1571.73	1353.05	1266.55	1228.01	1209.94
200000	3510.38	3303.86	3143.46	2706.10	2533.10	2456.02	2419.88
300000	5265.57	4955.79	4715.19	4059.15	3799.65	3684.03	3629.82
400000	7020.76	6607.72	6286.92	5412.20	5066.19	4912.05	4839.76
500000	8775.96	8259.66	7858.65	6765.25	6332.74	6140.06	6049.70
1000000	17551.91	16519.31	15717.30	13530.50	12665.49	12280.12	12099.40

14.875%

MONTHLY PAYMENT
NECESSARY TO AMORTIZE A LOAN

Amortization Amount	1 Year	2 Years	3 Years	4 Years	5 Years	6 Years	7 Years
25	2.25	1.21	0.86	0.69	0.59	0.52	0.47
50	4.50	2.41	1.72	1.38	1.17	1.04	0.95
100	9.00	4.82	3.44	2.75	2.35	2.08	1.90
200	18.00	9.64	6.88	5.51	4.70	4.17	3.80
300	27.00	14.47	10.32	8.26	7.05	6.25	5.69
400	36.00	19.29	13.76	11.02	9.40	8.34	7.59
500	45.00	24.11	17.19	13.77	11.75	10.42	9.49
600	53.99	28.93	20.63	16.53	14.10	12.50	11.39
700	62.99	33.75	24.07	19.28	16.45	14.59	13.29
800	71.99	38.57	27.51	22.04	18.80	16.67	15.18
900	80.99	43.40	30.95	24.79	21.14	18.75	17.08
1000	89.99	48.22	34.39	27.54	23.49	20.84	18.98
2000	179.98	96.44	68.78	55.09	46.99	41.68	37.96
3000	269.97	144.65	103.17	82.63	70.48	62.52	56.94
4000	359.97	192.87	137.56	110.18	93.98	83.36	75.92
5000	449.96	241.09	171.94	137.72	117.47	104.19	94.90
6000	539.95	289.31	206.33	165.27	140.96	125.03	113.88
7000	629.94	337.53	240.72	192.81	164.46	145.87	132.86
8000	719.93	385.75	275.11	220.36	187.95	166.71	151.84
9000	809.92	433.96	309.50	247.90	211.44	187.55	170.82
10000	899.91	482.18	343.89	275.45	234.94	208.39	189.81
11000	989.91	530.40	378.28	302.99	258.43	229.23	208.79
12000	1079.90	578.62	412.67	330.54	281.93	250.07	227.77
13000	1169.89	626.84	447.05	358.08	305.42	270.90	246.75
14000	1259.88	675.05	481.44	385.63	328.91	291.74	265.73
15000	1349.87	723.27	515.83	413.17	352.41	312.58	284.71
16000	1439.86	771.49	550.22	440.71	375.90	333.42	303.69
17000	1529.85	819.71	584.61	468.26	399.40	354.26	322.67
18000	1619.85	867.93	619.00	495.80	422.89	375.10	341.65
19000	1709.84	916.14	653.39	523.35	446.38	395.94	360.63
20000	1799.83	964.36	687.78	550.89	469.88	416.78	379.61
21000	1889.82	1012.58	722.16	578.44	493.37	437.62	398.59
22000	1979.81	1060.80	756.55	605.98	516.86	458.45	417.57
23000	2069.80	1109.02	790.94	633.53	540.36	479.29	436.55
24000	2159.79	1157.24	825.33	661.07	563.85	500.13	455.53
25000	2249.79	1205.45	859.72	688.62	587.35	520.97	474.51
26000	2339.78	1253.67	894.11	716.16	610.84	541.81	493.49
27000	2429.77	1301.89	928.50	743.71	634.33	562.65	512.47
28000	2519.76	1350.11	962.89	771.25	657.83	583.49	531.46
29000	2609.75	1398.33	997.27	798.79	681.32	604.33	550.44
30000	2699.74	1446.54	1031.66	826.34	704.81	625.16	569.42
35000	3149.70	1687.63	1203.61	964.06	822.28	729.36	664.32
40000	3599.66	1928.73	1375.55	1101.79	939.75	833.55	759.22
45000	4049.61	2169.82	1547.49	1239.51	1057.22	937.75	854.12
50000	4499.57	2410.91	1719.44	1377.23	1174.69	1041.94	949.03
55000	4949.53	2652.00	1891.38	1514.96	1292.16	1146.13	1043.93
60000	5399.49	2893.09	2063.33	1652.68	1409.63	1250.33	1138.83
65000	5849.44	3134.18	2235.27	1790.40	1527.10	1354.52	1233.74
70000	6299.40	3375.27	2407.21	1928.13	1644.57	1458.72	1328.64
75000	6749.36	3616.36	2579.16	2065.85	1762.04	1562.91	1423.54
80000	7199.31	3857.45	2751.10	2203.57	1879.51	1667.11	1518.44
85000	7649.27	4098.54	2923.05	2341.30	1996.98	1771.30	1613.35
90000	8099.23	4339.63	3094.99	2479.02	2114.44	1875.49	1708.25
95000	8549.18	4580.72	3266.93	2616.74	2231.91	1979.69	1803.15
100000	8999.14	4821.81	3438.88	2754.47	2349.38	2083.88	1898.05
200000	17998.28	9643.63	6877.75	5508.93	4698.77	4167.76	3796.11
300000	26997.43	14465.44	10316.63	8263.40	7048.15	6251.65	5694.16
400000	35996.57	19287.25	13755.51	11017.86	9397.53	8335.53	7592.22
500000	44995.71	24109.07	17194.38	13772.33	11746.92	10419.41	9490.27
1000000	89991.42	48218.14	34388.77	27544.65	23493.83	20838.82	18980.54

Amortization Amount	8 Years	9 Years	10 Years	15 Years	20 Years	25 Years	30 Years
25	0.44	0.41	0.39	0.34	0.32	0.31	0.30
50	0.88	0.83	0.79	0.68	0.64	0.62	0.61
100	1.76	1.66	1.58	1.36	1.28	1.24	1.22
200	3.52	3.32	3.16	2.72	2.55	2.47	2.44
300	5.29	4.98	4.74	4.08	3.83	3.71	3.66
400	7.05	6.64	6.32	5.44	5.10	4.95	4.88
500	8.81	8.29	7.89	6.81	6.38	6.19	6.10
600	10.57	9.95	9.47	8.17	7.65	7.42	7.32
700	12.33	11.61	11.05	9.53	8.93	8.66	8.54
800	14.10	13.27	12.63	10.89	10.20	9.90	9.75
900	15.86	14.93	14.21	12.25	11.48	11.13	10.97
1000	17.62	16.59	15.79	13.61	12.75	12.37	12.19
2000	35.24	33.18	31.58	27.22	25.50	24.74	24.39
3000	52.86	49.77	47.37	40.83	38.25	37.11	36.58
4000	70.48	66.35	63.15	54.44	51.01	49.48	48.77
5000	88.10	82.94	78.94	68.05	63.76	61.85	60.97
6000	105.72	99.53	94.73	81.66	76.51	74.22	73.16
7000	123.34	116.12	110.52	95.27	89.26	86.60	85.35
8000	140.95	132.71	126.31	108.88	102.01	98.97	97.54
9000	158.57	149.30	142.10	122.49	114.76	111.34	109.74
10000	176.19	165.89	157.89	136.10	127.52	123.71	121.93
11000	193.81	182.48	173.67	149.71	140.27	136.08	134.12
12000	211.43	199.06	189.46	163.32	153.02	148.45	146.32
13000	229.05	215.65	205.25	176.93	165.77	160.82	158.51
14000	246.67	232.24	221.04	190.54	178.52	173.19	170.70
15000	264.29	248.83	236.83	204.15	191.27	185.56	182.90
16000	281.91	265.42	252.62	217.76	204.03	197.93	195.09
17000	299.53	282.01	268.41	231.37	216.78	210.30	207.28
18000	317.15	298.60	284.20	244.98	229.53	222.67	219.47
19000	334.77	315.19	299.98	258.59	242.28	235.04	231.67
20000	352.39	331.77	315.77	272.20	255.03	247.41	243.86
21000	370.01	348.36	331.56	285.81	267.78	259.79	256.05
22000	387.63	364.95	347.35	299.42	280.54	272.16	268.25
23000	405.25	381.54	363.14	313.03	293.29	284.53	280.44
24000	422.86	398.13	378.93	326.65	306.04	296.90	292.63
25000	440.48	414.72	394.72	340.26	318.79	309.27	304.83
26000	458.10	431.31	410.50	353.87	331.54	321.64	317.02
27000	475.72	447.90	426.29	367.48	344.29	334.01	329.21
28000	493.34	464.48	442.08	381.09	357.04	346.38	341.40
29000	510.96	481.07	457.87	394.70	369.80	358.75	353.60
30000	528.58	497.66	473.66	408.31	382.55	371.12	365.79
35000	616.68	580.61	552.60	476.36	446.31	432.98	426.76
40000	704.77	663.55	631.54	544.41	510.06	494.83	487.72
45000	792.87	746.49	710.49	612.46	573.82	556.68	548.69
50000	880.97	829.44	789.43	680.51	637.58	618.54	609.65
55000	969.07	912.38	868.37	748.56	701.34	680.39	670.62
60000	1057.16	995.32	947.32	816.61	765.10	742.24	731.58
65000	1145.26	1078.27	1026.26	884.66	828.85	804.10	792.55
70000	1233.36	1161.21	1105.20	952.71	892.61	865.95	853.51
75000	1321.45	1244.15	1184.15	1020.77	956.37	927.81	914.48
80000	1409.55	1327.10	1263.09	1088.82	1020.13	989.66	975.44
85000	1497.65	1410.04	1342.03	1156.87	1083.89	1051.51	1036.41
90000	1585.74	1492.98	1420.98	1224.92	1147.64	1113.37	1097.37
95000	1673.84	1575.93	1499.92	1292.97	1211.40	1175.22	1158.34
100000	1761.94	1658.87	1578.86	1361.02	1275.16	1237.07	1219.30
200000	3523.87	3317.74	3157.72	2722.04	2550.32	2474.15	2438.60
300000	5285.81	4976.62	4736.58	4083.06	3825.48	3711.22	3657.90
400000	7047.75	6635.49	6315.44	5444.09	5100.64	4948.29	4877.20
500000	8809.68	8294.36	7894.31	6805.11	6375.80	6185.37	6096.50
1000000	17619.36	16588.72	15788.61	13610.21	12751.60	12370.73	12193.01

15%

MONTHLY PAYMENT
NECESSARY TO AMORTIZE A LOAN

Amortization Amount	1 Year	2 Years	3 Years	4 Years	5 Years	6 Years	7 Years
25	2.25	1.21	0.86	0.69	0.59	0.52	0.48
50	4.50	2.41	1.72	1.38	1.18	1.05	0.95
100	9.00	4.83	3.44	2.76	2.36	2.09	1.90
200	18.01	9.65	6.89	5.52	4.71	4.18	3.81
300	27.01	14.48	10.33	8.28	7.07	6.27	5.71
400	36.02	19.31	13.78	11.04	9.42	8.36	7.62
500	45.02	24.14	17.22	13.80	11.78	10.45	9.52
600	54.03	28.96	20.67	16.56	14.13	12.54	11.43
700	63.03	33.79	24.11	19.32	16.49	14.63	13.33
800	72.04	38.62	27.56	22.08	18.84	16.72	15.24
900	81.04	43.45	31.00	24.84	21.20	18.81	17.14
1000	90.05	48.27	34.45	27.60	23.56	20.90	19.05
2000	180.09	96.55	68.89	55.21	47.11	41.80	38.09
3000	270.14	144.82	103.34	82.81	70.67	62.71	57.14
4000	360.19	193.10	137.78	110.42	94.22	83.61	76.18
5000	450.23	241.37	172.23	138.02	117.78	104.51	95.23
6000	540.28	289.64	206.68	165.62	141.33	125.41	114.28
7000	630.33	337.92	241.12	193.23	164.89	146.32	133.32
8000	720.38	386.19	275.57	220.83	188.44	167.22	152.37
9000	810.42	434.47	310.02	248.44	212.00	188.12	171.41
10000	900.47	482.74	344.46	276.04	235.55	209.02	190.46
11000	990.52	531.01	378.91	303.64	259.11	229.93	209.51
12000	1080.56	579.29	413.35	331.25	282.66	250.83	228.55
13000	1170.61	627.56	447.80	358.85	306.22	271.73	247.60
14000	1260.66	675.83	482.25	386.46	329.77	292.63	266.65
15000	1350.70	724.11	516.69	414.06	353.33	313.53	285.69
16000	1440.75	772.38	551.14	441.66	376.88	334.44	304.74
17000	1530.80	820.66	585.58	469.27	400.44	355.34	323.78
18000	1620.84	868.93	620.03	496.87	423.99	376.24	342.83
19000	1710.89	917.20	654.48	524.48	447.55	397.14	361.88
20000	1800.94	965.48	688.92	552.08	471.10	418.05	380.92
21000	1890.98	1013.75	723.37	579.68	494.66	438.95	399.97
22000	1981.03	1062.03	757.82	607.29	518.22	459.85	419.01
23000	2071.08	1110.30	792.26	634.89	541.77	480.75	438.06
24000	2161.13	1158.57	826.71	662.50	565.33	501.66	457.11
25000	2251.17	1206.85	861.15	690.10	588.88	522.56	476.15
26000	2341.22	1255.12	895.60	717.70	612.44	543.46	495.20
27000	2431.27	1303.40	930.05	745.31	635.99	564.36	514.24
28000	2521.31	1351.67	964.49	772.91	659.55	585.26	533.29
29000	2611.36	1399.94	998.94	800.52	683.10	606.17	552.34
30000	2701.41	1448.22	1033.39	828.12	706.66	627.07	571.38
35000	3151.64	1689.59	1205.62	966.14	824.43	731.58	666.61
40000	3601.88	1930.96	1377.85	1104.16	942.21	836.09	761.84
45000	4052.11	2172.33	1550.08	1242.18	1059.99	940.60	857.07
50000	4502.34	2413.70	1722.31	1380.20	1177.76	1045.11	952.30
55000	4952.58	2655.06	1894.54	1518.22	1295.54	1149.63	1047.53
60000	5402.81	2896.43	2066.77	1656.24	1413.31	1254.14	1142.76
65000	5853.05	3137.80	2239.00	1794.26	1531.09	1358.65	1237.99
70000	6303.28	3379.17	2411.23	1932.28	1648.87	1463.16	1333.23
75000	6753.52	3620.54	2583.46	2070.30	1766.64	1567.67	1428.46
80000	7203.75	3861.91	2755.69	2208.32	1884.42	1672.18	1523.69
85000	7653.99	4103.28	2927.92	2346.34	2002.20	1776.69	1618.92
90000	8104.22	4344.65	3100.16	2484.36	2119.97	1881.21	1714.15
95000	8554.45	4586.02	3272.39	2622.38	2237.75	1985.72	1809.38
100000	9004.69	4827.39	3444.62	2760.40	2355.52	2090.23	1904.61
200000	18009.38	9654.78	6889.23	5520.80	4711.05	4180.46	3809.21
300000	27014.07	14482.17	10333.85	8281.20	7066.57	6270.69	5713.82
400000	36018.75	19309.56	13778.47	11041.60	9422.09	8360.92	7618.43
500000	45023.44	24136.95	17223.09	13802.00	11777.62	10451.15	9523.04
1000000	90046.89	48273.90	34446.17	27604.01	23555.24	20902.29	19046.07

Amortization Amount	8 Years	9 Years	10 Years	15 Years	20 Years	25 Years	30 Years
25	0.44	0.42	0.40	0.34	0.32	0.31	0.31
50	0.88	0.83	0.79	0.68	0.64	0.62	0.61
100	1.77	1.67	1.59	1.37	1.28	1.25	1.23
200	3.54	3.33	3.17	2.74	2.57	2.49	2.46
300	5.31	5.00	4.76	4.11	3.85	3.74	3.69
400	7.07	6.66	6.34	5.48	5.14	4.98	4.91
500	8.84	8.33	7.93	6.85	6.42	6.23	6.14
600	10.61	9.99	9.52	8.21	7.70	7.48	7.37
700	12.38	11.66	11.10	9.58	8.99	8.72	8.60
800	14.15	13.33	12.69	10.95	10.27	9.97	9.83
900	15.92	14.99	14.27	12.32	11.55	11.22	11.06
1000	17.69	16.66	15.86	13.69	12.84	12.46	12.29
2000	35.37	33.32	31.72	27.38	25.68	24.92	24.57
3000	53.06	49.97	47.58	41.07	38.51	37.38	36.86
4000	70.75	66.63	63.44	54.76	51.35	49.85	49.15
5000	88.43	83.29	79.30	68.45	64.19	62.31	61.43
6000	106.12	99.95	95.16	82.14	77.03	74.77	73.72
7000	123.81	116.61	111.02	95.83	89.86	87.23	86.01
8000	141.50	133.27	126.88	109.52	102.70	99.69	98.29
9000	159.18	149.92	142.74	123.21	115.54	112.15	110.58
10000	176.87	166.58	158.60	136.90	128.38	124.61	122.87
11000	194.56	183.24	174.46	150.59	141.22	137.08	135.15
12000	212.24	199.90	190.32	164.28	154.05	149.54	147.44
13000	229.93	216.56	206.18	177.97	166.89	162.00	159.73
14000	247.62	233.22	222.04	191.66	179.73	174.46	172.01
15000	265.30	249.87	237.90	205.35	192.57	186.92	184.30
16000	282.99	266.53	253.76	219.04	205.41	199.38	196.59
17000	300.68	283.19	269.62	232.73	218.24	211.84	208.87
18000	318.36	299.85	285.48	246.42	231.08	224.31	221.16
19000	336.05	316.51	301.34	260.11	243.92	236.77	233.45
20000	353.74	333.16	317.20	273.80	256.76	249.23	245.73
21000	371.43	349.82	333.06	287.49	269.59	261.69	258.02
22000	389.11	366.48	348.92	301.18	282.43	274.15	270.31
23000	406.80	383.14	364.78	314.87	295.27	286.61	282.59
24000	424.49	399.80	380.64	328.56	308.11	299.07	294.88
25000	442.17	416.46	396.50	342.25	320.95	311.54	307.17
26000	459.86	433.11	412.36	355.94	333.78	324.00	319.45
27000	477.55	449.77	428.22	369.63	346.62	336.46	331.74
28000	495.23	466.43	444.08	383.32	359.46	348.92	344.03
29000	512.92	483.09	459.94	397.01	372.30	361.38	356.31
30000	530.61	499.75	475.80	410.70	385.14	373.84	368.60
35000	619.04	583.04	555.10	479.15	449.32	436.15	430.03
40000	707.48	666.33	634.40	547.60	513.51	498.46	491.47
45000	795.91	749.62	713.70	616.05	577.70	560.77	552.90
50000	884.35	832.91	793.00	684.50	641.89	623.07	614.33
55000	972.78	916.20	872.30	752.95	706.08	685.38	675.77
60000	1061.21	999.49	951.60	821.40	770.27	747.69	737.20
65000	1149.65	1082.79	1030.90	889.85	834.46	809.99	798.63
70000	1238.08	1166.08	1110.20	958.31	898.65	872.30	860.07
75000	1326.52	1249.37	1189.50	1026.76	962.84	934.61	921.50
80000	1414.95	1332.66	1268.80	1095.21	1027.03	996.92	982.93
85000	1503.39	1415.95	1348.10	1163.66	1091.22	1059.22	1044.37
90000	1591.82	1499.24	1427.40	1232.11	1155.41	1121.53	1105.80
95000	1680.26	1582.53	1506.70	1300.56	1219.60	1183.84	1167.23
100000	1768.69	1665.82	1586.00	1369.01	1283.78	1246.15	1228.67
200000	3537.38	3331.65	3172.01	2738.01	2567.57	2492.29	2457.34
300000	5306.07	4997.47	4758.01	4107.02	3851.35	3738.44	3686.00
400000	7074.77	6663.30	6344.02	5476.03	5135.14	4984.58	4914.67
500000	8843.46	8329.12	7930.02	6845.04	6418.92	6230.73	6143.34
1000000	17686.92	16658.24	15860.04	13690.07	12837.84	12461.46	12286.68

15.125%

Amortization Amount	1 Year	2 Years	3 Years	4 Years	5 Years	6 Years	7 Years
25	2.25	1.21	0.86	0.69	0.59	0.52	0.48
50	4.51	2.42	1.73	1.38	1.18	1.05	0.96
100	9.01	4.83	3.45	2.77	2.36	2.10	1.91
200	18.02	9.67	6.90	5.53	4.72	4.19	3.82
300	27.03	14.50	10.35	8.30	7.09	6.29	5.73
400	36.04	19.33	13.80	11.07	9.45	8.39	7.64
500	45.05	24.16	17.25	13.83	11.81	10.48	9.56
600	54.06	29.00	20.70	16.60	14.17	12.58	11.47
700	63.07	33.83	24.15	19.36	16.53	14.68	13.38
800	72.08	38.66	27.60	22.13	18.89	16.77	15.29
900	81.09	43.50	31.05	24.90	21.26	18.87	17.20
1000	90.10	48.33	34.50	27.66	23.62	20.97	19.11
2000	180.20	96.66	69.01	55.33	47.23	41.93	38.22
3000	270.31	144.99	103.51	82.99	70.85	62.90	57.34
4000	360.41	193.32	138.01	110.65	94.47	83.86	76.45
5000	450.51	241.65	172.52	138.32	118.08	104.83	95.56
6000	540.61	289.98	207.02	165.98	141.70	125.80	114.67
7000	630.72	338.31	241.53	193.64	165.32	146.76	133.78
8000	720.82	386.64	276.03	221.31	188.93	167.73	152.89
9000	810.92	434.97	310.53	248.97	212.55	188.69	172.01
10000	901.02	483.30	345.04	276.63	236.17	209.66	191.12
11000	991.13	531.63	379.54	304.30	259.78	230.62	210.23
12000	1081.23	579.96	414.04	331.96	283.40	251.59	229.34
13000	1171.33	628.29	448.55	359.62	307.02	272.56	248.45
14000	1261.43	676.62	483.05	387.29	330.63	293.52	267.56
15000	1351.54	724.95	517.55	414.95	354.25	314.49	286.68
16000	1441.64	773.27	552.06	442.61	377.87	335.45	305.79
17000	1531.74	821.60	586.56	470.28	401.48	356.42	324.90
18000	1621.84	869.93	621.06	497.94	425.10	377.39	344.01
19000	1711.94	918.26	655.57	525.60	448.72	398.35	363.12
20000	1802.05	966.59	690.07	553.27	472.33	419.32	382.23
21000	1892.15	1014.92	724.58	580.93	495.95	440.28	401.35
22000	1982.25	1063.25	759.08	608.60	519.57	461.25	420.46
23000	2072.35	1111.58	793.58	636.26	543.18	482.21	439.57
24000	2162.46	1159.91	828.09	663.92	566.80	503.18	458.68
25000	2252.56	1208.24	862.59	691.59	590.42	524.15	477.79
26000	2342.66	1256.57	897.09	719.25	614.03	545.11	496.90
27000	2432.76	1304.90	931.60	746.91	637.65	566.08	516.02
28000	2522.87	1353.23	966.10	774.58	661.27	587.04	535.13
29000	2612.97	1401.56	1000.60	802.24	684.88	608.01	554.24
30000	2703.07	1449.89	1035.11	829.90	708.50	628.98	573.35
35000	3153.58	1691.54	1207.63	968.22	826.58	733.80	668.91
40000	3604.09	1933.19	1380.14	1106.54	944.67	838.63	764.47
45000	4054.61	2174.84	1552.66	1244.85	1062.75	943.46	860.03
50000	4505.12	2416.48	1725.18	1383.17	1180.84	1048.29	955.58
55000	4955.63	2658.13	1897.70	1521.49	1298.92	1153.12	1051.14
60000	5406.14	2899.78	2070.21	1659.80	1417.00	1257.95	1146.70
65000	5856.65	3141.43	2242.73	1798.12	1535.09	1362.78	1242.26
70000	6307.16	3383.08	2415.25	1936.44	1653.17	1467.61	1337.82
75000	6757.68	3624.73	2587.77	2074.76	1771.25	1572.44	1433.38
80000	7208.19	3866.37	2760.29	2213.07	1889.34	1677.27	1528.94
85000	7658.70	4108.02	2932.81	2351.39	2007.42	1782.10	1624.49
90000	8109.21	4349.67	3105.32	2489.71	2125.50	1886.93	1720.05
95000	8559.72	4591.32	3277.84	2628.02	2243.59	1991.76	1815.61
100000	9010.23	4832.97	3450.36	2766.34	2361.67	2096.58	1911.17
200000	18020.47	9665.94	6900.72	5532.68	4723.34	4193.17	3822.34
300000	27030.70	14498.90	10351.08	8299.02	7085.01	6289.75	5733.51
400000	36040.94	19331.87	13801.44	11065.36	9446.68	8386.34	7644.68
500000	45051.17	24164.84	17251.81	13831.70	11808.35	10482.92	9555.85
1000000	90102.35	48329.68	34503.61	27663.41	23616.70	20965.84	19111.69

Amortization Amount	8 Years	9 Years	10 Years	15 Years	20 Years	25 Years	30 Years
25	0.44	0.42	0.40	0.34	0.32	0.31	0.31
50	0.89	0.84	0.80	0.69	0.65	0.63	0.62
100	1.78	1.67	1.59	1.38	1.29	1.26	1.24
200	3.55	3.35	3.19	2.75	2.58	2.51	2.48
300	5.33	5.02	4.78	4.13	3.88	3.77	3.71
400	7.10	6.69	6.37	5.51	5.17	5.02	4.95
500	8.88	8.36	7.97	6.89	6.46	6.28	6.19
600	10.65	10.04	9.56	8.26	7.75	7.53	7.43
700	12.43	11.71	11.15	9.64	9.05	8.79	8.67
800	14.20	13.38	12.75	11.02	10.34	10.04	9.90
900	15.98	15.06	14.34	12.39	11.63	11.30	11.14
1000	17.75	16.73	15.93	13.77	12.92	12.55	12.38
2000	35.51	33.46	31.86	27.54	25.85	25.10	24.76
3000	53.26	50.18	47.79	41.31	38.77	37.66	37.14
4000	71.02	66.91	63.73	55.08	51.70	50.21	49.52
5000	88.77	83.64	79.66	68.85	64.62	62.76	61.90
6000	106.53	100.37	95.59	82.62	77.55	75.31	74.28
7000	124.28	117.10	111.52	96.39	90.47	87.87	86.66
8000	142.04	133.82	127.45	110.16	103.39	100.42	99.04
9000	159.79	150.55	143.38	123.93	116.32	112.97	111.42
10000	177.55	167.28	159.32	137.70	129.24	125.52	123.80
11000	195.30	184.01	175.25	151.47	142.17	138.08	136.18
12000	213.05	200.73	191.18	165.24	155.09	150.63	148.56
13000	230.81	217.46	207.11	179.01	168.01	163.18	160.95
14000	248.56	234.19	223.04	192.78	180.94	175.73	173.33
15000	266.32	250.92	238.97	206.55	193.86	188.28	185.71
16000	284.07	267.65	254.91	220.32	206.79	200.84	198.09
17000	301.83	284.37	270.84	234.09	219.71	213.39	210.47
18000	319.58	301.10	286.77	247.86	232.64	225.94	222.85
19000	337.34	317.83	302.70	261.63	245.56	238.49	235.23
20000	355.09	334.56	318.63	275.40	258.48	251.05	247.61
21000	372.85	351.29	334.56	289.17	271.41	263.60	259.99
22000	390.60	368.01	350.49	302.94	284.33	276.15	272.37
23000	408.36	384.74	366.43	316.71	297.26	288.70	284.75
24000	426.11	401.47	382.36	330.48	310.18	301.25	297.13
25000	443.86	418.20	398.29	344.25	323.11	313.81	309.51
26000	461.62	434.92	414.22	358.02	336.03	326.36	321.89
27000	479.37	451.65	430.15	371.79	348.95	338.91	334.27
28000	497.13	468.38	446.08	385.56	361.88	351.46	346.65
29000	514.88	485.11	462.02	399.33	374.80	364.02	359.03
30000	532.64	501.84	477.95	413.10	387.73	376.57	371.41
35000	621.41	585.48	557.61	481.95	452.35	439.33	433.31
40000	710.18	669.11	637.26	550.80	516.97	502.09	495.22
45000	798.96	752.75	716.92	619.65	581.59	564.85	557.12
50000	887.73	836.39	796.58	688.50	646.21	627.61	619.02
55000	976.50	920.03	876.24	757.35	710.83	690.38	680.92
60000	1065.27	1003.67	955.90	826.20	775.45	753.14	742.82
65000	1154.05	1087.31	1035.55	895.05	840.07	815.90	804.73
70000	1242.82	1170.95	1115.21	963.91	904.70	878.66	866.63
75000	1331.59	1254.59	1194.87	1032.76	969.32	941.42	928.53
80000	1420.37	1338.23	1274.53	1101.61	1033.94	1004.18	990.43
85000	1509.14	1421.87	1354.19	1170.46	1098.56	1066.94	1052.34
90000	1597.91	1505.51	1433.84	1239.31	1163.18	1129.71	1114.24
95000	1686.68	1589.15	1513.50	1308.16	1227.80	1192.47	1176.14
100000	1775.46	1672.79	1593.16	1377.01	1292.42	1255.23	1238.04
200000	3550.91	3345.57	3186.32	2754.01	2584.84	2510.46	2476.08
300000	5326.37	5018.36	4779.48	4131.02	3877.27	3765.68	3714.12
400000	7101.83	6691.15	6372.64	5508.03	5169.69	5020.91	4952.17
500000	8877.28	8363.94	7965.79	6885.04	6462.11	6276.14	6190.21
1000000	17754.57	16727.87	15931.59	13770.07	12924.22	12552.28	12380.41

15.25%

MONTHLY PAYMENT
NECESSARY TO AMORTIZE A LOAN

Amortization Amount	1 Year	2 Years	3 Years	4 Years	5 Years	6 Years	7 Years
25	2.25	1.21	0.86	0.69	0.59	0.53	0.48
50	4.51	2.42	1.73	1.39	1.18	1.05	0.96
100	9.02	4.84	3.46	2.77	2.37	2.10	1.92
200	18.03	9.68	6.91	5.54	4.74	4.21	3.84
300	27.05	14.52	10.37	8.32	7.10	6.31	5.75
400	36.06	19.35	13.82	11.09	9.47	8.41	7.67
500	45.08	24.19	17.28	13.86	11.84	10.51	9.59
600	54.09	29.03	20.74	16.63	14.21	12.62	11.51
700	63.11	33.87	24.19	19.41	16.57	14.72	13.42
800	72.13	38.71	27.65	22.18	18.94	16.82	15.34
900	81.14	43.55	31.10	24.95	21.31	18.93	17.26
1000	90.16	48.39	34.56	27.72	23.68	21.03	19.18
2000	180.32	96.77	69.12	55.45	47.36	42.06	38.35
3000	270.47	145.16	103.68	83.17	71.03	63.09	57.53
4000	360.63	193.54	138.24	110.89	94.71	84.12	76.71
5000	450.79	241.93	172.81	138.61	118.39	105.15	95.89
6000	540.95	290.31	207.37	166.34	142.07	126.18	115.06
7000	631.10	338.70	241.93	194.06	165.75	147.21	134.24
8000	721.26	387.08	276.49	221.78	189.43	168.24	153.42
9000	811.42	435.47	311.05	249.51	213.10	189.27	172.60
10000	901.58	483.85	345.61	277.23	236.78	210.29	191.77
11000	991.74	532.24	380.17	304.95	260.46	231.32	210.95
12000	1081.89	580.63	414.73	332.67	284.14	252.35	230.13
13000	1172.05	629.01	449.29	360.40	307.82	273.38	249.31
14000	1262.21	677.40	483.86	388.12	331.50	294.41	268.48
15000	1352.37	725.78	518.42	415.84	355.17	315.44	287.66
16000	1442.52	774.17	552.98	443.57	378.85	336.47	306.84
17000	1532.68	822.55	587.54	471.29	402.53	357.50	326.02
18000	1622.84	870.94	622.10	499.01	426.21	378.53	345.19
19000	1713.00	919.32	656.66	526.73	449.89	399.56	364.37
20000	1803.16	967.71	691.22	554.46	473.56	420.59	383.55
21000	1893.31	1016.09	725.78	582.18	497.24	441.62	402.73
22000	1983.47	1064.48	760.34	609.90	520.92	462.65	421.90
23000	2073.63	1112.87	794.90	637.63	544.60	483.68	441.08
24000	2163.79	1161.25	829.47	665.35	568.28	504.71	460.26
25000	2253.94	1209.64	864.03	693.07	591.96	525.74	479.44
26000	2344.10	1258.02	898.59	720.79	615.63	546.77	498.61
27000	2434.26	1306.41	933.15	748.52	639.31	567.80	517.79
28000	2524.42	1354.79	967.71	776.24	662.99	588.83	536.97
29000	2614.58	1403.18	1002.27	803.96	686.67	609.85	556.14
30000	2704.73	1451.56	1036.83	831.69	710.35	630.88	575.32
35000	3155.52	1693.49	1209.64	970.30	828.74	736.03	671.21
40000	3606.31	1935.42	1382.44	1108.91	947.13	841.18	767.10
45000	4057.10	2177.35	1555.25	1247.53	1065.52	946.33	862.98
50000	4507.89	2419.27	1728.05	1386.14	1183.91	1051.47	958.87
55000	4958.68	2661.20	1900.86	1524.78	1302.30	1156.62	1054.76
60000	5409.47	2903.13	2073.66	1663.37	1420.69	1261.77	1150.64
65000	5860.26	3145.06	2246.47	1801.99	1539.08	1366.92	1246.53
70000	6311.05	3386.98	2419.28	1940.60	1657.48	1472.06	1342.42
75000	6761.83	3628.91	2592.08	2079.21	1775.87	1577.21	1438.31
80000	7212.62	3870.84	2764.89	2217.83	1894.26	1682.36	1534.19
85000	7663.41	4112.77	2937.69	2356.44	2012.65	1787.50	1630.08
90000	8114.20	4354.69	3110.50	2495.06	2131.04	1892.65	1725.97
95000	8564.99	4596.62	3283.30	2633.67	2249.43	1997.80	1821.85
100000	9015.78	4838.55	3456.11	2772.29	2367.82	2102.95	1917.74
200000	18031.56	9677.09	6912.21	5544.57	4735.65	4205.89	3835.48
300000	27047.34	14515.64	10368.32	8316.86	7103.47	6308.84	5753.22
400000	36063.12	19354.19	13824.43	11089.14	9471.29	8411.79	7670.96
500000	45078.90	24192.74	17280.54	13861.43	11839.11	10514.73	9588.70
1000000	90157.80	48385.47	34561.07	27722.86	23678.23	21029.47	19177.40

Amortization Amount	8 Years	9 Years	10 Years	15 Years	20 Years	25 Years	30 Years
25	0.45	0.42	0.40	0.35	0.33	0.32	0.31
50	0.89	0.84	0.80	0.69	0.65	0.63	0.62
100	1.78	1.68	1.60	1.39	1.30	1.26	1.25
200	3.56	3.36	3.20	2.77	2.60	2.53	2.49
300	5.35	5.04	4.80	4.16	3.90	3.79	3.74
400	7.13	6.72	6.40	5.54	5.20	5.06	4.99
500	8.91	8.40	8.00	6.93	6.51	6.32	6.24
600	10.69	10.08	9.60	8.31	7.81	7.59	7.48
700	12.48	11.76	11.20	9.70	9.11	8.85	8.73
800	14.26	13.44	12.80	11.08	10.41	10.11	9.98
900	16.04	15.12	14.40	12.47	11.71	11.38	11.23
1000	17.82	16.80	16.00	13.85	13.01	12.64	12.47
2000	35.64	33.60	32.01	27.70	26.02	25.29	24.95
3000	53.47	50.39	48.01	41.55	39.03	37.93	37.42
4000	71.29	67.19	64.01	55.40	52.04	50.57	49.90
5000	89.11	83.99	80.02	69.25	65.05	63.22	62.37
6000	106.93	100.79	96.02	83.10	78.06	75.86	74.85
7000	124.76	117.58	112.02	96.95	91.08	88.50	87.32
8000	142.58	134.38	128.03	110.80	104.09	101.15	99.79
9000	160.40	151.18	144.03	124.65	117.10	113.79	112.27
10000	178.22	167.98	160.03	138.50	130.11	126.43	124.74
11000	196.05	184.77	176.04	152.35	143.12	139.08	137.22
12000	213.87	201.57	192.04	166.20	156.13	151.72	149.69
13000	231.69	218.37	208.04	180.05	169.14	164.36	162.16
14000	249.51	235.17	224.05	193.90	182.15	177.00	174.64
15000	267.33	251.96	240.05	207.75	195.16	189.65	187.11
16000	285.16	268.76	256.05	221.60	208.17	202.29	199.59
17000	302.98	285.56	272.06	235.45	221.18	214.93	212.06
18000	320.80	302.36	288.06	249.30	234.19	227.58	224.54
19000	338.62	319.15	304.06	263.15	247.20	240.22	237.01
20000	356.45	335.95	320.07	277.00	260.21	252.86	249.48
21000	374.27	352.75	336.07	290.85	273.23	265.51	261.96
22000	392.09	369.55	352.07	304.70	286.24	278.15	274.43
23000	409.91	386.35	368.07	318.55	299.25	290.79	286.91
24000	427.74	403.14	384.08	332.41	312.26	303.44	299.38
25000	445.56	419.94	400.08	346.26	325.27	316.08	311.86
26000	463.38	436.74	416.08	360.11	338.28	328.72	324.33
27000	481.20	453.54	432.09	373.96	351.29	341.37	336.80
28000	499.02	470.33	448.09	387.81	364.30	354.01	349.28
29000	516.85	487.13	464.09	401.66	377.31	366.65	361.75
30000	534.67	503.93	480.10	415.51	390.32	379.30	374.23
35000	623.78	587.92	560.11	484.76	455.38	442.51	436.60
40000	712.89	671.90	640.13	554.01	520.43	505.73	498.97
45000	802.00	755.89	720.15	623.26	585.48	568.94	561.34
50000	891.12	839.88	800.16	692.51	650.54	632.16	623.71
55000	980.23	923.87	880.18	761.76	715.59	695.38	688.08
60000	1069.34	1007.86	960.20	831.01	780.64	758.59	748.45
65000	1158.45	1091.84	1040.21	900.26	845.70	821.81	810.82
70000	1247.56	1175.83	1120.23	969.52	910.75	885.02	873.20
75000	1336.67	1259.82	1200.24	1038.77	975.80	948.24	935.57
80000	1425.79	1343.81	1280.26	1108.02	1040.86	1011.46	997.94
85000	1514.90	1427.80	1360.28	1177.27	1105.91	1074.67	1060.31
90000	1604.01	1511.79	1440.29	1246.52	1170.97	1137.89	1122.68
95000	1693.12	1595.77	1520.31	1315.77	1236.02	1201.10	1185.05
100000	1782.23	1679.76	1600.33	1385.02	1301.07	1264.32	1247.42
200000	3564.46	3359.52	3200.65	2770.04	2602.15	2528.64	2494.84
300000	5346.69	5039.28	4800.98	4155.06	3903.22	3792.96	3742.26
400000	7128.93	6719.05	6401.30	5540.09	5204.29	5057.28	4989.69
500000	8911.16	8398.81	8001.63	6925.11	6505.36	6321.60	6237.11
1000000	17822.32	16797.61	16003.26	13850.22	13010.73	12643.21	12474.22

15.375%

MONTHLY PAYMENT
NECESSARY TO AMORTIZE A LOAN

Amortization Amount	1 Year	2 Years	3 Years	4 Years	5 Years	6 Years	7 Years
25	2.26	1.21	0.87	0.69	0.59	0.53	0.48
50	4.51	2.42	1.73	1.39	1.19	1.05	0.96
100	9.02	4.84	3.46	2.78	2.37	2.11	1.92
200	18.04	9.69	6.92	5.56	4.75	4.22	3.85
300	27.06	14.53	10.39	8.33	7.12	6.33	5.77
400	36.09	19.38	13.85	11.11	9.50	8.44	7.70
500	45.11	24.22	17.31	13.89	11.87	10.55	9.62
600	54.13	29.06	20.77	16.67	14.24	12.66	11.55
700	63.15	33.91	24.23	19.45	16.62	14.77	13.47
800	72.17	38.75	27.69	22.23	18.99	16.87	15.39
900	81.19	43.60	31.16	25.00	21.37	18.98	17.32
1000	90.21	48.44	34.62	27.78	23.74	21.09	19.24
2000	180.43	96.88	69.24	55.56	47.48	42.19	38.49
3000	270.64	145.32	103.86	83.35	71.22	63.28	57.73
4000	360.85	193.77	138.47	111.13	94.96	84.37	76.97
5000	451.07	242.21	173.09	138.91	118.70	105.47	96.22
6000	541.28	290.65	207.71	166.69	142.44	126.56	115.46
7000	631.49	339.09	242.33	194.48	166.18	147.65	134.70
8000	721.71	387.53	276.95	222.26	189.92	168.75	153.95
9000	811.92	435.97	311.57	250.04	213.66	189.84	173.19
10000	902.13	484.41	346.19	277.82	237.40	210.93	192.43
11000	992.35	532.85	380.80	305.61	261.14	232.02	211.68
12000	1082.56	581.30	415.42	333.39	284.88	253.12	230.92
13000	1172.77	629.74	450.04	361.17	308.62	274.21	250.16
14000	1262.99	678.18	484.66	388.95	332.36	295.30	269.40
15000	1353.20	726.62	519.28	416.74	356.10	316.40	288.65
16000	1443.41	775.06	553.90	444.52	379.84	337.49	307.89
17000	1533.63	823.50	588.52	472.30	403.58	358.58	327.13
18000	1623.84	871.94	623.13	500.08	427.32	379.68	346.38
19000	1714.05	920.38	657.75	527.86	451.06	400.77	365.62
20000	1804.26	968.83	692.37	555.65	474.80	421.86	384.86
21000	1894.48	1017.27	726.99	583.43	498.54	442.96	404.11
22000	1984.69	1065.71	761.61	611.21	522.28	464.05	423.35
23000	2074.90	1114.15	796.23	638.99	546.02	485.14	442.59
24000	2165.12	1162.59	830.85	666.78	569.76	506.24	461.84
25000	2255.33	1211.03	865.46	694.56	593.50	527.33	481.08
26000	2345.54	1259.47	900.08	722.34	617.24	548.42	500.32
27000	2435.76	1307.91	934.70	750.12	640.97	569.52	519.57
28000	2525.97	1356.36	969.32	777.91	664.71	590.61	538.81
29000	2616.18	1404.80	1003.94	805.69	688.45	611.70	558.05
30000	2706.40	1453.24	1038.56	833.47	712.19	632.79	577.30
35000	3157.46	1695.44	1211.65	972.38	830.89	738.26	673.51
40000	3608.53	1937.65	1384.74	1111.29	949.59	843.73	769.73
45000	4059.60	2179.86	1557.84	1250.21	1068.29	949.19	865.94
50000	4510.66	2422.06	1730.93	1389.12	1186.99	1054.66	962.16
55000	4961.73	2664.27	1904.02	1528.03	1305.69	1160.12	1058.38
60000	5412.79	2906.48	2077.11	1666.94	1424.39	1265.59	1154.59
65000	5863.86	3148.68	2250.21	1805.85	1543.09	1371.06	1250.81
70000	6314.93	3390.89	2423.30	1944.76	1661.79	1476.52	1347.02
75000	6765.99	3633.10	2596.39	2083.68	1780.49	1581.99	1443.24
80000	7217.06	3875.30	2769.49	2222.59	1899.19	1687.45	1539.46
85000	7668.13	4117.51	2942.58	2361.50	2017.88	1792.92	1635.67
90000	8119.19	4359.71	3115.67	2500.41	2136.58	1898.38	1731.89
95000	8570.26	4601.92	3288.76	2639.32	2255.28	2003.85	1828.10
100000	9021.32	4844.13	3461.86	2778.23	2373.98	2109.32	1924.32
200000	18042.65	9688.25	6923.71	5556.47	4747.96	4218.63	3848.64
300000	27063.97	14532.38	10385.57	8334.70	7121.94	6327.95	5772.96
400000	36085.30	19376.51	13847.43	11112.94	9495.93	8437.27	7697.28
500000	45106.62	24220.64	17309.28	13891.17	11869.91	10546.58	9621.60
1000000	90213.24	48441.27	34618.56	27782.35	23739.81	21093.17	19243.19

Amortization Amount	8 Years	9 Years	10 Years	15 Years	20 Years	25 Years	30 Years
25	0.45	0.42	0.40	0.35	0.33	0.32	0.31
50	0.89	0.84	0.80	0.70	0.65	0.64	0.63
100	1.79	1.69	1.61	1.39	1.31	1.27	1.26
200	3.58	3.37	3.22	2.79	2.62	2.55	2.51
300	5.37	5.06	4.82	4.18	3.93	3.82	3.77
400	7.16	6.75	6.43	5.57	5.24	5.09	5.03
500	8.95	8.43	8.04	6.97	6.55	6.37	6.28
600	10.73	10.12	9.65	8.36	7.86	7.64	7.54
700	12.52	11.81	11.25	9.75	9.17	8.91	8.80
800	14.31	13.49	12.86	11.14	10.48	10.19	10.05
900	16.10	15.18	14.47	12.54	11.79	11.46	11.31
1000	17.89	16.87	16.08	13.93	13.10	12.73	12.57
2000	35.78	33.73	32.15	27.86	26.19	25.47	25.14
3000	53.67	50.60	48.23	41.79	39.29	38.20	37.70
4000	71.56	67.47	64.30	55.72	52.39	50.94	50.27
5000	89.45	84.34	80.38	69.65	65.49	63.67	62.84
6000	107.34	101.20	96.45	83.58	78.58	76.41	75.41
7000	125.23	118.07	112.53	97.51	91.68	89.14	87.98
8000	143.12	134.94	128.60	111.44	104.78	101.87	100.54
9000	161.01	151.81	144.68	125.37	117.88	114.61	113.11
10000	178.90	168.67	160.75	139.30	130.97	127.34	125.68
11000	196.79	185.54	176.83	153.24	144.07	140.08	138.25
12000	214.68	202.41	192.90	167.17	157.17	152.81	150.82
13000	232.57	219.28	208.98	181.10	170.27	165.54	163.39
14000	250.46	236.14	225.05	195.03	183.36	178.28	175.95
15000	268.35	253.01	241.13	208.96	196.46	191.01	188.52
16000	286.24	269.88	257.20	222.89	209.56	203.75	201.09
17000	304.13	286.75	273.28	236.82	222.66	216.48	213.66
18000	322.02	303.61	289.35	250.75	235.75	229.22	226.23
19000	339.91	320.48	305.43	264.68	248.85	241.95	238.79
20000	357.80	337.35	321.50	278.61	261.95	254.68	251.36
21000	375.69	354.22	337.58	292.54	275.04	267.42	263.93
22000	393.58	371.08	353.65	306.47	288.14	280.15	276.50
23000	411.47	387.95	369.73	320.40	301.24	292.89	289.07
24000	429.36	404.82	385.80	334.33	314.34	305.62	301.63
25000	447.25	421.69	401.88	348.26	327.43	318.36	314.20
26000	465.14	438.55	417.95	362.19	340.53	331.09	326.77
27000	483.03	455.42	434.03	376.12	353.63	343.82	339.34
28000	500.92	472.29	450.10	390.05	366.73	356.56	351.91
29000	518.81	489.16	466.18	403.98	379.82	369.29	364.47
30000	536.70	506.02	482.25	417.91	392.92	382.03	377.04
35000	626.16	590.36	562.63	487.57	458.41	445.70	439.88
40000	715.61	674.70	643.00	557.22	523.89	509.37	502.72
45000	805.06	759.04	723.38	626.87	589.38	573.04	565.56
50000	894.51	843.37	803.75	696.52	654.87	636.71	628.40
55000	983.96	927.71	884.13	766.18	720.35	700.38	691.24
60000	1073.41	1012.05	964.50	835.83	785.84	764.05	754.08
65000	1162.86	1096.39	1044.88	905.48	851.33	827.72	816.93
70000	1252.31	1180.72	1125.25	975.13	916.82	891.40	879.77
75000	1341.76	1265.06	1205.63	1044.79	982.30	955.07	942.61
80000	1431.21	1349.40	1286.00	1114.44	1047.79	1018.74	1005.45
85000	1520.66	1433.73	1366.38	1184.09	1113.28	1082.41	1068.29
90000	1610.11	1518.07	1446.75	1253.74	1178.76	1146.08	1131.13
95000	1699.57	1602.41	1527.13	1323.40	1244.25	1209.75	1193.97
100000	1789.02	1686.75	1607.50	1393.05	1309.74	1273.42	1256.81
200000	3578.03	3373.49	3215.01	2786.10	2619.47	2546.85	2513.62
300000	5367.05	5060.24	4822.51	4179.15	3929.21	3820.27	3770.42
400000	7156.07	6746.99	6430.02	5572.20	5238.94	5093.69	5027.23
500000	8945.08	8433.73	8037.52	6965.25	6548.68	6367.11	6284.04
1000000	17890.17	16867.46	16075.04	13930.50	13097.36	12734.23	12568.08

15.5%

Amortization Amount	1 Year	2 Years	3 Years	4 Years	5 Years	6 Years	7 Years
25	2.26	1.21	0.87	0.70	0.60	0.53	0.48
50	4.51	2.42	1.73	1.39	1.19	1.06	0.97
100	9.03	4.85	3.47	2.78	2.38	2.12	1.93
200	18.05	9.70	6.94	5.57	4.76	4.23	3.86
300	27.08	14.55	10.40	8.35	7.14	6.35	5.79
400	36.11	19.40	13.87	11.14	9.52	8.46	7.72
500	45.13	24.25	17.34	13.92	11.90	10.58	9.65
600	54.16	29.10	20.81	16.71	14.28	12.69	11.59
700	63.19	33.95	24.27	19.49	16.66	14.81	13.52
800	72.21	38.80	27.74	22.27	19.04	16.93	15.45
900	81.24	43.65	31.21	25.06	21.42	19.04	17.38
1000	90.27	48.50	34.68	27.84	23.80	21.16	19.31
2000	180.54	98.99	69.35	55.68	47.60	42.31	38.62
3000	270.81	145.49	104.03	83.53	71.40	63.47	57.93
4000	361.07	193.99	138.70	111.37	95.21	84.63	77.24
5000	451.34	242.49	173.38	139.21	119.01	105.78	96.55
6000	541.61	290.98	208.06	167.05	142.81	126.94	115.85
7000	631.88	339.48	242.73	194.89	166.61	148.10	135.16
8000	722.15	387.98	277.41	222.74	190.41	169.26	154.47
9000	812.42	436.47	312.08	250.58	214.21	190.41	173.78
10000	902.69	484.97	346.76	278.42	238.01	211.57	193.09
11000	992.96	533.47	381.44	306.26	261.82	232.73	212.40
12000	1083.22	581.96	416.11	334.10	285.62	253.88	231.71
13000	1173.49	630.46	450.79	361.94	309.42	275.04	251.02
14000	1263.76	678.96	485.47	389.79	333.22	296.20	270.33
15000	1354.03	727.46	520.14	417.63	357.02	317.35	289.64
16000	1444.30	775.95	554.82	445.47	380.82	338.51	308.95
17000	1534.57	824.45	589.49	473.31	404.62	359.67	328.25
18000	1624.84	872.95	624.17	501.15	428.43	380.82	347.56
19000	1715.10	921.44	658.85	529.00	452.23	401.98	366.87
20000	1805.37	969.94	693.52	556.84	476.03	423.14	386.18
21000	1895.64	1018.44	728.20	584.68	499.83	444.30	405.49
22000	1985.91	1066.94	762.87	612.52	523.63	465.45	424.80
23000	2076.18	1115.43	797.55	640.36	547.43	486.61	444.11
24000	2166.45	1163.93	832.23	668.21	571.23	507.77	463.42
25000	2256.72	1212.43	866.90	696.05	595.04	528.92	482.73
26000	2346.99	1260.92	901.58	723.89	618.84	550.08	502.04
27000	2437.25	1309.42	936.25	751.73	642.64	571.24	521.35
28000	2527.52	1357.92	970.93	779.57	666.44	592.39	540.65
29000	2617.79	1406.42	1005.61	807.41	690.24	613.55	559.96
30000	2708.06	1454.91	1040.28	835.26	714.04	634.71	579.27
35000	3159.40	1697.40	1213.66	974.47	833.05	740.49	675.82
40000	3610.75	1939.88	1387.04	1113.68	952.06	846.28	772.36
45000	4062.09	2182.37	1560.42	1252.88	1071.07	952.06	868.91
50000	4513.43	2424.85	1733.80	1392.09	1190.07	1057.85	965.45
55000	4964.78	2667.34	1907.18	1531.30	1309.08	1163.63	1062.00
60000	5416.12	2909.82	2080.56	1670.51	1428.09	1269.42	1158.54
65000	5867.46	3152.31	2253.95	1809.72	1547.09	1375.20	1255.09
70000	6318.81	3394.80	2427.33	1948.93	1666.10	1480.99	1351.64
75000	6770.15	3637.28	2600.71	2088.14	1785.11	1586.77	1448.18
80000	7221.49	3879.77	2774.09	2227.35	1904.12	1692.56	1544.73
85000	7672.84	4122.25	2947.47	2366.56	2023.12	1798.34	1641.27
90000	8124.18	4364.74	3120.85	2505.77	2142.13	1904.12	1737.82
95000	8575.52	4607.22	3294.23	2644.98	2261.14	2009.91	1834.36
100000	9026.87	4849.71	3467.61	2784.19	2380.15	2115.69	1930.91
200000	18053.73	9699.42	6935.22	5568.38	4760.29	4231.39	3861.82
300000	27080.60	14549.12	10402.82	8352.56	7140.44	6347.08	5792.72
400000	36107.47	19398.83	13870.43	11136.75	9520.58	8462.78	7723.63
500000	45134.34	24248.54	17338.04	13920.94	11900.73	10578.47	9654.54
1000000	90268.67	48497.08	34676.08	27841.88	23801.46	21156.94	19309.08

Amortization Amount	8 Years	9 Years	10 Years	15 Years	20 Years	25 Years	30 Years
25	0.45	0.42	0.40	0.35	0.33	0.32	0.32
50	0.90	0.85	0.81	0.70	0.66	0.64	0.63
100	1.80	1.69	1.61	1.40	1.32	1.28	1.27
200	3.59	3.39	3.23	2.80	2.64	2.57	2.53
300	5.39	5.08	4.84	4.20	3.96	3.85	3.80
400	7.18	6.77	6.46	5.60	5.27	5.13	5.06
500	8.98	8.47	8.07	7.01	6.59	6.41	6.33
600	10.77	10.16	9.69	8.41	7.91	7.70	7.60
700	12.57	11.86	11.30	9.81	9.23	8.98	8.86
800	14.37	13.55	12.92	11.21	10.55	10.26	10.13
900	16.16	15.24	14.53	12.61	11.87	11.54	11.40
1000	17.96	16.94	16.15	14.01	13.18	12.83	12.66
2000	35.92	33.87	32.29	28.02	26.37	25.65	25.32
3000	53.87	50.81	48.44	42.03	39.55	38.48	37.99
4000	71.83	67.75	64.59	56.04	52.74	51.30	50.65
5000	89.79	84.69	80.73	70.05	65.92	64.13	63.31
6000	107.75	101.62	96.88	84.07	79.10	76.95	75.97
7000	125.71	118.56	113.03	98.08	92.29	89.78	88.63
8000	143.66	135.50	129.18	112.09	105.47	102.60	101.30
9000	161.62	152.44	145.32	126.10	118.66	115.43	113.96
10000	179.58	169.37	161.47	140.11	131.84	128.25	126.62
11000	197.54	186.31	177.62	154.12	145.03	141.08	139.28
12000	215.50	203.25	193.76	168.13	158.21	153.90	151.94
13000	233.46	220.19	209.91	182.14	171.39	166.73	164.61
14000	251.41	237.12	226.06	196.15	184.58	179.55	177.27
15000	269.37	254.06	242.20	210.16	197.76	192.38	189.93
16000	287.33	271.00	258.35	224.17	210.95	205.21	202.59
17000	305.29	287.94	274.50	238.19	224.13	218.03	215.25
18000	323.25	304.87	290.64	252.20	237.31	230.86	227.92
19000	341.20	321.81	306.79	266.21	250.50	243.68	240.58
20000	359.16	338.75	322.94	280.22	263.68	256.51	253.24
21000	377.12	355.69	339.09	294.23	276.87	269.33	265.90
22000	395.08	372.62	355.23	308.24	290.05	282.16	278.56
23000	413.04	389.56	371.38	322.25	303.23	294.98	291.23
24000	430.99	406.50	387.53	336.26	316.42	307.81	303.89
25000	448.95	423.44	403.67	350.27	329.60	320.63	316.55
26000	466.91	440.37	419.82	364.28	342.79	333.46	329.21
27000	484.87	457.31	435.97	378.29	355.97	346.28	341.87
28000	502.83	474.25	452.11	392.31	369.16	359.11	354.54
29000	520.79	491.19	468.26	406.32	382.34	371.93	367.20
30000	538.74	508.12	484.41	420.33	395.52	384.76	379.86
35000	628.53	592.81	565.14	490.38	461.44	448.89	443.17
40000	718.32	677.50	645.88	560.44	527.36	513.01	506.48
45000	808.12	762.18	726.61	630.49	593.29	577.14	569.79
50000	897.91	846.87	807.35	700.55	659.21	641.27	633.10
55000	987.70	931.56	888.08	770.60	725.13	705.39	696.41
60000	1077.49	1016.25	968.82	840.65	791.05	769.52	759.72
65000	1167.28	1100.93	1049.55	910.71	856.97	833.65	823.03
70000	1257.07	1185.62	1130.29	980.76	922.89	897.77	886.34
75000	1346.86	1270.31	1211.02	1050.82	988.81	961.90	949.65
80000	1436.65	1354.99	1291.76	1120.87	1054.73	1026.03	1012.96
85000	1526.44	1439.68	1372.49	1190.93	1120.65	1090.15	1076.27
90000	1616.23	1524.37	1453.22	1260.98	1186.57	1154.28	1139.58
95000	1706.02	1609.06	1533.96	1331.04	1252.49	1218.41	1202.89
100000	1795.81	1693.74	1614.69	1401.09	1318.41	1282.53	1266.20
200000	3591.62	3387.48	3229.39	2802.18	2636.82	2565.07	2532.40
300000	5387.43	5081.23	4844.08	4203.27	3955.24	3847.60	3798.60
400000	7183.25	6774.97	6458.78	5604.36	5273.65	5130.14	5064.80
500000	8979.06	8468.71	8073.47	7005.46	6592.06	6412.67	6331.00
1000000	17958.11	16937.42	16146.94	14010.91	13184.12	12825.34	12662.00

15.625%

Amortization Amount	1 Year	2 Years	3 Years	4 Years	5 Years	6 Years	7 Years
25	2.26	1.21	0.87	0.70	0.60	0.53	0.48
50	4.52	2.43	1.74	1.40	1.19	1.06	0.97
100	9.03	4.86	3.47	2.79	2.39	2.12	1.94
200	18.06	9.71	6.95	5.58	4.77	4.24	3.88
300	27.10	14.57	10.42	8.37	7.16	6.37	5.81
400	36.13	19.42	13.89	11.16	9.55	8.49	7.75
500	45.16	24.28	17.37	13.95	11.93	10.61	9.69
600	54.19	29.13	20.84	16.74	14.32	12.73	11.63
700	63.23	33.99	24.31	19.53	16.70	14.85	13.56
800	72.26	38.84	27.79	22.32	19.09	16.98	15.50
900	81.29	43.70	31.26	25.11	21.48	19.10	17.44
1000	90.32	48.55	34.73	27.90	23.86	21.22	19.38
2000	180.65	97.11	69.47	55.80	47.73	42.44	38.75
3000	270.97	145.66	104.20	83.70	71.59	63.66	58.13
4000	361.30	194.21	138.93	111.61	95.45	84.88	77.50
5000	451.62	242.76	173.67	139.51	119.32	106.10	96.88
6000	541.94	291.32	208.40	167.41	143.18	127.32	116.25
7000	632.27	339.87	243.14	195.31	167.04	148.55	135.63
8000	722.59	388.42	277.87	223.21	190.91	169.77	155.00
9000	812.92	436.98	312.60	251.11	214.77	190.99	174.38
10000	903.24	485.53	347.34	279.00	238.63	212.21	193.75
11000	993.57	534.08	382.07	306.92	262.49	233.43	213.13
12000	1083.89	582.63	416.80	334.82	286.36	254.65	232.50
13000	1174.21	631.19	451.54	362.72	310.22	275.87	251.88
14000	1264.54	679.74	486.27	390.62	334.08	297.09	271.25
15000	1354.86	728.29	521.00	418.52	357.95	318.31	290.63
16000	1445.19	776.85	555.74	446.42	381.81	339.53	310.00
17000	1535.51	825.40	590.47	474.32	405.67	360.75	329.38
18000	1625.83	873.95	625.21	502.23	429.54	381.97	348.75
19000	1716.16	922.51	659.94	530.13	453.40	403.19	368.13
20000	1806.48	971.06	694.67	558.03	477.26	424.42	387.50
21000	1896.81	1019.61	729.41	585.93	501.13	445.64	406.88
22000	1987.13	1068.16	764.14	613.83	524.99	466.86	426.25
23000	2077.45	1116.72	798.87	641.73	548.85	488.08	445.63
24000	2167.78	1165.27	833.61	669.63	572.72	509.30	465.00
25000	2258.10	1213.82	868.34	697.54	596.58	530.52	484.38
26000	2348.43	1262.38	903.07	725.44	620.44	551.74	503.75
27000	2438.75	1310.93	937.81	753.34	644.31	572.96	523.13
28000	2529.07	1359.48	972.54	781.24	668.17	594.18	542.50
29000	2619.40	1408.03	1007.28	809.14	692.03	615.40	561.88
30000	2709.72	1456.59	1042.01	837.04	715.89	636.62	581.25
35000	3161.34	1699.35	1215.68	976.55	835.21	742.73	678.13
40000	3612.96	1942.12	1389.35	1116.06	954.53	848.83	775.00
45000	4064.58	2184.88	1563.01	1255.57	1073.84	954.94	871.88
50000	4516.20	2427.65	1736.68	1395.07	1193.16	1061.04	968.75
55000	4967.83	2670.41	1910.35	1534.58	1312.47	1167.14	1065.63
60000	5419.45	2913.17	2084.02	1674.09	1431.79	1273.25	1162.50
65000	5871.07	3155.94	2257.69	1813.59	1551.11	1379.35	1259.38
70000	6322.69	3398.70	2431.35	1953.10	1670.42	1485.45	1356.25
75000	6774.31	3641.47	2605.02	2092.61	1789.74	1591.56	1453.13
80000	7225.93	3884.23	2778.69	2232.12	1909.05	1697.66	1550.00
85000	7677.55	4127.00	2952.36	2371.62	2028.37	1803.77	1646.88
90000	8129.17	4369.76	3126.03	2511.13	2147.68	1909.87	1743.75
95000	8580.79	4612.53	3299.69	2650.64	2267.00	2015.97	1840.63
100000	9032.41	4855.29	3473.36	2790.15	2386.32	2122.08	1937.50
200000	18064.82	9710.58	6946.73	5580.29	4772.63	4244.16	3875.01
300000	27097.23	14565.87	10420.09	8370.44	7158.95	6366.24	5812.51
400000	36129.64	19421.16	13893.45	11160.58	9545.26	8488.31	7750.02
500000	45162.05	24276.45	17366.81	13950.73	11931.58	10610.39	9687.52
1000000	90324.10	48552.90	34733.63	27901.46	23863.16	21220.78	19375.04

Amortization Amount	8 Years	9 Years	10 Years	15 Years	20 Years	25 Years	30 Years
25	0.45	0.43	0.41	0.35	0.33	0.32	0.32
50	0.90	0.85	0.81	0.70	0.66	0.65	0.64
100	1.80	1.70	1.62	1.41	1.33	1.29	1.28
200	3.61	3.40	3.24	2.82	2.65	2.58	2.55
300	5.41	5.10	4.87	4.23	3.98	3.87	3.83
400	7.21	6.80	6.49	5.64	5.31	5.17	5.10
500	9.01	8.50	8.11	7.05	6.64	6.46	6.38
600	10.82	10.20	9.73	8.45	7.96	7.75	7.65
700	12.62	11.91	11.35	9.86	9.29	9.04	8.93
800	14.42	13.61	12.98	11.27	10.62	10.33	10.20
900	16.22	15.31	14.60	12.68	11.94	11.62	11.48
1000	18.03	17.01	16.22	14.09	13.27	12.92	12.76
2000	36.05	34.01	32.44	28.18	26.54	25.83	25.51
3000	54.08	51.02	48.66	42.27	39.81	38.75	38.27
4000	72.10	68.03	64.88	56.37	53.08	51.67	51.02
5000	90.13	85.04	81.09	70.46	66.36	64.58	63.78
6000	108.16	102.04	97.31	84.55	79.63	77.50	76.54
7000	126.18	119.05	113.53	98.64	92.90	90.42	89.29
8000	144.21	136.06	129.75	112.73	106.17	103.33	102.05
9000	162.24	153.07	145.97	126.82	119.44	116.25	114.80
10000	180.26	170.07	162.19	140.91	132.71	129.17	127.56
11000	198.29	187.08	178.41	155.01	145.98	142.08	140.32
12000	216.31	204.09	194.63	169.10	159.25	155.00	153.07
13000	234.34	221.10	210.85	183.19	172.52	167.92	165.83
14000	252.37	238.10	227.07	197.28	185.79	180.83	178.58
15000	270.39	255.11	243.28	211.37	199.07	193.75	191.34
16000	288.42	272.12	259.50	225.46	212.34	206.66	204.10
17000	306.44	289.13	275.72	239.55	225.61	219.58	216.85
18000	324.47	306.13	291.94	253.65	238.88	232.50	229.61
19000	342.50	323.14	308.16	267.74	252.15	245.41	242.36
20000	360.52	340.15	324.38	281.83	265.42	258.33	255.12
21000	378.55	357.16	340.60	295.92	278.69	271.25	267.88
22000	396.58	374.16	356.82	310.01	291.96	284.16	280.63
23000	414.60	391.17	373.04	324.10	305.23	297.08	293.39
24000	432.63	408.18	389.26	338.20	318.50	310.00	306.14
25000	450.65	425.19	405.47	352.29	331.78	322.91	318.90
26000	468.68	442.19	421.69	366.38	345.05	335.83	331.66
27000	486.71	459.20	437.91	380.47	358.32	348.75	344.41
28000	504.73	476.21	454.13	394.56	371.59	361.66	357.17
29000	522.76	493.22	470.35	408.65	384.86	374.58	369.92
30000	540.78	510.22	486.57	422.74	398.13	387.50	382.68
35000	630.92	595.26	567.66	493.20	464.49	452.08	446.46
40000	721.05	680.30	648.76	563.66	530.84	516.66	510.24
45000	811.18	765.34	729.85	634.12	597.20	581.24	574.02
50000	901.31	850.37	810.95	704.57	663.55	645.83	637.80
55000	991.44	935.41	892.04	775.03	729.91	710.41	701.58
60000	1081.57	1020.45	973.14	845.49	796.26	774.99	765.36
65000	1171.70	1105.49	1054.23	915.95	862.62	839.58	829.14
70000	1261.83	1190.52	1135.33	986.40	928.97	904.16	892.92
75000	1351.96	1275.56	1216.42	1056.86	995.33	968.74	956.70
80000	1442.09	1360.60	1297.52	1127.32	1061.68	1033.32	1020.48
85000	1532.22	1445.64	1378.61	1197.77	1128.04	1097.91	1084.26
90000	1622.35	1530.67	1459.71	1268.23	1194.39	1162.49	1148.04
95000	1712.49	1615.71	1540.80	1338.69	1260.75	1227.07	1211.82
100000	1802.62	1700.75	1621.90	1409.15	1327.10	1291.66	1275.60
200000	3605.23	3401.50	3243.79	2818.29	2654.20	2583.31	2551.20
300000	5407.85	5102.25	4865.69	4227.44	3981.30	3874.97	3826.79
400000	7210.46	6802.99	6487.58	5636.59	5308.40	5166.62	5102.39
500000	9013.08	8503.74	8109.48	7045.73	6635.50	6458.28	6377.99
1000000	18026.16	17007.49	16218.96	14091.47	13271.00	12916.55	12755.98

15.75%

MONTHLY PAYMENT
NECESSARY TO AMORTIZE A LOAN

Amortization Amount	1 Year	2 Years	3 Years	4 Years	5 Years	6 Years	7 Years
25	2.26	1.22	0.87	0.70	0.60	0.53	0.49
50	4.52	2.43	1.74	1.40	1.20	1.06	0.97
100	9.04	4.86	3.48	2.80	2.39	2.13	1.94
200	18.08	9.72	6.96	5.59	4.78	4.26	3.89
300	27.11	14.58	10.44	8.39	7.18	6.39	5.83
400	36.15	19.44	13.92	11.18	9.57	8.51	7.78
500	45.19	24.30	17.40	13.98	11.96	10.64	9.72
600	54.23	29.17	20.87	16.78	14.35	12.77	11.66
700	63.27	34.03	24.35	19.57	16.75	14.90	13.61
800	72.30	38.89	27.83	22.37	19.14	17.03	15.55
900	81.34	43.75	31.31	25.16	21.53	19.16	17.50
1000	90.38	48.61	34.79	27.96	23.92	21.28	19.44
2000	180.76	97.22	69.58	55.92	47.85	42.57	38.88
3000	271.14	145.83	104.37	83.88	71.77	63.85	58.32
4000	361.52	194.43	139.16	111.84	95.70	85.14	77.76
5000	451.90	243.04	173.96	139.81	119.62	106.42	97.21
6000	542.28	291.65	208.75	167.77	143.55	127.71	116.65
7000	632.66	340.26	243.54	195.73	167.47	148.99	136.09
8000	723.04	388.87	278.33	223.69	191.40	170.28	155.53
9000	813.42	437.48	313.12	251.65	215.32	191.56	174.97
10000	903.80	486.09	347.91	279.61	239.25	212.85	194.41
11000	994.17	534.70	382.70	307.57	263.17	234.13	213.85
12000	1084.55	583.30	417.49	335.53	287.10	255.42	233.29
13000	1174.93	631.91	452.29	363.49	311.02	276.70	252.73
14000	1265.31	680.52	487.08	391.46	334.95	297.99	272.18
15000	1355.69	729.13	521.87	419.42	358.87	319.27	291.62
16000	1446.07	777.74	556.66	447.38	382.80	340.56	311.06
17000	1536.45	826.35	591.45	475.34	406.72	361.84	330.50
18000	1626.83	874.96	626.24	503.30	430.65	383.12	349.94
19000	1717.21	923.57	661.03	531.26	454.57	404.41	369.38
20000	1807.59	972.17	695.82	559.22	478.50	425.69	388.82
21000	1897.97	1020.78	730.62	587.18	502.42	446.98	408.26
22000	1988.35	1069.39	765.41	615.14	526.35	468.26	427.70
23000	2078.73	1118.00	800.20	643.10	550.27	489.55	447.15
24000	2169.11	1166.61	834.99	671.07	574.20	510.83	466.59
25000	2259.49	1215.22	869.78	699.03	598.12	532.12	486.03
26000	2349.87	1263.83	904.57	726.99	622.05	553.40	505.47
27000	2440.25	1312.44	939.36	754.95	645.97	574.69	524.91
28000	2530.63	1361.04	974.15	782.91	669.90	595.97	544.35
29000	2621.01	1409.65	1008.94	810.87	693.82	617.26	563.79
30000	2711.39	1458.26	1043.74	838.83	717.75	638.54	583.23
35000	3163.28	1701.31	1217.69	978.64	837.37	744.96	680.44
40000	3615.18	1944.35	1391.65	1118.44	957.00	851.39	777.64
45000	4067.08	2187.39	1565.60	1258.25	1076.62	957.81	874.85
50000	4518.98	2430.44	1739.56	1398.05	1196.25	1064.24	972.05
55000	4970.87	2673.48	1913.52	1537.86	1315.87	1170.66	1069.26
60000	5422.77	2916.52	2087.47	1677.66	1435.50	1277.08	1166.47
65000	5874.67	3159.57	2261.43	1817.47	1555.12	1383.51	1263.67
70000	6326.57	3402.61	2435.38	1957.28	1674.74	1489.93	1360.88
75000	6778.46	3645.65	2609.34	2097.08	1794.37	1596.35	1458.08
80000	7230.36	3888.70	2783.30	2236.89	1913.99	1702.78	1555.29
85000	7682.26	4131.74	2957.25	2376.69	2033.62	1809.20	1652.49
90000	8134.16	4374.79	3131.21	2516.50	2153.24	1915.62	1749.70
95000	8586.05	4617.83	3305.16	2656.30	2272.87	2022.05	1846.90
100000	9037.95	4860.87	3479.12	2796.11	2392.49	2128.47	1944.11
200000	18075.90	9721.75	6958.24	5592.22	4784.98	4256.94	3888.22
300000	27113.86	14582.62	10437.36	8388.32	7177.48	6385.41	5832.33
400000	36151.81	19443.49	13916.48	11184.43	9569.97	8513.88	7776.44
500000	45189.76	24304.36	17395.60	13980.54	11962.46	10642.35	9720.55
1000000	90379.52	48608.73	34791.20	27961.08	23924.92	21284.70	19441.09

Amortization Amount	8 Years	9 Years	10 Years	15 Years	20 Years	25 Years	30 Years
25	0.45	0.43	0.41	0.35	0.33	0.33	0.32
50	0.90	0.85	0.81	0.71	0.67	0.65	0.64
100	1.81	1.71	1.63	1.42	1.34	1.30	1.29
200	3.62	3.42	3.26	2.83	2.67	2.60	2.57
300	5.43	5.12	4.89	4.25	4.01	3.90	3.86
400	7.24	6.83	6.52	5.67	5.34	5.20	5.14
500	9.05	8.54	8.15	7.09	6.68	6.50	6.43
600	10.86	10.25	9.77	8.50	8.01	7.80	7.71
700	12.67	11.95	11.40	9.92	9.35	9.11	9.00
800	14.48	13.66	13.03	11.34	10.69	10.41	10.28
900	16.28	15.37	14.66	12.75	12.02	11.71	11.57
1000	18.09	17.08	16.29	14.17	13.36	13.01	12.85
2000	36.19	34.16	32.58	28.34	26.72	26.02	25.70
3000	54.28	51.23	48.87	42.52	40.07	39.02	38.55
4000	72.38	68.31	65.16	56.69	53.43	52.03	51.40
5000	90.47	85.39	81.46	70.86	66.79	65.04	64.25
6000	108.57	102.47	97.75	85.03	80.15	78.05	77.10
7000	126.66	119.54	114.04	99.21	93.51	91.05	89.95
8000	144.75	136.62	130.33	113.38	106.86	104.06	102.80
9000	162.85	153.70	146.62	127.55	120.22	117.07	115.65
10000	180.94	170.78	162.91	141.72	133.58	130.08	128.50
11000	199.04	187.85	179.20	155.89	146.94	143.09	141.35
12000	217.13	204.93	195.49	170.07	160.30	156.09	154.20
13000	235.23	222.01	211.78	184.24	173.65	169.10	167.05
14000	253.32	239.09	228.08	198.41	187.01	182.11	179.90
15000	271.41	256.16	244.37	212.58	200.37	195.12	192.75
16000	289.51	273.24	260.66	226.75	213.73	208.13	205.60
17000	307.60	290.32	276.95	240.93	227.09	221.13	218.45
18000	325.70	307.40	293.24	255.10	240.44	234.14	231.30
19000	343.79	324.48	309.53	269.27	253.80	247.15	244.15
20000	361.89	341.55	325.82	283.44	267.16	260.16	257.00
21000	379.98	358.63	342.11	297.62	280.52	273.16	269.85
22000	398.07	375.71	358.40	311.79	293.88	286.17	282.70
23000	416.17	392.79	374.70	325.96	307.23	299.18	295.55
24000	434.26	409.86	390.99	340.13	320.59	312.19	308.40
25000	452.36	426.94	407.28	354.30	333.95	325.20	321.25
26000	470.45	444.02	423.57	368.48	347.31	338.20	334.10
27000	488.55	461.10	439.86	382.65	360.67	351.21	346.95
28000	506.64	478.17	456.15	396.82	374.02	364.22	359.80
29000	524.73	495.25	472.44	410.99	387.38	377.23	372.65
30000	542.83	512.33	488.73	425.16	400.74	390.24	385.50
35000	633.30	597.72	570.19	496.03	467.53	455.27	449.75
40000	723.77	683.11	651.64	566.89	534.32	520.31	514.00
45000	814.24	768.49	733.10	637.75	601.11	585.35	578.25
50000	904.72	853.88	814.55	708.61	667.90	650.39	642.50
55000	995.19	939.27	896.01	779.47	734.69	715.43	706.75
60000	1085.66	1024.66	977.47	850.33	801.48	780.47	771.00
65000	1176.13	1110.05	1058.92	921.19	868.27	845.51	835.25
70000	1266.60	1195.44	1140.38	992.05	935.06	910.55	899.50
75000	1357.07	1280.82	1221.83	1062.91	1001.85	975.59	963.75
80000	1447.54	1366.21	1303.29	1133.77	1068.64	1040.63	1028.00
85000	1538.02	1451.60	1384.74	1204.63	1135.43	1105.67	1092.25
90000	1628.49	1536.99	1466.20	1275.49	1202.22	1170.71	1156.50
95000	1718.96	1622.38	1547.65	1346.35	1269.01	1235.75	1220.75
100000	1809.43	1707.77	1629.11	1417.22	1335.80	1300.78	1285.00
200000	3618.86	3415.53	3258.22	2834.43	2671.60	2601.57	2570.00
300000	5428.29	5123.30	4887.33	4251.65	4007.40	3902.35	3855.00
400000	7237.72	6831.06	6516.44	5668.86	5343.20	5203.14	5140.00
500000	9047.15	8538.83	8145.55	7086.08	6679.00	6503.92	6425.00
1000000	18094.30	17077.66	16291.10	14172.15	13358.01	13007.85	12850.01

15.875%

Amortization Amount	1 Year	2 Years	3 Years	4 Years	5 Years	6 Years	7 Years
25	2.26	1.22	0.87	0.70	0.60	0.53	0.49
50	4.52	2.43	1.74	1.40	1.20	1.07	0.98
100	9.04	4.87	3.48	2.80	2.40	2.13	1.95
200	18.09	9.73	6.97	5.60	4.80	4.27	3.90
300	27.13	14.60	10.45	8.41	7.20	6.40	5.85
400	36.17	19.47	13.94	11.21	9.59	8.54	7.80
500	45.22	24.33	17.42	14.01	11.99	10.67	9.75
600	54.26	29.20	20.91	16.81	14.39	12.81	11.70
700	63.30	34.07	24.39	19.61	16.79	14.94	13.66
800	72.35	38.93	27.88	22.42	19.19	17.08	15.61
900	81.39	43.80	31.36	25.22	21.59	19.21	17.56
1000	90.43	48.66	34.85	28.02	23.99	21.35	19.51
2000	180.87	97.33	69.70	56.04	47.97	42.70	39.01
3000	271.30	145.99	104.55	84.06	71.96	64.05	58.52
4000	361.74	194.66	139.40	112.08	95.95	85.39	78.03
5000	452.17	243.32	174.24	140.10	119.93	106.74	97.54
6000	542.61	291.99	209.09	168.12	143.92	128.09	117.04
7000	633.04	340.65	243.94	196.15	167.91	149.44	136.55
8000	723.48	389.32	278.79	224.17	191.89	170.79	156.06
9000	813.91	437.98	313.64	252.19	215.88	192.14	175.57
10000	904.35	486.65	348.49	280.21	239.87	213.49	195.07
11000	994.78	535.31	383.34	308.23	263.85	234.84	214.58
12000	1085.22	583.97	418.19	336.25	287.84	256.18	234.09
13000	1175.66	632.64	453.03	364.27	311.83	277.53	253.59
14000	1266.09	681.30	487.88	392.29	335.81	298.88	273.10
15000	1356.52	729.97	522.73	420.31	359.80	320.23	292.61
16000	1446.96	778.63	557.58	448.33	383.79	341.58	312.12
17000	1537.39	827.30	592.43	476.35	407.77	362.93	331.62
18000	1627.83	875.96	627.28	504.37	431.76	384.28	351.13
19000	1718.26	924.63	662.13	532.39	455.75	405.63	370.64
20000	1808.70	973.29	696.98	560.41	479.73	426.97	390.14
21000	1899.13	1021.96	731.82	588.44	503.72	448.32	409.65
22000	1989.57	1070.62	766.67	616.46	527.71	469.67	429.16
23000	2080.00	1119.29	801.52	644.48	551.70	491.02	448.67
24000	2170.44	1167.95	836.37	672.50	575.68	512.37	468.17
25000	2260.87	1216.61	871.22	700.52	599.67	533.72	487.68
26000	2351.31	1265.28	906.07	728.54	623.66	555.07	507.19
27000	2441.74	1313.94	940.92	756.56	647.64	576.41	526.70
28000	2532.18	1362.61	975.77	784.58	671.63	597.76	546.20
29000	2622.61	1411.27	1010.62	812.60	695.62	619.11	565.71
30000	2713.05	1459.94	1045.46	840.62	719.60	640.46	585.22
35000	3165.22	1703.26	1219.71	980.73	839.54	747.20	682.75
40000	3617.40	1946.58	1393.95	1120.83	959.47	853.95	780.29
45000	4069.57	2189.91	1568.20	1260.93	1079.40	960.69	877.83
50000	4521.75	2433.23	1742.44	1401.04	1199.34	1067.43	975.36
55000	4973.92	2676.55	1916.68	1541.14	1319.27	1174.18	1072.90
60000	5426.10	2919.87	2090.93	1681.24	1439.20	1280.92	1170.43
65000	5878.27	3163.20	2265.17	1821.35	1559.14	1387.67	1267.97
70000	6330.44	3406.52	2439.42	1961.45	1679.07	1494.41	1365.51
75000	6782.62	3649.84	2613.66	2101.56	1799.01	1601.15	1463.04
80000	7234.79	3893.17	2787.90	2241.66	1918.94	1707.90	1560.58
85000	7686.97	4136.49	2962.15	2381.76	2038.87	1814.64	1658.11
90000	8139.14	4379.81	3136.39	2521.87	2158.81	1921.38	1755.65
95000	8591.32	4623.13	3310.64	2661.97	2278.74	2028.13	1853.19
100000	9043.49	4866.46	3484.88	2802.07	2398.67	2134.87	1950.72
200000	18086.99	9732.91	6969.76	5604.15	4797.35	4269.74	3901.45
300000	27130.48	14599.37	10454.64	8406.22	7196.02	6404.61	5852.17
400000	36173.97	19465.83	13939.52	11208.30	9594.70	8539.48	7802.89
500000	45217.46	24332.29	17424.40	14010.37	11993.37	10674.35	9753.62
1000000	90434.93	48664.57	34848.80	28020.74	23986.74	21348.69	19507.23

Amortization Amount	8 Years	9 Years	10 Years	15 Years	20 Years	25 Years	30 Years
25	0.45	0.43	0.41	0.36	0.34	0.33	0.32
50	0.91	0.86	0.82	0.71	0.67	0.65	0.65
100	1.82	1.71	1.64	1.43	1.34	1.31	1.29
200	3.63	3.43	3.27	2.85	2.69	2.62	2.59
300	5.45	5.14	4.91	4.28	4.03	3.93	3.88
400	7.27	6.86	6.55	5.70	5.38	5.24	5.18
500	9.08	8.57	8.18	7.13	6.72	6.55	6.47
600	10.90	10.29	9.82	8.55	8.07	7.86	7.77
700	12.71	12.00	11.45	9.98	9.41	9.17	9.06
800	14.53	13.72	13.09	11.40	10.76	10.48	10.36
900	16.35	15.43	14.73	12.83	12.10	11.79	11.65
1000	18.16	17.15	16.36	14.25	13.45	13.10	12.94
2000	36.33	34.30	32.73	28.51	26.89	26.20	25.89
3000	54.49	51.44	49.09	42.76	40.34	39.30	38.83
4000	72.65	68.59	65.45	57.01	53.78	52.40	51.78
5000	90.81	85.74	81.82	71.26	67.23	65.50	64.72
6000	108.98	102.89	98.18	85.52	80.67	78.60	77.66
7000	127.14	120.04	114.54	99.77	94.12	91.69	90.61
8000	145.30	137.18	130.91	114.02	107.56	104.79	103.55
9000	163.46	154.33	147.27	128.28	121.01	117.89	116.50
10000	181.63	171.48	163.63	142.53	134.45	130.99	129.44
11000	199.79	188.63	180.00	156.78	147.90	144.09	142.38
12000	217.95	205.78	196.36	171.04	161.34	157.19	155.33
13000	236.11	222.92	212.72	185.29	174.79	170.29	168.27
14000	254.28	240.07	229.09	199.54	188.23	183.39	181.22
15000	272.44	257.22	245.45	213.79	201.68	196.49	194.16
16000	290.60	274.37	261.81	228.05	215.12	209.59	207.11
17000	308.76	291.51	278.18	242.30	228.57	222.69	220.05
18000	326.93	308.66	294.54	256.55	242.01	235.79	232.99
19000	345.09	325.81	310.90	270.81	255.46	248.89	245.94
20000	363.25	342.96	327.27	285.06	268.90	261.98	258.88
21000	381.41	360.11	343.63	299.31	282.35	275.08	271.83
22000	399.58	377.25	359.99	313.57	295.79	288.18	284.77
23000	417.74	394.40	376.36	327.82	309.24	301.28	297.71
24000	435.90	411.55	392.72	342.07	322.68	314.38	310.66
25000	454.06	428.70	409.08	356.32	336.13	327.48	323.60
26000	472.23	445.85	425.45	370.58	349.57	340.58	336.55
27000	490.39	462.99	441.81	384.83	363.02	353.68	349.49
28000	508.55	480.14	458.17	399.08	376.46	366.78	362.43
29000	526.71	497.29	474.54	413.34	389.91	379.88	375.38
30000	544.88	514.44	490.90	427.59	403.35	392.98	388.32
35000	635.69	600.18	572.72	498.85	470.58	458.47	453.04
40000	726.50	685.92	654.53	570.12	537.81	523.97	517.76
45000	817.31	771.66	736.35	641.38	605.03	589.47	582.48
50000	908.13	857.40	818.17	712.65	672.26	654.96	647.20
55000	998.94	943.14	899.98	783.91	739.48	720.46	711.92
60000	1089.75	1028.88	981.80	855.18	806.71	785.95	776.65
65000	1180.57	1114.62	1063.62	926.44	873.93	851.45	841.37
70000	1271.38	1200.36	1145.43	997.71	941.16	916.95	906.09
75000	1362.19	1286.10	1227.25	1068.97	1008.38	982.44	970.81
80000	1453.00	1371.84	1309.07	1140.24	1075.61	1047.94	1035.53
85000	1543.82	1457.57	1390.88	1211.50	1142.84	1113.43	1100.25
90000	1634.63	1543.31	1472.70	1282.77	1210.06	1178.93	1164.97
95000	1725.44	1629.05	1554.52	1354.03	1277.29	1244.43	1229.69
100000	1816.25	1714.79	1636.33	1425.30	1344.51	1309.92	1294.41
200000	3632.51	3429.59	3272.67	2850.59	2689.03	2619.85	2588.82
300000	5448.76	5144.38	4909.00	4275.89	4033.54	3929.77	3883.23
400000	7265.02	6859.18	6545.34	5701.19	5378.05	5239.69	5177.64
500000	9081.27	8573.97	8181.67	7126.49	6722.56	6549.62	6472.04
1000000	18162.54	17147.94	16363.35	14252.97	13445.13	13099.23	12944.09

16%

MONTHLY PAYMENT
NECESSARY TO AMORTIZE A LOAN

Amortization Amount	1 Year	2 Years	3 Years	4 Years	5 Years	6 Years	7 Years
25	2.26	1.22	0.87	0.70	0.60	0.54	0.49
50	4.52	2.44	1.75	1.40	1.20	1.07	0.98
100	9.05	4.87	3.49	2.81	2.40	2.14	1.96
200	18.10	9.74	6.98	5.62	4.81	4.28	3.91
300	27.15	14.62	10.47	8.42	7.21	6.42	5.87
400	36.20	19.49	13.96	11.23	9.62	8.57	7.83
500	45.25	24.36	17.45	14.04	12.02	10.71	9.79
600	54.29	29.23	20.94	16.85	14.43	12.85	11.74
700	63.34	34.10	24.43	19.66	16.83	14.99	13.70
800	72.39	38.98	27.93	22.46	19.24	17.13	15.66
900	81.44	43.85	31.42	25.27	21.64	19.27	17.62
1000	90.49	48.72	34.91	28.08	24.05	21.41	19.57
2000	180.98	97.44	69.81	56.16	48.10	42.83	39.15
3000	271.47	146.16	104.72	84.24	72.15	64.24	58.72
4000	361.96	194.88	139.63	112.32	96.19	85.65	78.29
5000	452.45	243.60	174.53	140.40	120.24	107.06	97.87
6000	542.94	292.32	209.44	168.48	144.29	128.48	117.44
7000	633.43	341.04	244.34	196.56	168.34	149.89	137.01
8000	723.92	389.76	279.25	224.64	192.39	171.30	156.59
9000	814.41	438.48	314.16	252.72	216.44	192.71	176.16
10000	904.90	487.20	349.06	280.80	240.49	214.13	195.73
11000	995.39	535.92	383.97	308.88	264.53	235.54	215.31
12000	1085.88	584.65	418.88	336.97	288.58	256.95	234.88
13000	1176.37	633.37	453.78	365.05	312.63	278.37	254.45
14000	1266.86	682.09	488.69	393.13	336.68	299.78	274.03
15000	1357.35	730.81	523.60	421.21	360.73	321.19	293.60
16000	1447.85	779.53	558.50	449.29	384.78	342.60	313.18
17000	1538.34	828.25	593.41	477.37	408.83	364.02	332.75
18000	1628.83	876.97	628.32	505.45	432.88	385.43	352.32
19000	1719.32	925.69	663.22	533.53	456.92	406.84	371.90
20000	1809.81	974.41	698.13	561.61	480.97	428.26	391.47
21000	1900.30	1023.13	733.03	589.69	505.02	449.67	411.04
22000	1990.79	1071.85	767.94	617.77	529.07	471.08	430.62
23000	2081.28	1120.57	802.85	645.85	553.12	492.49	450.19
24000	2171.77	1169.29	837.75	673.93	577.17	513.91	469.76
25000	2262.26	1218.01	872.66	702.01	601.22	535.32	489.34
26000	2352.75	1266.73	907.57	730.09	625.26	556.73	508.91
27000	2443.24	1315.45	942.47	758.17	649.31	578.14	528.48
28000	2533.73	1364.17	977.38	786.25	673.36	599.56	548.06
29000	2624.22	1412.89	1012.29	814.33	697.41	620.97	567.63
30000	2714.71	1461.61	1047.19	842.41	721.46	642.38	587.20
35000	3167.16	1705.21	1221.72	982.82	841.70	749.45	685.07
40000	3619.61	1948.82	1396.26	1123.22	961.94	856.51	782.94
45000	4072.06	2192.42	1570.79	1263.62	1082.19	963.57	880.81
50000	4524.52	2436.02	1745.32	1404.02	1202.43	1070.64	978.67
55000	4976.97	2679.62	1919.85	1544.42	1322.67	1177.70	1076.54
60000	5429.42	2923.23	2094.39	1684.83	1442.92	1284.77	1174.41
65000	5881.87	3166.83	2268.92	1825.23	1563.16	1391.83	1272.27
70000	6334.32	3410.43	2443.45	1965.63	1683.40	1498.89	1370.14
75000	6786.77	3654.03	2617.98	2106.03	1803.65	1605.96	1468.01
80000	7239.23	3897.63	2792.51	2246.44	1923.89	1713.02	1565.88
85000	7691.68	4141.24	2967.05	2386.84	2044.13	1820.08	1663.74
90000	8144.13	4384.84	3141.58	2527.24	2164.38	1927.15	1761.61
95000	8596.58	4628.44	3316.11	2667.64	2284.62	2034.21	1859.48
100000	9049.03	4872.04	3490.64	2808.05	2404.86	2141.28	1957.35
200000	18098.07	9744.08	6981.29	5616.09	4809.72	4282.55	3914.69
300000	27147.10	14616.13	10471.93	8424.14	7214.59	6423.83	5872.04
400000	36196.13	19488.17	13962.57	11232.18	9619.45	8565.10	7829.38
500000	45245.16	24360.21	17453.21	14040.23	12024.31	10706.38	9786.73
1000000	90490.33	48720.42	34906.43	28080.45	24048.62	21412.76	19573.46

194

Amortization Amount	8 Years	9 Years	10 Years	15 Years	20 Years	25 Years	30 Years
25	0.46	0.43	0.41	0.36	0.34	0.33	0.33
50	0.91	0.86	0.82	0.72	0.68	0.66	0.65
100	1.82	1.72	1.64	1.43	1.35	1.32	1.30
200	3.65	3.44	3.29	2.87	2.71	2.64	2.61
300	5.47	5.17	4.93	4.30	4.06	3.96	3.91
400	7.29	6.89	6.57	5.73	5.41	5.28	5.22
500	9.12	8.61	8.22	7.17	6.77	6.60	6.52
600	10.94	10.33	9.86	8.60	8.12	7.91	7.82
700	12.76	12.05	11.50	10.03	9.47	9.23	9.13
800	14.58	13.77	13.15	11.47	10.83	10.55	10.43
900	16.41	15.50	14.79	12.90	12.18	11.87	11.73
1000	18.23	17.22	16.44	14.33	13.53	13.19	13.04
2000	36.46	34.44	32.87	28.67	27.06	26.38	26.08
3000	54.69	51.65	49.31	43.00	40.60	39.57	39.11
4000	72.92	68.87	65.74	57.34	54.13	52.76	52.15
5000	91.15	86.09	82.18	71.67	67.66	65.95	65.19
6000	109.39	103.31	98.61	86.00	81.19	79.14	78.23
7000	127.62	120.53	115.05	100.34	94.73	92.33	91.27
8000	145.85	137.75	131.49	114.67	108.26	105.53	104.31
9000	164.08	154.96	147.92	129.01	121.79	118.72	117.34
10000	182.31	172.18	164.36	143.34	135.32	131.91	130.38
11000	200.54	189.40	180.79	157.67	148.86	145.10	143.42
12000	218.77	206.62	197.23	172.01	162.39	158.29	156.46
13000	237.00	223.84	213.66	186.34	175.92	171.48	169.50
14000	255.23	241.06	230.10	200.67	189.45	184.67	182.54
15000	273.46	258.27	246.54	215.01	202.99	197.86	195.57
16000	291.69	275.49	262.97	229.34	216.52	211.05	208.61
17000	309.92	292.71	279.41	243.68	230.05	224.24	221.65
18000	328.16	309.93	295.84	258.01	243.58	237.43	234.69
19000	346.39	327.15	312.28	272.34	257.11	250.62	247.73
20000	364.62	344.37	328.71	286.68	270.65	263.81	260.76
21000	382.85	361.58	345.15	301.01	284.18	277.00	273.80
22000	401.08	378.80	361.59	315.35	297.71	290.20	286.84
23000	419.31	396.02	378.02	329.68	311.24	303.39	299.88
24000	437.54	413.24	394.46	344.01	324.78	316.58	312.92
25000	455.77	430.46	410.89	358.35	338.31	329.77	325.96
26000	474.00	447.68	427.33	372.68	351.84	342.96	338.99
27000	492.23	464.89	443.76	387.02	365.37	356.15	352.03
28000	510.46	482.11	460.20	401.35	378.91	369.34	365.07
29000	528.70	499.33	476.64	415.68	392.44	382.53	378.11
30000	546.93	516.55	493.07	430.02	405.97	395.72	391.15
35000	638.08	602.64	575.25	501.69	473.63	461.67	456.34
40000	729.24	688.73	657.43	573.36	541.29	527.63	521.53
45000	820.39	774.82	739.61	645.03	608.96	593.58	586.72
50000	911.54	860.92	821.79	716.70	676.62	659.53	651.91
55000	1002.70	947.01	903.96	788.37	744.28	725.49	717.10
60000	1093.85	1033.10	986.14	860.04	811.94	791.44	782.29
65000	1185.01	1119.19	1068.32	931.71	879.60	857.40	847.48
70000	1276.16	1205.28	1150.50	1003.37	947.27	923.35	912.68
75000	1367.32	1291.37	1232.68	1075.04	1014.93	989.30	977.87
80000	1458.47	1377.47	1314.86	1146.71	1082.59	1055.26	1043.06
85000	1549.62	1463.56	1397.04	1218.38	1150.25	1121.21	1108.25
90000	1640.78	1549.65	1479.21	1290.05	1217.91	1187.16	1173.44
95000	1731.93	1635.74	1561.39	1361.72	1285.57	1253.12	1238.63
100000	1823.09	1721.83	1643.57	1433.39	1353.24	1319.07	1303.82
200000	3646.18	3443.67	3287.14	2866.78	2706.47	2638.14	2607.64
300000	5469.26	5165.50	4930.71	4300.18	4059.71	3957.21	3911.47
400000	7292.35	6887.33	6574.28	5733.57	5412.95	5276.28	5215.29
500000	9115.44	8609.16	8217.85	7166.96	6766.18	6595.35	6519.11
1000000	18230.88	17218.33	16435.71	14333.92	13532.36	13190.70	13038.22

16.125%

MONTHLY PAYMENT
NECESSARY TO AMORTIZE A LOAN

Amortization Amount	1 Year	2 Years	3 Years	4 Years	5 Years	6 Years	7 Years
25	2.26	1.22	0.87	0.70	0.60	0.54	0.49
50	4.53	2.44	1.75	1.41	1.21	1.07	0.98
100	9.05	4.88	3.50	2.81	2.41	2.15	1.96
200	18.11	9.76	6.99	5.63	4.82	4.30	3.93
300	27.16	14.63	10.49	8.44	7.23	6.44	5.89
400	36.22	19.51	13.99	11.26	9.64	8.59	7.86
500	45.27	24.39	17.48	14.07	12.06	10.74	9.82
600	54.33	29.27	20.98	16.88	14.47	12.89	11.78
700	63.38	34.14	24.47	19.70	16.88	15.03	13.75
800	72.44	39.02	27.97	22.51	19.29	17.18	15.71
900	81.49	43.90	31.47	25.33	21.70	19.33	17.68
1000	90.55	48.78	34.96	28.14	24.11	21.48	19.64
2000	181.09	97.55	69.93	56.28	48.22	42.95	39.28
3000	271.64	146.33	104.89	84.42	72.33	64.43	58.92
4000	362.18	195.11	139.86	112.56	96.44	85.91	78.56
5000	452.73	243.88	174.82	140.70	120.55	107.38	98.20
6000	543.27	292.66	209.78	168.84	144.66	128.86	117.84
7000	633.82	341.43	244.75	196.98	168.77	150.34	137.48
8000	724.37	390.21	279.71	225.12	192.88	171.82	157.12
9000	814.91	438.99	314.68	253.26	217.00	193.29	176.76
10000	905.46	487.76	349.64	281.40	241.11	214.77	196.40
11000	996.00	536.54	384.60	309.54	265.22	236.25	216.04
12000	1086.55	585.32	419.57	337.68	289.33	257.72	235.68
13000	1177.09	634.09	454.53	365.82	313.44	279.20	255.32
14000	1267.64	682.87	489.50	393.96	337.55	300.68	274.96
15000	1358.19	731.64	524.46	422.10	361.66	322.15	294.60
16000	1448.73	780.42	559.43	450.24	385.77	343.63	314.24
17000	1539.28	829.20	594.39	478.38	409.88	365.11	333.88
18000	1629.82	877.97	629.35	506.52	433.99	386.58	353.52
19000	1720.37	926.75	664.32	534.66	458.10	408.06	373.16
20000	1810.91	975.53	699.28	562.80	482.21	429.54	392.80
21000	1901.46	1024.30	734.25	590.94	506.32	451.01	412.44
22000	1992.01	1073.08	769.21	619.08	530.43	472.49	432.07
23000	2082.55	1121.85	804.17	647.22	554.54	493.97	451.71
24000	2173.10	1170.63	839.14	675.36	578.65	515.45	471.35
25000	2263.64	1219.41	874.10	703.51	602.76	536.92	490.99
26000	2354.19	1268.18	909.07	731.65	626.87	558.40	510.63
27000	2444.73	1316.96	944.03	759.79	650.99	579.88	530.27
28000	2535.28	1365.74	978.99	787.93	675.10	601.35	549.91
29000	2625.83	1414.51	1013.96	816.07	699.21	622.83	569.55
30000	2716.37	1463.29	1048.92	844.21	723.32	644.31	589.19
35000	3169.10	1707.17	1223.74	984.91	843.87	751.69	687.39
40000	3621.83	1951.05	1398.56	1125.61	964.42	859.08	785.59
45000	4074.56	2194.93	1573.38	1266.31	1084.98	966.46	883.79
50000	4527.29	2438.81	1748.20	1407.01	1205.53	1073.84	981.99
55000	4980.01	2682.70	1923.02	1547.71	1326.08	1181.23	1080.19
60000	5432.74	2926.58	2097.84	1688.41	1446.63	1288.61	1178.39
65000	5885.47	3170.46	2272.67	1829.11	1567.19	1396.00	1276.58
70000	6338.20	3414.34	2447.49	1969.81	1687.74	1503.38	1374.78
75000	6790.93	3658.22	2622.31	2110.52	1808.29	1610.77	1472.98
80000	7243.66	3902.10	2797.13	2251.22	1928.84	1718.15	1571.18
85000	7696.39	4145.98	2971.95	2391.92	2049.40	1825.54	1669.38
90000	8149.11	4389.87	3146.77	2532.62	2169.95	1932.92	1767.58
95000	8601.84	4633.75	3321.59	2673.32	2290.50	2040.30	1865.78
100000	9054.57	4877.63	3496.41	2814.02	2411.06	2147.69	1963.98
200000	18109.14	9755.26	6992.82	5628.04	4822.11	4295.38	3927.95
300000	27163.72	14632.88	10489.22	8442.06	7233.17	6443.07	5891.93
400000	36218.29	19510.51	13985.63	11256.08	9644.22	8590.76	7855.91
500000	45272.86	24388.14	17482.04	14070.10	12055.28	10738.45	9819.88
1000000	90545.72	48776.28	34964.08	28140.20	24110.56	21476.89	19639.76

Amortization Amount	8 Years	9 Years	10 Years	15 Years	20 Years	25 Years	30 Years
25	0.46	0.43	0.41	0.36	0.34	0.33	0.33
50	0.91	0.86	0.83	0.72	0.68	0.66	0.66
100	1.83	1.73	1.65	1.44	1.36	1.33	1.31
200	3.66	3.46	3.30	2.88	2.72	2.66	2.63
300	5.49	5.19	4.95	4.32	4.09	3.98	3.94
400	7.32	6.92	6.60	5.77	5.45	5.31	5.25
500	9.15	8.64	8.25	7.21	6.81	6.64	6.57
600	10.98	10.37	9.90	8.65	8.17	7.97	7.88
700	12.81	12.10	11.56	10.09	9.53	9.30	9.19
800	14.64	13.83	13.21	11.53	10.90	10.63	10.51
900	16.47	15.56	14.86	12.97	12.26	11.95	11.82
1000	18.30	17.29	16.51	14.42	13.62	13.28	13.13
2000	36.60	34.58	33.02	28.83	27.24	26.56	26.26
3000	54.90	51.87	49.52	43.25	40.86	39.85	39.40
4000	73.20	69.16	66.03	57.66	54.48	53.13	52.53
5000	91.50	86.44	82.54	72.08	68.10	66.41	65.66
6000	109.80	103.73	99.05	86.49	81.72	79.69	78.79
7000	128.10	121.02	115.56	100.91	95.34	92.98	91.93
8000	146.39	138.31	132.07	115.32	108.96	106.26	105.06
9000	164.69	155.60	148.57	129.74	122.58	119.54	118.19
10000	182.99	172.89	165.08	144.15	136.20	132.82	131.32
11000	201.29	190.18	181.59	158.57	149.82	146.10	144.46
12000	219.59	207.47	198.10	172.98	163.44	159.39	157.59
13000	237.89	224.75	214.61	187.40	177.06	172.67	170.72
14000	256.19	242.04	231.11	201.81	190.68	185.95	183.85
15000	274.49	259.33	247.62	216.23	204.30	199.23	196.99
16000	292.79	276.62	264.13	230.64	217.92	212.52	210.12
17000	311.09	293.91	280.64	245.06	231.54	225.80	223.25
18000	329.39	311.20	297.15	259.47	245.15	239.08	236.38
19000	347.69	328.49	313.66	273.89	258.77	252.36	249.52
20000	365.99	345.78	330.16	288.30	272.39	265.64	262.65
21000	384.29	363.07	346.67	302.72	286.01	278.93	275.78
22000	402.58	380.35	363.18	317.13	299.63	292.21	288.91
23000	420.88	397.64	379.69	331.55	313.25	305.49	302.05
24000	439.18	414.93	396.20	345.96	326.87	318.77	315.18
25000	457.48	432.22	412.70	360.38	340.49	332.06	328.31
26000	475.78	449.51	429.21	374.79	354.11	345.34	341.44
27000	494.08	466.80	445.72	389.21	367.73	358.62	354.57
28000	512.38	484.09	462.23	403.62	381.35	371.90	367.71
29000	530.68	501.38	478.74	418.04	394.97	385.19	380.84
30000	548.98	518.66	495.25	432.45	408.59	398.47	393.97
35000	640.48	605.11	577.79	504.53	476.69	464.88	459.63
40000	731.97	691.55	660.33	576.60	544.79	531.29	525.30
45000	823.47	778.00	742.87	648.68	612.89	597.70	590.96
50000	914.97	864.44	825.41	720.75	680.99	664.11	656.62
55000	1006.46	950.88	907.95	792.83	749.08	730.52	722.28
60000	1097.96	1037.33	990.49	864.90	817.18	796.93	787.94
65000	1189.46	1123.77	1073.03	936.98	885.28	863.35	853.61
70000	1280.95	1210.22	1155.57	1009.05	953.38	929.76	919.27
75000	1372.45	1296.66	1238.11	1081.13	1021.48	996.17	984.93
80000	1463.94	1383.11	1320.65	1153.20	1089.58	1062.58	1050.59
85000	1555.44	1469.55	1403.20	1225.28	1157.68	1128.99	1116.25
90000	1646.94	1555.99	1485.74	1297.35	1225.77	1195.40	1181.92
95000	1738.43	1642.44	1568.28	1369.43	1293.87	1261.81	1247.58
100000	1829.93	1728.88	1650.82	1441.50	1361.97	1328.22	1313.24
200000	3659.86	3457.76	3301.64	2883.00	2723.94	2656.45	2626.48
300000	5489.79	5186.65	4952.46	4324.50	4085.91	3984.67	3939.72
400000	7319.72	6915.53	6603.27	5766.00	5447.89	5312.90	5252.96
500000	9149.65	8644.41	8254.09	7207.50	6809.86	6641.12	6566.20
1000000	18299.31	17288.82	16508.19	14415.01	13619.72	13282.25	13132.40

16.25%

Amortization Amount	1 Year	2 Years	3 Years	4 Years	5 Years	6 Years	7 Years
25	2.27	1.22	0.88	0.70	0.60	0.54	0.49
50	4.53	2.44	1.75	1.41	1.21	1.08	0.99
100	9.06	4.88	3.50	2.82	2.42	2.15	1.97
200	18.12	9.77	7.00	5.64	4.83	4.31	3.94
300	27.18	14.65	10.51	8.46	7.25	6.46	5.91
400	36.24	19.53	14.01	11.28	9.67	8.62	7.88
500	45.30	24.42	17.51	14.10	12.09	10.77	9.85
600	54.36	29.30	21.01	16.92	14.50	12.92	11.82
700	63.42	34.18	24.52	19.74	16.92	15.08	13.79
800	72.48	39.07	28.02	22.56	19.34	17.23	15.76
900	81.54	43.95	31.52	25.38	21.76	19.39	17.74
1000	90.60	48.83	35.02	28.20	24.17	21.54	19.71
2000	181.20	97.66	70.04	56.40	48.35	43.08	39.41
3000	271.80	146.50	105.07	84.60	72.52	64.62	59.12
4000	362.40	195.33	140.09	112.80	96.69	86.16	78.82
5000	453.01	244.16	175.11	141.00	120.86	107.71	98.53
6000	543.61	292.99	210.13	169.20	145.04	129.25	118.24
7000	634.21	341.83	245.15	197.40	169.21	150.79	137.94
8000	724.81	390.66	280.17	225.60	193.38	172.33	157.65
9000	815.41	439.49	315.20	253.80	217.55	193.87	177.36
10000	906.01	488.32	350.22	282.00	241.73	215.41	197.06
11000	996.61	537.15	385.24	310.20	265.90	236.95	216.77
12000	1087.21	585.99	420.26	338.40	290.07	258.49	236.47
13000	1177.81	634.82	455.28	366.60	314.24	280.03	256.18
14000	1268.42	683.65	490.30	394.80	338.42	301.58	275.89
15000	1359.02	732.48	525.33	423.00	362.59	323.12	295.59
16000	1449.62	781.31	560.35	451.20	386.76	344.66	315.30
17000	1540.22	830.15	595.37	479.40	410.93	366.20	335.00
18000	1630.82	878.98	630.39	507.60	435.11	387.74	354.71
19000	1721.42	927.81	665.41	535.80	459.28	409.28	374.42
20000	1812.02	976.64	700.44	564.00	483.45	430.82	394.12
21000	1902.62	1025.48	735.46	592.20	507.62	452.36	413.83
22000	1993.22	1074.31	770.48	620.40	531.80	473.90	433.54
23000	2083.83	1123.14	805.50	648.60	555.97	495.45	453.24
24000	2174.43	1171.97	840.52	676.80	580.14	516.99	472.95
25000	2265.03	1220.80	875.54	705.00	604.31	538.53	492.65
26000	2355.63	1269.64	910.57	733.20	628.49	560.07	512.36
27000	2446.23	1318.47	945.59	761.40	652.66	581.61	532.07
28000	2536.83	1367.30	980.61	789.60	676.83	603.15	551.77
29000	2627.43	1416.13	1015.63	817.80	701.00	624.69	571.48
30000	2718.03	1464.96	1050.65	846.00	725.18	646.23	591.18
35000	3171.04	1709.13	1225.76	987.00	846.04	753.94	689.72
40000	3624.04	1953.29	1400.87	1128.00	966.90	861.64	788.25
45000	4077.05	2197.45	1575.98	1269.00	1087.77	969.35	886.78
50000	4530.06	2441.61	1751.09	1410.00	1208.63	1077.06	985.31
55000	4983.06	2685.77	1926.20	1551.00	1329.49	1184.76	1083.84
60000	5436.07	2929.93	2101.31	1692.00	1450.35	1292.47	1182.37
65000	5889.07	3174.09	2276.41	1833.00	1571.22	1400.17	1280.90
70000	6342.08	3418.25	2451.52	1974.00	1692.08	1507.88	1379.43
75000	6795.08	3662.41	2626.63	2115.00	1812.94	1615.58	1477.96
80000	7248.09	3906.57	2801.74	2256.00	1933.80	1723.29	1576.49
85000	7701.09	4150.73	2976.85	2397.00	2054.67	1830.99	1675.02
90000	8154.10	4394.89	3151.96	2538.00	2175.53	1938.70	1773.55
95000	8607.11	4639.05	3327.07	2679.00	2296.39	2046.40	1872.08
100000	9060.11	4883.22	3502.18	2820.00	2417.26	2154.11	1970.62
200000	18120.22	9766.43	7004.35	5640.00	4834.51	4308.22	3941.23
300000	27180.33	14649.65	10506.53	8460.00	7251.77	6462.33	5911.85
400000	36240.44	19532.86	14008.71	11280.00	9669.02	8616.44	7882.46
500000	45300.55	24416.08	17510.88	14100.00	12086.28	10770.55	9853.08
1000000	90601.11	48832.15	35021.76	28200.00	24172.56	21541.10	19706.16

Amortization Amount	8 Years	9 Years	10 Years	15 Years	20 Years	25 Years	30 Years
25	0.46	0.43	0.41	0.36	0.34	0.33	0.33
50	0.92	0.87	0.83	0.72	0.69	0.67	0.66
100	1.84	1.74	1.66	1.45	1.37	1.34	1.32
200	3.67	3.47	3.32	2.90	2.74	2.67	2.65
300	5.51	5.21	4.97	4.35	4.11	4.01	3.97
400	7.35	6.94	6.63	5.80	5.48	5.35	5.29
500	9.18	8.68	8.29	7.25	6.85	6.69	6.61
600	11.02	10.42	9.95	8.70	8.22	8.02	7.94
700	12.86	12.15	11.61	10.15	9.60	9.36	9.26
800	14.69	13.89	13.26	11.60	10.97	10.70	10.58
900	16.53	15.62	14.92	13.05	12.34	12.04	11.90
1000	18.37	17.36	16.58	14.50	13.71	13.37	13.23
2000	36.74	34.72	33.16	28.99	27.41	26.75	26.45
3000	55.10	52.08	49.74	43.49	41.12	40.12	39.68
4000	73.47	69.44	66.32	57.98	54.83	53.50	52.91
5000	91.84	86.80	82.90	72.48	68.54	66.87	66.13
6000	110.21	104.16	99.48	86.98	82.24	80.24	79.36
7000	128.57	121.52	116.07	101.47	95.95	93.62	92.59
8000	146.94	138.88	132.65	115.97	109.66	106.99	105.81
9000	165.31	156.23	149.23	130.47	123.36	120.36	119.04
10000	183.68	173.59	165.81	144.96	137.07	133.74	132.27
11000	202.05	190.95	182.39	159.46	150.78	147.11	145.49
12000	220.41	208.31	198.97	173.95	164.49	160.49	158.72
13000	238.78	225.67	215.55	188.45	178.19	173.86	171.95
14000	257.15	243.03	232.13	202.95	191.90	187.23	185.17
15000	275.52	260.39	248.71	217.44	205.61	200.61	198.40
16000	293.89	277.75	265.29	231.94	219.31	213.98	211.63
17000	312.25	295.11	281.87	246.44	233.02	227.36	224.85
18000	330.62	312.47	298.45	260.93	246.73	240.73	238.08
19000	348.99	329.83	315.03	275.43	260.44	254.10	251.31
20000	367.36	347.19	331.62	289.92	274.14	267.48	264.53
21000	385.72	364.55	348.20	304.42	287.85	280.85	277.76
22000	404.09	381.91	364.78	318.92	301.56	294.23	290.99
23000	422.46	399.27	381.36	333.41	315.27	307.60	304.21
24000	440.83	416.63	397.94	347.91	328.97	320.97	317.44
25000	459.20	433.99	414.52	362.41	342.68	334.35	330.67
26000	477.56	451.34	431.10	376.90	356.39	347.72	343.89
27000	495.93	468.70	447.68	391.40	370.09	361.09	357.12
28000	514.30	486.06	464.26	405.89	383.80	374.47	370.35
29000	532.67	503.42	480.84	420.39	397.51	387.84	383.57
30000	551.04	520.78	497.42	434.89	411.22	401.22	396.80
35000	642.87	607.58	580.33	507.37	479.75	468.09	462.93
40000	734.71	694.38	663.23	579.85	548.29	534.96	529.06
45000	826.55	781.17	746.13	652.33	616.82	601.82	595.20
50000	918.39	867.97	829.04	724.81	685.36	668.69	661.33
55000	1010.23	954.77	911.94	797.29	753.89	735.56	727.46
60000	1102.07	1041.56	994.85	869.77	822.43	802.43	793.60
65000	1193.91	1128.36	1077.75	942.25	890.97	869.30	859.73
70000	1285.75	1215.16	1160.65	1014.74	959.50	936.17	925.86
75000	1377.59	1301.96	1243.56	1087.22	1028.04	1003.04	992.00
80000	1469.43	1388.75	1326.46	1159.70	1096.57	1069.91	1058.13
85000	1561.27	1475.55	1409.37	1232.18	1165.11	1136.78	1124.26
90000	1653.11	1562.35	1492.27	1304.66	1233.65	1203.65	1190.40
95000	1744.94	1649.14	1575.17	1377.14	1302.18	1270.52	1256.53
100000	1836.78	1735.94	1658.08	1449.62	1370.72	1337.39	1322.66
200000	3673.57	3471.88	3316.16	2899.24	2741.44	2674.78	2645.32
300000	5510.35	5207.82	4974.23	4348.86	4112.15	4012.16	3967.99
400000	7347.13	6943.77	6632.31	5798.49	5482.87	5349.55	5290.65
500000	9183.92	8679.71	8290.39	7248.11	6853.59	6686.94	6613.31
1000000	18367.84	17359.41	16580.78	14496.22	13707.18	13373.88	13226.62

16.375%

MONTHLY PAYMENT
NECESSARY TO AMORTIZE A LOAN

Amortization Amount	1 Year	2 Years	3 Years	4 Years	5 Years	6 Years	7 Years
25	2.27	1.22	0.88	0.71	0.61	0.54	0.49
50	4.53	2.44	1.75	1.41	1.21	1.08	0.99
100	9.07	4.89	3.51	2.83	2.42	2.16	1.98
200	18.13	9.78	7.02	5.65	4.85	4.32	3.95
300	27.20	14.67	10.52	8.48	7.27	6.48	5.93
400	36.26	19.56	14.03	11.30	9.69	8.64	7.91
500	45.33	24.44	17.54	14.13	12.12	10.80	9.89
600	54.39	29.33	21.05	16.96	14.54	12.96	11.86
700	63.46	34.22	24.56	19.78	16.96	15.12	13.84
800	72.53	39.11	28.06	22.61	19.39	17.28	15.82
900	81.59	44.00	31.57	25.43	21.81	19.44	17.80
1000	90.66	48.89	35.08	28.26	24.23	21.61	19.77
2000	181.31	97.78	70.16	56.52	48.47	43.21	39.55
3000	271.97	146.66	105.24	84.78	72.70	64.82	59.32
4000	362.63	195.55	140.32	113.04	96.94	86.42	79.09
5000	453.28	244.44	175.40	141.30	121.17	108.03	98.86
6000	543.94	293.33	210.48	169.56	145.41	129.63	118.64
7000	634.60	342.22	245.56	197.82	169.64	151.24	138.41
8000	725.25	391.10	280.64	226.08	193.88	172.84	158.18
9000	815.91	439.99	315.72	254.34	218.11	194.45	177.95
10000	906.56	488.88	350.79	282.60	242.35	216.05	197.73
11000	997.22	537.77	385.87	310.86	266.58	237.66	217.50
12000	1087.88	586.66	420.95	339.12	290.82	259.26	237.27
13000	1178.53	635.54	456.03	367.38	315.05	280.87	257.04
14000	1269.19	684.43	491.11	395.64	339.28	302.48	276.82
15000	1359.85	733.32	526.19	423.90	363.52	324.08	296.59
16000	1450.50	782.21	561.27	452.16	387.75	345.69	316.36
17000	1541.16	831.10	596.35	480.42	411.99	367.29	336.13
18000	1631.82	879.98	631.43	508.68	436.22	388.90	355.91
19000	1722.47	928.87	666.51	536.94	460.46	410.50	375.68
20000	1813.13	977.76	701.59	565.20	484.69	432.11	395.45
21000	1903.79	1026.65	736.67	593.46	508.93	453.71	415.23
22000	1994.44	1075.54	771.75	621.72	533.16	475.32	435.00
23000	2085.10	1124.42	806.83	649.98	557.40	496.92	454.77
24000	2175.76	1173.31	841.91	678.24	581.63	518.53	474.54
25000	2266.41	1222.20	876.99	706.50	605.87	540.13	494.32
26000	2357.07	1271.09	912.07	734.76	630.10	561.74	514.09
27000	2447.73	1319.98	947.15	763.02	654.33	583.35	533.86
28000	2538.38	1368.86	982.23	791.28	678.57	604.95	553.63
29000	2629.04	1417.75	1017.30	819.54	702.80	626.56	573.41
30000	2719.69	1466.64	1052.38	847.80	727.04	648.16	593.18
35000	3172.98	1711.08	1227.78	989.09	848.21	756.19	692.04
40000	3626.26	1955.52	1403.18	1130.39	969.38	864.22	790.91
45000	4079.54	2199.96	1578.58	1271.69	1090.56	972.24	889.77
50000	4532.82	2444.40	1753.97	1412.99	1211.73	1080.27	988.63
55000	4986.11	2688.84	1929.37	1554.29	1332.90	1188.30	1087.49
60000	5439.39	2933.28	2104.77	1695.59	1454.08	1296.32	1186.36
65000	5892.67	3177.72	2280.17	1836.89	1575.25	1404.35	1285.22
70000	6345.95	3422.16	2455.56	1978.19	1696.42	1512.38	1384.08
75000	6799.24	3666.60	2630.96	2119.49	1817.60	1620.40	1482.95
80000	7252.52	3911.04	2806.36	2260.79	1938.77	1728.43	1581.81
85000	7705.80	4155.48	2981.76	2402.09	2059.94	1836.46	1680.67
90000	8159.08	4399.92	3157.15	2543.39	2181.11	1944.48	1779.54
95000	8612.37	4644.36	3332.55	2684.68	2302.29	2052.51	1878.40
100000	9065.65	4888.80	3507.95	2825.98	2423.46	2160.54	1977.26
200000	18131.30	9777.61	7015.89	5651.97	4846.92	4321.08	3954.53
300000	27196.95	14666.41	10523.84	8477.95	7270.38	6481.61	5931.79
400000	36262.59	19555.21	14031.79	11303.93	9693.84	8642.15	7909.05
500000	45328.24	24444.02	17539.74	14129.92	12117.31	10802.69	9886.32
1000000	90656.48	48888.03	35079.47	28259.83	24234.61	21605.38	19772.63

200

Amortization Amount	8 Years	9 Years	10 Years	15 Years	20 Years	25 Years	30 Years
25	0.46	0.44	0.42	0.36	0.34	0.34	0.33
50	0.92	0.87	0.83	0.73	0.69	0.67	0.67
100	1.84	1.74	1.67	1.46	1.38	1.35	1.33
200	3.69	3.49	3.33	2.92	2.76	2.69	2.66
300	5.53	5.23	5.00	4.37	4.14	4.04	4.00
400	7.37	6.97	6.66	5.83	5.52	5.39	5.33
500	9.22	8.72	8.33	7.29	6.90	6.73	6.66
600	11.06	10.46	9.99	8.75	8.28	8.08	7.99
700	12.91	12.20	11.66	10.20	9.66	9.43	9.32
800	14.75	13.94	13.32	11.66	11.04	10.77	10.66
900	16.59	15.69	14.99	13.12	12.42	12.12	11.99
1000	18.44	17.43	16.65	14.58	13.79	13.47	13.32
2000	36.87	34.86	33.31	29.16	27.59	26.93	26.64
3000	55.31	52.29	49.96	43.73	41.38	40.40	39.96
4000	73.75	69.72	66.61	58.31	55.18	53.86	53.28
5000	92.18	87.15	83.27	72.89	68.97	67.33	66.60
6000	110.62	104.58	99.92	87.47	82.77	80.79	79.93
7000	129.06	122.01	116.57	102.04	96.56	94.26	93.25
8000	147.49	139.44	133.23	116.62	110.36	107.72	106.57
9000	165.93	156.87	149.88	131.20	124.15	121.19	119.89
10000	184.36	174.30	166.53	145.78	137.95	134.66	133.21
11000	202.80	191.73	183.19	160.35	151.74	148.12	146.53
12000	221.24	209.16	199.84	174.93	165.54	161.59	159.85
13000	239.67	226.59	216.50	189.51	179.33	175.05	173.17
14000	258.11	244.02	233.15	204.09	193.13	188.52	186.49
15000	276.55	261.45	249.80	218.66	206.92	201.98	199.81
16000	294.98	278.88	266.46	233.24	220.72	215.45	213.13
17000	313.42	296.31	283.11	247.82	234.51	228.91	226.46
18000	331.86	313.74	299.76	262.40	248.31	242.38	239.78
19000	350.29	331.17	316.42	276.97	262.10	255.85	253.10
20000	368.73	348.60	333.07	291.55	275.90	269.31	266.42
21000	387.17	366.03	349.72	306.13	289.69	282.78	279.74
22000	405.60	383.46	366.38	320.71	303.48	296.24	293.06
23000	424.04	400.89	383.03	335.28	317.28	309.71	306.38
24000	442.47	418.32	399.68	349.86	331.07	323.17	319.70
25000	460.91	435.75	416.34	364.44	344.87	336.64	333.02
26000	479.35	453.18	432.99	379.02	358.66	350.11	346.34
27000	497.78	470.61	449.64	393.59	372.46	363.57	359.66
28000	516.22	488.04	466.30	408.17	386.25	377.04	372.98
29000	534.66	505.47	482.95	422.75	400.05	390.50	386.31
30000	553.09	522.90	499.60	437.33	413.84	403.97	399.63
35000	645.28	610.05	582.87	510.21	482.82	471.30	466.23
40000	737.46	697.20	666.14	583.10	551.79	538.62	532.84
45000	829.64	784.36	749.41	655.99	620.76	605.95	599.44
50000	921.82	871.51	832.67	728.88	689.74	673.28	666.04
55000	1014.01	958.66	915.94	801.77	758.71	740.61	732.65
60000	1106.19	1045.81	999.21	874.65	827.69	807.94	799.25
65000	1198.37	1132.96	1082.48	947.54	896.66	875.26	865.86
70000	1290.55	1220.11	1165.74	1020.43	965.63	942.59	932.46
75000	1382.73	1307.26	1249.01	1093.32	1034.61	1009.92	999.07
80000	1474.92	1394.41	1332.28	1166.20	1103.58	1077.25	1065.67
85000	1567.10	1481.56	1415.55	1239.09	1172.55	1144.57	1132.28
90000	1659.28	1568.71	1498.81	1311.98	1241.53	1211.90	1198.88
95000	1751.46	1655.86	1582.08	1384.87	1310.50	1279.23	1265.48
100000	1843.65	1743.01	1665.35	1457.76	1379.48	1346.56	1332.09
200000	3687.29	3486.02	3330.70	2915.51	2758.95	2693.12	2664.18
300000	5530.94	5229.03	4996.04	4373.27	4138.43	4039.68	3996.27
400000	7374.58	6972.05	6661.39	5831.02	5517.90	5386.23	5328.35
500000	9218.23	8715.06	8326.74	7288.78	6897.38	6732.79	6660.44
1000000	18436.46	17430.12	16653.48	14577.55	13794.75	13465.58	13320.88

16.5%

Amortization Amount	1 Year	2 Years	3 Years	4 Years	5 Years	6 Years	7 Years
25	2.27	1.22	0.88	0.71	0.61	0.54	0.50
50	4.54	2.45	1.76	1.42	1.21	1.08	0.99
100	9.07	4.89	3.51	2.83	2.43	2.17	1.98
200	18.14	9.79	7.03	5.66	4.86	4.33	3.97
300	27.21	14.68	10.54	8.50	7.29	6.50	5.95
400	36.28	19.58	14.05	11.33	9.72	8.67	7.94
500	45.36	24.47	17.57	14.16	12.15	10.83	9.92
600	54.43	29.37	21.08	16.99	14.58	13.00	11.90
700	63.50	34.26	24.60	19.82	17.01	15.17	13.89
800	72.57	39.16	28.11	22.66	19.44	17.34	15.87
900	81.64	44.05	31.62	25.49	21.87	19.50	17.86
1000	90.71	48.94	35.14	28.32	24.30	21.67	19.84
2000	181.42	97.89	70.27	56.64	48.59	43.34	39.68
3000	272.14	146.83	105.41	84.96	72.89	65.01	59.52
4000	362.85	195.78	140.55	113.28	97.19	86.68	79.36
5000	453.56	244.72	175.69	141.60	121.48	108.35	99.20
6000	544.27	293.66	210.82	169.92	145.78	130.02	119.04
7000	634.98	342.61	245.96	198.24	170.08	151.69	138.87
8000	725.69	391.55	281.10	226.56	194.37	173.36	158.71
9000	816.41	440.50	316.23	254.88	218.67	195.03	178.55
10000	907.12	489.44	351.37	283.20	242.97	216.70	198.39
11000	997.83	538.38	386.51	311.52	267.26	238.37	218.23
12000	1088.54	587.33	421.65	339.84	291.56	260.04	238.07
13000	1179.25	636.27	456.78	368.16	315.86	281.71	257.91
14000	1269.97	685.21	491.92	396.48	340.15	303.38	277.75
15000	1360.68	734.16	527.06	424.80	364.45	325.05	297.59
16000	1451.39	783.10	562.20	453.12	388.75	346.72	317.43
17000	1542.10	832.05	597.33	481.44	413.04	368.39	337.27
18000	1632.81	880.99	632.47	509.75	437.34	390.06	357.11
19000	1723.53	929.93	667.61	538.07	461.64	411.72	376.94
20000	1814.24	978.88	702.74	566.39	485.93	433.39	396.78
21000	1904.95	1027.82	737.88	594.71	510.23	455.06	416.62
22000	1995.66	1076.77	773.02	623.03	534.53	476.73	436.46
23000	2086.37	1125.71	808.16	651.35	558.82	498.40	456.30
24000	2177.08	1174.65	843.29	679.67	583.12	520.07	476.14
25000	2267.80	1223.60	878.43	707.99	607.42	541.74	495.98
26000	2358.51	1272.54	913.57	736.31	631.71	563.41	515.82
27000	2449.22	1321.49	948.70	764.63	656.01	585.08	535.66
28000	2539.93	1370.43	983.84	792.95	680.31	606.75	555.50
29000	2630.64	1419.37	1018.98	821.27	704.60	628.42	575.34
30000	2721.36	1468.32	1054.12	849.59	728.90	650.09	595.18
35000	3174.91	1713.04	1229.80	991.19	850.39	758.44	694.37
40000	3628.47	1957.76	1405.49	1132.79	971.87	866.79	793.57
45000	4082.03	2202.48	1581.17	1274.39	1093.35	975.14	892.76
50000	4535.59	2447.20	1756.86	1415.99	1214.84	1083.49	991.96
55000	4989.15	2691.92	1932.55	1557.58	1336.32	1191.84	1091.16
60000	5442.71	2936.64	2108.23	1699.18	1457.80	1300.18	1190.35
65000	5896.27	3181.35	2283.92	1840.78	1579.29	1408.53	1289.55
70000	6349.83	3426.07	2459.60	1982.38	1700.77	1516.88	1388.74
75000	6803.39	3670.79	2635.29	2123.98	1822.25	1625.23	1487.94
80000	7256.95	3915.51	2810.98	2265.58	1943.74	1733.58	1587.14
85000	7710.51	4160.23	2986.66	2407.18	2065.22	1841.93	1686.33
90000	8164.07	4404.95	3162.35	2548.77	2186.70	1950.28	1785.53
95000	8617.63	4649.67	3338.03	2690.37	2308.19	2058.62	1884.72
100000	9071.19	4894.39	3513.72	2831.97	2429.67	2166.97	1983.92
200000	18142.37	9788.78	7027.44	5663.94	4859.34	4333.95	3967.84
300000	27213.56	14683.18	10541.16	8495.91	7289.02	6500.92	5951.76
400000	36284.74	19577.57	14054.88	11327.89	9718.69	8667.89	7935.68
500000	45355.93	24471.96	17568.60	14159.86	12148.36	10834.87	9919.60
1000000	90711.85	48943.92	35137.21	28319.72	24296.72	21669.73	19839.20

Amortization Amount	8 Years	9 Years	10 Years	15 Years	20 Years	25 Years	30 Years
25	0.46	0.44	0.42	0.37	0.35	0.34	0.34
50	0.93	0.88	0.84	0.73	0.69	0.68	0.67
100	1.85	1.75	1.67	1.47	1.39	1.36	1.34
200	3.70	3.50	3.35	2.93	2.78	2.71	2.68
300	5.55	5.25	5.02	4.40	4.16	4.07	4.02
400	7.40	7.00	6.69	5.86	5.55	5.42	5.37
500	9.25	8.75	8.36	7.33	6.94	6.78	6.71
600	11.10	10.50	10.04	8.80	8.33	8.13	8.05
700	12.95	12.25	11.71	10.26	9.72	9.49	9.39
800	14.80	14.00	13.38	11.73	11.11	10.85	10.73
900	16.65	15.75	15.05	13.19	12.49	12.20	12.07
1000	18.51	17.50	16.73	14.66	13.88	13.56	13.42
2000	37.01	35.00	33.45	29.32	27.76	27.11	26.83
3000	55.52	52.50	50.18	43.98	41.65	40.67	40.25
4000	74.02	70.00	66.91	58.64	55.53	54.23	53.66
5000	92.53	87.50	83.63	73.30	69.41	67.79	67.08
6000	111.03	105.01	100.36	87.95	83.29	81.34	80.49
7000	129.54	122.51	117.08	102.61	97.18	94.90	93.91
8000	148.04	140.01	133.81	117.27	111.06	108.46	107.32
9000	166.55	157.51	150.54	131.93	124.94	122.02	120.74
10000	185.05	175.01	167.26	146.59	138.82	135.57	134.15
11000	203.56	192.51	183.99	161.25	152.71	149.13	147.57
12000	222.06	210.01	200.72	175.91	166.59	162.69	160.98
13000	240.57	227.51	217.44	190.57	180.47	176.25	174.40
14000	259.07	245.01	234.17	205.23	194.35	189.80	187.81
15000	277.58	262.51	250.89	219.89	208.24	203.36	201.23
16000	296.08	280.01	267.62	234.54	222.12	216.92	214.64
17000	314.59	297.52	284.35	249.20	236.00	230.48	228.06
18000	333.09	315.02	301.07	263.86	249.88	244.03	241.47
19000	351.60	332.52	317.80	278.52	263.77	257.59	254.89
20000	370.10	350.02	334.53	293.18	277.65	271.15	268.30
21000	388.61	367.52	351.25	307.84	291.53	284.70	281.72
22000	407.11	385.02	367.98	322.50	305.41	298.26	295.13
23000	425.62	402.52	384.70	337.16	319.30	311.82	308.55
24000	444.12	420.02	401.43	351.82	333.18	325.38	321.96
25000	462.63	437.52	418.16	366.48	347.06	338.93	335.38
26000	481.13	455.02	434.88	381.13	360.94	352.49	348.79
27000	499.64	472.52	451.61	395.79	374.83	366.05	362.21
28000	518.14	490.03	468.34	410.45	388.71	379.61	375.63
29000	536.65	507.53	485.06	425.11	402.59	393.16	389.04
30000	555.16	525.03	501.79	439.77	416.47	406.72	402.46
35000	647.68	612.53	585.42	513.07	485.89	474.51	469.53
40000	740.21	700.04	669.05	586.36	555.30	542.29	536.61
45000	832.73	787.54	752.68	659.66	624.71	610.08	603.68
50000	925.26	875.05	836.31	732.95	694.12	677.87	670.76
55000	1017.78	962.55	919.95	806.25	763.53	745.66	737.84
60000	1110.31	1050.06	1003.58	879.54	832.95	813.44	804.91
65000	1202.84	1137.56	1087.21	952.84	902.36	881.23	871.99
70000	1295.36	1225.06	1170.84	1026.13	971.77	949.02	939.06
75000	1387.89	1312.57	1254.47	1099.43	1041.18	1016.80	1006.14
80000	1480.41	1400.07	1338.10	1172.72	1110.59	1084.59	1073.22
85000	1572.94	1487.58	1421.73	1246.02	1180.01	1152.38	1140.29
90000	1665.47	1575.08	1505.37	1319.31	1249.42	1220.16	1207.37
95000	1757.99	1662.59	1589.00	1392.61	1318.83	1287.95	1274.44
100000	1850.52	1750.09	1672.63	1465.90	1388.24	1355.74	1341.52
200000	3701.03	3500.18	3345.26	2931.80	2776.49	2711.47	2683.04
300000	5551.55	5250.28	5017.89	4397.70	4164.73	4067.21	4024.56
400000	7402.07	7000.37	6690.52	5863.61	5552.97	5422.95	5366.08
500000	9252.59	8750.46	8363.15	7329.51	6941.22	6778.68	6707.59
1000000	18505.17	17500.92	16726.29	14659.01	13882.44	13557.37	13415.19

16.625%

MONTHLY PAYMENT
NECESSARY TO AMORTIZE A LOAN

Amortization Amount	1 Year	2 Years	3 Years	4 Years	5 Years	6 Years	7 Years
25	2.27	1.22	0.88	0.71	0.61	0.54	0.50
50	4.54	2.45	1.76	1.42	1.22	1.09	1.00
100	9.08	4.90	3.52	2.84	2.44	2.17	1.99
200	18.15	9.80	7.04	5.68	4.87	4.35	3.98
300	27.23	14.70	10.56	8.51	7.31	6.52	5.97
400	36.31	19.60	14.08	11.35	9.74	8.69	7.96
500	45.38	24.50	17.60	14.19	12.18	10.87	9.95
600	54.46	29.40	21.12	17.03	14.62	13.04	11.94
700	63.54	34.30	24.64	19.87	17.05	15.21	13.93
800	72.61	39.20	28.16	22.70	19.49	17.39	15.92
900	81.69	44.10	31.68	25.54	21.92	19.56	17.92
1000	90.77	49.00	35.19	28.38	24.36	21.73	19.91
2000	181.53	98.00	70.39	56.76	48.72	43.47	39.81
3000	272.30	147.00	105.58	85.14	73.08	65.20	59.72
4000	363.07	196.00	140.78	113.52	97.44	86.94	79.62
5000	453.84	245.00	175.97	141.90	121.79	108.67	99.53
6000	544.60	294.00	211.17	170.28	146.15	130.40	119.44
7000	635.37	343.00	246.36	198.66	170.51	152.14	139.34
8000	726.14	392.00	281.56	227.04	194.87	173.87	159.25
9000	816.90	441.00	316.75	255.42	219.23	195.61	179.15
10000	907.67	490.00	351.95	283.80	243.59	217.34	199.06
11000	998.44	539.00	387.14	312.18	267.95	239.08	218.96
12000	1089.21	588.00	422.34	340.56	292.31	260.81	238.87
13000	1179.97	637.00	457.53	368.94	316.67	282.54	258.78
14000	1270.74	686.00	492.73	397.31	341.02	304.28	278.68
15000	1361.51	735.00	527.92	425.69	365.38	326.01	298.59
16000	1452.28	784.00	563.12	454.07	389.74	347.75	318.49
17000	1543.04	833.00	598.31	482.45	414.10	369.48	338.40
18000	1633.81	882.00	633.51	510.83	438.46	391.21	358.31
19000	1724.58	931.00	668.70	539.21	462.82	412.95	378.21
20000	1815.34	980.00	703.90	567.59	487.18	434.68	398.12
21000	1906.11	1029.00	739.09	595.97	511.54	456.42	418.02
22000	1996.88	1078.00	774.29	624.35	535.90	478.15	437.93
23000	2087.65	1127.00	809.48	652.73	560.25	499.89	457.83
24000	2178.41	1176.00	844.68	681.11	584.61	521.62	477.74
25000	2269.18	1225.00	879.87	709.49	608.97	543.35	497.65
26000	2359.95	1274.00	915.07	737.87	633.33	565.09	517.55
27000	2450.71	1323.00	950.26	766.25	657.69	586.82	537.46
28000	2541.48	1372.00	985.46	794.63	682.05	608.56	557.36
29000	2632.25	1420.99	1020.65	823.01	706.41	630.29	577.27
30000	2723.02	1469.99	1055.85	851.39	730.77	652.02	597.18
35000	3176.85	1714.99	1231.82	993.29	852.56	760.70	696.70
40000	3630.69	1959.99	1407.80	1135.19	974.36	869.37	796.23
45000	4084.52	2204.99	1583.77	1277.08	1096.15	978.04	895.76
50000	4538.36	2449.99	1759.75	1418.98	1217.94	1086.71	995.29
55000	4992.20	2694.99	1935.72	1560.88	1339.74	1195.38	1094.82
60000	5446.03	2939.99	2111.70	1702.78	1461.53	1304.05	1194.35
65000	5899.87	3184.99	2287.67	1844.68	1583.33	1412.72	1293.88
70000	6353.70	3429.99	2463.65	1986.57	1705.12	1521.39	1393.41
75000	6807.54	3674.99	2639.62	2128.47	1826.92	1630.06	1492.94
80000	7261.38	3919.99	2815.60	2270.37	1948.71	1738.73	1592.47
85000	7715.21	4164.98	2991.57	2412.27	2070.51	1847.40	1692.00
90000	8169.05	4409.98	3167.55	2554.17	2192.30	1956.07	1791.53
95000	8622.89	4654.98	3343.52	2696.07	2314.09	2064.74	1891.05
100000	9076.72	4899.98	3519.50	2837.96	2435.89	2173.42	1990.58
200000	18153.44	9799.96	7038.99	5675.93	4871.78	4346.83	3981.17
300000	27230.16	14699.95	10558.49	8513.89	7307.67	6520.25	5971.75
400000	36306.89	19599.93	14077.99	11351.86	9743.56	8693.66	7962.34
500000	45383.61	24499.91	17597.48	14189.82	12179.45	10867.08	9952.92
1000000	90767.21	48999.82	35194.97	28379.64	24358.89	21734.16	19905.84

Amortization Amount	8 Years	9 Years	10 Years	15 Years	20 Years	25 Years	30 Years
25	0.46	0.44	0.42	0.37	0.35	0.34	0.34
50	0.93	0.88	0.84	0.74	0.70	0.68	0.68
100	1.86	1.76	1.68	1.47	1.40	1.36	1.35
200	3.71	3.51	3.36	2.95	2.79	2.73	2.70
300	5.57	5.27	5.04	4.42	4.19	4.09	4.05
400	7.43	7.03	6.72	5.90	5.59	5.46	5.40
500	9.29	8.79	8.40	7.37	6.99	6.82	6.75
600	11.14	10.54	10.08	8.84	8.38	8.19	8.11
700	13.00	12.30	11.76	10.32	9.78	9.55	9.46
800	14.86	14.06	13.44	11.79	11.18	10.92	10.81
900	16.72	15.81	15.12	13.27	12.57	12.28	12.16
1000	18.57	17.57	16.80	14.74	13.97	13.65	13.51
2000	37.15	35.14	33.60	29.48	27.94	27.30	27.02
3000	55.72	52.72	50.40	44.22	41.91	40.95	40.53
4000	74.30	70.29	67.20	58.96	55.88	54.60	54.04
5000	92.87	87.86	84.00	73.70	69.85	68.25	67.55
6000	111.44	105.43	100.80	88.44	83.82	81.90	81.06
7000	130.02	123.00	117.59	103.18	97.79	95.54	94.57
8000	148.59	140.57	134.39	117.92	111.76	109.19	108.08
9000	167.17	158.15	151.19	132.67	125.73	122.84	121.59
10000	185.74	175.72	167.99	147.41	139.70	136.49	135.10
11000	204.31	193.29	184.79	162.15	153.67	150.14	148.60
12000	222.89	210.86	201.59	176.89	167.64	163.79	162.11
13000	241.46	228.43	218.39	191.63	181.61	177.44	175.62
14000	260.04	246.01	235.19	206.37	195.58	191.09	189.13
15000	278.61	263.58	251.99	221.11	209.55	204.74	202.64
16000	297.18	281.15	268.79	235.85	223.52	218.39	216.15
17000	315.76	298.72	285.59	250.59	237.49	232.04	229.66
18000	334.33	316.29	302.39	265.33	251.46	245.69	243.17
19000	352.91	333.86	319.19	280.07	265.43	259.34	256.68
20000	371.48	351.44	335.98	294.81	279.40	272.98	270.19
21000	390.05	369.01	352.78	309.55	293.37	286.63	283.70
22000	408.63	386.58	369.58	324.29	307.34	300.28	297.21
23000	427.20	404.15	386.38	339.03	321.32	313.93	310.72
24000	445.78	421.72	403.18	353.77	335.29	327.58	324.23
25000	464.35	439.30	419.98	368.52	349.26	341.23	337.74
26000	482.92	456.87	436.78	383.26	363.23	354.88	351.25
27000	501.50	474.44	453.58	398.00	377.20	368.53	364.76
28000	520.07	492.01	470.38	412.74	391.17	382.18	378.27
29000	538.65	509.58	487.18	427.48	405.14	395.83	391.78
30000	557.22	527.15	503.98	442.22	419.11	409.48	405.29
35000	650.09	615.01	587.97	515.92	488.96	477.72	472.83
40000	742.96	702.87	671.97	589.62	558.81	545.97	540.38
45000	835.83	790.73	755.96	663.33	628.66	614.21	607.93
50000	928.70	878.59	839.96	737.03	698.51	682.46	675.48
55000	1021.57	966.45	923.96	810.73	768.36	750.71	743.02
60000	1114.44	1054.31	1007.95	884.44	838.21	818.95	810.57
65000	1207.31	1142.17	1091.95	958.14	908.06	887.20	878.12
70000	1300.18	1230.03	1175.95	1031.84	977.92	955.45	945.67
75000	1393.05	1317.89	1259.94	1105.55	1047.77	1023.69	1013.21
80000	1485.92	1405.75	1343.94	1179.25	1117.62	1091.94	1080.76
85000	1578.79	1493.61	1427.93	1252.95	1187.47	1160.18	1148.31
90000	1671.66	1581.46	1511.93	1326.65	1257.32	1228.43	1215.86
95000	1764.53	1669.32	1595.93	1400.36	1327.17	1296.68	1283.41
100000	1857.40	1757.18	1679.92	1474.06	1397.02	1364.92	1350.95
200000	3714.80	3514.37	3359.84	2948.12	2794.04	2729.84	2701.91
300000	5572.20	5271.55	5039.76	4422.18	4191.07	4094.77	4052.86
400000	7429.59	7028.73	6719.69	5896.24	5588.09	5459.69	5403.81
500000	9286.99	8785.91	8399.61	7370.30	6985.11	6824.61	6754.77
1000000	18573.99	17571.83	16799.22	14740.60	13970.22	13649.22	13509.53

16.75%

MONTHLY PAYMENT
NECESSARY TO AMORTIZE A LOAN

Amortization Amount	1 Year	2 Years	3 Years	4 Years	5 Years	6 Years	7 Years
25	2.27	1.23	0.88	0.71	0.61	0.54	0.50
50	4.54	2.45	1.76	1.42	1.22	1.09	1.00
100	9.08	4.91	3.53	2.84	2.44	2.18	2.00
200	18.16	9.81	7.05	5.69	4.88	4.36	3.99
300	27.25	14.72	10.58	8.53	7.33	6.54	5.99
400	36.33	19.62	14.10	11.38	9.77	8.72	7.99
500	45.41	24.53	17.63	14.22	12.21	10.90	9.99
600	54.49	29.43	21.15	17.06	14.65	13.08	11.98
700	63.58	34.34	24.68	19.91	17.09	15.26	13.98
800	72.66	39.24	28.20	22.75	19.54	17.44	15.98
900	81.74	44.15	31.73	25.60	21.98	19.62	17.98
1000	90.82	49.06	35.25	28.44	24.42	21.80	19.97
2000	181.65	98.11	70.51	56.88	48.84	43.60	39.95
3000	272.47	147.17	105.76	85.32	73.26	65.40	59.92
4000	363.29	196.22	141.01	113.76	97.68	87.19	79.89
5000	454.11	245.28	176.26	142.20	122.11	108.99	99.86
6000	544.94	294.33	211.52	170.64	146.53	130.79	119.84
7000	635.76	343.39	246.77	199.08	170.95	152.59	139.81
8000	726.58	392.45	282.02	227.52	195.37	174.39	159.78
9000	817.40	441.50	317.27	255.96	219.79	196.19	179.75
10000	908.23	490.56	352.53	284.40	244.21	217.99	199.73
11000	999.05	539.61	387.78	312.84	268.63	239.79	219.70
12000	1089.87	588.67	423.03	341.28	293.05	261.58	239.67
13000	1180.69	637.72	458.29	369.71	317.47	283.38	259.64
14000	1271.52	686.78	493.54	398.15	341.90	305.18	279.62
15000	1362.34	735.84	528.79	426.59	366.32	326.98	299.59
16000	1453.16	784.89	564.04	455.03	390.74	348.78	319.56
17000	1543.98	833.95	599.30	483.47	415.16	370.58	339.53
18000	1634.81	883.00	634.55	511.91	439.58	392.38	359.51
19000	1725.63	932.06	669.80	540.35	464.00	414.17	379.48
20000	1816.45	981.11	705.06	568.79	488.42	435.97	399.45
21000	1907.27	1030.17	740.31	597.23	512.84	457.77	419.42
22000	1998.10	1079.23	775.56	625.67	537.26	479.57	439.40
23000	2088.92	1128.28	810.81	654.11	561.69	501.37	459.37
24000	2179.74	1177.34	846.07	682.55	586.11	523.17	479.34
25000	2270.56	1226.39	881.32	710.99	610.53	544.97	499.31
26000	2361.39	1275.45	916.57	739.43	634.95	566.76	519.29
27000	2452.21	1324.50	951.82	767.87	659.37	588.56	539.26
28000	2543.03	1373.56	987.08	796.31	683.79	610.36	559.23
29000	2633.85	1422.62	1022.33	824.75	708.21	632.16	579.20
30000	2724.68	1471.67	1057.58	853.19	732.63	653.96	599.18
35000	3178.79	1716.95	1233.85	995.39	854.74	762.95	699.04
40000	3632.90	1962.23	1410.11	1137.58	976.84	871.95	798.90
45000	4087.02	2207.51	1586.37	1279.78	1098.95	980.94	898.77
50000	4541.13	2452.79	1762.64	1421.98	1221.06	1089.93	998.63
55000	4995.24	2698.07	1938.90	1564.18	1343.16	1198.93	1098.49
60000	5449.35	2943.34	2115.17	1706.38	1465.27	1307.92	1198.35
65000	5903.47	3188.62	2291.43	1848.57	1587.37	1416.91	1298.22
70000	6357.58	3433.90	2467.69	1990.77	1709.48	1525.91	1398.08
75000	6811.69	3679.18	2643.96	2132.97	1831.58	1634.90	1497.94
80000	7265.81	3924.46	2820.22	2275.17	1953.69	1743.89	1597.81
85000	7719.92	4169.74	2996.48	2417.37	2075.80	1852.89	1697.67
90000	8174.03	4415.02	3172.75	2559.56	2197.90	1961.88	1797.53
95000	8628.14	4660.29	3349.01	2701.76	2320.01	2070.87	1897.39
100000	9082.26	4905.57	3525.28	2843.96	2442.11	2179.87	1997.26
200000	18164.51	9811.15	7050.55	5687.92	4884.22	4359.73	3994.51
300000	27246.77	14716.72	10575.83	8531.88	7326.34	6539.60	5991.77
400000	36329.03	19622.29	14101.10	11375.84	9768.45	8719.46	7989.03
500000	45411.28	24527.87	17626.38	14219.80	12210.56	10899.33	9986.28
1000000	90822.57	49055.73	35252.76	28439.60	24421.12	21798.65	19972.57

206

Amortization Amount	8 Years	9 Years	10 Years	15 Years	20 Years	25 Years	30 Years
25	0.47	0.44	0.42	0.37	0.35	0.34	0.34
50	0.93	0.88	0.84	0.74	0.70	0.69	0.68
100	1.86	1.76	1.69	1.48	1.41	1.37	1.36
200	3.73	3.53	3.37	2.96	2.81	2.75	2.72
300	5.59	5.29	5.06	4.45	4.22	4.12	4.08
400	7.46	7.06	6.75	5.93	5.62	5.50	5.44
500	9.32	8.82	8.44	7.41	7.03	6.87	6.80
600	11.19	10.59	10.12	8.89	8.43	8.24	8.16
700	13.05	12.35	11.81	10.38	9.84	9.62	9.52
800	14.91	14.11	13.50	11.86	11.25	10.99	10.88
900	16.78	15.88	15.19	13.34	12.65	12.37	12.24
1000	18.64	17.64	16.87	14.82	14.06	13.74	13.60
2000	37.29	35.29	33.74	29.64	28.12	27.48	27.21
3000	55.93	52.93	50.62	44.47	42.17	41.22	40.81
4000	74.57	70.57	67.49	59.29	56.23	54.96	54.42
5000	93.21	88.21	84.36	74.11	70.29	68.71	68.02
6000	111.86	105.86	101.23	88.93	84.35	82.45	81.62
7000	130.50	123.50	118.11	103.76	98.41	96.19	95.23
8000	149.14	141.14	134.98	118.58	112.46	109.93	108.83
9000	167.79	158.79	151.85	133.40	126.52	123.67	122.44
10000	186.43	176.43	168.72	148.22	140.58	137.41	136.04
11000	205.07	194.07	185.59	163.05	154.64	151.15	149.64
12000	223.71	211.71	202.47	177.87	168.70	164.89	163.25
13000	242.36	229.36	219.34	192.69	182.76	178.63	176.85
14000	261.00	247.00	236.21	207.51	196.81	192.38	190.45
15000	279.64	264.64	253.08	222.33	210.87	206.12	204.06
16000	298.29	282.29	269.96	237.16	224.93	219.86	217.66
17000	316.93	299.93	286.83	251.98	238.99	233.60	231.27
18000	335.57	317.57	303.70	266.80	253.05	247.34	244.87
19000	354.21	335.21	320.57	281.62	267.10	261.08	258.47
20000	372.86	352.86	337.44	296.45	281.16	274.82	272.08
21000	391.50	370.50	354.32	311.27	295.22	288.56	285.68
22000	410.14	388.14	371.19	326.09	309.28	302.31	299.29
23000	428.79	405.79	388.06	340.91	323.34	316.05	312.89
24000	447.43	423.43	404.93	355.74	337.39	329.79	326.49
25000	466.07	441.07	421.81	370.56	351.45	343.53	340.10
26000	484.72	458.71	438.68	385.38	365.51	357.27	353.70
27000	503.36	476.36	455.55	400.20	379.57	371.01	367.31
28000	522.00	494.00	472.42	415.02	393.63	384.75	380.91
29000	540.64	511.64	489.30	429.85	407.69	398.49	394.51
30000	559.29	529.29	506.17	444.67	421.74	412.23	408.12
35000	652.50	617.50	590.53	518.78	492.03	480.94	476.14
40000	745.72	705.71	674.89	592.89	562.32	549.65	544.16
45000	838.93	793.93	759.25	667.00	632.62	618.35	612.18
50000	932.14	882.14	843.61	741.12	702.91	687.06	680.20
55000	1025.36	970.36	927.97	815.23	773.20	755.76	748.21
60000	1118.57	1058.57	1012.33	889.34	843.49	824.47	816.23
65000	1211.79	1146.78	1096.70	963.45	913.78	893.17	884.25
70000	1305.00	1235.00	1181.06	1037.56	984.07	961.88	952.27
75000	1398.22	1323.21	1265.42	1111.67	1054.36	1030.59	1020.29
80000	1491.43	1411.43	1349.78	1185.78	1124.65	1099.29	1088.31
85000	1584.65	1499.64	1434.14	1259.90	1194.94	1168.00	1156.33
90000	1677.86	1587.86	1518.50	1334.01	1265.23	1236.70	1224.35
95000	1771.07	1676.07	1602.86	1408.12	1335.52	1305.41	1292.37
100000	1864.29	1764.28	1687.22	1482.23	1405.81	1374.11	1360.39
200000	3728.58	3528.57	3374.45	2964.46	2811.62	2748.23	2720.78
300000	5592.87	5292.85	5061.67	4446.69	4217.43	4122.34	4081.17
400000	7457.16	7057.14	6748.90	5928.92	5623.25	5496.46	5441.56
500000	9321.45	8821.42	8436.12	7411.15	7029.06	6870.57	6801.95
1000000	18642.89	17642.84	16872.25	14822.31	14058.11	13741.14	13603.91

16.875%

MONTHLY PAYMENT
NECESSARY TO AMORTIZE A LOAN

Amortization Amount	1 Year	2 Years	3 Years	4 Years	5 Years	6 Years	7 Years
25	2.27	1.23	0.88	0.71	0.61	0.55	0.50
50	4.54	2.46	1.77	1.42	1.22	1.09	1.00
100	9.09	4.91	3.53	2.85	2.45	2.19	2.00
200	18.18	9.82	7.06	5.70	4.90	4.37	4.01
300	27.26	14.73	10.59	8.55	7.35	6.56	6.01
400	36.35	19.64	14.12	11.40	9.79	8.75	8.02
500	45.44	24.56	17.66	14.25	12.24	10.93	10.02
600	54.53	29.47	21.19	17.10	14.69	13.12	12.02
700	63.61	34.38	24.72	19.95	17.14	15.30	14.03
800	72.70	39.29	28.25	22.80	19.59	17.49	16.03
900	81.79	44.20	31.78	25.65	22.04	19.68	18.04
1000	90.88	49.11	35.31	28.50	24.48	21.86	20.04
2000	181.76	98.22	70.62	57.00	48.97	43.73	40.08
3000	272.63	147.33	105.93	85.50	73.45	65.59	60.12
4000	363.51	196.45	141.24	114.00	97.93	87.45	80.16
5000	454.39	245.56	176.55	142.50	122.42	109.32	100.20
6000	545.27	294.67	211.86	171.00	146.90	131.18	120.24
7000	636.15	343.78	247.17	199.50	171.38	153.04	140.28
8000	727.02	392.89	282.48	228.00	195.87	174.91	160.32
9000	817.90	442.00	317.80	256.50	220.35	196.77	180.35
10000	908.78	491.12	353.11	285.00	244.83	218.63	200.39
11000	999.66	540.23	388.42	313.50	269.32	240.50	220.43
12000	1090.53	589.34	423.73	342.00	293.80	262.36	240.47
13000	1181.41	638.45	459.04	370.49	318.28	284.22	260.51
14000	1272.29	687.56	494.35	398.99	342.77	306.09	280.55
15000	1363.17	736.67	529.66	427.49	367.25	327.95	300.59
16000	1454.05	785.79	564.97	455.99	391.73	349.81	320.63
17000	1544.92	834.90	600.28	484.49	416.22	371.67	340.67
18000	1635.80	884.01	635.59	512.99	440.70	393.54	360.71
19000	1726.68	933.12	670.90	541.49	465.18	415.40	380.75
20000	1817.56	982.23	706.21	569.99	489.67	437.26	400.79
21000	1908.44	1031.34	741.52	598.49	514.15	459.13	420.83
22000	1999.31	1080.46	776.83	626.99	538.63	480.99	440.87
23000	2090.19	1129.57	812.14	655.49	563.12	502.85	460.91
24000	2181.07	1178.68	847.45	683.99	587.60	524.72	480.95
25000	2271.95	1227.79	882.76	712.49	612.09	546.58	500.98
26000	2362.83	1276.90	918.07	740.99	636.57	568.44	521.02
27000	2453.70	1326.01	953.39	769.49	661.05	590.31	541.06
28000	2544.58	1375.13	988.70	797.99	685.54	612.17	561.10
29000	2635.46	1424.24	1024.01	826.49	710.02	634.03	581.14
30000	2726.34	1473.35	1059.32	854.99	734.50	655.90	601.18
35000	3180.73	1718.91	1235.87	997.49	856.92	765.21	701.38
40000	3635.12	1964.47	1412.42	1139.98	979.34	874.53	801.58
45000	4089.51	2210.02	1588.98	1282.48	1101.75	983.84	901.77
50000	4543.90	2455.58	1765.53	1424.98	1224.17	1093.16	1001.97
55000	4998.29	2701.14	1942.08	1567.48	1346.59	1202.48	1102.17
60000	5452.67	2946.70	2118.63	1709.98	1469.00	1311.79	1202.36
65000	5907.06	3192.26	2295.19	1852.47	1591.42	1421.11	1302.56
70000	6361.45	3437.82	2471.74	1994.97	1713.84	1530.43	1402.76
75000	6815.84	3683.37	2648.29	2137.47	1836.26	1639.74	1502.95
80000	7270.23	3928.93	2824.85	2279.97	1958.67	1749.06	1603.15
85000	7724.62	4174.49	3001.40	2422.47	2081.09	1858.37	1703.35
90000	8179.01	4420.05	3177.95	2564.96	2203.51	1967.69	1803.54
95000	8633.40	4665.61	3354.50	2707.46	2325.92	2077.01	1903.74
100000	9087.79	4911.17	3531.06	2849.96	2448.34	2186.32	2003.94
200000	18175.58	9822.33	7062.11	5699.92	4896.68	4372.64	4007.88
300000	27263.37	14733.50	10593.17	8549.88	7345.02	6558.96	6011.81
400000	36351.16	19644.66	14124.23	11399.85	9793.36	8745.29	8015.75
500000	45438.96	24555.83	17655.29	14249.81	12241.70	10931.61	10019.69
1000000	90877.91	49111.65	35310.57	28499.61	24483.40	21863.21	20039.38

208

Amortization Amount	8 Years	9 Years	10 Years	15 Years	20 Years	25 Years	30 Years
25	0.47	0.44	0.42	0.37	0.35	0.35	0.34
50	0.94	0.89	0.85	0.75	0.71	0.69	0.68
100	1.87	1.77	1.69	1.49	1.41	1.38	1.37
200	3.74	3.54	3.39	2.98	2.83	2.77	2.74
300	5.61	5.31	5.08	4.47	4.24	4.15	4.11
400	7.48	7.09	6.78	5.96	5.66	5.53	5.48
500	9.36	8.86	8.47	7.45	7.07	6.92	6.85
600	11.23	10.63	10.17	8.94	8.49	8.30	8.22
700	13.10	12.40	11.86	10.43	9.90	9.68	9.59
800	14.97	14.17	13.56	11.92	11.32	11.07	10.96
900	16.84	15.94	15.25	13.41	12.73	12.45	12.33
1000	18.71	17.71	16.95	14.90	14.15	13.83	13.70
2000	37.42	35.43	33.89	29.81	28.29	27.67	27.40
3000	56.14	53.14	50.84	44.71	42.44	41.50	41.09
4000	74.85	70.86	67.78	59.62	56.58	55.33	54.79
5000	93.56	88.57	84.73	74.52	70.73	69.17	68.49
6000	112.27	106.28	101.67	89.42	84.88	83.00	82.19
7000	130.98	124.00	118.62	104.33	99.02	96.83	95.89
8000	149.70	141.71	135.56	119.23	113.17	110.67	109.59
9000	168.41	159.43	152.51	134.14	127.31	124.50	123.28
10000	187.12	177.14	169.45	149.04	141.46	138.33	136.98
11000	205.83	194.85	186.40	163.95	155.61	152.16	150.68
12000	224.54	212.57	203.34	178.85	169.75	166.00	164.38
13000	243.25	230.28	220.29	193.75	183.90	179.83	178.08
14000	261.97	248.00	237.24	208.66	198.05	193.66	191.78
15000	280.68	265.71	254.18	223.56	212.19	207.50	205.47
16000	299.39	283.42	271.13	238.47	226.34	221.33	219.17
17000	318.10	301.14	288.07	253.37	240.48	235.16	232.87
18000	336.81	318.85	305.02	268.27	254.63	249.00	246.57
19000	355.53	336.57	321.96	283.18	268.78	262.83	260.27
20000	374.24	354.28	338.91	298.08	282.92	276.66	273.97
21000	392.95	371.99	355.85	312.99	297.07	290.50	287.66
22000	411.66	389.71	372.80	327.89	311.21	304.33	301.36
23000	430.37	407.42	389.74	342.80	325.36	318.16	315.06
24000	449.09	425.13	406.69	357.70	339.51	332.00	328.76
25000	467.80	442.85	423.63	372.60	353.65	345.83	342.46
26000	486.51	460.56	440.58	387.51	367.80	359.66	356.16
27000	505.22	478.28	457.53	402.41	381.94	373.49	369.85
28000	523.93	495.99	474.47	417.32	396.09	387.33	383.55
29000	542.64	513.70	491.42	432.22	410.24	401.16	397.25
30000	561.36	531.42	508.36	447.12	424.38	414.99	410.95
35000	654.92	619.99	593.09	521.64	495.11	484.16	479.44
40000	748.48	708.56	677.82	596.17	565.84	553.33	547.93
45000	842.04	797.13	762.54	670.69	636.57	622.49	616.42
50000	935.59	885.70	847.27	745.21	707.31	691.66	684.92
55000	1029.15	974.27	932.00	819.73	778.04	760.82	753.41
60000	1122.71	1062.84	1016.72	894.25	848.77	829.99	821.90
65000	1216.27	1151.41	1101.45	968.77	919.50	899.15	890.39
70000	1309.83	1239.98	1186.18	1043.29	990.23	968.32	958.88
75000	1403.39	1328.55	1270.90	1117.81	1060.96	1037.49	1027.37
80000	1496.95	1417.12	1355.63	1192.33	1131.69	1106.65	1095.87
85000	1590.51	1505.69	1440.36	1266.85	1202.42	1175.82	1164.36
90000	1684.07	1594.26	1525.09	1341.37	1273.15	1244.98	1232.85
95000	1777.63	1682.83	1609.81	1415.89	1343.88	1314.15	1301.34
100000	1871.19	1771.40	1694.54	1490.41	1414.61	1383.31	1369.83
200000	3742.38	3542.79	3389.08	2980.83	2829.22	2766.63	2739.66
300000	5613.57	5314.19	5083.62	4471.24	4243.83	4149.94	4109.50
400000	7484.76	7085.58	6778.16	5961.66	5658.44	5533.25	5479.33
500000	9355.94	8856.98	8472.70	7452.07	7073.05	6916.57	6849.16
1000000	18711.89	17713.95	16945.39	14904.14	14146.11	13833.14	13698.32

17%
MONTHLY PAYMENT
NECESSARY TO AMORTIZE A LOAN

Amortization Amount	1 Year	2 Years	3 Years	4 Years	5 Years	6 Years	7 Years
25	2.27	1.23	0.88	0.71	0.61	0.55	0.50
50	4.55	2.46	1.77	1.43	1.23	1.10	1.01
100	9.09	4.92	3.54	2.86	2.45	2.19	2.01
200	18.19	9.83	7.07	5.71	4.91	4.39	4.02
300	27.28	14.75	10.61	8.57	7.36	6.58	6.03
400	36.37	19.67	14.15	11.42	9.82	8.77	8.04
500	45.47	24.58	17.68	14.28	12.27	10.96	10.05
600	54.56	29.50	21.22	17.14	14.73	13.16	12.06
700	63.65	34.42	24.76	19.99	17.18	15.35	14.07
800	72.75	39.33	28.29	22.85	19.64	17.54	16.09
900	81.84	44.25	31.83	25.70	22.09	19.74	18.10
1000	90.93	49.17	35.37	28.56	24.55	21.93	20.11
2000	181.87	98.34	70.74	57.12	49.09	43.86	40.21
3000	272.80	147.50	106.11	85.68	73.64	65.78	60.32
4000	363.73	196.67	141.47	114.24	98.18	87.71	80.43
5000	454.67	245.84	176.84	142.80	122.73	109.64	100.53
6000	545.60	295.01	212.21	171.36	147.27	131.57	120.64
7000	636.53	344.17	247.58	199.92	171.82	153.49	140.74
8000	727.47	393.34	282.95	228.48	196.37	175.42	160.85
9000	818.40	442.51	318.31	257.04	220.91	197.35	180.96
10000	909.33	491.68	353.68	285.60	245.46	219.28	201.06
11000	1000.27	540.84	389.05	314.16	270.00	241.21	221.17
12000	1091.20	590.01	424.42	342.72	294.55	263.13	241.28
13000	1182.13	639.18	459.79	371.28	319.09	285.06	261.38
14000	1273.07	688.35	495.16	399.84	343.64	306.99	281.49
15000	1364.00	737.51	530.53	428.39	368.19	328.92	301.59
16000	1454.93	786.68	565.89	456.95	392.73	350.85	321.70
17000	1545.87	835.85	601.26	485.51	417.28	372.77	341.81
18000	1636.80	885.02	636.63	514.07	441.82	394.70	361.91
19000	1727.73	934.18	672.00	542.63	466.37	416.63	382.02
20000	1818.66	983.35	707.37	571.19	490.91	438.56	402.13
21000	1909.60	1032.52	742.74	599.75	515.46	460.48	422.23
22000	2000.53	1081.69	778.11	628.31	540.01	482.41	442.34
23000	2091.46	1130.85	813.47	656.87	564.55	504.34	462.44
24000	2182.40	1180.02	848.84	685.43	589.10	526.27	482.55
25000	2273.33	1229.19	884.21	713.99	613.64	548.20	502.66
26000	2364.26	1278.36	919.58	742.55	638.19	570.12	522.76
27000	2455.20	1327.52	954.95	771.11	662.74	592.05	542.87
28000	2546.13	1376.69	990.32	799.67	687.28	613.98	562.98
29000	2637.06	1425.86	1025.68	828.23	711.83	635.91	583.08
30000	2728.00	1475.03	1061.05	856.79	736.37	657.84	603.19
35000	3182.66	1720.87	1237.89	999.59	859.10	767.47	703.72
40000	3637.33	1966.70	1414.74	1142.39	981.83	877.11	804.25
45000	4092.00	2212.54	1591.58	1285.18	1104.56	986.75	904.78
50000	4546.66	2458.38	1768.42	1427.98	1227.29	1096.39	1005.31
55000	5001.33	2704.22	1945.26	1570.78	1350.02	1206.03	1105.84
60000	5455.99	2950.05	2122.11	1713.58	1472.74	1315.67	1206.38
65000	5910.66	3195.89	2298.95	1856.38	1595.47	1425.31	1306.91
70000	6365.33	3441.73	2475.79	1999.18	1718.20	1534.95	1407.44
75000	6819.99	3687.57	2652.63	2141.97	1840.93	1644.59	1507.97
80000	7274.66	3933.41	2829.47	2284.77	1963.66	1754.23	1608.50
85000	7729.33	4179.24	3006.32	2427.57	2086.39	1863.87	1709.03
90000	8183.99	4425.08	3183.16	2570.37	2209.12	1973.51	1809.56
95000	8638.66	4670.92	3360.00	2713.17	2331.85	2083.15	1910.10
100000	9093.32	4916.76	3536.84	2855.97	2454.57	2192.78	2010.63
200000	18186.65	9833.52	7073.68	5711.93	4909.15	4385.57	4021.25
300000	27279.97	14750.27	10610.53	8567.90	7363.72	6578.35	6031.88
400000	36373.30	19667.03	14147.37	11423.87	9818.30	8771.14	8042.51
500000	45466.62	24583.79	17684.21	14279.83	12272.87	10963.92	10053.14
1000000	90933.25	49167.58	35368.42	28559.66	24545.74	21927.85	20106.27

Amortization Amount	8 Years	9 Years	10 Years	15 Years	20 Years	25 Years	30 Years
25	0.47	0.44	0.43	0.37	0.36	0.35	0.34
50	0.94	0.89	0.85	0.75	0.71	0.70	0.69
100	1.88	1.78	1.70	1.50	1.42	1.39	1.38
200	3.76	3.56	3.40	3.00	2.85	2.79	2.76
300	5.63	5.34	5.11	4.50	4.27	4.18	4.14
400	7.51	7.11	6.81	5.99	5.69	5.57	5.52
500	9.39	8.89	8.51	7.49	7.12	6.96	6.90
600	11.27	10.67	10.21	8.99	8.54	8.36	8.28
700	13.15	12.45	11.91	10.49	9.96	9.75	9.65
800	15.02	14.23	13.61	11.99	11.39	11.14	11.03
900	16.90	16.01	15.32	13.49	12.81	12.53	12.41
1000	18.78	17.79	17.02	14.99	14.23	13.93	13.79
2000	37.56	35.57	34.04	29.97	28.47	27.85	27.59
3000	56.34	53.36	51.06	44.96	42.70	41.78	41.38
4000	75.12	71.14	68.07	59.94	56.94	55.70	55.17
5000	93.90	88.93	85.09	74.93	71.17	69.63	68.96
6000	112.69	106.71	102.11	89.92	85.41	83.55	82.76
7000	131.47	124.50	119.13	104.90	99.64	97.48	96.55
8000	150.25	142.28	136.15	119.89	113.87	111.40	110.34
9000	169.03	160.07	153.17	134.87	128.11	125.33	124.13
10000	187.81	177.85	170.19	149.86	142.34	139.25	137.93
11000	206.59	195.64	187.21	164.85	156.58	153.18	151.72
12000	225.37	213.42	204.22	179.83	170.81	167.10	165.51
13000	244.15	231.21	221.24	194.82	185.04	181.03	179.31
14000	262.93	248.99	238.26	209.81	199.28	194.95	193.10
15000	281.71	266.78	255.28	224.79	213.51	208.88	206.89
16000	300.50	284.56	272.30	239.78	227.75	222.80	220.68
17000	319.28	302.35	289.32	254.76	241.98	236.73	234.48
18000	338.06	320.13	306.34	269.75	256.22	250.65	248.27
19000	356.84	337.92	323.35	284.74	270.45	264.58	262.06
20000	375.62	355.70	340.37	299.72	284.68	278.50	275.86
21000	394.40	373.49	357.39	314.71	298.92	292.43	289.65
22000	413.18	391.27	374.41	329.69	313.15	306.35	303.44
23000	431.96	409.06	391.43	344.68	327.39	320.28	317.23
24000	450.74	426.84	408.45	359.67	341.62	334.20	331.03
25000	469.52	444.63	425.47	374.65	355.86	348.13	344.82
26000	488.31	462.41	442.48	389.64	370.09	362.06	358.61
27000	507.09	480.20	459.50	404.62	384.32	375.98	372.40
28000	525.87	497.98	476.52	419.61	398.56	389.91	386.20
29000	544.65	515.77	493.54	434.60	412.79	403.83	399.99
30000	563.43	533.56	510.56	449.58	427.03	417.76	413.78
35000	657.33	622.48	595.65	524.51	498.20	487.38	482.75
40000	751.24	711.41	680.75	599.44	569.37	557.01	551.71
45000	845.14	800.33	765.84	674.37	640.54	626.63	620.67
50000	939.05	889.26	850.93	749.30	711.71	696.26	689.64
55000	1032.95	978.18	936.03	824.23	782.88	765.89	758.60
60000	1126.86	1067.11	1021.12	899.17	854.05	835.51	827.57
65000	1220.76	1156.04	1106.21	974.10	925.22	905.14	896.53
70000	1314.67	1244.96	1191.31	1049.03	996.39	974.76	965.49
75000	1408.57	1333.89	1276.40	1123.96	1067.57	1044.39	1034.46
80000	1502.48	1422.81	1361.49	1198.89	1138.74	1114.02	1103.42
85000	1596.38	1511.74	1446.58	1273.82	1209.91	1183.64	1172.38
90000	1690.29	1600.67	1531.68	1348.75	1281.08	1253.27	1241.35
95000	1784.19	1689.59	1616.77	1423.68	1352.25	1322.89	1310.31
100000	1878.10	1778.52	1701.86	1498.61	1423.42	1392.52	1379.28
200000	3756.20	3557.03	3403.73	2997.22	2846.84	2785.04	2758.55
300000	5634.29	5335.55	5105.59	4495.83	4270.26	4177.56	4137.83
400000	7512.39	7114.07	6807.46	5994.44	5693.68	5570.08	5517.11
500000	9390.49	8892.58	8509.32	7493.05	7117.10	6962.60	6896.38
1000000	18780.98	17785.17	17018.65	14986.09	14234.20	13925.19	13792.76

17.125%

MONTHLY PAYMENT
NECESSARY TO AMORTIZE A LOAN

Amortization Amount	1 Year	2 Years	3 Years	4 Years	5 Years	6 Years	7 Years
25	2.27	1.23	0.89	0.72	0.62	0.55	0.50
50	4.55	2.46	1.77	1.43	1.23	1.10	1.01
100	9.10	4.92	3.54	2.86	2.46	2.20	2.02
200	18.20	9.84	7.09	5.72	4.92	4.40	4.03
300	27.30	14.77	10.63	8.59	7.38	6.60	6.05
400	36.40	19.69	14.17	11.45	9.84	8.80	8.07
500	45.49	24.61	17.71	14.31	12.30	11.00	10.09
600	54.59	29.53	21.26	17.17	14.76	13.20	12.10
700	63.69	34.46	24.80	20.03	17.23	15.39	14.12
800	72.79	39.38	28.34	22.90	19.69	17.59	16.14
900	81.89	44.30	31.88	25.76	22.15	19.79	18.16
1000	90.99	49.22	35.43	28.62	24.61	21.99	20.17
2000	181.98	98.45	70.85	57.24	49.22	43.99	40.35
3000	272.97	147.67	106.28	85.86	73.82	65.98	60.52
4000	363.95	196.89	141.71	114.48	98.43	87.97	80.69
5000	454.94	246.12	177.13	143.10	123.04	109.96	100.87
6000	545.93	295.34	212.56	171.72	147.65	131.96	121.04
7000	636.92	344.56	247.98	200.34	172.26	153.95	141.21
8000	727.91	393.79	283.41	228.96	196.87	175.94	161.39
9000	818.90	443.01	318.84	257.58	221.47	197.93	181.56
10000	909.89	492.24	354.26	286.20	246.08	219.93	201.73
11000	1000.87	541.46	389.69	314.82	270.69	241.92	221.91
12000	1091.86	590.68	425.12	343.44	295.30	263.91	242.08
13000	1182.85	639.91	460.54	372.06	319.91	285.90	262.25
14000	1273.84	689.13	495.97	400.68	344.51	307.90	282.43
15000	1364.83	738.35	531.39	429.30	369.12	329.89	302.60
16000	1455.82	787.58	566.82	457.92	393.73	351.88	322.77
17000	1546.81	836.80	602.25	486.54	418.34	373.87	342.95
18000	1637.79	886.02	637.67	515.16	442.95	395.87	363.12
19000	1728.78	935.25	673.10	543.78	467.55	417.86	383.29
20000	1819.77	984.47	708.53	572.40	492.16	439.85	403.46
21000	1910.76	1033.69	743.95	601.01	516.77	461.84	423.64
22000	2001.75	1082.92	779.38	629.63	541.38	483.84	443.81
23000	2092.74	1132.14	814.80	658.25	565.99	505.83	463.98
24000	2183.73	1181.36	850.23	686.87	590.60	527.82	484.16
25000	2274.71	1230.59	885.66	715.49	615.20	549.81	504.33
26000	2365.70	1279.81	921.08	744.11	639.81	571.81	524.50
27000	2456.69	1329.04	956.51	772.73	664.42	593.80	544.68
28000	2547.68	1378.26	991.94	801.35	689.03	615.79	564.85
29000	2638.67	1427.48	1027.36	829.97	713.64	637.78	585.02
30000	2729.66	1476.71	1062.79	858.59	738.24	659.78	605.20
35000	3184.60	1722.82	1239.92	1001.69	861.28	769.74	706.06
40000	3639.54	1968.94	1417.05	1144.79	984.33	879.70	806.93
45000	4094.49	2215.06	1594.18	1287.89	1107.37	989.66	907.80
50000	4549.43	2461.18	1771.31	1430.99	1230.41	1099.63	1008.66
55000	5004.37	2707.29	1948.45	1574.09	1353.45	1209.59	1109.53
60000	5459.31	2953.41	2125.58	1717.19	1476.49	1319.55	1210.39
65000	5914.26	3199.53	2302.71	1860.28	1599.53	1429.52	1311.26
70000	6369.20	3445.65	2479.84	2003.38	1722.57	1539.48	1412.13
75000	6824.14	3691.76	2656.97	2146.48	1845.61	1649.44	1512.99
80000	7279.09	3937.88	2834.10	2289.58	1968.65	1759.40	1613.86
85000	7734.03	4184.00	3011.23	2432.68	2091.69	1869.37	1714.73
90000	8188.97	4430.12	3188.37	2575.78	2214.73	1979.33	1815.59
95000	8643.91	4676.23	3365.50	2718.88	2337.77	2089.29	1916.46
100000	9098.86	4922.35	3542.63	2861.98	2460.81	2199.26	2017.32
200000	18197.71	9844.70	7085.26	5723.95	4921.63	4398.51	4034.65
300000	27296.57	14767.06	10627.89	8585.93	7382.44	6597.77	6051.97
400000	36395.43	19689.41	14170.51	11447.90	9843.26	8797.02	8069.30
500000	45494.29	24611.76	17713.14	14309.88	12304.07	10996.28	10086.62
1000000	90988.57	49223.52	35426.29	28619.76	24608.14	21992.55	20173.25

212

MONTHLY PAYMENT
NECESSARY TO AMORTIZE A LOAN **17.125%**

Amortization Amount	8 Years	9 Years	10 Years	15 Years	20 Years	25 Years	30 Years
25	0.47	0.45	0.43	0.38	0.36	0.35	0.35
50	0.94	0.89	0.85	0.75	0.72	0.70	0.69
100	1.89	1.79	1.71	1.51	1.43	1.40	1.39
200	3.77	3.57	3.42	3.01	2.86	2.80	2.78
300	5.66	5.36	5.13	4.52	4.30	4.21	4.17
400	7.54	7.14	6.84	6.03	5.73	5.61	5.55
500	9.43	8.93	8.55	7.53	7.16	7.01	6.94
600	11.31	10.71	10.26	9.04	8.59	8.41	8.33
700	13.20	12.50	11.96	10.55	10.03	9.81	9.72
800	15.08	14.29	13.67	12.05	11.46	11.21	11.11
900	16.97	16.07	15.38	13.56	12.89	12.62	12.50
1000	18.85	17.86	17.09	15.07	14.32	14.02	13.89
2000	37.70	35.71	34.18	30.14	28.64	28.03	27.77
3000	56.55	53.57	51.28	45.20	42.97	42.05	41.66
4000	75.40	71.43	68.37	60.27	57.29	56.07	55.55
5000	94.25	89.28	85.46	75.34	71.61	70.09	69.44
6000	113.10	107.14	102.55	90.41	85.93	84.10	83.32
7000	131.95	125.00	119.64	105.48	100.26	98.12	97.21
8000	150.80	142.85	136.74	120.55	114.58	112.14	111.10
9000	169.65	160.71	153.83	135.61	128.90	126.16	124.99
10000	188.50	178.56	170.92	150.68	143.22	140.17	138.87
11000	207.35	196.42	188.01	165.75	157.55	154.19	152.76
12000	226.20	214.28	205.10	180.82	171.87	168.21	166.65
13000	245.05	232.13	222.20	195.89	186.19	182.23	180.53
14000	263.90	249.99	239.29	210.95	200.51	196.24	194.42
15000	282.75	267.85	256.38	226.02	214.84	210.26	208.31
16000	301.60	285.70	273.47	241.09	229.16	224.28	222.20
17000	320.45	303.56	290.56	256.16	243.48	238.29	236.08
18000	339.30	321.42	307.66	271.23	257.80	252.31	249.97
19000	358.15	339.27	324.75	286.30	272.13	266.33	263.86
20000	377.00	357.13	341.84	301.36	286.45	280.35	277.74
21000	395.85	374.99	358.93	316.43	300.77	294.36	291.63
22000	414.70	392.84	376.02	331.50	315.09	308.38	305.52
23000	433.55	410.70	393.12	346.57	329.42	322.40	319.41
24000	452.40	428.56	410.21	361.64	343.74	336.42	333.29
25000	471.25	446.41	427.30	376.70	358.06	350.43	347.18
26000	490.10	464.27	444.39	391.77	372.38	364.45	361.07
27000	508.95	482.13	461.48	406.84	386.70	378.47	374.96
28000	527.80	499.98	478.58	421.91	401.03	392.48	388.84
29000	546.65	517.84	495.67	436.98	415.35	406.50	402.73
30000	565.50	535.69	512.76	452.04	429.67	420.52	416.62
35000	659.76	624.98	598.22	527.39	501.28	490.61	486.05
40000	754.01	714.26	683.68	602.73	572.90	560.69	555.49
45000	848.26	803.54	769.14	678.07	644.51	630.78	624.93
50000	942.51	892.82	854.60	753.41	716.12	700.87	694.36
55000	1036.76	982.11	940.06	828.75	787.73	770.95	763.80
60000	1131.01	1071.39	1025.52	904.09	859.34	841.04	833.23
65000	1225.26	1160.67	1110.98	979.43	930.96	911.13	902.67
70000	1319.51	1249.95	1196.44	1054.77	1002.57	981.21	972.11
75000	1413.76	1339.24	1281.90	1130.11	1074.18	1051.30	1041.54
80000	1508.01	1428.52	1367.36	1205.45	1145.79	1121.39	1110.98
85000	1602.26	1517.80	1452.82	1280.79	1217.40	1191.47	1180.42
90000	1696.51	1607.08	1538.28	1356.13	1289.02	1261.56	1249.85
95000	1790.77	1696.37	1623.74	1431.48	1360.63	1331.65	1319.29
100000	1885.02	1785.65	1709.20	1506.82	1432.24	1401.73	1388.72
200000	3770.03	3571.30	3418.40	3013.63	2864.48	2803.46	2777.45
300000	5655.05	5356.95	5127.60	4520.45	4296.72	4205.20	4166.17
400000	7540.07	7142.59	6836.80	6027.26	5728.96	5606.93	5554.90
500000	9425.08	8928.24	8546.00	7534.08	7161.20	7008.66	6943.62
1000000	18850.16	17856.48	17092.01	15068.16	14322.39	14017.32	13887.24

213

17.25%

MONTHLY PAYMENT
NECESSARY TO AMORTIZE A LOAN

Amortization Amount	1 Year	2 Years	3 Years	4 Years	5 Years	6 Years	7 Years
25	2.28	1.23	0.89	0.72	0.62	0.55	0.51
50	4.55	2.46	1.77	1.43	1.23	1.10	1.01
100	9.10	4.93	3.55	2.87	2.47	2.21	2.02
200	18.21	9.86	7.10	5.74	4.93	4.41	4.05
300	27.31	14.78	10.65	8.60	7.40	6.62	6.07
400	36.42	19.71	14.19	11.47	9.87	8.82	8.10
500	45.52	24.64	17.74	14.34	12.34	11.03	10.12
600	54.63	29.57	21.29	17.21	14.80	13.23	12.14
700	63.73	34.50	24.84	20.08	17.27	15.44	14.17
800	72.84	39.42	28.39	22.94	19.74	17.65	16.19
900	81.94	44.35	31.94	25.81	22.20	19.85	18.22
1000	91.04	49.28	35.48	28.68	24.67	22.06	20.24
2000	182.09	98.56	70.97	57.36	49.34	44.11	40.48
3000	273.13	147.84	106.45	86.04	74.01	66.17	60.72
4000	364.18	197.12	141.94	114.72	98.68	88.23	80.96
5000	455.22	246.40	177.42	143.40	123.35	110.29	101.20
6000	546.26	295.68	212.91	172.08	148.02	132.34	121.44
7000	637.31	344.96	248.39	200.76	172.69	154.40	141.68
8000	728.35	394.24	283.87	229.44	197.36	176.46	161.92
9000	819.40	443.52	319.36	258.12	222.04	198.52	182.16
10000	910.44	492.79	354.84	286.80	246.71	220.57	202.40
11000	1001.48	542.07	390.33	315.48	271.38	242.63	222.64
12000	1092.53	591.35	425.81	344.16	296.05	264.69	242.88
13000	1183.57	640.63	461.29	372.84	320.72	286.75	263.12
14000	1274.61	689.91	496.78	401.52	345.39	308.80	283.36
15000	1365.66	739.19	532.26	430.20	370.06	330.86	303.60
16000	1456.70	788.47	567.75	458.88	394.73	352.92	323.84
17000	1547.75	837.75	603.23	487.56	419.40	374.97	344.09
18000	1638.79	887.03	638.72	516.24	444.07	397.03	364.33
19000	1729.83	936.31	674.20	544.92	468.74	419.09	384.57
20000	1820.88	985.59	709.68	573.60	493.41	441.15	404.81
21000	1911.92	1034.87	745.17	602.28	518.08	463.20	425.05
22000	2002.97	1084.15	780.65	630.96	542.75	485.26	445.29
23000	2094.01	1133.43	816.14	659.64	567.42	507.32	465.53
24000	2185.05	1182.71	851.62	688.32	592.09	529.38	485.77
25000	2276.10	1231.99	887.10	717.00	616.78	551.43	506.01
26000	2367.14	1281.27	922.59	745.68	641.44	573.49	526.25
27000	2458.19	1330.55	958.07	774.36	666.11	595.55	546.49
28000	2549.23	1379.83	993.56	803.04	690.78	617.61	566.73
29000	2640.27	1429.10	1029.04	831.72	715.45	639.66	586.97
30000	2731.32	1478.38	1064.53	860.40	740.12	661.72	607.21
35000	3186.54	1724.78	1241.95	1003.80	863.47	772.01	708.41
40000	3641.76	1971.18	1419.37	1147.20	986.82	882.29	809.61
45000	4096.98	2217.58	1596.79	1290.60	1110.18	992.58	910.81
50000	4552.19	2463.97	1774.21	1433.99	1233.53	1102.87	1012.02
55000	5007.41	2710.37	1951.63	1577.39	1356.88	1213.15	1113.22
60000	5462.63	2956.77	2129.05	1720.79	1480.24	1323.44	1214.42
65000	5917.85	3203.17	2306.47	1864.19	1603.59	1433.73	1315.62
70000	6373.07	3449.56	2483.89	2007.59	1726.94	1544.01	1416.82
75000	6828.29	3695.96	2661.31	2150.99	1850.29	1654.30	1518.02
80000	7283.51	3942.36	2838.73	2294.39	1973.65	1764.59	1619.22
85000	7738.73	4188.76	3016.16	2437.79	2097.00	1874.87	1720.43
90000	8193.95	4435.15	3193.58	2581.19	2220.35	1985.16	1821.63
95000	8649.17	4681.55	3371.00	2724.59	2343.71	2095.45	1922.83
100000	9104.39	4927.95	3548.42	2867.99	2467.06	2205.73	2024.03
200000	18208.78	9855.89	7096.84	5735.98	4934.12	4411.47	4048.06
300000	27313.17	14783.84	10645.25	8603.97	7401.18	6617.20	6072.09
400000	36417.56	19711.79	14193.67	11471.96	9868.24	8822.93	8096.12
500000	45521.95	24639.74	17742.09	14339.95	12335.30	11028.66	10120.15
1000000	91043.89	49279.47	35484.18	28679.89	24670.60	22057.33	20240.30

Amortization Amount	8 Years	9 Years	10 Years	15 Years	20 Years	25 Years	30 Years
25	0.47	0.45	0.43	0.38	0.36	0.35	0.35
50	0.95	0.90	0.86	0.76	0.72	0.71	0.70
100	1.89	1.79	1.72	1.52	1.44	1.41	1.40
200	3.78	3.59	3.43	3.03	2.88	2.82	2.80
300	5.68	5.38	5.15	4.55	4.32	4.23	4.19
400	7.57	7.17	6.87	6.06	5.76	5.64	5.59
500	9.46	8.96	8.58	7.58	7.21	7.05	6.99
600	11.35	10.76	10.30	9.09	8.65	8.47	8.39
700	13.24	12.55	12.02	10.61	10.09	9.88	9.79
800	15.14	14.34	13.73	12.12	11.53	11.29	11.19
900	17.03	16.14	15.45	13.64	12.97	12.70	12.58
1000	18.92	17.93	17.17	15.15	14.41	14.11	13.98
2000	37.84	35.86	34.33	30.30	28.82	28.22	27.96
3000	56.76	53.78	51.50	45.45	43.23	42.33	41.95
4000	75.68	71.71	68.66	60.60	57.64	56.44	55.93
5000	94.60	89.64	85.83	75.75	72.05	70.55	69.91
6000	113.52	107.57	102.99	90.90	86.46	84.66	83.89
7000	132.44	125.50	120.16	106.05	100.87	98.77	97.87
8000	151.36	143.42	137.32	121.20	115.29	112.88	111.85
9000	170.27	161.35	154.49	136.35	129.70	126.99	125.84
10000	189.19	179.28	171.65	151.50	144.11	141.10	139.82
11000	208.11	197.21	188.82	166.65	158.52	155.20	153.80
12000	227.03	215.13	205.99	181.80	172.93	169.31	167.78
13000	245.95	233.06	223.15	196.95	187.34	183.42	181.76
14000	264.87	250.99	240.32	212.10	201.75	197.53	195.74
15000	283.79	268.92	257.48	227.26	216.16	211.64	209.73
16000	302.71	286.85	274.65	242.41	230.57	225.75	223.71
17000	321.63	304.77	291.81	257.56	244.98	239.86	237.69
18000	340.55	322.70	308.98	272.71	259.39	253.97	251.67
19000	359.47	340.63	326.14	287.86	273.80	268.08	265.65
20000	378.39	358.56	343.31	303.01	288.21	282.19	279.63
21000	397.31	376.49	360.47	318.16	302.62	296.30	293.62
22000	416.23	394.41	377.64	333.31	317.03	310.41	307.60
23000	435.15	412.34	394.81	348.46	331.45	324.52	321.58
24000	454.07	430.27	411.97	363.61	345.86	338.63	335.56
25000	472.99	448.20	429.14	378.76	360.27	352.74	349.54
26000	491.91	466.13	446.30	393.91	374.68	366.85	363.53
27000	510.82	484.05	463.47	409.06	389.09	380.96	377.51
28000	529.74	501.98	480.63	424.21	403.50	395.07	391.49
29000	548.66	519.91	497.80	439.36	417.91	409.18	405.47
30000	567.58	537.84	514.96	454.51	432.32	423.29	419.45
35000	662.18	627.48	600.79	530.26	504.37	493.83	489.36
40000	756.78	717.12	686.62	606.01	576.43	564.38	559.27
45000	851.37	806.76	772.45	681.77	648.48	634.93	629.18
50000	945.97	896.39	858.27	757.52	720.53	705.48	699.09
55000	1040.57	986.03	944.10	833.27	792.59	776.02	769.00
60000	1135.17	1075.67	1029.93	909.02	864.64	846.57	838.90
65000	1229.76	1165.31	1115.76	984.77	936.69	917.12	908.81
70000	1324.36	1254.95	1201.58	1060.52	1008.75	987.67	978.72
75000	1418.96	1344.59	1287.41	1136.28	1080.80	1058.21	1048.63
80000	1513.56	1434.23	1373.24	1212.03	1152.85	1128.76	1118.54
85000	1608.15	1523.87	1459.07	1287.78	1224.91	1199.31	1188.45
90000	1702.75	1613.51	1544.89	1363.53	1296.96	1269.86	1258.36
95000	1797.35	1703.15	1630.72	1439.28	1369.01	1340.40	1328.27
100000	1891.94	1792.79	1716.55	1515.03	1441.07	1410.95	1398.17
200000	3783.89	3585.58	3433.09	3030.07	2882.14	2821.90	2796.35
300000	5675.83	5378.37	5149.64	4545.10	4323.20	4232.85	4194.52
400000	7567.78	7171.16	6866.19	6060.14	5764.27	5643.80	5592.70
500000	9459.72	8963.95	8582.74	7575.17	7205.34	7054.75	6990.87
1000000	18919.44	17927.90	17165.47	15150.34	14410.68	14109.50	13981.74

17.375%

Amortization Amount	1 Year	2 Years	3 Years	4 Years	5 Years	6 Years	7 Years
25	2.28	1.23	0.89	0.72	0.62	0.55	0.51
50	4.55	2.47	1.78	1.44	1.24	1.11	1.02
100	9.11	4.93	3.55	2.87	2.47	2.21	2.03
200	18.22	9.87	7.11	5.75	4.95	4.42	4.06
300	27.33	14.80	10.66	8.62	7.42	6.64	6.09
400	36.44	19.73	14.22	11.50	9.89	8.85	8.12
500	45.55	24.67	17.77	14.37	12.37	11.06	10.15
600	54.66	29.60	21.33	17.24	14.84	13.27	12.18
700	63.77	34.53	24.88	20.12	17.31	15.49	14.22
800	72.88	39.47	28.43	22.99	19.79	17.70	16.25
900	81.99	44.40	31.99	25.87	22.26	19.91	18.28
1000	91.10	49.34	35.54	28.74	24.73	22.12	20.31
2000	182.20	98.67	71.08	57.48	49.47	44.24	40.61
3000	273.30	148.01	106.63	86.22	74.20	66.37	60.92
4000	364.40	197.34	142.17	114.96	98.93	88.49	81.23
5000	455.50	246.68	177.71	143.70	123.67	110.61	101.54
6000	546.60	296.01	213.25	172.44	148.40	132.73	121.84
7000	637.69	345.35	248.79	201.18	173.13	154.86	142.15
8000	728.79	394.68	284.34	229.92	197.86	176.98	162.46
9000	819.89	444.02	319.88	258.66	222.60	199.10	182.77
10000	910.99	493.35	355.42	287.40	247.33	221.22	203.07
11000	1002.09	542.69	390.96	316.14	272.06	243.34	223.38
12000	1093.19	592.03	426.51	344.88	296.80	265.47	243.69
13000	1184.29	641.36	462.05	373.62	321.53	287.59	264.00
14000	1275.39	690.70	497.59	402.36	346.26	309.71	284.30
15000	1366.49	740.03	533.13	431.10	371.00	331.83	304.61
16000	1457.59	789.37	568.67	459.84	395.73	353.95	324.92
17000	1548.69	838.70	604.22	488.58	420.46	376.08	345.23
18000	1639.79	888.04	639.76	517.32	445.20	398.20	365.53
19000	1730.88	937.37	675.30	546.06	469.93	420.32	385.84
20000	1821.98	986.71	710.84	574.80	494.66	442.44	406.15
21000	1913.08	1036.04	746.38	603.54	519.40	464.57	426.46
22000	2004.18	1085.38	781.93	632.28	544.13	486.69	446.76
23000	2095.28	1134.71	817.47	661.02	568.86	508.81	467.07
24000	2186.38	1184.05	853.01	689.76	593.59	530.93	487.38
25000	2277.48	1233.39	888.55	718.50	618.33	553.05	507.69
26000	2368.58	1282.72	924.09	747.24	643.06	575.18	527.99
27000	2459.68	1332.06	959.64	775.98	667.79	597.30	548.30
28000	2550.78	1381.39	995.18	804.72	692.53	619.42	568.61
29000	2641.88	1430.73	1030.72	833.46	717.26	641.54	588.92
30000	2732.98	1480.06	1066.26	862.20	741.99	663.67	609.22
35000	3188.47	1726.74	1243.97	1005.90	865.66	774.28	710.76
40000	3643.97	1973.42	1421.68	1149.60	989.32	884.89	812.30
45000	4099.46	2220.09	1599.39	1293.30	1112.99	995.50	913.83
50000	4554.96	2466.77	1777.11	1437.00	1236.66	1106.11	1015.37
55000	5010.46	2713.45	1954.82	1580.70	1360.32	1216.72	1116.91
60000	5465.95	2960.13	2132.53	1724.40	1483.99	1327.33	1218.45
65000	5921.45	3206.80	2310.24	1868.10	1607.65	1437.94	1319.98
70000	6376.94	3453.48	2487.95	2011.80	1731.32	1548.55	1421.52
75000	6832.44	3700.16	2665.66	2155.51	1854.98	1659.16	1523.06
80000	7287.94	3946.83	2843.37	2299.21	1978.65	1769.77	1624.60
85000	7743.43	4193.51	3021.08	2442.91	2102.31	1880.38	1726.13
90000	8198.93	4440.19	3198.79	2586.61	2225.98	1991.00	1827.67
95000	8654.42	4686.87	3376.50	2730.31	2349.65	2101.61	1929.21
100000	9109.92	4933.54	3554.21	2874.01	2473.31	2212.22	2030.74
200000	18219.84	9867.09	7108.42	5748.01	4946.62	4424.43	4061.49
300000	27329.76	14800.63	10662.63	8622.02	7419.93	6636.65	6092.23
400000	36439.68	19734.17	14216.84	11496.03	9893.24	8848.87	8122.98
500000	45549.60	24667.72	17771.05	14370.04	12366.55	11061.09	10153.72
1000000	91099.21	49335.43	35542.10	28740.07	24733.11	22122.17	20307.44

216

Amortization Amount	8 Years	9 Years	10 Years	15 Years	20 Years	25 Years	30 Years
25	0.47	0.45	0.43	0.38	0.36	0.36	0.35
50	0.95	0.90	0.86	0.76	0.72	0.71	0.70
100	1.90	1.80	1.72	1.52	1.45	1.42	1.41
200	3.80	3.60	3.45	3.05	2.90	2.84	2.82
300	5.70	5.40	5.17	4.57	4.35	4.26	4.22
400	7.60	7.20	6.90	6.09	5.80	5.68	5.63
500	9.49	9.00	8.62	7.62	7.25	7.10	7.04
600	11.39	10.80	10.34	9.14	8.70	8.52	8.45
700	13.29	12.60	12.07	10.66	10.15	9.94	9.85
800	15.19	14.40	13.79	12.19	11.60	11.36	11.26
900	17.09	16.20	15.52	13.71	13.05	12.78	12.67
1000	18.99	18.00	17.24	15.23	14.50	14.20	14.08
2000	37.98	36.00	34.48	30.47	29.00	28.40	28.15
3000	56.97	54.00	51.72	45.70	43.50	42.61	42.23
4000	75.96	72.00	68.96	60.93	58.00	56.81	56.31
5000	94.94	90.00	86.20	76.16	72.50	71.01	70.38
6000	113.93	108.00	103.43	91.40	86.99	85.21	84.46
7000	132.92	126.00	120.67	106.63	101.49	99.41	98.53
8000	151.91	144.00	137.91	121.86	115.99	113.61	112.61
9000	170.90	161.99	155.15	137.09	130.49	127.82	126.69
10000	189.89	179.99	172.39	152.33	144.99	142.02	140.76
11000	208.88	197.99	189.63	167.56	159.49	156.22	154.84
12000	227.87	215.99	206.87	182.79	173.99	170.42	168.92
13000	246.85	233.99	224.11	198.02	188.49	184.62	182.99
14000	265.84	251.99	241.35	213.26	202.99	198.82	197.07
15000	284.83	269.99	258.59	228.49	217.49	213.03	211.14
16000	303.82	287.99	275.82	243.72	231.99	227.23	225.22
17000	322.81	305.99	293.06	258.95	246.48	241.43	239.30
18000	341.80	323.99	310.30	274.19	260.98	255.63	253.37
19000	360.79	341.99	327.54	289.42	275.48	269.83	267.45
20000	379.78	359.99	344.78	304.65	289.98	284.03	281.53
21000	398.76	377.99	362.02	319.89	304.48	298.24	295.60
22000	417.75	395.99	379.26	335.12	318.98	312.44	309.68
23000	436.74	413.99	396.50	350.35	333.48	326.64	323.75
24000	455.73	431.99	413.74	365.58	347.98	340.84	337.83
25000	474.72	449.99	430.98	380.82	362.48	355.04	351.91
26000	493.71	467.98	448.22	396.05	376.98	369.25	365.98
27000	512.70	485.98	465.45	411.28	391.47	383.45	380.06
28000	531.69	503.98	482.69	426.51	405.97	397.65	394.14
29000	550.68	521.98	499.93	441.75	420.47	411.85	408.21
30000	569.66	539.98	517.17	456.98	434.97	426.05	422.29
35000	664.61	629.98	603.37	533.14	507.47	497.06	492.67
40000	759.55	719.98	689.56	609.31	579.96	568.07	563.05
45000	854.50	809.97	775.76	685.47	652.46	639.08	633.43
50000	949.44	899.97	861.95	761.63	724.95	710.09	703.81
55000	1044.38	989.97	948.15	837.80	797.45	781.10	774.19
60000	1139.33	1079.96	1034.34	913.96	869.94	852.09	844.58
65000	1234.27	1169.96	1120.54	990.12	942.44	923.11	914.96
70000	1329.22	1259.96	1206.73	1066.29	1014.93	994.12	985.34
75000	1424.16	1349.96	1292.93	1142.45	1087.43	1065.13	1055.72
80000	1519.10	1439.95	1379.12	1218.61	1159.93	1136.14	1126.10
85000	1614.05	1529.95	1465.32	1294.77	1232.42	1207.15	1196.48
90000	1708.99	1619.95	1551.51	1370.94	1304.92	1278.16	1266.86
95000	1803.94	1709.94	1637.71	1447.10	1377.41	1349.17	1337.25
100000	1898.88	1799.94	1723.90	1523.26	1449.91	1420.17	1407.63
200000	3797.76	3599.88	3447.81	3046.53	2899.81	2840.35	2815.25
300000	5696.64	5399.82	5171.71	4569.79	4349.72	4260.52	4222.88
400000	7595.52	7199.77	6895.62	6093.06	5799.63	5680.70	5630.51
500000	9494.40	8999.71	8619.52	7616.32	7249.53	7100.87	7038.13
1000000	18988.81	17999.42	17239.05	15232.65	14499.06	14201.75	14076.27

217

17.5%

Amortization Amount	1 Year	2 Years	3 Years	4 Years	5 Years	6 Years	7 Years
25	2.28	1.23	0.89	0.72	0.62	0.55	0.51
50	4.56	2.47	1.78	1.44	1.24	1.11	1.02
100	9.12	4.94	3.56	2.88	2.48	2.22	2.04
200	18.23	9.88	7.12	5.76	4.96	4.44	4.07
300	27.35	14.82	10.68	8.64	7.44	6.66	6.11
400	36.46	19.76	14.24	11.52	9.92	8.87	8.15
500	45.58	24.70	17.80	14.40	12.40	11.09	10.19
600	54.69	29.63	21.36	17.28	14.88	13.31	12.22
700	63.81	34.57	24.92	20.16	17.36	15.53	14.26
800	72.92	39.51	28.48	23.04	19.84	17.75	16.30
900	82.04	44.45	32.04	25.92	22.32	19.97	18.34
1000	91.15	49.39	35.60	28.80	24.80	22.19	20.37
2000	182.31	98.78	71.20	57.60	49.59	44.37	40.75
3000	273.46	148.17	106.80	86.40	74.39	66.56	61.12
4000	364.62	197.57	142.40	115.20	99.18	88.75	81.50
5000	455.77	246.96	178.00	144.00	123.98	110.94	101.87
6000	546.93	296.35	213.60	172.80	148.77	133.12	122.25
7000	638.08	345.74	249.20	201.60	173.57	155.31	142.62
8000	729.24	395.13	284.80	230.40	198.37	177.50	163.00
9000	820.39	444.52	320.40	259.20	223.16	199.68	183.37
10000	911.55	493.91	356.00	288.00	247.96	221.87	203.75
11000	1002.70	543.31	391.60	316.80	272.75	244.06	224.12
12000	1093.85	592.70	427.20	345.60	297.55	266.25	244.50
13000	1185.01	642.09	462.80	374.40	322.34	288.43	264.87
14000	1276.16	691.48	498.40	403.20	347.14	310.62	285.25
15000	1367.32	740.87	534.00	432.00	371.94	332.81	305.62
16000	1458.47	790.26	569.60	460.80	396.73	354.99	325.99
17000	1549.63	839.65	605.20	489.60	421.53	377.18	346.37
18000	1640.78	889.05	640.80	518.41	446.32	399.37	366.74
19000	1731.94	938.44	676.40	547.21	471.12	421.55	387.12
20000	1823.09	987.83	712.00	576.01	495.91	443.74	407.49
21000	1914.24	1037.22	747.60	604.81	520.71	465.93	427.87
22000	2005.40	1086.61	783.20	633.61	545.50	488.12	448.24
23000	2096.55	1136.00	818.80	662.41	570.30	510.30	468.62
24000	2187.71	1185.39	854.40	691.21	595.10	532.49	488.99
25000	2278.86	1234.79	890.00	720.01	619.89	554.68	509.37
26000	2370.02	1284.18	925.60	748.81	644.69	576.86	529.74
27000	2461.17	1333.57	961.20	777.61	669.48	599.05	550.12
28000	2552.33	1382.96	996.80	806.41	694.28	621.24	570.49
29000	2643.48	1432.35	1032.40	835.21	719.07	643.43	590.87
30000	2734.64	1481.74	1068.00	864.01	743.87	665.61	611.24
35000	3190.41	1728.70	1246.00	1008.01	867.85	776.55	713.11
40000	3646.18	1975.66	1424.00	1152.01	991.83	887.48	814.99
45000	4101.95	2222.61	1602.00	1296.01	1115.81	998.42	916.86
50000	4557.73	2469.57	1780.00	1440.01	1239.78	1109.35	1018.73
55000	5013.50	2716.53	1958.00	1584.02	1363.76	1220.29	1120.61
60000	5469.27	2963.48	2136.00	1728.02	1487.74	1331.23	1222.48
65000	5925.04	3210.44	2314.00	1872.02	1611.72	1442.16	1324.35
70000	6380.82	3457.40	2492.00	2016.02	1735.70	1553.10	1426.23
75000	6836.59	3704.36	2670.00	2160.02	1859.68	1664.03	1528.10
80000	7292.36	3951.31	2848.00	2304.02	1983.65	1774.97	1629.97
85000	7748.13	4198.27	3026.00	2448.02	2107.63	1885.90	1731.85
90000	8203.91	4445.23	3204.00	2592.03	2231.61	1996.84	1833.72
95000	8659.68	4692.18	3382.00	2736.03	2355.59	2107.77	1935.59
100000	9115.45	4939.14	3560.01	2880.03	2479.57	2218.71	2037.47
200000	18230.90	9878.28	7120.01	5760.06	4959.14	4437.42	4074.93
300000	27346.35	14817.42	10680.02	8640.09	7438.70	6656.13	6112.40
400000	36461.80	19756.56	14240.02	11520.12	9918.27	8874.84	8149.86
500000	45577.25	24695.70	17800.03	14400.14	12397.84	11093.54	10187.33
1000000	91154.51	49391.40	35600.05	28800.29	24795.68	22187.09	20374.66

Amortization Amount	8 Years	9 Years	10 Years	15 Years	20 Years	25 Years	30 Years
25	0.48	0.45	0.43	0.38	0.36	0.36	0.35
50	0.95	0.90	0.87	0.77	0.73	0.71	0.71
100	1.91	1.81	1.73	1.53	1.46	1.43	1.42
200	3.81	3.61	3.46	3.06	2.92	2.86	2.83
300	5.72	5.42	5.19	4.59	4.38	4.29	4.25
400	7.62	7.23	6.93	6.13	5.84	5.72	5.67
500	9.53	9.04	8.66	7.66	7.29	7.15	7.09
600	11.43	10.84	10.39	9.19	8.75	8.58	8.50
700	13.34	12.65	12.12	10.72	10.21	10.01	9.92
800	15.25	14.46	13.85	12.25	11.67	11.44	11.34
900	17.15	16.26	15.58	13.78	13.13	12.86	12.75
1000	19.06	18.07	17.31	15.32	14.59	14.29	14.17
2000	38.12	36.14	34.63	30.63	29.18	28.59	28.34
3000	57.17	54.21	51.94	45.95	43.76	42.88	42.51
4000	76.23	72.28	69.25	61.28	58.35	57.18	56.68
5000	95.29	90.36	86.56	76.58	72.94	71.47	70.85
6000	114.35	108.43	103.88	91.89	87.53	85.76	85.02
7000	133.41	126.50	121.19	107.21	102.11	100.06	99.20
8000	152.47	144.57	138.50	122.52	116.70	114.35	113.37
9000	171.52	162.64	155.81	137.84	131.29	128.65	127.54
10000	190.58	180.71	173.13	153.15	145.88	142.94	141.71
11000	209.64	198.78	190.44	168.47	160.46	157.23	155.88
12000	228.70	216.85	207.75	183.78	175.05	171.53	170.05
13000	247.76	234.92	225.07	199.10	189.64	185.82	184.22
14000	266.82	252.99	242.38	214.41	204.23	200.12	198.39
15000	285.87	271.07	259.69	229.73	218.81	214.41	212.56
16000	304.93	289.14	277.00	245.04	233.40	228.70	226.73
17000	323.99	307.21	294.32	280.36	247.99	243.00	240.90
18000	343.05	325.28	311.63	275.67	262.58	257.29	255.07
19000	362.11	343.35	328.94	290.99	277.16	271.59	269.25
20000	381.17	361.42	346.25	306.30	291.75	285.88	283.42
21000	400.22	379.49	363.57	321.62	306.34	300.18	297.59
22000	419.28	397.56	380.88	336.93	320.93	314.47	311.76
23000	438.34	415.63	398.19	352.25	335.51	328.76	325.93
24000	457.40	433.70	415.51	367.56	350.10	343.06	340.10
25000	476.46	451.78	432.82	382.88	364.69	357.35	354.27
26000	495.51	469.85	450.13	398.19	379.28	371.65	368.44
27000	514.57	487.92	467.44	413.51	393.86	385.94	382.61
28000	533.63	505.99	484.76	428.82	408.45	400.23	396.78
29000	552.69	524.06	502.07	444.14	423.04	414.53	410.95
30000	571.75	542.13	519.38	459.45	437.63	428.82	425.12
35000	667.04	632.49	605.95	536.03	510.56	500.29	495.98
40000	762.33	722.84	692.51	612.60	583.50	571.76	566.83
45000	857.62	813.20	779.07	689.18	656.44	643.23	637.69
50000	952.91	903.55	865.64	765.75	729.38	714.70	708.54
55000	1048.20	993.91	952.20	842.33	802.31	786.17	779.40
60000	1143.50	1084.26	1038.76	918.90	875.25	857.64	850.25
65000	1238.79	1174.62	1125.33	995.48	948.19	929.11	921.10
70000	1334.08	1264.97	1211.89	1072.05	1021.13	1000.58	991.96
75000	1429.37	1355.33	1298.45	1148.63	1094.07	1072.05	1062.81
80000	1524.66	1445.68	1385.02	1225.20	1167.00	1143.52	1133.67
85000	1619.95	1536.04	1471.58	1301.78	1239.94	1214.99	1204.52
90000	1715.24	1626.39	1558.15	1378.36	1312.88	1286.46	1275.37
95000	1810.54	1716.75	1644.71	1454.93	1385.82	1357.93	1346.23
100000	1905.83	1807.10	1731.27	1531.51	1458.75	1429.40	1417.08
200000	3811.65	3614.21	3462.55	3063.01	2917.51	2858.81	2834.16
300000	5717.48	5421.31	5193.82	4594.52	4376.26	4288.21	4251.25
400000	7623.31	7228.41	6925.09	6126.03	5835.02	5717.62	5668.33
500000	9529.13	9035.52	8656.36	7657.53	7293.77	7147.02	7085.41
1000000	19058.26	18071.03	17312.73	15315.06	14587.54	14294.05	14170.82

17.625%

Amortization Amount	1 Year	2 Years	3 Years	4 Years	5 Years	6 Years	7 Years
25	2.28	1.24	0.89	0.72	0.62	0.56	0.51
50	4.56	2.47	1.78	1.44	1.24	1.11	1.02
100	9.12	4.94	3.57	2.89	2.49	2.23	2.04
200	18.24	9.89	7.13	5.77	4.97	4.45	4.09
300	27.36	14.83	10.70	8.66	7.46	6.68	6.13
400	36.48	19.78	14.26	11.54	9.94	8.90	8.18
500	45.60	24.72	17.83	14.43	12.43	11.13	10.22
600	54.73	29.67	21.39	17.32	14.91	13.35	12.27
700	63.85	34.61	24.96	20.20	17.40	15.58	14.31
800	72.97	39.56	28.53	23.09	19.89	17.80	16.35
900	82.09	44.50	32.09	25.97	22.37	20.03	18.40
1000	91.21	49.45	35.66	28.86	24.86	22.25	20.44
2000	182.42	98.89	71.32	57.72	49.72	44.50	40.88
3000	273.63	148.34	106.97	86.58	74.57	66.76	61.33
4000	364.84	197.79	142.63	115.44	99.43	89.01	81.77
5000	456.05	247.24	178.29	144.30	124.29	111.26	102.21
6000	547.26	296.68	213.95	173.16	149.15	133.51	122.65
7000	638.47	346.13	249.61	202.02	174.01	155.76	143.09
8000	729.68	395.58	285.26	230.88	198.87	178.02	163.54
9000	820.89	445.03	320.92	259.74	223.72	200.27	183.98
10000	912.10	494.47	356.58	288.61	248.58	222.52	204.42
11000	1003.31	543.92	392.24	317.47	273.44	244.77	224.86
12000	1094.52	593.37	427.90	346.33	298.30	267.02	245.30
13000	1185.73	642.82	463.55	375.19	323.16	289.28	265.75
14000	1276.94	692.26	499.21	404.05	348.02	311.53	286.19
15000	1368.15	741.71	534.87	432.91	372.87	333.78	306.63
16000	1459.36	791.16	570.53	461.77	397.73	356.03	327.07
17000	1550.57	840.61	606.19	490.63	422.59	378.29	347.51
18000	1641.78	890.05	641.84	519.49	447.45	400.54	367.96
19000	1732.99	939.50	677.50	548.35	472.31	422.79	388.40
20000	1824.20	988.95	713.16	577.21	497.17	445.04	408.84
21000	1915.41	1038.39	748.82	606.07	522.02	467.29	429.28
22000	2006.62	1087.84	784.48	634.93	546.88	489.55	449.72
23000	2097.83	1137.29	820.13	663.79	571.74	511.80	470.17
24000	2189.04	1186.74	855.79	692.65	596.60	534.05	490.61
25000	2280.25	1236.18	891.45	721.51	621.46	556.30	511.05
26000	2371.45	1285.63	927.11	750.37	646.32	578.55	531.49
27000	2462.66	1335.08	962.77	779.23	671.17	600.81	551.93
28000	2553.87	1384.53	998.42	808.10	696.03	623.06	572.37
29000	2645.08	1433.97	1034.08	836.96	720.89	645.31	592.82
30000	2736.29	1483.42	1069.74	865.82	745.75	667.56	613.26
35000	3192.34	1730.66	1248.03	1010.12	870.04	778.82	715.47
40000	3648.39	1977.90	1426.32	1154.42	994.33	890.08	817.68
45000	4104.44	2225.13	1604.61	1298.72	1118.62	1001.34	919.89
50000	4560.49	2472.37	1782.90	1443.03	1242.92	1112.60	1022.10
55000	5016.54	2719.61	1961.19	1587.33	1367.21	1223.86	1124.31
60000	5472.59	2966.84	2139.48	1731.63	1491.50	1335.12	1226.52
65000	5928.64	3214.08	2317.77	1875.94	1615.79	1446.38	1328.73
70000	6384.69	3461.32	2496.06	2020.24	1740.08	1557.65	1430.94
75000	6840.74	3708.55	2674.35	2164.54	1864.37	1668.91	1533.15
80000	7296.78	3955.79	2852.64	2308.84	1988.66	1780.17	1635.36
85000	7752.83	4203.03	3030.93	2453.15	2112.96	1891.43	1737.57
90000	8208.88	4450.26	3209.22	2597.45	2237.25	2002.69	1839.78
95000	8664.93	4697.50	3387.51	2741.75	2361.54	2113.95	1941.99
100000	9120.98	4944.74	3565.80	2886.06	2485.83	2225.21	2044.20
200000	18241.96	9889.48	7131.61	5772.11	4971.66	4450.41	4088.39
300000	27362.94	14834.21	10697.41	8658.17	7457.49	6675.62	6132.59
400000	36483.92	19778.95	14263.21	11544.22	9943.32	8900.83	8176.78
500000	45604.90	24723.69	17829.01	14430.28	12429.15	11126.04	10220.98
1000000	91209.80	49447.38	35658.03	28860.55	24858.30	22252.07	20441.96

Amortization Amount	8 Years	9 Years	10 Years	15 Years	20 Years	25 Years	30 Years
25	0.48	0.45	0.43	0.38	0.37	0.36	0.36
50	0.96	0.91	0.87	0.77	0.73	0.72	0.71
100	1.91	1.81	1.74	1.54	1.47	1.44	1.43
200	3.83	3.63	3.48	3.08	2.94	2.88	2.85
300	5.74	5.44	5.22	4.62	4.40	4.32	4.28
400	7.65	7.26	6.95	6.16	5.87	5.75	5.71
500	9.56	9.07	8.69	7.70	7.34	7.19	7.13
600	11.48	10.89	10.43	9.24	8.81	8.63	8.56
700	13.39	12.70	12.17	10.78	10.27	10.07	9.99
800	15.30	14.51	13.91	12.32	11.74	11.51	11.41
900	17.22	16.33	15.65	13.86	13.21	12.95	12.84
1000	19.13	18.14	17.39	15.40	14.68	14.39	14.27
2000	38.26	36.29	34.77	30.80	29.35	28.77	28.53
3000	57.38	54.43	52.16	46.19	44.03	43.16	42.80
4000	76.51	72.57	69.55	61.59	58.70	57.55	57.06
5000	95.64	90.71	86.93	76.99	73.38	71.93	71.33
6000	114.77	108.86	104.32	92.39	88.06	86.32	85.59
7000	133.89	127.00	121.71	107.78	102.73	100.70	99.86
8000	153.02	145.14	139.09	123.18	117.41	115.09	114.12
9000	172.15	163.28	156.48	138.58	132.08	129.48	128.39
10000	191.28	181.43	173.87	153.98	146.76	143.86	142.65
11000	210.41	199.57	191.25	169.37	161.44	158.25	156.92
12000	229.53	217.71	208.64	184.77	176.11	172.64	171.18
13000	248.66	235.86	226.02	200.17	190.79	187.02	185.45
14000	267.79	254.00	243.41	215.57	205.47	201.41	199.72
15000	286.92	272.14	260.80	230.96	220.14	215.80	213.98
16000	306.05	290.28	278.18	246.36	234.82	230.18	228.25
17000	325.17	308.43	295.57	261.76	249.49	244.57	242.51
18000	344.30	326.57	312.96	277.16	264.17	258.96	256.78
19000	363.43	344.71	330.34	292.55	278.85	273.34	271.04
20000	382.56	362.85	347.73	307.95	293.52	287.73	285.31
21000	401.68	381.00	365.12	323.35	308.20	302.11	299.57
22000	420.81	399.14	382.50	338.75	322.87	316.50	313.84
23000	439.94	417.28	399.89	354.14	337.55	330.89	328.10
24000	459.07	435.43	417.28	369.54	352.23	345.27	342.37
25000	478.20	453.57	434.66	384.94	366.90	359.66	356.63
26000	497.32	471.71	452.05	400.34	381.58	374.05	370.90
27000	516.45	489.85	469.44	415.73	396.25	388.43	385.17
28000	535.58	508.00	486.82	431.13	410.93	402.82	399.43
29000	554.71	526.14	504.21	446.53	425.61	417.21	413.70
30000	573.83	544.28	521.60	461.93	440.28	431.59	427.96
35000	669.47	635.00	608.53	538.92	513.66	503.52	499.29
40000	765.11	725.71	695.46	615.90	587.04	575.46	570.62
45000	860.75	816.42	782.39	692.89	660.42	647.39	641.94
50000	956.39	907.14	869.33	769.88	733.81	719.32	713.27
55000	1052.03	997.85	956.26	846.87	807.19	791.25	784.60
60000	1147.67	1088.56	1043.19	923.86	880.57	863.18	855.92
65000	1243.31	1179.28	1130.12	1000.84	953.95	935.12	927.25
70000	1338.95	1269.99	1217.06	1077.83	1027.33	1007.05	998.58
75000	1434.59	1360.71	1303.99	1154.82	1100.71	1078.98	1069.90
80000	1530.23	1451.42	1390.92	1231.81	1174.09	1150.91	1141.23
85000	1625.86	1542.13	1477.85	1308.80	1247.47	1222.84	1212.56
90000	1721.50	1632.85	1564.78	1385.78	1320.85	1294.78	1283.89
95000	1817.14	1723.56	1651.72	1462.77	1394.23	1366.71	1355.21
100000	1912.78	1814.27	1738.65	1539.76	1467.61	1438.64	1426.54
200000	3825.56	3628.55	3477.30	3079.52	2935.22	2877.28	2853.08
300000	5738.34	5442.82	5215.95	4619.28	4402.83	4315.92	4279.62
400000	7651.13	7257.10	6954.60	6159.04	5870.44	5754.56	5706.16
500000	9563.91	9071.37	8693.26	7698.79	7338.05	7193.20	7132.70
1000000	19127.81	18142.75	17386.51	15397.59	14676.10	14386.41	14265.40

17.75%

MONTHLY PAYMENT
NECESSARY TO AMORTIZE A LOAN

Amortization Amount	1 Year	2 Years	3 Years	4 Years	5 Years	6 Years	7 Years
25	2.28	1.24	0.89	0.72	0.62	0.56	0.51
50	4.56	2.48	1.79	1.45	1.25	1.12	1.03
100	9.13	4.95	3.57	2.89	2.49	2.23	2.05
200	18.25	9.90	7.14	5.78	4.98	4.46	4.10
300	27.38	14.85	10.71	8.68	7.48	6.70	6.15
400	36.51	19.80	14.29	11.57	9.97	8.93	8.20
500	45.63	24.75	17.86	14.46	12.46	11.16	10.25
600	54.76	29.70	21.43	17.35	14.95	13.39	12.31
700	63.89	34.65	25.00	20.24	17.44	15.62	14.36
800	73.01	39.60	28.57	23.14	19.94	17.85	16.41
900	82.14	44.55	32.14	26.03	22.43	20.09	18.46
1000	91.27	49.50	35.72	28.92	24.92	22.32	20.51
2000	182.53	99.01	71.43	57.84	49.84	44.63	41.02
3000	273.80	148.51	107.15	86.76	74.76	66.95	61.53
4000	365.06	198.01	142.86	115.68	99.68	89.27	82.04
5000	456.33	247.52	178.58	144.60	124.60	111.59	102.55
6000	547.59	297.02	214.30	173.53	149.53	133.90	123.06
7000	638.86	346.52	250.01	202.45	174.45	156.22	143.57
8000	730.12	396.03	285.73	231.37	199.37	178.54	164.07
9000	821.39	445.53	321.44	260.29	224.29	200.85	184.58
10000	912.65	495.03	357.16	289.21	249.21	223.17	205.09
11000	1003.92	544.54	392.88	318.13	274.13	245.49	225.60
12000	1095.18	594.04	428.59	347.05	299.05	267.81	246.11
13000	1186.45	643.54	464.31	375.97	323.97	290.12	266.62
14000	1277.71	693.05	500.02	404.89	348.89	312.44	287.13
15000	1368.98	742.55	535.74	433.81	373.81	334.76	307.64
16000	1460.24	792.05	571.46	462.73	398.74	357.07	328.15
17000	1551.51	841.56	607.17	491.65	423.66	379.39	348.66
18000	1642.77	891.06	642.89	520.58	448.58	401.71	369.17
19000	1734.04	940.56	678.60	549.50	473.50	424.03	389.68
20000	1825.30	990.07	714.32	578.42	498.42	446.34	410.19
21000	1916.57	1039.57	750.04	607.34	523.34	468.66	430.70
22000	2007.83	1089.07	785.75	636.26	548.26	490.98	451.21
23000	2099.10	1138.58	821.47	665.18	573.18	513.29	471.71
24000	2190.36	1188.08	857.18	694.10	598.10	535.61	492.22
25000	2281.63	1237.58	892.90	723.02	623.02	557.93	512.73
26000	2372.89	1287.09	928.62	751.94	647.95	580.25	533.24
27000	2464.16	1336.59	964.33	780.86	672.87	602.56	553.75
28000	2555.42	1386.09	1000.05	809.78	697.79	624.88	574.26
29000	2646.69	1435.60	1035.76	838.70	722.71	647.20	594.77
30000	2737.95	1485.10	1071.48	867.63	747.63	669.51	615.28
35000	3194.28	1732.62	1250.06	1012.23	872.23	781.10	717.83
40000	3650.60	1980.13	1428.64	1156.83	996.84	892.68	820.37
45000	4106.93	2227.65	1607.22	1301.44	1121.44	1004.27	922.92
50000	4563.25	2475.17	1785.80	1446.04	1246.05	1115.86	1025.47
55000	5019.58	2722.69	1964.38	1590.65	1370.65	1227.44	1128.01
60000	5475.91	2970.20	2142.96	1735.25	1495.26	1339.03	1230.56
65000	5932.23	3217.72	2321.54	1879.86	1619.86	1450.61	1333.11
70000	6388.56	3465.24	2500.12	2024.46	1744.47	1562.20	1435.65
75000	6844.88	3712.75	2678.70	2169.06	1869.07	1673.78	1538.20
80000	7301.21	3960.27	2857.28	2313.67	1993.68	1785.37	1640.75
85000	7757.53	4207.79	3035.86	2458.27	2118.28	1896.96	1743.29
90000	8213.86	4455.30	3214.44	2602.88	2242.89	2008.54	1845.84
95000	8670.18	4702.82	3393.02	2747.48	2367.49	2120.13	1948.39
100000	9126.51	4950.34	3571.60	2892.09	2492.10	2231.71	2050.93
200000	18253.02	9900.67	7143.21	5784.17	4984.20	4463.42	4101.87
300000	27379.53	14851.01	10714.81	8676.26	7476.29	6695.14	6152.80
400000	36508.04	19801.35	14286.41	11568.34	9968.39	8926.85	8203.74
500000	45632.55	24751.68	17858.01	14460.43	12460.49	11158.56	10254.67
1000000	91265.09	49503.37	35716.03	28920.85	24920.98	22317.12	20509.34

Amortization Amount	8 Years	9 Years	10 Years	15 Years	20 Years	25 Years	30 Years
25	0.48	0.46	0.44	0.39	0.37	0.36	0.36
50	0.96	0.91	0.87	0.77	0.74	0.72	0.72
100	1.92	1.82	1.75	1.55	1.48	1.45	1.44
200	3.84	3.64	3.49	3.10	2.95	2.90	2.87
300	5.76	5.46	5.24	4.64	4.43	4.34	4.31
400	7.68	7.29	6.98	6.19	5.91	5.79	5.74
500	9.60	9.11	8.73	7.74	7.38	7.24	7.18
600	11.52	10.93	10.48	9.29	8.86	8.69	8.62
700	13.44	12.75	12.22	10.84	10.34	10.14	10.05
800	15.36	14.57	13.97	12.38	11.81	11.58	11.49
900	17.28	16.39	15.71	13.93	13.29	13.03	12.92
1000	19.20	18.21	17.46	15.48	14.76	14.48	14.36
2000	38.39	36.43	34.92	30.96	29.53	28.96	28.72
3000	57.59	54.64	52.38	46.44	44.29	43.44	43.08
4000	76.79	72.86	69.84	61.92	59.06	57.92	57.44
5000	95.99	91.07	87.30	77.40	73.82	72.39	71.80
6000	115.18	109.29	104.76	92.88	88.59	86.87	86.16
7000	134.38	127.50	122.22	108.36	103.35	101.35	100.52
8000	153.58	145.72	139.68	123.84	118.12	115.83	114.88
9000	172.78	163.93	157.14	139.32	132.88	130.31	129.24
10000	191.97	182.15	174.60	154.80	147.65	144.79	143.60
11000	211.17	200.36	192.06	170.28	162.41	159.27	157.96
12000	230.37	218.57	209.52	185.76	177.18	173.75	172.32
13000	249.57	236.79	226.99	201.24	191.94	188.22	186.68
14000	268.76	255.00	244.45	216.72	206.71	202.70	201.04
15000	287.96	273.22	261.91	232.20	221.47	217.18	215.40
16000	307.16	291.43	279.37	247.68	236.24	231.66	229.76
17000	326.36	309.65	296.83	263.16	251.00	246.14	244.12
18000	345.55	327.86	314.29	278.64	265.77	260.62	258.48
19000	364.75	346.08	331.75	294.12	280.53	275.10	272.84
20000	383.95	364.29	349.21	309.60	295.30	289.58	287.20
21000	403.15	382.51	366.67	325.08	310.06	304.06	301.56
22000	422.34	400.72	384.13	340.57	324.82	318.53	315.92
23000	441.54	418.93	401.59	356.05	339.59	333.01	330.28
24000	460.74	437.15	419.05	371.53	354.35	347.49	344.64
25000	479.94	455.36	436.51	387.01	369.12	361.97	359.00
26000	499.13	473.58	453.97	402.49	383.88	376.45	373.36
27000	518.33	491.79	471.43	417.97	398.65	390.93	387.72
28000	537.53	510.01	488.89	433.45	413.41	405.41	402.08
29000	556.73	528.22	506.35	448.93	428.18	419.89	416.44
30000	575.92	546.44	523.81	464.41	442.94	434.38	430.80
35000	671.91	637.51	611.11	541.81	516.77	506.76	502.60
40000	767.90	728.58	698.42	619.21	590.59	579.15	574.40
45000	863.89	819.66	785.72	696.61	664.41	651.55	646.20
50000	959.87	910.73	873.02	774.01	738.24	723.94	718.00
55000	1055.86	1001.80	960.32	851.41	812.06	796.34	789.80
60000	1151.85	1092.87	1047.62	928.81	885.89	868.73	861.60
65000	1247.83	1183.95	1134.93	1006.21	959.71	941.12	933.40
70000	1343.82	1275.02	1222.23	1083.62	1033.53	1013.52	1005.20
75000	1439.81	1366.09	1309.53	1161.02	1107.36	1085.91	1077.00
80000	1535.80	1457.16	1396.83	1238.42	1181.18	1158.31	1148.80
85000	1631.78	1548.24	1484.13	1315.82	1255.00	1230.70	1220.60
90000	1727.77	1639.31	1571.44	1393.22	1328.83	1303.09	1292.40
95000	1823.76	1730.38	1658.74	1470.62	1402.65	1375.49	1364.20
100000	1919.75	1821.46	1746.04	1548.02	1476.48	1447.88	1436.00
200000	3839.49	3642.91	3492.08	3096.05	2952.95	2895.76	2872.00
300000	5759.24	5464.37	5238.12	4644.07	4429.43	4343.65	4308.00
400000	7678.98	7285.82	6984.16	6192.09	5905.90	5791.53	5744.00
500000	9598.73	9107.28	8730.20	7740.11	7382.38	7239.41	7180.00
1000000	19197.45	18214.56	17460.40	15480.23	14764.76	14478.82	14359.99

17.875%

MONTHLY PAYMENT
NECESSARY TO AMORTIZE A LOAN

Amortization Amount	1 Year	2 Years	3 Years	4 Years	5 Years	6 Years	7 Years
25	2.28	1.24	0.89	0.72	0.62	0.56	0.51
50	4.57	2.48	1.79	1.45	1.25	1.12	1.03
100	9.13	4.96	3.58	2.90	2.50	2.24	2.06
200	18.26	9.91	7.15	5.80	5.00	4.48	4.12
300	27.40	14.87	10.73	8.69	7.50	6.71	6.17
400	36.53	19.82	14.31	11.59	9.99	8.95	8.23
500	45.66	24.78	17.89	14.49	12.49	11.19	10.29
600	54.79	29.74	21.46	17.39	14.99	13.43	12.35
700	63.92	34.69	25.04	20.29	17.49	15.67	14.40
800	73.06	39.65	28.62	23.18	19.99	17.91	16.46
900	82.19	44.60	32.20	26.08	22.49	20.14	18.52
1000	91.32	49.56	35.77	28.98	24.98	22.38	20.58
2000	182.64	99.12	71.55	57.96	49.97	44.76	41.15
3000	273.96	148.68	107.32	86.94	74.95	67.15	61.73
4000	365.28	198.24	143.10	115.92	99.93	89.53	82.31
5000	456.60	247.80	178.87	144.91	124.92	111.91	102.88
6000	547.92	297.36	214.64	173.89	149.90	134.29	123.46
7000	639.24	346.92	250.42	202.87	174.89	156.68	144.04
8000	730.56	396.47	286.19	231.85	199.87	179.06	164.61
9000	821.88	446.03	321.97	260.83	224.85	201.44	185.19
10000	913.20	495.59	357.74	289.81	249.84	223.82	205.77
11000	1004.52	545.15	393.51	318.79	274.82	246.20	226.34
12000	1095.84	594.71	429.29	347.77	299.80	268.59	246.92
13000	1187.16	644.27	465.06	376.76	324.79	290.97	267.50
14000	1278.49	693.83	500.84	405.74	349.77	313.35	288.08
15000	1369.81	743.39	536.61	434.72	374.76	335.73	308.65
16000	1461.13	792.95	572.38	463.70	399.74	358.12	329.23
17000	1552.45	842.51	608.16	492.68	424.72	380.50	349.81
18000	1643.77	892.07	643.93	521.66	449.71	402.88	370.38
19000	1735.09	941.63	679.71	550.64	474.69	425.26	390.96
20000	1826.41	991.19	715.48	579.62	499.67	447.64	411.54
21000	1917.73	1040.75	751.26	608.61	524.66	470.03	432.11
22000	2009.05	1090.31	787.03	637.59	549.64	492.41	452.69
23000	2100.37	1139.87	822.80	666.57	574.63	514.79	473.27
24000	2191.69	1189.42	858.58	695.55	599.61	537.17	493.84
25000	2283.01	1238.98	894.35	724.53	624.59	559.56	514.42
26000	2374.33	1288.54	930.13	753.51	649.58	581.94	535.00
27000	2465.65	1338.10	965.90	782.49	674.56	604.32	555.57
28000	2556.97	1387.66	1001.67	811.47	699.54	626.70	576.15
29000	2648.29	1437.22	1037.45	840.45	724.53	649.09	596.73
30000	2739.61	1486.78	1073.22	869.44	749.51	671.47	617.30
35000	3196.21	1734.58	1252.09	1014.34	874.43	783.38	720.19
40000	3652.81	1982.37	1430.96	1159.25	999.35	895.29	823.07
45000	4109.42	2230.17	1609.83	1304.15	1124.27	1007.20	925.96
50000	4566.02	2477.97	1788.70	1449.06	1249.19	1119.11	1028.84
55000	5022.62	2725.77	1967.57	1593.97	1374.10	1231.02	1131.72
60000	5479.22	2973.56	2146.44	1738.87	1499.02	1342.93	1234.61
65000	5935.82	3221.36	2325.31	1883.78	1623.94	1454.85	1337.49
70000	6392.43	3469.16	2504.18	2028.68	1748.86	1566.76	1440.38
75000	6849.03	3716.95	2683.05	2173.59	1873.78	1678.67	1543.26
80000	7305.63	3964.75	2861.92	2318.50	1998.70	1790.58	1646.14
85000	7762.23	4212.55	3040.79	2463.40	2123.62	1902.49	1749.03
90000	8218.83	4460.34	3219.66	2608.31	2248.53	2014.40	1851.91
95000	8675.44	4708.14	3398.54	2753.21	2373.45	2126.31	1954.80
100000	9132.04	4955.94	3577.41	2898.12	2498.37	2238.22	2057.68
200000	18264.07	9911.87	7154.81	5796.24	4996.74	4476.45	4115.36
300000	27396.11	14867.81	10732.22	8694.36	7495.11	6714.67	6173.04
400000	36528.15	19823.75	14309.62	11592.48	9993.49	8952.90	8230.72
500000	45660.19	24779.68	17887.03	14490.60	12491.86	11191.12	10288.40
1000000	91320.37	49559.37	35774.05	28981.20	24983.72	22382.25	20576.80

Amortization Amount	8 Years	9 Years	10 Years	15 Years	20 Years	25 Years	30 Years
25	0.48	0.46	0.44	0.39	0.37	0.36	0.36
50	0.96	0.91	0.88	0.78	0.74	0.73	0.72
100	1.93	1.83	1.75	1.56	1.49	1.46	1.45
200	3.85	3.66	3.51	3.11	2.97	2.91	2.89
300	5.78	5.49	5.26	4.67	4.46	4.37	4.34
400	7.71	7.31	7.01	6.23	5.94	5.83	5.78
500	9.63	9.14	8.77	7.78	7.43	7.29	7.23
600	11.56	10.97	10.52	9.34	8.91	8.74	8.67
700	13.49	12.80	12.27	10.89	10.40	10.20	10.12
800	15.41	14.63	14.03	12.45	11.88	11.66	11.56
900	17.34	16.46	15.78	14.01	13.37	13.11	13.01
1000	19.27	18.29	17.53	15.56	14.85	14.57	14.45
2000	38.53	36.57	35.07	31.13	29.71	29.14	28.91
3000	57.80	54.86	52.60	46.69	44.56	43.71	43.36
4000	77.07	73.15	70.14	62.25	59.41	58.29	57.82
5000	96.34	91.43	87.67	77.81	74.27	72.86	72.27
6000	115.60	109.72	105.21	93.38	89.12	87.43	86.73
7000	134.87	128.01	122.74	108.94	103.97	102.00	101.18
8000	154.14	146.29	140.28	124.50	118.83	116.57	115.64
9000	173.40	164.58	157.81	140.07	133.68	131.14	130.09
10000	192.67	182.86	175.34	155.63	148.53	145.71	144.55
11000	211.94	201.15	192.88	171.19	163.39	160.28	159.00
12000	231.21	219.44	210.41	186.76	178.24	174.86	173.46
13000	250.47	237.72	227.95	202.32	193.10	189.43	187.91
14000	269.74	256.01	245.48	217.88	207.95	204.00	202.36
15000	289.01	274.30	263.02	233.44	222.80	218.57	216.82
16000	308.27	292.58	280.55	249.01	237.66	233.14	231.27
17000	327.54	310.87	298.08	264.57	252.51	247.71	245.73
18000	346.81	329.16	315.62	280.13	267.36	262.28	260.18
19000	366.08	347.44	333.15	295.70	282.22	276.85	274.64
20000	385.34	365.73	350.69	311.26	297.07	291.43	289.09
21000	404.61	384.02	368.22	326.82	311.92	306.00	303.55
22000	423.88	402.30	385.76	342.39	326.78	320.57	318.00
23000	443.15	420.59	403.29	357.95	341.63	335.14	332.46
24000	462.41	438.88	420.83	373.51	356.48	349.71	346.91
25000	481.68	457.16	438.36	389.07	371.34	364.28	361.37
26000	500.95	475.45	455.89	404.64	386.19	378.85	375.82
27000	520.21	493.73	473.43	420.20	401.04	393.42	390.27
28000	539.48	512.02	490.96	435.76	415.90	408.00	404.73
29000	558.75	530.31	508.50	451.33	430.75	422.57	419.18
30000	578.02	548.59	526.03	466.89	445.60	437.14	433.64
35000	674.35	640.03	613.70	544.70	519.87	509.99	505.91
40000	770.69	731.46	701.38	622.52	594.14	582.85	578.18
45000	867.02	822.89	789.05	700.33	668.41	655.71	650.46
50000	963.36	914.32	876.72	778.15	742.67	728.56	722.73
55000	1059.69	1005.76	964.39	855.96	816.94	801.42	795.00
60000	1156.03	1097.19	1052.06	933.78	891.21	874.28	867.28
65000	1252.37	1188.62	1139.74	1011.59	965.48	947.13	939.55
70000	1348.70	1280.05	1227.41	1089.41	1039.74	1019.99	1011.82
75000	1445.04	1371.49	1315.08	1167.22	1114.01	1092.85	1084.10
80000	1541.37	1462.92	1402.75	1245.04	1188.28	1165.70	1156.37
85000	1637.71	1554.35	1490.42	1322.85	1262.55	1238.56	1228.64
90000	1734.05	1645.78	1578.10	1400.67	1336.81	1311.42	1300.91
95000	1830.38	1737.21	1665.77	1478.48	1411.08	1384.27	1373.19
100000	1926.72	1828.65	1753.44	1556.30	1485.35	1457.13	1445.46
200000	3853.44	3657.29	3506.88	3112.60	2970.70	2914.26	2890.92
300000	5780.15	5485.94	5260.32	4668.89	4456.05	4371.39	4336.38
400000	7706.87	7314.59	7013.76	6225.19	5941.40	5828.52	5781.84
500000	9633.59	9143.23	8767.20	7781.49	7426.75	7285.64	7227.30
1000000	19267.18	18286.47	17534.39	15562.98	14853.49	14571.28	14454.61

18%

Amortization Amount	1 Year	2 Years	3 Years	4 Years	5 Years	6 Years	7 Years
25	2.28	1.24	0.90	0.73	0.63	0.56	0.52
50	4.57	2.48	1.79	1.45	1.25	1.12	1.03
100	9.14	4.96	3.58	2.90	2.50	2.24	2.06
200	18.28	9.92	7.17	5.81	5.01	4.49	4.13
300	27.41	14.88	10.75	8.71	7.51	6.73	6.19
400	36.55	19.85	14.33	11.62	10.02	8.98	8.26
500	45.69	24.81	17.92	14.52	12.52	11.22	10.32
600	54.83	29.77	21.50	17.42	15.03	13.47	12.39
700	63.96	34.73	25.08	20.33	17.53	15.71	14.45
800	73.10	39.69	28.67	23.23	20.04	17.96	16.52
900	82.24	44.65	32.25	26.14	22.54	20.20	18.58
1000	91.38	49.62	35.83	29.04	25.05	22.45	20.64
2000	182.75	99.23	71.66	58.08	50.09	44.89	41.29
3000	274.13	148.85	107.50	87.12	75.14	67.34	61.93
4000	365.50	198.46	143.33	116.17	100.19	89.79	82.58
5000	456.88	248.08	179.16	145.21	125.23	112.24	103.22
6000	548.25	297.69	214.99	174.25	150.28	134.68	123.87
7000	639.63	347.31	250.82	203.29	175.33	157.13	144.51
8000	731.01	396.92	286.66	232.33	200.37	179.58	165.15
9000	822.38	446.54	322.49	261.37	225.42	202.03	185.80
10000	913.76	496.15	358.32	290.42	250.47	224.47	206.44
11000	1005.13	545.77	394.15	319.46	275.51	246.92	227.09
12000	1096.51	595.38	429.99	348.50	300.56	269.37	247.73
13000	1187.88	645.00	465.82	377.54	325.60	291.82	268.38
14000	1279.26	694.62	501.65	406.58	350.65	314.26	289.02
15000	1370.63	744.23	537.48	435.62	375.70	336.71	309.67
16000	1462.01	793.85	573.31	464.67	400.74	359.16	330.31
17000	1553.39	843.46	609.15	493.71	425.79	381.61	350.95
18000	1644.76	893.08	644.98	522.75	450.84	404.05	371.60
19000	1736.14	942.69	680.81	551.79	475.88	426.50	392.24
20000	1827.51	992.31	716.64	580.83	500.93	448.95	412.89
21000	1918.89	1041.92	752.47	609.87	525.98	471.40	433.53
22000	2010.26	1091.54	788.31	638.91	551.02	493.84	454.18
23000	2101.64	1141.15	824.14	667.96	576.07	516.29	474.82
24000	2193.02	1190.77	859.97	697.00	601.12	538.74	495.46
25000	2284.39	1240.38	895.80	726.04	626.16	561.19	516.11
26000	2375.77	1290.00	931.63	755.08	651.21	583.63	536.75
27000	2467.14	1339.62	967.47	784.12	676.26	606.08	557.40
28000	2558.52	1389.23	1003.30	813.16	701.30	628.53	578.04
29000	2649.89	1438.85	1039.13	842.21	726.35	650.98	598.69
30000	2741.27	1488.46	1074.96	871.25	751.40	673.42	619.33
35000	3198.15	1736.54	1254.12	1016.46	876.63	785.66	722.55
40000	3655.03	1984.61	1433.28	1161.66	1001.86	897.90	825.77
45000	4111.90	2232.69	1612.44	1306.87	1127.09	1010.13	929.00
50000	4568.78	2480.77	1791.61	1452.08	1252.33	1122.37	1032.22
55000	5025.66	2728.85	1970.77	1597.29	1377.56	1234.61	1135.44
60000	5482.54	2976.92	2149.93	1742.50	1502.79	1346.85	1238.66
65000	5939.42	3225.00	2329.09	1887.70	1628.02	1459.08	1341.88
70000	6396.29	3473.08	2508.25	2032.91	1753.26	1571.32	1445.10
75000	6853.17	3721.15	2687.41	2178.12	1878.49	1683.56	1548.33
80000	7310.05	3969.23	2866.57	2323.33	2003.72	1795.79	1651.55
85000	7766.93	4217.31	3045.73	2468.53	2128.95	1908.03	1754.77
90000	8223.81	4465.38	3224.89	2613.74	2254.19	2020.27	1857.99
95000	8680.69	4713.46	3404.05	2758.95	2379.42	2132.51	1961.21
100000	9137.56	4961.54	3583.21	2904.16	2504.65	2244.74	2064.43
200000	18275.13	9923.07	7166.42	5808.32	5009.30	4489.49	4128.87
300000	27412.69	14884.61	10749.63	8712.48	7513.95	6734.23	6193.30
400000	36550.26	19846.15	14332.84	11616.63	10018.60	8978.97	8257.73
500000	45687.82	24807.69	17916.05	14520.79	12523.25	11223.72	10322.17
1000000	91375.64	49615.37	35832.11	29041.58	25046.51	22447.43	20644.34

MONTHLY PAYMENT
NECESSARY TO AMORTIZE A LOAN
18%

Amortization Amount	8 Years	9 Years	10 Years	15 Years	20 Years	25 Years	30 Years
25	0.48	0.46	0.44	0.39	0.37	0.37	0.36
50	0.97	0.92	0.88	0.78	0.75	0.73	0.73
100	1.93	1.84	1.76	1.56	1.49	1.47	1.45
200	3.87	3.67	3.52	3.13	2.99	2.93	2.91
300	5.80	5.51	5.28	4.69	4.48	4.40	4.36
400	7.73	7.34	7.04	6.26	5.98	5.87	5.82
500	9.67	9.18	8.80	7.82	7.47	7.33	7.27
600	11.60	11.02	10.57	9.39	8.97	8.80	8.73
700	13.54	12.85	12.33	10.95	10.46	10.26	10.18
800	15.47	14.69	14.09	12.52	11.95	11.73	11.64
900	17.40	16.52	15.85	14.08	13.45	13.20	13.09
1000	19.34	18.36	17.61	15.65	14.94	14.66	14.55
2000	38.67	36.72	35.22	31.29	29.88	29.33	29.10
3000	58.01	55.08	52.83	46.94	44.83	43.99	43.65
4000	77.35	73.43	70.43	62.58	59.77	58.66	58.20
5000	96.68	91.79	88.04	78.23	74.71	73.32	72.75
6000	116.02	110.15	105.65	93.88	89.65	87.98	87.30
7000	135.36	128.51	123.26	109.52	104.60	102.65	101.84
8000	154.70	146.87	140.87	125.17	119.54	117.31	116.39
9000	174.03	165.23	158.48	140.81	134.48	131.97	130.94
10000	193.37	183.58	176.08	156.46	149.42	146.64	145.49
11000	212.71	201.94	193.69	172.10	164.37	161.30	160.04
12000	232.04	220.30	211.30	187.75	179.31	175.97	174.59
13000	251.38	238.66	228.91	203.40	194.25	190.63	189.14
14000	270.72	257.02	246.52	219.04	209.19	205.29	203.69
15000	290.05	275.38	264.13	234.69	224.13	219.96	218.24
16000	309.39	293.74	281.74	250.33	239.08	234.62	232.79
17000	328.73	312.09	299.34	265.98	254.02	249.28	247.34
18000	348.07	330.45	316.95	281.63	268.96	263.95	261.89
19000	367.40	348.81	334.56	297.27	283.90	278.61	276.44
20000	386.74	367.17	352.17	312.92	298.85	293.28	290.98
21000	406.08	385.53	369.78	328.56	313.79	307.94	305.53
22000	425.41	403.89	387.39	344.21	328.73	322.60	320.08
23000	444.75	422.24	405.00	359.85	343.67	337.27	334.63
24000	464.09	440.60	422.60	375.50	358.62	351.93	349.18
25000	483.42	458.96	440.21	391.15	373.56	366.59	363.73
26000	502.76	477.32	457.82	406.79	388.50	381.26	378.28
27000	522.10	495.68	475.43	422.44	403.44	395.92	392.83
28000	541.44	514.04	493.04	438.08	418.38	410.59	407.38
29000	560.77	532.40	510.65	453.73	433.33	425.25	421.93
30000	580.11	550.75	528.25	469.38	448.27	439.91	436.48
35000	676.79	642.55	616.30	547.60	522.98	513.23	509.22
40000	773.48	734.34	704.34	625.83	597.69	586.55	581.97
45000	870.16	826.13	792.38	704.06	672.40	659.87	654.72
50000	966.85	917.92	880.42	782.29	747.12	733.19	727.46
55000	1063.53	1009.72	968.47	860.52	821.83	806.51	800.21
60000	1160.22	1101.51	1056.51	938.75	896.54	879.83	872.95
65000	1256.90	1193.30	1144.55	1016.98	971.25	953.15	945.70
70000	1353.59	1285.09	1232.59	1095.21	1045.96	1026.47	1018.45
75000	1450.27	1376.89	1320.64	1173.44	1120.67	1099.78	1091.19
80000	1546.96	1468.68	1408.68	1251.67	1195.39	1173.10	1163.94
85000	1643.64	1560.47	1496.72	1329.90	1270.10	1246.42	1236.69
90000	1740.33	1652.26	1584.76	1408.13	1344.81	1319.74	1309.43
95000	1837.01	1744.05	1672.81	1486.35	1419.52	1393.06	1382.18
100000	1933.70	1835.85	1760.85	1564.58	1494.23	1466.38	1454.92
200000	3867.40	3671.69	3521.70	3129.17	2988.46	2932.76	2909.85
300000	5801.10	5507.54	5282.55	4693.75	4482.70	4399.14	4364.77
400000	7734.80	7343.39	7043.40	6258.33	5976.93	5865.52	5819.70
500000	9668.50	9179.24	8804.25	7822.92	7471.16	7331.90	7274.62
1000000	19337.00	18358.47	17608.49	15645.84	14942.32	14663.80	14549.24

227

18.125%

Amortization Amount	1 Year	2 Years	3 Years	4 Years	5 Years	6 Years	7 Years
25	2.29	1.24	0.90	0.73	0.63	0.56	0.52
50	4.57	2.48	1.79	1.46	1.26	1.13	1.04
100	9.14	4.97	3.59	2.91	2.51	2.25	2.07
200	18.29	9.93	7.18	5.82	5.02	4.50	4.14
300	27.43	14.90	10.77	8.73	7.53	6.75	6.21
400	36.57	19.87	14.36	11.64	10.04	9.01	8.28
500	45.72	24.84	17.95	14.55	12.55	11.26	10.36
600	54.86	29.80	21.53	17.46	15.07	13.51	12.43
700	64.00	34.77	25.12	20.37	17.58	15.76	14.50
800	73.14	39.74	28.71	23.28	20.09	18.01	16.57
900	82.29	44.70	32.30	26.19	22.60	20.26	18.64
1000	91.43	49.67	35.89	29.10	25.11	22.51	20.71
2000	182.86	99.34	71.78	58.20	50.22	45.03	41.42
3000	274.29	149.01	107.67	87.31	75.33	67.54	62.14
4000	365.72	198.69	143.56	116.41	100.44	90.05	82.85
5000	457.15	248.36	179.45	145.51	125.55	112.56	103.56
6000	548.59	298.03	215.34	174.61	150.66	135.08	124.27
7000	640.02	347.70	251.23	203.71	175.77	157.59	144.98
8000	731.45	397.37	287.12	232.82	200.87	180.10	165.70
9000	822.88	447.04	323.01	261.92	225.98	202.61	186.41
10000	914.31	496.71	358.90	291.02	251.09	225.13	207.12
11000	1005.74	546.39	394.79	320.12	276.20	247.64	227.83
12000	1097.17	596.06	430.68	349.22	301.31	270.15	248.54
13000	1188.60	645.73	466.57	378.33	326.42	292.66	269.26
14000	1280.03	695.40	502.46	407.43	351.53	315.18	289.97
15000	1371.46	745.07	538.35	436.53	376.64	337.69	310.68
16000	1462.89	794.74	574.24	465.63	401.75	360.20	331.39
17000	1554.33	844.41	610.13	494.73	426.86	382.72	352.10
18000	1645.76	894.09	646.02	523.84	451.97	405.23	372.82
19000	1737.19	943.76	681.91	552.94	477.08	427.74	393.53
20000	1828.62	993.43	717.80	582.04	502.19	450.25	414.24
21000	1920.05	1043.10	753.69	611.14	527.30	472.77	434.95
22000	2011.48	1092.77	789.58	640.24	552.41	495.28	455.66
23000	2102.91	1142.44	825.47	669.35	577.52	517.79	476.37
24000	2194.34	1192.11	861.36	698.45	602.62	540.30	497.09
25000	2285.77	1241.78	897.25	727.55	627.73	562.82	517.80
26000	2377.20	1291.46	933.14	756.65	652.84	585.33	538.51
27000	2468.63	1341.13	969.04	785.75	677.95	607.84	559.22
28000	2560.07	1390.80	1004.93	814.86	703.06	630.36	579.93
29000	2651.50	1440.47	1040.82	843.96	728.17	652.87	600.65
30000	2742.93	1490.14	1076.71	873.06	753.28	675.38	621.36
35000	3200.08	1738.50	1256.16	1018.57	878.83	787.94	724.92
40000	3657.24	1986.86	1435.61	1164.08	1004.37	900.51	828.48
45000	4114.39	2235.21	1615.06	1309.59	1129.92	1013.07	932.04
50000	4571.55	2483.57	1794.51	1455.10	1255.47	1125.63	1035.60
55000	5028.70	2731.93	1973.96	1600.61	1381.01	1238.20	1139.16
60000	5485.85	2980.28	2153.41	1746.12	1506.56	1350.76	1242.72
65000	5943.01	3228.64	2332.86	1891.63	1632.11	1463.32	1346.28
70000	6400.16	3477.00	2512.31	2037.14	1757.65	1575.89	1449.84
75000	6857.32	3725.35	2691.76	2182.65	1883.20	1688.45	1553.40
80000	7314.47	3973.71	2871.21	2328.16	2008.75	1801.02	1656.96
85000	7771.63	4222.07	3050.67	2473.67	2134.30	1913.58	1760.52
90000	8228.78	4470.43	3230.12	2619.18	2259.84	2026.14	1864.08
95000	8685.94	4718.78	3409.57	2764.69	2385.39	2138.71	1967.64
100000	9143.09	4967.14	3589.02	2910.20	2510.94	2251.27	2071.20
200000	18286.18	9934.28	7178.04	5820.40	5021.87	4502.54	4142.39
300000	27429.27	14901.42	10767.06	8730.60	7532.81	6753.81	6213.59
400000	36572.36	19868.56	14356.07	11640.80	10043.74	9005.08	8284.78
500000	45715.45	24835.70	17945.09	14551.01	12554.68	11256.35	10355.98
1000000	91430.90	49671.39	35890.19	29102.01	25109.35	22512.69	20711.96

Amortization Amount	8 Years	9 Years	10 Years	15 Years	20 Years	25 Years	30 Years
25	0.49	0.46	0.44	0.39	0.38	0.37	0.37
50	0.97	0.92	0.88	0.79	0.75	0.74	0.73
100	1.94	1.84	1.77	1.57	1.50	1.48	1.46
200	3.88	3.69	3.54	3.15	3.01	2.95	2.93
300	5.82	5.53	5.30	4.72	4.51	4.43	4.39
400	7.76	7.37	7.07	6.29	6.01	5.90	5.86
500	9.70	9.22	8.84	7.86	7.52	7.38	7.32
600	11.64	11.06	10.61	9.44	9.02	8.85	8.79
700	13.58	12.90	12.38	11.01	10.52	10.33	10.25
800	15.53	14.74	14.15	12.58	12.02	11.81	11.72
900	17.47	16.59	15.91	14.16	13.53	13.28	13.18
1000	19.41	18.43	17.68	15.73	15.03	14.76	14.64
2000	38.81	36.86	35.37	31.46	30.06	29.51	29.29
3000	58.22	55.29	53.05	47.19	45.09	44.27	43.93
4000	77.63	73.72	70.73	62.92	60.12	59.03	58.58
5000	97.03	92.15	88.41	78.64	75.16	73.78	73.22
6000	116.44	110.58	106.10	94.37	90.19	88.54	87.86
7000	135.85	129.00	123.78	110.10	105.22	103.29	102.51
8000	155.26	147.44	141.46	125.83	120.25	118.05	117.15
9000	174.66	165.88	159.14	141.56	135.28	132.81	131.80
10000	194.07	184.31	176.83	157.29	150.31	147.56	146.44
11000	213.48	202.74	194.51	173.02	165.34	162.32	161.08
12000	232.88	221.17	212.19	188.75	180.37	177.08	175.73
13000	252.29	239.60	229.87	204.47	195.41	191.83	190.37
14000	271.70	258.03	247.56	220.20	210.44	206.59	205.01
15000	291.10	276.46	265.24	235.93	225.47	221.35	219.66
16000	310.51	294.89	282.92	251.66	240.50	236.10	234.30
17000	329.92	313.32	300.61	267.39	255.53	250.86	248.95
18000	349.32	331.75	318.29	283.12	270.56	265.61	263.59
19000	368.73	350.18	335.97	298.85	285.59	280.37	278.23
20000	388.14	368.61	353.65	314.58	300.62	295.13	292.88
21000	407.54	387.04	371.34	330.30	315.65	309.88	307.52
22000	426.95	405.47	389.02	346.03	330.69	324.64	322.17
23000	446.36	423.90	406.70	361.76	345.72	339.40	336.81
24000	465.77	442.33	424.38	377.49	360.75	354.15	351.45
25000	485.17	460.76	442.07	393.22	375.78	368.91	366.10
26000	504.58	479.19	459.75	408.95	390.81	383.67	380.74
27000	523.99	497.63	477.43	424.68	405.84	398.42	395.39
28000	543.39	516.06	495.12	440.41	420.87	413.18	410.03
29000	562.80	534.49	512.80	456.14	435.91	427.93	424.67
30000	582.21	552.92	530.48	471.86	450.94	442.69	439.32
35000	679.24	645.07	618.89	550.51	526.09	516.47	512.54
40000	776.28	737.22	707.31	629.15	601.25	590.25	585.76
45000	873.31	829.38	795.72	707.80	676.41	664.04	658.98
50000	970.35	921.53	884.13	786.44	751.56	737.82	732.19
55000	1067.38	1013.68	972.55	865.08	826.72	811.60	805.41
60000	1164.41	1105.83	1060.96	943.73	901.87	885.38	878.63
65000	1261.45	1197.99	1149.37	1022.37	977.03	959.16	951.85
70000	1358.48	1290.14	1237.79	1101.02	1052.19	1032.95	1025.07
75000	1455.52	1382.29	1326.20	1179.66	1127.34	1106.73	1098.29
80000	1552.55	1474.45	1414.62	1258.30	1202.50	1180.51	1171.51
85000	1649.59	1566.60	1503.03	1336.95	1277.65	1254.29	1244.73
90000	1746.62	1658.75	1591.44	1415.59	1352.81	1328.07	1317.95
95000	1843.66	1750.90	1679.86	1494.24	1427.97	1401.85	1391.17
100000	1940.69	1843.06	1768.27	1572.88	1503.12	1475.64	1464.39
200000	3881.38	3686.12	3536.54	3145.76	3006.25	2951.27	2928.78
300000	5822.07	5529.17	5304.81	4718.64	4509.37	4426.91	4393.17
400000	7762.76	7372.23	7073.08	6291.52	6012.49	5902.54	5857.56
500000	9703.45	9215.29	8841.34	7864.40	7515.61	7378.18	7321.95
1000000	19406.90	18430.58	17682.69	15728.80	15031.23	14756.36	14643.89

18.25%

Amortization Amount	1 Year	2 Years	3 Years	4 Years	5 Years	6 Years	7 Years
25	2.29	1.24	0.90	0.73	0.63	0.56	0.52
50	4.57	2.49	1.80	1.46	1.26	1.13	1.04
100	9.15	4.97	3.59	2.92	2.52	2.26	2.08
200	18.30	9.95	7.19	5.83	5.03	4.52	4.16
300	27.45	14.92	10.78	8.75	7.55	6.77	6.23
400	36.59	19.89	14.38	11.66	10.07	9.03	8.31
500	45.74	24.86	17.97	14.58	12.59	11.29	10.39
600	54.89	29.84	21.57	17.50	15.10	13.55	12.47
700	64.04	34.81	25.16	20.41	17.62	15.80	14.55
800	73.19	39.78	28.76	23.33	20.14	18.06	16.62
900	82.34	44.75	32.35	26.25	22.66	20.32	18.70
1000	91.49	49.73	35.95	29.16	25.17	22.58	20.78
2000	182.97	99.45	71.90	58.32	50.34	45.16	41.56
3000	274.46	149.18	107.84	87.49	75.52	67.73	62.34
4000	365.94	198.91	143.79	116.65	100.69	90.31	83.12
5000	457.43	248.64	179.74	145.81	125.86	112.89	103.90
6000	548.92	298.36	215.69	174.97	151.03	135.47	124.68
7000	640.40	348.09	251.64	204.14	176.21	158.05	145.46
8000	731.89	397.82	287.59	233.30	201.38	180.62	166.24
9000	823.38	447.55	323.53	262.46	226.55	203.20	187.02
10000	914.86	497.27	359.48	291.62	251.72	225.78	207.80
11000	1006.35	547.00	395.43	320.79	276.89	248.36	228.58
12000	1097.83	596.73	431.38	349.95	302.07	270.94	249.36
13000	1189.32	646.46	467.33	379.11	327.24	293.51	270.14
14000	1280.81	696.18	503.28	408.27	352.41	316.09	290.92
15000	1372.29	745.91	539.22	437.44	377.58	338.67	311.69
16000	1463.78	795.64	575.17	466.60	402.76	361.25	332.47
17000	1555.26	845.37	611.12	495.76	427.93	383.83	353.25
18000	1646.75	895.09	647.07	524.92	453.10	406.40	374.03
19000	1738.24	944.82	683.02	554.09	478.27	428.98	394.81
20000	1829.72	994.55	718.97	583.25	503.45	451.56	415.59
21000	1921.21	1044.28	754.91	612.41	528.62	474.14	436.37
22000	2012.70	1094.00	790.86	641.57	553.79	496.72	457.15
23000	2104.18	1143.73	826.81	670.74	578.96	519.29	477.93
24000	2195.67	1193.46	862.76	699.90	604.13	541.87	498.71
25000	2287.15	1243.19	898.71	729.06	629.31	564.45	519.49
26000	2378.64	1292.91	934.66	758.22	654.48	587.03	540.27
27000	2470.13	1342.64	970.60	787.39	679.65	609.61	561.05
28000	2561.61	1392.37	1006.55	816.55	704.82	632.18	581.83
29000	2653.10	1442.10	1042.50	845.71	730.00	654.76	602.61
30000	2744.58	1491.82	1078.45	874.87	755.17	677.34	623.39
35000	3202.02	1740.46	1258.19	1020.69	881.03	790.23	727.29
40000	3659.45	1989.10	1437.93	1166.50	1006.89	903.12	831.19
45000	4116.88	2237.73	1617.67	1312.31	1132.75	1016.01	935.08
50000	4574.31	2486.37	1797.41	1458.12	1258.61	1128.90	1038.98
55000	5031.74	2735.01	1977.16	1603.94	1384.47	1241.79	1142.88
60000	5489.17	2983.65	2156.90	1749.75	1510.34	1354.68	1246.78
65000	5946.60	3232.28	2336.64	1895.56	1636.20	1467.51	1350.68
70000	6404.03	3480.92	2516.38	2041.37	1762.06	1580.46	1454.58
75000	6861.46	3729.56	2696.12	2187.19	1887.92	1693.35	1558.47
80000	7318.89	3978.19	2875.86	2333.00	2013.78	1806.24	1662.37
85000	7776.32	4226.83	3055.60	2478.81	2139.64	1919.13	1766.27
90000	8233.75	4475.47	3235.35	2624.62	2265.50	2032.02	1870.17
95000	8691.19	4724.10	3415.09	2770.44	2391.36	2144.91	1974.07
100000	9148.62	4972.74	3594.83	2916.25	2517.23	2257.80	2077.97
200000	18297.23	9945.48	7189.66	5832.50	5034.45	4515.60	4155.93
300000	27445.85	14918.23	10784.49	8748.74	7551.68	6773.41	6233.90
400000	36594.46	19890.97	14379.32	11664.99	10088.90	9031.21	8311.86
500000	45743.08	24863.71	17974.14	14581.24	12586.13	11289.01	10389.83
1000000	91486.16	49727.42	35948.29	29162.48	25172.26	22578.02	20779.65

Amortization Amount	8 Years	9 Years	10 Years	15 Years	20 Years	25 Years	30 Years
25	0.49	0.46	0.44	0.40	0.38	0.37	0.37
50	0.97	0.93	0.89	0.79	0.76	0.74	0.74
100	1.95	1.85	1.78	1.58	1.51	1.48	1.47
200	3.90	3.70	3.55	3.16	3.02	2.97	2.95
300	5.84	5.55	5.33	4.74	4.54	4.45	4.42
400	7.79	7.40	7.10	6.32	6.05	5.94	5.90
500	9.74	9.25	8.88	7.91	7.56	7.42	7.37
600	11.69	11.10	10.65	9.49	9.07	8.91	8.84
700	13.63	12.95	12.43	11.07	10.58	10.39	10.32
800	15.58	14.80	14.21	12.65	12.10	11.88	11.79
900	17.53	16.65	15.98	14.23	13.61	13.36	13.26
1000	19.48	18.50	17.76	15.81	15.12	14.85	14.74
2000	38.95	37.01	35.51	31.62	30.24	29.70	29.48
3000	58.43	55.51	53.27	47.44	45.36	44.55	44.22
4000	77.91	74.01	71.03	63.25	60.48	59.40	58.95
5000	97.38	92.51	88.78	79.06	75.60	74.24	73.69
6000	116.86	111.02	106.54	94.87	90.72	89.09	88.43
7000	136.34	129.52	124.30	110.68	105.84	103.94	103.17
8000	155.82	148.02	142.06	126.49	120.96	118.79	117.91
9000	175.29	166.52	159.81	142.31	136.08	133.64	132.65
10000	194.77	185.03	177.57	158.12	151.20	148.49	147.39
11000	214.25	203.53	195.33	173.93	166.32	163.34	162.12
12000	233.72	222.03	213.08	189.74	181.44	178.19	176.86
13000	253.20	240.54	230.84	205.55	196.56	193.04	191.60
14000	272.68	259.04	248.60	221.37	211.68	207.89	206.34
15000	292.15	277.54	266.35	237.18	226.80	222.73	221.08
16000	311.63	296.04	284.11	252.99	241.92	237.58	235.82
17000	331.11	314.55	301.87	268.80	257.04	252.43	250.56
18000	350.58	333.05	319.63	284.61	272.16	267.28	265.29
19000	370.06	351.55	337.38	300.43	287.28	282.13	280.03
20000	389.54	370.06	355.14	316.24	302.40	296.98	294.77
21000	409.01	388.56	372.90	332.05	317.52	311.83	309.51
22000	428.49	407.06	390.65	347.86	332.64	326.68	324.25
23000	447.97	425.56	408.41	363.67	347.76	341.53	338.99
24000	467.45	444.07	426.17	379.48	362.89	356.38	353.73
25000	486.92	462.57	443.92	395.30	378.01	371.22	368.46
26000	506.40	481.07	461.68	411.11	393.13	386.07	383.20
27000	525.88	499.57	479.44	426.92	408.25	400.92	397.94
28000	545.35	518.08	497.20	442.73	423.37	415.77	412.68
29000	564.83	536.58	514.95	458.54	438.49	430.62	427.42
30000	584.31	555.08	532.71	474.36	453.61	445.47	442.16
35000	681.69	647.60	621.49	553.42	529.21	519.71	515.85
40000	779.08	740.11	710.28	632.47	604.81	593.96	589.54
45000	876.46	832.62	799.06	711.53	680.41	668.20	663.24
50000	973.84	925.14	887.85	790.59	756.01	742.45	736.93
55000	1071.23	1017.65	976.63	869.65	831.61	816.69	810.62
60000	1168.61	1110.17	1065.42	948.71	907.21	890.94	884.31
65000	1266.00	1202.68	1154.20	1027.77	982.81	965.18	958.01
70000	1363.38	1295.19	1242.99	1106.83	1058.42	1039.43	1031.70
75000	1460.77	1387.71	1331.77	1185.89	1134.02	1113.67	1105.39
80000	1558.15	1480.22	1420.56	1264.95	1209.62	1187.92	1179.08
85000	1655.54	1572.74	1509.34	1344.01	1285.22	1262.16	1252.78
90000	1752.92	1665.25	1598.13	1423.07	1360.82	1336.41	1326.47
95000	1850.31	1757.76	1686.91	1502.13	1436.42	1410.65	1400.16
100000	1947.69	1850.28	1775.70	1581.19	1512.02	1484.90	1473.86
200000	3895.38	3700.56	3551.40	3162.37	3024.04	2969.79	2947.71
300000	5843.07	5550.83	5327.10	4743.56	4536.06	4454.69	4421.57
400000	7790.76	7401.11	7102.80	6324.75	6048.09	5939.59	5895.42
500000	9738.45	9251.39	8878.49	7905.94	7560.11	7424.49	7369.28
1000000	19476.90	18502.78	17756.99	15811.87	15120.22	14848.97	14738.56

18.375%
MONTHLY PAYMENT
NECESSARY TO AMORTIZE A LOAN

Amortization Amount	1 Year	2 Years	3 Years	4 Years	5 Years	6 Years	7 Years
25	2.29	1.24	0.90	0.73	0.63	0.57	0.52
50	4.58	2.49	1.80	1.46	1.26	1.13	1.04
100	9.15	4.98	3.60	2.92	2.52	2.26	2.08
200	18.31	9.96	7.20	5.84	5.05	4.53	4.17
300	27.46	14.94	10.80	8.77	7.57	6.79	6.25
400	36.62	19.91	14.40	11.69	10.09	9.06	8.34
500	45.77	24.89	18.00	14.61	12.62	11.32	10.42
600	54.92	29.87	21.60	17.53	15.14	13.59	12.51
700	64.08	34.85	25.20	20.46	17.66	15.85	14.59
800	73.23	39.83	28.81	23.38	20.19	18.11	16.68
900	82.39	44.81	32.41	26.30	22.71	20.38	18.76
1000	91.54	49.78	36.01	29.22	25.24	22.64	20.85
2000	183.08	99.57	72.01	58.45	50.47	45.29	41.69
3000	274.62	149.35	108.02	87.67	75.71	67.93	62.54
4000	366.17	199.13	144.03	116.89	100.94	90.57	83.39
5000	457.71	248.92	180.03	146.11	126.18	113.22	104.24
6000	549.25	298.70	216.04	175.34	151.41	135.86	125.08
7000	640.79	348.48	252.04	204.56	176.65	158.50	145.93
8000	732.33	398.27	288.05	233.78	201.88	181.15	166.78
9000	823.87	448.05	324.06	263.01	227.12	203.79	187.63
10000	915.41	497.83	360.06	292.23	252.35	226.43	208.47
11000	1006.96	547.62	396.07	321.45	277.59	249.08	229.32
12000	1098.50	597.40	432.08	350.68	302.82	271.72	250.17
13000	1190.04	647.18	468.08	379.90	328.06	294.36	271.02
14000	1281.58	696.97	504.09	409.12	353.29	317.01	291.86
15000	1373.12	746.75	540.10	438.34	378.53	339.65	312.71
16000	1464.66	796.54	576.10	467.57	403.76	362.29	333.56
17000	1556.20	846.32	612.11	496.79	429.00	384.94	354.41
18000	1647.75	896.10	648.12	526.01	454.23	407.58	375.25
19000	1739.29	945.89	684.12	555.24	479.47	430.22	396.10
20000	1830.83	995.67	720.13	584.46	504.70	452.87	416.95
21000	1922.37	1045.45	756.13	613.68	529.94	475.51	437.80
22000	2013.91	1095.24	792.14	642.91	555.17	498.16	458.64
23000	2105.45	1145.02	828.15	672.13	580.41	520.80	479.49
24000	2196.99	1194.80	864.15	701.35	605.65	543.44	500.34
25000	2288.54	1244.59	900.16	730.57	630.88	566.09	521.19
26000	2380.08	1294.37	936.17	759.80	656.12	588.73	542.03
27000	2471.62	1344.15	972.17	789.02	681.35	611.37	562.88
28000	2563.16	1393.94	1008.18	818.24	706.59	634.02	583.73
29000	2654.70	1443.72	1044.19	847.47	731.82	656.66	604.58
30000	2746.24	1493.50	1080.19	876.69	757.06	679.30	625.42
35000	3203.95	1742.42	1260.22	1022.80	883.23	792.52	729.66
40000	3661.66	1991.34	1440.26	1168.92	1009.41	905.74	833.90
45000	4119.36	2240.26	1620.29	1315.03	1135.58	1018.95	938.13
50000	4577.07	2489.17	1800.32	1461.15	1261.76	1132.17	1042.37
55000	5034.78	2738.09	1980.35	1607.26	1387.94	1245.39	1146.61
60000	5492.48	2987.01	2160.39	1753.38	1514.11	1358.60	1250.85
65000	5950.19	3235.92	2340.42	1899.49	1640.29	1471.82	1355.08
70000	6407.90	3484.84	2520.45	2045.61	1766.46	1585.04	1459.32
75000	6865.61	3733.76	2700.48	2191.72	1892.64	1698.26	1563.56
80000	7323.31	3982.68	2880.51	2337.84	2018.82	1811.47	1667.79
85000	7781.02	4231.59	3060.55	2483.95	2144.99	1924.69	1772.03
90000	8238.73	4480.51	3240.58	2630.07	2271.17	2037.91	1876.27
95000	8696.43	4729.43	3420.61	2776.18	2397.35	2151.12	1980.51
100000	9154.14	4978.35	3600.64	2922.30	2523.52	2264.34	2084.74
200000	18308.28	9956.69	7201.28	5844.60	5047.04	4528.68	4169.49
300000	27462.42	14935.04	10801.92	8766.90	7570.56	6793.02	6254.23
400000	36616.56	19913.38	14402.57	11689.20	10094.09	9057.36	8338.97
500000	45770.70	24891.73	18003.21	14611.49	12617.61	11321.71	10423.71
1000000	91541.40	49783.45	36006.42	29222.99	25235.21	22643.41	20847.43

232

Amortization Amount	8 Years	9 Years	10 Years	15 Years	20 Years	25 Years	30 Years
25	0.49	0.46	0.45	0.40	0.38	0.37	0.37
50	0.98	0.93	0.89	0.79	0.76	0.75	0.74
100	1.95	1.86	1.78	1.59	1.52	1.49	1.48
200	3.91	3.72	3.57	3.18	3.04	2.99	2.97
300	5.86	5.57	5.35	4.77	4.56	4.48	4.45
400	7.82	7.43	7.13	6.36	6.08	5.98	5.93
500	9.77	9.29	8.92	7.95	7.60	7.47	7.42
600	11.73	11.15	10.70	9.54	9.13	8.96	8.90
700	13.68	13.00	12.48	11.13	10.65	10.46	10.38
800	15.64	14.86	14.27	12.72	12.17	11.95	11.87
900	17.59	16.72	16.05	14.31	13.69	13.45	13.35
1000	19.55	18.58	17.83	15.90	15.21	14.94	14.83
2000	39.09	37.15	35.66	31.79	30.42	29.88	29.67
3000	58.64	55.73	53.49	47.69	45.63	44.82	44.50
4000	78.19	74.30	71.33	63.58	60.84	59.77	59.33
5000	97.73	92.88	89.16	79.48	76.05	74.71	74.17
6000	117.28	111.45	106.99	95.37	91.26	89.65	89.00
7000	136.83	130.03	124.82	111.27	106.46	104.59	103.83
8000	156.38	148.60	142.65	127.16	121.67	119.53	118.67
9000	175.92	167.18	160.48	143.06	136.88	134.47	133.50
10000	195.47	185.75	178.31	158.95	152.09	149.42	148.33
11000	215.02	204.33	196.15	174.85	167.30	164.36	163.17
12000	234.56	222.90	213.98	190.74	182.51	179.30	178.00
13000	254.11	241.48	231.81	206.64	197.72	194.24	192.83
14000	273.66	260.05	249.64	222.53	212.93	209.18	207.67
15000	293.20	278.63	267.47	238.43	228.14	224.12	222.50
16000	312.75	297.20	285.30	254.32	243.35	239.07	237.33
17000	332.30	315.78	303.13	270.22	258.56	254.01	252.17
18000	351.85	334.35	320.97	286.11	273.77	268.95	267.00
19000	371.39	352.93	338.80	302.01	288.98	283.89	281.83
20000	390.94	371.50	356.63	317.90	304.19	298.83	296.66
21000	410.49	390.08	374.46	333.80	319.39	313.77	311.50
22000	430.03	408.65	392.29	349.69	334.60	328.72	326.33
23000	449.58	427.23	410.12	365.59	349.81	343.66	341.16
24000	469.13	445.80	427.95	381.48	365.02	358.60	356.00
25000	488.67	464.38	445.78	397.38	380.23	373.54	370.83
26000	508.22	482.95	463.62	413.27	395.44	388.48	385.66
27000	527.77	501.53	481.45	429.17	410.65	403.42	400.50
28000	547.32	520.10	499.28	445.06	425.86	418.37	415.33
29000	566.86	538.68	517.11	460.96	441.07	433.31	430.16
30000	586.41	557.25	534.94	476.85	456.28	448.25	445.00
35000	684.14	650.13	624.10	556.33	532.32	522.96	519.16
40000	781.88	743.00	713.26	635.80	608.37	597.66	593.33
45000	879.61	835.88	802.41	715.28	684.42	672.37	667.50
50000	977.35	928.75	891.57	794.75	760.46	747.08	741.66
55000	1075.08	1021.63	980.73	874.23	836.51	821.79	815.83
60000	1172.82	1114.50	1069.88	953.70	912.56	896.50	889.99
65000	1270.55	1207.38	1159.04	1033.18	988.60	971.21	964.16
70000	1368.29	1300.25	1248.20	1112.65	1064.65	1045.91	1038.33
75000	1466.02	1393.13	1337.35	1192.13	1140.70	1120.62	1112.49
80000	1563.76	1486.01	1426.51	1271.60	1216.74	1195.33	1186.66
85000	1661.49	1578.88	1515.67	1351.08	1292.79	1270.04	1260.83
90000	1759.23	1671.76	1604.83	1430.55	1368.84	1344.75	1334.99
95000	1856.96	1764.63	1693.98	1510.03	1444.88	1419.45	1409.16
100000	1954.70	1857.51	1783.14	1589.51	1520.93	1494.16	1483.32
200000	3909.40	3715.01	3566.28	3179.01	3041.86	2988.32	2966.65
300000	5864.09	5572.52	5349.42	4768.52	4562.79	4482.49	4449.97
400000	7818.79	7430.03	7132.56	6358.02	6083.71	5976.65	5933.29
500000	9773.49	9287.53	8915.70	7947.53	7604.64	7470.81	7416.62
1000000	19546.98	18575.07	17831.39	15895.05	15209.28	14941.62	14833.24

18.5%

MONTHLY PAYMENT
NECESSARY TO AMORTIZE A LOAN

Amortization Amount	1 Year	2 Years	3 Years	4 Years	5 Years	6 Years	7 Years
25	2.29	1.25	0.90	0.73	0.63	0.57	0.52
50	4.58	2.49	1.80	1.46	1.26	1.14	1.05
100	9.16	4.98	3.61	2.93	2.53	2.27	2.09
200	18.32	9.97	7.21	5.86	5.06	4.54	4.18
300	27.48	14.95	10.82	8.79	7.59	6.81	6.27
400	36.64	19.94	14.43	11.71	10.12	9.08	8.37
500	45.80	24.92	18.03	14.64	12.65	11.35	10.46
600	54.96	29.90	21.64	17.57	15.18	13.63	12.55
700	64.12	34.89	25.25	20.50	17.71	15.90	14.64
800	73.28	39.87	28.85	23.43	20.24	18.17	16.73
900	82.44	44.86	32.46	26.36	22.77	20.44	18.82
1000	91.60	49.84	36.06	29.28	25.30	22.71	20.92
2000	183.19	99.68	72.13	58.57	50.60	45.42	41.83
3000	274.79	149.52	108.19	87.85	75.89	68.13	62.75
4000	366.39	199.36	144.26	117.13	101.19	90.84	83.66
5000	457.98	249.20	180.32	146.42	126.49	113.54	104.58
6000	549.58	299.04	216.39	175.70	151.79	136.25	125.49
7000	641.18	348.88	252.45	204.98	177.09	158.96	146.41
8000	732.77	398.72	288.52	234.27	202.39	181.67	167.32
9000	824.37	448.56	324.58	263.55	227.68	204.38	188.24
10000	915.97	498.39	360.65	292.84	252.98	227.09	209.15
11000	1007.56	548.23	396.71	322.12	278.28	249.80	230.07
12000	1099.16	598.07	432.77	351.40	303.58	272.51	250.98
13000	1190.76	647.91	468.84	380.69	328.88	295.22	271.90
14000	1282.35	697.75	504.90	409.97	354.18	317.92	292.81
15000	1373.95	747.59	540.97	439.25	379.47	340.63	313.73
16000	1465.55	797.43	577.03	468.54	404.77	363.34	334.64
17000	1557.14	847.27	613.10	497.82	430.07	386.05	355.56
18000	1648.74	897.11	649.16	527.10	455.37	408.76	376.48
19000	1740.34	946.95	685.23	556.39	480.67	431.47	397.39
20000	1831.93	996.79	721.29	585.67	505.96	454.18	418.31
21000	1923.53	1046.63	757.36	614.95	531.26	476.89	439.22
22000	2015.13	1096.47	793.42	644.24	556.56	499.60	460.14
23000	2106.72	1146.31	829.49	673.52	581.86	522.30	481.05
24000	2198.32	1196.15	865.55	702.80	607.16	545.01	501.97
25000	2289.92	1245.99	901.61	732.09	632.46	567.72	522.88
26000	2381.51	1295.83	937.68	761.37	657.75	590.43	543.80
27000	2473.11	1345.67	973.74	790.66	683.05	613.14	564.71
28000	2564.71	1395.51	1009.81	819.94	708.35	635.85	585.63
29000	2656.30	1445.35	1045.87	849.22	733.65	658.56	606.54
30000	2747.90	1495.18	1081.94	878.51	758.95	681.27	627.46
35000	3205.88	1744.38	1262.26	1024.92	885.44	794.81	732.03
40000	3663.87	1993.58	1442.58	1171.34	1011.93	908.35	836.61
45000	4121.85	2242.78	1622.91	1317.76	1138.42	1021.90	941.19
50000	4579.83	2491.97	1803.23	1464.18	1264.91	1135.44	1045.76
55000	5037.82	2741.17	1983.55	1610.59	1391.40	1248.99	1150.34
60000	5495.80	2990.37	2163.87	1757.01	1517.89	1362.53	1254.92
65000	5953.78	3239.57	2344.20	1903.43	1644.38	1476.08	1359.49
70000	6411.76	3488.76	2524.52	2049.85	1770.88	1589.62	1464.07
75000	6869.75	3737.96	2704.84	2196.27	1897.37	1703.17	1568.65
80000	7327.73	3987.16	2885.17	2342.68	2023.86	1816.71	1673.22
85000	7785.71	4236.36	3065.49	2489.10	2150.35	1930.25	1777.80
90000	8243.70	4485.55	3245.81	2635.52	2276.84	2043.80	1882.38
95000	8701.68	4734.75	3426.13	2781.94	2403.33	2157.34	1986.95
100000	9159.66	4983.95	3606.46	2928.35	2529.82	2270.89	2091.53
200000	18319.33	9967.90	7212.92	5856.71	5059.65	4541.77	4183.06
300000	27478.99	14951.85	10819.37	8785.06	7589.47	6812.66	6274.59
400000	36638.66	19935.80	14425.83	11713.42	10119.29	9083.55	8366.11
500000	45798.32	24919.75	18032.29	14641.77	12649.11	11354.44	10457.64
1000000	91596.64	49839.50	36064.58	29283.54	25298.23	22708.87	20915.28

MONTHLY PAYMENT
NECESSARY TO AMORTIZE A LOAN   **18.5%**

Amortization Amount	8 Years	9 Years	10 Years	15 Years	20 Years	25 Years	30 Years
25	0.49	0.47	0.45	0.40	0.38	0.38	0.37
50	0.98	0.93	0.90	0.80	0.76	0.75	0.75
100	1.96	1.86	1.79	1.60	1.53	1.50	1.49
200	3.92	3.73	3.58	3.20	3.06	3.01	2.99
300	5.89	5.59	5.37	4.79	4.59	4.51	4.48
400	7.85	7.46	7.16	6.39	6.12	6.01	5.97
500	9.81	9.32	8.95	7.99	7.65	7.52	7.46
600	11.77	11.19	10.74	9.59	9.18	9.02	8.96
700	13.73	13.05	12.53	11.18	10.71	10.52	10.45
800	15.69	14.92	14.32	12.78	12.24	12.03	11.94
900	17.66	16.78	16.12	14.38	13.77	13.53	13.44
1000	19.62	18.65	17.91	15.98	15.30	15.03	14.93
2000	39.23	37.29	35.81	31.96	30.60	30.07	29.86
3000	58.85	55.94	53.72	47.93	45.90	45.10	44.78
4000	78.47	74.59	71.62	63.91	61.19	60.14	59.71
5000	98.09	93.24	89.53	79.89	76.49	75.17	74.64
6000	117.70	111.88	107.44	95.87	91.79	90.21	89.57
7000	137.32	130.53	125.34	111.85	107.09	105.24	104.50
8000	156.94	149.18	143.25	127.83	122.39	120.27	119.42
9000	176.55	167.83	161.15	143.80	137.69	135.31	134.35
10000	196.17	186.47	179.06	159.78	152.98	150.34	149.28
11000	215.79	205.12	196.96	175.76	168.28	165.38	164.21
12000	235.41	223.77	214.87	191.74	183.58	180.41	179.14
13000	255.02	242.42	232.78	207.72	198.88	195.45	194.06
14000	274.64	261.06	250.68	223.70	214.18	210.48	208.99
15000	294.26	279.71	268.59	239.67	229.48	225.51	223.92
16000	313.87	298.36	286.49	255.65	244.77	240.55	238.85
17000	333.49	317.01	304.40	271.63	260.07	255.58	253.77
18000	353.11	335.65	322.31	287.61	275.37	270.62	268.70
19000	372.73	354.30	340.21	303.59	290.67	285.65	283.63
20000	392.34	372.95	358.12	319.57	305.97	300.69	298.56
21000	411.96	391.60	376.02	335.54	321.27	315.72	313.49
22000	431.58	410.24	393.93	351.52	336.57	330.76	328.41
23000	451.19	428.89	411.84	367.50	351.86	345.79	343.34
24000	470.81	447.54	429.74	383.48	367.16	360.82	358.27
25000	490.43	466.19	447.65	399.46	382.46	375.86	373.20
26000	510.05	484.83	465.55	415.44	397.76	390.89	388.13
27000	529.66	503.48	483.46	431.41	413.06	405.93	403.05
28000	549.28	522.13	501.36	447.39	428.36	420.96	417.98
29000	568.90	540.78	519.27	463.37	443.65	436.00	432.91
30000	588.51	559.42	537.18	479.35	458.95	451.03	447.84
35000	686.60	652.66	626.71	559.24	535.45	526.20	522.48
40000	784.69	745.90	716.24	639.13	611.94	601.37	597.12
45000	882.77	839.14	805.77	719.02	688.43	676.54	671.76
50000	980.86	932.37	895.29	798.92	764.92	751.72	746.40
55000	1078.94	1025.61	984.82	878.81	841.41	826.89	821.04
60000	1177.03	1118.85	1074.35	958.70	917.91	902.06	895.68
65000	1275.11	1212.08	1163.88	1038.59	994.40	977.23	970.32
70000	1373.20	1305.32	1253.41	1118.48	1070.89	1052.40	1044.95
75000	1471.29	1398.56	1342.94	1198.37	1147.38	1127.57	1119.59
80000	1569.37	1491.80	1432.47	1278.27	1223.87	1202.75	1194.23
85000	1667.46	1585.03	1522.00	1358.16	1300.37	1277.92	1268.87
90000	1765.54	1678.27	1611.53	1438.05	1376.86	1353.09	1343.51
95000	1863.63	1771.51	1701.06	1517.94	1453.35	1428.26	1418.15
100000	1961.71	1864.75	1790.59	1597.83	1529.84	1503.43	1492.79
200000	3923.43	3729.49	3581.18	3195.67	3059.69	3006.86	2985.59
300000	5885.14	5594.24	5371.77	4793.50	4589.53	4510.30	4478.38
400000	7846.86	7458.98	7162.36	6391.33	6119.37	6013.73	5971.17
500000	9808.57	9323.73	8952.95	7989.17	7649.22	7517.16	7463.96
1000000	19617.15	18647.46	17905.89	15978.33	15298.43	15034.32	14927.93

MONTHLY INTEREST FACTORS

Interest for one month at nominal annual rates shown
based upon interest compounded semiannually

4.000%	0.00330589	11.000%	0.00896339
4.125%	0.00340833	11.125%	0.00906299
4.250%	0.00351071	11.250%	0.00916254
4.375%	0.00361304	11.375%	0.00926204
4.500%	0.00371532	11.500%	0.00936149
4.625%	0.00381755	11.625%	0.00946089
4.750%	0.00391972	11.750%	0.00956024
4.875%	0.00402184	11.875%	0.00965954
5.000%	0.00412392	12.000%	0.00975879
5.125%	0.00422593	12.125%	0.00985800
5.250%	0.00432790	12.250%	0.00995716
5.375%	0.00442982	12.375%	0.01005626
5.500%	0.00453168	12.500%	0.01015532
5.625%	0.00463349	12.625%	0.01025433
5.750%	0.00473525	12.750%	0.01035330
5.875%	0.00483696	12.875%	0.01045221
6.000%	0.00493862	13.000%	0.01055107
6.125%	0.00504023	13.125%	0.01064989
6.250%	0.00514178	13.250%	0.01074866
6.375%	0.00524329	13.375%	0.01084738
6.500%	0.00534474	13.500%	0.01094605
6.625%	0.00544614	13.625%	0.01104468
6.750%	0.00554749	13.750%	0.01114325
6.875%	0.00564879	13.875%	0.01124178
7.000%	0.00575004	14.000%	0.01134026
7.125%	0.00585124	14.125%	0.01143869
7.250%	0.00595238	14.250%	0.01153708
7.375%	0.00605348	14.375%	0.01163541
7.500%	0.00615452	14.500%	0.01173370
7.625%	0.00625552	14.625%	0.01183194
7.750%	0.00635646	14.750%	0.01193014
7.875%	0.00645735	14.875%	0.01202828
8.000%	0.00655820	15.000%	0.01212638
8.125%	0.00665899	15.125%	0.01222443
8.250%	0.00675973	15.250%	0.01232243
8.375%	0.00686042	15.375%	0.01242039
8.500%	0.00696106	15.500%	0.01251830
8.625%	0.00706165	15.625%	0.01261616
8.750%	0.00716219	15.750%	0.01271397
8.875%	0.00726268	15.875%	0.01281174
9.000%	0.00736312	16.000%	0.01290946
9.125%	0.00746351	16.125%	0.01300713
9.250%	0.00756385	16.250%	0.01310475
9.375%	0.00766414	16.375%	0.01320233
9.500%	0.00776438	16.500%	0.01329986
9.625%	0.00786457	16.625%	0.01339735
9.750%	0.00796471	16.750%	0.01349479
9.875%	0.00806480	16.875%	0.01359218
10.000%	0.00816485	17.000%	0.01368952
10.125%	0.00826484	17.125%	0.01378682
10.250%	0.00836478	17.250%	0.01388407
10.375%	0.00846467	17.375%	0.01398127
10.500%	0.00856452	17.500%	0.01407843
10.625%	0.00866431	17.625%	0.01417554
10.750%	0.00876405	17.750%	0.01427260
10.875%	0.00886375	17.875%	0.01436962

LOAN PROGRESS TABLE
Showing the dollar balance remaining on a $1000 loan

Rate (%)	Amort. Years	Elapsed Time in Years										
		2	3	4	5	8	10	12	15	20	25
4	10	830	740	647	549	233					
	15	898	845	788	730	541	401	250			
	20	932	896	858	819	692	598	497	329		
	25	951	925	899	871	780	713	640	520	286	
	30	964	945	924	904	836	786	732	643	469	256
4.25	10	832	743	649	552	235					
	15	900	847	792	734	546	406	254			
	20	934	898	861	823	697	604	503	334		
	25	953	928	901	874	785	719	647	527	290	
	30	965	947	928	907	842	793	740	652	478	263
4.5	10	834	745	653	556	238					
	15	902	850	795	737	549	409	256			
	20	935	901	864	827	703	610	509	340		
	25	955	930	905	878	791	726	655	536	299	
	30	967	949	931	911	848	800	748	661	488	272
4.75	10	836	748	655	559	239					
	15	904	852	798	741	555	415	261			
	20	937	903	867	830	707	615	514	343		
	25	956	932	908	882	796	732	662	544	305	
	30	968	951	933	914	852	806	755	669	495	276
5	10	837	750	658	562	241					
	15	905	855	801	745	559	418	263			
	20	938	905	870	834	713	621	520	349		
	25	957	934	910	885	801	737	667	549	307	
	30	969	953	936	917	857	812	762	676	503	281
5.25	10	839	752	661	565	244					
	15	907	857	804	748	563	422	266			
	20	940	907	873	837	717	626	525	353		
	25	959	937	913	888	806	744	675	557	314	
	30	971	955	938	921	862	818	768	684	512	288
5.5	10	841	755	664	568	246					
	15	909	859	807	752	567	426	269			
	20	942	910	877	841	723	633	533	360		
	25	960	939	916	892	812	751	682	565	322	
	30	972	857	941	924	867	824	776	693	521	295
5.75	10	843	757	666	571	248					
	15	910	862	810	755	572	431	273			
	20	943	912	879	845	728	638	538	365		
	25	962	941	919	895	816	756	688	571	326	
	30	973	959	943	927	872	830	783	701	531	304
6	10	844	759	669	573	249					
	15	912	864	813	759	576	435	276			
	20	945	914	882	848	733	644	544	370		
	25	963	943	921	898	821	761	694	578	331	
	30	974	960	945	930	876	835	788	708	537	307
6.25	10	846	761	672	576	252					
	15	914	866	816	763	581	440	280			
	20	946	916	885	852	738	650	550	375		
	25	964	944	924	901	826	767	701	584	336	
	30	975	962	947	932	880	840	794	714	544	311

LOAN PROGRESS TABLE
Showing the dollar balance remaining on a $1000 loan

Rate (%)	Amort. Years	Elapsed Time in Years									
		2	3	4	5	8	10	12	15	20	25
6.5	10	848	764	675	579	254					
	15	915	869	819	766	586	444	284			
	20	947	918	887	854	742	654	554	378		
	25	965	946	926	904	831	773	707	592	342	
	30	977	964	950	935	886	847	802	724	556	324
6.75	10	849	766	677	583	257					
	15	917	871	822	769	589	448	286			
	20	949	920	890	858	747	660	560	384		
	25	967	948	929	908	835	779	714	599	349	
	30	978	965	952	938	890	852	808	732	564	330
7	10	851	768	680	585	258					
	15	918	873	825	773	594	453	290			
	20	950	923	893	861	752	666	567	390		
	25	968	950	931	911	840	785	721	607	357	
	30	978	967	954	940	893	855	813	736	568	330
7.25	10	853	771	683	588	261					
	15	920	875	827	776	598	456	293			
	20	951	924	895	864	757	671	572	394		
	25	969	952	933	913	844	789	726	612	360	
	30	979	968	956	943	897	861	819	744	577	339
7.5	10	854	773	685	591	263					
	15	921	877	830	779	602	460	295			
	20	953	926	898	867	761	675	577	398		
	25	970	953	935	916	848	794	731	618	364	
	30	981	970	958	945	902	866	826	752	588	349
7.75	10	856	775	688	594	265					
	15	923	880	833	783	607	465	300			
	20	954	929	901	871	766	682	584	406		
	25	971	955	938	919	853	800	739	627	374	
	30	981	971	960	947	905	870	830	758	593	352
8	10	858	777	691	597	268					
	15	924	882	836	786	611	469	304			
	20	955	930	903	874	771	687	590	411		
	25	972	957	940	922	857	805	745	633	379	
	30	982	972	961	949	908	874	835	763	599	356
8.25	10	859	780	693	600	270					
	15	926	884	838	789	615	473	307			
	20	957	932	906	877	775	693	595	416		
	25	973	958	942	924	861	810	750	640	385	
	30	983	973	963	951	911	878	840	769	606	361
8.5	10	861	782	696	603	271					
	15	927	886	841	792	619	478	310			
	20	958	934	908	879	779	696	599	418		
	25	974	960	944	927	866	815	756	647	391	
	30	984	974	964	953	914	883	845	775	613	366
8.75	10	862	784	698	605	274					
	15	929	888	844	796	624	482	314			
	20	959	935	910	882	783	702	605	424		
	25	975	961	945	929	868	819	760	651	392	
	30	984	976	966	955	918	887	850	782	621	373

LOAN PROGRESS TABLE
Showing the dollar balance remaining on a $1000 loan

Rate (%)	Amort. Years	Elapsed Time in Years										
		2	3	4	5	8	10	12	15	20	25
9	10	864	786	701	608	276					
	15	930	890	846	798	627	485	315			
	20	960	937	912	885	788	707	611	431		
	25	976	962	947	931	873	824	766	658	400	
	30	985	977	968	957	921	891	856	789	629	382
9.25	10	865	788	704	611	278					
	15	931	892	849	802	631	490	320			
	20	961	939	914	888	791	711	615	434		
	25	977	964	950	934	877	830	773	666	409	
	30	986	978	969	959	925	896	861	796	638	391
9.5	10	867	790	706	614	280					
	15	933	894	851	805	636	495	324			
	20	962	941	917	891	796	717	622	441		
	25	978	965	951	936	880	833	777	671	412	
	30	986	979	970	961	927	898	864	799	641	390
9.75	10	868	792	709	617	283					
	15	934	896	854	807	639	498	326			
	20	963	942	919	893	800	721	626	445		
	25	979	966	953	938	883	837	782	675	415	
	30	987	980	972	963	930	903	870	807	652	403
10	10	870	794	711	620	285					
	15	935	898	856	811	644	503	331			
	20	964	944	921	896	804	726	631	449		
	25	980	968	955	940	888	843	789	685	427	
	30	988	981	973	964	933	906	873	811	656	404
10.25	10	871	796	713	622	286					
	15	936	899	859	814	648	506	333			
	20	965	945	923	898	807	730	635	453		
	25	980	969	956	942	891	847	793	690	431	
	30	988	982	974	966	936	911	879	819	668	419
10.5	10	873	798	716	625	289					
	15	938	901	861	816	651	510	336			
	20	966	947	925	901	813	737	643	462		
	25	981	970	958	944	894	851	798	696	437	
	30	989	983	975	968	939	914	883	823	673	422
10.75	10	874	801	719	628	292					
	15	939	903	864	820	657	516	342			
	20	967	948	927	903	815	739	646	463		
	25	982	971	959	946	897	855	803	702	443	
	30	989	983	976	969	941	916	886	828	678	426
11	10	875	802	721	631	293					
	15	940	905	866	823	660	519	345			
	20	968	949	929	905	819	744	651	468		
	25	982	972	960	947	899	857	806	704	441	
	30	990	984	978	970	943	919	890	833	684	431
11.25	10	877	805	724	634	296					
	15	941	907	868	825	664	523	348			
	20	969	951	931	908	823	749	657	474		
	25	983	973	962	949	903	862	811	710	449	
	30	990	985	979	972	945	922	894	838	691	437

LOAN PROGRESS TABLE
Showing the dollar balance remaining on a $1000 loan

Rate (%)	Amort. Years	Elapsed Time in Years									
		2	3	4	5	8	10	12	15	20	25
11.5	10	878	806	726	636	297					
	15	942	909	871	828	668	527	351			
	20	970	952	933	911	827	754	662	480		
	25	984	974	963	951	906	866	816	717	457	
	30	991	986	980	973	948	926	898	843	698	444
11.75	10	880	809	729	639	300					
	15	944	910	873	831	672	532	355			
	20	971	953	934	912	830	757	665	482		
	25	984	975	965	953	909	871	822	724	466	
	30	991	986	981	974	950	929	902	848	705	453
12	10	881	810	731	642	302					
	15	945	912	875	833	675	534	356			
	20	972	955	936	915	834	762	672	489		
	25	985	976	966	955	911	873	825	727	466	
	30	992	987	982	976	952	932	906	854	713	462
12.25	10	882	812	733	644	304					
	15	946	913	877	836	679	538	360			
	20	972	956	937	917	837	765	675	491		
	25	986	977	967	957	915	878	831	735	477	
	30	992	987	982	976	953	933	907	854	712	455
12.5	10	884	814	735	647	306					
	15	947	915	879	839	683	543	365			
	20	973	957	939	919	841	771	682	499		
	25	986	978	968	958	917	880	834	738	478	
	30	993	988	983	977	956	936	911	860	721	467
12.75	10	885	816	738	650	309					
	15	948	916	881	841	686	546	366			
	20	974	959	941	921	844	774	685	502		
	25	987	978	969	959	919	883	837	742	480	
	30	993	989	984	979	958	939	916	866	731	480
13	10	887	818	741	653	311					
	15	949	918	883	844	690	551	371			
	20	975	960	942	923	847	778	689	506		
	25	987	980	971	961	923	888	843	750	493	
	30	993	989	985	979	959	940	917	868	731	474
13.25	10	888	820	743	655	313					
	15	950	920	885	846	693	553	373			
	20	976	961	944	925	851	784	696	515		
	25	988	980	972	962	925	891	846	754	496	
	30	994	990	986	981	961	944	921	874	741	490
13.5	10	889	822	745	658	315					
	15	951	921	888	849	698	559	378			
	20	976	962	946	927	854	787	700	519		
	25	988	981	973	963	927	893	850	758	499	
	30	994	990	986	981	962	945	922	875	741	484
13.75	10	890	824	748	660	318					
	15	952	923	889	851	701	562	380			
	20	977	963	947	929	858	791	705	523		
	25	989	982	974	965	929	896	853	763	503	
	30	994	991	987	982	965	948	927	882	753	503

LOAN PROGRESS TABLE
Showing the dollar balance remaining on a $1000 loan

Rate (%)	Amort. Years	2	3	4	5	8	10	12	15	20	25
						Elapsed Time in Years					
14	10	892	826	750	663	320					
	15	953	924	891	853	704	565	382			
	20	978	964	949	931	861	795	709	528		
	25	989	982	975	966	931	899	856	767	507	
	30	995	991	987	983	966	949	928	884	754	499
14.25	10	893	827	752	666	323					
	15	954	926	894	856	709	571	389			
	20	978	965	950	933	864	799	714	533		
	25	989	983	976	967	933	902	860	772	512	
	30	995	991	988	983	966	950	929	885	754	495
14.5	10	894	829	754	668	323					
	15	955	927	895	859	712	574	391			
	20	979	966	952	935	867	803	719	538		
	25	990	984	977	968	936	905	864	776	518	
	30	995	992	989	985	969	954	934	892	768	518
14.75	10	895	831	756	671	326					
	15	956	929	897	861	715	578	394			
	20	980	967	952	936	868	805	720	538		
	25	990	984	978	970	938	908	868	781	524	
	30	995	992	989	985	970	955	936	894	769	515
15	10	897	833	759	673	329					
	15	957	930	899	863	719	581	397			
	20	980	968	954	938	872	809	725	544		
	25	991	985	978	971	940	911	871	787	531	
	30	995	993	989	986	971	956	937	895	770	512
15.25	10	898	835	761	676	331					
	15	958	931	901	865	722	585	401			
	20	981	969	955	939	875	813	730	550		
	25	991	986	979	972	942	914	875	792	539	
	30	996	993	990	987	973	960	942	903	786	540
15.5	10	899	836	763	678	332					
	15	959	933	903	868	726	589	404			
	20	982	970	957	941	878	818	736	557		
	25	991	986	980	972	943	914	876	791	532	
	30	996	994	991	987	974	961	943	905	787	538
15.75	10	900	838	765	681	335					
	15	959	934	905	870	729	593	408			
	20	982	971	958	942	880	819	737	557		
	25	992	987	981	974	945	917	880	797	540	
	30	996	994	991	988	975	962	945	907	789	537
16	10	901	839	767	683	337					
	15	960	935	906	872	733	597	412			
	20	983	972	959	944	883	824	743	564		
	25	992	987	982	975	947	920	884	803	550	
	30	996	994	991	988	975	963	946	908	790	536
16.25	10	903	841	770	686	340					
	15	961	936	908	874	735	599	412			
	20	983	972	960	945	885	826	745	565		
	25	993	988	982	976	950	924	888	809	560	
	30	996	994	992	989	976	964	947	910	792	535

LOAN PROGRESS TABLE
Showing the dollar balance remaining on a $1000 loan

Rate (%)	Amort. Years	Elapsed Time in Years									
		2	3	4	5	8	10	12	15	20	25
16.5	10	904	843	772	688	341					
	15	962	938	909	876	739	603	417			
	20	984	973	961	947	889	831	751	573		
	25	993	988	983	976	950	924	888	809	553	
	30	997	994	992	989	977	965	948	912	794	533
16.75	10	905	845	774	691	344					
	15	963	939	911	879	743	608	421			
	20	984	974	962	948	890	833	753	574		
	25	993	989	984	978	952	927	893	815	565	
	30	997	995	993	990	980	969	954	921	813	573
17	10	906	846	776	693	346					
	15	963	940	913	880	745	609	422			
	20	985	975	964	950	894	838	760	583		
	25	993	989	984	978	953	928	893	815	558	
	30	997	995	993	991	980	970	955	923	816	574
17.25	10	907	848	778	695	347					
	15	964	941	914	883	749	614	427			
	20	985	976	964	951	896	840	762	585		
	25	994	990	985	979	955	931	898	822	571	
	30	997	996	994	991	981	971	957	924	818	574
17.5	10	908	850	780	698	351					
	15	965	942	916	884	751	616	428			
	20	986	976	965	952	897	842	764	586		
	25	994	990	986	980	958	935	903	829	584	
	30	997	996	994	991	982	972	958	926	820	575
17.75	10	910	851	782	701	353					
	15	966	944	918	887	755	621	434			
	20	986	977	967	954	901	847	771	596		
	25	994	990	986	981	958	935	903	828	579	
	30	998	996	994	992	982	973	959	928	822	576
18	10	911	853	784	703	355					
	15	966	945	919	888	757	623	435			
	20	987	978	968	955	903	849	774	599		
	25	994	991	987	982	960	938	908	836	593	
	30	998	996	994	992	983	973	960	929	825	577
18.25	10	912	854	786	705	356					
	15	967	946	921	891	761	629	441			
	20	987	978	968	956	905	852	776	601		
	25	995	991	987	982	961	939	908	835	588	
	30	998	996	995	992	983	974	961	931	827	578
18.5	10	913	856	788	707	358					
	15	968	947	922	892	764	631	442			
	20	987	979	969	957	906	854	779	603		
	25	995	992	988	983	963	942	913	843	604	
	30	998	996	995	993	984	975	962	932	829	579
18.75	10	914	857	790	710	360					
	15	968	948	923	894	766	633	444			
	20	988	980	970	958	908	856	782	606		
	25	995	992	988	983	963	943	913	843	598	
	30	998	997	995	993	985	976	963	934	831	579

WEEKLY PAYMENT
NECESSARY TO AMORTIZE A LOAN OF $1000

Rate (%)	5 Years	10 Years	15 Years	20 Years	25 Years	30 Years
4	4.2465	2.3328	1.7032	1.3944	1.2139	1.0974
4.25	4.2722	2.3598	1.7317	1.4244	1.2454	1.1302
4.5	4.2979	2.3870	1.7605	1.4548	1.2772	1.1636
4.75	4.3236	2.4144	1.7895	1.4855	1.3095	1.1974
5	4.3495	2.4419	1.8187	1.5164	1.3422	1.2316
5.25	4.3754	2.4695	1.8483	1.5477	1.3752	1.2662
5.5	4.4014	2.4974	1.8780	1.5794	1.4086	1.3013
5.75	4.4274	2.5254	1.9080	1.6113	1.4424	1.3368
6	4.4535	2.5535	1.9382	1.6435	1.4765	1.3727
6.25	4.4797	2.5818	1.9686	1.6760	1.5109	1.4089
6.5	4.5059	2.6102	1.9993	1.7088	1.5457	1.4455
6.75	4.5323	2.6388	2.0302	1.7419	1.5809	1.4825
7	4.5586	2.6676	2.0613	1.7753	1.6163	1.5199
7.25	4.5851	2.6964	2.0927	1.8090	1.6521	1.5575
7.5	4.6116	2.7255	2.1243	1.8429	1.6882	1.5955
7.75	4.6382	2.7547	2.1560	1.8771	1.7246	1.6338
8	4.6648	2.7840	2.1880	1.9116	1.7613	1.6724
8.25	4.6915	2.8135	2.2203	1.9463	1.7982	1.7113
8.5	4.7183	2.8431	2.2527	1.9813	1.8355	1.7505
8.75	4.7451	2.8729	2.2853	2.0165	1.8730	1.7899
9	4.7720	2.9028	2.3181	2.0520	1.9107	1.8296
9.25	4.7990	2.9329	2.3511	2.0877	1.9487	1.8696
9.5	4.8260	2.9631	2.3844	2.1236	1.9870	1.9097
9.75	4.8531	2.9934	2.4178	2.1598	2.0255	1.9501
10	4.8802	3.0239	2.4514	2.1961	2.0642	1.9908
10.25	4.9075	3.0545	2.4852	2.2327	2.1031	2.0316
10.5	4.9347	3.0852	2.5192	2.2696	2.1423	2.0726
10.75	4.9621	3.1161	2.5533	2.3066	2.1817	2.1138
11	4.9895	3.1471	2.5877	2.3438	2.2212	2.1552
11.25	5.0169	3.1782	2.6222	2.3812	2.2610	2.1968
11.5	5.0444	3.2095	2.6569	2.4188	2.3009	2.2385
11.75	5.0720	3.2409	2.6918	2.4566	2.3410	2.2804
12	5.0996	3.2724	2.7268	2.4946	2.3813	2.3224
12.25	5.1273	3.3040	2.7620	2.5327	2.4218	2.3646
12.5	5.1551	3.3358	2.7974	2.5710	2.4624	2.4069
12.75	5.1829	3.3677	2.8329	2.6095	2.5031	2.4493
13	5.2108	3.3997	2.8685	2.6481	2.5440	2.4918
13.25	5.2387	3.4318	2.9044	2.6869	2.5851	2.5345
13.5	5.2667	3.4641	2.9404	2.7259	2.6262	2.5772
13.75	5.2947	3.4964	2.9765	2.7650	2.6675	2.6200

WEEKLY PAYMENT
NECESSARY TO AMORTIZE A LOAN OF $1000

Rate (%)	5 Years	10 Years	15 Years	20 Years	25 Years	30 Years
14	5.3229	3.5289	3.0128	2.8043	2.7089	2.6629
14.25	5.3510	3.5615	3.0492	2.8436	2.7505	2.7059
14.5	5.3792	3.5942	3.0857	2.8832	2.7921	2.7490
14.75	5.4075	3.6271	3.1224	2.9228	2.8339	2.7922
15	5.4358	3.6600	3.1592	2.9626	2.8757	2.8354
15.25	5.4642	3.6931	3.1962	3.0025	2.9177	2.8787
15.5	5.4926	3.7262	3.2333	3.0425	2.9597	2.9220
15.75	5.5211	3.7595	3.2705	3.0826	3.0018	2.9654
16	5.5497	3.7929	3.3078	3.1229	3.0440	3.0088
16.25	5.5783	3.8263	3.3453	3.1632	3.0863	3.0523
16.5	5.6069	3.8599	3.3828	3.2036	3.1286	3.0958
16.75	5.6356	3.8936	3.4205	3.2442	3.1710	3.1394
17	5.6644	3.9274	3.4583	3.2848	3.2135	3.1829
17.25	5.6932	3.9613	3.4962	3.3255	3.2560	3.2266
17.5	5.7221	3.9952	3.5342	3.3664	3.2986	3.2702
17.75	5.7510	4.0293	3.5724	3.4073	3.3413	3.3138
18	5.7800	4.0635	3.6106	3.4482	3.3840	3.3575
18.25	5.8090	4.0978	3.6489	3.4893	3.4267	3.4012
18.5	5.8381	4.1321	3.6873	3.5304	3.4695	3.4449
18.75	5.8672	4.1666	3.7258	3.5716	3.5123	3.4886

BIWEEKLY PAYMENT
NECESSARY TO AMORTIZE A LOAN OF $1000

Rate (%)	5 Years	10 Years	15 Years	20 Years	25 Years	30 Years
4	8.4931	4.6656	3.4063	2.7888	2.4278	2.1947
4.25	8.5443	4.7197	3.4634	2.8489	2.4907	2.2605
4.5	8.5957	4.7741	3.5209	2.9096	2.5545	2.3271
4.75	8.6473	4.8288	3.5790	2.9709	2.6190	2.3947
5	8.6990	4.8838	3.6375	3.0329	2.6843	2.4632
5.25	8.7508	4.9391	3.6965	3.0955	2.7504	2.5325
5.5	8.8027	4.9947	3.7560	3.1587	2.8172	2.6026
5.75	8.8548	5.0507	3.8160	3.2226	2.8847	2.6736
6	8.9070	5.1070	3.8764	3.2870	2.9530	2.7453
6.25	8.9594	5.1635	3.9373	3.3521	3.0219	2.8178
6.5	9.0119	5.2204	3.9986	3.4177	3.0915	2.8911
6.75	9.0645	5.2776	4.0604	3.4839	3.1618	2.9651
7	9.1173	5.3351	4.1227	3.5507	3.2327	3.0397
7.25	9.1702	5.3929	4.1854	3.6180	3.3042	3.1150
7.5	9.2232	5.4510	4.2485	3.6859	3.3764	3.1910
7.75	9.2763	5.5094	4.3121	3.7543	3.4492	3.2676
8	9.3296	5.5680	4.3761	3.8232	3.5225	3.3448
8.25	9.3830	5.6270	4.4405	3.8926	3.5964	3.4226
8.5	9.4366	5.6863	4.5053	3.9626	3.6709	3.5010
8.75	9.4902	5.7458	4.5706	4.0330	3.7459	3.5798
9	9.5440	5.8056	4.6362	4.1040	3.8214	3.6592
9.25	9.5980	5.8657	4.7023	4.1754	3.8975	3.7391
9.5	9.6520	5.9261	4.7687	4.2472	3.9740	3.8195
9.75	9.7062	5.9868	4.8356	4.3195	4.0510	3.9003
10	9.7605	6.0477	4.9028	4.3923	4.1284	3.9815
10.25	9.8149	6.1089	4.9704	4.4655	4.2063	4.0632
10.5	9.8694	6.1704	5.0383	4.5391	4.2846	4.1453
10.75	9.9241	6.2321	5.1067	4.6131	4.3633	4.2277
11	9.9789	6.2941	5.1754	4.6876	4.4424	4.3105
11.25	10.0338	6.3564	5.2444	4.7624	4.5219	4.3936
11.5	10.0889	6.4189	5.3138	4.8376	4.6018	4.4771
11.75	10.1440	6.4817	5.3835	4.9132	4.6820	4.5608
12	10.1993	6.5447	5.4536	4.9891	4.7626	4.6449
12.25	10.2547	6.6080	5.5240	5.0654	4.8435	4.7292
12.5	10.3102	6.6716	5.5947	5.1420	4.9247	4.8138
12.75	10.3658	6.7353	5.6657	5.2190	5.0062	4.8986
13	10.4216	6.7994	5.7371	5.2963	5.0880	4.9836
13.25	10.4774	6.8636	5.8088	5.3739	5.1701	5.0689
13.5	10.5334	6.9281	5.8807	5.4518	5.2525	5.1544
13.75	10.5895	6.9929	5.9530	5.5300	5.3351	5.2400

BIWEEKLY PAYMENT
NECESSARY TO AMORTIZE A LOAN OF $1000

Rate (%)	5 Years	10 Years	15 Years	20 Years	25 Years	30 Years
14	10.6457	7.0578	6.0255	5.6085	5.4179	5.3259
14.25	10.7020	7.1231	6.0984	5.6873	5.5010	5.4119
14.5	10.7585	7.1885	6.1715	5.7663	5.5842	5.4980
14.75	10.8150	7.2541	6.2448	5.8456	5.6677	5.5843
15	10.8716	7.3200	6.3185	5.9252	5.7514	5.6708
15.25	10.9284	7.3861	6.3924	6.0050	5.8353	5.7573
15.5	10.9853	7.4524	6.4666	6.0850	5.9194	5.8440
15.75	11.0423	7.5190	6.5410	6.1652	6.0036	5.9308
16	11.0994	7.5857	6.6157	6.2457	6.0880	6.0176
16.25	11.1566	7.6527	6.6906	6.3264	6.1726	6.1046
16.5	11.2139	7.7198	6.7657	6.4073	6.2572	6.1916
16.75	11.2713	7.7872	6.8411	6.4884	6.3421	6.2787
17	11.3288	7.8548	6.9167	6.5696	6.4270	6.3659
17.25	11.3864	7.9225	6.9925	6.6511	6.5121	6.4531
17.5	11.4442	7.9905	7.0685	6.7327	6.5973	6.5404
17.75	11.5020	8.0586	7.1447	6.8145	6.6825	6.6277
18	11.5599	8.1270	7.2212	6.8965	6.7679	6.7150
18.25	11.6180	8.1955	7.2978	6.9786	6.8534	6.8024
18.5	11.6761	8.2643	7.3746	7.0608	6.9389	6.8898
18.75	11.7343	8.3332	7.4516	7.1432	7.0245	6.9772

SEMIMONTHLY PAYMENT
NECESSARY TO AMORTIZE A LOAN OF $1000

Rate (%)	5 Years	10 Years	15 Years	20 Years	25 Years	30 Years
4	9.2008	5.0544	3.6902	3.0212	2.6301	2.3776
4.25	9.2564	5.1130	3.7520	3.0863	2.6983	2.4488
4.5	9.3121	5.1719	3.8143	3.1520	2.7674	2.5211
4.75	9.3679	5.2311	3.8772	3.2185	2.8373	2.5943
5	9.4239	5.2907	3.9406	3.2856	2.9080	2.6685
5.25	9.4800	5.3507	4.0045	3.3535	2.9796	2.7435
5.5	9.5363	5.4110	4.0690	3.4220	3.0520	2.8195
5.75	9.5927	5.4716	4.1339	3.4911	3.1251	2.8964
6	9.6493	5.5325	4.1994	3.5609	3.1990	2.9741
6.25	9.7060	5.5938	4.2654	3.6314	3.2737	3.0527
6.5	9.7629	5.6555	4.3318	3.7025	3.3491	3.1320
6.75	9.8199	5.7174	4.3988	3.7742	3.4252	3.2121
7	9.8770	5.7797	4.4662	3.8466	3.5021	3.2930
7.25	9.9343	5.8423	4.5342	3.9195	3.5796	3.3746
7.5	9.9918	5.9052	4.6026	3.9930	3.6578	3.4569
7.75	10.0494	5.9685	4.6714	4.0671	3.7366	3.5399
8	10.1071	6.0320	4.7408	4.1418	3.8161	3.6236
8.25	10.1649	6.0959	4.8106	4.2170	3.8961	3.7078
8.5	10.2229	6.1601	4.8808	4.2928	3.9768	3.7927
8.75	10.2811	6.2246	4.9515	4.3691	4.0581	3.8782
9	10.3394	6.2894	5.0226	4.4459	4.1399	3.9642
9.25	10.3978	6.3545	5.0941	4.5233	4.2222	4.0507
9.5	10.4563	6.4200	5.1661	4.6012	4.3051	4.1378
9.75	10.5150	6.4857	5.2385	4.6795	4.3885	4.2253
10	10.5738	6.5517	5.3113	4.7583	4.4724	4.3133
10.25	10.6328	6.6180	5.3846	4.8376	4.5568	4.4018
10.5	10.6919	6.6846	5.4582	4.9174	4.6416	4.4907
10.75	10.7511	6.7515	5.5322	4.9976	4.7269	4.5800
11	10.8105	6.8186	5.6066	5.0782	4.8126	4.6697
11.25	10.8700	6.8861	5.6814	5.1593	4.8988	4.7597
11.5	10.9296	6.9538	5.7566	5.2407	4.9853	4.8502
11.75	10.9893	7.0218	5.8321	5.3226	5.0722	4.9409
12	11.0492	7.0901	5.9080	5.4049	5.1595	5.0319
12.25	11.1092	7.1587	5.9843	5.4875	5.2471	5.1233
12.5	11.1694	7.2275	6.0609	5.5705	5.3351	5.2149
12.75	11.2296	7.2966	6.1379	5.6539	5.4234	5.3068
13	11.2900	7.3660	6.2152	5.7377	5.5120	5.3989
13.25	11.3505	7.4356	6.2928	5.8217	5.6010	5.4913
13.5	11.4112	7.5055	6.3708	5.9061	5.6902	5.5839
13.75	11.4720	7.5756	6.4491	5.9908	5.7796	5.6767

SEMIMONTHLY PAYMENT
NECESSARY TO AMORTIZE A LOAN OF $1000

Rate (%)	5 Years	10 Years	15 Years	20 Years	25 Years	30 Years
14	11.5328	7.6460	6.5276	6.0759	5.8694	5.7697
14.25	11.5939	7.7166	6.6065	6.1612	5.9594	5.8629
14.5	11.6550	7.7875	6.6858	6.2468	6.0496	5.9562
14.75	11.7162	7.8587	6.7652	6.3327	6.1401	6.0497
15	11.7776	7.9300	6.8450	6.4189	6.2307	6.1433
15.25	11.8391	8.0016	6.9251	6.5054	6.3216	6.2371
15.5	11.9007	8.0735	7.0055	6.5921	6.4127	6.3310
15.75	11.9625	8.1455	7.0861	6.6790	6.5039	6.4250
16	12.0243	8.2179	7.1670	6.7662	6.5953	6.5191
16.25	12.0863	8.2904	7.2481	6.8536	6.6869	6.6133
16.5	12.1484	8.3631	7.3295	6.9412	6.7787	6.7076
16.75	12.2106	8.4361	7.4112	7.0291	6.8706	6.8020
17	12.2729	8.5093	7.4930	7.1171	6.9626	6.8964
17.25	12.3353	8.5827	7.5752	7.2053	7.0548	6.9909
17.5	12.3978	8.6564	7.6575	7.2938	7.1470	7.0854
17.75	12.4605	8.7302	7.7401	7.3824	7.2394	7.1800
18	12.5233	8.8042	7.8229	7.4712	7.3319	7.2746
18.25	12.5861	8.8785	7.9059	7.5601	7.4245	7.3693
18.5	12.6491	8.9529	7.9892	7.6492	7.5172	7.4640
18.75	12.7122	9.0276	8.0726	7.7385	7.6099	7.5587

MONTHLY PAYMENT
NECESSARY TO AMORTIZE A LOAN OF $1000

Rate (%)	5 Years	10 Years	15 Years	20 Years	25 Years	30 Years
4	18.4017	10.1089	7.3804	6.0425	5.2602	4.7552
4.25	18.5127	10.2260	7.5040	6.1725	5.3966	4.8977
4.5	18.6241	10.3438	7.6287	6.3041	5.5347	5.0422
4.75	18.7358	10.4623	7.7544	6.4370	5.6746	5.1886
5	18.8477	10.5815	7.8812	6.5713	5.8160	5.3369
5.25	18.9600	10.7014	8.0091	6.7069	5.9592	5.4871
5.5	19.0726	10.8219	8.1380	6.8439	6.1039	5.6391
5.75	19.1854	10.9432	8.2679	6.9822	6.2502	5.7928
6	19.2986	11.0651	8.3988	7.1219	6.3981	5.9482
6.25	19.4120	11.1877	8.5308	7.2628	6.5474	6.1053
6.5	19.5257	11.3109	8.6637	7.4050	6.6982	6.2640
6.75	19.6398	11.4348	8.7976	7.5484	6.8505	6.4243
7	19.7541	11.5594	8.9325	7.6931	7.0042	6.5860
7.25	19.8687	11.6846	9.0683	7.8390	7.1592	6.7492
7.5	19.9835	11.8105	9.2051	7.9860	7.3155	6.9139
7.75	20.0987	11.9370	9.3429	8.1342	7.4732	7.0798
8	20.2142	12.0641	9.4815	8.2836	7.6321	7.2471
8.25	20.3299	12.1918	9.6211	8.4340	7.7923	7.4156
8.5	20.4459	12.3202	9.7616	8.5856	7.9536	7.5854
8.75	20.5622	12.4492	9.9029	8.7382	8.1161	7.7563
9	20.6787	12.5789	10.0452	8.8919	8.2798	7.9283
9.25	20.7956	12.7091	10.1883	9.0466	8.4445	8.1014
9.5	20.9127	12.8399	10.3323	9.2023	8.6103	8.2755
9.75	21.0300	12.9713	10.4771	9.3590	8.7771	8.4506
10	21.1477	13.1034	10.6227	9.5166	8.9449	8.6267
10.25	21.2656	13.2360	10.7691	9.6752	9.1136	8.8036
10.5	21.3838	13.3692	10.9164	9.8347	9.2833	8.9814
10.75	21.5023	13.5029	11.0644	9.9951	9.4539	9.1600
11	21.6210	13.6373	11.2133	10.1564	9.6253	9.3394
11.25	21.7400	13.7722	11.3629	10.3185	9.7975	9.5195
11.5	21.8592	13.9077	11.5132	10.4815	9.9706	9.7003
11.75	21.9787	14.0437	11.6643	10.6452	10.1444	9.8818
12	22.0985	14.1803	11.8161	10.8097	10.3190	10.0639
12.25	22.2185	14.3174	11.9686	10.9750	10.4943	10.2466
12.5	22.3387	14.4550	12.1219	11.1411	10.6702	10.4298
12.75	22.4593	14.5932	12.2758	11.3078	10.8468	10.6136
13	22.5801	14.7320	12.4304	11.4753	11.0241	10.7979
13.25	22.7011	14.8712	12.5856	11.6434	11.2019	10.9826
13.5	22.8224	15.0110	12.7416	11.8123	11.3803	11.1678
13.75	22.9439	15.1512	12.8981	11.9817	11.5593	11.3534

MONTHLY PAYMENT
NECESSARY TO AMORTIZE A LOAN OF $1000

Rate (%)	5 Years	10 Years	15 Years	20 Years	25 Years	30 Years
14	23.0657	15.2920	13.0553	12.1518	11.7388	11.5394
14.25	23.1877	15.4333	13.2131	12.3224	11.9187	11.7257
14.5	23.3100	15.5750	13.3715	12.4937	12.0992	11.9124
14.75	23.4325	15.7173	13.5305	12.6655	12.2801	12.0994
15	23.5552	15.8600	13.6901	12.8378	12.4615	12.2867
15.25	23.6782	16.0033	13.8502	13.0107	12.6432	12.4742
15.5	23.8015	16.1469	14.0109	13.1841	12.8253	12.6620
15.75	23.9249	16.2911	14.1722	13.3580	13.0078	12.8500
16	24.0486	16.4357	14.3339	13.5324	13.1907	13.0382
16.25	24.1726	16.5808	14.4962	13.7072	13.3739	13.2266
16.5	24.2967	16.7263	14.6590	13.8824	13.5574	13.4152
16.75	24.4211	16.8722	14.8223	14.0581	13.7411	13.6039
17	24.5457	17.0186	14.9861	14.2342	13.9252	13.7928
17.25	24.6706	17.1655	15.1503	14.4107	14.1095	13.9817
17.5	24.7957	17.3127	15.3151	14.5875	14.2940	14.1708
17.75	24.9210	17.4604	15.4802	14.7648	14.4788	14.3600
18	25.0465	17.6085	15.6458	14.9423	14.6638	14.5492
18.25	25.1723	17.7570	15.8119	15.1202	14.8490	14.7386
18.5	25.2982	17.9059	15.9783	15.2984	15.0343	14.9279
18.75	25.4244	18.0552	16.1452	15.4769	15.2198	15.1173